LENI RIEFENSTAHL

LENI RIEFENSTAHL

A Memoir

Picador USA
New York

ISBN 0-312-11926-7

First published in the United States by St. Martin's Press
Originally published in German under the title *Memoiren*

First published in Great Britain under the title *The Sieve of Time*
by Quartet Books Limited 1992

First Picador USA Edition: February 1995
10 9 8 7 6 5 4 3 2 1

So many things have been written about me, masses of insolent lies and inventions, that I would have perished long ago, had I paid any attention. One must take comfort in the fact that time has a sieve, through which most trivia run off into the sea of oblivion.

Albert Einstein

CONTENTS

DANCE AND FILM

INDEX

657

LENI RIEFENSTAHL

DANCE AND FILM

SUN, MOON AND STARS

It is not easy for me to leave the present behind and to immerse myself in the past in order to understand my life in all its strangeness. I feel as though I have lived many lives, experienced the heights and depths of each and, like the waves of the ocean, never known rest. Throughout the years I have looked always for the unusual, for the wonderful, for the mysteries at the heart of life.

As a young girl I was happy, growing up amid trees and bushes, plants and insects; a veritable child of nature, shielded and protected in an era undisturbed by radio and television. By the time I was four or five years old, however, I was beginning to enjoy dressing up and playing games of fantasy. I clearly remember an evening in the apartment on Prinz-Eugen-Strasse, in the Wedding district of Berlin, where I was born. My parents were out. With the help of bed-sheets, I transformed my brother Heinz, three years my junior, into an Egyptian mummy, binding him so tightly that he could not move, while I turned myself into an Indian dancing-girl by wrapping tulle round my body and donning my mother's long lilac evening gloves. The moment I rather dreaded came when my parents returned and my astonished mother stood staring at this scene, especially at the mummified body of my baby brother. She confessed to me later, however, that she too had wanted to be an actress but instead had married at the age of twenty-two; 'Dear God, give me a beautiful daughter who will become a famous actress.'

Unfortunately, or so it seemed, the girl born to her on 22 August 1902, was ugliness itself – wizened, cross-eyed and with thin wispy hair. Having been told that my mother wept bitterly when she first saw me, I found small comfort in the assurances of cameramen later on that my slightly squinting gaze was perfect for the two-dimensional medium of film.

My father, Alfred Riefenstahl, was a businessman, the owner of a large heating and ventilation firm, who, where work was concerned, was modern and far-sighted. Before World War I, for example, he installed modern sanitation in many of Berlin's buildings. He met my mother, Bertha Scherlack, at a fancy-dress party, and, like her, he loved the theatre. Yet, although they went often to plays, he considered the acting profession to be not quite respectable. Actresses, especially, were held in deep suspicion of being no better than they should be. The one exception to this was Fritzi Massary, a famous soubrette, whom he adored and whose performances he never willingly missed.

My father was a tall, powerful man, with blond hair and blue eyes, full of *joie de vivre*, an impetuous nature and a very strong will. He could easily lose his temper if he did not get his own way, especially with my mother and me, but people as a rule did not dare to contradict him. He took charge everywhere, among his relatives or among the friends he hunted with, bowled with, played cards with. He had the final say about anything concerning his wife and children, no matter how strongly my mother argued her own point of view. As a young man he had dabbled in acting and had a good voice, but he never dreamed that his daughter might develop similar inclinations.

The first play I ever saw, as a child of four or five, was an unforgettable experience. It was at Christmas and the play was *Snow White* but I can't remember the name of the theatre in Berlin. My excitement was at fever pitch on the trainride home, and I can still recall how the other passengers finally covered their ears and begged my mother to make her hysterical child stop babbling. I was fascinated by the very idea of the theatre and of all that mysterious world behind the curtain. As I grew, so did my curiosity and I would bombard with questions anyone I could find who had anything at all to do with the stage. In fact I was generally inquisitive. At school, I was probably the only pupil who constantly earned bad marks for conduct because I so often interrupted the teacher with questions; and my poor father was stuck for an answer when I insisted that he tell me exactly how many stars there were in the sky.

My love for the theatre and my empathy with the dramatic arts has, of course, been a driving force throughout my life, at times an uncomfortable one. At the age of thirty-five I was forced to run from a performance of *Othello* at the Deutsches Theater. When the drama reached its climax, during the scene in which Iago's web of lies has driven the Moor to kill his beloved Desdemona, I could not bear it, and fled, screaming, for the exit.

My favourite pastime was reading fairy-tales and this taste lasted well beyond childhood. At fifteen I was still buying a weekly magazine entitled *Fairy-Tale World*, and I used to lock myself in my room to read it undisturbed. Some of the stories I read and re-read, over and over again. I have never forgotten, for example, *The Girl with the Three Walnuts* which tells of a young girl who, wandering through a wood, discovers a poor bent old woman who can't walk any more because her feet are bleeding and she is too exhausted even to stand up. Pitying the old creature, the girl takes off her own dress, tears it in two and wraps the pieces round the woman's bleeding feet. Then the crone takes the girl to her hut and, by way of gratitude, gives her three walnuts. The first contains a beautiful frock, the colour and texture of moonlight; in the second she finds another dress, even more lovely than the first, woven out of sparkling starlight; and when the girl opens the third walnut, golden beams of light, shining and glittering like the sun, envelop her. Moon, stars, sun . . . gradations of unearthly light. I have never forgotten that series of images.

It seems that the heavenly bodies were always to have an influence over me. It might even be said that in my childhood I was literally moonstruck . . . At weekends, we usually went to our country cottage in Rauchfangswerder, south of Berlin. Twice, when the moon was full, my mother had to get me down from the roof where I was walking in my sleep. After that, at the time of the full moon I had to sleep in my parents' bedroom until eventually I recovered from my somnambulism, though not from the lunar influence. When I filmed *The Blue Light*, the moon played the leading part in the fantasy – the blue light coming from the moonbeams refracted in mountain crystals. Some of the most sublime moments of my life were experienced during the starry nights on Mont Blanc and on the Nile. However, as I have written in my last book of photographs, it was the sun that made me succumb to the magic of Africa.

MY PARENTS AND MY HOME

In the years before World War I, sport did not feature much in the lives of ordinary people, and men such as Jahn, the father of gymnastics, were mocked by intellectuals and caricatured by cartoonists. My father, however, saw some of his performances and greatly admired him; so, although I was a dreamy child, I was encouraged from a very early age to be athletic. In his own youth, my father played soccer in Rixdorf and, in later life, became interested in boxing and in horse-racing. I was only five years old when he made me a life-belt out of reeds and threw me into the water.

Before we moved into the cottage in Rauchfangswerder, we used to spend weekends in the small, idyllic village of Petz, in Brandenburg, about an hour's trainride from Berlin. The banks of the lake were lined with dense reeds and pussy willows. It was alive with frogs, and sometimes otters could be seen in the dark waters. Once, while trying to swim, I nearly drowned when I swallowed too much water; strangely enough, although I nearly passed out, I was not afraid. It all happened very quickly but it is still a vivid memory, and ever since I have been perfectly at home in the water. In Rauchfangswerder, I often swam long distances, usually to the other side of the lake where, with the help of her husband, Aunt Olga, an older sister of my mother, ran a huge garden restaurant. During these long-distance swims I was usually accompanied by my mother in the family rowing boat.

When I was twelve I was allowed to join a swimming club where I swam competitively with other children and won several prizes, before an accident forced me to take a long rest from swimming. At the Hallensee swimming-pool in Berlin, the girls practised diving from the ten-foot board, but one day I summoned up enough nerve to climb to the fifteen-foot board; I was standing there looking timidly down when I was pushed violently from behind and did a belly-flop on to the surface of the water. The pain was so acute that I never again stood on a fifteen-foot board.

Without asking my father's permission, I joined a gymnastics club and gymnastics soon became my great passion. Bars and rings were my favourite equipment but I had another accident there. While I was doing a headstand on the rings, someone inadvertently loosened the rope hooked to the wall. I plunged down vertically, nearly bit off my tongue and suffered serious concussion. In addition, I was punished by my father in accordance with the way children were brought up in those days – I was no longer allowed to do gymnastics. Thus, one more pleasure vanished from my childhood, to be replaced at once by something else – this time roller-skating and ice-skating – for I had a need to fulfil my love of movement and to use my boundless energy. Despite the pleasure and physical satisfaction of these activities, however, I remained at heart a dreamer, still vaguely searching for something more meaningful in my life.

I found it difficult to accept the views and ideas of the grown-ups around me since they were so often at odds with each other. How was I to know who was right if two people, of equal authority in my eyes, propounded diametrically opposed opinions? I remember going through a period of great mental agony at that time, tormenting myself about religion, issues of personal freedom and, because of a series of child sex-murders, the moral pros and cons of the death penalty. I could not talk to people of my own age, for they were simply not interested, and I believe my tendency to be solitary stems from that time. A terrible accident which I witnessed at the age of twelve did nothing to calm the turmoil in my mind: a little girl was run over in a Berlin street and even today I can still hear the desperate screams of her mother. How could God allow something like this to happen? I asked myself. What if this happened to me? What if I lost my eyesight and could no longer delight in the beauties of nature? What if I could no longer walk? For weeks on end I could hardly eat or sleep and my parents became very worried about me.

Eventually, however, immature as I was, I began to work out some kind of hopeful answer to all my questions. If evil was indeed the dominant force in the world then in the millions of years since creation, it had had plenty of time to destroy all that is good in nature and in mankind; and clearly this it had not done. The green grass, the flowers and the trees died and revived again; human life went on. I began at first to have more faith and confidence and then quite suddenly I felt liberated. I knew that no matter what might happen to me, as long as I lived, I would say yes to life. Every evening thereafter I prayed that God would give me the strength to endure everything that fate held in store for me, that I would never again condemn life but always thank God for it. Throughout all my later life, the knowledge of myself that I gained then has been an inexhaustible source of strength.

RAUCHFANGSWERDER

Rauchfangswerder is a peninsula on Lake Zeuthen, to the south-east of Berlin. Across from it on the railway line between Berlin and Königswuster-hausen lies the village of Zeuthen, part of one of the most beautiful areas in the environs of the capital city of what was the German Empire. My parents owned a property there, right on the lake and with a marvellously overgrown meadow attached . . . Luckily the meadow had been left in its primeval condition; huge weeping willows bordered the shore, their branches trailing in the water, and nearby I built a tiny straw hut encircled by an equally tiny garden. In a small area of the property, my parents planted all sorts of useful fruits and vegetables, and I noticed that my father was a lot more amiable here than he was in the city. He fished tirelessly for hours on end and often invited me to play chess or billiards with him. Sometimes I was even allowed to join a game of Skat, a card game popular in Germany. To protect my privacy in my little hut, I planted a hedge of tall sunflowers all around, and within that enclosure I dreamed my dreams.

I enjoyed the thought of cloistered seclusion in the peaceful garden of a convent and I toyed with the idea of becoming a nun. On the other hand, I loved the wildest games, and with the neighbours' children, a gang of boys and girls, I climbed trees, and joined in swimming, rowing and sailing races. Nothing was too high for me, nothing too steep or too perilous; but between games I was drawn back to my little garden hut where I wrote poems and plays. In love with nature, I allowed no people into my verses, only trees, birds and even insects – bees, caterpillars, anything that moved.

We moved house to Hermannsplatz in Berlin-Neukölln, and during my first year in school there, I was caught stealing apples from the fruit and

7

vegetable market. I was the ringleader in this escapade which involved knocking over the baskets in the hope of grabbing a few of the rolling apples. When my father found out, I was severely beaten and locked in a dark room for an entire day. This was not the only occasion in which I suffered from my father's strict ideas about discipline.

When we lived on Hermannsplatz I had a truly terrible experience. At that time a particularly brutal sex-murderer of children was at large in Berlin, a man who mutilated children before killing them and of whom everyone was mortally afraid. One evening my father sent me out for beer to a tavern only a few minutes' walk from our flat. I ran downstairs with a 'syphon' – that is what we called the type of beer tankard with a lid of white porcelain – and I saw a man standing at the staircase window with his back to me. He looked somehow menacing because, of course, the window was in darkness and nothing could be seen from it, so why was he there? I scurried past him hoping he would be gone when I returned, but once back with the filled tankard I did not dare enter the building. I stood outside, terrified, all too aware that since we had no telephone there was no way of notifying my parents, yet not wanting to stay out in the streets at night. At last I made up my mind; I started for the stairs – and there he stood, straddle-legged as before, silently gazing into the darkness beyond the window. Clutching the beer syphon, I dashed past him and took the stairs two at a time, but I did not get very far before he grabbed me by the coat collar. I dropped the beer and screamed for help. Next, his hands were round my throat and I was choking but at the same instant doors were being pulled open by neighbours alarmed by the noise and the man released me and fled. To this day I feel a chill of horror when I hear footsteps behind me.

My maternal grandparents came from West Prussia but moved to Poland because my grandfather, a master builder, found a good job there. When his first wife died after giving birth to my mother, her eighteenth child, he married the children's nanny and they had three more children. When eastern Poland was annexed by Russia, he moved back to Berlin, having no desire to become a Russian citizen. The family had to live very frugally for, by now, my grandfather was too old to find work, though he looked marvellous to me and seemed always very lively. His youngest daughter, my Aunt Toni, never forgave him for fathering twenty-one children, but I loved him because he was always kind to me. My mother, a good needlewoman, supported her parents by making and selling blouses; but I also recall some other kind of work. I can dimly see us sitting at a long wide table glueing cigarette papers. Some of my mother's older brothers and sisters remained in Russia and married there. We never heard from any of them and they may have perished in the Russian Revolution.

My father's parents and their ancestors came from Brandenburg. His father was a locksmith who had three sons and one daughter. My grandmothers on both sides were quiet, gentlewomen who lived only for their families and for the values of their middle-class milieu. It was a world in which I never felt quite at home.

In that era it was always thought necessary for a young girl of good background to take piano lessons; accordingly, twice a week for five years, my father took me to a piano teacher who lived on Genthiner-Strasse. I must confess that I did not enjoy the lessons at all; I hated practising even though I loved music and later, as a dancer, I never missed a good concert. With the piano as with painting, I had some talent but not enough. I was actually chosen to participate in a student concert and performed a Beethoven sonata quite successfully, but I lacked the passion that I felt so deeply for the art of dance.

When I look back to the wonderful concerts I heard at the Berlin Philharmonie, I remember particularly Ferruccio Busoni, the brilliant pianist and composer whom I met during my training as a dancer. Busoni belonged to a group of musicians who played once a week at the salon of the von Baumback family. Once, during a recital, I began to dance to the music and when he had finished playing and the guests were applauding, he came over to me, touched my hair and said, 'My dear girl, you have a gift; some day you will be a great dancer. I am going to compose something for you.' Just a few days later I received a score from him, accompanied by a note: 'For the dancer, Leni Riefenstahl. Busoni.' This *Valse Caprice*, composed especially for me, eventually became one of my greatest successes.

ADOLESCENCE

I had to live with my parents until I was twenty-one, during which time I was never allowed to go out with young men, nor could I go to a cinema without my parents. It is impossible to convey accurately the difference between adolescence then and that of young people today. My mother always made a beautiful dress for me to wear at Whitsun but it always seemed to annoy my father slightly. If a man looked back at me in the street, he would fly into a rage and yell, crimson-faced: 'Keep your eyes down; don't look at men in that way!' His rebukes were quite unfair for it had not entered my head to flirt with men. 'Don't get so excited, Papa,' my mother would say soothingly; 'Leni doesn't ever look at men.' She was both right and wrong.

From the age of fourteen I always had to be in love with someone even though I didn't know my idol personally. For two years I worshipped a young man I had happened to see only once, but had never spoken to. Every day after school I walked up and down the street where I'd seen him, hoping to catch another glimpse, but without success. No other male creature existed, only this one while it lasted.

About then we moved to Goltzstrasse, but we spent hardly more than a year in that apartment which my father found too small and we moved again to a much nicer one in Yorkstrasse; from there I could roller-skate to school in fifteen minutes. After school, I liked to go to the Tiergarten, the huge park containing the Zoo, where I would annoy the public with my skating antics until the police arrived and I had to dash away.

My friend Alice, with whom I lost touch for a while after her marriage, has reminded me of all sorts of pranks. For example, we climbed up on to the school roof and removed the flag, which was flying there in honour of the Kaiser's birthday; and one day when there was not the Kaiser's birthday nor any victory of any kind to celebrate, we ran up the flag in the hope of getting the day off school. I wasn't afraid of high places and could climb like a monkey. Another time, in order to play truant, I painted Alice's throat, arms and face with red dots and, as there was an epidemic of rubella raging, she was immediately sent home. Two days later she actually did get rubella.

According to Alice, I was incredibly naïve at fifteen, coming to her after my first kiss to ask if a baby would result. It is true that for a long time I was not as mature as my girlfriends. I was embarrassed when Alice showed me her breasts, for I had none; so, to look as if I did, I stuffed the front of my blouse with stockings. Alice was already engaged at fifteen and married by the time she was nineteen; I, on the other hand, was still undeveloped at twenty-one and looked years younger.

Despite the silly pranks I got up to with my schoolmates, I was becoming more and more aware of a serious side to my character, and very often I would shut myself up in my room to meditate, undisturbed. I was already absorbed in doing something untypical of girls or, I suppose, of many people of either sex. There was no civilian air travel of any sort as yet, but I began to draw aeroplanes that could carry a large number of people. It was the last year of the war and great numbers of the planes being used at the front were being shot down in flames and their pilots burned to death. How much better it would be, I thought, if these machines could carry people peacefully from city to city. I worked out a precise schedule interconnecting the most important German cities, and I estimated the cost of plane manufacture, airfield construction, and fuel, in order to calculate the possible price of tickets. I found this work fascinating and noted that there was in me some organizational talent struggling to emerge. When my father caught me doing this, he said, as he often did: 'Too bad you were not the boy, and your brother the girl.'

My father was not altogether wrong, for Heinz's character was almost the opposite of mine. Where I was active and outgoing, he was quiet and withdrawn; but, nevertheless, we had in common a love of art and of all things beautiful; this to the chagrin of my father who wanted his son to be his partner and eventual successor in the firm. My brother's hobby was interior decorating, for which he had a great talent, but he wanted most of all to be an architect. Heinz did not get his way; he was forced to study engineering and then enter my father's company. Yet it must be said that despite his undoubted strictness, my father idolized us just as much as my mother did.

In spite of frequent truancy, I left school with a good enough record to satisfy my father. I did not get an A in all subjects, but I was best in mathematics and algebra as well as in gymnastics and painting. On the other hand I was the worst in history and in singing . . .

Shortly afterwards, on Easter Sunday 1918, when I was almost sixteen, I was confirmed at the Kaiser Wilhelm Memorial Church. I can still remember the minister's name – Nithak-Stahn. He was very handsome and all the girls had a crush on him. My mother had made me a wonderful dress of black ruffled tulle, lined with silk, in which Alice claimed that I looked more like a *femme fatale* than a candidate for confirmation.

THE GRIMM-REITER SCHOOL

That year when I was sixteen brought a turning point in my life, heralded by an advertisement in a newspaper, the *Berliner-Zeitung am Mittag*. It read:

> Wanted: twenty young girls for the film *Opium*.
> Apply at the Grimm-Reiter School of Dance,
> Berlin-W., Budapester Strasse 6.

I went to the audition purely out of curiosity, with no serious intention of going on the stage. If I were chosen I could easily think up some excuse to turn the offer down. When I entered the auditorium, I found it thronged with young girls, each of whom had to go up to the table where Frau Grimm was sitting. She sized up every applicant with a brief glance, jotting down her name and address. Sometimes she ticked a name and I was glad to see that she put a tick after mine. I expected to be informed there and then if I had been chosen but, to my disappointment, we were told that they would get in touch with us later.

Just as I was leaving, I paused at a slightly open door through which I glimpsed several young dancers. I heard a piano and a voice commanding, 'One, two, three; one, two, three,' amid much hopping and stamping. The desire to rush inside and join in was almost uncontrollable. Against all the rules of commonsense, for I knew my father would never consent to it, I asked about the qualifications required and the cost of lessons; then, without hesitation, I signed up for the beginners' class, two hours a week. Apart from the low fees which I could easily afford, all I needed was a dance smock. That would be no problem but keeping the lessons secret from my father would be a major difficulty. Fortunately he would be at the office during the hours in question, but there was still a danger of being found out. My poor mother, who could not resist my passionate insistence, became my confidante and accomplice, and, since the lessons were purely for my own pleasure with no professional goal in mind, we had few scruples of conscience.

Now I had to lie in wait for the postman every morning, lest the longed-for letter should fall into my father's hands. In the event it was intercepted quite soon, without difficulty; the selected girls were to report back to the Grimm-Reiter School. This time, however, I found a much smaller number of applicants, each of whom had to dance a waltz before the casting jury. Delighted as I was to be selected along with several others, I knew I could not take advantage of this opportunity, and I said so at once to the disappointed director.

The secret dance class was my compensation, however, and my enthusiasm grew with every lesson. At first I was too tense and not particularly skilful but technically I found it all very easy because of my training in gymnastics and in various sports. After five or six lessons, my muscles relaxed and my limbs and body began to respond to the music. From then on my progress was very rapid and I became one of the best pupils in a very short time. When I had been attending classes for three months, my father still knew nothing and, encouraged by this, I decided to take ballet lessons too, which would mean going to the school four times a week. This I did, and soon I was dancing on points. No pain or strain was too great for me: I practised many hours a day outside school time, using every rail or bannister for that purpose; I made my friends flex my limbs so that they could move as easily as those of a rubber doll. Even in the street I would do great leaps and entrechats, paying no heed to the stares and shaking heads of passers-by. I could always concentrate entirely on whatever interested me, quite indifferent to what others might say or think about it, and during those weeks and months I cocooned myself into a world of my own.

Already each of my friends had a boyfriend, and the experiences which excited them most were all about flirting with men. I showed not the least interest in any of that. Of course, I had thought myself deeply in love several times but these were mere infatuations, with boys I was never even close to in any sense. My feelings were poured into my dancing.

It was now 1918 and the war was over. We had lost. There had been a revolution and there was no Kaiser, no king. But I experienced all these things in a cloud of unknowing. My mind was turned in on a tiny exclusive world.

During that period, in the winter of 1918 or the spring of 1919, I was once briefly involved in street fighting when an elevated train on which my mother and I were travelling, was spattered with bullets. We all had to lie down and the lights went out; as we hurried home later, shots whistled past us and we had to dash from entrance hall to entrance hall, seeking cover. I had not the faintest notion why this was happening or what it meant; the word 'politics' was not yet part of my vocabulary, and my reaction to anything connected with war was a shudder of revulsion. To my shame, I must confess that patriotism as such was alien to me in my youth. For me, war was the ultimate evil and extreme nationalism was usually responsible for war's very existence. All human beings, black, white or red, had the same value for me and I had never even heard of racist theories. It could be said that my head was in the clouds, for my interests, apart from dancing, were in the mysteries of outer space and in the planets, in the cosmos itself. The stars, and especially the moon still exercised an irresistable fascination.

AFTER LEAVING SCHOOL

Now that I was sixteen and had completed my schooling, a decision had to be made about my future. My father, determined to cure me of my obsession with acting, wished to send me to a domestic-science college, the prestigious Lettehaus in Berlin, and then to finishing school. All my appeals for training in drama made him so furious that, for my mother's sake, I gave up, and concentrated instead on finding some way to prevent my exile to a boarding-school. The very thought of that was unendurable.

The last thing I wanted was to leave Berlin where I was happy. It was an exciting place at that time and I was of an age to enjoy it all. Several times I was approached by film directors at the Romanische Café or at Schwanecke on Rankestrasse, and asked if I would be willing to take screen tests or to appear in films, but I knew better than to accept these tempting offers. There was one director, however, who simply would not take no for an answer, and so persistent was he that I finally gave in. Unbeknown to my father and with my mother's connivance, I acted a small part for several days, no doubt very badly since I was so nervous about my father finding out; and that was really my film debut.

My desire to be independent was growing stronger and stronger. When I saw how my mother was treated sometimes by my father, how he would stamp about, roaring like a rogue elephant for no reason other than that he could not unbutton the starched collar of his shirt, I swore to myself that, as long as I lived, I would never allow myself to become dependent on another human being. My decisions would always be my own. My mother was a wonderful person, yet she was my father's willing slave and I suffered to see what she had to put up with from a man whom she loved very much. Nevertheless, I could not hate my father who had many good qualities. He took good care of his family, worked very hard to provide for them and, whenever he smashed china in his temper tantrums, it was touching to see how he tried to glue it together again. But he made it so difficult for us to get along well with him. When I was allowed to play chess, I had to let him win; once when I foolishly checkmated him, he lost his temper and stopped me going to a party I had been looking forward to for weeks. Fortunately for us, he went away hunting rather a lot and these were the good times when we all felt completely free. My mother and I would go off to the cinema, sometimes even to dances, leaving my brother at home, well aware of the need for secrecy but too young to join us. He was a good boy.

THE RACE TRACK

My father loved horse-racing and was a frequent visitor to race courses where, though he was not a heavy gambler, he bet and lost rather more than he should. He preferred the flat-races at Grunewald and Hoppegarten – steeple-chasing was of no interest to him – and he allowed me and my mother to accompany him. I had neither money to bet nor any interest in doing so, but I loved the horses and the jockeys, who were the darlings of the crowd. The most popular jockey in Berlin was Otto Schmidt; every win by him sent the race-goers into a delirium, and he soon became my favourite too. He rode exclusively for the Von Weinberg stable and he could be picked out easily by their colours of blue and white stripes on his shirt. This stable also had a so-called miracle horse named Pergolese which had never been beaten over short distances of 1000 to 1200 metres. He lost only once when his owners made the mistake of running him in a race twice that length, and his defeat desolated his fans. I actually wept.

My best friend, Hertha, usually came to the races with us and, wearing the blue and white ribbons of the Weinberg stable, we cheered and suffered with Otto Schmidt. Sometimes I asked Hertha whether she thought that Otto Schmidt, sitting high on his mount, ever happened to look at my adoring eyes, and she usually said that of course he had. I did not believe it for a minute, for jockeys, just like performers on stage, seldom see clearly anyone in the audience. Several times I had tried to make contact with this demi-god, but to no avail; he was too shy and retiring.

There was, however, another well-known and popular jockey, named Rastenberger, in personality utterly different from Schmidt: lively and gregarious, he often talked to members of the public and one day, after eyeing me for some time, he came over and spoke to me; my father being nowhere about, I was free to chat. Rastenberger was astonished by my knowledge of thoroughbreds and their pedigrees, not only those of the Weinberg stable but those of all the major stables and stud farms. I had studied the subject because of Otto Schmidt and processed statistically all the information I collected. It was practically a doctoral dissertation, and I still have it today, the thick black notebook with the calico cover in which for years I entered the ancestry and the successes of the horses. It is one of the few relics of my very early youth that has remained with me.

Rastenberger, very impressed, suggested that we meet sometime and, rather nervously, I agreed, though I stipulated that I could see him only in the afternoon. The rendezvous was at a restaurant on Friedrichstrasse and he was waiting for me outside on the pavement. I was seventeen and this was my first date, yet when I found myself in a room with no other diners, the walls, sofa and even the table, covered in red velvet, I knew at once what kind of room it was and what I had let myself in for.

Rastenberger had ordered champagne and, as our glasses clinked, he put his arm round me. Carefully I extricated myself and began to chatter about Otto Schmidt, who was the only reason I had agreed to see his fellow jockey. Rastenberger had no interest whatsoever in talking about Schmidt, or in my lying disclosure that I was Otto's cousin. Dismissing my suggestion that we should visit my 'cousin', he seized me roughly in his arms and tried to kiss me; then as I pulled away and fled, he pursued me downstairs and into the street. Outside it was raining heavily and, as a perfect end to this adventure, I found myself being beaten about the head by a woman I had never seen before. It was Frau Rastenberger.

Several years later I had a similar experience, though with rather more reason. I was sitting in the stand at the Rot-Weiss tennis club and one row behind me sat the film actress, Pola Negri, who was very famous at that time. We had never met before but we were both there that day for the same reason – to see Otto Froitzheim, Germany's best tennis player, with whom, I learned later, Miss Negri was having an affair. What *she* didn't know was that I had recently become engaged to him. During the game, Froitzheim kept looking fondly up at me, until, finding this too irritating, the actress rose and struck me hard with her parasol, before storming out. The engagement did not last.

MY FIRST PUBLIC PERFORMANCE

My father still knew nothing about my dance classes. Every Tuesday and Friday I roller-skated all the way to the entrance of the school and I got away with my deception until a terrible day of reckoning. Every year Frau Grimm-Reiter's students gave a display and, this particular year, she was delighted to have a star attraction. Anita Berber, a former student and now a famous dancer who sometimes practised at the school, had agreed to perform. I had so often watched her practising and, in private, had so often imitated her every movement that when, three days before the recital, she dropped out through illness, it occurred to me that I might do as a replacement.

Frau Grimm-Reiter was doubtful at first but, after I performed one or two of Berber's dances, she agreed, providing we could find suitable costumes. This was no problem and it was only when everything was arranged that I thought of my father. There being no hope of obtaining his permission, my mother contrived to have him invited to a card party with friends. The only other person who knew the secret was my brother and he was to be in the audience for my first public performance as a dancer. Nearly all the spectators were friends and relatives of the students.

Oddly enough, although I was trembling with excitement, I felt no stage fright, and, when my cue finally came, I glided across the stage as though I had been performing all my life. The applause was so loud and insistent that I had to respond with several encores. I was numb with happiness, when it was over. I knew that this alone must be my life and my world. But my delight was short-lived.

THE EXPLOSION

Having seen my performance, a family friend innocently congratulated my father on having so gifted a daughter. My father's anger was such that the first thing he did was to instruct a lawyer to initiate divorce proceedings against my mother. Only now did I begin to realize the extent of the crisis I had provoked by my desire to go on the stage. My mother had assisted me in deceiving my father and had secretly made my costume. She was to suffer and I could not bear to see it. I decided to give up. I begged him to stop the divorce and I would bury all my dreams and longings. But he did not trust me; I was to be sent to boarding-school.

From the age of thirteen I had suffered from bilious colic, and this illness helped me in my efforts to avoid being sent away from home. Perhaps it was the distress I was causing in the family that brought on my attacks of colic, but, for whatever reason, I was in agony for several days and my father saw it and suffered with me. I began to feel very sorry for him and to realize how deeply he loved me, for he was in such a state that he could not enjoy anything. He knew that I was ill with longing to be allowed to train for the theatre but, to him, the stage was one step up from the gutter and he could not yield.

My awareness that the happiness of an entire family was being destroyed because of me, that my brother, my father and, most of all, my mother, were victims of my obsession, sent me to my father in penitence. I told him that for his sake I would study painting and, though at first he eyed me doubtfully, my sincerity convinced him and he sighed with relief. The very next day he enrolled me at the State School of Arts and Crafts on Prinz-Albrecht-Strasse. Listlessly I presented myself to sit the qualifying examination among a hundred other young applicants, male and female. We had to do several nude drawings, some portraits and one other work of our own choosing. Only two of the hundred were accepted and I was one of them, but I felt no joy in an honour which would probably seal my fate. I went faithfully to college every day, but fell deeper and deeper into a profound depression which my father could not fail to notice.

BOARDING SCHOOL IN THE HARZ MOUNTAINS

Without saying a word to anyone, my father began to send away for brochures from boarding-school for girls all over Germany; he chose the Lohmann School in Thale, in the Harz Mountains, and enrolled me there. This time there was no escape and in the spring of 1919 my parents delivered me to Thale, and to Fräulein Lohmann, the headmistress. 'Be very strict with my daughter,' he cautioned her. 'Above all, never encourage her in her ambitions to be either a dancer or an actress. I have brought her here to be cured of these desires forever. I trust you to do all that you can to help me.'

All the same, I had secretly packed my ballet slippers, stifling pangs of conscience by telling myself that practice would be for my own pleasure only. And practise I did. I trained secretly in every spare moment, rising at 5 a.m. to have three hours' ballet before breakfast. I became close friends with my room-mate, Hela Gruel, who also wanted to be an actress, and had been sent here for the same reason as I had.

It hadn't occurred to my father that in such a finishing school staging plays is usually part of the curriculum, nor apparently had anybody told him. I became a leading performer, played all kinds of parts and directed dramas myself. I appeared as a hunch-backed woman in *The Pied Piper of Hamelin*; I played Faust in the old German play *The Descent of Doctor Faust into Hell*. Furthermore, we were allowed to attend the outdoor theatre in Thale every weekend to see such classics as Schiller's *The Brigand*, Lessing's *Minna Von Barnhelm* and Goethe's *Faust*. Had Fräulein had any suspicion of how these performances were stirring up all my repressed desires, she would never have allowed me to go. Neither would she or my father have approved of the letter I sent to my friend in Berlin, during my time at Thale:

Dear Alice,

I'm afraid I'm growing more and more serious, and I don't know why. I think too much and sometimes feel that I'm going mad, yet I can't do foolish things any more and really I'm becoming too sensible. I feel as if I am already twenty to thirty years old, but can't decide whether this is to my advantage or disadvantage. Everything seems so ridiculous – and people most of all.

I've actually started to write – can you imagine? Already I've penned a few articles that I'd like to send to *Sports World*, if only I could pluck up the courage, and I hope to write a few short stories for *Film Week*. I am also working on a film scenario, but I intend to keep that to myself for, someday, I'd like to play the leading role. The title is to be *Queen of the*

Turf and it consists of a prologue and six acts. I do hope I succeed in this. I have also worked out something about civilian air travel, which I think is to come soon, and I've done several drawings in this connection. Of course, it's all just fantasy. How I wish I were a man; it would be so much easier to carry out all my plans . . .

Your Leni

I quote this letter, which Alice returned to me some years ago, only because it reveals my early inclinations towards my later profession.

Before I left boarding-school, my father demanded that I come to some decision about what kind of professional training I wished to take up, for I seemed unable to make up my mind about what was to be my next step. My heroine was the Polish scientist, Madame Curie, whom I admired for her willpower and her almost obsessive devotion to her work. A life of such self-sacrifice seemed to me to be an ideal worth striving for yet, interested as I was in science, I worried lest because of my love of art and my strongly emotional nature I would fail to find fulfilment in a purely scientific career. The real reason, however, for my indecision was probably my inability to contemplate giving up dancing, which by now was more important to me than acting.

Then I had a rather clever idea. My father had always nursed a desire to have me work in his office as his private secretary and confidante, and it occurred to me that if I suggested doing this, he might very well be prepared to allow me to go on with my dancing, provided, of course, that I promised never to go on the stage. I thought it all out very carefully and then wrote a tactful letter to my father. His reply when it came sent me into ecstasies. He agreed to everything.

ON THE TENNIS COURT

What I remember most about my first day in father's office is that I was put in charge of the petty cash and had to work an hour's overtime to clear up a deficit of five pfennigs. I set to work to learn typing, shorthand and book-keeping and, while my father was well satisfied, I was delighted; not only was I permitted to go to dancing lessons three times a week, but he also allowed me to take part in a dance recital staged by the Grimm-Reiter School at the Blüthner Hall.

Another mark of his approval was that he raised no objections to my taking tennis lessons at the Berlin ice-skating club where he had friends who would keep an eye on me. From then on I spent many hours on the tennis courts and made many friends there, two of whom were my tennis coaches. Many years later, I cast one of them, Max Holzboer, a man of striking appearance, in two of my films: *The Blue Light* and *Tiefland*. My other teacher, Günther Rahn, had once been an adjutant to HRH the Crown Prince Wilhelm, and he gave me lessons really because he had fallen in love with me. With their help, I was soon at the stage of playing in easy tournaments.

Around that time, something very strange occurred. I was in the locker room when a man opened the door and gazed at me for a long time with rather vague, grey eyes, and then closed the door. For some reason I found the incident very disturbing and it took me some time to recover from the tension that followed and from a feeling that I can only describe as being like an electric shock. Nothing like it had ever happened before. The finals of the national tennis championships were held at the ice-skating club, and, when I saw Otto Froitzheim, the top German tennis player, I recognized the man whose appearance at the locker-room door had so confused me. He was much gossiped about, not only because of his prowess at tennis, but also because of his innumerable love affairs. I made up my mind to avoid him as best I could, having no desire to be counted among the conquests of this Lothario.

FIRST OPERATION

Early each summer, my father, who had a heart condition, went to the spa at Bad Nauheim, and that year I was allowed to go too. There being no dance lessons to attend, I played a lot of tennis, particularly with two handsome young men who wooed me and sent flowers, vying with each other in their attentions to me. Surprisingly, my father who had never permitted this sort of thing, seemed to look kindly on their courtship, mainly I suspected because he thought my admirers might be rather wealthy. The black-haired one was a Chilean who owned silver mines and was reputed to be one of the richest men in South America. The other was a blond Spanish aristocrat who had rented an entire floor of the best hotel for himself and his retinue. I could see that my father would have welcomed either suitor as a son-in-law. When he asked what I thought of my beaux, I replied, 'They're all right, but I wouldn't marry either of them.' Greatly disappointed, he frowned and snapped, 'How can you talk such nonsense? Who else would be so foolish?' He seemed to be quite dazzled by the wealth and social status of these young men and, since I was nearly nineteen, he would have liked to hurry me to the altar. My mother remained tactfully neutral.

Suddenly, however, the vacation and all the thoughts of romance that went with it, came to an abrupt end. While playing with my Chilean partner I suffered such an intense attack of abdominal pain that I fell to the ground in agony. When I regained consciousness, I was being wheeled into the operating theatre at the hospital in Giessen, where they removed my gall bladder, the cause, apparently, of my old 'bilious colic' trouble. The gallstones, two of them the size of walnuts, lay on the locker beside my bed when I awoke from the anaesthetic. Still drowsy, I recognized my mother and then, to my amazement, Walter Lubovski, a young man whom I had met as a schoolgirl at the ice-rink. He had helped me on with my skates and had fallen madly in love with me. At first I thought it was a mirage, but it wasn't. Walter continued to show up every morning and sit in silence next to my mother at my bedside. Now and then, I heard him whisper my name. Despite my mother's urging that he leave when visiting hours were over, he remained, and when darkness fell would jump from my second-floor balcony since the main hospital entrance was locked. My mother seemed to feel sorry for this crazy boy, but he was beginning to irritate me.

I was released from hospital within a week and we went home, not to Yorkstrassse, but to the house by the lakeside at Zeuthen, which my father had just bought and which I loved at first sight. It was quite a long way from father's office but well worth the daily journey. Within a few days of being discharged from hospital, I was well enough to resume my dancing lessons, freed at last from attacks of colic.

FORCED TO LEAVE HOME

Ever since our return from Bad Nauheim, my father had been behaving strangely, not addressing a word to me if he could avoid doing so; even in the train to town, he would read his newspaper and ignore me completely, though, as far as I knew, he had been given not the slightest cause for anger or resentment. The whole family suffered from this cold silence but none of us had any inkling as to the reason for it. His business was doing well, otherwise he would not have been able to afford the house at Zeuthen, but we did not dare to ask him what the matter was. Then one evening his feelings simply boiled over and he roared at me like a madman. 'I know you have been lying to me; you are still planning to go on the stage; the job as my secretary is only to fool me and you have never had any intention of keeping your promise. You are no daughter of mine!'

The injustice of this was just too much; my resolve to give up the idea of a stage career had been as sincere as it was firm, and I had done nothing to deserve this. Upset, yet with a sense of liberation, I ran from the room, hastily packed a bag and left my parents' house, after kissing and comforting my poor weeping mother. I felt rather like a hunted animal as I ran through the forest to the railway station, afraid of hearing pursuing footsteps and of being dragged back to the house.

Now, I thought, I have reached the point of no return. I went to my grandmother (my mother's stepmother) who had a modest apartment in Berlin-Charlottenburg and, though it was very late when I arrived, she was sweet to me and sympathized with my situation. In bed that night I felt as though an enormous load had dropped from my shoulders. Something irrevocable had occurred and my destiny was now in my own hands. I would work and train as hard as I knew how, for years if necessary, to prove to my father that I could become a great dancer, that I would never bring on him or on his name the shame that he feared.

As so often happens, however, things worked out very differently. The very next day, one of my father's clerks appeared and asked me to report to the office where my father wished to see me; my mother had guessed where I might be found. He looked composed as I faced him, with wildly beating heart, determined to hold on fiercely to my new-won freedom. But he was forcing himself to be calm, exercising great self-control, as he spoke the words I had expected never to hear. 'You are as stubborn as I am,' he told me, 'and, for your mother's sake only, I am willing to consent to your training as a dancer. Personally, I am convinced that you have little talent, and will never be more than mediocre; but you will have no cause to say later on that I destroyed your life, or ruined your chances of a career. You will receive the best possible training and everything else will depend on you and on you alone.'

He paused, and I pitied him, for I could see what it cost him to make this speech. I heard the bitterness in his voice as he went on: 'I hope that I shall never suffer the mortification, some day, of seeing your name among newspaper advertisements.' I flinched at this, and yet I was deeply grateful; even as he spoke these harsh words, I swore in my heart that I would never do anything to disappoint him. That very day, he took me to an excellent ballet teacher, Eugenie Eduardova, a once famous ballerina from St Petersburg, to whom he repeated his belief that I lacked any talent worth speaking of, and that he was merely indulging my whim. His parting advice to her was that she should exercise great severity when instructing me.

Nobody was happier than my mother when I came home to Zeuthen with my father that evening. And now a wonderful time began for me, even though the dancing lessons and the exercises were exceedingly strenuous. At nineteen, I was really too old to be training for the ballet among students who had started at the age of six or eight; I had to try and close the enormous gap between them and me. I trained and practised until only my willpower prevented me from passing out and, thanks again to my early training in athletics, I succeeded so well that within a few months I could stay on points for several minutes, and by the end of the year, I was among the best. Madame Edouardova, a remarkable woman and a marvellous teacher, was satisfied with me, and, for my part, I truly revered her, then and always.

A TRAGEDY OF YOUNG LOVE

During this busy period of my life, my daily schedule was more or less as follows: in the morning I travelled from Zeuthen to Berlin with my father, attended ballet class in Regensburger Strasse and then went to lunch at the home of my Uncle Hermann, my father's older brother who owned a draper's shop in Prager Strasse. After lunch and a two-hour nap, I went to the Jutta Klamt School, where expressive dance was taught, before returning in the evening to Zeuthen with my father.

Quite soon, these evening train journeys became a nerve-wracking ordeal because of Walter Lubovski's obsession with me. I had done everything to avoid arousing any hope in him, yet every evening when we took the train to Zeuthen, Walter entered our compartment and sat facing me, dressed always in black and wearing huge dark sunglasses. It frightened me. My father did not know him but he noticed that the same young man in sunglasses sat with us on each evening trip. We never exchanged a word and this behaviour could not have been more foolish, since it only made me dislike Walter more and more.

One winter evening, we were all at home; my friend, Hertha, had come to stay, and she chatted happily with my mother while my father and I played billiards. There was a storm howling outside and eventually my parents said good-night and went upstairs to bed. I could hear the shutters in my bedroom banging to and fro, and we were about to follow my parents upstairs, when there was a knock at the door. We looked at each other in alarm. Who could be there at this time of night? We stood by the door, petrified. After a while, there was another knock and I thought I heard a plaintive voice. I was reluctant to disturb my father at midnight, so I opened the door a crack and, to my horror, I saw Walter standing in the snowstorm, rigid with cold. We pulled him inside, though I knew I would be beaten if my father came down and found him there; but he would have frozen to death if we had left him outside.

We dragged him upstairs to my room, took off his wet outer clothes, dried him as best we could and got him into bed. Hertha made some tea which we poured into him through his chattering teeth; between swallows, he whimpered but was unable to speak. After about an hour, he appeared to fall asleep and we tiptoed to the room next to mine, to try to work out what was to be done with him, without my father finding out. Suddenly we heard moans and rushed back to my room. Walter's right arm dangled out of the bed almost to the floor where a pool of blood had collected, and there was blood on the bed covers. He had cut his wrist and then passed out. In our fright and horror, we did what we could; I ripped up a towel and bound up the wound, while Hertha tried to bring him round by applying compresses to his face and body. After some time he began to moan; he was still alive.

When dawn came, we managed to carry him into the next room, place him under the couch and shut the door; then having wiped away all traces of blood, we waited anxiously for my parents to rise. My father noticed nothing amiss and we were so terrified of him that we said nothing. In the kitchen, we told my mother and left her to take in the dreadful events of the night and to shoulder responsibility for saving Walter's life, since Hertha and I, willy-nilly, must travel to Berlin with my father. My mother whispered that she would immediately fetch a doctor and have Walter taken to hospital, while we must notify Walter's family. He did not die, but was sent for a long period of time to a mental hospital and never allowed to see me again, lest it bring about a relapse. Later, his family moved to America where he slowly recovered and was eventually able to resume his studies and become a professor of mathematics in San Francisco. Many years later, after the war, he did visit me and my mother in Kitzbühel, for he never forgot me as long as he lived. At the end of his days, he was almost totally blind.

THE MAGICIAN

In July 1923, before inflation plunged the country into ruin, my parents allowed me to join Hertha in taking a summer course in dance, run by the Jutta Klamt School at a resort on Lake Constance. Imagine the joy and excitement we felt on our first trip together without parents! We were seen off by both sets of parents at the railway station and, along with a great deal of advice, we received third-class return tickets and a generous allowance in the currency of the day. We were delirious with happiness until we reached the station at Ulm, where we were informed that the course was cancelled because Frau Klamt had fallen ill; unfortunately, it had not been possible to notify us in time.

Were we to give up this freedom before it had even been tasted? We thought not and, in the best of spirits, with only a touch of uneasiness, we travelled on to Lindau where we rented a nice room in a professor's house. We hoped our parents would not find out about the cancellation. We enjoyed our freedom and the splendid landscape with the shores of the lake still deserted. It was wonderful.

One evening we were attracted by a poster announcing a magician of international fame – as had been almost a thousand other people who filled the large auditorium. The performance was sold out, but luckily Hertha and I found seats in one of the front rows. During the first half of the programme only magic tricks were to be performed, to be followed after the intermission by experiments with hypnosis.

The magician, who had an athletic black man as his assistant, seemed very skilful. He whisked the usual things out of a top hat: flowers, handkerchiefs, pigeons, chickens, but performed these tricks so well that no one could have guessed how he did it.

However, what happened in the second half of the evening was not scheduled. The magician stood in front of the stage and asked the spectators to stretch their arms over their heads, make fists, turn the outsides of their hands upwards, and remain like that for a while. Then he said something unintelligible, waved his arms, and called loudly into the auditorium: 'Now try to unclench your fists; some of you will be unable to do so. These people are suitable for hypnotic experiments, and they are the only ones who can come on stage.'

Hertha and I exchanged glances. I instantly suspected trickery. I could easily have unclenched my fists, but I wanted to go on stage in order to find out more; so I pretended I couldn't relax my hands and nudged Hertha to do the same. The powerful Negro tried to unclench each person's fists, and if he managed to do it, then he sent the person back. When it was my turn I clenched my fists so tightly that he let me through and to my amazement Hertha succeeded in fooling him too. Now, some twenty people were standing on the stage and the master told us that we could unclench our hands, which we did. I had no idea whether the other people were merely pretending, as we were, or really acting under compulsion.

First, he placed a box of matches on the floor and called over one young man, saying: 'This box weighs five hundred pounds. You cannot lift it.' The man made strenuous efforts to pick up the box – but failed, and similarly, a girl couldn't move it from its spot. When it was my turn, the magician seemed to give me a slightly nervous glance. I wondered whether I ought to go along with the trick. Rather than be a spoilsport I acted as if I too could not move the box. Then he said: 'It is now minus forty degrees centigrade.' We all began shaking our arms, massaging our legs, and patting one another to keep warm. Next, he said, 'Now you are in the desert, at the equator, it is unendurably hot, the temperature is almost fifty degrees centigrade.' We began to moan, our heads drooped, some of us lay down on the floor; the audience roared with laughter; they were having a wonderful time. Meanwhile, when I made eye contact with some of the 'hypnotized' subjects, I realized that they were all just going along with it for fun. Nobody was acting under hypnosis.

The master was delighted that everything was working out as he wanted it to and not at all disconcerted when, winking and whispering, I said: 'Let me dance, I know how.' He understood, but didn't suspect what I had in mind. He had the band play a fanfare as he stepped up to the ramp and announced: 'Ladies and gentlemen, you are now going to witness an extraordinary example of the power of my hypnotic abilities. I will hypnotize one of the young ladies and get her to perform a dance, as if she were a professional.'

There was a stir of excitement among the audience as he took me by the hand and led me to the centre of the stage. I lowered my eyes demurely as he called to the band: 'The Strauss waltz'. When the music began I started to move slowly as if under a spell, then to sway like a dancer, increasing my rhythm and doing spins and jetés such as only a ballerina could perform. Enchanted, the audience rose, applauding wildly even before the music stopped. I bowed over and over again, but remained where I was. I had made up my mind to reveal the truth to the spectators, for I was annoyed that the magician was making such fools of them. When the applause died down, I shouted into the auditorium: 'Ladies and gentlemen, I'm sorry to have to disappoint you. What you have seen on stage is nothing but a huge swindle . . .'

I got no further! The Negro yanked me off stage into an adjacent dressing room where I could still hear the shouts of the spectators and the cries of protest as well as some clapping. Then I saw the 'master' dashing towards me. I thought he was about to kill me, but instead he shook my hands and said: 'My dear girl, you were great. You simply must come and work with me. I'd really like to work with you!'

Meanwhile he kept running back out on to the stage to bow to the audience – I don't know what he had told them. My head was whirling – for my intention had been something very different. I must get some fresh air, I thought. Amid the tumult I managed to run out of the room, and when I found Hertha she whispered: 'Leni, you were wonderful!'

But the greatest surprise was awaiting us in our rented room. Our landlord, the professor, had also been at the performance and we could not convince him that we had not been under the master's hyponosis from beginning to end.

INFLATION

The next morning brought us an awful shock. We were in the grip of the inflation – our money was worthless. The professor and his wife shared their meagre food with us and allowed us to stay on without paying. We didn't dare send a telegram to our parents for money in case they made us come home.

I hawked crayon drawings of Lake Constance landscapes among the patrons in the garden restaurants, but the money I earned for each drawing was not even enough to pay for a hot meal.

To our surprise we met up with two men, my friend Willy Jaeckel, whom I knew from the Berlin Secession, and Nuschka, who was also a painter. They had come to Lindau for only a few hours to try to raise some money. Jaeckel had a summer cottage in the village of Gunzesried in Allgäu, and he taught painting there. They couldn't give us any money, but Jaeckel told us we could get by in Gunzesried. He said he had just traded a painting for a gigantic cheese, and bread and milk were easy to get. He had just enough petrol in his tiny car so that we soon arrived safe and sound in the village. We spent somed unforgettable days in that splendid Allgäu landscape. Jaeckel was working on etchings for a new edition of the Bible. He also sketched me in every conceivable pose.

After a day or two we returned to Berlin by train and from there we went to Warnemünde on the Baltic where we swam and sunbathed and, when the sun wasn't too strong, I practised on the beach. I had set myself a goal: I wanted to perform at a concert hall that autumn and I would ask my father to finance it. I had been taking classes for only two years, not counting the

Grimm-Reiter School, and I intended to keep studying, but I wanted to know how an audience would react and what I had to work on most.

While practising on the beach I was continually watched by a young man with dark hair and a narrow, aristocratic face. One day he spoke to me, introducing himself as Harry Sokal from Innsbruck. He complimented me on my improvised beach dancing and, during our very first conversation, he said: 'If you like, I can sign you up for several dance recitals at the Innsbruck City Theatre.'

Rather distantly I said: 'I'm not ready yet, I still have to train for a few more years.'

'Do you play tennis?' he asked. I said I did, and that evening he invited us to dinner at a picturesque seafood restaurant. It was a pleasant diversion in our holiday, and I had never seen Hertha so relaxed. She liked Sokal.

From then on the three of us were always together. He was an excellent tennis player, which I found exciting, and we were on the courts almost daily. I realized he was crazy about me, but I couldn't return his interest, alas. I liked him – and that was all.

And then our stay was over. On the last day Harry asked me outright to marry him. I was always embarrassed when a man fell in love with me and I couldn't reciprocate his feelings. But Sokal didn't give up hope. He seemed determined to fight for me.

When we returned to Berlin my parents were still in Bad Hauheim, and Hertha's parents were also still on holiday. We had been lucky.

A BEAUTY CONTEST

A beauty contest was to be held at the Zoo Banquet Hall in Berlin. My father was away hunting for the weekend, and so I was able to attend the festivities with my mother. She had made me a lovely silvery green silk gown trimmed with a border of white swan feathers. The posters said that the competitors would include film stars, such as Lee Parry, a well-known and very beautiful blonde screen actress from Munich. I was becoming more and more fascinated by the theatre and the cinema, because my life had always been so narrowly bourgeois.

Not unexpectedly, Lee Parry, wearing a white tulle dress trimmed with silver spangles, won first prize. The second prize, and I thought I would sink through the floor, was awarded to me. Amid thunderous applause, I was taken down from the stage and, to my mother's dismay, two men hoisted me on their shoulders and carried me through the room. I feared the photographers' flashes even more than the dangerous throng, for there was no telling what my father would do if he saw my picture in the papers.

Flowers and calling cards were handed to me and many people asked for my name and address. I had a very difficult time extricating myself from the crowd and getting back to my mother. We both felt very guilty, but luckily my father never found out about the beauty contest.

Among the cards I received I noticed two names, which I knew from magazines. One was F. W. Koebner, editor-in-chief of a renowned fashion journal, called *Dame* I think. The other was Karl Vollmoeller, author of the play *Miracle*, staged so opulently by Max Reinhardt. He was known to be friendly with Reinhardt.

Vollmoeller had scrawled something on his card: 'I would be delighted to meet you and to help you professionally.' Koebner's message read: 'You are very beautiful, I can promise you a great career.'

One afternoon I visited Herr Koebner, who lived in a ground-floor apartment in the western area of Berlin. A young maid opened the door and led me to a room which came as quite a surprise. All four walls were covered with photographs showing nothing but legs – no bodies, no faces, just legs. Then Koebner came in, slender, rather tall, his clothes elegantly casual, and greeted me with a slightly leering smile that instantly aroused my antipathy. The first thing he said was: 'Show me your legs, my lovely.'

I was stunned, for I was wearing a fairly short skirt.

'But you can see my legs,' I said.

'Please, just pull your skirt a little higher, over your knees.'

Foolishly I drew it halfway up my thighs, then dropped it again.

'What's all this about?' I asked in annoyance. Condescendingly he motioned me to a chair and said, as if offering me a magnificent present: 'I have something special in mind for you. If you can dance only half as well as your legs suggest, I'll get you a solo dance number at La Scala.'

La Scala was Berlin's biggest vaudeville theatre, and its international programme was world-famous. If Herr Koebner thought I would be so overjoyed that I would throw my arms around him or let out a shriek of delight, he must have been very disappointed. I reflected for an instant, then said with a rather conceited grin: 'But Herr Koebner, I've never had any intention of appearing at a vaudeville house, even one as famous as La Scala. I am going to dance only in concert halls and on theatre platforms.'

He stared at me as if I were a freak. Then, offended, he opened the door. 'Goodbye and good luck,' he said, as I left.

My visit to Herr Dr Vollmoeller was entirely different. Actually, after my encounter with Herr Koebner, I didn't feel much like meeting any other strange men from the world of the Zoo Banquet Hall. Yet I felt it was worth seeing this playwright because of his collaboration with Max Reinhardt, whose productions at the Deutsche Theater and the Kammerspiele I hardly ever missed. So one afternoon I stood on Pariser Platz, outside a luxurious building near the Brandenburg Gate. It was on the side where, ten years later, Goebbels would occupy his ministerial offices, and I would be in much the same situation as I was now with Dr Vollmoeller.

A butler led me to an elegant, thickly-carpeted room full of antique furniture and costly paintings; everything was in perfect harmony and taste. Nothing was overdone. Softly, almost inaudibly, Dr Vollmoeller entered the room. He had an air of refinement and, in this ambience, I could picture him in the costume of a bygone age. His face was lean, his eyes bright, and he had sparse light-brown hair. He greeted me with a kiss on my hand – the first I had ever received. The butler served tea and cake and I was offered a cigarette, which I declined with thanks.

'You don't smoke?'

I shook my head.

'May I offer you a liqueur?'

This too I declined. 'I don't like alcohol: it makes me feel tired and dizzy,' I said apologetically.

'Don't you have any bad habits?'

I shrugged. 'I have my weaknesses, but they are of a different nature.'

'What are they?'

'I am very self-willed and I often don't do what other people demand of me. I'm also very undiplomatic.'

'How do you mean?'

'I'm often tempted to say things people don't wish to hear.'

'One couldn't tell from your appearance. You look rather gentle.'

After this exchange we got down to talking about the theatre, about dancing and future plans.

'How do you envisage your future?'

'I am going to dance.'

'And how and where do you want to dance?'

'Like Impekhoven, like Gert, like Wigman, in concert halls and on stages.'

'Do you have a rich friend to finance you?'

I laughed. 'I don't need a rich friend. I'll succeed on my own.'

Smiling, he broke in. 'Dear little Fräulein, Leni Riefenstahl – that's your name, isn't it? – you strike me as very naïve. You need a rich friend. Otherwise you'll never get anywhere. Never.'

'Would you care to bet on it?' I said.

'Yes, I would,' he said, and tried to put his arms around me. I pulled away, stood up, and walked quickly to the door.

'What a pity!' I said, 'I was looking forward to chatting with you.'

He tried to hold me, but I hurried out. Before closing the door, I called back: 'I'll send you an invitation to my first recital – that's a promise. Goodbye!'

He got his invitation – six months later.

INJURIES

My dance training was severely disrupted when I broke bones in my feet no fewer than three times. The first time, I slipped on orange peel after ballet class. Unable to stand, I was taken to hospital. My right ankle was fractured – but I was able to dance again after only three weeks. My second accident occurred six months later. Walking home through the woods in the darkness, I stepped into a hole. This time I fractured my left ankle. The third accident was more serious. My bedroom floor had been painted the previous day and, in order to reach the hallway without touching the floor, I took a gigantic leap from the bed. The bed slid back, I lost my balance and came down lopsided. Now my metatarsal bone was broken, and I had to stop training for six weeks. I could still feel the pain years later.

During this time of enforced rest I saw a film about Albert Einstein and his theory of relativity. It was an important discovery for me. I don't think I am exaggerating when I say that the moment I began to understand this theory, many things changed for me and I seemed to undergo an expansion of consciousness. For someone with my ideas, Einstein's concept of the 'relative' was revolutionary.

MY FIRST MAN

At the age of twenty-one I had my first experience with a man. Even though I wouldn't admit it to myself, my feelings for Otto Froitzheim were growing deeper until at times they were almost overpowering; and yet I managed to avoid seeing him for two years. I could live with it only because I was completely fulfilled by my passion for dancing.

All my girlfriends were already having love affairs. Some were engaged, and Alice, my best friend, had already married. I was the only one who was still sexually inexperienced. Eventually I did feel that I was missing something and I often toyed with the idea of having an adventure. But with whom? I had many quiet admirers, but didn't like any of them much. So, almost against my will, my thoughts concentrated more and more on the man whom I almost feared. My most ardent suitor was Günther Rahn, a kind-hearted man who was friendly with Otto Froitzheim. Somehow I managed to tell Günther about my secret fantasies and, although I realized that he would be very distressed, I also said that I thought of him as a very dear friend, but nothing more. It was he who told me that Froitzheim had left Berlin and was living in Cologne, where he had become deputy police commissioner. He still kept his apartment in Berlin however, and, according to Günther, visited the capital every two weeks. I began to nag poor Günther to arrange a date for me and Froitzheim, perhaps an invitation to tea, or something similar. This was not so easy, since a meeting was possible only at weekends, when Papa was off hunting. I was still a carefully sheltered girl.

There was great excitement when Günther told me several weeks later that Otto Froitzheim would be expecting me at his apartment. Only now did I become fully aware of how reckless my plan was. There was no going back, but I was very apprehensive about what was to come. Alice was experienced in matters of love, so I shared my secret with her and asked her for advice.

'The most important thing,' she said, 'is to wear beautiful lingerie. You can't go in your woollen underwear. I'll lend you my set of silk undies.'

Punctually at five in the afternoon, I stood in front of the house, an old and elegant patrician mansion on Rauchstrasse. Inside, a broad marble staircase, luxuriously carpeted, led to the first floor. Slowly, very slowly, I climbed the steps as if going to my execution. I rang the bell. Then the man, whom I didn't even know, and whom I had been dreaming about for two years, stood in the doorway. Since the light was behind him, I could't see his face clearly, but he held out his hand, and his deep, gentle voice made me shiver: 'Please come in, Fräulein Leni, if I may call you that. I am delighted to make your acquaintance.' Then he helped me out of my black velvet coat, trimmed – alas! – with fake ermine. After arranging my hair, I stepped into a living room, softly lit to suggest intimacy, I thought. I sat down in a comfortable armchair, while he poured me a cup of tea. A faltering conversation developed, small talk about tennis, dancing and various trivia.

I grew more and more embarrassed. Günther had told me that Froitzheim was eighteen years my senior. At thirty-nine he was already an elderly man, according to the notions of those days. The longer he gazed at me the more nervous I became, especially when his gaze rested on my legs. By now I just wanted to run home, but he put a record on the gramophone, a tango. Unresisting, I let him draw me out of the chair, and, as if hypnotized, I danced several steps with him, nestling happily against him. My dreams and yearnings were coming true. Then as he lifted me bodily up in his arms and gently placed me on a couch, my happiness abruptly fled. All I could feel was fear, a terror of the unknown, as he virtually ripped the clothes from my body and, with almost brutal violence, tried to possess me quickly and totally.

The experience was traumatic. Was this love? I felt nothing but pain and disappointment. How far it was from my dreams and hopes. All I had wanted was tenderness, just to be with him, to cuddle with him or to lie at his feet. I endured it to the end, then covered my tearful face with a pillow. A short while later he tossed me a towel and pointed to the bathroom: 'You can wash in there.' Profoundly ashamed and humiliated, I walked into the bathroom, where I wept bitter tears. For the first time in my life feelings of hatred rose in me.

When I came back to the living room he was already dressed. Glancing at his watch, he said with insulting indifference: 'I have an appointment.' Then, incredibly, he pressed a banknote into my hand: twenty American dollars – a fortune at that time. 'If you get pregnant, you can use this to get rid of it.' I tore up the banknote and threw the pieces at his feet. 'You are a monster!' I shouted, and ran from the apartment, filled with rage and despair.

Outside it was cold and foggy. I wandered through the streets until I came to the Landwehrkanal, which flows nearby, and for many hours I stood and stared down at the water. I had only one wish: to die. The experience had been so shocking that I didn't think I could go on living.

But the cold, clammy air gradually brought me back to reality. I arrived home in Zeuthen late in the evening. That same night I wrote a letter to Froitzheim, telling him about the love I once had for him and my boundless repugnance now.

Eager to get out of Berlin, I asked my father to register me at the Mary Wigman School in Dresden, and, to my surprise, he agreed. My mother took me to Dresden, renting a small room for me in the home of a family, near the Wigman School.

The very next day I was allowed to audition for Frau Wigman, who accepted me into her master class. I studied along with Palucca, Yvonne Georgi and Vera Skoronell. I was lonely in Dresden, and I had a very hard time integrating into the group dancing of the Wigman School. I found the style too abstract, too rigorous, and too ascetic, where my own urge was to surrender completely to the rhythms of the music. I suffered in part because I was tormented by doubts about my talent, and eventually I rented a small room in a boarding-house and tried to choreograph my own dance.

In Dresden the memory of Froitzheim was sublimated into some of my later dances, including the cycle *The Three Dances of Eros*. I called the first one 'Fire', a passionate dance to music by Tchaikovsky; for the second one, 'Surrender', I chose Chopin; and I used a piece by Grieg for the third dance, 'Release', which was inspired by Gothic sculptures.

One day, to my astonishment, I found exquisite flowers in my room and a card which said: 'Forgive me, I love you, I have to see you again – Your Otto.' I had never expected an answer to my desperate letter and I never wanted to see that man again. Yet now he was sending me flowers. Why didn't I hurl them from the window? Why did I clutch them in my arms? Why did I kiss the card? I locked myself in my room and wept, wept, wept.

Several days later he appeared in person. I had felt all along that I would not have the strength to resist his insolence; that in some mysterious way I was a slave to him. He ran his hand over my hair. 'I was shaken by your letter,' he told me. 'Can you forgive me? I didn't realize how wonderful you are.'

He remained all day and all night, and I found him much changed; he had become more tender. Again, I was hypnotized by his eyes, and even more by his voice; yet physically, I could feel nothing for him. He came back two weeks later, then a third time, treating me as if I had become his property while I could think only of escape from this bondage.

DANCE AND PAINTING

I terminated my dance lessons in Dresden and resumed studying with Eduardova and Jutta Klamt more intensely than ever and almost beyond reason. I launched into an extremely creative phase, choreographing two of my best-known dances. Schubert's Unfinished Symphony and *The Dance to the Sea* to the music of Beethoven's Fifth Symphony. I never missed a single production by Niddy Impekoven, Mary Wigman or Valesca Gert. They were goddesses to me, unattainable beings. The dancer who made the deepest impact on me, however, was Harald Kreutzberg; he was a genius, a magician. I found his powers of expression incredible and his dances quite brilliant. The spectators were so enthralled that they refused to leave the theatre until Kreutzberg had danced several scores.

Painting too played a special role in my life during that period. My friendships with Jaeckel and other artists helped me attain a great understanding of music and of modern art. I am thinking now of Kandinsky, Pechstein, Nolde and others. I was especially fascinated by Franz Marc, whose *Tower of Blue Horses* was one of my favourite paintings.

As often as possible I visited the Crown Prince Palace, a marvellous museum, full of works by contemporary painters and sculptors. I made a hobby of picking out my favourite painting in each room and regarding it as 'mine'. This 'personal' collection included Impressionists like Manet and Monet, as well as Cézanne, Degas and Klee. Once I was affected to an extraordinary degree by a painting of flowers in colours so muted as to be almost unnoticeable. Yet, strangely enough, I was so excited that I nearly burst into tears. I have often wondered why that work in particular had such a powerful effect on me. It was not the subject, not the flowers as such, but the artist himself: Vincent Van Gogh. This was the first Van Gogh painting I ever saw. After that I studied him in detail, researching both his life and his work, for he struck me as the most passionate of all painters, an artist who utterly consumed himself. That passion which expressed his genius and madness so overwhelmingly must have ignited something inside me when I gazed at his painting.

Before the start of World War II, I wrote a screenplay about Van Gogh. I would have loved to make a film of his highly unusual, tragic life story, but that dream, like so many others, never came true.

MY FIRST DANCE RECITAL

I was training harder than ever, for several hours a day. At night I fell into bed exhausted, and it was difficult getting up the next morning. My darling mother spoiled me terribly, even putting my shoes and stockings on me in bed.

Then came the day I had to prove myself. On 23 October 1923, I stood on the stage of Munich's Tonhalle, waiting for the music to begin. At that time inflation was at such a height that Harry Sokal had to shell out only one US dollar to pay for the hall and the necessary publicity. My first recital, financed by my father, was to take place four days later in Berlin, but Sokal felt I should have some previous experience, and had arranged for me to have a kind of dress rehearsal here.

The room was barely one third full, for of course I was unknown and the few spectators had probably obtained free passes from the manager's office;

the emptiness of the room didn't bother me, however. I was simply happy to be dancing in front of an audience and I could hardly wait to get on stage.

My very first dance, *Study after a Gavotte*, was applauded enthusiastically and I had to encore the third. The clapping became louder and louder until, during my final dances, the audience demanded repeated encores. I danced on until I was too exhausted to continue. *Die Münchner Neusten Nachrichten* said: 'This is a marvellously gifted dancer; her artistry is utterly authentic and original, for instance in *Valse Caprice* and in the delightful final dance in which she had all the grace of a swaying poppy, a bending cornflower . . .'

And then I stood on stage in Berlin, once again at Blüthner Hall. The place was almost sold out. Friends had made sure of that. This time I had to prove to my father that there was no other future for me. I had to convince him, conquer him, triumph over him, once and for all. I was dancing purely for him and I gave it my all.

At the end of the recital a wave of applause came crashing towards me and, as I curtsied, I felt my father's eyes upon me. Had he forgiven me? That night I won my first great victory. Not only had my father forgiven me, he was deeply moved. Kissing me, he said: 'Now I believe you.' That was my finest reward. The evening was more than a success; it was a triumph beyond my wildest dreams.

The next day I sat in a pastry shop on Kurfürstendamm, reading the headline: A NEW DANCER. At first it didn't even cross my mind that this referred to me. Then I noticed that the review was about my performance and that it was a hymn of praise, to be repeated in every Berlin newspaper. John Schikovski, the most knowledgeable and most feared dance critic in Berlin, wrote in *Der Vorwärts*: 'It was a revelation. An almost total realization of the heights of artistry which can be achieved in the realm of dance. Fräulein Riefenstahl came very close to the goal towards which her most famous colleagues have striven in vain: the fulfilment of our hopes for dance in the future; that new spirit and supreme style.' Fred Hildenbrandt wrote in the *Berliner Tageblatt*: 'When one sees this girl move to the music, one has an awareness that here is a dancer who will appear perhaps once in a thousand years, an artiste of consummate grace and unparalleled beauty . . .'

Overnight my life veered off in an entirely new direction. I received offers from all sides and, inexperienced as I was, I accepted everything without an impresario's help, regardless of whether it made sense or not.

One of the first people to engage me was Max Reinhardt. I did six evening performances at his Deutsches Theater and several matinées at his Kammerspiele. I had no idea how Max Reinhardt came to notice me so soon. Only later did I learn that I owed this to Dr Vollmoeller, with whom I had wagered that I would achieve my goal without a rich friend. I hadn't forgotten that and sent him two tickets for the Blüthner Hall, but heard nothing more from him. As he subsequently told me, he had taken Reinhardt along to my opening night, and Reinhardt had been so enthusiastic that he engaged me for his Deutsches Theater. This was the first time that a dancer had appeared as a sole performer at the most famous theatre in Germany.

Next I received numerous offers from agencies. I danced in a different city almost every evening. Frankfurt, Leipzig, Düsseldorf, Cologne, Dresden, Kiel and Stettin. And everywhere I experienced the same success with the public and the press. My mother accompanied me on all these trips. After just a few months I also received offers from abroad. Before the year ended I had danced at Zurich's Schauspielhaus, at Innsbruck's Municipal Theatre and at Prague's Central Concert Hall. It was intoxicating. Even in Zurich, among the restrained Swiss, I had to encore my first dance, a *Caucasian March* by Ippolitov. That hadn't happened in any other city. And in Prague I had to break off *Oriental Fairy Tale* and start again three times because the audience applauded my very first movements so enthusiastically that I couldn't hear the music.

The physical strain of dancing alone all evening was tremendous. During the intermission, bathed in sweat, I would lie on a couch, unable to speak, but my youth and my hard training helped me overcome all exhaustion. My programme consisted of ten dances, five in the first half, five in the second, and at some recitals my encores increased the total to fourteen.

I designed the costumes myself, and my mother made them. The backdrop of the stage was black, always ideal because nothing then diverts the audience's eyes from the dancer as she moves in the cones of light. I named one of my most successful creations *Dream Blossom*. Danced to music by Chopin, it was based on Anna Pavlova's *Dying Swan*; but, being barefoot, I did not dance on points. I wore a leotard of silver lamé under chiffon draperies shimmering in intense autumn colours, the effect intensified by reddish and violet spotlights. However, the dance in which I expressed myself most powerfully was Schubert's Unfinished Symphony.

Was I happy during that period? I believe I was, even though I didn't fully appreciate my unusual success. After my première in Berlin every single one of my recitals was sold out. Apart from expenses, I was paid five hundred to one thousand marks for each appearance and just after the end of inflation that was a huge amount of money. It was wonderful, and yet I wasn't entirely satisfied. I suffered from having broken off my studies prematurely. I would have preferred to continue to develop myself both technically and artistically; but it would have been very difficult to turn my back on this flush of triumphs.

I also received various film offers, but I did not even consider them; I wanted to live only for the dance. My passion involved sacrifices and I had to give up many things, especially a private life. The training was hard, and my performances demanded the unlimited commitment of all my energy. I certainly was interested in the screen, but the thought of interrupting my dance training for weeks or perhaps even for months was inconceivable. However, one film offer was very difficult to turn down. I was asked by the director Artur Robison to play the lead in the UFA film *Pietro the Corsair*. What appealed to me about it was that the part called for a dancer. Paul Richter was supposed to star opposite me. I couldn't resist temptation, so I had a screen test and they must have liked it: I stood before one of the UFA bigwigs, Erich Pommer, and he offered me thirty thousand marks, an astronomical sum in those days. I was unable to dismiss it right away, so I asked if I could have a few days to think it over. But after a difficult struggle with my conscience I declined Herr Pommer's offer and thereby turned down a unique opportunity.

GUEST APPEARANCE IN ZURICH

When I became twenty-one I was allowed to leave my parents' home and I rented a small apartment on Fasanenstrasse, near Kurfürstendamm. However, I maintained almost daily contact with my mother. This was the period in which we bought the fabrics for my costumes. She knew about my relationship with Otto Froitzheim and was rather unhappy about it, especially because of the great difference in our ages. She knew nothing, however, about his bohemian lifestyle. She was always my best friend, even if I could not tell her everything.

Once, in February 1924, when she was unable to accompany me on my tour, my friend Hertha replaced her. I was to perform in Zurich, Paris and London, and Harry Sokal, who still hadn't given up hope of conquering me, was going to meet me in Zurich. When I entered the hotel room I walked into a sea of flowers, his way of welcoming me.

I had two guest appearances schedules at Zurich's Schauspielhaus where I was to alternate with Tolstoy's play *The Living Corpse* starring Alexander Moissi, a marvellous actor with whom I quickly became friends. After spending an evening with him I returned to the hotel quite late. I had already undressed when I heard a knock at the door. It was Sokal asking to come in. I refused.

'I'm tired,' I said, 'and I don't want to let a man into my room so late at night.'

'Come into my room then. I won't do anything. I just want to be with you.' I almost pitied him and tried to calm him down.

'Be reasonable, Harry, I can't come to you. I would never be able to make you happy.'

He wept, shouted, threatened to shoot himself, and said so many dreadful things that I became quite afraid, threw my clothes on, left my room, and hurried downstairs to Hertha. We didn't dare leave her room until the next afternoon when, to our great relief, we learned that Sokal had left town. The concierge handed me a letter in which Sokal apologized for his conduct. He did not wish to lose my friendship and he promised never to harass me like that again. He wrote that he only wanted to make me happy, which was why he had arranged my dance recitals in Paris and London.

This was a shock; I had no idea that he had organized and probably also financed the offers from Paris and London. Profoundly disappointed, I dropped the letter. No other dancer had performed solo in Paris after World War I. I had been so proud, so ecstatic, to receive those invitations; and now this disappointment! When I picked up the letter and read it to the end I lost all desire to dance in Paris and London. Sokal continued: 'Since you don't have the proper clothes to appear in these big cities, I have ordered a suitable wardrobe to be sent to your hotel room. You can take whatever you like.'

At that moment my doorbell rang, and a messenger brought in two armfuls of fur coats. Hertha signed the receipt for two mink coats, an ermine, and a sporty leopard coat trimmed with black leather. They were all beautiful, but I was not tempted, for the whole thing felt like a slap in the face. It would have been wonderful dancing in Paris and London and owning such furs, but what would it cost me? I would have had to pretend love, put on an act. I could not and I would not.

'Hertha,' I said impulsively, 'let's take the next train back to Berlin.' I wrote a few comforting lines of farewell to Sokal, asking him to try and understand, and then Hertha and I fled from the hotel. In the train compartment I hugged Hertha, saying: 'You can't imagine how happy I feel after my decision. Now I'm free again.'

MY MISFORTUNE IN PRAGUE

My next recital took place in Prague, at a theatre that could hold three thousand spectators. Anna Pavlova was the only other dancer who had ever performed here, and tonight the house was sold out down to the last seat. My evening was a triumph, but perhaps my last. While making one of my leaps I felt a crack in my knee. The pain was so sharp that I could barely finish the dance.

It was still too early to assess how serious the accident had been, but the pain grew worse and worse. I had to muster every last ounce of willpower to make it through a few more performances; but then I had to stop. Cancelling all further appearances, I consulted several doctors.

First I went to the famous orthopaedic surgeon Professor Lexer in Freiburg. His diagnosis was that I had strained ligaments and no surgery was necessary. His prescription was simply to take a great deal of rest. Despairing, I went to see the equally renowned Professor Lange in Munich whose diagnosis was the same. Neither doctor could tell me how long I would have to rest from dancing, or whether the pain would eventually subside.

I began to doubt their diagnoses and consulted several other internationally recognized specialists in Holland and Zurich, but they couldn't help me either. Every doctor prescribed rest, rest, and more rest.

I was helpless. Retrospectively it sounds utterly incredible that in the year 1924, thirty years after the discovery of X-rays, my knee was not X-rayed, even though my dance career was totally dependent on the correct diagnosis of my condition. So I had no other choice but to wait and hope that the pain in my knee would go away.

During that miserable period, when I could walk only with the help of a stick, Otto Froitzheim looked after me. Although before the accident my tours had allowed me to meet him only very rarely, he insisted that we become officially engaged. He had introduced me to his mother who lived in Wiesbaden, and had begun preparations for our wedding. I agreed to everything, for he still had great power over me, and I couldn't contradict him to his face. But I was secretly determined not to marry him. I knew we could only be unhappy.

MOUNTAIN OF DESTINY

Then something unexpected happened which changed my life completely. It was June, just a few days after the Whitsuntide tennis tournament, in which Froitzheim had been as successful as ever. After spending every free hour with me, he had left town. Somewhat breathless, I stood alone on the elevated subway platform at Nollendorfplatz. I was going to a doctor, a friend of my father's, not an orthopaedic surgeon this time, but an outstanding physician whom I saw as my last chance. I waited impatiently for the train which wouldn't come and I was in such a state of nerves that my few minutes of waiting seemed like hours.

My eyes darted cross the advertising posters on the walls of the station. My thoughts were elsewhere, reviewing the recent past. Six months ago, in Munich, I had made my début at my first dance recital. Three days later came the second performance in Berlin. My memories whirled through my head like a merry-go-round. I felt as if I still couldn't grasp everything that had happened in just a few weeks. After my Berlin première I had been swept up on a wave of success, an unexpected, incomprehensible, unbelievable success which had made the unknown dance student famous overnight. Reality had left my most ambitious dreams far behind. Everything that I saw in that time, paintings, statues, all the music I heard, related purely to the dance. I felt destined to devote my life, today and forever, purely to dancing, which I had conquered after a gruelling struggle. Yet now this cruel stroke of fate!

Tired, exhausted, I stood waiting on the platform, gritting my teeth as my knee began to throb again. My eyes wandered over the colours of the posters on the opposite wall until abruptly they focused on something: a male figure clambering over a towering mountain chimney. Underneath, the poster said: 'Mountain of Destiny – a film about the Dolomites by Dr Arnold Fanck'. Still tormented by thoughts about my future, I stared as if hypnotized at the poster, at those steep walls of rock, at the man swinging from one wall to the next.

The train arrived at last and came to a halt between the poster and me. It was the train that I had been waiting for so impatiently, but I let it steam off again, to unblock my view of the poster. As if awakening from a trance, I saw the train vanish into the tunnel of Kleistrasse.

Mountain of Destiny was running at the Mozart Hall, on the other side of the square, so I forgot about going to the doctor and instead went out into the street. Several minutes later I was sitting in the cinema. During the era of the silent screen you could enter and leave a German film theatre at any time.

The very first images of mountains, clouds, alpine slopes and towering rock fascinated me. I was experiencing a world that I did not know, for I had never seen such mountains. I knew them only from postcards, on which they looked rigid and lifeless. But here, on the screen, they were alive, mysterious, and more entrancingly beautiful than I had ever dreamed mountains could be. As the film went on I became more and more spellbound. I was so excited that even before it ended I had made up my mind to get to know those mountains.

Filled with a new yearning, I left the theatre. That night it took me a long time to fall asleep as I debated with myself through the wakeful hours whether I was really enthralled by nature or by the artistry of the film. I dreamed of wild mountain crags, I saw myself running across talus slopes, and always, the leading performer in the film, the symbol of all the feelings aroused in me, seemed to be a steep tower of rock: the Guglia.

A DREAM COMES TRUE

Several weeks later I stood in front of those walls of rock for the first time. After viewing *Mountain of Destiny* every evening for a week, I couldn't stand Berlin any more. Since leaving home I had unfortunately seen little of my brother; but now he accompanied me on my trip to support me as I walked. i headed towards Lake Caro in the Dolomites, foolishly hoping to meet the performers and directors of *Mountain of Destiny*. I was not disappointed by reality. The red rock fortresses, the green mountain forests, the slender, light-green larches, and Lake Caro, shining like an iridescent butterfly amid the dark-green fir trees – the whole landscape brought back to mind all the long-forgotten fairy tales of my childhood.

I spent four weeks discovering an enchanted world; then, on the day of my depature, I met someone at the hotel. It was a meeting that I had greatly hoped for. In the lobby I had come upon a poster announcing that the motion picture *Mountain of Destiny* would be shown that evening at the hotel, and that the leading actor, Luis Trenker, would be present at the screening.

After dinner I nervously watched the film, though I knew almost every sequence of images by heart. Nevertheless, the effect on me was as powerful as it had been in Berlin. As soon as it had ended and the lights had gone up, I hobbled back to where the projector was set up and found, standing next to it, a man whom I recognized as the star of the movie.

'Are you Herr Trenker?' I asked somewhat diffidently. His eyes slid over my elegant clothes; then he nodded and said, 'Yes, I am.' My embarrassment evaporated. My enthusiasm for the film, the mountains, and the performers simply bubbled out of me.

'I'm going to be in your next picture,' I said self-confidently, as if this were the most obvious thing in the world.

Trenker eyed me in astonishment and began to laugh: 'Can you mountain-climb? An elegant little lady like you shouldn't be traipsing around mountains.'

'I'll learn how. I will definitely learn how; I can do it if I make up my mind to.' Again I felt a sharp pain in my knee. An ironic smile flitted across Trenker's face. Gesturing goodbye, he turned away.

I called after him: 'Where can I write to you?'

'Trenker, Bolzano, that's enough.'

Immediately after returning to Berlin I wrote him a letter, asking him to forward the enclosed photographs and newspaper clippings to Dr Fanck. I waited impatiently for a reply from Trenker or Dr Fanck; but I waited in vain. Günther Rahn, always a true friend, informed me that Dr Fanck would soon be coming to Berlin from Freiburg, his home town in the Black Forest, to negotiate with UFA about his new movie. Now I wouldn't give Gunther a moment's peace. He didn't know Dr Fanck personally, but a good friend of his, Dr Bader, had appeared in Fanck's sensational sports film *The Miracle of the Snowshoe*, and eventually Günther managed to arrange a meeting between me and Dr Fanck.

One sunny autumn day I entered the Rumpelmeyer pastry shop on Kurfürstendamm where I was supposed to meet the director. We had not agreed on any signs by which we were to recognize each other but, as my eyes darted around the room, I thought I recognized Dr Fanck, a middle-aged man sitting alone at a round table, stirring his coffee.

'Excuse me, are you Dr Fanck?' I asked, stepping towards him. He stood up and asked in return: 'Are you Fräulein Riefenstahl?' We sat down, and I opened the conversation. At first I was inhibited by Dr Fanck's timidity, but little by little I grew livelier, almost rapturous. Dr Fanck sat opposite me, mute, his eyes almost constantly lowered to his coffee cup. He asked me only one question: what kind of work did I do. Trenker had obviously not sent him my letter and my photographs. Dr Fanck knew nothing whatever about me, but hesitantly he began to talk. He was supposed to do a picture for UFA but had no subject as yet. I didn't dare ask him for a part; I simply told him that I would love to be involved in his next film, if only as a spectator.

As we said goodbye he asked me to send him pictures and reviews of my dance recitals, and I gave him my address. Now I stood alone again on Kurfürstendamm. It was seven in the evening and my feelings were in a ferment, for I sensed that something fateful was developing. After that meeting, the pain in my knee, which was still no better, forced me to seek immediate treatment. I had no time to lose. I thought of Dr Pribram, a young surgeon and assistant to the famous Professor Bier. I had met him at the tennis club, and discussed my complaints with him several times. He had promised to X-ray my knee, and as there was a telephone booth next to the pastry shop I tried to call him, but he was in the hospital and couldn't be disturbed. Hoping to catch him before he went home, I hurried there in a taxi and begged him to X-ray my knee that very evening. He refused, but I pleaded, wept, implored, until he finally gave in and, at long last, I found out for certain what was wrong. His diagnosis, based on the X-ray, was that a tear had caused a growth of cartilage the size of a walnut which could be removed only by surgery.

In those days, however, surgeons did not perform that type of operation, and in any case Dr Pribram and his superior were specialists in removing gallstones. But now that I finally knew what was really wrong with my knee, I was eager to have surgery as soon as possible. I can't remember how I did it, but I managed to talk him into operating the next morning. He had explained all the risks, but I dug in my heels. It would mean at least ten weeks in a cast, he said, and, even worse, my leg might remain stiff. But at this point I had no choice. It was kill or cure, for otherwise I had no chance of going to the mountains with Dr Fanck, to whom I had sent the promised photographs and reviews.

That same night I arrived at the hospital, and at eight the following morning I was lying on the operating table. As the ether began to take effect, visions danced behind my closed eyes: I saw images from *Mountain of Destiny*, precipices, clouds, and, over and over again, the Guglia, the needle of destiny. It suddenly loomed before me and then slowly retreated, faded, dissolved.

I sank into the deep sleep of unconsciousness.

THE HOLY MOUNTAIN

The third day after my operation, when the nurse announced that I had a visitor, I was incredulous, for no one knew where I was; and who should it be but Dr Fanck! He looked pale and exhausted and, as the nurse left us, he said: 'I brought you something. I spent the last three nights writing it for you.' And he handed me a bundle wrapped in paper. I unpacked it slowly. Inside was a manuscript, and on the first page I read:

The Holy Mountain

Written for the dancer Leni Riefenstahl

I cannot put into words my feelings at that moment. I laughed and wept with delight. How was it possible, I wondered, that a wish could come true so quickly, a wish that I had never even uttered.

I had to stay in bed for three months, three endless months, not knowing whether I would ever be able to move my leg as before, and during that time Dr Fanck went through the entire film with me, scene by scene. His faith and confidence were unshakable, as if there was no doubt that the operation would be a success. In the thirteenth week I was finally allowed to stand up. The physician and the nurse hovered near to help me take my first steps. And, I was in luck: I could bend and move my knee without pain. Dr Pribram was radiant and, as for me, my feelings of gratitude were beyond his imaginings and are still impossible to convey.

Meanwhile, the first snowflakes were falling in the streets. They slowly fluttered down, rather wet Berlin snow, utterly useless, but the only snow I had ever known. However, things were about to change for me very radically.

A change occurred in my private life too. I learned from tennis friends that Otto Froitzheim, my fiancé, was having an affair with a tennis colleague. They had shared a room for a whole week! Painful in a way as this news was, I saw it as a stroke of providence. I could finally break off all connection with that man – a decision for which I had previously been unable to muster enough courage – yet I still suffered at the thought of the final parting.

Froitzheim wouldn't hear of it. He kept sending me letters and flowers daily and one day he stood outside my door, asking if he could come in. I knew that if I let him enter, I would be at his mercy again, but I still found it hard not to open the door to him. He must have heard my sobs for he did not go away. He kept knocking and begging me in his gentle, seductive voice: 'Leni, let me in – Leni, Leni . . .' I did not yield, however, although it was the most painful decision I had ever made. After his footsteps faded I wept all night.

Fanck, who visited me daily, was surprised at my melancholy and my tear-stained face. He pestered me with questions, and finally I told him the whole story. When he gave me a comforting hug I sensed that, contrary to what I had hoped, his feelings for me were not paternal. I drew away from him and tactfully made it clear that he shouldn't embrace me.

Shortly before Christmas I was able to plan a trip to Freiburg, where Dr Fanck wanted to give me a screen-test at his studio. I was very nervous because my playing the female lead depended solely on the outcome of this test.

I made up my face as I was accustomed to do for my recitals, but I was relieved and rather pleased when Dr Fanck explained that his performers had to do without make-up, for he preferred to have natural faces, not film-star glamour. The next day, when I saw myself on the screen for the first time, I was devastated to find myself strange and ugly, a disappointment experienced by many film actors. The screen-test was repeated, but this time, to my surprise, it was successful. Dr Fanck explained why. The change was caused quite simply by different lighting and that was how I learned about the decisive role of light in any film. The right lighting can add years to a face, or take them off, even a face without make-up.

The director was satisfied with the new rushes and I received a contract with a star's salary of twenty thousand marks. In addition, UFA would have a pianist available for me throughout the shooting. As if that were not enough, they transported a piano to the mountain lodge (where he would be living for weeks) so that, while filming, I would not have to interrupt my dance training, which I had resumed. After my successful operation I had not even considered giving up my dance career. I wanted to act in this film purely for the sake of getting to know the mountain world, especially Dr Fanck's.

Three months were scheduled for the shooting.

TRENKER AND FANCK

Dr Fanck invited me to spend a few days in Freiburg until the arrival of his male lead, Luis Trenker, with whom we were to discuss the project in detail. Meanwhile, in the home of Dr Fanck's mother, I came to know his unusually rich and interesting library, from which almost no important poet, writer or philosopher was missing. It was an aesthetic delight just to hold the books, most of which were beautifully bound in leather.

Dr Fanck's sister was a very talented bookbinder. She later designed his film subtitles, a device that was crucial to the silent screen, since they made the plot intelligible to the audience. Aside from his library, Dr Fanck also had a large collection of original drawings and etchings by modern artists, chiefly those who pursued socialist themes like Käthe Kollwitz, George Grosz and others. Dr Fanck in fact became my intellectual mentor. As a film director he was an outsider, for his real profession was geology which he had studied at the University of Zurich at the same time as Lenin, whom he knew slightly. His passions, however, were mountains and photography.

In his childhood he had suffered so badly from asthma that, as he told me, he had had to learn how to walk over and over again. At eleven he was sent to Davos where, amazingly, he immediately became well. This had moved him so profoundly that he had made the mountains his world. He attended boarding-school in Zuoz, Switzerland, remaining there until his graduation and spending his free time skiing, climbing mountains and photographing. He was twenty-six at the outbreak of World War I and for the duration of the war worked for German military intelligence, at times with the famous German spy Mademoiselle Docteur.

After the war, in Freiburg, he and several friends started the Freiburg Mountain and Sports Film Company. Here he made his first documentaries, which ultimately became famous: *The Fight with the Mountain, The Miracle of the Snowshoe* and the latter's second part, *The Foxhunt in Engadin*. The novelty of these films was that they had no plot; yet the revolutionary impact of their fantastic photography and ingenious editing made them more thrilling than many feature films. Dr Fanck was a pioneer in his field. He was also the first screen director to use slow motion and fast motion as cinematic devices.

The gathering of storm clouds, the intensity of sunlight, and the shadows falling across precipices and mountain tops could first be seen only in his films, yet he had to fight hard for recognition. No distributor was willing to handle his early works, and no one in the business believed in his eventual success, for it was an article of faith that a suspenseful plot was a necessity for any film. But Dr Fanck had faith in his work. He rented auditoriums, screened his films himself, and eventually his great success proved him right. Suddenly, UFA itself offered him three hundred thousand marks for a mountain film – but only if it had a plot. The result was *The Holy Mountain*.

I grew closer and closer to Dr Fanck, but although I greatly respected and admired him as a brilliant film pioneer and intellectual, as a potential lover he had no effect on me. I was unsettled therefore by the fact that Fanck grew more deeply in love with me day by day. He showered me with presents, especially editions of Hölderlin and Nietzsche, woodcuts by Käthe Kollwitz, and graphics of contemporary artists such as Heinrich Zille and George Grosz. He wouldn't accept my rejection even though I remained adamant.

When Luis Trenker arrived he had already learned that I would be playing opposite him and, in contrast to his behaviour at the Lake Caro Hotel, he was pleasant, cheerful and witty. We took to each other as if we'd been friends for years. Dr Fanck brought a few special wines from the cellar, and we were supposed to try out each bottle in turn. This was risky for me, since I can hold only small amounts of liquor and I become sleepy after just one glass of beer. But I was so happy, so joyful to be with Fanck and Trenker and to be talking about our film that I exuberantly joined in the wine-tasting from beginning to end.

It was already past midnight when Fanck opened a bottle of champagne, and we pledged our friendship and drank to the success of our film. Then, when Fanck stepped out for a few moments, Trenker hugged and kissed me. It may have been the champagne, the delightful prospect of our future work, or just the atmosphere of goodwill, but all I know is that this was the first time that I ever lay in a man's arms under the spell of a happiness I had never known before. When Fanck returned and saw us embracing he looked thunderstruck, and his face was ashen as I pulled away from Trenker. What worried me most was that this incident might endanger our project. Would this destroy my dream of playing in *The Holy Mountain*? There was an instant of tension, then Trenker stood up and said: 'It's late. I'll see Leni back to her hotel.'

'No, I'll take Leni to the Zähringer Hof,' said Fanck.

Trenker, happy to withdraw, murmured as he shook my hand: 'I'll stop by to see you in the morning, before I head back to Bolzano.'

I would have given anything to leave with him, but I felt too sorry for Fanck. No sooner were we alone than he collapsed, sobbing and burying his face in his hands. From his incoherent, almost unintelligible words, I learned how deeply he cared for me, how much he had hoped and dreamed about me, and how terribly wounded he had been by seeing us embrace. I tried to comfort him while he caressed my hands, saying: 'You – my Diotima,' which was the name of my role in *The Holy Mountain*. Eventually he stood up, handed me my coat, and said: 'I'll take you back to your hotel; you've got to rest. Forgive me.'

Silently we walked through the streets in the cold night air until Fanck halted abruptly at a small bridge and, with a low cry, ran down the slope towards the river, apparently to jump in. I threw my arms around him, desperately trying to hold him back while I shouted for help, but Fanck was already up to his hips in water and I wasn't strong enough to pull him out. Then I heard footsteps and voices. Some men came running and hauled Fanck out of the water. He was shaking with cold, but offered no resistance.

We took him in a taxi to the Freiburg Hospital. He was feverish and delirious but they allowed me to stay with him until he fell asleep. Dejected and unspeakably sad, I went to my hotel. What would happen now? What was I to do? The film couldn't possibly be made. There were no answers to any of my questions and the situation gnawed at me through the few hours until dawn.

In the morning there was a knock at my door. When I opened it, Trenker stood there, and I let him in. For a moment we exchanged embarrassed looks; then he hugged me, and I began to sob as I told him what I had gone through with Fanck.

'He's crazy,' Trenker said angrily. 'He'll come round. I know him. He went mad once before while we were shooting *Mountain of Destiny*.'

'What about our film?'

Trenker shrugged. 'Let's wait,' he said, 'he'll calm down.' At that instant there was a loud knock at the door which I had carelessly forgotten to lock. The door flew open and Fanck entered the room. Raving like a madman, he jumped on Trenker who, being a stronger man, grabbed and held him. But Fanck was beyond control. He tore loose and a brutal fistfight began, growing more and more violent. I tried to pull them apart but it was no use. I ran to the window, opened it, and climbed on to the window-sill as if I were going to jump. My ploy worked. The men stopped fighting, Trenker lifted me down into his arms and Fanck stormed out of the room.

I boarded the next train back to Berlin without seeing Fanck, convinced that the project was destroyed. But my fear was groundless, for soon after my arrival flowers arrived from Fanck and letters from both men. My director seemed to have resigned himself to the fact that I revered him as an artist only. Nevertheless, one did not have to be a prophet to sense that there would be difficulties during the shooting which was scheduled to begin during early January in Switzerland.

Meanwhile Trenker and Schneeberger, the cameraman, prepared to give me skiing instruction. Skis and poles were selected for my first lesson at the Falzarego Pass where they showed me how to turn according to the prevailing style; I spent more time on the ground than on my feet. Finally, I was allowed to risk a small downhill run. I skiied down the flat slope, relishing the delight of skimming gently along – until I noticed that I was picking up speed. I tried to stop – but couldn't. The slope grew steeper, and I went faster and faster – until at last I came crashing down. Buried deep in the snow, I tried to burrow my way out, but Trenker and Schneeberger were already there, helping me. Alas, I felt sharp pains in my left foot and I couldn't stand. No doubt about it: my ankle was broken, a terrible misfortune. What would I say to Fanck? The most important and also most expensive shooting was to begin in Lenzerheide in just a few days. Fantastic ice palaces had been built on the frozen lake and had already devoured a third of the budget.

Trenker went down to Cortina to get a sledge. The night set in, and it was bitterly cold as Schneeberger carried me piggyback, wading through the snow. A storm blew up, my ankle bones ached; we kept breaking through the snow cover and plunging down into hidden hollows so that we finally gave up our descent. Frozen stiff, we waited for the sledge. I was sick with disappointment.

The next morning, in Cortina, my leg was put in a cast. Both ankle bones in my left foot were broken. It must be a record, I thought, five fractures within a single year. I was sure that when Fanck learned what had happened he would wipe the floor with me. Miserably we drove to the railway station, then boarded the train to Lenzerheide. In Chur we telephoned our director, but he didn't get the bad news until he picked us up at the station and, as I expected, his face turned deathly pale. The film had been written with me in mind. What would happen if I had to drop out? We realized the full scope of the disaster when we got to the lake. The ice palaces, some fifty feet high, were completed; the frost had been shaping them for weeks. The shooting should have started immediately, and here I was wearing a cast. We despaired.

The situation got even worse, for the weather warmed up, and within six days, four weeks of work melted away. Only the skeletons now stood on the still frozen lake. Then the next catastrophe started brewing. Hannes Schneider, who was also playing a major role in the film, skidded over an icy area while skiing, causing a qudruple fracture of his thigh. For weeks he hovered been life and death, so the scenes he was to appear in could not be shot. As if that were not enough, Ernst Petersen, a nephew of Dr Fanck's, dropped out. He was to play the second male lead but while doing a wild downhill run for the film, he plunged over a snowy rock right in front of the camera and, whirling fifty feet through the air, he crashed down, breaking his foot. Finally, Schneeberger, our cameraman, also had an accident. Granted a holiday by our series of calamities, Snowflea – Schneeberger's nickname because of his wild leaps – had gone to Kitzbühel in order to participate as a hot favourite in the Austrian ski championships. The snow conditions were atrocious: rocks, underbush, and sandy areas were sticking out on all slopes. One of the finest downhill skiers in Austria and Switzerland, he tried at a furious speed to leap over those obstacles but instead whirled through the air and fell, cracking his spine.

So our film camp turned into a field hospital. For weeks it was questionable whether The Holy Mountain would ever be made. UFA, we heard, wanted to abandon the project. We felt hopeless. For six weeks we hung around in Lenzerheide, unable to shoot a single frame while the Föhn blew more and more of the snow away. It was a bleak, treacherous winter.

Then the wind suddenly came from the north-east, and the frost returned. The temperature dropped, and the workers started rebuilding the ice sets, labouring day and night. The doctor took off my cast, and I could at least hobble.

The first scenes were shot – at night – on the lake. The spotlights flared up, illuminating the ice palaces, but it was so dreadfully cold that the cables were split apart and the sockets and cameras froze up. In the teeth of adversity, we slogged on. I admired Fanck's calm and self control during these troubles and I was fascinated by the work. Fanck gave me insights into his directorial method. He taught me that everything has to be equally well photographed: people, animals, clouds, water, ice. Every single shot, said Fanck, had to be above mere mediocrity; the most important thing was to avoid routine and to see everything with absolutely fresh eyes.

I was allowed to peer through the camera and to select views; I learned about negative and positive stock, different focal lengths, and the effects of lenses and colour filters. It occurred to me that film-making might be a possibility, a new thing of substance in my life. At the same time I realized that in a film the individual means nothing; everything worthwhile results from a collective effort. The best actor is ineffectual if the cameraman is worthless; he, in turn, depends on the best possible work in the printing laboratory, and the best development is useless if the camerawork is inadequate. If only one member of the team fails, then he imperils the whole project.

Two weeks later we were still working in Lenzerheide. Then we stopped, though *The Holy Mountain* was not yet completed. Fanck had chosen Sils Maria in the Engadine Valley as our next shooting site and we were billeted there in a small pension. It was already early April, all the hotels were shut and the village deserted. The stress of the last few months, when we constantly feared a cancellation of the film, had overshadowed our private problems. But they hadn't vanished. Harry Sokal often visited Lenzerheide, trying to approach me at every opportunity. I wanted to know whether he had actually changed professions (he had been a banker at the Austrian Loan Bank in Innsbruck) or whether his activity in the film industry was merely a guest appearance. He declared himself fascinated by film-making, which he thought was a thousand times more interesting than banking, but I had no doubt that his primary motive was to be near me.

Dr Fanck also kept trying to win my affection. Because we sensed how dreadfully he suffered, Trenker and I attempted to hide our feelings which by now amounted to more than friendship. All these things created tensions that were hard to endure, especially for me. I hoped that Trenker would liberate me from my dependence on Froitzheim, my ex-fiancé, whom, in a strange way, I still loved.

When Sokal and Trenker were out of town, Trenker for only a short time, Fanck's mood changed: he became more cheerful again. Now that there were only seven of us, and I was already part of the 'old staff', I quickly grew used to this new, simple life, and I enjoyed it. More than anything else I now had to learn how to ski seriously in Sils Maria. Fanck asked our cameraman to give me more skiing lessons. My ankle fractures had made me unsure of myself, and Schneeberger had to show a lot of patience; but I improved with every passing day.

Meanwhile, they photographed sequences that were full of atmosphere. I learned how much perseverance it takes to do nature shots. Usually the sun did not cooperate. It would peek out for a few seconds – and then, as soon as we tried to shoot, it would vanish again. This went on for hours, until we finally packed up the cameras and, with blue noses and ears, went back down the crusted slopes. But there were other days when we were lucky and produced marvellous footage.

Until then I had known the mountains only from below, but this soon changed. We were supposed to shoot at the Forno hut, and the route there from Maloja went through a very long valley. Our group was made up of five people: Fanck, Trenker, who had returned from Bolzano, Schneeberger, a carrier, and myself. During this, my first mountain hike, sealskins were attached to the bottoms of our skis, but I was soon worn out by the countless zigzags; the sweat was pouring from my forehead, and my legs grew heavier and heavier. Finally, we reached the last, steep slope, and then we were at the top. The panorama of an endlessly vast horizon was overwhelming. The shelter hut, a very neglected place, was just big enough for us to squeeze in together. We unpacked our bread and bacon, built a fire, and told mountain-climbing stories; then we all felt the same urge – to get to bed as soon as possible.

Since the hut was still too cold, and we had few blankets, we took off only our hiking boots. The carrier had to sleep on the bench but there was also a bunk. How would Fanck determine the sleeping arrangements? Normally two people would have slept on each bed but, as Fanck insisted on taking the upper bunk for himself, Trenker, Schneeberger, and I had to share the lower mattress. As a result the room was filled with nervous tension and I couldn't fall asleep, nor could Trenker. Now and then, when Fanck fitfully rolled about overhead, I could hear the creaking of the wooden boards. The first person to doze off was Schneeberger, but, lying between him and Trenker, I didn't dare move. After remaining awake for hours on end, however, I must have been overwhelmed at last by fatigue.

At one point I thought I heard noises, but I slept on until, waking up, I noticed that my head was on Schneeberger's arm, and he was fast asleep. I sat up and was surprised to discover that the space to my left was empty. I searched the room with my torch, but couldn't find Trenker anywhere. What had happened? Had I rolled over towards Schneeberger while sleeping, and could Trenker have misunderstood and grown jealous? Could he really have taken off? That would have been sheer madness. I woke Schneeberger and Fanck, who discovered that Trenker's knapsack and skis were missing. Fanck reproached himself because, just for the fun of it, he had tried to make Trenker jealous of Schneeberger during the past few days. I had often noticed a small streak of sado-masochism in Fanck. Now we were in an impossible predicament, but I didn't think I had done anything wrong. My feelings for Trenker were still undimmed, and the only thing I felt for Schneeberger was friendship. I was furious with Fanck, for if he hadn't provoked Trenker so maliciously none of this would have happened.

Grumpy and still freezing, we were drinking our morning coffee, when the door flew open, sunshine poured into our hut, and Trenker walked in, laughing and saying 'Hello!' It was a tremendous relief. Trenker appeared to be in high spirits. He teased Fanck, calling to him: 'You really thought I'd never come back, didn't you? I really fooled you!'

Trenker ignored me, but Fanck had only one thought in mind: to get the scene with me and Trenker finished as fast as possible. The shooting was completed by sunset, and we prepared for our descent.

Trenker skied down ahead of us. While Schneeberger and Fanck packed the camera equipment and the knapsacks, a storm blew up. For the first time I witnessed how quickly and radically mountain weather can change. The sun was hardly visible and now an icy blizzard was lashing the cabin. There was no possibility of skiing down. The blizzard had probably overtaken Trenker during his descent but, as an experienced alpinist, he was certain to find his way down. Fanck tried to cheer us up with his black humour when we realized we would have to spend another night in the hut. At least the sleeping arrangements were no longer a problem. I slept below, Fanck and Schneeberger above, while the blizzard ranged more and more fiercely. After two days and two nights our food and wood were running out. We were not equipped for a long stay and, even though we ate very little, we eventually consumed the last crumb of bread.

I know that I alone had prevented them from descending. If it hadn't been for me, the men would have skied down long ago. My insecurity on skis was the reason why the four of us had had to remain in the hut. But they could no longer be so considerate. We got ready to make a start, for there was no other possibility. Fanck and the carrier went on ahead, and Snowflea, the best skier, was detailed to take care of me. Our meeting-point would be Maloja.

The two figures in front of us vanished within a few seconds, swallowed up by the blizzard. Schneeberger and I stood outside the door of the hut. The storm swept through our clothes, and our hair and eyelashes were instantly coated with ice. Snowflea took my arm, and we glided out into the unknown. We could see nothing, and I couldn't believe we would ever find the way.

'Keep your legs together!' Snowflea shouted. I realized we were sliding over snowhills which might become avalanches. Then the ground under our feet levelled out. All at once I felt as if I were standing still. That same instant I soared headfirst at a furious speed, turned a few somersaults and landed next to a boulder. I felt snow shifting across my face, and my body started sliding with a mass of snow. 'Avalanche!' I shrieked as loudly as I could. But luckily it was only a brief snowslide which buried me up to my neck. I could just make out a shadow – Schneeberger – flitting nearby and heading towards me. He dug me out and rubbed my hands warm. But now I really was terrified and I didn't want to go on. I was afraid of avalanches and boulders, and especially of another fractured leg. I wanted to go back to the hut. But Snowflea grabbed my arm and we sped on down the glacier, often nearly grazing the rocks which loomed up out of the darkness only at the last moment. I hung in Schneeberger's arms like a rag doll until, as we came to a forest, the raging of the storm abated and visibility improved.

A few more meadows and roads later we arrived in Maloja to find that Trenker had already left on the train.

DANCE OR MOVIES

Our next destination was Interlaken. We were supposed to shoot the springtime scenes there and, in contrast to the blizzards at the Forno shelter, the meadows here were bright with narcissus.

But, once again, we encountered the bad luck that had been dogging our picture. The shooting had to be interrupted because Dr Fanck was ordered to report to UFA in Berlin. The project was to be cancelled because, as a result of all the accidents, the winter shooting was incomplete, and they didn't care to risk a second winter in the high mountains. I stayed on in Interlaken with Snowflea and Benitz, our young assistant cameraman.

Dejected, we watched day by day as the blossom fell from the trees. Not only had we lost half a winter, but now the spring was passing us by. I resolved to act on my own, since we still had two thousand feet of stock and an empty till. I pawned my jewels, took charge, and did my best to replace Dr Fanck. My first job as a screen director!

In Les Avants, where we found the most beautiful narcissus meadows, we shot all the scenes within three days and, expecting a rebuke, we nervously dispatched the rushes to Berlin. Instead we received a wire from Fanck: 'Congratulations! UFA wild about rushes. Film to be completed.' We cheered.

The money arrived to pay our hotel bills, and we returned to Freiburg. Here I rented a tiny garret and went to the printing laboratory every day. In a small screening room Fanck checked the footage he had shot during the past five months, and it was there that I learned about developing and printing. In those days rushes were developed frame by frame, which had the advantage that each cut could be treated individually. In this way a director could achieve first-class results as well as saving underexposed or overexposed scenes. Fanck taught me how to edit a film, a job that enthralled me. It is an unbelievably fascinating creative process. At twenty-three I was already making great progress in hitherto unknown territory.

Although I appeared totally absorbed in my new profession, a painful struggle was raging inside me. Should I give up dancing? The thought was unendurable. When I took the film part I had no intention whatsoever of abandoning the dance; my film work was to last three months at most and I had been willing to sacrifice that much time; but now, six months had already elapsed, and no end to the shooting seemed imminent. What was I to do? Was there any possibility of pursuing both careers? My situation looked almost hopeless. The original plan to practise dancing in shelter huts turned out to be naïve and impracticable. It was too strenuous climbing mountains and then training as a dancer every day.

I asked Herr Klamt, my pianist, who had accompanied me at all my recitals, to come to Freiburg; and here I resumed my training. My first practice sessions after my knee operation and a hiatus of one year were very difficult; I had to grit my teeth and to get through them; yet no sooner had I overcome the worst than I was called back to the film.

The dance sequences were to be shot in Helgoland, under the steep rocky coastline where the surf is strongest. These dances were meant to be the opening scenes of the film, a romantic idea favoured by Fanck, and I was to choregraph the *Dance to the Sea* to the music of Beethoven's Fifth Symphony. Fanck wanted the waves and breakers to be precisely synchronized to the dancer's movements, which could be done by using appropriate cuts and slow motion. To fit the dancing to the rhythm of the music, a violinist was lowered down the cliff by a rope, but it was horribly difficult dancing on the slippery rocks in that wild surf. Film-making was a perilous business in an era that did not yet have soundtracks. At times the roar of the surf was so loud that I could hear only occasional notes of music, and so powerful that it knocked me into the ocean several times.

The location filming in Helgoland was followed by studio shooting in Berlin-Babelsberg. Fritz Lang was there at the same time, filming *Metropolis* with Brigitte Helm; and Murnau was directing his famous *Faust*, with Gosta Ekman in the title role, Camilla Horn as Gretchen, and Emil Jannings as Mephisto. These were silent pictures which are both still internationally admired today. Acting in the studio was a lot less difficult than competing with the sea, and it was easier to concentrate in closed rooms.

That autumn came the shooting in Zermatt, probably the most beautiful mountain landscape in all of Europe. Overwhelmed, I gazed up at the peaks of the Matterhorn, Monte Rosa and Weisshorn and felt myself drawn to them irresistibly. Some day, I knew, I would stand on such mountain tops.

Ever since Trenker had left the Forno hut that night a coolness had developed between us; a gap which grew deeper and deeper. At the start of our acquaintanceship I had, above all, admired Trenker the actor in his role, the hero of the mountains, but I knew too little about his real character. It was only when he returned to the Forno hut, trying so hard to disguise his feelings, that I sensed another Trenker existed, and I become more critical of him. During the shooting I noticed several things that annoyed me. More than anything else I was bothered by his colossal ambition. He could easily fly off the handle if he thought that Fanck had shot a few more feet of me than of him and his jealousy of the bond between Fanck and me grew more and more intense. I realized that my feelings for him had never gone very deep and were fading fast.

When the shooting in Zermatt was done, I immediately resumed my dance training, but I was on the horns of a dilemma. I saw dance as the fulfilment of my life, yet I had always been fascinated by the cinema. Nevertheless, I tried to go back to dancing.

After an interval of one and a half years I was back on stage again and my first recital took place at Düsseldorf's Schauspielhaus; then I performed at Frankfurt's Schauspielhaus, again at the Deutsches Theater in Berlin, followed by appearances in Dresden, Leipzig, Kassel and Cologne. I was successful, but I sensed that I had made no progress. The interruption had been too lengthy. However, my dancing grew more relaxed and, from evening to evening, more supple; yet just as I was beginning to feel I could make it again, I was summoned back to the film, and had to break off my tour and return to the mountains. For the first time I didn't want to have anything more to do with the film, but I could neither break my contract nor leave Dr Fanck in the lurch. He still felt very deeply for me, though he kept trying to disguise his emotions with sarcastic humour, usually in the form of poems which he wrote on small slips of paper, handing them to me almost daily.

BURIED BY AVALANCHES

In January 1926 – the second winter of the film – we worked on the Feldberg (the highest point in the Black Forest) but the weather was too awful and the work advanced at an excruciatingly slow pace. Two, even three weeks dragged by, and we couldn't complete a single foot. Either the sun didn't shine, or else it blazed so intensely that the snow became heavy, not powdery enough for the camera. It is hard to describe what strenuous lengths we went to for our outdoor shooting. We used no gimmickry, and any sensational events were usually a lot more dangerous in reality than they looked on the screen.

For example, the script called for a scene in which the female lead is buried by an avalanche *en route* to the cabin. Schneeberger and I went alone to Zürs on the Arlberg, where we hoped to shoot on Flexen Pass (its tunnel had not yet been built). It had been snowing non-stop for five days and the Flexen Pass was blocked so that no sleigh, no horse, no human being could get through, and there was an extreme danger of avalanches. That was precisely what we needed, but we couldn't talk anyone into accompanying us. The mountain guides thought we were crazy; yet it was already April and the snow could get wet any day, so we decided to do it on our own. Schneeberger took the camera and the tripod, while I carried the suitcases containing the optics. The blizzard was so awful that we could not even see thirty feet ahead. Slowly we struggled against the storm; small and large avalanches kept rolling down from the heights. We had to locate a suitable place and find cover under overhanging boulders so that we wouldn't be swept into the chasm. The camera was set up, and we waited and froze. Two hours went by, and still not even the tiniest snowslide. Our feet were numb, our noses were running, our eyelashes were coated with ice. At last we heard a roaring overhead and Snowflea leaped over to the camera, I to the prepared place, where my hands could cling to the rock. Suddenly all was darkness, I felt the snow piling up on me, solid and heavy – I was buried! Now I really was afraid. I felt my heart hammering as I tried to push my way out with my arms, head and shoulders. Then I felt Snowflea's hands digging above me. I could breathe again.

'We got terrific shots,' he said. 'Fanck is going to be really excited.'

I could scarcely listen; I was still too dazed. Worst of all was the realization that the scene would have to be repeated a number of times, since Fanck wanted everything in distant shots, closer shots, and closeups. I went on strike, for my body was a lump of ice. Later on, I was furious when I read in several newspapers: 'The avalanche shots of the leading actress were inauthentic. They should have been filmed in the mountains and not in the studio.'

THE MIRACLE CURE IN ST ANTON

The next assignment Fanck had for me was, together with Hannes Schneider and several skiers, to shoot torchlight scenes in a snowy forest, and to do the directing myself since Fanck could not come to St Anton.

We found the right location at a creek and set up the camera on a small bridge. Schneeberger had to join the cast since we didn't have enough skiers, so this left me to crank the camera myself; as it was already twilight, each performer, including a little boy from the village who was standing right next to me, held a magnesium torch. In the torchlight the snowy fir trees glittered in a thousand reflections; it was a beautiful scene and I began to shoot. All at once I saw a harsh burst of light which cracked and flashed. The torch held by the little boy had exploded and I could hear him screaming as I felt my own face burning. I tried to put out the flames with my left hand and keep cranking the camera with my right until the scene was done; only then did I see that the boy had vanished. I left the camera and, with my face stinging, I dashed into the house and up the stairs to find a mirror. One half of my face was black, the skin tattered and dangling and my brows and lashes were scorched. My hair, however, protected by a leather cap was only partly singed.

Then I looked for the child. He lay in bed in a neighbour's house with burns all over his body and was screaming so dreadfully that I forgot my own pain. The doctor came, but he couldn't help. Then I witnessed a bizarre scene. The peasants brought a little old woman who sat down on the boy's bed and breathed on him. Just a few minutes later, the boy quietened down, stretched out and calmly fell asleep. I was speechless, for I had never believed in miracle cures.

Now I felt my own pain and I ran outdoors to cool the burns with snow which only increased the pain. In my despair I too consulted the old woman who lived in an ancient farmhouse a short distance from St Anton. She didn't even want to open the door but I begged and begged until she finally let me in; then she murmured something to herself and as her face came very close to mine, I could feel her breath as cool as ice and my pain vanished. I can imagine that this sounds incredible. The dermatologist whom I consulted in Innsbruck the next day didn't believe me either. He said I had a third-degree burn, and scars would remain on my face. Had his diagnosis been correct, my film career would have been over, but no scars remained. There is no scientific explanation for this entire incident.

A FRIENDSHIP CRUMBLES

Shortly before the première of *The Holy Mountain*, Fanck and Trenker had another serious argument. The relationships between the two men and between Trenker and me were still terribly strained.

On 14 December 1926, at the première of *The Holy Mountain*, we all sat in the box at the UFA Zoo Palace. Before the screening I had danced to Schubert's Unfinished Symphony. And then I saw the film on a huge screen for the first time. I was not the only one to be so deeply affected, for the audience was enthralled; they kept applauding throughout, and afterwards we took innumerable bows on stage. Outwardly no one could sense our conflicts. But I had no more doubts: my friendship with Trenker was at an end.

The Holy Mountain was a huge success for all of us. The day after the première my telephone rang incessantly, and I received innumerable congratulations and flowers. Dr Servaes, a well-known Berlin theatre critic, was one of those who rang me up. He indignantly told me about a press conference at which Trenker had made very derogatory remarks about me and Fanck. He had descended to vulgar abuse of me, calling me 'a nanny-goat' and informing the journalists that I had such a negative influence on Fanck that his artistic faculties suffered. According to Dr Servaes, Trenker had looked so artless and genuine that some of the critics were more than willing to believe him. I was speechless. Then, when Dr Servaes read me a review of our film by Dr Roland Schacht, one of the most influential film crticis in Berlin, I was even more alarmed. His review detailed everything about me that Trenker had so venomously spouted at the press conference. Not even the personal insults were missing.

I was furious. I hadn't thought Trenker capable of so much meanness, and Fanck too was beside himself, especially when this review reached UFA. Although most of the journalists wrote in praise, and the film was a hit, this hostile critique by a man of Dr Schacht's reputation had made the UFA people very suspicious of Fanck and myself. In fact UFA badly wanted to break their new contract with Fanck, or at least they hoped to reduce the risk of doing any further expensive projects with him. The budget for *A Winter's Tale* was as high as *Metropolis*, the most expensive film that UFA had ever made. In the end they asked Fanck to pen a new script, for a cheaper production, which would cost at most half as much.

After recovering from the initial shock and much comforted by record box-office returns for *The Holy Mountain*, Fanck wrote a new screenplay in an astonishingly short time. The title was *The Great Leap*, a comedy set in the mountains, and quite unlike *A Winter's Tale*. I was supposed to play a goatherd and, since humour was one of the positive sides of my director's character, he planned to have me accompanied by a little nanny-goat – as a 'homage' to Dr Schacht, who had seen fit to repeat Trenker's gross description of me.

THE GREAT LEAP

Before letting Dr Fanck know whether or not I would play the female lead in his new picture, I had to make my decision once and for all: was it to be film-making? Finally I chose motion pictures and signed the contract. What tipped the balance was that my accident and the long hiatus had set my dancing back too far and at the age of twenty-four I felt I was too old to make up for the two years lost.

While Fanck was making the preparations for his film I rented a three-room flat in a new building in Berlin-Wilmersdorf. It was on the sixth storey, and it had a penthouse as well as a large studio where I could if I wished practise dance routines. I was overjoyed to have my own flat at last. But my happiness was dimmed by the fact that Harry Sokal rented the other flat on the same floor. It was a signal that he still hadn't given up on me. Furthermore, he liked film-making so much that he had started his own company and produced various successful pictures. His best-known films were *The Golem* with Paul Wegener and *The Student from Prague* with

Dagny Servaes, Werner Krauss and Conrad Veidt, all of them artists of stature.

Fanck's cameraman Schneeberger was asked to star in *The Great Leap*; he wouldn't hear of it, but his resistance was useless. No one else could have performed the acrobatic feats on skis that Fanck had conceived for his male lead. Snowflea had to sacrifice himself for our movie.

And it was a sacrifice in the truest sense of the word. Wearing an inflated rubber suit, as demanded by the comic role, he had to ski the most difficult routes, leap over precipitous slopes and cabins, while pretending that he couldn't ski at all. Stripping off his rubber suit after the daily shooting, he gave off steam like a race horse. Thin already, he gradually lost more than twenty pounds.

Despite the fierce tensions between Fanck and Trenker, they managed to work together again, one last time. I had asked Fanck to give Trenker at least some kind of part after all and as Fanck didn't hold grudges, he had Trenker play a peasant lad; typecasting in my opinion.

Meanwhile Fanck had moved house from Freiburg to Berlin, where he rented a beautiful villa on Kaiserdamm with a garden, just a few minutes from my flat. He installed an editing room in his home, completely different from any I had ever known. The walls were lined with racks containing huge, illuminated opal glass panes, through which one could comfortably view the many film strips hanging from them. Later on I took over this system which helped me greatly when I came to edit my own films.

One day Fanck told me to go to the Dolomites with Snowflea – a superb climber as well as skier – to be trained in mountain-climbing. I greatly looked forward to this. I had been good friends with Snowflea for a long time, and after we had begun shooting in Stuben our friendship had turned into love. We were virtually inseparable and Fanck and Sokal had to resign themselves to the situation. Nevertheless Fanck still sent me love letters, and he even gave me a grand piano for my dance studio. It was as if neither Fanck nor Sokal believed that Schneeberger and I would remain together for long. As it turned out, they were mistaken.

When we said goodbye to Fanck, he told me: 'Remember, you have to learn to climb barefoot, as your part demands.' This was a new and unusual task given by our director, who, contrary to his normally gentle nature, now brooked no contradiction.

As the starting-point for our climbing practice we picked the Sella Pass shelter hut. Stone blocks of all sizes lay in front of the Langkofel but I began to climb with enthusiasm; not only was climbing lots of fun, but I found it very easy, as if I had been doing it for years. In these early stages I wore shoes. My dance training had developed my sense of balance, and dancing on points had strengthened my toes. Snowflea was so satisfied with my progress that he suggested we try some real mountain-climbing, and selected the Vajolette Towers.

As I stood before those rocks I thought I could never scale the lofty vertical walls. The view from below was terrifying, but Snowflea didn't give me much time to reflect. He tied a rope around my waist, and several minutes later I was ascending the wall. At first I avoided glancing down, but the rock allowed a firm grip, and the whole thing wasn't as difficult as I had imagined.

I ascended further and further, losing all fear as we climbed slowly and steadily. At last we rested on a narrow ledge and I looked down for the first time. I didn't get dizzy, but I didn't care to peer down for long either. Then on we climbed, through small chimneys and across tiny ledges. We reached the top fairly soon, and I stood, delighted, on my first peak. It was a marvellous feeling to be so free, so remote from the world, and so near the clouds. More climbs followed, increasingly difficult ones, and sometimes, while climbing, I truly believed I couldn't go on. But once at the top I looked forward to the next climb. I learned to scale overhangs, to insert and extract hooks and to traverse steep walls. I particularly enjoyed being lowered by a rope.

Now we had to start my barefoot training; not much fun, for my soles could never get used to these piercing Dolomite rocks. I spent weeks walking barefoot over the rocks and climbing daily without shoes. Later on, however, once the shooting began, my feet bled anyway. It was a terrible grind and, in my opinion, quite unnecessary, but Fanck remained adamant. I was very glad when this shooting was over.

There were further unpleasant days, when we had to spend hours acting in icy mountain brooks. Fanck also wanted me to swim across Lake Caro, dressed only in a thin shirt, when the temperature was just a few degrees above freezing – simply because our director wanted to include the romantic, shimmering green lake in his film.

Fascinating and enthralling as I found my work in the mountains with Fanck, it did not fulfil me as an artist. The long production schedule of these difficult films and the small number of my scenes, shot at widely spaced intervals, could not challenge me artistically. When I was a dancer every day was full, not only with practice, but also with choreographing new dances. My director was aware of my frustration and tried to get me other film parts; but he didn't manage to do so, and neither did I, for we heard the same thing on all sides: Riefenstahl is a mountain-climber and a dancer. I suffered from being typecast. A difficult period began for me during which I even attempted to write screenplays.

My first script was titled *Maria*, a love story with a tragic ending. Actually I had written it for myself, showing it to no one, not even Snowflea, with whom I was now living very happily. My love for him had developed slowly, but then all the more intensely, becoming so powerful that we couldn't stay apart. Although Schneeberger was seven years my senior, he liked being led. He was the passive partner, I the active one, yet our life together was harmonious for we both loved nature and sports, and above all our work. We were not the sort of people who liked parties or social obligations and were happiest when we could be alone together.

ABEL GANCE

The world of the cinema expanded my horizons and I met many exciting people, especially directors and cameramen such as Lupu Pick, G.W. Pabst and, above all, Abel Gance. He was a wonderful film-maker and also a likeable man. In contrast with some of his famous colleagues he was never smug or arrogant; yet he had achieved a sensational triumph with his *Napoleon*, a film lasting several hours. It made him famous not only because of its new technique (this was the first time that a film was shot by three cameras and shown by three projectors), but also because of its artistic pioneering. I had witnessed his triumph at the UFA Palace and celebrated it with him. Sixty years later his film has enthralled a whole new generation of filmgoers, proving that its director is one of the great men in screen history. We owe the current version of *Napoleon* to the British director Kevin Brownlow, an admirer of Abel Gance: he discovered the footage, which had been lost for decades, and restored it, sequence by sequence.

Shortly before Abel Gance died in Paris at the age of ninety, Kevin Brownlow was able to screen the new print of *Napoleon* for him. Abel Gance heard the ovations at the New York première on the telephone shortly before he died.

ERICH MARIA REMARQUE

Around this time I met Erich Maria Remarque, as yet unknown as a writer. One day he rang my doorbell, introducing himself as a journalist who wanted to have a photograph of me for *Scherl-Magazin*. Shortly afterwards I also met Frau Remarque. I saw her for the first time at a première in the Gloria Palace on Kurfürstendamm, and was greatly impressed by her looks. She was not only beautiful, but also very intelligent. Tall, slender as a fashion model, and strikingly dressed, she had a sphinx-like quality, similar to that of the vamp roles later played by Marlene Dietrich. I believe that many men envied Remarque his wife. She liked me, and we became friends.

Whenever she came to see me, and she visited often, she always had the manuscript of a novel that her husband had written. Since he was overburdened, she said, she was working on it for him, revising it and also completing the final chapter. I wasn't surprised, for she was very gifted. It was only later, when this book became world-famous as *All Quiet on the Western Front*, that I recalled the period when Frau Remarque was working on it so intensively. Remarque would often pick her up at my flat, and I had the impression that they had a good marriage, but I soon became witness to a terrible drama.

Remarque wanted to meet a good friend of mine, Walter Ruttmann, a film director, so I promised to arrange a pleasant evening at my home. Schneeberger was on location, and so there were just the four of us. I was surprised when I greeted Frau Remarque, for she was wearing an elegant evening gown, as if she were going to a gala. She looked wonderful with her red curls, held in place by jewelled combs, and an almost pure white complexion. She appealed not only to me and to her husband, but also, and most of all, to Walter Ruttmann – as soon became apparent.

At first it was a lively and cheerful evening. We drank wine and champagne, and, perhaps as a result, Frau Remarque behaved so seductively that she completely turned Ruttmann's head. At first I thought it was only harmless flirting, but as the mood grew more animated, Ruttman and Frau Remarque got up, leaving me alone with her husband. They retreated to a dimly lit corner while I remained with Remarque, who tried to drown his jealousy in liquor. Ruttmann and Frau Remarque behaved as if they were alone and I became more and more distressed, not knowing what to do in this embarrassing situation. Remarque sat on the couch with downcast eyes, his head drooping sadly, and I felt so very sorry for him. All at once Frau Remarque and Ruttmann were standing in front of us. 'You've been drinking too much,' she said accusingly, 'Herr Ruttmann is taking me home. I'll see you later.'

I squeezed poor Remarque's hands, then, followed by the other two, I went to the lift and saw them down to the front door. As we said goodnight, I pleaded: 'Don't make your husband suffer so much,' but she merely smiled and blew me a kiss. I did not shake Ruttmann's hand for I considered his

behaviour as awful as hers, if not worse. When I went back upstairs I found a
sobbing man whom I tried in vain to comfort. 'I love my wife, I love her
madly. I can't lose her, I can't live without her.' He kept repeating these
words, his whole body shaking, and when I offered to call a taxi, he refused;
so I stayed up with him until dawn. In the morning light he looked a human
wreck but he didn't resist when I put him in a cab, utterly exhausted. As
with Fanck I had again witnessed a man reduced to a pitiful state. Both men
were alike in being unusually gifted, yet hypersensitive, vulnerable.

Two days later Remarque called me. His voice sounded hoarse and
agitated: 'Leni, is my wife there? Have you seen her, has she called you?'
Barely waiting for me to say no, he shouted into the telephone: 'She hasn't
come home, I can't find her anywhere.' Then he hung up.

That evening he came to my flat and wept without restraint, drinking one
cognac after another. He kept answering me that his marriage had been
unruffled, indeed very happy, until this meeting with Ruttmann, and he was
at a loss to understand his wife's conduct. He blamed it on some spell, but
was certain she'd come back; and of course, he would forgive her
completely, so long as she came back. However, she didn't come back. Nor
did she get in touch with me. I tried for some time to call Ruttmann, but no
one answered the telephone.

For almost two weeks a desperate Remarque came to my place almost
every day. Then, unexpectedly, he told me he couldn't stand being in Berlin
any more and was going to a spa; he simply had to get away. He never got in
touch with me again, nor did I hear from his wife for many years. Some time
after Remarque's last visit – it may have been a few weeks later – I read a
newspaper report that Frau Ruttmann had killed herself by jumping out of a
window.

Eventually I learned about Remarque's great triumphs from the press. *All
Quiet on the Western Front* came out by the end of the following year, in
November 1928. The film version, produced in America, was shown in
Germany in 1930, triggering such widespread demonstrations that, as I
learned, several countries stopped showing the film by December of that
same year.

When I attended the première in Berlin's Mozart Cinema on Nollendorfplatz, I saw the methods used to disrupt the showings. Quite suddenly
the theatre was ringing with screams so that at first I thought a fire had
started. Panic broke out and girls and women were standing on their seats,
shrieking. The film was halted, and it was only when I was out on the street
again that I learned from the bystanders that a certain Dr Goebbels, whose

name I had never heard before, had caused the pandemonium by releasing hundreds of white mice at the start of the movie.

According to the newspapers, Remarque moved to Switzerland in 1929, then emigrated to the United States in 1939. He died in Locarno, Switzerland, on 25 September 1970.

It may have been during the seventies that Frau Remarque telephoned me in Munich. I was just about to leave for Africa, and we were both sorry that we couldn't get together again.

BERLIN – A METROPOLIS

In Berlin one could bump into all the film and theatre VIPs. The city vibrated with life. There were parties, premières and invitations almost every day. Once a week artists got together in the home of Betty Stern, near Kurfürstendamm. Her rooms were so crowded that you couldn't find a place to sit down and it was there that I first met Elisabeth Bergner and her husband Paul Czinner. Bergner was loved and honoured in Berlin as was no other actress, except perhaps Käthe Dorsch. Bergner was a true sorceress. No one who saw her playing Shaw's *Saint Joan*, directed by Max Reinhardt at the Deutsches Theater, will ever forget her. At Betty Stern's home I also met the Russian director Tairov, who, like Max Reinhardt and Dr Fanck, wanted me to play the title role in a film version of Kleist's *Penthesilea*. But this was still the era of the silent screen, and I couldn't imagine this play without Kleist's language. Along with Bergner I also met other great stars, for instance Maria Orska, who had enjoyed such a great triumph in Wedekind's *Lulu*, as well as Fritzi Massari and her husband Max Pallenberg, both incomparable in their sparkling operettas.

I was particularly charmed by Josephine Baker's performance at the Nelson Theater on Kurfürstendamm, where she did her banana dance, which later became so famous; the Berliners lionized the young, coffee-brown beauty. The immortal Anna Pavlova also came to Berlin; I had the good fortune not only to see her as the dying swan, but I also met her in person – the greatest of all ballerinas – at the Berlin Press Ball. She looked so frail and delicate that I scarcely dared to touch her hand.

During this period I saw the film that completely overshadowed all previous films: Sergei M. Eisenstein's *Potemkin*. When I left the theatre on Kurfürstendamm I was dazed. The effect was tremendous, its cast and the photography quite revolutionary. For the first time I realized that a film could be a work of art.

THE WHITE HELL OF PIZ PALÜ

Dr Fanck was now working on a new script, inspired by a newspaper version of a mountain drama based on a true story. He wrote day and night. Once again Harry Sokal was to produce it, and I was to be cast in a good part. Although I would much rather have worked with a feature film director, I was glad to be in a picture again. Sokal, aware of my predicament, tried to take financial advantage of me by offering a fee amounting to only ten per cent of what I had received for any previous role. For two thousand marks I was suppposed to be available for seven months, five of them for the most difficult and perilous shooting in ice and snow! Earlier I had been paid twenty thousand marks per film, but Sokal wanted to get even with me, for he had never forgiven me for rejecting him as a lover and possible husband. Yet he did not want to do without my participation in the project and he knew he wouldn't find anyone else who could ski and climb and play those dangerous scenes without a stand-in. With a sense of outrage I turned down his offer.

During this period I met G.W. Pabst, a film-maker whom I greatly admired and whose films I had seen several times. We had an instant rapport and it became my great desire to appear in one of his pictures. Suddenly I had a rather crazy idea. If I could talk Sokal and Fanck into allowing Pabst to direct the acting scenes of their film while Fanck shot the outdoor and sports sequences, the combination would be fabulous. Fanck was unbeatable as a director of nature films, but he paid too little attention to the performers. Pabst respected Dr Fanck and was willing to accept my idea, so I went ahead and in fact the matter was less difficult than I had imagined. Fanck was still ready to agree to anything I wanted, and Sokal was smart enough to see that this collaboration would greatly boost the project, which was to be titled *The White Hell of Piz Palü*. Since I refused to play the role for two thousand marks, Sokal raised my fee to four thousand, but at Fanck's expense for he subtracted these extra two thousand marks from Fanck's salary. No one told me and I didn't find out about it until much later, from Fanck himself.

A chance meeting helped me to add something sensational to the project. One day I was standing in pouring rain, waiting for a cab outside the film studio on Cicerostrasse, near Kurfürstendamm, when a man hurried forward and offered me his umbrella.

'Are you Fräulein Riefenstahl?'

'Yes, and who are you?' I gave him a querying look.

'I am Ernst Udet,' he said almost shyly. 'May I drive you home?'

'How very nice of you, I'd love it.' I was overjoyed, for Ernst Udet was famous. Who didn't know the most renowned stunt pilot in the world? He accepted my invitation to have a cognac and, as our conversation grew more and more lively, I felt as if we had known each other for years. Then I had another mad idea. 'How would you like to be in a film and perform your stunts in the mountains?'

'It sounds great,' said Udet, his eyes shining. He had already downed a few cognacs.

'Fine,' I said, 'I'll introduce you to Dr Fanck. He's writing a scenerio now, your stunt flying would fit in nicely with it.'

And so it came about that Ernst Udet joined the project, which was great for the film, although it initiated a private tragedy.

Schneeberger also met Udet, and was so taken with him that a friendship soon developed between the two men. For Schneeberger, Udet was the great hero of World War I, the most successful German fighter pilot, who as a member of the Richthofen Squadron had been awarded all sorts of decorations. Schneeberger, as a young Austrian lieutenant, had participated in the mountain fighting against the Italians, and had been awarded the Gold Medal for Courage. The two of them soon became close friends.

Erni, as we called Udet, was amused that Schneeberger and I clung so closely together. If Snowflea and I were separated for even a few hours we had to telephone each other, and our feelings had so deepened over the years that a break-up would have seemed inconceivable; no other man had the slightest chance with me, although I had had many admirers. Udet, however, couldn't understand such profound emotions. He was a playboy; and he enjoyed life, liked being surrounded by beautiful women, but never took anything too seriously. He was a regular patron at Horcher, an expensive restaurant, and he frequented all the good nightclubs. Although he drank a lot, he was always cheerful and full of humour. Having flown with Göring in the famous Richtofen Squadron, he would draw delightful cartoons of Göring with satirical captions. Udet's caricatures were masterly.

One day he took me aside and seriously tried to convince me that my life with Snowflea would spell the end of my career. It was unforgivable, he said, that I was cutting myself off from everything because of my love for his friend. He had learned from Snowflea that we were in financial difficulties, that our money was dwindling. 'I'll introduce you to some of my rich friends. Maybe you'll like one of them, and then you won't have to live like Cinderella any more.'

I laughed. 'You're out of your mind,' I said. 'I couldn't be any happier than I am with my Snowflea, and my career takes second place. As for money, we'll find a way.'

Meanwhile the preparations for the *Piz Palü* film were done, and in late January 1929 we moved into settled quarters on the Morteratsch Glacier in the Engadine Valley. First, all the acting scenes were to be shot by Pabst in as brief a time as possible. The valley was in the grip of a Siberian cold such as it hadn't experienced in decades. The temperatures hovered between minus 28 and 30 degrees centigrade for weeks on end. Pabst did not have an easy time working under these conditions and, without Fanck, he would have been incapable of tracking down the right locations. We needed an ice wall and electricity for the acting sequences, many of which took place at night, but no electric current was to be found near an ice wall, so the settings had to be created artificially. Not far from the Hotel Mortertsch, Fanck found a precipice as high as a house which they kept spraying with water until it was coated with ice. For close-ups they were able to build a ledge of rock, covered with deep snow, near the hotel.

It took Pabst a month to complete his shooting. Throughout the bitter cold we had to sit buried in snow for hours on end, while the cutting wind drove ice crystals into our faces and ice needles tore our skin. My upper thighs were frost-bitten and, worst of all, I contracted a severe bladder problem that I have never managed to get rid of. My two fellow actors, Gustav Diessl and Ernst Petersen, also suffered from the cold, but Diessl the more acutely as in some scenes he wore only a shirt. At times propellors were used to augment the wind, making the blizzard all the harder to bear. Often we had to stop working in order to warm up at a kitchen stove; then we changed clothes and back we went out into the cold. At such moments we envied our fellow performers who worked in wind-proof and weather-proof studios and were generally cosseted.

My close-ups were shot only when I was exhausted and at the end of my strength after many hours of climbing. In addition, they were usually shot in the grim cold, which notched sharp creases in my face. At this temperature I was forced to drink cognac, for without alcohol I could never have endured the awful stress and strain.

It was a new experience for me to be directed by G.W. Pabst. I felt for the first time that I too was an actress. I couldn't perform as well under Dr Fanck's direction because he completely misunderstood me and projected on to me his own female ideal – to which I did not correspond. His ideal girl was a naïve, gentle type, a sort of *ingénue*, very different from me.

It was also Pabst, and not Fanck, who first realized that I had a talent for directing. During one scene Pabst said: 'Leni, look to the left.'

But I looked to the right, and I did it several times until Pabst figured out the reason. He called to me: 'You're an actress now, not a director.'

'What do you mean?' I asked him.

'You look at everything as if you were peering through the camera. The directions are reversed, left is right, and right is left.' Pabst was correct. Dr Fanck had accustomed me to looking at scenes through a viewfinder.

The frostbite on my legs was so bad that I had to drop out for several weeks in order to have radiotherapy. During this period they shot Udet's aerial stunts. This was his first job in films, and he was so enthusiastic about it that he wanted Schneeberger to shoot directly from the plane, no easy task since Schneeberger was under contract to UFA as assistant cameraman: but Udet managed to talk the studio into letting him go for a few weeks.

We all found Udet wonderful. Not only did he pull off the wildest acrobatic stunts, but he was also punctual and agreeable to work with. We held our breath whenever we watched his silvery red Flamingo zoom just a hair's breadth away from the rock walls.

Although I really liked Udet, I was very annoyed with him for having induced Sokal to put Snowflea up at the St Moritz Palace, where Udet had a suite, instead of with the rest of us at the Hotel Morteratsch. This was the first time that Snowflea and I had been parted. We saw each other daily, but when Udet's scenes were completed, Schneeberger flew back to St Moritz with him. I suffered more from this separation than did Snowflea, who now entered a new and unfamiliar world among the beautiful and elegant women who always surrounded Udet. Hearing about wild parties that lasted until dawn, I gradually became uneasy, and for the first time felt something like jealousy, though it was really more a fear of losing him.

Once the Udet sequences were finished UFA called Schneeberger back to Berlin and those were the last happy days with him.

In March Fanck began shooting at the Diavolezza shelter hut. There was of course no such thing as a cable car and the hut was in such a state of neglect that we switched headquarters to the Bernina Houses. From here we had to spend hours every day hiking up to the ice and rock walls of Piz Palü. It became more and more precipitous and increasingly difficult.

In order to shorten the route Fanck decided that we ought to put up at the Diavolezza hut for a while, which in size and comfort bore no relation to today's Diavolezza hut. When we awoke before sunrise the water in the basins was frozen. Drinking our morning coffee, we warmed up a little. Then we had to go out and shoot; often we skied down the glacier to our main work area. The speed at which we worked made it impossible to lower and raise the crew on ropes, so most of the shooting had to be done without

70

them. Sometimes the glacier boomed eerily, filling me with fear that the ground might open up beneath me and I would fall into one of the deep crevasses.

Conditions while shooting on Piz Palü were so harsh and draining that my hair still stands on end when I recall certain episodes. For example, the script said that I was to be hauled up along an ice wall as avalanches plunged over me. I was really afraid during this scene. Fanck had found a wall seventy feet high on the Morteratsch Glacier. For three days they piled up huge amounts of snow and ice fragments at the edge of this wall and I eyed these preparations with suspicion. I also knew Fanck too well; he didn't mind manoeuvring his performers into difficult situations so long as he obtained good shots.

When everything was all set for the shooting, Fanck, noticing my anxiety, promised me that I would be hoisted only a few yards. They attached the rope to me. 'Wind,' came the order, and I was pulled upward. Then I saw the snow cornice falling away from the edge of the ice wall. The sky darkened and the snowy masses went hurtling past me. Since my arms were roped up I couldn't shield myself against the snow powder and my ears, nose and mouth filled with snow and ice. I screamed at the crew to lower me, but it was no use; contrary to Fanck's promise, they hoisted me all the way up the ice wall. Nor did they stop when I reached the sharp icy edge: I was pulled over it, and I arrived at the top, weeping in pain and rage at my director's brutality. Fanck's only response was his delight at the excellent footage.

A blizzard imprisoned us for about a week, so powerful that it was impossible to leave the hut. At night the blizzard raged so violently that we were afraid it would tear off the roof and hurl it into the glacier. We were all sick of the winter and yearned for spring. For five months now we hadn't left the ice even once.

Meanwhile Fanck was driving me mad. Every night I found poems and love letters under my pillow and it was extremely annoying. Since Snowflea and I were apart, Fanck assumed that he could get me to change my mind, but it had the opposite effect – I couldn't even look at him. All I wanted was to get away from there, far away, and this became an obsession. One of our mountain guides was a young Swiss, renowned for his boldness, and I managed to talk him into escaping with me. The very next day, while the others were innocently taking their afternoon naps, we two, dressed out of all recognition, charged out into the blizzard.

Never before had I experienced such a fury of the elements. We were literally hurled into the air and just a few minutes later the hut was nowhere to be seen. Deafened, we found ourselves in a seething witches' cauldron and had to hold hands in order not to lose one another as our skis bore us into the unknown. We promptly regretted our reckless decision, but didn't have the nerve to admit it. My face was paralysed, icicles hung from my hair, my hands ached. But there was no going back; we were completely unable to get our bearings, and we could easily have stumbled on to avalanche slopes.

At that instant of maximum distress something happened which seemed like a miracle. Three people came towards us out of the grey fog. I thought at first it was a mirage, but they were really coming our way. When they were close to us I recognized the Engadine guide Caspar Grass who, together with two tourists, had been travelling to the Diavolezza hut for the previous seven hours. Caspar Grass shouted to us: 'Are you out of your minds! You'll never make it down! The entire route is threatened by avalanches. We barely managed to escape one ourselves!'

We were delighted to be forced to obey and, joining the other three, we got back to the hut two hours later. If we hadn't bumped into Caspar Grass we would never have emerged from the White Hell. Instead of the row we feared, everyone was delighted that we were still alive, having almost given up hope of ever seeing us again.

As if the god of weather wanted to make up for all his destruction, the blizzard suddenly stopped and the sun shone in a clear blue sky. My last scenes were filmed in a great hurry and finally I was able to leave the world of ice.

THE BLACK CAT

Happy as I was to be home again, I felt terribly lonely. For several weeks Snowflea had been on location in Hungary where UFA was making *Hungarian Rhapsody*. Fanck also was back in Berlin. After his abortive *Winter's Tale* he was working on his best screenplay, *The Black Cat*. This story about the war in the Dolomites was based on an experience of Schneeberger's involving the great explosion at Castaletto.

Schneeberger, a lieutenant, had held the position with sixty men until the very last moment. Then it was blown up by the Italians. All the men were buried but Schneeberger and eight others managed to dig their way out from the ruins, and with this tiny squad of soldiers he succeeded in holding the position until relief arrived. For this achievement he was awarded a high decoration.

Snowflea had written down his experiences on the Dolomite front and given Fanck the manuscript. A further true incident of this Austrian-Italian mountain warfare was the tragic experience of the daughter of Innerkofler, a well-known mountain guide. Fanck's scenerio tied the two stories together and at last I had a chance to play a dramatic part.

Because of her climbing skills, Innerkofler's daughter was known as the Black Cat. In the script she and her father climb near the Italian military base in order to scout for the Austrians. Her father is shot, but the Black Cat gets her revenge. Becoming a spy, she finds out when the Italians intend to set off the explosion and warns the Austrians in time, but she herself dies in the explosion. That was the basic plot of the film.

Fanck offered the scenerio to UFA, but it was turned down. They wanted no war films at that time and other studios had the same qualms. The script went through countless hands; everyone was enthralled by the theme, but no one had the courage to do a war film. Then Harry Sokal got hold of it. He was the only one who realized how successful the project could be. Since the production would be very expensive he did not care to risk it by himself and he looked for another backer, and found it in Homfilm. The contracts were signed, and the preparations were in progress. I was happy that at last I would be playing a suitable part.

Then came the bombshell. Fanck called me up: 'Our film's in danger. Trenker must have read my script and copied it. He's ahead of us, his project's called *Mountains in Flames*, and he's already announced it in the *Film-Kurier*.' Fanck found out that Trenker had probably obtained the script from Albert Benitz, a cameraman who had been Fanck's second assistant and now thought he had a great opportunity: to work as Trenker's cinematographer. Furthermore, Benitz didn't like Fanck and was jealous because the director had been harmlessly flirting with Benitz's wife. Sokal flew into a rage and sued Trenker for plagiarism, but when the court decided in Sokal's favour Trenker appealed against the verdict and won.

The two screenplays were indeed very similar; both had mountain warfare and the same dramatic main story – the explosion in which Hans Schneeberger had been involved – although Trenker's film did not include the Black Cat. Trenker was helped by Albert Benitz's declaration in court that he had never given Fanck's script to Trenker. Also, an actress to whom Trenker had promised a part in his film testified in his favour. (He never kept his promise, however, as she herself declared after the war.) In any case neither Sokal nor Fanck could prove that Trenker had plagiarized the script, so *The Black Cat* had to be put to sleep. Another excellent screenplay by Fanck could not be filmed, and in both cases it was Trenker's fault.

Once again I faced ruin. I had forfeited my career as a dancer, good film opportunities had disintegrated, my money was running out, and I saw no hope anywhere. I had reached a low point in my life and I was only twenty-six.

Although I couldn't even pay my rent, I refused to tell my father, or even my mother, about my plight. In this mood of depression my separation from Snowflea became more and more painful. One night I awoke from a nightmare, bathed in sweat. I had dreamed that an elegant but no longer young woman was hugging and kissing Snowflea. Next to her stood a young man, and she said to Snowflea: 'This is my son.' I couldn't possibly go back to sleep. I paced up and down my apartment until finally I reached a decision which brought me a little peace of mind: tomorrow I would go to Hungary where Snowflea was on location. I didn't know exactly where he was, so I sent him a telegram announcing my proposed visit. After a day of almost unendurable waiting I received his answer: 'Don't come. Wait for my letter.'

I was tormented by jealousy for three days and nights until the letter arrived. I kept staring at the envelope as if the text were written on it, so afraid that for several minutes I dared not open it. I had a premonition of disaster and I will never forget that letter which destroyed our happy life together.

I'm very sorry about what I have to tell you today. I don't love you any more. I have met a woman whom I love and I am now living with her. Please don't come. It won't change anything and I don't want to see you again. Snowflea.

It was so cruel that I couldn't grasp it. Throughout those years we had always been a happy couple, without fights or friction. If we were separated only for a few hours we yearned to be together again. But this letter? There must have been some black magic – someone had put a spell on him – I couldn't believe it. The pain crept into every cell of my body, paralysing me. I tried to relieve the tension by screaming aloud. Weeping, yelling, biting my hands; I reeled from one room to the next then grabbed a paper-knife and cut myself – my arms, legs and hips. I didn't feel physical pain but my mental anguish burned like the fires of hell.

I don't know how I managed to survive those weeks and months, the worst in my life, during which I wanted to jump out of every window, throw myself in front of every train. Why didn't I do it? I suppose I hoped I could get Snowflea back by talking to him, but I was deluding myself, for he gave me no chance to see him again. He did everything he could to avoid a meeting. I begged Udet, but Snowflea resisted him too. He did not want to see me again.

I lived with that pain for more than five months until, little by little, I stifled my love and became a different person. Never again, I swore to myself, never again would I love a man so deeply.

JOSEF VON STERNBERG

The only way I could take my mind off my sorrow was to see good films. And there were several very good ones, with stars like Charlie Chaplin, Harold Lloyd and Buster Keaton. It was the great final period of silent pictures before they were replaced by talkies.

One day I saw a motion picture that simply mesmerized me. I went back to see it again. I was convinced that, like Fanck's *Mountain of Destiny*, it could only have been made by an unusually gifted director. It was not the theme that enthralled me but the artistry of the film-maker and his camera. This is hard to put into words but a true work of art exerts a charisma. I remember how deeply moved I was by paintings by Van Gogh, Franz Marc and Paul Klee.

The movie was *The Docks of New York*, its director, Josef von Sternberg. The *Berliner Zeitung* printed a brief report that he was coming to Germany to make a film at UFA. I wanted to meet him just as I had wanted to meet Fanck. Sternberg was coming from Hollywood, and that was all I knew about him. Later on, when I learned from the press that he had arrived in Berlin and was negotiating with UFA, I decided to go and see him at the studio.

I wanted to dress with as much chic as I could and chose a Russian-green woollen dress and coat trimmed with red fox, and a matching green felt hat. To judge by his film, Sternberg liked to see women well dressed. I had to make inquiries all over the UFA building until I finally tracked down his office, but there I was told emphatically not to disturb him: he was in an important meeting with Erich Pommer, the novelist Heinrich Mann, and the playwright Carl Zuckmayer, names that commanded great respect. Apprehensively I stood at the door of the conference room, from which a clamour of loud voices could be heard. I wavered: should I knock or go away? I decided to knock. The door opened, a thick cloud of cigar smoke billowed into my face and a voice said: 'What do you want?'

With suddenly inexplicable courage I managed to squeak: 'I would like to speak to Herr von Sternberg.'

The voice: 'Impossible.'

The door slammed in my face. I stood there, numb. All at once, the door opened again, and a stranger, a man with extremely beautiful large, light-grey eyes, stuck his head through the crack.

'What can I do for you?' he asked pleasantly enough, though his voice had an ironic intonation.

'I would like to speak to you. I've seen your films, and *The Docks of New York* is simply brilliant.'

Sternberg looked me up and down, then opened the door a bit wider, so that I could see all of him. 'Well,' he said, again somewhat ironically, 'well, so you like my picture?' For a brief instant he seemed at a loss to know what to do next. Then, glancing at his watch, he said: 'Why don't you come to the Hotel Bristol at 2 p.m. We could have lunch there.'

An hour before our appointment I arrived at the Bristol on the Unter den Linden and waited patiently. I was not certain whether he would really come, and he did show up. I can still remember what we ate: tender beef with kale and horseradish, a speciality of the house.

Now I could finally introduce myself. He was unfamiliar with my name as a dancer and screen actress, nor was he interested. All he wanted to know was why I had liked his film so much that I had actually tried to visit him during an important meeting. It was not easy for me to explain what I had felt while watching his movie. 'I think that everything in your film is marked by a highly personal touch,' I said hesitantly, 'and I noticed that you do not let a scene play out all the way. The viewer has to complete the events in his own imagination.'

Sternberg showed no reaction, so somewhat uncertainly I went on: 'I like the fact that you never make too much of a kissing scene. Instead, you just let a love scene develop. You merely hint at things, and that makes their impact more powerful – at least, as I see it. You leave out a lot; that heightens the suspense. And another thing: your visual technique creates a special ambience. One senses atmosphere in every room.'

At this point Sternberg broke in. 'You say you sense the atmosphere in my film. No critic has ever observed that. You have a very sharp eye.' And with no ironic undertone he continued, 'I like you.' Then he began to talk about his project at UFA. The title of the film was to be *The Blue Angel*, and the big problem at the moment was whom to cast as the female lead. Emil Jannings was already chosen for the male lead – 'Professor Unrat', after the novel of the same name by Heinrich Mann. The book was to be adapted for the screen by Carl Zuckmayer and Sternberg. 'I haven't yet found anyone for the female lead,' Sternberg said nervously. 'They're trying to talk me into casting women I don't like.' He paused, ordered a glass of water, then went on: 'But I have almost no hope of finding my Lola. I've been shown photos of some actress named Marlene Dietrich, but they're awful.'

'Marlene Dietrich? I've only seen her once, but she caught my eye at Schwanecke, a small artists' cafe on Rankestrasse. She was sitting there with several young actresses. I noticed her deep, husky voice, which sounded sexy and slightly vulgar. Maybe she was a bit tipsy. I heard her saying loudly: "Why does a woman always have to have beautiful breasts? Her bosom can sag a little, can't it?" Then she lifted her left breast slightly and enjoyed the startled faces of the young girls sitting around her. I think Marlene Dietrich is the woman you're looking for.'

The very next day Sternberg wanted to see me again to show me the various photographs and again we met at the Bristol. He said he had gone to the theatre the previous evening because UFA had suggested Hans Albers for the second male lead in his movie and that had been a stroke of luck. Not only did Albers strike him as ideal for the part, but Sternberg had found his Lola – Marlene Dietrich. 'I was fascinated,' he told me. 'She only had a tiny part, but when she appeared on stage I couldn't take my eyes off her. I'm meeting her tomorrow.'

From then on we met every day. He liked me, and I liked him, but it was not a romance; we were developing a friendship. Sternberg told me everything about *The Blue Angel*, and I almost felt as if I were working with him. That was how I found out about his battle to cast Dietrich. He had to struggle mainly against Emil Jannings and a group of other actors hired for the production. Sternberg was convinced that he had found the ideal actress, and I encouraged him, since I liked her a lot too. One day I received a huge bouquet of lilies of the valley, bound in white silk ribbons. There was a card, which said: 'For Du-Du, from Jo.'

Those lilies of the valley were the beginning of an unfortunately one-sided romance. I would have liked to feel more for Sternberg than warmth and admiration, for not only was he good looking, but his company and his conversation made him one of the most fascinating personalities I have ever met. However, I still hadn't overcome my painful rejection by Schneeberger – and I wouldn't get over him for a long time. Sternberg visited me on Hindenburgstrasse almost every evening, and we had supper together. Often it was late at night before he left, sometimes taking me along with him to Babelsberg to show me his rushes. He was interested in my opinion, and wanted to hear it before Pommer got to see the footage.

As luck would have it Marlene lived in my block. Her building entrance was on Hildegardstrasse, which ran parallel to Hindenburgstrasse. I lived on the fifth landing, Marlene on the third, and I could look into her windows from my roof garden, which faced the back courtyard. However, she was still in the dark about my friendship with Sternberg. This would have made no difference to her at the start of the shooting; but soon everything changed.

At weekends Sternberg would pick me up in a rented car and we would drive out to idyllic places in the suburbs of Berlin. Those were lyrical and enchanting hours. Sternberg was a brilliant raconteur. He always called me 'Du-Du', never 'Leni', and I called him 'Jo'. He spoiled me with the most marvellous and unusual flowers, and I just didn't know how to thank him. However, the nicest present of all was when he let me visit his set. It was an experience watching him shoot. He directed his performers with the authority of an animal trainer, and they hung on his every look.

It was on the set of *The Blue Angel* that I first met Emil Jannings, who, for once, was in a good mood and willing to talk to me. Sternberg was rehearsing with Marlene. It was the scene that later became so famous: Marlene, flaunting her beautiful legs, was sitting with her right knee drawn up to her breasts and singing her famous hit by Friedrich Holländer: 'Falling in love again . . . What am I to do, I can't help it.' Sternberg rehearsed and rehearsed, but it wasn't working. Marlene seemed irritated by my presence. She wasn't listening to Sternberg. Bored and piqued, she began tugging at her knickers, and sat in such a way as to offer an unobstructed view of everything she was suppposed to hide. She did it so blatantly that only a blind man could have failed to see that she was trying to tease. Sternberg suddenly lost his temper and yelled: 'Marlene, behave yourself!' With a defiant pout, she tugged her panties down a little, and the rehearsal went on, and I was so embarrassed by the situation that I said goodbye to Sternberg and left.

That evening he told me that when the shooting was done Marlene had thrown a tantrum, threatening to walk out for good if I ever showed up on the set again. I was surprised by her behaviour. Jo had told me she was in love with him but, since I was neither in love with Sternberg nor having an affair with him, any romance between them would have meant nothing to me. Jo said that Marlene was being positively motherly, even cooking for him every day. Nevertheless, for Sternberg she was simply the raw material out of which he was creating his Lola. The atmosphere was already charged, especially because of Jannings' conduct, so to keep things from getting even more explosive I never went back to the set of *The Blue Angel*.

Harry Sokal, now having an affair with the beautiful Countess Agnes Esterhazy, one of the most attractive stars of silent pictures, came to me with a surprising request. 'Could you possibly go to Paris for two or three weeks? I'd like you to cut fifteen hundred feet from the German version of *The White Hell of Piz Palü*. Fanck's done the editing, but the picture is simply much too long for the French distribution.'

'But you know I've never edited a film,' I told him.

'Fanck can't part with even a single inch of celluloid. But you could, I know you could.' He was very insistent, and naturally I was tremendously tempted by the thought of suddenly getting to know Paris. I also felt quite capable of trimming *Piz Palü*.

'And what will you pay me?' I asked.

'All expenses, plus three hundred marks.'

'Don't be silly,' I said, and we began to negotiate. I couldn't squeeze more than five hundred marks out of him, but finally I agreed.

In a side street off the Champs Elysées there was a small editing laboratory opposite a tiny hotel, where I rented a modest room. When I moved in I found my dreary room enhanced by a wonderful basket of flowers. It came from Sternberg, but I had no idea how he had ferreted out my address. Sokal had probably revealed it to him.

That very first evening I strolled along the Champs Elysées. What a marvellous avenue it seemed, even more beautiful than Berlin's Kurfürsten-damm. I wandered like a sleepwalker through crowds of people, admiring the precious displays in the boutique windows. It was good to be in this foreign city where all my problems faded to the back of my mind.

The cutting was a lot of fun, and, to my surprise, I found it easy. A woman had been hired to help me with the splicing, and ten days later I had snipped out the fifteen hundred feet from the print. This tightened version made a more powerful impact and Sokal was satisfied, but Fanck never forgave me.

When I returned to Berlin Sternberg was already waiting for me. Everything was still the same as before, except that I no longer drove out to Babelsberg.

On a grey November day *The White Hell of Piz Palü* had its première at Berlin's UFA Palace by the Zoo. This was the greatest of Fanck's successes. And it was also a triumph for Pabst and me. The Berlin press outdid itself in praise, and even newspapers that had criticized Fanck's earlier movies wrote: 'No film has ever been more touching, no cinematic experience more bitter, no motion picture more poignant than this one.' Sternberg came to see it with me.

'You're very good,' he said, 'I could make you into a big star. Come to

Hollywood with me!' Too bad, I thought, for I knew I couldn't take advantage of this unique opportunity. I still didn't have the strength to end my attachment to Schneeberger.

'You're so different from Marlene,' Sternberg continued. 'But both of you are extraordinary creatures. I'll work my magic on Marlene, and I'll transform you too. Why, you haven't even been discovered yet.' He said a lot more, but those words stuck in my memory. After the war I often regretted that I hadn't gone to America with Sternberg.

Despite the tremendous success of *Piz Palü* wherever it was shown, my financial situation was desperate. On 1 December, unable to pay my rent, I went to Sokal's office on Friedrichstrasse and, with a heavy heart, I blurted out my predicament. Could he lend me three hundred marks? I will never forget the way Sokal looked at me and said: 'You're a pretty girl. You could earn your money in the street.'

I was aghast. What was he saying? It was the hatred of a rejected suitor. 'You disgust me.' And I spat at him.

Often in my life when I have reached rock bottom something delightful has happened. This time it was a letter from AAFA, the film company that was distributing Sokal's *Piz Palü*. To my surprise AAFA was offering me twenty thousand marks to play the female lead in Fanck's next movie, *Storms over Mont Blanc*. Their offer was, no doubt, inspired by the great success of *Piz Palü*. Its success endured and I was invited to the premières in Paris and London. The great acclaim I received there from the public and the press was very encouraging.

Before my return to the white mountain world Sternberg invited me to the Berlin Press Ball. He said he would call for me and I was still dressing when he arrived – one hour early. This was the first time I had ever seen him so agitated. He begged me to forgive him, he couldn't take me to the ball. When Marlene had found out she had threatened to kill herself. I couldn't understand, but naturally I told him it was all right with me. Too bad the three of us can't go, I thought to myself.

There is a special photograph of this press ball, which I then attended with G.W. Pabst and his wife. Taken by the American photographer Alfred Eisenstädt, it shows me together with Marlene and the Chinese actress Anna May Wong, who had achieved international stardom in Hollywood. Later I spent an exciting evening with Sternberg in the home of the stage director Erwin Piscator. His apartment was festively decorated with flowers and candles, and champagne and caviare were served. Sternberg knew that I was very fond of caviare. I had once told him that when I was still a dance student I had received a very meagre allowance, but nevertheless I had managed to scrimp and save enough to buy a small tin of caviare for three marks.

'Today you shall have all the caviare you can eat,' said Jo. He was glad I didn't hold that unfortunate Press Ball incident against him, and again tried to talk me into following him to Hollywood.

'What about Marlene?' I asked.

'She hasn't made up her mind yet,' he said. 'Marlene is going to be a star, but the UFA people are so dim, that they still don't believe my film's going to be a hit. And they have even less faith in Marlene. They're so stupid that they've actually dropped her option.' I told Sternberg that I had had a somewhat similar experience with Garbo. In 1925, in Berlin, I had seen *The Joyless Street* with Asta Nielsen, Werner Krauss and Garbo. I was so fascinated by Garbo that I dragged Fanck and Sokal to the cinema to have a look at her, and begged Sokal to hire Garbo. I was absolutely captivated by her aristocratic beauty, and convinced she would become world-famous. But neither Fanck nor Sokal could see anything whatsoever in her. I was sad and furious. Only a few days later I saw her on the front page of *Berliner Illustrierte*: she had just signed a Hollywood contract.

When I finally said farewell to Sternberg – it was in January 1930 – we still weren't sure whether Marlene or I would be following him to Hollywood.

MONT BLANC

In February I arrived in Arosa, Switzerland, where we completed the skiing sequences for Fanck's Mont Blanc film within three weeks. Then we went to St Moritz for a few days. Udet, who was featured in this movie too, was waiting for us. I had often admired him for his daredevil flights over Piz Palü, but I had never flown with him myself. This was to be my maiden effort, though the flying conditions were anything but ideal. By now the frozen surface of Lake St Moritz was softening, and some parts were already open. I climbed into the plane, Udet's famous Motte (Moth). The tiny silvery monoplane had to strain in order to lift off from the heavy, sticky layer of snow. No sooner were we in the air than Udet did a sudden loop. Since I wasn't wearing a safety belt I was sure I'd tumble right out and naturally I was terrified, but that was the whole point of it for Udet. He looked back at me and guffawed like a mischievious little boy. Then we had to fly several low circles around the movie camera. It wasn't the safest stunt in the world, and when we touched down we nearly crash-landed.

From St Moritz our caravan travelled to the Bernina Hospiz, a lodge some seven thousand feet high on the Bernina Pass, from where a year earlier we had often climbed up to Piz Palü. There harsh weather is the order of the day – usually a blizzard. It was early April and we remained there for six weeks.

Nearby they built the interior of a Mont Blanc observatory – a real studio with spotlights. This too was a pioneer feat of Dr Fanck's. Under conditions of great hardship he constructed this room in an almost Arctic landscape, where it had to freeze over at the mercy of blizzards. The cold was almost unendurable. Day and night the cameramen, lighting technicians, director, and above all, Sepp Rist, the male lead, had to work in this ice hole for hours on end.

Luckily I didn't have too many scenes there, so I used every spare day to climb up to high altitudes with the Lantschner brothers – a necessary training for the coming alpine shooting in the Mont Blanc area.

But first we spent several days in Lausanne where it was already spring. Udet wanted to start his Mont Blanc flights from here, so on the first nice day we took off on my first alpine flight. It was the most exciting thing I had ever experienced. After passing Lake Geneva we suddenly headed straight towards the Dent de Midi. The second plane which contained Schneeberger and his camera was trailing us. Fanck had had to hire him because Udet insisted that Schneeberger shoot his flying scenes. My feelings for him had died, so meeting him again made no difference to me. Strangely enough, when I saw him I felt neither sadness nor hatred.

Plunging through thick cumuli, we saw the French mountains down below and towering over everything was the peak of Mont Blanc. The snow-covered range lay beneath us like so many sleeping polar bears. In a single moment, however, the scenery changed. Violent squalls whirled us topsy-turvy like a piece of paper, past razor-sharp ridges. We flew over several glaciers and peered into the immeasurably deep, blue-black crevasses. A high jagged crest zoomed directly towards us. The icy wind storming down from the peak grabbed us and whirled us closer and closer to the rocks. I screamed as the walls of ice seemed to be collapsing upon us. I saw the sky over me and then, a second later, a chasm beneath. I could only close my eyes. Some fifteen hundred feet ahead of us the escort plane sank down. Now we ourselves were in an air pocket, plummeting like a stone. Somehow Udet managed to pull out, then he soared through the clouds and landed on the glacier like a huge bird. It was the first time an aircraft had ever landed on Mont Blanc, and I was there.

After the shooting we finally reached Chamonix. There it towered above

As Hella, the woman pilot in *SOS Iceberg*, 1932

My mother Bertha Riefenstahl,
née Scherlach

My father Alfred Riefenstahl
in 1902, the year of my birth

As a child of four,
the age at which I began to
write my first poems

With my brother Heinz, six years old
– three and a half years younger than I

I called this dance 'Dream Blossom'. Max Reinhardt had
engaged me to perform at his *Deutsches Theater*. I first danced on
this world-famous stage on 20 December 1923.

'Study after a gavotte'
A knee injury forced me to give up my successful dancing career
after more than seventy recitals in Germany and abroad.

The Holy Mountain, 1925/6
A dream-like vision made of ice which the director
Dr Fanck constructed on the frozen lake in Lenzerheide.

As Diotima the dancer in *The Holy Mountain*

A night shot from *The White Hell of Piz Palü*, 1929
We worked on this film for weeks at a temperature below minus
thirty degrees centigrade and suffered serious frostbite. The still
shows Ernst Petersen. Directed by Dr Arnold Fanck and
G.W. Pabst, the film enjoyed world–wide success.

This still from *The White Hell of Piz Palü* shows me with the
male lead Gustav Diessl desperately trying to signal to a rescue
plane looking for us on the icy walls of the mountain.

us, our star, the massive giant, Mont Blanc. Its white glacier paws reached all the way down through the green forests into the valley. We all stood in front of our hotel, the Gourmet, scanning the white mass through our binoculars. Far above us we saw the Vallot shelter hut standing on a ridge, 14,000 feet above sea level. Later on we would bivouac there for a long time but first we looked for a suitable landing place for Udet. That evening he rang up from Lausanne and explained that he couldn't land in the area near Grand Mulets designated by Fanck, so a different spot was chosen. Then we left Chamonix and began climbing. Dr Fanck, who was suffering from flu, was forced to remain behind temporarily.

Our goal was the neglected Dupuis shelter hut and the ascent to it was strenuous. It took us two hours to climb between precipitous talus slopes and rocks, carrying our skis, which was uncomfortable and tiring. Even before we reached the snow line a knapsack fell over the edge and as each of our backpacks contained valuable material we had to try to retrieve it. It had fallen a thousand feet and a rescue operation would be difficult. Unfortunately our efforts were in vain – the camera inside was shattered. We clambered on through the silent solitude and, after a long, arduous ascent, supper and hot grog tasted delicious.

The shelter hut was more primitive than any I had ever seen and that first night sleep was out of the question. Wrapped in filthy blankets, we lay on hard mattresses. It was cold, and anyone who had expected something romantic was deeply disappointed. Here are a few notes from my diary.

Day 1 In the Dupuis hut. Weather very foggy – no visibility. We are spending the day lazily, some of us are playing cards – I find a chess player and kill half the day playing. The boredom makes us nervous.

Day 2 Slept a few hours last night. But my body is stiff. The weather is the same as yesterday: we are all fairly depressed. It is awful always having fog around us. And Udet has to get back to Berlin in two days. What will happen if we can't shoot his landing on the glacier?

Day 3 We've been dozing since early morning but the weather seems to be improving – at least, outlines are appearing through the fog. Then we hear the noise of propellors – it can only be Udet. Everyone dashes outside, the humming comes nearer, then vanishes again. Snow begins to fall – the wind gets stronger, and fog again floats about us. We can barely see fifty feet ahead. What is Udet planning? He can't land in this weather – suddenly a gust blasts from the valley, and for a few seconds the entire cloud mass lies over us, with an aeroplane flying into the grey. We shout, we wave, and we realize it's not Udet; it's the second plane, the one piloted by Klaus von Suchotzky. The plane sinks, pulls out, then circles over our roof. The two men wave, and now a package falls, and another. What a delight, they are bringing food. And then something else comes fluttering down, a small nosegay of carnations. From an altitude of seven thousand feet they are tossing carnations at me. Then the plane vanishes again in the fog.

Day 4 The clouds slowly begin to lift. If Udet doesn't come soon it will be too late to shoot. The sun is drawing water, and that is always suspicious. We've been waiting four hours. Then, at 9 a.m., we hear the roar of propellors. Fifteen pairs of eyes scan the heavens without sighting anything. But then, in the distance, a black dot emerges over the clouds. There he is – it has to be Udet. Sepp Allgeier quickly climbs up to a snow peak. Angst, the cameraman, sets up his camera, and the rest of us lie down so that we won't get into the picture. The cameramen focus. Don't get excited; don't do anything clumsy. Missing this unique opportunity would mean an irreparable loss.

Then the two planes whirr over us. And everything happens like lightning. Udet's craft drops so quickly that it looks as if it were collapsing. Then it lands on the glacier. And the cameramen crank and crank. This is the first time ever that anyone has filmed a landing on the glacier. Five minutes later we are back in the middle of a fog. The clouds are drifting over us as if a curtain had been drawn. The landing took place in the last second of light. But how will Udet get away again? He has to take off through the fog, away from the glacier. The darkness becomes thicker and thicker until it is quite black. Finally Udet decides to risk it; he can't wait until night. After swinging the propeller he allows the plane to glide into the soupy obscurity. We hear the noise fade away into the distance and then stop altogether. Udet is gone – will he get back? Will he find his way through the countless crags?

He did find his way. We were told days later, when we arrived back in Chamonix, that he had landed safely in Lausanne.

Now we began to climb up Mont Blanc. This climb is no major event, it is merely strenuous. The alpinists who were part of the expedition made sure that everything went smoothly and the only thing they couldn't control was the weather.

We wanted to start shooting at the Vallot hut. At two o'clock in the morning we climbed up from the Grand Mulet hut. The snow was frozen, but we made good progress with our crampons and we reached our destination by six o'clock. I had no problems with the thin air, probably only because I have very low blood pressure, but it was different for Fanck and the other men who had to carry heavy loads. They were short of breath and suffered from headaches.

This hut too was a wretched hole. Twelve people managed to fit in only if they lay squeezed together like sardines. There was nothing but ice and snow and frozen blankets. We had lugged up everything, even pots and tableware, but the Vallot hut didn't even have a stove.

The surrounding landscape was magnificent. The hut is framed by the wildest and most dangerous crevasses and ice walls to be found in Europe. There was a constant roaring as avalanches and ice blocks plunged down with an almost regular rhythm. The glacier changed every day. It was June by now, the snow was melting, and the cracks were opening appreciably. Just a few days earlier the ground had been covered with vast stretches of snow, but now crevasses were becoming visible, wide enough and deep enough to swallow Cologne cathedral or the temple at Carnac.

Fanck, obsessed with capturing these unique images on film, paid scant heed to the dangers confronting us. And that proved to be a bad mistake. The cameras having been unpacked hundreds of feet below the Vallot hut, he walked several steps ahead in order to find the best locations. All at once we saw him – only seventy feet away – silently vanishing. The glacier had swallowed him up. Our tiny group was deathly quiet, but only for an instant or two. Then I saw with what wonderful presence of mind the staff operated in such emergencies. Within seconds a rope was plunging into the fissure. As everyone listened and it dropped foot by foot, the faces of our men grew darker and darker. Half the rope had already uncoiled, seventy feet hung into the crevasse. Finally a sound came up, and we breathed a sigh of relief. The men felt a tug on the rope and everyone pulled with all his might. At last, Fanck's head popped up, his mouth still holding the cigarette he had clenched in his teeth when falling. Utterly calm, as if nothing had happened, he clambered out of the crevasse, and shooting resumed.

A sudden, nasty drop in the temperature imprisoned us in the hut. We were running out of food. All we had left were a few crusts of bread and some ersatz coffee that had already been heated three times. Soon the mood among the men became difficult, something I felt keenly as the only woman. No one could get too close to me for comfort, but the young men had to give vent to their long frustration. They all tried to outdo one another with obscene jokes. Some of them constructed blatant sexual symbols of ice and snow around the hut. Naturally, I was pestered, and for me the situation became impossible. One of the young men imagined he was so deeply in love with me that he threatened to kill himself by jumping into a crevasse. Nor had Fanck expelled me from his fantasies; every day he kept slipping me notes in prose or verse, and they grew more and more erotic. It was a great relief when we could finally go down to Chamonix for two days.

Without ropes, as in nearly all of Fanck's location shooting, we swooped from the seven-thousand-foot altitude down to the mountain station, past gigantic crevasses, over narrow bridges, precipitous slopes, across powder snow and ice. The men skied so furiously that I couldn't follow them. But one of our guides, Beni Führer, a Swiss, remained with me.

The final steep gradient above the Grand Mulet shelter hut was pure ice. Despite their steel edges, the skis had no hold. I flew down over one hundred and sixty feet and crash-landed on a snowbridge spanning a gigantic fissure. I saw one of my ski poles hurtling into the abyss, and was frightened out of my wits. I didn't dare stir. The bridge could give way any second. Beni flopped down on his belly, held his ski poles out towards me, and gradually pulled me off the bridge.

'That was a close call!' Those were the only words he blurted out in his terror.

Two days later we climbed back up. Avalanches could still be shot, especially around the Bosson Glacier. By this time so much ice and snow had melted that we had to lay ladders eight times during our ascent in order to cross the crevasses. Little by little we grew indifferent to the incessant dangers confronting us. We had only one wish: to get out of the glacier world as soon as possible.

Although the month of avalanches had arrived, Sepp Rist, playing a meteorological observer with frozen hands, had to ski down without poles. He had to concentrate hard to keep clear of the crevasses. While filming such a scene with Rist, we saw a gigantic ice cornice break away from the substratum of rock and, with tremendous force, crash over the rocks, towards our glacier. The cameramen, relentless and unflappable, kept cranking. They shot Rist fleeing the avalanche as it thundered towards him. For us it was too late to escape. Tremendous masses of ice rolled down the glacier towards us. We could only hope that the avalanche would halt before it reached us.

Shrouded more and more densely in snow powder, no one dared to speak. The spell was broken only after several minutes of silence. Almost a quarter of an hour passed before the snow powder finished settling and we had some visibility. We stopped working that day. All of us had had enough of our adventures in the snow.

Fanck had discovered a huge ice cornice. It was already tilting forward, about to break off at any moment. Nothing like this had ever been filmed before. Smaller cornices could be blown up, but not one this big. Fanck told Schneeberger to keep watch until the cornice loosened and Schneeberger didn't move from the spot for hours and hours. But then he did have to desert his post after all – certain needs always get the better of us – and right then the avalanche broke loose. Schneeberger dashed from the outhouse, grabbed the camera – but the moment had passed. He did not share our amusement; he was furious.

For the final shots in the Mont Blanc ice, I was supposed to cross a ladder spanning a crevasse fifty feet wide. For the maximum cinematic effect the director had chosen a very deep crevasse. I was afraid of doing this scene, and wanted to get out of it. My comrades had already placed bets that I wouldn't go across the ladder, and usually I would take such dares, for they knew I was more afraid of looking weak. Even as we were heading towards the crevasse I pictured how simple it must be to walk across such a ladder. What can happen? I asked myself. After all, I'm roped up, so I can't fall very far. But that little word 'far' says everything. I could still plummet forty or fifty feet and shatter my head against the ice walls. I tried to dismiss that horrible thought, and kept telling myself I wouldn't fall if I didn't look down.

The time had come. The director shouted 'Action!' Ignoring my fear, I started out, and felt the ladder swaying under my feet. This was something I hadn't counted on. It rocked more and more the closer I got to the middle. To make things even more difficult, the script demanded that while crossing the ladder I had to turn back and shout something at the people behind me. I mustered every ounce of my willpower to keep from collapsing on the ladder in utter terror. Somehow I made it, and the final shot of me was completed just as Fanck wanted it.

That evening I leafed through the album of the shelter hut. I had never looked at it because it records the accidents that have occurred on Mont Blanc and its glaciers. I felt something akin to gratitude that a lucky star had prevented us from adding one more accident to this sad alpine chronicle.

THE ARRIVAL OF THE SOUND FILM

When sound came it was a revolution. Although *Storms over Mont Blanc* had been planned as a talkie, the soundtrack was still dubbed; in 1930 it was technically impossible to do difficult mountain shooting with the first, heavy sound cameras. The new technology demanded a complete revamping of production, and screenwriting and directing required entirely different methods.

After returning from Mont Blanc I looked for a good speech teacher. Colleagues recommended Herr Kuchenbuch, a scrawny man with a birdlike face. He was an excellent teacher, and I greatly enjoyed working with him. I took daily lessons and we concentrated on intense breath training. I had a lot of trouble rolling my Rs. I practised and practised, and sometimes I felt hopeless because I barely noticed any progress. Again, I learned that one should never give up easily, and that a great deal can be achieved with hard work and tenacity, with patience and self-confidence. Eventually I had no difficulties whatsoever in my first sound scenes for the Mont Blanc film.

Before talkies reached the German movie theatre I had watched a sound newsreel in London, the first time I'd heard a talking picture. It seemed to me a technological miracle. But although I was excited by this new dimension of cinema, I was saddened by the inevitable death of the silent screen which retained some great advantages over talkies, especially artistically. If language was missing, then it had to be replaced by other forms of expression. The art of photography had attained great heights in this respect. Silent films often had more atmosphere than sound films because the dialogue became the crucial plot device in most of them, and there was sometimes a great deal of superfluous chit-chat.

Thus, sound movies that made sparing use of dialogue and still emphasized the visual form became masterpieces. They were created by Josef von Sternberg, Luis Buñuel, Elia Kazan, Rene Clément, Vittorio de Sica, Federico Fellini, Kurosawa – to name just a few.

But the silent films with Asta Nielsen, Henny Porten, Greta Garbo, Charlie Chaplin, Harold Lloyd, Buster Keaton, Lillian Gish, Douglas Fairbanks Sr, Conrad Veidt, and Emil Jannings, remain unforgettable. Films like *The Golem, The Cabinet of Dr Caligari* or *The Nibelungs*, and their directors – 'they only happen once . . .' The same is true of the works of the great Russian directors such as Pudovkin or Eisenstein, whose original version of *Potemkin* was silent.

THE BLUE LIGHT

Once again a great project was over, and once again I asked myself whether it had satisfied me. I could not answer yes. It was not just the performance I cared about. There was something else. I had started to become excited about working with the camera, I was interested in lenses, in celluloid, in the filter technique. Furthermore, I had watched Fanck editing his films. I was fascinated by the effects that could be achieved by means of editing. The editing room became a magic workshop for me, and Fanck was a past master of film editing.

Almost against my will I was diverted more and more to the actual process of film-making. At first I resisted. I was an actress and I didn't want to be side-tracked, but now I couldn't help seeing everything with a film-maker's eyes. I translated every room, every face, into images and movements. I longed more and more to create something of my own.

I was dissatisfied with the part I had played in my last mountain film, for it wasn't a real part at all. My work had been extremely arduous and dangerous, but now I felt that I'd had enough of the icy cold, the storms and glaciers. I yearned for the mountains, but without ice and snow. I began to dream and my dreams turned into images of a young girl who lived in the mountains, a creature of nature. I saw her climbing, saw her in the moonlight; I watched her being chased and pelted with stones, and finally I dreamed of this girl as she fell away from a wall of rock and slowly plunged into the depths.

These images seized hold of me and, as they grew ever more vivid, I wrote everything down as a treatment, eighteen pages long, which I named *The Blue Light*. I called the girl Junta but I don't know how the name came to me since I had never consciously heard it before.

When I showed the screenplay to my friends they liked it, so I submitted it to several film producers who found the plot too boring. Finally I showed it to my director and eagerly waited for his opinion. He felt the story wasn't so bad, but it would require major backing.

'Why major backing?' I asked, surprised. 'Nearly all the shooting can be done outdoors, and besides, the cast is very small.'

'But imagine the picture in the form of a legend or fairy tale,' said Fanck. 'To get that effect all the nature shots have to be stylized, the way Fritz Lang did it in his *Nibelungs*. He spent a fortune building the forest and the other natural settings in the studio. That was the only way he could create an unrealistic nature.'

I disagreed: 'That's exactly what I want to avoid, I don't want anything to look like a studio or cardboard. I do see the natural locations as stylized, but not with artificial sets. We can stylize them with the angles and cuts, and especially the way we use lighting. With light you can turn the camera into a magic instrument, and if you also use colour filters to change the tonal values you can succeed in altering the outdoors and stylizing nature.'

Fanck, smiling indulgently and ironically, then said: 'How do you intend to do unrealistic shots of the rock walls that you'll have to keep climbing? Rock will always look like rock.' It was a weighty and cogent argument, and it silenced me. Fanck was triumphant. 'Forget about all this. It's pure fantasy.'

Was it really impossible to make my dream come true? For days and nights on end I mulled it over: how could I involve the real rock walls in such a way that they would fit in with the other images in my dream world? Within just a few days I found the solution – a very simple one. I would veil the walls in patches of fog, which would soften their outlines and make them look mysterious. The idea dispelled my depression and made me even more eager to tackle the project, but I was determined to carry it out exactly as I saw it. But how? I had a small nest egg, but nowhere near the amount I needed. I could do without an expensive studio – all the scenes took place out of doors anyway – and the few interior sequences could be shot on location with the help of a light van. Since I would be playing the female lead I wouldn't have to pay myself a fee.

The chief financial problem would be to hire a director. Would I find one who wouldn't mind waiting for his fee until the picture started making money? So far, it hadn't even occurred to me that I could direct the film myself. The cast was small, and I was going to use amateurs, which was still customary in 1931. The ideal actor for the part of Vigo was Mathias Wieman, who was almost unknown on the screen, but had already made a name for himself on the stage. He was no matinée idol but a rather rugged young man with considerable charisma. It was still too early to contact him, however.

What struck me as most important of all was to find a good collaborator for the script. I approached Bela Balazs, one of the best screenwriters of the period who had also done the libretto for operas such as *Bluebeard's Castle* by Béla Bartók. To my delight Belazs was so excited about the outline that he was willing to co-author the script without a fee. As cameraman Schneeberger would of course be the best choice, but could I endure working so closely with him? Only two years had passed since our break-up, yet despite the shock it had caused me my scars appeared to have healed and no bitterness remained on my part.

Schneeberger was ready to work without a fee. For his assistant I had decided on Heinz von Javorsky, my secretary. He was delirious at the thought of an apprenticeship with a master like Schneeberger, even at a salary of only fifty marks a month. I hoped I could manage with a crew of only six – and for a ten-week schedule. Everyone had to do without their daily expenses, and I had to do without a producer, assistant director, secretary, wardrobe mistress and make-up man.

Drawing up one budget after another, I realized that we needed at least ninety thousand marks in cash for film stock, work at the printing lab, renting the light van, building a crystal grotto, and the dubbing, including the music track. No matter how often I added up my figures the end result was the same. I wondered if I would finally have to give up my project. But all was not yet lost. Fanck was shooting a new winter-sports movie, *The White Flame*, a comedy in the snow. I accepted his invitation to play the lead, since I wanted to invest my fee in *The Blue Light*.

The filming took place at St Anton and Zürs on the Arlberg. Wonderful as it was to ski with Hannes Schneider, Rudi Matt, the Lantschner brothers and other racers, I couldn't devote myself fully to this pleasure; all my thoughts were on *The Blue Light*. Furthermore, I considered the part I had to play in *The White Flame* really rather silly. At almost every moment the director asked me to cry out 'Oh, great!' I found this silly phrase repugnant and I just couldn't get it across my lips. The results were tears – and also fights with Fanck, which he revelled in. He loved making me furious. Needless to say, he was supported in this by Sokal, who was producing the film for AAFA Film Distributors.

Sokal, who had switched completely to the screen, had made a fortune with *The White Hell of Piz Palü*. Unlike Fanck he had managed to resign himself to the fact that he would never win me. He had developed a powerful interest in film-making, and he turned out to be extremely talented. Like G.W. Pabst, he too believed that I could direct films. Nevertheless, he did not yet want to risk backing me in my own project.

While I was tormenting myself in *The White Flame*, falling down in all sorts of ways in my role as a beginner on skis, I had a very agreeable surprise. Bela Balazs visited me in St Anton to work with me on scripting my fantasy film, and I found this very inspiring. We complemented one another ideally. While he was a master of dialogue and scene distribution, I could translate everything visually. In less than four weeks we completed a remarkable screenplay. I could hardly wait to finish my shooting on the Arlberg.

At last, after five months – it was May by now – I was back in Berlin. Since I was going to invest the twenty thousand marks I had received for *The White Flame* in my own project, I now needed only seventy thousand more. To avoid drawing on my nest egg, I lived as frugally as a monk. I didn't even buy stockings, any more; I wore only slacks.

Despite the impressive script, almost no one had any faith in the material. The main objections were that the film was too quiet, too romantic; it didn't offer even the most harmless excitement. I had no illusions about the real reasons for these rejections. Aside from these arguments, which were quite understandable, the main cause of the reluctance was that no one could actually empathize with my visual fantasies which would constitute the special quality of the film. Nothing similar had ever been previously attempted, especially the depiction of such a theme in the style that I was striving for. *The Blue Light* could not have been more different from the films made by Dr Fanck. Let me explain this with an example.

All of Fanck's subjects were realistic, but not his photography; the sun always had to be shining and the shots had to be primarily 'beautiful', even if this didn't suit the scene. This often bothered me, for I considered it a defect in his style. But since I too liked 'beautiful' shots, I decided on a story that required visually marvellous photography because of the subject matter, whether as a fairy tale, a legend or a poem. Stylistic unity emerges only when the theme and the visual creation express one and the same thing. And that was what I was aiming for. But how was I to proceed? I contracted AGFA, thinking specifically about a film emulsion that is insensitive to certain colours but, when used with special filters, can produce colour transformations and unusual visual effects. AGFA was very cooperative; they did some experiments, and the result was R-material. Later on it was used universally, especially in day-for-night shooting.

Grateful for my inspiration, AGFA promised to make the film stock available to me, and when the Geyer printing lab offered me a cutting room and a splicing assistant available at no cost, I took the risk. I sold jewellery given to me by my parents and an original etching that I had received from Fanck – in fact, almost everything I owned. I even mortgaged my flat. In early summer 1931 I established my first film company in which I was the sole shareholder: L.R. Studio-Film Inc. Within just a few weeks I had completed my preparations and could begin scouting locations in June. Because of my severely limited budget, I had decided to direct the film myself.

The tiny hamlet of Foroglia lies at the foot of a huge waterfall, at the end of the Maggia Valley in Ticino, Switzerland, and this was to be the setting of the movie. In the Brenta Group of the Dolomites I found the Crozzon, called Monte Cristallo in the film. On its peak, according to the legend, the blue light shimmers on nights when the moon is full.

Now my biggest problem was that I still lacked peasants. I wanted to have particular faces: strange, rugged types, as immortalized in the paintings of Segantini. I visited numerous villages in the most remote valleys, but I grew more and more frustrated and was on the verge of giving up hope. None of the peasants matched the style I was aiming at in my film.

In Bolzano I met a friend of mine, a painter, and I told him about my predicament.

'I know the peasants you're looking for; they do exist,' he said, 'but it's hopeless trying to talk them into being in a film. For years now I've been trying to paint them; they're unusual types, extremely shy and stubborn, and they wouldn't sit for me for money or presents.'

His words electrified me. 'Where can I find them?'

'Not too far from here. You can get there in less than an hour. You'll find them in the Sarn Valley. If you want to see them you have to go to Sarentino on a Sunday morning; every week they come down from their cottages and go to church there.'

I went there the very next Sunday. The little hamlet of Sarentino is only eighteen miles from Bolzano. The tiny streets were dead. The church stood in the centre of the village, opposite a small tavern. I stepped inside in order to observe the peasants coming out of the church. I was on edge – what would they look like? Would I be able to talk with them?

At last the church doors opened and the first peasants appeared. I was delighted. They looked exactly as I had pictured them: severe figures in black, with lean faces and a proud, unapproachable bearing. The men all wore large, black felt hats, which made them appear even more impressive.

Grabbing my Leica, I went out, trembling with excitement. Meanwhile, various groups were gathering in front of the church, including elderly women, also dressed in forbidding black. When I approached the first group of men and greeted them, they all turned away from me. Then I tried another group – with the same result. After greeting only chilly glares and turned backs from a third group, I gave up. I hadn't imagined it would be this hard. According to the tavern-keeper, who had told me many not very encouraging things about these peasants, they had never seen a photo of themselves, for they lived completely isolated on their mountain farms. I snatched at this straw; I would achieve my goal by photographing them, and when I managed to take a few shots, unobserved, heads emerged that could have been drawn by Dürer. Renting a room in the tavern, I remained several days in order to get to know the people. It was worth the trouble, for quite soon I noticed that their looks were no longer so chilly.

The next Sunday, after church, I showed the photographs to them. At first nothing happened, then one of them began to laugh. Now all of them studied the photos, and launched into lively chatter. I ordered several pitchers of red wine, and the spell seemed to be broken; the photos and the wine worked wonders. I sat among them, trying to communicate with them. Most had never been out of this valley, and they didn't have the remotest idea about films.

I was rather worried when I thought of the difficult scenes in the script – for instance, a chase along a village street, some boisterous revelry, and certain dramatic sequences. A further difficulty was the fact that the peasants wouldn't be free until September. Until then they would be busy with their hay and their harvest; but the ice was broken. They promised to take some time off when I returned in the autumn. Nevertheless, I realized that using these peasants constituted a big risk for my film.

In early June, our little crew left Berlin, six of us, including myself. Along with Schneeberger and his assistant Heinz von Javorsky, there was Waldi Traut whom I entrusted with my modest cash. He was a young student at that time, but later a successful producer at Ilse Kubashewski's Gloria-Film. He had agreed to a monthly salary of two hundred marks. Our fifth crew member was Karl Buchholz, an able production manager. Buchholz was a real treasure who always worked out a solution even to the worst problems; and our sixth member was Walter Riml, a tall, skinny cameraman from Hamburg, who was to shoot the stills. He had never done this before, but I couldn't afford a professional.

Before we began filming something infuriating happened. *En route* from Innsbruck we wanted to take the Brenner Pass to Bolzano. The Italian customs man, finding 70,000 feet of unexposed celluloid in our baggage and a complete professional camera outfit, demanded that we pay duty and surety. This would have been the death-blow to our entire enterprise, for we simply didn't have the money. We assured them we would take everything back with us; we begged and pleaded, but to no avail. The train left without us and, desperate and despondent, I sat on a rock. It was all too much; I could not face the thought of giving up everything just before the starting point. My friends too were losing heart, and in my despair I decided to wire an SOS to Mussolini, describing our situation and asking for a dispensation from customs duty. The answer came in only six hours, and it was positive. The customs inspectors gaped, but we were speedily ushered across the border. In Bolzano, we celebrated our victory at the Hotel Zum Mondschein. I hadn't been in such high spirits for a long time, and, the wine being so incredibly cheap there, we could all drink to our hearts' content.

A short time later we were in Ticino and, in order to reach our hamlet by the waterfall, we had to hike for two hours, our baggage carried by natives of the Maggia Valley. In Foroglia we were almost completely secluded from the rest of the world. Without mail, telephone or newspapers we felt carefree and able to concentrate entirely on our work. I believe that no smaller film crew has ever existed for a full-length feature – and no thriftier one. We didn't have to spend a penny on a hotel, for there was no hotel, and no inn either for that matter. The entire village had nine adult inhabitants, a few children, two cows, a sheep, a goat and several cats, and most of the houses were empty since many people had emigrated to America years before.

Thus each of us could live in a house of his own. A mattress and a basin were all the luxury we needed. What a wonderful feeling it was when we got down to work and discussed the first scenes at the waterfall. We could create in peace and quiet, without being rushed. No one stood behind us, pressuring us; no studio had set up a watchman. We were our own bosses. Often we filmed only a few minutes a day in order to catch a particular light effect at the waterfall.

Every day of shooting we would develop a bit of footage as a test, to see if we had captured the mood correctly. In the evening we would sit at the fireplace in one of the ruined houses and discuss the scenes; it was true teamwork. We had good shooting weather for four weeks, so we could film almost every day; then we sent the first ten thousand feet to be developed in Berlin and waited in suspense for the outcome. A few days later I received a wire which I almost didn't have the nerve to open – too much depended on it. But then I tore off the envelope. First I saw the signature: 'Arnold'. That could only be Fanck.

'Congrats! The rushes are indescribable – I've never seen such images.' What a miracle it was to read these words from Fanck, who had almost discouraged me from making the film. I was jubilant. Then came an even greater surprise. A second telegram, from Sokal: 'After viewing rushes I am ready to be your partner and take over the final financing of the picture on condition that you pay for the production costs. Harry Sokal.'

We joyfully embraced one another and danced in front of the post office like over-excited children. I was so thoroughly convinced of the success of this film that no risk seemed too great. I cabled Sokal: 'Agreed. Send me contract draft. Leni.'

We worked now with even stronger motivation. We could not disappoint the people who had put their trust in us. It also became more and more an issue of my very livelihood since I had taken responsibility for the production budget without knowing how high the final expenses would be. We had not yet calculated the outlay for the crystal grotto, for the dubbing and for recording the music. I would never have managed without the sacrifices of my fellow workers. We were a family; everything was paid from a collective fund, and everyone tried to spend as little as possible in order to stretch our funds. If someone had holes in his shoes or needed something equally urgent, it was taken care of from this treasury. In early August, Mathias Wieman arrived; two weeks later came Bela Balazs, who wanted to supervise a few of the scenes that I acted in. It was an ideal collaboration. There was never any bad temper or argument.

In the Brenta Group of the Dolomites we mainly shot the climbing scenes. One morning we had a strange experience there. Far above on a narrow ledge, we saw a flock of forty chamois, led by a huge, snow-white male. It was like a fairy tale, and the hut keeper said it was rare to see this legendary creature.

We lived in a primitive farmhouse high on the rocks and our daily fare was bread and cheese. Even here we continued developing the rushes, though not in the farmhouse. Two of our people had to go down to the valley every day after sunset and develop the footage in Madonna di Campiglio. Often they didn't return until after midnight, but at five the next morning I could already see the rushes. This was necessary, because we were experimenting with different colour filters.

In order to shoot as much authentic footage as possible, I wanted to film the interiors of the cottages, farmhouses, and village church on their original sites. For this we used a light van I had ordered from Vienna, but we weren't sure whether the experiment would work, for we didn't have the necessary experience. In those days interior shooting was always done in studios. But Papa John, the owner of the light van, did a great job. The spotlights never failed even once, though this in itself was no simple matter. Cables up to three hundred feet in length had to be pulled up the walls of rock to the Castle of Runkelstein, where the first scenes with the peasants were to be shot.

The night before, I slept fitfully. We were staying at the Sarentino Inn and I had asked the innkeeper to tell some forty of the peasants, whom I had chosen on the basis of my photos, to meet me at the marketplace at 7 a.m. But would they come? The completion of our film was in their hands, yet what could we do if they didn't show up? I tossed and turned in my bed. This film was a worrying project. Unfortunately the weather changed. I stood up and peered out of the window at torrents of country rain. In this awful weather I was sure no one would show up. Yet I couldn't afford to lose another day. Mathias Weiman, my male lead, had to return to his theatre in Berlin.

From my window at dawn I could look down right into the marketplace, but not a soul could be seen. But before seven o'clock the first peasants arrived, then more turned up and, armed with gigantic umbrellas, they stood in the square. Among them I saw a limping old man and two old women, wearing their Sunday best, huge, shiny satin aprons. Then another group approached; it looked like an entire family. More and more drifted in. I was overjoyed and felt like hugging all of them. Despite the pouring rain they had kept their word. I dashed down and shook hands with each and every one.

The peasants waited patiently for whatever was to come. Meanwhile the two post vans I had ordered drove up to bring them all to Runkelstein Castle. At first several, especially the old people, did not want to get in, for they had never ridden in such a monster. After I had coaxed all the timid ones, with the support of the younger peasants, their resistance vanished, and in the end no one cared to remain behind. In the end the vehicles were crammed full: more peasants had come than I had asked for.

After driving over ten miles we reached our destination, the overgrown ruins of Runkelstein Castle. Everything was well prepared: wooden tables and benches had been set up for the peasants under the ancient oaks and shady beeches, and they were given as much wine as they wanted. They quickly lost their inhibitions and even became very interested in our film equipment. Rather than intimidate the peasants, we began with some easy scenes, and as actors they were completely ingenuous. Things went so smoothly that we could begin more difficult shooting that very same day. With amazing acumen they realized better than some professionals do that the aim was to be natural. One of them, who had never left his valley, and was somewhat tipsy from several pints of wine, said: 'I shall light my pipe, that always looks good.'

The first day we filmed until late in the evening, when the peasants had to be driven back to their village. Dead tired, but happy, I drifted off into a deep sleep. There was only another week to get through, then the most difficult part would be behind us. It was unbelievable what my crew managed to pull off in that time. Until 3 or 4 a.m. every day they hauled cables and spotlights up high to the castle ruins.

On the last day at Runkelstein Castle we began very early in the morning. The shooting had to be completed, since the following day the peasants would no longer be free. It was good that these people were accustomed to hard work, but midnight came, and we still weren't done. We hadn't yet shot the big revelry. Everyone was exhausted; I myself could barely stand up. Clutching my script, I sat down on an empty beer keg, on the verge of tears. For a week now I had hardly slept a wink and eaten next to nothing. I could barely concentrate any more. Peasants were dozing in every corner, yet now I was supposed to photograph them carousing wildly.

My crew dragged over the spotlights, tables, benches, barrels, everything we needed for the rustic revelry; then the musicians were called and they woke up the entire company with an earsplitting polka. Wine and fresh beer helped to conjure up an atmosphere of gaiety. I danced with the peasant lads, and everyone laughed and sang and capered, while my men were cranking away from every angle. Schneeberger had given Walter Riml a hand camera, and Riml climbed into an empty barrel in order to be as inconspicuous as possible while shooting.

By 2 a.m. the carnival was over. While the peasants were driven home and my boys rolled up the cables, I was sitting on my beer keg again, making thick red strokes on a whole script page. The next day we could sleep as long as we liked. Wieman and Balazs had already left. We packed another twenty-five thousand feet of rushes into a crate, quickly nailed it shut and put it ready to be dispatched to Berlin to be developed. The only things missing were the shots of the peasants in their homes, streets and church.

I feel very nostalgic whenever I recall that time. Unapproachable as the people were initially, they proved to be as cooperative as possible, so willing to do anything we wanted that we could actually film them during their church service, with even the minister joining in. We had succeeded in winning their hearts.

However, they did not make our departure easy. At the crack of dawn the peasants came and serenaded us, and a little old lady pressed home-made wax flowers into my hands – flowers that would never fade. Several peasants didn't even want to leave us and accompanied us all the way to Bolzano.

It was autumn now, mid-September. Our crew had shrunk back down to six people again, and the light van had returned to Vienna. It was time to go back to the Brenta for my climbing scenes. The first snow was already lying in the mountains, and we certainly couldn't use it in our summer scenes. Furthermore, I had to climb barefoot, dressed only in rags and unsecured (the almost invisible steel rope hadn't been invented yet). Luckily, the weather blessed us with a few more warm days, so we finally got all our shots.

After ten weeks to the very day, I could return to Berlin where the most exciting thing that awaited me was viewing the rushes. I watched breathlessly in the screening room: the rushes were more powerful than I had imagined.

All the business aspects were settled with Harry Sokal. Our contract stipulated that from now on all financial and organizational matters would be handled by his firm, which was a great relief to me. Unencumbered by worries, I could now tackle the studio shooting. We needed only two work days to build the crystal grotto – our only studio set, and the art director did a marvellous job. He had ordered a lorry-load of huge glass fragments, probably remnants from a glass factory, and had them polished into what looked like authentic crystals. This set cost ten thousand marks – one third of the budget of all the location shooting.

I could have spent the rest of my life in that editing room, so fascinating was the work. But since I had never edited a film (aside from shortening *Piz Palü* in Paris), and since I couldn't afford an editor, I had a difficult time. The results didn't satisfy me. I kept changing the film, lengthening or abbreviating the scenes; but the suspense was missing. Finally I decided to ask Fanck for help. One evening I brought my edited print to his home on Kaiserallee. He promised that we'd improve the edited version together, but when I came back to him the next afternoon, he said, 'You can see your film now. I re-edited it last night, I changed and shifted almost every scene.'

I stared at Fanck in utter dismay.

'You cut my film without me – have you gone out of your mind?' I stammered.

'But you wanted me to help you,' he said.

'Only together with me,' I whispered, before bursting into tears. It was my first nervous collapse.

After Fanck left the room and I slowly calmed down, I gathered the hundreds of celluloid snippets dangling from Fanck's glass walls and tossed them into a huge basket standing in the room.

Days passed before I had the courage to look at Fanck's re-edited print. Maybe it wouldn't be as bad as I feared; but what I saw was a mutilation. I never found out whether he was getting even with me or simply didn't understand the subject matter. After all, he hadn't liked the first draft and had been enthusiastic only about the rushes.

Now our friendship had cooled and I was no longer under his influence. My new, independent career had begun.

In order to salvage my picture, I began editing it from scratch. From the thousands of tiny snippets, which I had to splice back together, I gradually wove a real film, which became more visible week by week. At last the legend of *The Blue Light*, which had been a dream just one year earlier, lay before me: completed.

The première took place at Berlin's UFA Palace on 24 March 1932, and it was an undreamt-of success, a triumph beyond my wildest dreams – a sensation. The Berlin critics outdid one another with their accolades. *The Blue Light* was celebrated as the best film of recent years and the press wrote that it deserved the highest award that the movie industry could bestow. *Film-Kurier* wrote: 'The audience was entranced; when the lights went on again the spectators had been living in a different world. A courageous woman, faithful to her work and to her obsession, has turned the film world upside down.'

What effect did this unexpected and unparalleled success have on me? I could barely think; it simply rolled over me. Every day the mailman brought enthusiastic letters, as well as congratulatory telegrams from Charlie Chaplin and Douglas Fairbanks, who had seen a print of the movie in Hollywood.

The Paris and London premières were just around the corner; the Venice Biennale was to take place for the first time that year, and, a few months later, it awarded the silver medal to *The Blue Light* as the second-best film. Behind this success was the plot, a romantic legend without sensational effects, which had been sneered at and rejected by the entire film industry.

As if it were a premonition, *The Blue Light* told of my ultimate fate: Junta, the strange mountain girl, living in a dream world, persecuted and driven out of society, dies because her ideals are destroyed. In the film these ideals are symbolized by the shimmering mountain crystals. Until the early summer of 1932 I too had lived in a dream world, ignoring the harsh reality of the era, not comprehending events like the First World War or its dramatic aftermath.

My friends used to say to me afterwards, 'You must surely remember the day the war ended – Berlin was in such total chaos: the streets were full of people, soldiers, and red flags.' The truth is that I was sixteen, went to school near the Kaiser Wilhelm Memorial Church, and saw and heard little of the final days of the war. I didn't even know why there was shooting in the streets.

It was only after the première of *The Blue Light*, when I toured the length and breadth of Germany with my film, that I had any contact with the people. Here I heard the name Adolf Hitler for the first time. When I was asked what I expected of this man, I could only give the embarrassing answer: 'I have no idea.' I was asked this question more and more often, until I started to become interested in him. Wherever I went, people were passionately discussing Hitler. Many of them obviously viewed him as Germany's saviour, others made fun of him. But I was unable to form an opinion; politically I was so ignorant that I wasn't even quite sure what concepts like 'right' and 'left' meant.

I knew we had over six million unemployed, and my parents believed that the poverty and despair were growing more and more ominous, that the hope for any improvement of conditions was constantly shrinking. My father had dismissed two-thirds of his employees and could barely keep his business afloat, even though it had previously been thriving. He sold our house on Lake Zeuthen and rented a small apartment near the Schöneberg town hall. The social welfare system broke down, unable to deal with all the hardship. Starvation was already rampant among the poor. Wherever I went people were talking about Adolf Hitler; and many expected him to end this misery. I did not like the photographs and newspaper lithographs I saw of him, and could scarcely imagine that this man could fulfil the hopes that people were pinning on him.

I wanted to form my own image.

A FATEFUL MEETING

When I returned to Berlin after touring with *The Blue Light*, the city was filled with posters announcing that Adolf Hitler would be giving a speech at the Berlin Sports Palace. On the spur of the moment I decided to attend. I think it was late February 1932. I had never before been to a political rally.

The Sports Palace was so mobbed that it was hard to find a seat. Finally I managed to squeeze in among people so excited and noisy that already I regretted coming; but it was almost impossible to leave, for the crowds blocked the exits. At last, after a brass band played march after march, Hitler appeared, very late. The spectators jumped from their seats, shouting wildly for several minutes: 'Heil, Heil, Heil!' I was too far away to see Hitler's face but, after the shouts died down, I heard his voice: 'Fellow Germans!' That very same instant I had an almost apocalyptic vision that I was never able to forget. It seemed as if the earth's surface were spreading out in front of me, like a hemisphere that suddenly splits apart in the middle, spewing out an enormous jet of water, so powerful that it touched the sky and shook the earth. I felt quite paralysed. Although there was a great deal in his speech that I didn't understand, I was still fascinated, and I sensed that the audience was in bondage to this man.

Two hours later I stood freezing on Potsdamer Strasse. The rally had had such a profound impact on me that I felt unable to hail a cab. No doubt about it, I was deeply affected. New and unexpected thoughts shot through my mind. Would this man play a role in Germany's history, and would the results be good or bad? As I slowly walked towards Hindenburgstrasse, my mind was in a turmoil.

The next day, simply in order to talk about Hitler, I met my friend

Manfred George, editor of the Berlin evening newspaper *Tempo*, at the Ullstein publishing house. (Ten years later, during World War II, he became publisher and editor-in-chief of the German-Jewish newspaper *Der Aufbau* in New York.) Until that day I had no idea what it meant to be a Jew. It was never talked about in my family or among my friends. Had I not been friends with Manfred George, I might have become more entangled in the National-Socialist ideas. Although an ardent Zionist, he too failed to foresee the full scope of the imminent danger, and his verdict on Hitler was: brilliant, but dangerous.

Many people will not understand how I could trust Hitler for years despite my friendship with Manfred George. I will try to answer this difficult question with absolute honesty. In our conversation George quite understood that I was impressed by Hitler's personality. However, I made a crucial distinction between Hitler's political notions and his personality. Those were two entirely different things, as far as I was concerned. I unreservedly rejected his racist ideas; and therefore I could never have joined the National Socialist Party. However, I welcomed his socialist plans. The deciding factor for me was the possibility that Hitler could reduce the tremendous unemployment that had already made over six million Germans unhappy and desperate. In any case, his racism, many people thought, was only a theory and nothing but campaign rhetoric.

Despite the confusion caused in me by Hitler's appearance at the Sports Palace, the impression of that evening soon receded. Around this time, spring 1932, I was more involved in my future film plans than in any politics. I received a wire from Hollywood, an interesting offer from Universal. They wanted me to play the female lead in Fanck's new film – not only the German version, but also the American one. This would be a German-American co-production, and it would be filmed in the Arctic.

I felt a deep conflict when I read the telegram, and also the subsequent ones. Universal awaited my answer more and more impatiently, but I couldn't make up my mind. No doubt about it, Greenland would be quite an experience. But the success of *The Blue Light* gave me a chance to keep making my own independent movies. Was I to miss that opportunity? Attractive as the Hollywood offer was, I turned it down; which, I believe, pleased Dr Fanck, for the triumph of my film had driven us further and further apart, and he never got over my success.

However, Universal wanted to have me at any price, and now they dangled before me an unbelievable fee; though ultimately it was not the money that made me accept the offer. I was more attracted to the unique opportunity of getting to know Greenland, and there was something else that contributed to my decision: the hope that the American version might help to establish my reputation in the United States. However, the last and deciding factor was an emotional one: the chance of going on another and perhaps final expedition with my former colleagues.

I was cast as a woman pilot whose husband, a scientist, is lost in the Greenland ice. The shooting would be extraordinarily difficult. Knud Rasmussen, the uncrowned king of the Eskimos, half Dane, half Eskimo, was also talked into participating. His knowledge of Greenland – his native country – and his relations with the Eskimos were invaluable for the success of this movie. Paul Kohner, the producer, also succeeded in hiring two members of the Wegener expedition: the scientists Dr Loewe and Dr Sorge.

While the pre-production work was going full speed ahead, I was obsessed with another very different idea. After hearing Hitler's speech at the Sports Palace I wanted to meet him personally; I wanted to form my own opinion of him. Was he a charlatan or truly a genius? I simply wished to learn more about him. The closer we got to the day of departure for Greenland, the stronger became my desire to meet this controversial man before I left.

Although I apparently had little hope of receiving an answer in time, I wrote Hitler a letter, every word of which I still remember, for I have often had to quote the text. I posted my letter on 18 May 1932, and it read:

Dear Herr Hitler,

Recently I attended a political rally for the first time in my life. You were giving a speech at the Sports Palace and I must confess that I was so impressed by you and by the enthusiasm of the spectators that I would like to meet you personally. Unfortunately, I have to leave Germany in the next few days in order to make a film in Greenland so a meeting with you prior to my depature will scarcely be possible: nor indeed do I know whether this letter will ever reach you. I would be very glad to receive an answer from you.

Cordially,

Leni Riefenstahl

In the Nazi Party newspaper *Völkischer Beobachter*, I found the address of the 'Brown House' in Munich to which I sent the letter. However, the newspaper said that Hitler was not in Munich at the time; he was campaigning in Oldenburg, North Germany. I therefore could not count on a response before I sailed.

During those days before my departure I was surprised by an unusual visitor, a very senior Catholic priest, who later became Cardinal of Cologne, Monsignor Frings. He had already written that he had been asked by his superiors in Rome to meet with me, and now I learned why. Monsignor Frings asked me whether I would be willing to make films for the Catholic Church. As a Protestant I was absolutely amazed by this offer. From my conversation with the priest I learned that *The Blue Light* had had a strong impact on the Vatican, and more than anything it was the mystical character of the film that so appealed.

I found the priest very likeable and I did not want to disappoint him, but I didn't care for the idea of making films with prescribed themes; so I thanked him for the honour and asked him if I could think it over until after my return from Greenland.

Universal was sponsoring a going-away party at Dr Fanck's home for the press and the members of the expedition, and only now did we obtain details about our venture. Udet was to take along three stunt planes, the small Klemm, his famous Moth and a seaplane. A British ship would take us to the Arctic and back. Two motorboats, forty tents, and two tons of luggage were part of our equipment – along with two polar bears from the Hamburg Zoo.

'We can't wait for local Greenland bears,' said Fanck. Eventually, I learned how right he was.

One day before our trip my telephone rang and a voice said: 'This is Brückner, adjutant to the Führer.' I held my breath. 'The Führer has read your letter, and has told me to ask you whether you could possibly come to Wilhelmshaven tomorrow for the day. We would pick you up at the railway station and drive you to Horumersiel, where the Führer is currently staying.' There was a pause. Then I heard: 'You could leave Berlin tomorrow morning and arrive in Wilhelmshaven at 4 p.m.' I thought someone was playing a prank on me, so I shouted down the telephone: 'Who is this? Are you still there?'

'Wilhelm Brückner,' I heard. 'What shall I tell the Führer?'

'I don't know who you are. You say you're Hitler's adjutant?' I asked, still sceptical.

Laughing, he said: 'Yes, I am, of course I am. You can believe me.'

My doubts began to vanish, but suddenly it hit me that I was expected at Berlin's Lehrter Station tomorrow at that same time in order to go to Hamburg with the others. Universal had rented a private railway carriage and invited the Berlin press. Inside the train the director and the lead actors were to give interviews, and they set great store by my presence. All this flashed through my head and I realized that I could not possibly leave our crew in the lurch. But I heard myself saying: 'Yes . . . I'll come.'

'Thank you, I will tell the Führer.'

I hung up, feeling as if I'd been turned to stone.

What had happened to me? How could I do this? Wasn't I risking my entire career? Uneasy as I was, my curiosity and the exciting prospect of meeting Hitler were stronger. I wired Fanck a few lines, saying I wouldn't come to Lehrter Station because something unexpected had come up, but I would certainly arrive in Hamburg before the ship sailed. 'Don't worry, I'll definitely be there.' I knew our steamer wouldn't leave the harbour for two days.

The next morning, while the Universal people, the members of the expedition, and the journalists were waiting in vain at the railway station and finally had to take off without me, I boarded a train at a different station and headed towards Wilhelmshaven. I was in such a state of confusion that I could read neither a book nor a newspaper during the journey. Why had I become involved in this? I didn't know. Something was driving me, but the closer the train got to Wilhelmshaven, the more nervous I became. I swore to myself I would not let Hitler influence me under any circumstances, even if he made a good impression. Strong lights cast deep shadows, I thought, and I recalled Manfred George's words: 'The man's a genius – but dangerous.'

At 4 p.m. I got out at Wilhelmshaven and looked around the platform. A tall man came towards me and introduced himself as Brückner, adjutant to the Führer. He wore plain clothes, since, as I later found out, the SA was not permitted to wear uniforms. He took me to a black Mercedes in which sat several other men, also in plain clothes. The driver was a Herr Schreck and the two other men were introduced as Sepp Dietrich and Dr Otto Dietrich.

During the drive, which lasted barely half an hour, I asked Herr Brückner why I had been honoured by such a quick response.

'It was really quite a coincidence. Just a few hours before I received the mail from Munich, I was strolling on the beach with the Führer. We were talking about films, and he said: 'The most beautiful thing I have ever seen in a film was Riefenstahl's dance on the sea in *The Holy Mountain*.' Then, when I was sorting the mail at the hotel and found a letter from you, I brought it to the Führer. After reading it he said, "Try to reach Fräulein Riefenstahl anyway. I would really like to meet her." That was exactly what happened.'

Was this chance or fate?

The car stopped near the beach. Hitler came over and, as he greeted me, a man sprang out from the group of people standing in the background; he obviously wanted to photograph the welcome, but Hitler waved him off. 'Don't, Hoffmann, this could harm Fräulein Riefenstahl.' I didn't understand. How could it harm me?

Hitler wore a dark-blue suit with a white shirt and an unobtrusive necktie. His head was bare and he looked natural and uninhibited, like a completely normal person; in no sense like a future dictator. Indeed, he seemed unexpectedly modest. This Hitler appeared to have nothing in common with the one I had seen at the Sports Palace.

We walked on the beach, Brückner and Schaub following a short distance behind. The sea was calm and the air unseasonably warm. Hitler looked out to the horizon through his binoculars and told me about the various types of boats he could see, and I had the impression that he was quite knowledgeable about them. Soon, however, he began to speak about my films. He made enthusiastic comments about my 'dance on the sea' and told me he had seen all the films I had appeared in. 'The film that made the strongest impact on me was *The Blue Light* – above all, because it is unusual for a young woman to win out against the hostility and prejudices of the motion-picture industry.'

Now that the ice was broken Hitler asked many questions, and I could tell he was well informed about the latest films. As I began to talk, he listened patiently for a long time, then suddenly he said: 'Once we come to power, you must make my films.'

'I can't,' I said impulsively. Hitler looked at me calmly, displaying no reaction. 'I really can't,' I said, now almost apologetically. 'Just two days ago I turned down a very prestigious offer from the Catholic Church on the grounds that I will never make prescribed films. I don't have the knack for it – I have to have a very personal relationship with my subject matter. Otherwise I can't be creative.' Hitler was still silent. Encouraged, I went on after a pause. 'Please do not misunderstand my visit. I have no interest whatsoever in politics; I could never be a member of your party.'

Now Hitler looked at me in surprise. 'I would never force anyone to join my party,' he said, 'but when you become older and more mature perhaps you will be able to understand my ideas.'

Hesitantly I said: 'After all, you have racial prejudices. If I had been born an Indian or a Jew you wouldn't even speak to me, so how can I work for someone who makes such distinctions among people?'

'I wish the people around me would be as uninhibited as you,' he said quietly, and that was the conversation that took place between us.

Meanwhile, Brückner and Schaub had come over to us several times, reminding Hitler that he had to attend an election rally. I also wanted to say goodbye since I was planning to leave for Hamburg that night, but

Hitler said: 'Please stay here. I seldom get the chance to speak to a real artist.'

'I'm sorry,' I insisted, 'I have to board our ship in time tomorrow.'

'Don't worry about it,' he broke in. 'You will be there tomorrow morning. I will arrange for a plane.'

He told Schaub to find me a room and, before I could protest, the cars arrived and everyone crowded in. They were already very late for the election rally. Perplexed, I remained behind with Schaub. The tiny fishing village of Horumersiel had an inn, with a bar, and some guest rooms in which Hitler and his men were staying. Since Schaub could not dig up a free room, he gave me his and bedded down somewhere else.

Before dark Hitler came back with his retinue, their cars loaded with flowers. At dinner everyone, including Hitler, was in excellent spirits. He said no woman had ever been present at any such function and for him it was agreeable not to be surrounded only by men.

After dinner we all went outdoors, most of us strolling towards the sea, but Hitler waited a while, then asked me to accompany him, which I thought a little strange, but I didn't want to be impolite by refusing. Again the two adjutants trailed at a short distance. Hitler was entirely relaxed; he talked about his private life and about things that greatly interested him, especially architecture and music. He spoke about Wagner, about King Ludwig of Bavaria, and about Bayreuth, but after a while he suddenly changed his expression and his voice. With great passion he declared: 'More than anything else I am filled with my political mission. I feel that I have been called to save Germany – I cannot and must not refuse this calling.'

This is the other Hitler, I thought, the one I saw at the Sports Palace. It was dark, and I couldn't see the men behind us now. We walked silently, side by side until, after a long silence, he halted, looked at me, slowly put his arms around me, and drew me to him. I had certainly not wished for such a development. He stared at me in some excitement but when he noticed my lack of response he instantly let go and turned away. Then I saw him raise his hands beseechingly: 'How can I love a woman until I have completed my task?' Bewildered, I made no reply and, still without exchanging a word, we walked back to the inn; there, somewhat distantly, he said, 'Good night.' I felt that I had offended him and regretted that I had come in the first place.

The next morning, when we all had breakfast together, Hitler asked whether I had slept well, but remained rather taciturn, and his mind seemed to be elsewhere. Then he asked Brückner whether the plane was ready, and when he heard that it was he walked me down the steps. Kissing my hand, he said goodbye. 'Come back safe and sound and tell me about your experiences in Greenland.'

'I'll get in touch when I return,' I said. 'Be careful about assassination attempts.'

His voice was cutting in reply. 'I will never be the victim of an assassin's bullet.'

We left and as the car rounded a bend in the road, I looked back. Hitler was still standing in the same place, gazing after us.

SOS ICEBERG

On the morning of 24 May I found myself on the deck of our British liner, the *Borodino*, where I was greeted with great relief by the members of the expedition. Everybody wanted to know why I hadn't caught the train with them, but for the moment I told no one my secret. Dr Fanck was very angry with me; but he soon calmed down, burdened as he was with work and problems. Besides, my lateness had caused no harm since the *Borodino* weighed anchor one day later than scheduled anyway. Paul Kohner, our nice producer (later, the successful Hollywood agent of great stars) never forgave me for the sympathies with Hitler that I felt at that time. The next morning, when the ship put to sea, we were all troubled by the same question: What would Germany be like when we got back?

The film people were the only passengers on the *Borodino*, apart from the ship's crew. The skipper told me that it was very unusual for the Danish government to have given us permission to go to Greenland. Not even Danes were allowed to travel there, because the Eskimos had to be protected against disease and a civilization that was harmful to them. Normally only scientific expeditions were permitted to enter.

As mountain people we found the ocean marvellous. After the first three days we had recovered from our seasickness and begun to enjoy the peace and quiet on deck. It was then I revealed my secret and told the others about my encounter with Hitler. Opinions about him were divided; several people were enthusiastic followers, others sceptical, but most were uninterested.

There was great excitement on deck when the first whales were spotted, their fins emerging behind the stern. This was wonderful for us landlubbers, but an even stronger impact was made by the first iceberg, which seemed to be sailing towards us from the horizon. It was more than just an unfamiliar sight, for we felt that our film was floating there. We would be spending the next few months on just such an icy platform as the one drifting past us. Now more and more and icebergs appeared; their forms were fantastic, yet they looked unshakeably solid. Meanwhile the nights kept growing shorter till eventually the sun shone both day and night.

One morning I was peering through the porthole of my cabin when, to my great astonishment, I saw that we were close to land and I could already hear shouts: 'Umanak! Umanak!' We had reached our destination after travelling eleven days. I quickly extricated myself from my blankets and dashed out to the railing. What a sight met my eyes: a huge, rocky mountain towered at least thirty-five hundred feet above sea level, with a tiny settlement at its foot. The Eskimos came darting towards the ship in narrow kayaks, and soon they were scurrying up the ladder and grinning at us, little realizing that we would be living among them for many months.

So this was Greenland. Not unfriendly, not at all grey; on the contrary, we saw a soft, green land. Neither was it ice-cold; in fact we could stroll about in lightweight coats. Our ship seemed fenced in by huge icebergs and it was a great achievement of our English skipper to have steered the two-thousand-ton freighter unscathed through this labyrinth of ice. The Eskimo administrator of Umanak, a colony with only two hundred and fifty inhabitants, came to welcome us and we accompanied him ashore. How pleasant to have solid ground underfoot again! A horde of dogs dashed towards us. There were dogs everywhere, and they all looked starved.

My eyes were refreshed by the wonderful enchantment of colours, but my nose picked up the dreadful smell of fish oil. Fish waste lay everywhere, and the dogs also left their mark. The air was heavy with the stench of stale fish.

We had landed at the right time. An enormous whale was being hauled ashore by a whaler, and we learned that such a catch is made only every few years. The Eskimos were very excited, for they would be all able to live on that one whale for months on end. Its tremendous body was pulled in as far as possible; then the inhabitants ran over and set about slicing it up into large cubes until their boots were blood-soaked and their faces sweaty and radiant with the zeal of working. The famished dogs greedily devoured the entrails, so greedily that the next day some of them lay dead with over-stuffed bellies. When the whale meat was salted and hung up to dry, the smell hung over the entire coast like a cloud of gas.

We fled back to the ship where the unloading had already begun, and for the first time we saw the huge number of crates that had been stowed in the belly of the *Borodino*. It took a week to bring everything ashore and during that time we were allowed to remain on board.

When Udet's three aeroplanes were unpacked and re-assembled, the Eskimos were transfixed with wonder. The first aquaplane was seaworthy in just a few days, and Udet zoomed off on a test flight. It was splendid watching him taxi across the water, take off in between icebergs, and then loop elegantly around the drifting ice castles. The Eskimos couldn't believe what they were seeing.

When the entire cargo was unloaded, we had to say farewell to the *Borodino*. It was almost painful watching her steam off, knowing that we were left on this northern coast of Greenland for almost five months with no link to Europe; in a strange country, among people who were utterly remote from our world. We didn't even have a hut here. We had to sleep in small tents and we couldn't hurry back to civilization if we felt like taking a hot bath like we could when we were in the mountains. We gazed wistfully at the plume of smoke from our ship until she vanished beyond the icebergs.

On our campsite, twenty minutes from the fish stench of Umanak, countless wooden crates were heaped up. First, the tents and tools were unpacked, so that we could set up our sleeping places. Then there was a rush to grab the best and most windless tent site with the most beautiful view. We didn't know whether it was day or night, for the sun shone non-stop. Primitive furniture was made from the empty wooden crates: tables, chairs, small dressers emerged, and many of them were attractively covered with waxcloth. An Eskimo traded me a dogskin which I used as a bedside rug.

Eventually our tent city became ever more grand. We even had our own kitchen. Two small tents were equipped as darkrooms and two large ones as dining rooms, where we ate our meals together. Our clever production manager used empty, floating gasoline drums to build a fabulous gangplank, while Dr Sorge, assisted by a score of helpful Eskimos, was to construct a pit for the polar bears.

Laymen will wonder why we had to take polar bears along to Greenland, which had polar bears galore. But it would be impossible to film dramatic sequences with wild polar bears. We could spend days hunting for one and at best our camera would capture a swimming or climbing polar bear, but no one in the world would be able to direct polar bears swimming in the Arctic Ocean and get them to follow a script.

Our three bears were fierce creatures, perhaps even fiercer than bears living in the wild. Not even their Hamburg keeper dared to reach into their cage, much less open its door, so we didn't even know whether the scheduled scenes would work out. However, rather than keep the bears in a cage the whole time, we tried to build them an outdoor pit. On three sides there were rocks, which loomed only six feet above the water when the tide was in. The fourth side of the 'cage' was the open sea and we had to cover this exit with a huge wire net. The net reached thirteen feet below the surface of the water, right down to the floor of the bay. In this way we would be sure that the bears wouldn't escape.

The big moment came for Tommy, the largest of our bears, when his cage door was opened. Cautiously he stuck out his head, shook a bit, and then plopped into the water where, with understandable relish, he washed the dirt of his long captivity out of his fur while his two colleagues in the other cages eyed him enviously. But we soon realized we had underestimated Tommy. First he tried to clamber up the rock and stones had to be thrown to force him back into the water. We saw that our bearpit wouldn't work, for we couldn't have someone perch on the rock twenty-four hours a day, chasing the bear back down. Tommy, however, had already found an escape hatch. He had dived down and looked for a place to slip through, but had found the wire net reached all the way down to the ground; unable to discover a hole, Tommy had dug into the soft mud with his paws and swun out. Although we whooped like Indians on the warpath, Tommy paddled out all the more swiftly into the Arctic Ocean; losing no time, Tobias, a bold Eskimo bear-hunter who had been a member of the Wegener Expedition, went after him in his kayak. He was quick enough to catch up with Tommy and drive him back, but the bear refused to re-enter the cage; not even the choicest piece of seal meat could lure him in. Apparently enjoying himself, he swam around, and two men had to stand guard and thwart any escape efforts.

We all slept badly during those days, because the slightest rustle could have been our polar bear. At last, on the fourth day, Tommy gave up the struggle against his growling stomach, trotted back into his cage, and that same instant the door slammed shut.

Aside from a few Eskimo scenes, all our shooting had to be done on icebergs and ice floes; so we had to find an iceberg that we could climb with the least amount of danger. Since innumerable icebergs drifted past Umanak every hour, we had more than enough to choose from; except that they drifted on and never stayed around. They floated so quickly that within just a few hours, they were sixty miles beyond our campsite. Another problem was that we had to shoot on the iceberg for several weeks, not just one day, but no iceberg remained alive that long. Huge pieces of ice kept plunging into the sea, making it change its position, tilt over, wobble – or simply turn upside down.

Icebergs do not offer solid ground, and I regard them as more perilous than glaciers. Sometimes the roars of their splinterings and calvings are so loud that they sound like the booming cannon of a battleship. None of us could imagine setting foot on such a treacherous support, much less working on it, and our director's face grew more anxious by the day. He began to realize that he had underestimated the danger; each take would jeopardize the lives of his crew.

One morning Dr Fanck called us together and announced that after conferring with our scientists he had decided to shift our base of operations further inland, to the fjords of Greenland. He said that the icebergs there, which broke off freshly from the glaciers, were harder and more stable than those in the open sea and it might be possible to find a stranded iceberg that would not yield to its wanderlust as easily as those out here.

As we had only two small motorboats we could not take down the entire camp. The food and the tents were to remain in Umanak, to be sent to our work camp at the inner fjord only when needed.

Fanck was accompanied by twelve people, while the rest stayed at the camp in Umanak. Incidentally, this time, unlike with Fanck's other film projects, I was not the only female; nine of our thirty-seven members were women. The scientists had taken along their wives, Udet his classy, red-haired girlfriend (nicknamed Louse), and our director his secretary Lisa, whom he later married. There was also an American girl, the wife of Marton, the American director.

Since I wasn't needed for the early shooting, I enjoyed my freedom and relished the surrounding Arctic landscape. The air was as soft as silk and so warm that one could run about in a bathing suit. However, a plague of mosquitoes descended and to escape them I assembled my collapsible boat and paddled out to sea, where I drifted around, hour after hour, whiling away half the day. I glided through gates of ice, past glittering and towering icebergs, through shimmering grottoes, whose walls were reflected all the way down into the water – green, pink, blue and violet. A few times I encountered Eskimos in their nimble kayaks, returning from the hunt, and always they greeted me with smiles.

One day, unnoticed by anyone else, I took a rubber mattress along in my paddle boat and searched until I found an iceberg with a flat base, which I could easily climb. It was the first iceberg I had ever stepped on. Water from the melting ice had formed a small lake, which lay in the ice like an emerald, and even on the iceberg it was so warm that I took a refreshing swim in the small lake. Then I stretched out on my mattress and began to sunbathe. I had seldom felt so carefree and liberated as the iceberg slowly drifted through the fjord.

All at once an earsplitting crash tore me out of my reverie. My iceberg shuddered, the lake washed over me, I slid down the slope on my belly and grabbed hold of my paddleboat, which I could not lose at any price. Luckily the iceberg didn't capsize, but merely heaved and pitched to and fro until gradually it calmed down. Now at last I could see what had happened. It was not my iceberg that had calved, but a neighbouring one that had broken apart, and was rolling about in the water like a wounded monster. More chunks of ice kept tumbling off, creating huge waves and keeping my little iceberg in constant agitation as I paddled away. It was the first and last time that I visited an iceberg for my own pleasure. Naturally I told the director nothing about my adventure.

Although I had sworn after my break-up with Hans Schneeberger that I would never fall in love again, I nevertheless succumbed once more. A pair of eyes, green like a cat's, had been attracting me for several days. They belonged to Hans Ertl, whom Fanck had taken along, together with the Swiss mountain guide David Zogg, as a specialist for cutting the ice steps, necessary for climbing icebergs. Ertl was, without a doubt, the most attractive male member of the expedition and, impetuous and enthusiastic, he could fascinate people for hours on end with his stories.

Once, when I wanted to paddle out in my boat, he accompanied me, in order, as he said, to teach me how to paddle correctly, but a casual flirtation suddenly turned into passion. I forgot all my resolutions and was happy to be in love again. We were both visual people who loved nature, so as long as we still had time we hunted and fished together – and soon we were inseparable. We could enjoy that paradise of undimmed happiness for nearly a week. Then Hans was summoned by our director to a new camp which was to be set up further north. I had to remain at the base camp in Umanak with the others.

Our expedition now consisted of three units: the base camp here, Fanck's work camp in Nuljarfik, and Udet's flying camp in Igloswid, sixty miles from Umanak. Udet was bivouacked there with the aviator Schrieck, his mechanic Bayer, and Schneeberger, who again did the flight shooting, as he had done at Piz Palü and Mont Blanc. Flying in Greenland was not as easy as it had seemed on the first day. Initially the ocean around Umanak was fairly free of icebergs, but now the bay was filling up with floes. The seaplanes no longer had a landing place, and since Udet's Moth couldn't possibly touch down on the hilly terrain, he had gone looking for a take-off and landing point that was free of ice. The only one he could find, Igloswid, was far away from Umanak. But how were we to communicate with Igloswid? Udet hit on a practical solution, but one which could be carried out only by a brilliant flyer like himself. Fanck accepted the plan and wrote out detailed instructions for what Udet was to do in the air. He established precise directions and also did a few sketches. The letter was then placed in a mailbag, which was suspended at the tip of a long pole. Udet then had to fish up the bag by means of a hook attached to a rope hanging from his plane. He kept flying around the pole until he caught the mailbag. Without his skill the flying sequences wouldn't have come off.

At last we received a report from Fanck which Udet tossed down in a bag over Umanak. What we read wasn't exactly cheerful. Fanck had penetrated a fjord, where they were working on an ice floe; but the fjord was very dangerous. Two large glaciers, the Umaniako and the Rinks, coming from the interior ice, had wound up in this fjord and both glaciers calved horrendously every week or two. The huge ice masses breaking off from the inland glaciers are so gigantic that they cause a turmoil throughout the fjord and during those hours no boat can venture near. Even large icebergs are hurled about and shattered by the waves stirred up by the calvings, and a boat was sure to be crushed. Nevertheless we had to sail across the fjord in order to reach Fanck's camp. But we could risk it only if we travelled between two calvings. There was of course no computation available to predict the exact time of the breaking, and we had to travel twenty-five miles across the dangerous fjord.

After a few days our boat, the *Per*, came to pick me up, along with two of the three polar bears. The dangerous crossing was imminent. Frau Sorge came along because she missed her husband. The motor-launch contained its steersman Krauss, two women, two polar bears, many crates of provisions and petroleum; thus laden we chugged across the Arctic Sea. I realized that Fanck had once again manoeuvred us into an insane adventure.

The bitter cold drove Frau Sorge and me into the tiny cabin; but inside there was no room to stretch out. We found a sort of mattress, about as wide as an ironing board, but we had to embrace one another in order to lie down. As soon as one of us fell asleep, and loosened an arm, the other would fall down on to our sardine provisions which lay on the floor of the cabin. The place smelled of damp wood, bears, food leftovers and oil, and the ice floes beat against the sides.

On we sailed for many hours, first in milky dawn, then in harsh sunshine. When we got hungry we pulled a can of liverwurst out of the provisions and brewed a few cups of tea on the alcohol burner. Then, exhausted and greasy, we climbed on deck to get a breath of fresh air. But here our sleepiness instantly vanished, for we were overwhelmed by the extraordinary appearance of the fjord. The shoreline consisted of vertical coal-black walls, and a shimmering mass of ice moved all around us as our little boat tried to push its way through. Everything surrounding us was shrouded in soft blue veils of fog. Silent and deeply moved, Frau Sorge and I sat on the ropes, peering out at this inconceivably beautiful sight.

The voice of Krauss, our pilot, aroused us from our reverie.

'We can't possibly go any further,' he said.

'What are we going to do?' I asked uneasily, but he only shrugged.

'That's Greenland for you,' he said. He tried again to get through. Every time a tiny gully opened up between the ice floes he promptly nosed the boat in, but soon the cleft in the barrier closed tight and we knew it was hopeless. Our pilot felt that advancing any further was too dangerous because we might be unable to turn back – a terrifying thought. After twenty-four hours of travelling we were at most only one hour from Dr Fanck and yet separated by many days.

All at once a tremendous block of ice surfaced right in front of us and towered between the floes. Now our boat was stuck for good. We were trapped in the ice. Gazing at the shore very close by, I wondered whether we could risk dashing across the floes and hiking to the camp after reaching the shore. This was our only possible salvation, and Gerda Sorge was all for it, so we decided to try. Krauss had to remain in the boat with his bears, but once we arrived at the camp we would send help.

Gerda and I scurried across the ice floes, and by great good luck we made it to shore; then we trudged over hills and rocks until, an hour later, far below us, we recognized a tiny mushroom – Dr Fanck's white tent. We shouted, we yodelled, we yelled, until someone actually came out of the white mushroom and peered up. Then more people gathered as we ran down the slope and were jubilantly welcomed at the bottom. Our little boat remained far away, among the ice floes, but the very next day a favourable current drove the blocks apart, freeing the boat from its predicament.

In Nuljarfik we had three tents in which fifteen people slept, but the weather was warm, thank goodness, and we could finally work. The ice-floe shooting was more difficult than Fanck had imagined; the floes often broke, and the performers had perforce to take one cold bath after another. Our cameras were especially in jeopardy for, if they fell into the water, our film would be doomed, there being no possibility of sending to Europe for new cameras.

We were delighted when Knud Rasmussen, whom the Eskimos looked upon as their king, arrived in order to help with the Eskimo scenes. He knew their language since his mother was a Greenlander, and with him we moved to the small Eskimo settlement of Nugatsiak, where we were given a welcoming feast. Here we got to know other aspects of the smiling Eskimos. They were big children who admired everything foreign. They were carefree, kind-hearted and dedicated, but nothing in the world, not even twenty whales, could get them to paddle their kayaks past an iceberg. If they were asked to do it, they would say: 'Aiyapok, aiyapok' (Very, very bad). Even Rasmussen, their idol and compatriot, could not get them to change their minds. Unfortunately, however, all the scenes in Fanck's script took place on icebergs and floes. He himself was unhappy about the possible dangers, and we all knew very well that disaster could strike any day. Nevertheless, Fanck wanted to attempt shooting on the iceberg. Otherwise we would have had to cancel our film. Day after day, using binoculars, he scoured the area for a relatively stable iceberg with one side sloping flat into the sea, so that we could board it from our boats. At last he found one suitable for his purpose. Only the key people came along, as well as the polar bears, who were needed for this shooting. I too had to go, for my first scenes were to be filmed.

We steered towards the iceberg, a giant at least two hundred and fifty feet high. As we drew up close we saw that the wall descending into the water was still fifteen or twenty feet above us. It was too high for us to pull up the terribly heavy cages containing the bears, though Ertl and Zogg could cut steps and wedge hooks into the walls and hoist up the equipment. I scaled the ice wall with the first group and it was only when I reached the top that I could scan the breadth and height of this monstrous chunk of ice, which moved so silently through the polar sea. It took half an hour to walk to the highest point. Standing with a few of our people some fifteen yards from the edge, I suddenly felt a quivering and a dull roaring inside the colossus. Before I could run to the edge there was a second tremor. To my horror I saw a broad stretch of ice split off and four of our men, who were perched on it, plunged into the ocean. Deafening crashes and booms filled the air, along with screams and cries for help. We were petrified as huge columns of water spouted upwards. We crept to the edge of the break-off place and saw our boat pitching and rocking amid the ice masses, tossed about like a nutshell between the ice blocks. Our people desperately struggled for their lives, some of them unable to swim. Ropes were thrown out to them from the boat and, helplessly, I watched Hans Ertl, David Zogg, Richard Angst and Schneeberger disappear under the ice blocks, then re-surface, as they attempted to cling to the chunks of ice. The first to be rescued was Hans: a long pole was held out to him from the boat. Then the others, the non-swimmers, were hauled in.

Meanwhile the boat had sailed very close to the break-off point, and we were hurriedly brought down with ropes and ladders, for more ice massses could have split off at any moment. We breathed sighs of relief once we got out of the danger zone, grateful that we hadn't taken cameras or polar bears on to the iceberg.

For days on end we felt the terror of that experience in our bones. Now nobody felt like gambling his life for the sake of a film. Not a single frame of the iceberg scenes had been shot, and the polar summer was almost over. The air grew cooler, the nights longer, twilight settled over land and sea and our spirits sank with the sun.

DR SORGE

Nine days earlier Dr Sorge had gone to the fjord in order to measure the calvings of the Rinks Glacier. It was important for scientists to determine how fast glaciers move. He had paddled off alone in a tiny kayak, not even packing a tent. We hadn't heard from him for nine days, and his provisions must have run out long since. Gerda and the rest of us were very uneasy. Fanck was arranging a rescue operation when an Eskimo, who had been hunting seals in the fjord, brought back the middle piece of Dr Sorge's collapsible kayak after fishing it up. This fragment could only mean that the boat had been shattered by ice masses, yet not a muscle twitched in Gerda's pale face. It was only when, amid the deathly silence of our crew, she handed Dr Fanck her husband's sketches that the tears poured from her eyes.

Boats were set out to hunt for Dr Sorge, and Udet also flew off, not returning until four hours later. He had scoured the entire twenty-five miles of the fjord, but had not found the slightest trace of Dr Sorge. Any further search seemed futile; Dr Sorge was given up for lost. Then Udet decided to take another stab at it, and again we waited for hours.

It was already growing dark when we heard the roar of Udet's plane. It almost grazed our heads, and we could see him wave, so we sensed that he was bringing us good news. Udet had indeed found Dr Sorge at the very end of the fjord, at the foot of the Rinks Glacier. Although Udet had very little fuel left in the plane, he wanted to attempt a third flight in order to throw down food and clothes. Meanwhile, he had tossed a rough map down to our people in the rescue boats, which would enable them to find our lost colleague and bring him back.

Precisely twenty-four hours later our two search boats returned with Dr Sorge and, despite his exhaustion, he gave an immediate account of his adventure. He had paddled for thirty hours through the ice blocks of the fjord until he reached the foot of the glacier. There he had clambered up the steep rocks with his instruments and provisions until he had found the right spot. The instant he peered through his telescope it happened – the catastrophe that probably no human being had ever lived through before. The entire front of the glacier broke loose in a chunk about three miles wide and half a mile in from the inland ice mass and thundered down into the fjord. Water columns hundreds of feet high were hurled into the air by the pressure of the ice masses. The mass of the crumbling glacier ice, as he calculated, was greater than the cubic contents of all the buildings in Berlin.

The tremendous spring tide had swept Dr Sorge's boat away, but he had never lost faith that he would be rescued. He went on with his scientific observations, carefully rationing the food which had been meant to last only five days, and built stone figures so that his whereabouts could be identified from the air. It was only on his second flight that Udet discovered the stone pyramids and also the small column of smoke that Dr Sorge had barely managed to keep going with burning moss.

THE POLAR WINTER APPROACHES

The bad weather caused us a great many problems. Cold winds swept over the tents, and one night I was woken by my whole tent collapsing upon me, along with the poles, sticks and strings. When I finally struggled out of the network of safety ropes, I discovered that all the other tents had done the same.

We also had a lot of trouble with the dogs. They had already broken into our kitchen tent one night and pounced on our valuable provisions, but now they began ripping the tents and devouring our leathers and furs. My mountain boots had already fallen victim to them, and not even my Leica, whose leather case attracted the dogs, was safe from their greed. We built large stone walls around the tents, yet nevertheless one day I missed my seal trousers, my beautiful film costume. I had assumed they'd be safe under my sleeping bags, but the dogs had found them anyway.

Another two weeks of bleak weather dragged by as the days grew shorter, the nights icier, and slowly we got a sense of the loneliness of the polar nights. When the weather improved we shot our first scenes with Tommy. The polar bear inside his cage was lowered into the boat and with rifles aboard we chugged out to sea for several hours so that when the bear was let go he wouldn't swim back to shore. He would then have to be caught again since he was needed for further sequences. Besides, we had promised the Danish government not to release any bears in Greenland. Bears that had been in Europe might be carriers of trichina, which would have had disastrous consequences if the animal had been caught by an Eskimo.

Finding a suitable iceberg, we opened the trap-door of the cage, and Tommy leaped eagerly from the boat. At first he was still a bit weak but then his form improved and he clambered up to the highest peak of the iceberg, so that we got good shots of him. Next, lured by the water, he swam off faster than we could follow and continued to elude us. We pursued him for hours, but couldn't bag him. After trailing him for a whole day without success, we were totally worn out. While Tommy went to sleep on an iceberg, we dozed off in our boat. When we awoke, the bear was gone – great for Tommy, but bad news for us. Again we scoured the water for many hours, and finally, on a tiny rock islet, very close to shore, we found him – again fast asleep. Our Eskimo, Tobias, managed to lasso the bear and lock him back in his cage.

I had caught such a cold during this long bear-hunt in the polar autumn that I developed a high fever and my body shook with rigors. This was a calamity, for we had not yet shot a single one of my scenes, and our Danish physician had no morphine or painkillers or any medicaments that could help me. 'That idiot,' Fanck snapped furiously, 'he has only rusty hypodermics for the clap!' He decided to have me flown to Umanak where at least there was a small paediatric hospital. After an hour of flying, the plane descended towards the settlement. We soared over the hospital roof and were about to touch down when a sudden storm prevented our landing. The waves were so violent that they shattered the floats of the seaplane and we had no choice but to turn around. My aches and pains grew more and more hard to bear.

I had no option but to try and defy my illness and do the most important scenes, especially the ones with Udet. Despite my condition, those Arctic flights were an unforgettable experience. Udet soared through ice gates and straight up ice walls only to plunge down again. On one occasion my breath almost failed me. Udet wanted to fly in between two gigantic vertical ice towers that stood right next to one another, but it was only in the last moment that he saw a third tower behind them. He yanked the plane around in a fraction of a second and swooped through the narrow space at a sharp angle. I thought my heart would stop.

After those sequences one last stunt was left for me and Udet. It was the most difficult scene, but as it was crucial to the story Fanck refused to omit it and, though they might have used a stand-in for me, he wouldn't hear of it. The script required that I fly my plane right into the wall of an iceberg and jump out just as the aircraft goes up in flames. Not only was I terrified of this scene, but Udet too was nervous. He was supposed to be concealed inside the plane in order to pilot it so that it would be damaged by the collision but not totally destroyed; otherwise it wouldn't burn. Furthermore, Udet was not a good swimmer.

We took off, Udet flew a couple of loops, then throttled down the engine, and whizzed towards the iceberg, losing more and more speed. I closed my eyes, and when I opened them for an instant the iceberg looked as if it were heading straight towards us. Then we crashed – flames darted up and the plane was soon burning furiously. I leaped into the icy water and Udet jumped a bit later to avoid being filmed.

Fanck had his rushes in the can and we were all very relieved that the scene was over and done with. But it was sad that Udet's famous Moth had to be sacrificed for this breathtaking stunt. She lies at the bottom of the sea under the ice of Greenland.

The final days were once again to show us the terrors of the Arctic, for no day passed without a struggle with nature. The next scene was the one in which I was to be unroped. The boat was hooked to the iceberg and I had already wound the rope around me. Ertl and Zogg were the first to climb the iceberg in order to wedge in hooks and snap links. Suddenly Tobias shouted, 'Start the engine!' And then we saw our boat being scooped up by a large ice fragment and the iceberg to which we were moored began to wobble. In the last second our steersman managed to prevent the boat from capsizing by letting it slide down the ice column. We were saved.

Ertl and Zogg had been standing on the teetering iceberg only twenty-five feet above water level. An instant later, as the ice colossus rose from the sea, they were one hundred feet above us. They were hurled up and down as if on a gigantic swing, but never low enough to jump safely into the water. This was awful for David Zogg, who couldn't swim. Ertl, losing his crampon, began to slide, but managed to cling to the ice and, as the iceberg sank back down to the sea, he dived into the water. While we pulled him into the boat, Sepp Rist rowed a small boat close to the see-sawing iceberg so that Zogg could leap in at the right instant. We watched, helpless and with nerves on edge, until Zogg shouted, and we saw him perform a ski-jumper's forward leap directly into the boat. He landed with his head in the pit of Rist's stomach.

This time Fanck was shocked into full awareness of the dangers. He ordered a rest period of several days, and learning that the *Disco*, a Danish freighter, would shortly be arriving in Umanak, he decided with a heavy heart to shoot my acting scenes in the Swiss Alps. I was to go ahead on the *Disco*.

FAREWELL TO GREENLAND

I packed in great haste. In an hour the motorboat was to take me to Umanak, where the Danish freighter had already docked, and it was only when my iron valises had been deposited in the tiny boat and I sat, all bundled up in thick blankets on a mountain of old, empty petrol drums, that I realized this was a farewell. Everyone shook my hand and sent greetings to Germany.

In the grey twilight I could hardly make out the faces of my comrades, and when I heard the farewell salute I began to weep for the first time in years. Through a veil of tears I watched the shore moving further and further away. The petrol drums wobbled and I was freezing in my dogskin suit, but when the night came it was a real night. I saw a star for the first time in months. A blood-red strip glowed on the horizon and there was a beautiful play of lights and colours. The icebergs drifted by like ghosts in the moonlight. Wrapped in green veils of fog they heaved and waved as if trying to hold me back. Sadness engulfed me. Would I ever see Greenland again? The boat chugged softly through the stillness and I slowly drifted off to sleep.

The shrill wail of a siren woke me up. It came from my freighter. Someone took my luggage and I followed numbly. The water rushed up in front of the keel, the *Disco* headed south. We left Greenland.

I still shudder today when I recall that voyage. For a month we ploughed through stormy seas. Most of the passengers, as well as a large number of crewmen, were seasick, and waves thirty feet high swept across the deck. The storm grew into a hurricane with wind speed Beaufort 12 and I was horribly nauseated. In addition I was afflicted by bladder colics and I had a sharp pain in my big toe. Since my days as a ballet dancer, my toenails tended to grow into my skin unless I went for regular pedicures, and I had already been operated on three times for this condition. When the captain saw my foot he immediately said: 'That looks bad; you can't wait until we reach Europe. We'll put in at the harbour in southern Greenland, and you can get surgery there.' And so the *Disco* changed course.

When I awoke from the ether I heard the Danish physician say: 'Before you went under you whispered twice: "Life is beautiful."' From then on I felt better, since the hospital had also given me painkillers for my colics.

Before reaching our final destination, Copenhagen, the *Disco* anchored in Stockholm where the captain immediately sent me to a urological hospital. The diagnosis was devastating: 'Your bladder is so badly damaged that you will never be fully rid of this painful ailment.' At the time I didn't realize how correct the doctor was. For decades I have been a martyr to this disease.

In the last week of September the *Disco* docked in Copenhagen where I was greeted, to my great surprise, by my parents, who threw their arms lovingly around me. A reporter asked me: 'Are you glad to be back? Wasn't it awful in those icy waters? And how did you endure all the strain and exertion?' Certainly the vicissitudes had been great, but only because, thanks to Dr Fanck, we had to film on icebergs. Greenland itself was marvellous – so splendid that almost none of us was happy to be leaving it. Even Udet, who loved the pleasures of night-life with beautiful women, wanted to stay on. We all felt certain we would go back in two or three years. Nor were we the only ones who felt that way; everyone who had ever lived in that environment felt and spoke as we did, and a few have remained there forever.

What is the miracle that casts such a spell on this land without trees, without flowers, without vegetation, except for the swamp grass during the summer months? I believe it is inexplicable. No real miracle ever can be explained. The magic of Greenland is spun like a veil from thousands of invisible silk threads. We see differently there, we feel differently. Europe's issues and problems lose their meanings – they fade away. In Greenland we were barely conscious of the things that agitated us at home. We carry a gigantic ballast of superfluous, unproductive things that can never make us happy, and that seemed to vanish in the ocean – no telephone, no radio, no mail, no car. We find we can do without all those things. And we had time. Our real lives were restored to us.

HOTEL KAISERHOF

I was back in Berlin. Hitler was not yet in power, and his party had suffered setbacks. The posters announced that he would be giving another speech at the Sports Palace. I had promised to tell him about Greenland, so I called the Hotel Kaiserhof and asked for Herr Schaub or Herr Brückner. This time Schaub came to the phone and seemed rather disgruntled. I asked him to tell Hitler that I was back from Greenland. A call came just a few hours later; it was Brückner on the line, wondering whether I had time that same afternoon to have tea with Hitler. We settled on five o'clock.

As I went up in the lift at the Hotel Kaiserhof, I noticed a short man with a thin face and big, dark eyes, wearing a raincoat and a felt hat. He kept staring at me unabashedly. As I subsequently learned, it was Dr Goebbels, later to be propaganda minister. He got out on the same floor as I did and Herr Brückner, who was expecting me, also greeted the short man and said:

'Doctor, the Führer is still busy. Please be seated in the salon.' Then Brückner took me to Hitler's office. Hitler came towards me and greeted me warmly and without ceremony. His first words were: 'Tell me all about your experience in Greenland.'

Enthusiastically I described my impressions and experiences, and as I was showing him photographs Brückner came back and said: 'Dr Goebbels is waiting in the salon.'

Hitler broke in, 'Tell the doctor I'll come soon.'

He wanted to know more, and I was still so filled with the memories of our expedition that I kept talking as if I were giving a lecture on Greenland. When Brückner reappeared and urged Hitler to come with him, Hitler stood up and said politely, 'Excuse me, Fräulein Riefenstahl, but your description was so riveting that I am almost late for my election rally.'

Meanwhile Schaub appeared with Hitler's coat and, as he put it on, Hitler said to Brückner: 'Take Fräulein Riefenstahl along to the Sports Palace in your car. I'll see the doctor quickly.'

Surprised, I asked: 'What does this mean?'

Brückner replied, 'The Führer assumed that you are going to the Sports Palace too, but won't be able to make it on time; so I am to take you along. Wait here for one moment, I'll come right back for you.' Everything happened very quickly. I was put in a car in which two other women were sitting, though I no longer recall their names.

Nor do I remember any details of the rally at the Sports Palace. I only recollect that everything was quite similar to the first occasion of its kind I had attended before my trip to Greenland. The same enthusiastic masses, the same passionate appeals for support from Hitler. He spoke without a script and with such force that his words seemed to lash the spectators. He appeared demonic as he swore to them that he would create a new Germany and put an end to unemployment and poverty. When he said: 'Collective good takes precedence over individual good,' his words struck at my heart. I had always been preoccupied with my personal interests and given little thought to other people. I had lived very egocentrically. I felt ashamed and at this point I felt ready to make the sacrifices he called for. Perhaps I wasn't the only person to respond in that way. His ability to arouse such feelings may have been the reason why so many people were unable to escape Hitler's persuasive powers. After the speech, however, I had only one idea in mind: to get home as fast as possible. It was almost a flight from danger. I did not want to get dragged into something that could jeopardize my independence.

The next day I was amazed to receive an invitation from Frau Goebbels, whom I did not yet know. I was reluctant to accept, but my interest in learning more about Hitler got the better of me, and my instinct was not wrong, for when I entered the apartment at Reichskanzlerplatz, Hitler was among the numerous guests. Nothing about him recalled the fanatical speaker of the previous day.

As I found out from Frau Goebbels, whom one could ungrudgingly call a beauty, such a social gathering was always arranged whenever Hitler wanted to relax in the home of the Goebbels family after his strenuous campaign trips. Artists in particular were invited to such functions.

It was here I met Hermann Göring, who was not yet as fat as he became later on when he was Reich Marshall. He had read stories about my flights with Udet in Greenland and he wanted to know more about our work together. Göring really was very interested; he and Udet had been in the same squadron during the war, though they hadn't been in contact since 1918.

Then Dr Goebbels discovered me and again I felt his strange stare as he introduced me to several artists. He was himself witty and a brilliant conversationalist, capable of sparkling repartee. Nevertheless, although I was unable to account for it, I always felt uneasy in his presence. His face was not uninteresting: the large dark eyes were striking, as were his high forehead, thick dark hair and well-manicured hands. The lower half of his face, however, especially the mouth, seemed somewhat coarse. It was odd that this man had such a beautiful wife. Magda Goebbels was a lady, aloof and self-assured, a perfect hostess whom I instantly liked. I did not know any of the forty or fifty guests but there was almost no political talk, the main topics of conversation being the theatre and various cultural events.

Trying to avoid Hitler, I exchanged only a few words with him. He spent most of the evening on a small sofa, conversing intently with Gretl Slezak, daughter of the opera singer Leo Slezak. She was a well-known young singer in her own right and Hitler had been friendly with her for some time. I knew her only from the stage, where I had seen her in a few operettas. She was blonde, a bit plump, but pretty and highly vivacious.

Just before midnight, when I was about to leave, Hitler came over to me, and to my surprise asked whether he and his photographer Heinrich Hoffmann could briefly drop in at my place the next day, as he wanted me to show Hoffmann my stills from *The Blue Light*. Quite unprepared for such a visit, I asked nervously: 'Would the day after tomorrow suit?'

'Unfortunately not,' said Hitler, 'Hoffmann and I have to return to Munich tomorrow evening, and we won't be coming back to Berlin for some time.' I thought of my tiny lift and said: 'I live five flights up, and the lift in my building is very small.'

Hitler laughed: 'We'll manage quite well without a lift.' I had no business card with me, so I wrote my address on a slip of paper.

The very next day I anxiously awaited my visitors. My maid had prepared tea and baked the cake herself; punctually at 5 p.m. the doorbell rang. Hitler and Heinrich Hoffmann were accompanied by Dr Goebbels and a Herr Hanfstaengl. As they entered my studio, Hitler's eyes were drawn to Käthe Kollwitz's charcoal drawings.

'Do you like those?' he asked.

'Yes – don't you, Herr Hitler?'

'No,' he replied. 'Those pictures are too dismal, too negative.'

I disagreed. 'I find the drawings deeply moving; the expression of misery and hunger in the faces of the mother and the child is brilliantly done.' His reply to this was, 'When we come to power, there will be no more poverty or misery.' Then he turned away from the drawings, and my maid served tea. I didn't like what Hitler had said. I was taken aback by his words and I saw that he knew little or nothing about art. Fanck had given me these drawings, and when I'd told him about Hitler's imminent visit, he had advised me to take the Kollwitzes down, but I deliberately left them on the wall, because I wanted to see Hitler's reaction.

After a brief conversation, Hitler asked to look at my photographs. When I showed them to him he said, 'Look, Hoffmann, these photos are real compositions. You click around much too much. Better to aim for quality rather than quantity.' I turned crimson. It wasn't tactful of Hitler, and I defended Hoffmann. 'These photos cannot be compared with Herr Hoffmann's. His job is to snap current events. He can't spend time on composition.' Hoffmann winked at me in gratitude.

Meanwhile Hanfstaengl sat down at my piano and improvised a few melodies. I noticed that Hitler was glancing through a book on my desk. I saw that it was *Mein Kampf*. I had jotted such comments in the margins as 'Untrue ... Wrong ... Mistaken', though sometimes I'd put 'Good'. I didn't like Hitler reading these marginalia, but he seemed amused. He took hold of the book, sat down, and kept leafing through it. 'This is interesting,' he said. 'You're a sharp critic, but then we're dealing with an artist.' Hitler never forgot that episode. Even years later, just a few months before the outbreak of World War II, I was reminded of it in the Reich Chancellery.

Over a thousand artists had been invited for the annual get-together: musicians, sculptors, architects, stage and screen performers had come from all over Germany. I arrived rather late. Groups had formed throughout the various spacious rooms and I spotted a large cluster of people with Hitler in the middle. I was so alarmed when I heard him talk about the critical remarks he had found in my copy of *Mein Kampf* that I wanted the ground to swallow me up, especially when he described our first meeting on the coast of the North Sea, where I had told him I could never join the Nazi party. He recited it all as if he were on stage, imitating our dialogue like an actor; yet when my presence was noticed, I was swamped in embraces from my colleagues.

6 NOVEMBER 1932

Soon I received another invitation from Frau Goebbels. Arriving very late, I was surprised to see how few guests there were. Only now did I learn that this was a special Sunday, Election Day, 6 November 1932, when Germans were voting for a new Reichstag. The outcome, I was told, would be decisive for the Party. I had never voted, however, nor did I do so this time, so I couldn't understand why I had been invited.

It was evening already. One could tell from the faces around me that the news was bad. The tension was hardly bearable. The radio kept reporting further losses for the Nazi Party and gains by the Communists; everyone was very dejected. After the final announcements Dr Goebbels went into an adjacent room and could be heard telephoning Hitler in Munich; but I could make out only a few fragments of their conversation. Around midnight when the preliminary tallies were reported, Dr Goebbels looked worried. He told his wife, 'We're facing hard times – but we've overcome worse crises.' Yet I felt somehow that he didn't believe his own words.

The next evening I went to Munich. I was scheduled to give a talk in connection with a new screening of *The Blue Light* at the Atlantik Theater at the Isartor. Just as I was about to close the door to my sleeping compartment, I saw Dr Goebbels standing out in the corridor. He was as surprised as I and asked whether he could come in and sit down for a moment. He had an appointment with Hitler in Munich and he told me about his personal problems and the power struggles in the Party. When he noticed how little I knew about all those matters, he changed the topic and shifted, oddly enough, to the theme of homosexuality. He said Hitler had an extreme dislike of homosexual men; but he, Goebbels, was more tolerant, and did not condemn all equally.

'In my opinion,' I said, 'the characteristics of both sexes are present in every human being – perhaps especially so in artists – but that has absolutely nothing to do with a defective or inferior character.' Surprisingly, Goebbels agreed.

The next day, after returning to my hotel in Munich from a lighting rehearsal at the film theatre, I received a call from Dr Goebbels who asked whether I would care to accompany him to his meeting with Hitler. I hesitated. I was slowly getting to feel that I was being drawn into political matters in which I didn't want to be involved. On the other hand this was an opportunity to get Hitler's personal reaction to the election results.

Indeed, I witnessed an historic moment. The meeting took place in the back room of a restaurant appointed in Bavarian style – the Sternecker, as I later found out. When I entered the room with Goebbels, some eight or ten men, sitting around a circular wooden table, rose to their feet. Hitler, whose face was a deep crimson, greeted me as usual by kissing my hand. He introduced the others, but the name I recall is Wagner, a man who eventually became Gauleiter of Munich.

I had expected to find Hitler in low spirits, but I was mistaken. Amazingly, he spoke as if he had won the election, and the morose and depressed faces of the men gathered round him lit up visibly. Within a short time Hitler managed to imbue them with new courage and convince them that they would soon come to power despite this temporary defeat. 'For the next Landtag elections in Lippa,' he said, 'we have to enter every single home and struggle for every single vote – we will win that election and finally make it. Only the weak have deserted us, and that is good!'

Goebbels had looked completely disheartened, but Hitler succeeded in changing his mood. I had never met anyone with such power of persuasion, able to influence other minds so effectively. It was reason to avoid this man, despite the fascination he exerted over me.

HITLER UNDER PRESSURE

I was back in Berlin, determined to focus purely on my future work and not let myself be diverted by political adventures. I had received various offers, and a few were tempting, but I wasn't free as yet. The acting scenes for the Greenland film were to be completed at the Bernina Pass in just a few weeks.

By chance I met Hitler once more that same year, in an unusual situation. According to my calendar notes it was 8 December 1932. After attending a concert, I was heading home along Wilhelmstrasse when suddenly I heard newsvendors shouting: 'Gregor Strasser leaves Hitler', 'Nazi Party

Finished', 'Hitler's Star Falls'. I bought the newspapers and sat down in the lobby of the Hotel Kaiserhof to read the sensational reports. The news was devastating for Hitler and now I finally understood the things that Goebbels had told me in the train, his descriptions of the intrigues and power struggles inside the Party. How could everything change so quickly and so radically? Just one month earlier, in Munich, I had witnessed Hitler's optimism, and now I was learning about the disintegration of his hopes, perhaps their very end.

Lost in thought, I heard a man's voice saying: 'What are you doing here?' I looked up. It was Brückner, Hitler's tall assistant.

'Are these news stories correct?'

With a dismissive motion he said, 'A press campaign – that's all,' and he strode off towards the stairs. I felt quite shaken, as if something unusual were in the making; then I immersed myself in the newspapers again. I was unfamiliar with the names Gregor Strasser and General Schleicher; I had never consciously heard of either one, but now I saw them before me in front-page banner headlines. Strasser was evidently an important member of Hitler's retinue who had switched sides and was coming to terms with Hitler's opponents.

Brückner again stood in front of me. 'It's a good thing you're here,' he said, 'please come along, the Führer would like to see you.' The blood rushed to my head. I didn't wish to see Hitler in this critical situation. I hesitated, but then I followed Brückner, my heart beating loudly. We went up a wide, carpeted staircase to the first floor, walked down a hallway and around a corner, and then I stood in Hitler's room, where Brückner left us alone.

I am still baffled as to why Hitler sent for me in such a dramatic situation. He shook my hand and then paced up and down the room. His face was wan, his hair clung to his forehead which was covered in sweat. All at once he erupted. 'Those traitors, those cowards – and this shortly before the final victory – those fools – we've struggled and laboured and given our all for thirteen years – we've survived the worst crises, and now this betrayal just before the goal.'

While blurting out these words, he never once looked at me, but paced up and down, halted, clutched his forehead, and then, virtually soliloquizing, he said, 'If the Party crumbles, I'll have to put an end to my life.' After a brief pause he continued, in great agitation, 'But so long as I still have men like Hess and Göring around me I can't do it, I can't desert them, or the many loyal Party members. We will go on fighting, even if we have to start from scratch.'

Hitler was breathing heavily and clenching his hands together. Now I understood why he had sent for me. He obviously needed someone in whom he could confide. At this point he lapsed into an endless monologue about the genesis of the party and only gradually calmed down. Then, looking at me for the first time, he took my hand and said, 'Thank you for coming.'

Deeply moved, I couldn't speak. Without having uttered even a single word, I left the room.

DR GOEBBELS

According to the press, the power struggle in Hitler's party was still raging, and Dr Goebbels, as Gauleiter of Berlin, was playing a major part. It was astonishing to me how much physical energy that little man possessed as each militant speech was followed by another. I didn't like him, but to be fair he was very courageous. When he spoke to Communist workers in Wedding, a poor district of Berlin, beer mugs were hurled at him. He never left the platform on such occasions, even if he was injured, and he nearly always managed to gain control of the angry crowd and win it over. In Berlin he was indispensable to Hitler. I found it all the more incomprehensible that the same man, who had to devote his entire strength to this last phase of the struggle for power, also tried to win me at any price, and at such a time.

Goebbels telephoned me just a few days after I witnessed Hitler's despair. What I had suspected was now confirmed: no day went by without a phone call from Goebbels. On some days he even rang me several times, and kept insisting that we meet. One afternoon he stood at my door, unannounced. 'Please, just for one moment,' he asked apologetically. 'I happened to be in the neighbourhood.' I found this very disagreeable, but I didn't dare turn him away. When I asked my maid to prepare some tea, he begged to be excused: 'Please don't bother, I've got very little time – I'm due at a meeting tonight.'

'What brings you to me, Doctor?'

'I've got problems, and I wanted to tell you all about them.'

'I don't think I am the right person.'

Goebbels ignored my response and began to talk about his problems, especially his political activities, in a manner that seemed arrogant and overweening. Boastfully he assured me, 'I am the invisible wire-puller in the Reichstag, I have all the strings in my hand and I make the puppets dance.' This sounded so cynical that he appeared a real-life Mephistopheles at that moment, a man who would just as readily serve Stalin if circumstances demanded it. He was a dangerous man.

Although I asked Goebbels not to visit any more, his conduct didn't change. He must have noticed long ago that I did not care for him, but my rejection only encouraged him the more. Plainly he could not grasp that a woman could resist his courtship, and eventually we got into an embarrassing argument. I had refused to receive him at home any more, but when he promised to come just one last time, I unfortunately agreed, hoping he would finally give me peace. He was behaving like a schoolboy with a crush. His eyes shone as he said that in 1926, six years earlier, he had stood outside the UFA Palace in Berlin, at the première of *The Holy Mountain*, hoping to catch a glimpse of me.

Until then I had assumed that he was interested in me purely as an actress, but now I realized that he was after me chiefly as a woman. During all this flattery, he noticed an open book. It was Nietzsche's *Thus Spake Zarathustra*. He picked it up, leafed through the pages, and asked me whether I was an admirer of Nietzsche's. I said I was.

'I especially love his language, and above all his poetry. Do you know Nietzsche's poems?' I asked. He nodded and immersed himself in the book. Then, to my surprise, he began to declaim passages, like an actor. I was glad to see him sidetracked. But he put the book down, came over, and gazed at me as if trying to hypnotize me. 'Admit it,' he said, 'you love the Führer.'

'What nonsense,' I cried, 'Hitler is a phenomenon that I admire, not a man to fall in love with.'

Now Goebbels lost control. 'You must be my mistress, I need you – without you my life is a torment! I've been in love with you for such a long time!' He actually knelt down in front of me and began to sob. It was sheer madness. I felt quite stunned at the sight of Goebbels on his knees, but then, when he grabbed my ankles, it was too much for me and I ordered him to leave my apartment immediately. His face turned ashen, but when he still hesitated, I shouted: 'What kind of a man are you! You have a wonderful wife, a darling child! Your conduct is simply outrageous.'

'I love my wife and my child, don't you understand? But I love you too, and I would sacrifice anything for you.'

'Leave, Doctor,' I cried angrily, 'leave, you are quite mad.'

I opened the apartment door and pressed for the lift. With hanging head and without glancing at me again, he left.

The future Minister of Propaganda never forgave me for that humiliation.

ESCAPE TO THE MOUNTAINS

After that I had only one wish – to leave Berlin as soon as possible. I did not want to run into Dr Goebbels again or for that matter, Hitler. Christmas was only a few days off, however, and since my parents wanted to spend Christmas Eve with me I decided to remain in Berlin until then. Besides, I still hadn't finished my series of articles for Manfred George. The first few instalments had already come out in *Tempo*. After my return from Greenland, George had asked me to write a book about my experiences on location, and he had acquired the first serial rights for *Tempo*. My book was published in early 1933 by Hesse & Becker in Leipzig. Its title was *Struggle in Snow and Ice*.

One day, when I returned from shopping, I found a bouquet outside my door. The accompanying card said: 'Du-Du – I'm back again and I'm staying at the Hotel Eden.' Josef von Sternberg was in Berlin after a three-year absence. We met the next day and I found he had hardly changed at all. He told me that Erich Pommer had invited him to make another film.

Naturally, the conversation turned on Hitler and National Socialism, and I told him about our encounters. To my amazement Sternberg said, 'Hitler is a phenomenon – too bad that I'm a Jew and he's an anti-Semite. If he comes to power we'll see whether his anti-Semitism is genuine or just campaign rhetoric.' Incidentally, Sternberg was not the only one of my Jewish acquaintances to say such things. Harry Sokal and others made similar comments. I realize that today, when we know about the dreadful crimes that took place during the Hitler regime, all that sounds unbelievable, especially to younger people. But it is the truth.

Sternberg wanted to see *The Blue Light*. We drove to the Geyer printing lab in Neukölln where my film material was stored. I was eager to hear his opinion, for I knew that he was a severe critic. But I was not disappointed.

'It's a beautiful film,' he said, 'and you are wonderful. There is no greater antithesis than that between you as Junta in *The Blue Light* and Marlene as Lola in *The Blue Angel*. I made Marlene: she is my creature. Now she's an international star. And you – when are you coming?'

'I'll come as soon as I've completed the shooting for *SOS Iceberg*. I really hope it'll be by spring.' With this promise we parted after celebrating our second farewell until midnight, with lots of champagne at the Eden Bar. This separation was to last a long time.

The next day, Christmas Eve, I was still far behind in preparing for my trip to the Swiss mountains where the shooting would take several months. As I was packing my bags the doorbell rang several times with deliveries of

Christmas presents. When it rang again I yanked open the door and I stared aghast into the face of Dr Goebbels, wearing an embarrassed smile. Before I could utter a word, he said, 'Please excuse me, I wanted to wish you a merry Christmas and bring you a small Yuletide gift.'

I let him in, and when he saw the huge wardrobe trunk he asked in surprise: 'Are you going on a trip?'

I nodded.

'Will you be away for a long time?'

I nodded again.

'Where are you going – when are you coming back?'

'I'll be gone for a long time. First I'm going on a skiing vacation and then I have to do my scenes for *SOS Iceberg*.'

In some agitation Goebbels said, 'Please don't go away.' When I held up my hand to ward him off, he said, 'Don't be afraid, I won't get too close, but I'd at least like to talk to you now and then. I'm so alone, my wife is seriously ill. She's in hospital, and I'm afraid she may die.' He said this with such a poignant expression that I almost felt sorry for him, but I was much more sorry to hear that Magda Goebbels was in hospital.

'Listen, Doctor, your place is with your wife more than ever. You should spend every free moment with her.' I could not understand this man.

Goebbels was very depressed. Despondently he sat down on the couch without removing his coat. 'At least tell me where you can be reached, so that I can telephone you.'

'I don't know where I'll be. I'm going to a different winter resort, and I have no idea when the shooting will start.'

Once he realized how hopeless his efforts were, all human quality vanished from his features. His face now looked like a mask as he handed me two small packages, muttering, 'A Yuletide greeting.'

When the door shut behind him, I opened his gifts. One package contained a copy of Hitler's *Mein Kampf* bound in red leather, with a personal dedication from Goebbels. The second package contained a bronze medallion with a relief of Goebbels' head. What bad taste, I thought, to make me a present of himself.

It was good to be in the mountains again. In St Anton on the Arlberg I was able to improve my skiing with Hannes Schneider and learn the latest techniques at what was perhaps the finest skiing school in the world.

One afternoon, when I returned to the Hotel Post after skiing, the manager told me that a certain Dr Goebbels had rung me up several times. How had he tracked me down in St Anton? No sooner had I changed my clothes than I was summoned to the telephone. It was Goebbels again. I was upset, and asked him who had revealed my whereabouts to him, but he answered merely that he had called up several skiing resorts till he found me. I didn't know if I could believe him.

'What do you want from me?'

'I only wanted to find out when you'll be back in Berlin.' His stubbornness was beyond belief. Coldly I said, 'I won't be back for the time being, and please leave me in peace, Herr Goebbels, and don't telephone me any more.' I hung up. My mood was spoiled for the rest of the evening.

In mid-January I travelled to Davos, lured by the Parsenn skiing area – as a dream area for skiers, which surpassed all my expectations. There were miles of downhill terrain covered with powder snow, and so many routes that you could pick a different one every day, each more beautiful than the last.

On the Parsenn I ran into Walter Prager, whom I had first met in St Anton. Surprisingly this young Swiss had become the Kandahar champion. He offered to train me for the Parsenn-Derby race, and skiing was even more fun with him, for he was a first-class trainer. I made progress day after day and we now trained by the clock.

Walter Prager and I developed a friendship. In time it grew deeper, resulting in a romance that lasted for two years. Oddly enough, I have never fallen in love with men who were socially, politically or artistically prominent, or who spoiled women with expensive gifts. When my mother eventually met Walter she wasn't very happy about my choice.

'What do you see in the boy?' she asked. 'You never show up with an intelligent man. I don't understand you.' Poor Mama, how could I explain it to her? Walter was handsome, but did not make much of an impression at first. Soon, however, I was utterly entranced by his special charm, his vivacity, his personal appeal. It is not easy to make people understand sudden feelings of liking and love – not even people one is as close to as I was to my mother.

Our Swiss location shooting was delayed from week to week, but I didn't mind. I was in Davos in late January when I was surprised by the sensational news: Hitler had become Chancellor of Germany. So he had made it. I didn't know how, for I had read no newspapers for weeks. Since there was no television in those days, I didn't watch the day of Hitler's takeover and the torchlight parade until years after the war, in old newsreels. Hitler had achieved his goal, and as Chancellor he interested me a lot less than he did before the takeover.

In early February I was finally called to location shooting at the Bernina Lodge. At the time I was still in Davos. My bags were already packed when, without warning, Udet turned up.

'What are you doing here?' I asked, surprised.

'I'm calling for you,' he said impishly.

'How?' I asked, nonplussed. 'In your plane?'

'Of course in my plane.' Udet was unbelievable. I sent my mountains of luggage on by rail and climbed into the sports plane which Udet had landed on the small frozen lake in Davos.

At take-off we almost had an accident. The area for taxiing was small and there was a stiff tail wind. Terrified, I saw that our plane was dashing straight towards the hayricks at the end of the lake. But with his innate skill Udet pulled the plane aloft just before it reached the haystacks. After a brief flight we landed effortlessly and to a warm welcome on the small icy surface of Lake Bernina, right beside our sets. I greeted Fanck and his colleagues and also the movie people who had come from Hollywood. Tay Garnett was directing the American version, in which Rod la Roque was the male lead.

The ice sets were fantastic. The architects had built a genuine polar landscape containing huge ice caverns and I was pleased to see that working relationships were generally harmonious. Tay Garnett and Dr Fanck seemed to have a fine rapport. It was a real pleasure working with Garnett, although it was a pity the weather was so bitterly cold and the shooting prolonged for such a long time. Luckily I often had long breaks, and our executive producer, Paul Kohner, was generous enough to allow me to fly to Davos with Udet on my free days. I could continue my ski training on the Parsenn, and my efforts were crowned with success. I paticipated in the renowned Parsenn Derby, along with the best female racers in Switzerland and, after skiing down the long run, I won second prize.

It was already May, and the shooting still hadn't ended. The ice was starting to melt, so that we had to climb further up. As a result we transferred to the Jungfrau Pass, which looms ten thousand feet high in the Berne Alps, and it was here that, most important of all, the scenes with the sled dogs were to be shot. At last, in June, the final footage of the Greenland film was completed.

A VISIT TO THE REICH CHANCELLERY

After a six-month absence from Berlin I had to get used to the big city again and to the changes in Germany. We had already learned at the Bernina Pass that Hitler had become Chancellor, but we hadn't heard about the book burnings in front of the university in May or about the start of the persecution of the Jews with the first boycott in all cities. I was deeply disturbed and alarmed.

In my mail I found a letter from my friend Manfred George, who was now in Prague. He wrote that he had been forced to emigrate, like many of his Jewish acquaintances, since he could no longer work in Germany. He was going to try to move to the United States, and what moved me most of all was that he wished me luck. There was also a letter from my friend Bela Balazs in Moscow. An ardent Communist, he wanted to remain in Russia for the time being, then return to his native Hungary later on. I wept as I held these letters in my hand.

I heard from more and more friends and acquaintances that they had left Germany. Only my two doctors, Dr Lubovski, who was engaged to my friend Hertha, and Dr Cohn a well-known gynaecologist, were still in Berlin. Many great Jewish actors and actresses, such as Elisabeth Bergner, were no longer performing, and Max Reinhardt and Erich Pommer had also left Germany. I just couldn't understand the terrible things that had happened. I hadn't heard anything from Hitler since December nor, of course, from Goebbels, which I was very happy about. Now that Hitler was in power I didn't want to have any contact with him.

A year had passed since the successful première of *The Blue Light*. In Greenland and later in the Swiss Alps I had lost contact with the film industry and had therefore been unable to use the scenes of this film for my career. I had trustingly placed everything concerning *The Blue Light* in the hands of my partner Harry Sokal. During the long work in *SOS Iceberg*, I had used up my fee, even though I still had obligations towards my own firm. Once again I was penniless, with barely enough money to pay my back rent. But since I was supposed to receive fifty per cent of the profit on my film I wasn't the least bit worried.

When I tried to see Sokal, I learned from Herr Plehn, his assistant, that Sokal had left – understandably, since he was half-Jewish. What I couldn't grasp was why he had never sent me my half of the profits from the distribution both in Germany and abroad. The film had been an international triumph. I was depending on the receipts, but had not yet received a single penny. With a certain unease, I asked Herr Plehn if Sokal had left any money for me? 'No,' was the reply.

'How am I to get to my money?'

Herr Plehn shrugged and answered evasively, 'Herr Sokal will most certainly take care of it from abroad, but there's not much hope. The tax office says he owes them 275,000 marks.'

This bad news was followed by even worse news. At the Geyer printing lab I found out that Sokal had taken my original negative. Desperately I tried to reach him but I was told he was in France, and I couldn't locate him anywhere there.

During those days, when I was suffering from depression, I recalled a film that Fanck had suggested, to be named after its subject: *Mademoiselle Docteur*. It was a spy story set in Germany and France during World War I. Fanck had made some valuable documents available to me, for he had worked with Mademoiselle Docteur in the German espionage office. She had been given her nickname by the French in recognition of her excellent work, which they had greatly feared.

I presented the idea to UFA. They were excited by the subject and willing to produce and finance it. They also guaranteed me a say in the artistic control of the project. For the script they promised me their star writer, Gerhard Henzel, with whom I had already made contact. I wanted Frank Wisbar to direct and UFA was more than agreeable. For the first time since *The Blue Light*, I had a chance to prove myself in a dramatic screen role, which had been my most fervent wish for years.

But then I got a telephone call from the Reich Chancellery asking me to be there the next day at 4 p.m.; the Führer wanted to see me. I didn't have the courage to say no.

The next day I arrived punctually at the Chancellery where Hitler was already expecting me. It was a warm summer day with not a cloud in the sky. I wore a simple white dress and discreet makeup. The tea table was set on the terrace facing the garden. Only the butler was present. I had seen neither Schaub nor Brückner, the adjutants. Hitler looked relaxed and he was just as friendly as he had been a year earlier, when I had first met him by the North Sea.

'Please have a seat, Fräulein Riefenstahl.' He pulled out my chair and settled opposite me while the butler poured the tea and offered cake. I kept looking down and felt very inhibited – in contrast to our earlier meetings.

'We haven't met for a long time.' Hitler began. 'If memory serves me right it was last December, before I came to power. Back then you saw me in my worst moments. I was on the verge of shooting myself.' I sat with downcast eyes, saying nothing. 'But,' he went on, 'fate decreed otherwise, and for all those who easily lose heart, it is a lesson that one should never give up a struggle, no matter how hopeless it appears.' I didn't dare glance at him. 'When my Party disintegrated and my fellow fighters abandoned me, I would never have dreamed that six weeks later victory would drop into my lap like a ripe fruit.' He took a sip of tea, looked at my face, and asked encouragingly: 'And what about you, where have you been all this time and what have you been doing?'

I still hadn't uttered a single word, for I was thinking of Manfred George and my other friends, who had left Germany because of this man, but I was at a loss as to how I could broach this subject. There seemed to be a lump in my throat. At last, overcoming my inhibition, I said, 'I have been in Austria and Switzerland finishing the shooting for SOS Iceberg. I only came back to Germany a short while ago. But so much has changed here.'

'What do you mean?' he asked, becoming more distant.

'Some of my best friends have emigrated, and so have a number of great artists, for instance, the unique and irreplaceable Elisabeth Bergner.'

Hitler raised his hand as if to stem my flow of words. Rather angrily he said, 'Fräulein Riefenstahl, I know how you feel; you told me as much in Horumersiel. I respect you. But I would like to ask you not to talk to me about a topic that I find disagreeable. I have great esteem for you as an artist, you have a rare talent, and I do not wish to influence you. But I cannot discuss the Jewish problem with you.' His face relaxed again and then he continued with a more amiable expression: 'I have not yet told you why I invited you here. I would like to make you an honourable offer, consistent with your talent. As you know, Dr Goebbels, as Minister of Propaganda, is responsible not only for the press, but also for theatre and cinema. But since he has no experience in the area of films I thought of you. You could work at his side and be in charge of the artistic aspect of the German cinema.'

These words made me almost dizzy. 'You suddenly look so pale,' he said anxiously, 'do you feel all right?' If Hitler had had an inkling of what had gone on between Goebbels and me, he would never have made me that offer, and I couldn't possibly talk to him about it. But even aside from that business I would never have accepted such a position.

'My Führer,' I said, 'please forgive me, but I do not feel that I could take on this honourable task.'

Hitler looked at me in surprise.

'Why not, Fräulein Riefenstahl?'

'I do not have the ability. I have specific ideas of what I could do, but if I had to do something that I don't have a feel for, I would fail miserably.' Hitler gave me a long, scrutinizing look. Then he said, 'Good, I understand. You are a very self-willed person. But you could still make films for me.' This was the very thing that I had feared. 'I'm thinking of a film about Horst Wessel or one about my movement.' Now it was I who interrupted Hitler.

'I can't, I can't,' I said, almost pleadingly. 'Please don't forget I'm an actress – with all my heart and soul.'

I could tell from Hitler's expression how greatly I had disappointed him. He stood up, took leave of me, and said, 'I am sorry that I cannot win you over for my films, but I wish you luck and success.' Then he motioned to the servant in the next room. 'Please escort Fräulein Riefenstahl to her car.'

Confused and troubled, I drove home, upset that I had so deeply disappointed Hitler, whom I still respected at that time. But I was unable to do otherwise; I am what I am. When Fanck visited me, I told him about this conversation and my dilemma. He was appalled. 'Your behaviour was outrageous: you have to try to make up for it in some way.'

'But how?' I asked, crestfallen. Fanck thought hard. 'Years ago, when I had a terrible crush on you, I gave you a valuable first edition of the complete works of Fichte – my sister had bound it very beautifully in white leather. Why don't you part with it and give it to Hitler, along with a few lines explaining your conduct.'

'A good idea,' I said, and gratefully hugged my director.

MY CAR BREAKS DOWN IN GRUNEWALD

A few days later I had a visit from Walter Prager and Hans Ertl who told me about mountain tours they had made after the conclusion of the work on the Greenland film. As we were preparing supper in a cheerful mood, the telephone rang. Since it was very late I didn't want to answer it, but Prager was already holding the receiver and handing it to me. When I recognized the voice, I nearly dropped it. It was unmistakably Dr Goebbels.

'May I call on you for a few moments?'

'No,' I said brusquely, 'I'm sorry, Herr Minister, but I've got company.'

There was a pause. Then I heard: 'I have something very urgent to tell you.'

'You can't come here. My friends arrived from Switzerland today and they're spending the night here.'

Goebbels insisted. 'Just for a moment – I can be there in ten minutes – I'll hail a cab,' and without waiting for my answer he hung up. I was so furious that I didn't want to go downstairs. But my friends advised me not to show Goebbels too much hostility, so I went down. In any case our lovely evening was thoroughly spoiled.

When I stepped out into the street, Dr Goebbels was already standing there all alone. It was raining heavily and there was no taxi to be seen anywhere. Goebbels was wearing a raincoat, and his broad-brimmed hat was pulled down over his face. After greeting me and apologizing for his sudden appearance, he said, looking round the dark, deserted street: 'We can't stay here, you'll be drenched.' I glanced at my small Mercedes parked in front of the building and we took refuge inside the car.

'I must not be seen with you, we have to drive away from here.'

'Where to?' I asked, perplexed.

'Wherever you like, so long as we won't be seen.'

'What's this all about, Dr Goebbels? Just what do you want from me?'

'I didn't know you were back in town. I only learned about it yesterday, from the Führer.'

'You're still being very silly – you're going to get us both into terrible trouble.'

I switched on the engine and drove down Kaiserallee towards Grunewald. There was only one thing on my mind: nobody must see us. The rain was so heavy that I could barely make out anything through the car windows, and it looked as if it might start to hail any moment. The best thing to do, I thought, would be to drive into Grunewald. Nobody could possibly be strolling there in this weather. As we turned into the forest I saw Goebbels produce a gun from his raincoat pocket and thrust it into the glove compartment. Noticing my alarm, he smiled. 'I never go anywhere without a weapon.'

Now I was eager to find out what was so urgent. But he kept silent. I could only drive at a snail's pace. Huge paddles had formed on the road, splattering the car windows. Just don't drive into a tree, I told myself, as I left the main thoroughfare and drove straight through the woods, which became more and more dense so that I had to zigzag around the firs. It took all my concentration just to keep driving over that swampy ground. Suddenly Goebbels put his arm around my waist, the Mercedes jerked violently, the engine stalled, and to my horror I realized that it was leaning at a dangerous angle. We dared not stir lest the car overturn altogether. Goebbels, who remained astonishingly calm, cautiously removed his pistol from the glove compartment and thrust it into his raincoat pocket. Then he tried to open the car door and fortunately we managed to climb out unscathed. Because of the poor visibility I had driven into a mound of soft earth. The back part of the Mercedes was stuck in mud up to the left running board, while the front wheels dangled in the air. There was no way that the two of us could pull the car out of the quagmire.

Goebbels then told me to walk in the direction from which we had come. 'In a few minutes you'll arrive at a road where you can telephone for a cab. Unfortunately I can't accompany you. We must not be seen, no matter what.'

I was amazed that he knew his way around so well in this darkness; then he said goodnight, pulled up his coat collar, and started off in the opposite direction.

After wandering around for a long time I found a tavern. There I telephoned home and told my friends, who were very worried about my disappearance, to call a taxi and come immediately. Perhaps, with the driver's help, they could get my car going again. Soaked to the skin, I asked them to bring along some warm clothes, a raincoat, and any torches they could dig up.

As I sat there, wet and shivering, I warmed myself with a hot grog. The kind tavern-keeper gave me a knitted jacket and woollen scarf for my wet hair. I was afraid of Goebbels, who was still pursuing me shamefully. The tremendous secret he wanted to tell me was nothing but a rotten trick.

How relieved I was when my friends came, and how lucky that I hadn't been alone that evening. Together with the cabby we went looking for my Mercedes; but, when we found it, all our efforts at making it roadworthy again were useless. We had to take the taxi back home where we set about celebrating my 'rescue'.

MAGDA GOEBBELS' CONFESSION

My friends had left Berlin, my car was in the garage again, and I could now devote myself entirely to my new project. I was working with Gerhard Menzel almost daily on the script for *Mademoiselle Docteur* and having conferences with Frank Wisbar. The shooting was scheduled to begin in mid-September at the UFA studios in Babelsberg.

To my surprise I received an invitation from the Reich Chancellery for a Sunday excursion to Heiligendamm. The Führer would be participating, but I was given no further details. After my last meeting with Hitler I had assumed I would never hear from him again.

I can recall little of this outing. All I remember is that our group took two cars to Heiligendamm. Hitler sat in the first car, with Goebbels, the photographer Heinrich Hoffmann, and Brückner. I sat in the second with Frau Goebbels, and an aide of Goebbels' sat next to the driver.

I do, however, have an undimmed memory of my conversation with Magda Goebbels. After some chit-chat about fashions, cosmetics, and artists, she became more intimate and began to tell me about her life. She confessed that she had married Goebbels only in order to be near Hitler as much as possible.

'I do love my husband,' she said, 'but my love for Hitler is stronger. I would be willing to give up my life for him. I am so profoundly in love with the Führer that I divorced Günther Quandt, even though we had a good marriage and he spoiled me greatly. I did not mind giving up wealth and luxury for I only had one wish: to be near Hitler; and so I took the job as Dr Goebbels' secretary. Then, however, I realized that Hitler cannot love any woman aside from Geli, his niece – whose death he has never recovered from. He can only love "his Germany", as he says. And so I agreed to marry Dr Goebbels because this way I can be close to my Führer.'

At the end of the war I was reminded of Magda Goebbels' words when I heard about the tragic deaths of the Goebbels family in the Reich Chancellery. Upon learning that Hitler was about to shoot himself, Frau Goebbels killed herself and her six children, whom I know she adored.

To this day I do not know why Frau Goebbels confessed all this to me. My only other memory of that trip was that the cars stopped in front of a hotel – the Park Hotel, I believe – where I was greeted by Hitler and Goebbels, the latter smiling rather sheepishly. Frau Goebbels had told me that Frau von Dirksen, a patroness of Hitler's, had arranged this outing so that he could meet her niece, Baroness von Laffert. This young and very beautiful girl was by all accounts one of the few women whom Hitler admired.

THE PROPAGANDA MINISTER

Just a few days after that excursion, the Ministry of Propaganda, on behalf of the Minister, asked me to come to his office on Pariser Platz the next afternoon at four. How could I avoid another encounter with Goebbels? I thought of pretending to be sick, but that would do nothing to alter this unpleasant situation. The sooner a decision was reached the better.

I rang the doorbell punctually at 4 p.m. A servant led me to a large, beautifully furnished room which reminded me of Dr Vollmoeller's apartment. It could even have been the same apartment or a smaller one next door. Dr Goebbels came in almost soundlessly; elegantly dressed and very well groomed, he greeted me almost cheerfully and led me to a small table decorated with flowers.

'Will you have tea or coffee?'

I asked for coffee and tried to appear calm.

'As you know,' Goebbels began, 'the Führer has put me in charge of cinema, theatre, press and propaganda. I wanted to talk to you therefore about your future film projects. I read in the newspapers that you have been commissioned by UFA to do a motion picture that deals with espionage. How did you come to this subject?'

I told him about Dr Fanck and Mademoiselle Docteur's experiences during the war.

'What other plans do you have?'

'My most ardent wish is to play Kleist's Penthesilea.'

'That would be a good part for you,' said Goebbels. I can imagine you as an Amazon queen. Changing the topic, he asked, 'Didn't you want to visit the Führer some time ago and discuss your plans with him?'

'Not directly,' I said evasively. 'But I did tell him that I wanted to work only as an actress and not as a director. I directed *The Blue Light* purely as a stopgap measure, because I didn't have the money to hire a director.'

'It's a great pity you don't want to cultivate this talent. I have a wonderful subject for you, and that was what I wished to discuss with you.'

I looked at him uneasily.

'It's a film about the press. I would entitle it *The Seventh Great Power.*' Before I could even reply, he launched into an endless dissertation on the press, which he said could manipulate anything. Waxing enthusiastic, he explained, 'I would do a scenario and finance the production. You could then work directly with me.'

I broke in. 'I know nothing about that area: you'd be greatly disappointed in me. It would be an interesting assignment for Walter Ruttmann, who made that outstanding documentary *Berlin, Symphony of a Great City*.

Goebbels shook his head: 'Ruttmann is a Communist; we can't possibly consider him.'

'But he *is* talented,' I retorted.

The expression on Goebbels' face changed. In a soft voice he said, 'I like the fact that you have a mind of your own. You're an unusual woman, and you know I desire you. I will never stop fighting for you.'

Then he made the biggest mistake a man can make in such a situation. He grabbed my breast and tried to force himself on me. I had to wrestle my way out of his arms and dashed to the door, with Goebbels pursuing me. Beside himself with rage, he held me against the wall and tried to kiss me. His eyes were wide open and his face completely distorted. I desperately resisted and, moving along the wall, I managed to push my back against a buzzer and press it. Goebbels instantly let go of me and he seemed to pull himself together even before the servant arrived. When I left his offices I knew that the Propaganda Minister was now my enemy for sure.

VICTORY OF THE FAITH

In the last week of August 1933, I was invited to a luncheon at the Reich Chancellery. Full of forebodings, I drove over to Wilhelmstrasse where Brückner received me and indicated a place at a long table. Some thirty or forty people had already gathered, most of them in SA or SS uniforms, very few in civilian clothes and, being the only woman, I felt utterly out of place. Aside from Hitler's adjutants, Brückner and Schaub, I knew none of these men. When Hitler entered the room he was greeted by arms raised in salute. As soon as he sat down at the head of the table, the conversation became animated, but soon only Hitler's voice could be heard. All I could think was: Why have I been asked here?

After the meal, when the company broke up into small groups, Brückner came over to me and said, 'The Führer would like to speak to you,' and I was led to an adjacent room. There was no one else there except a servant who stood at a small table, serving coffee, tea and mineral water. A short time later Hitler came in and greeted me, apparently in high good humour. His very first question however put me in a quandary.

'I invited you here today in order to find out how far you've got with your preparations for the film on the Party rally, and whether you're getting enough support from the Ministry of Propaganda.'

I stared at him in amazement – what was he talking about? Surprised at my reaction, he said: 'Didn't the Propaganda Ministry inform you that I want you to make a film about the Party rally in Nuremberg?'

I shook my head and Hitler was clearly perplexed. 'You know nothing about it?' he asked angrily. 'Why, that's impossible. Brückner transmitted my request to Dr Goebbels weeks ago. Haven't you been notified?' Once again I had to say no and Hitler grew even more upset. He summoned Brückner and angrily asked him, 'Didn't you pass my request on to the doctor? Why wasn't Fräulein Riefenstahl informed?' As he spoke he clenched his fists, glaring with anger. Before his terrified aide could reply, Hitler jeered, 'I can imagine how the gentlemen at the Propaganda Ministry must envy this gifted young artist. They can't stand the fact that such an honour has been awarded to a woman – and, indeed, an artist who isn't even a member of the Party.' Neither Brückner nor I dared to respond. 'It's outrageous of them to boycott my request,' Hitler ranted. He snapped at Brückner to telephone Dr Goebbels and tell him to order the people in his cinema department to support me and my work in Nuremberg in every possible way.

I myself was by now very agitated, and I interrupted Hitler. 'My Führer, I cannot accept this – I have never seen a Party rally, I know nothing about what goes on there, and I have no experience in making documentaries. It would be better if such films were made by Party members who know the material and are happy to be given such assignments.' I talked to Hitler almost beseechingly, and slowly he relaxed and calmed down.

Looking at me, he said, 'Fräulein Riefenstahl, don't let me down. You would only have to take a few days off. I am convinced that you alone have the artistic ability to turn real-life events into more than ordinary newsreel footage – certainly the officials at the cinema department of the Propaganda Ministry do not. I stood before him, eyes lowered, as he went on urging me more and more insistently. 'The Party rally will begin in three days. Naturally you won't be able to make a really great film this year. But you can go to Nuremberg in order to gain some experience and try to film whatever can be filmed without preparations.' He took a few steps, then resumed. 'My wishes were probably never communicated to the doctor. I will personally ask him to support you.'

My God, I thought, if Hitler knew how impossible any collaboration would be between Goebbels and myself. But I had no desire to tell him about his minister's escapades. Besides, I felt less and less able to contradict him. I simply lacked the courage.

As Hitler took leave of me, his last words were: 'Hold your head up high, everything will work out. You will receive further information before the day is over.' Hitler had not understood how unhappy his project would make me. My most passionate desire was to work as an actress. This documentary would be a burden – very far from the temptation that it was so often made out to be in later years.

When I returned home I found a letter from UFA, informing me that the film project *Mademoiselle Docteur* was to be cancelled. It seemed that the Ministry of Defence had generally outlawed any production of spy films. I was sick at heart – desperately unhappy. Then I was notified that the people of the cinema department were all in Nuremberg and I was to contact them there. I felt angry but I decided to go to Nuremberg. I had neither a contract nor even a letter in my possession to indicate that Hitler had commissioned me to film at the Party rally. I assumed that this would all be worked out in Nuremberg by the cinema department people, but I didn't know anyone there personally, so I presented myself to Herr Fangauf – one of the responsible men in the cinema department of the Ministry of Propaganda – in order to discuss the project. But he claimed he knew nothing about it. How could this be possible? He didn't even want to make a cameraman or film stock available to me. I sensed his profound hostility and avoided getting into an argument. What was I to do? The best thing was to leave.

While reflecting on this and feeling rather helpless, I was approached by a young man. It was Albert Speer, the architect, who had designed the constructions for the Party rally. This was the first time I had ever met him, but I liked him at once, and we instantly got on very well. When I told him about Hitler's plan for me and the boycott at the Propaganda Ministry, Speer advised me not to admit defeat.

'You have to make an attempt at it. I'll help you.'

And indeed, he managed to get a young cameraman to come immediately. This cameraman had never worked on a major film and he possessed only a hand camera; but he was said to be talented, and he proved it too. His name was Walter Frentz and he eventually became a major cinematographer. Then, by telephone, I managed to hire two more cameramen, including Sepp Algeier, an experienced cameraman who had shot Fanck's first mountain films. I got some stock from the Agfa people, with whom I had had a good relationship ever since the days of *The Blue Light*. Since I had no one to help me and I didn't even have an assistant, I rang up my father and asked him to lend me my brother Heinz for six days. Furthermore my father had to loan me money just so that I could get started in the first place. When we began shooting, our staff consisted of five people: three cameramen, my brother who was in charge of expenses, and myself; not an ideal situation.

The first day we filmed only the constructions of the as yet incomplete stands for spectators, and, in the old part of town, the old, beautiful houses, decked out with flags and garlands for the occasion. By the second day the shooting had become extremely difficult. Wherever we stationed ourselves, we were thrown out by SA or SS men and, having no permits, there was nothing we could do. On the third day there was a very worrying incident. I was summoned by Rudolf Hess, who greeted me coolly and said: 'I was told by an SA man that you were sharing a table with Herr Speer and State Secretary Gutterer at the Rathaus Cellar and that you said aloud that the Führer would dance to your tune, and that you also made other derogatory remarks about him. I must warn you not to speak so disrespectfully about the Führer.'

'You actually believe I would?' I exclaimed indignantly.

'The SA man who reported this to me is someone I know personally, and he's no liar. He wouldn't make up such a story.'

'It's a vicious lie,' I snapped, absolutely furious. 'I didn't say a word about Hitler.'

'What else is to be expected of an actress,' Hess retorted somewhat disparagingly. Then, relenting slightly, he added, 'But naturally, I will ask Herr Speer and Herr Gutterer, as witnesses.'

Without saying goodbye I walked out, slamming the door behind me.

Until then I had had no experience of plots or intrigues, and I was so shaken by this incident that I didn't leave my hotel all day. Nor was I comforted when Speer and Gutterer told me the next day that Hess had believed them and would apologize to me. What was I becoming involved in? What kind of trouble was brewing for me? I suspected Goebbels of being behind it. My cameramen told me how difficult it had been to take shots of the minister. Whenever they tried to film him he would ostentatiously turn around to face away from the camera.

Because of all these problems and the resultant agitation, I finally collapsed and blacked out during my last evening in Nuremberg. When I came to, my brother, a physician and a man in Party uniform, were standing at my bedside. When the stranger introduced himself I felt my blood run cold. It was Julius Streicher, the leader of the Franks (Frankenführer) and publisher of that repulsive anti-Semitic newspaper *Der Stürmer*. He of all people had summoned the physician and professed himself very concerned about my state of health. When the doctor had finished examining me and left the room, I said to Streicher, 'How can you publish such a nasty newspaper as *Der Stürmer*?' Streicher laughed, in no way ashamed, and said, 'My newspaper isn't written for intelligent people like yourself. It's for the country populace, so that the peasant girls can tell the difference between Aryans and Jews.'

'I still find what you do loathsome,' I retorted.

Still laughing, he took his leave. 'I wish you a speedy recovery, Fräulein Riefenstahl.'

When the Party rally was over and my three cameramen had left Nuremberg, my doctor prescribed rest and relaxation; but how could I relax? My life was a shambles. My dazzling successes as a dancer, actress, and young producer in Germany seemed far behind me. I saw no chance of fighting the power of the Propaganda Minister, who was in charge of the entire German cinema, theatre and press, and who hated me for repelling his sexual advances.

On my return to Berlin I was summoned to the Reich Chancellery. As before, I was the only woman at the big luncheon table, and again Hitler had the floor, occasionally echoed by Dr Goebbels who, to my dismay, was also present. When the meal was over I was again invited into the adjacent room, by now familiar to me. A short time later Hitler appeared with Goebbels and an embarrassing scene ensued as Goebbels and I tried to hide the tension between us.

'Tell me,' said Hitler, 'about your work in Nuremberg.' I couldn't control myself any longer and I poured out all the humiliation, harassment, and trouble I had endured in Nuremberg. I also told him about the bizarre interrogation by Rudolf Hess, until, choking back tears, I could not go on. Hitler's face turned crimson, while Goebbels became chalky white as the Führer leaped up and snapped: 'Doctor, you are responsible for this. It is not to happen again. The motion picture about the national Party rally is to be made by Fräulein Riefenstahl and not by the Party film people. Those are my orders!'

Full of despair, I exclaimed: 'I can't, I absolutely can't!'

Hitler's voice became icy. 'You can and you will. I apologize for what you have been through. It will not happen again.' Then he said goodbye and left the room without so much as glancing at Goebbels. The Propaganda Minister, his face stony, went off without looking at me either.

Still utterly bewildered, I arrived home just as the telephone rang. I was to come to the Ministry of Propaganda immediately, where the Minister wished to speak to me. I was prepared for the worst, I called a taxi and raced to the ministry. When I entered Goebbels' huge office, he strode towards me, his face contorted with rage, and yelled: 'If you weren't a woman, I'd throw you down the stairs. How dare you tell Hitler such stories about my staff. I am the boss. You are to report to me.'

I tried to defend myself. 'Why? The Führer told me to report to him about my work in Nuremberg, and you were there, Herr Minister!'

Goebbels was furious. 'I can see you're a dangerous person. You tip the Führer off about everything. Get out! I can't bear the sight of you!'

I recall every single detail of that encounter, and also the date. It was 13 October 1933, the day Dr Goebbels went to the disarmament conference in Geneva to announce Germany's withdrawal from the League of Nations.

Several days after that scene I was visited by a Herr Quaas, an employee at the cinema department of the Ministry of Propaganda. He said he had been ordered to help me in the completion of the film on the Party rally and asked me also to draw up a list of all my expenditures so far; I was to be compensated for everything; the Party would cover all further outlays. This meant that I could not now withdraw from the project.

An office was placed at my disposal at the Tesch printing laboratory. The room was so small and primitive however that it didn't even have space for the editing table which had to be set up in an immobilized freight lift, whose doors had been removed. Luckily, I was given a likeable and capable

147

assistant, Erna Peters, who for decades became my most indispensable helper. She remained loyal to me even after the war, and we are still good friends today.

Unenthusiastically I began to sort out the rushes in order to cut them into something useful. Since the film had neither a plot nor a script, I could only try to collate the images in such a way as to create visual rhythm and variety. I have so often been accused of having made propaganda films, but such charges are misguided. This film was a factual documentary, which is something very different. No one, not even the Party, gave me any sort of instructions on what to do. Nor were the shots posed for the camera. We had only four thousand feet of celluloid at our disposal, and the rushes consisted of documentary footage made purely *in situ* during the Party rally. During my work I never thought of propaganda for even an instant.

While I was working on the film at the printing lab, I received an urgent telephone message from Rudolf Diels, chief of the Secret State Police, that he wanted to come and see me. What did that mean? What did the Gestapo want from me? It was late when Herr Diels arrived, but I was kept busy editing until far into the night.

'I apologize for visiting you at such a late hour,' he said, 'but it is so urgent that I didn't want to lose time.'

'What have I done?' I asked anxiously.

'You don't have to be afraid. Your safety isn't at stake. I've been told to take you under my protection forthwith.'

'Who told you to do this?'

'My boss,' he said, 'Reich Minister Göring.'

'He must be joking. Why would I need protection?'

'I can't tell you anything about that. You must trust me.'

'I don't know you, and I don't know if what you're telling me is correct. Perhaps you're only trying to sound me out . . . Excuse me,' I said, somewhat more politely, 'but I've had such odd experiences recently that I'm thoroughly confused and I've become distrustful – something I've never been in my life before.'

While offering Diels a drink, I recalled something that Udet had told me just a few days earlier: 'You have to be careful,' he had said, 'you've got enemies, including some who are after your life.'

'But why?' I had asked, sceptically. And Udet had said: 'Hitler likes you too much. People are afraid that you might get direct access to him, and they want to prevent that.'

'What people?'

'Rumour has it that they're in SS circles.' I then recalled my encounter with Hess, who had said that an SS man had accused me. Suddenly now I was afraid.

'How can you protect me?' I asked Diels.

'You will be watched day and night without noticing it or being bothered, until we know for sure who the people are who want to harm you.'

'Why am I being persecuted?' I asked, still incredulous. And then Diels said in effect almost the same thing as Udet. 'Because the Führer greatly respects you as an artist – which many Party members can't understand – and has honoured you with the task of making a film about the national Party rally. This has caused bad blood among the Party people, who have been waiting for such signs of favour for years – it is a slap in the face for them.'

'But everyone knows,' I replied, 'that I didn't want to make this film and that I don't want to make any in the future.'

'That's not the issue. The point is that Hitler admires you, and this arouses a great deal of envy and ill will, especially among the wives of the Party functionaries. There are rumours circulating that you are Hitler's mistress and that you could therefore become dangerous. People are doing everything they can to make you unpopular with the Führer. For instance, just a few days ago, he was shown a document that had circulated secretly through various offices of the Propaganda Ministry, according to which your mother is Jewish. When this document was submitted to Hitler, it appears that he swept it off his desk.'

I was taken aback, but it was not hard for me to guess who was behind such machinations. While Diels slowly slipped his wine, I gazed at him with interest. He was an extremely attractive man, still young, who could have played the lead in an American western. Tall and slender, his narrow, angular face was scarred, and his hair and eyes were dark. He was a type that would appeal to lots of women.

To take my mind off possible danger, Diels changed the subject and told me all about his work for the current trial in connection with the burning of the Reichstag. The trial had created a world-wide stir, and there were many fantastic versions about what had happened, with newspapers running front-page stories about it every day. The riddle seems to have been solved only recently, and not all historians agree with the Tobias thesis which Diels was advocating back then.

While the German press accused the Communists of perpetrating this crime, the foreign press maintained more or less unanimously that the National Socialists themselves had set fire to the building. Nowhere, however, could one read what I heard that evening from Herr Diels, the head of the Gestapo, who had so often interrogated Van der Lubbe, the principal defendant.

'It's odd,' said Diels, 'that no one wants to believe that Van der Lubbe set fire to the Reischstag by himself, without Communist accomplices. This man is a fanatic – he's obsessed. Understandably for the National Socialists there could be no better propaganda than the fact that this fire was prepared by the Communists and that Van der Lubbe was their tool, but that the fire could have been set by a madman acting alone is less acceptable.'

'Do you really believe that Van der Lubbe set the fire alone?'

'I know he did,' said Diels. At the time I could not tell whether Diels was a man of unusual acumen or of blind prejudice.

After that evening I would much rather have fled to the mountains; but unfortunately I had to complete the Party rally film. It was a thankless task but eventually I managed to see it through. The film ran a little longer than one hour and, at the request of the Party, I called it *Victory of the Faith*, for that was the official name of the fifth Party rally in the history of the National Socialist German Workers' Party.

The cinema department at the Ministry of Propaganda, which was officially the producer of the film, paid me a fee of twenty thousand marks for my work. The entire production costs, including the music, post-synchronization, and my fee, ran to only sixty thousand marks. I mention this purely as a reply to the nonsensical rumours that have been spread about this motion picture. I read just recently that Hitler had ordered me to destroy the negative and all the prints of the film because it contained several shots of Ernst Röhm, the then chief of staff of the SA, whom Hitler had ordered to be shot on 30 June 1934. Actually, even after the war, these duplicate negatives and lavender prints were still stored in bunkers in Kitzbühel and Berlin until they were removed or confiscated by the Allies. During the final days of the war the original negative, like that of *Triumph of the Will*, was lost during transport to Bolzano, where it was to be protected from air raids. Despite all efforts – also by the Allies – these original negatives have never been unearthed.

When I watched the film in a cinema I was anything but happy. What I .saw was only an imperfect fragment, not a motion picture. But the spectators appeared to like it; perhaps because it was more interesting than the usual newsreels. Sepp Allgeier, who had done most of the photography, did a good job. And Herbert Windt, whom I first met in connection with this project, composed a score that added to the effect of this modest film. I, for my part, never looked at it again. I have to smile whenever I read in the press that this film was made with a 'colossal' technical expertise and that I prevented it from being screened after 1945. Another of many legends.

However, the Party mounted a dazzling première which took place at the UFA Palace on 1 December 1933 and ran for only an hour or so. Hitler and the Party bigwigs are said to have been enthralled.

THE GRAND BALL

I was about to leave this disagreeable life for several months and retreat to the mountains but a few days before my departure I received another visit from Herr Diels, who asked me whether I had been invited to the grand ball being given by Dr Goebbels and Frau von Dirksen. Diels told me that this would be a major social event to which many artists and the most beautiful women in Germany were invited. He said that on this occasion Hitler was going to be partnered by a woman, since it was believed that this would make him appear less fanatical and improve his image generally. According to Diels, Frau von Dirksen had been trying for a long time to find him a suitable woman.

The evening of the grand ball – a Saturday – I was sitting at my small desk, making entries in my journal. I was concerned that I hadn't received an invitation; just as I was about to go to bed the telephone rang. It was a Herr Kannenberg, who identified himself as Hitler's head cook, and who asked me a question that struck me as very odd. 'Are you still up, Fräulein Riefenstahl?'

'Well, yes,' I said, not really caring to answer.

'Would it be inconvenient for you to come to the Reich Chancellery at such a late hour? The Führer knows nothing about my calling you, but I am certain he would be delighted if you could come.'

Nonplussed, I said, 'I don't understand. I thought the Führer was at a ball?'

'Yes, he should be, but at the last moment he decided not to go, although he was already dressed, so his aides went without him. He stayed behind alone, and when I brought him something to drink, he said: "It would be so nice if Fräulein Riefenstahl were here." ' For an instant I wavered. I remembered Udet's and Diel's warnings. But then I said: 'I'll come,' and dressing hurriedly, I sped to the Reich Chancellery in my little Mercedes.

When I stepped out of the lift, Hitler was already standing on the stairway and came to greet me. He kept thanking me for coming at such a late hour, and then he told me why he had decided at the last moment not to go to the ball. 'I had the impression,' he said, 'that they were trying to match me up with someone and I couldn't bear the thought.' We sat down in two comfortable armchairs as Kannenberg brought beverages, fruit and cake, then left us by ourselves.

'I'm no mysogynist,' said Hitler. 'I like having beautiful women around me. But I can't stand having anything forced on me.'

Then he began to talk about his youth, about his great love for his mother, about Vienna, about his disappointment at failing as an artist, about his political plans, about how he wanted to make Germany healthy and independent again, and about the difficulties of making his ideas come true. He never once touched upon the Jewish problem, and I felt I was being a coward, but I knew he would not enter into a dialogue under any circumstances. He would have instantly stood up and taken his leave.

Once again it amounted to a monologue. He asked me no questions, nor did he give me any opportunity to interrupt him with a question. The words flowed without a break, but I sensed that he enjoyed having someone listening to him. It was already late when he stood up, took my hand, and said, 'You must be tired. Thank you very much for coming.' Then he summoned Kannenberg, who took me downstairs.

A CHANCE ENCOUNTER WITH MAX REINHARDT

After completing my work in Berlin, I went for a long stay to Davos where I had rented an apartment in the Weber House, opposite the Parsenn Line. I hoped to relax, to forget about the intrigues in Berlin, and to have to worry no longer about being 'protected' by the Gestapo. I was not alone. Walter Prager came with me. Ours was not a tempestuous love, more a rather tender romance. I liked his diffidence and his sensitivity. Walter was not only an athlete but also an intellectual. We both shared a love of skiing, but despite my enthusiasm, my other wishes and plans had not faded, and after being thwarted in my desire to play Mademoiselle Docteur I now focused on another dream-part: Penthesilea, the last Amazon queen, in the tragedy by Heinrich von Kleist.

My desire to play this role had developed in a strange way. In 1925, when I was in a dining car *en route* to my first location shooting in the mountains, I was eyed rather obviously by a man sitting with a woman at the next table. When I stood up and was about to leave the dining car, the stranger blocked my path. Beaming at me, he spread out his arms and said: 'Penthesilea – at last I've found my Penthesilea.'

'A lunatic,' I thought to myself in alarm.

Noticing my reaction, he smiled. 'Don't you know me? You danced in my theatre. I'm Max Reinhardt, and this is Helene Thiemig, my wife.'

I was very embarrassed, for though I had never met Reinhardt personally I owed him my early fame as a dancer. Delighted by the encounter, I sat down with the great director while he enthused. 'You're the one, the perfect Penthesilea. I've been looking for her for years.'

When I confessed to him that I had never read this play by Kleist, he told me I'd be fascinated by it, and then he summed up the plot. He said it was an extremely difficult, but also extremely gripping, play. The three of us sat together for a long time, until I got out at Innsbruck. When we said goodbye I had to promise Reinhardt that I would visit him in Berlin after my location work was done.

When I arrived in Lenzerheide for the first shooting days of *The Holy Mountain*, I told Dr Fanck about this meeting; he said that Reinhardt was right, the part would fit me like a glove. I was enthralled when I read it, not only by the role, but by the entire play. One year later my enthusiasm increased when the Russian stage director Tairov first saw me at Betty Stern's salon. Just as Max Reinhardt had done, he cried out: 'Penthesilea.'

Tairov was so excited that he went to see Dr Fanck and talked him into collaborating on a screenplay. Unfortunately, the project came to nothing because of the astronomical costs. It was just as well, for films were still silent in those days and Kleist's verses would have appeared only as subtitles.

For me *Penthesilea* remained a dream.

TIEFLAND

During the last few days that I spent in Davos, I received a call from Terra Film in Berlin: they asked me to direct and play the lead in a movie to be called *Tiefland* (Lowland). The project interested me, and I went to Berlin.

Eugen d'Albert's opera *Tiefland* goes back to an old Spanish folk play by Angel Guimera. It is set in Spain, during the time of Goya, and the plot is simple. The mountain world with the shepherd Pedro embodies good, the lowland with Don Sebastian embodies evil. These two men fight over the heroine Martha.

My negotiations with Terra went well. They gave me a large amount of artistic and organizational control, so we decided on a co-production. Heinrich George was cast as Don Sebastian and Sepp Rist as Pedro, while the actor Hans Abel was hired to direct my scenes. The outdoor shots were to be done in Spain.

One of the reasons why I decided so quickly was that I wanted to escape any further involvement with Hitler's projects. I had not the slightest interest in a making another Party rally film, but in case he insisted – which was to be feared – I wanted to try and find a good surrogate director, so that the Führer would change his mind about having me. The best man for the job was, beyond any shadow of doubt, Walter Ruttmann, though this was a rather daring notion on my part. I hadn't seen him since his affair with Frau Remarque; and it was questionable whether Ruttmann, an ardent Communist, would agree. I was extremely surprised when he accepted my idea enthusiastically.

Since I refused to work with the Party, the film could only be funded privately, but I managed to get backing more quickly than I had imagined. UFA, which was not yet subordinate to the Ministry of Propaganda, was extremely taken with the project. After a conference with Ludwig Klitzsch, general manager of UFA, my firm, L.R. Studio-Film Inc. (which I renamed Reich Party Rally Film Inc. because of that production) received a distribution contract amounting to three hundred thousand marks. Using that sum, I could work as an independent producer and hire Walter Ruttmann. I knew that he would make an above-average picture, and I hoped that this would pacify Hitler.

I thought of the Party rally film purely in terms of documentary shots, but Ruttmann had a very different conception. He said it would be impossible to turn speeches and parades into an interesting full-length movie, and suggested that the parades should fill only the last third, while the main portion should show the rise of the Nazi Party; that is, the process by which seven men grew into a party of tremendous power within such a short time. I wasn't convinced, but Ruttmann assured me he could splice this part together out of newsreels, newspapers, posters and documents – in the style of Russian films – and the results would be impressive. My respect for Ruttmann's abilities was so great that he managed to assuage my doubts. We agreed that he would do his shooting in Germany with Sepp Allgeier, while I worked on *Tiefland* in Spain.

Meanwhile the pre-production work for *Tiefland* was going full steam ahead. Guzzi Lantschner and Walter Riml were scouting locations in Spain. I had to interrupt my own preparations because I was scheduled to speak at the universities of London, Cambridge and Oxford about my previous movies and about my experiences in Greenland. I have never forgotten my flight to England. There were such violent storms over the North Sea that I became airsick. When we landed I felt so wretched that I was on the verge of cancelling my speech at Oxford, which I was supposed to give on the day of my arrival. During the ride to Oxford I began to feel better, and so I agreed to talk after all. When I entered the auditorium the students were so enthusiastic that I was quite carried away. There was no room to squeeze in even one more chair, and most of the spectators sat on the floor. I didn't get to bed until dawn, for, after I spoke, the discussion continued in the Senior Common Room. My experiences were the same in Cambridge and London. I would never have believed that Englishmen could be even more enthusiastic than Italians.

In London I had the good fortune to meet the director Robert Flaherty and to attend the première of his film *Man of Aran*. This quiet picture touched me deeply with its simplicity and imagery. It is one of the most poignant films I have ever seen.

In Berlin I had my final production conference with Ruttmann about the Party rally film and with Willy Cleve, executive producer of Terra, about *Tiefland*. The shooting in Spain was risky because of the problem of supplies, and the schedule had to be followed precisely since, because of his theatrical obligations, Heinrich George, our lead actor, had only eighteen days.

Terra took over the pre-production work in Berlin, while I went to Spain to help seek out locations and to cast the Spanish performers. In Barcelona I met my assistants, Guzzi Lantschner and Walter Riml, who had done fine preliminary work, but were not in very high spirits. They hadn't received a single penny from Terra and had already spent their own modest funds long ago. I hadn't received any money either, although Terra had promised I would be able to withdraw cash at the bank in Barcelona.

The Spanish landscape was marvellously photogenic, and we couldn't have found a better cinematic background. I was also impressed by the people and the wonderful buildings. I gazed, astonished, at the ancient walls in Avila, the interior courtyards in Salamanca, the churches in Burgos and, above all, Cordova.

In Madrid my old tennis friend Günther Rahn, who had been living in Spain for a year, was waiting for me. Finally the news we had been hoping for came from Berlin, and so did some money, but not enough, alas. We were annoyed to hear that the scriptwriter was ill and that the light van would be two weeks late. How were we going to be able to shoot Heinrich George? I was very worried.

Having found my locations and suitable actors for the film, I waited impatiently, day after day, for our crew to arrive from Berlin. The first day of shooting was only a few days off. Finally, Schneeberger, our cameraman, arrived, but without film stock. What he told us about Terra was deeply worrying. Everything was at sixes and at sevens there, and the head of production was almost impossible to get hold of. I couldn't sleep, my nerves were on edge, as Terra kept stalling me day by day with telegrams and telephone calls. The situation was desperate.

The first day of shooting came but not the crew. I stood trembling in the phone booth of our hotel and heard the distant voice of our head of production: 'The shooting schedule has to be delayed for two weeks.' The receiver dropped from my hand and, feeling faint, I groped about to keep from collapsing, then felt my way along the walls until I reached the hotel lobby. Schneeberger stood there, and as I tried to walk towards him, the ceiling whirled and I crashed down on the marble floor of the hotel lobby.

When I came to, I found myself in the German hospital in Madrid. I assumed I had merely fainted, but I was mistaken. The diagnosis was so serious that I was not allowed to receive visitors for two weeks. I was told I had suffered a circulatory collapse, but I never really found out what that meant. All I know is that I had hypothermia for a long time and suffered from constant fatigue. Just speaking required a strenuous effort.

Only gradually did I learn what had happened. The entire film project had foundered after my admission to hospital, but luckily, although without letting me know, Terra had taken out an insurance policy on me at Lloyd's of London, so their losses were covered. But for me *Tiefland* had died – my second major setback within a year. After four weeks I was released from the hospital but the doctor advised me to wait one month before returning to Germany.

In the north of Mallorca I moved into the newly opened Hotel Formentor, which had very few guests, and there I found the necessary rest and quiet. My feebleness gradually subsided, and I could discuss work plans with Ruttmann, who after telephoning me had boarded an aquaplane in Barcelona and landed directly in the bay in front of my hotel. I was still afraid of any excitement, but my secret fear of receiving unpleasant news from him was groundless. Ruttmann was satisfied with his work. Above all, he praised the talent and zeal of his cameraman Allgeier, and hoped that he could show me most of the rushes as soon as I got back; but something irritated me, he seemed absent-minded, and I noticed how restless his eyes were. When he said goodbye I felt uneasy despite his optimism.

TRIUMPH OF THE WILL

It was around mid-August when I returned to the house on Hindenburg-strasse where baskets of unopened mail were waiting for me. But, afraid of bad news, I opened no letters during the first few days.

Finally I did have to make a start. After sorting out the fan mail, I noticed a large envelope with the return address: Brown House, Munich, and rather nervously I opened it. Hess wrote that he was surprised I had put Walter Ruttmann in charge of this year's Party rally film when the Führer had insisted that I alone was to make the film. Hess asked me to contact him as soon as possible.

This amounted almost to a threat. Even so, I was determined to resist taking on this assignment. First I tried to get in touch with Hess. I called up the Brown House, and was told Herr Hess would be coming to Berlin in two or three days; I could reach him then at the Reich Chancellery. I used the time to look at Walter Ruttmann's footage, and received a new shock. What I saw on the screen was, to put it mildly, useless. It was a jumble of shots of newspapers fluttering along a street, their front pages tracing the rise of the Nazi Party. I didn't understand how Ruttmann could present such work. I was miserable. I couldn't show these rushes to anyone, yet Ruttmann had already spent one hundred thousand marks – a third of my budget – on all this footage. He admitted to being depressed too and claimed that he hadn't realized how little newsreel material there was during the years prior to the Nazi takeover. I couldn't see myself assuming responsibility for this work, but I couldn't think of a way out, other than to discard Ruttmann's footage and to film only during the Party rally in Nuremberg. Ruttmann finally agreed with me.

After many attempts I eventually got through to Hess. In contrast to the previous year he was charming and showed some sympathy for my refusal to make the film. He promised he would discuss it with Hitler and then let me know. Two days later Hess called me back. He regretted that he had got nowhere with Hitler who, he said, had been annoyed that I hadn't begun my preparations, for the rally was to start in two weeks. I asked Hess to tell me where I could reach Hitler, for I absolutely had to speak to him personally in order to beg him not to force this project on me. Hesse said the Führer was in Nuremberg, inspecting the site where the Party rally was to take place.

One hour later I was in my car, speeding to Nuremberg, with only one thought in mind: to free myself from this project. That afternoon I found Hitler. He was at the rally site, surrounded by a group of men, including Speer, Brückner, and Hoffmann, and as I headed towards him I sensed that he knew what I wanted.

After our exchange of greetings he said amiably, but earnestly: 'Party Member Hess has told me why you wish to speak to me. I can assure you that your worries are groundless. You will have no problems this time.'

'That is not all, my Führer. I am afraid I cannot make this film.'

'Why not?'

'I am completely unfamiliar with all the subject matter. I can't even tell the SA from the SS.'

'That's an advantage. Then you'll see only the essentials. I don't want a boring Party rally film; I don't want newsreel shots. I want an artistic visual document. The Party people don't understand this. Your *Blue Light* proved that you can do it.'

I interrupted. 'That wasn't a documentary. How am I supposed to know what is politically important or unimportant, what should or shouldn't be shown? If my ignorance makes me leave out some personality or other, I'll make a lot of mistakes.'

Hitler listened attentively. Then he said, smiling, but in a resoluted tone, 'You're too sensitive. You're just imagining all these obstacles. Don't worry, and don't force me to keep asking you. It's only six days you'll be giving me.'

'Six days?' Again I interrupted him. 'It's going to take months. The main work starts in the editing room. But quite apart from the time factor,' I pleaded, 'I could never take responsibility for such a project.'

Then Hitler became insistent. 'Fräulein Riefenstahl, you have to have more self-confidence. You can and you will do this project.' It sounded almost like an order.

I realized I could not break Hitler's resolve. Now at least I had to try and obtain the best possible working conditions. I asked him, 'Will I have complete freedom in my work, or could Dr Goebbels and his people order me around?'

'Out of the question. The Party will exert no influence on you. I have discussed this with Dr Goebbels.'

'Not even financially?'

'If the Party were to finance the film,' he said sarcastically, 'it would obtain the money only after the Party rally was over. The Party agencies have received instruction from me to support you and your people.'

'Will I be given a deadline for the completion of the film?

At last, growing impatient, Hitler barked, 'No, you can take a year or several years. You are not to be under any time pressure!'

Abandoning my resistance, I ventured to make one last request. 'I'll try it. But I can do it only if I can be free after completing this project and do not have to make any more films to order. That must be my reward. I apologize for making this request. But I wouldn't want to go on living if I had to give up acting.'

Hitler, clearly satisfied that I had given in, took both my hands and said, 'Thank you, Fräulein Riefenstahl! I will keep my word. After this Party rally film you can make any films you like.'

Despite everything, once the decision was made, I felt a sense of relief, and tremendously encouraged by the thought that I would be completely free after this project and be able to do whatever I wished. Barely two weeks were left and the most important thing before the deadline was to find the right cameramen. The best ones were working for film companies or newsreels, so it would be difficult; but luckily, along with my head cinematographer Sepp Allgeier, I managed to hire Walter Frentz, a gifted young man. Both were particularly suitable for this new kind of documentary. Eventually we drummed up a total of eighteen cameramen, each of whom was given an assistant. Ruttmann and I parted on friendly terms.

I was greatly helped by Gutterer, a government official. Within twenty-four hours he managed to furnish an empty house for us in Nuremberg and have a telephone installed. We had our conferences there every morning and every evening. Kiekebusch, our production manager, who was nicknamed 'Mother of the Company', knew everybody and everything. First, he distributed the cars. Every cameraman got one. Then, white and red slips were handed out to be displayed on windscreens, allowing us free passage through all barriers. Finally each cameraman and each technician was given an armband. Counting the lighting men, sound men, cameramen, and drivers, our crew had grown to one hundred and seventy.

Now I could finally start with the directorial meetings at which each cameraman received his instructions for the next day. I had to work out how to raise the film above a newsreel level and it wasn't easy to transform speeches, pageants, and so many almost identical events into a motion picture that would not bore the spectators. A plot, of course, would be inappropriate. The only solution I hit upon was to shoot the documentary events in as versatile a manner as possible, with the emphasis on dynamic rather than static tasks, and I achieved this by having the cameramen practise rollerskating. Such effects were seldom employed in those days. Abel Gance, in his *Napoleon*, was the first screen director to use the mobile camera successfully in a feature film, but documentaries did not employ such mobile photography. I wanted to try it and so I built rails and tracks wherever I could at the rally site. I even wanted to install a tiny lift on a 140-foot flag pole in order to achieve intensely visual effects. At first the city fathers refused to grant me permission; but with Albert Speer's help it was finally installed on the flagpole.

We did not always get what we wanted. For instance, we provisionally

159

added a thirty-five-foot balcony, with tracks, to a house from which Hitler usually watched the parades. Here we could have made first-class tracking shots of the marching groups. But just a few minutes before the start of the parade, the track was shut down by SS men. We had to make do with shooting from roofs and windows.

I had a brainwave concerning Hitler's speech to the Hitler Youth on the Champ de Mars, and by sheer persistence I managed to get my way. In order to liven up the potentially monotonous shots of countless speeches, I had circular tracks built around the podium. The camera could circle Hitler at a suitable distance while he spoke. This resulted in new and lively images.

The atmosphere in our crew was very pleasant; but the obstacles we encountered were unpleasant. My assumption that this time things would be made easy for me proved to be quite wrong. If anything, the boycotts and resistance were even greater. Not a single one of the newsreel people paid any attention to my instructions; and the guards at the barriers always gave us the hardest possible time. Once some SS men pushed our sound van into a ditch; our tracks were dismantled, and I was not allowed into many of the functions. It was so annoying that several times I felt like dumping the whole film. However, during those days, I had no hope of getting to Hitler in order to tell him about the difficulties being put in our way.

Nevertheless, I gathered important experience during this project. I discovered that I had a definite talent for documentaries. I experienced the pleasure of a film-maker who gives cinematic shape to actual events without falsifying them. This pleasure induced me to forge ahead despite all the irritations and the sometimes almost insuperable technical problems. Thus we were unable to photograph the foreign diplomats, who lived in a special train at the main terminal of Nuremberg: the terminal was too dark even during the day. In those days we didn't have the highly sensitive stock that would now be used in such conditions. I assumed the diplomats would like to see themselves in the film, and so I asked them whether they would mind if the train went outdoors. Every last one of them was agreeable, and – most important of all – so was the engineer. The train pulled out of the station, and we could shoot in sunlight. The diplomats obviously enjoyed themselves, since they were probably very bored.

Things didn't always go so smoothly with the diplomats. To film the nocturnal last-post which ended the rally in front of Hitler's hotel, Der Deutsche Hof, we hurriedly got hold of some spotlights without obtaining anyone's permission. The band and the diplomats were briefly bathed in harsh light, and then the spotlights had to be switched off. I knew that this must be an order from Göring, and I had them switched back on, which triggered loud protests, and then they were off for good. What could we do? A member of our crew recalled that we had brought along magnesium torches, so I had them carried over and lit. But I hadn't reckoned with the devastating smoke that they produced. In the twinkling of an eye everything was shrouded in fumes. The diplomats, who were near the band, started to cough and a few even took to their heels. I realized too late what mischief we'd perpetrated, but we had shot some atmospheric footage, and that comforted me. Without waiting for the storm to break over me, I left the square as soon as possible and boarded the next train back to Berlin.

Before viewing the rushes I had an unpleasant and upsetting talk with Herr Klitzsch, general manager of UFA. At issue was the prestige of UFA, with whom my firm had signed a distribution contract. This did not stipulate that the prints were to be done at AFIFA, a printing lab belonging to UFA, and although this was normally a matter of course for films handled by UFA Distribution, it was different for me. I had always worked so closely with Herr Geyer that I had promised him this job too. I'd felt grateful to him ever since *The Blue Light*. He had always generously supported me and, for the rally film, he had built a house with modern editing rooms on his property.

I had vastly underestimated the importance of the printing lab issue. I sensed this when I stood in front of the senior executive of UFA. 'How could you even imagine,' he thundered at me, 'that if UFA financed a film it would be printed by Geyer?'

'I know that this is not pleasant for UFA,' I said, 'but please understand, I owe a great debt of gratitude to Herr Geyer. He helped me when I was in trouble, and now he's built me a wonderful editing house.'

Klitzsch broke in vehemently: 'We'll build you an even better one. We're even ready to pay Geyer the profit from the prints, but we cannot allow him to make them.'

The sweat was pouring down his face – and down mine too. I found myself in a terrible predicament. Naturally I understood Herr Klitzsch's demands: but on the other side, I did not feel I could break my promise to Herr Geyer.

'Talk to Herr Geyer yourself.' That was all I managed to blurt out before I was ungraciously dismissed.

Next, Herr Klitzsch and Herr Geyer had a meeting, but predictably to no avail. Herr Geyer was not willing to step aside, and I had the awful feeling that I had made another enemy in Herr Klitzsch.

I was now faced with the most difficult part of the works: editing the film. I had to sift through four hundred thousand feet of rushes, of which I wanted to use only about ten thousand feet. Although Hitler had given me no deadline for completing the picture, my contract with UFA stipulated that I had to deliver it at the least by mid-March of the following year. I had exactly five months left. This was rather tight, because in those days the splicing area of every single frame had to be scraped with a knife. I had no model for creating this film, nothing to go by, so I had to experiment. Nor did I have any adviser or other assistants except for the women who spliced and sorted. I had a cutter only for the sound editing.

The task seemed almost hopeless. I sealed myself off from the outside world and concentrated totally on my work in the editing room. I wouldn't talk to anyone, not even to my mother. During the first week I laboured twelve hours a day, and during the second week fourteen. Then came sixteen hours a day, and so it went on including weekends and holidays.

Before two months had passed we were exhausted. Some of my employees became ill, and in the final months I was left with only three people who could endure this pace: Frau Peters, who worked in the cutting room; Wolfgang Brüning, a boy on leave from high school who labelled the film clips; and our photographer, Herr Lantin, who voluntarily remained until five every morning in order to drive Frau Peters and me home.

Waldi Traut, my closest colleague (production manager and trustee of my firm), was supposed to stave off anything that could disrupt my work; it may have been in early December that he announced a visitor whom I had to receive: General von Reichenau. He was accompanied by a second general, whose name I have forgotten. They wanted to see the shots of the Wehrmacht in Nuremberg. Since the military exercises had taken place in bad weather, sometimes even rain, I had decided long ago to leave out this footage. I explained this to Herr von Reichenau, unaware of what I was getting myself into. I did not realize the vast significance of the fact that 1934 was the first year that the Wehrmacht had been involved in a Party rally. The general looked at me in utter consternation, as if I had indulged in a poor joke.

'You can't possibly exclude the Wehrmacht from the film – just who do you think you are!'

I tried to make him see that the shots weren't good enough, that they were grey, and useless for the film, but the general demanded to see them. I was shaken when he liked them. 'Why, they're wonderful,' he said, 'I don't know what's wrong with you.'

Now the matter was serious, for I had actually shown him only the worst parts, not expecting him to be delighted. He insisted that the Wehrmacht footage had to be inserted into the film no matter what, and I, equally firm, declared that I would not include it.

'I am sorry,' said General von Reichenau, 'but in that case I'll have to go to the Führer.' Taking his leave, he walked out of the screening room, leaving me very uneasy. This wasn't good: I had made yet another enemy. I wondered whether I might hit on some face-saving solution. But none occurred to me. It was my fault, for I was too uncompromising, but it would have gone against the grain to do as they demanded.

Several weeks after this incident, Brückner got in touch with me to say that Hitler wanted me to come to Munich on the first day of Christmas; he wished to speak to me in the home of the Hess family. I was expected for tea at 4 p.m. I hadn't seen Hitler since our brief conversation at the site of the Party rally. What did this invitation mean?

Somewhat late I arrived at the villa of the Hess family in Munich-Harlaching. Hitler was already there and benevolently inquired about my work. I told him about my problems in the editing room: for instance, how difficult it was to take a speech of his that actually lasted two hours and cut it down to just a few minutes in the film – but without changing its importance. Hitler nodded sympathetically. I liked Frau Hess, whom I met here for the first time. She chatted with us vivaciously, while her husband stayed silent.

Suddenly Hitler said, 'When I gave you the assignment for the Party rally film I promised you complete freedom for the production.' I looked at him tenderly. 'And I wish to keep my promise. But more than anything I would not want you to have any unpleasant repercussions from your work, or make any new enemies.' Now I had dark forebodings. 'I asked you to come here,' he went on, 'because I would like to ask you to make one single compromise. General von Reichenau came to see me. He complained that you do not wish to include the Wehrmacht in the film. I've been thinking about it and worked out a way that could allow you to change your film and, without having to make any artistic compromises, still incorporate all the people who deserve special credit. Human beings are more or less vain, and wishes have been voiced to me from various sides.'

This was the very thing I had feared, and why I had been so surprised at being promised a free hand.

'I would therefore like to make the following suggestion: I will ask the most important generals and members of the Party to come to a film studio – I will be present too. Then we will line up, and the camera will move slowly down the line. This will make it possible to emphasize the contributions of each person with a few words. That could be the opening credits of your film. No one will be offended, and you will not annoy anyone.' Hitler was growing more and more enthusiastic, but I was growing more and more upset. I gazed at him in disbelief.

'What's wrong?' he asked me in amazement. 'Don't you like my idea?'

My rough cut of the opening sequence flashed past my eyes: the sea of clouds at the start of the film, the spires and gables of Nuremberg looming through – I couldn't imagine any other beginning. This mood would be destroyed if I had to add the footage suggested by Hitler. Tears came to my eyes.

'For God's sake, what's wrong with you?' said Hitler. 'I'm only trying to help you.' And he again began to point out all the merits of his idea.

I forgot who was in front of me. All I could think of was my cinematic work, and I found Hitler's idea simply terrible. My reaction was so vehement that I lost all fear. I leaped up and stamped my foot, shouting, 'I can't do it.'

For the first time I saw Hitler angry with me. He snapped, 'Have you forgotten whom you're talking to?' He stood up and barked, 'You're behaving like a stubborn mule. I was only thinking of you. But if you don't want to do it, then let's drop it.'

I had turned away in order to hide my tears, but then I had an idea. 'Couldn't I make up for it,' I said, 'by doing a short film on the Wehrmacht next year? That might appease the generals.'

Hitler was already standing in the open doorway and, making an almost weary gesture, he said, 'I'll leave that up to you.' Then, accompanied by Frau Hess, he left the room.

The last few weeks in the editing room were a martyrdom. We couldn't get more than four or five hours sleep a night. During all those months, Frau Peters had slept in my home, but she too was at the end of her strength. When we came home at dawn, she would wrap wet, cold sheets around my legs to make me fall asleep more easily. I didn't dare take a sedative.

I could no longer view my work objectively, nor could I tell whether or not the film was turning out well. I re-edited it daily, changed sequences around, spliced in new scenes, cut out others, and shortened or lengthened them until I felt they were just right.

UFA had scheduled the première for the last week in March, and it dangled over my head like a sword of Damocles. I was afraid I wouldn't get the editing done by myself, so I hired Herr Schaad, one of the best film editors. I asked him to cut the parade sequence. These scenes were to run for twenty minutes, and we had almost thirty-five thousand feet of rushes. Herr Schaad was given his own editing room, an assistant, and a deadline of two months. I hoped we would succeed.

Prior to the post-synchronization, I screened his reel – and got quite a shock. I had counted on using it at least as a rough cut, but it was as useless as Ruttmann's film: again it looked more like a newsreel. I had no choice: I re-edited the entire footage. Luckily I was so practised by now that I managed to complete this task in three days, though we had to work seventy-two hours with almost no sleep.

I did my editing with a small Lytax instrument, like the one Fanck had used to cut his films – at least the silent ones. Primitive as this instrument was, I found it indispensable. I could not have worked so quickly with any other editing table, no matter how excellent. My Lytax had no screen, only a double magnifying lens, through which the frames could be pulled to and fro. Without this instrument, which was very hard on my eyes, I would have had to spend far more time cutting the footage.

Editing the sound was a different matter. In those days film-making normally used sound-film or union tables. Incidentally, Herr Gaede, my sound editor, eventually invented the Steenbeck editing table. While working together we kept racking our brains, trying to figure out how the sound tables could be improved, and the Steenbeck table became world-famous.

We had two days to do the post-synchronization. Now we were faced with a new problem, and once again it involved the parade. A special march had been written for the film, but neither the composer Herbert Windt nor the conductor succeeded in conducting the music so that it synchronized with the images. Cameras then did not have automatic speed; and they were still hand-cranked. Every cameraman worked at a different pace, which caused me tremendous difficulties at the editing table. In some rushes the people marched too quickly, in others too slowly. The rapid visual changes made it impossible for the conductors and musicians to cue in on time and to adjust their playing to groups marching at such different speeds. Despite hours of practice, neither the conductor nor Herr Windt was able to synchronize the music correctly; and Herr Windt even suggested that I simply leave out the entire parade. So I myself took over the task of conducting the eighty-man orchestra. I had every frame down pat, and I knew exactly when the music should be conducted faster and when slower. At last the sound was synchronized precisely.

It was 28 March 1935. We were still working on the print until a few short hours before the première. We didn't even have time to screen it for the censors – a highly unusual situation, since no film could be shown in public until it was passed by the censorship board. Aside from my staff no one had seen the film before the première, so I didn't even know how it would be received.

I worked on in the printing lab for such a long time that I didn't even have a chance to go to my hairdresser. In a great hurry, I combed my hair, made up my face, slipped into an evening gown, and, very behind schedule, drove with my parents and Heinz to the festively decorated UFA Palace. The manager of the theatre was already waiting impatiently to lead us to our seats.

It was rather an embarrassing outing, since Hitler and all the guests of honour, including the diplomats, were already sitting in their boxes. No sooner had we settled down than the talking died, the lights faded, an orchestra played a march, the curtains parted, the screen lit up and the film began.

I re-experienced my sleepless nights and the arduous efforts at each transition from one sequence to the next, all the anxieties that my staff and I might have done something wrong. I had omitted not only the military manoeuvres, but so many other events, including those of the Congress of Women.

Holding my eyes shut most of the time, I kept hearing more and more clapping. The end of the film was greeted by long, indeed almost endless, applause. At that moment my strength ran out altogether. When Hitler thanked me and handed me a lilac bouquet I felt faint – and then lost consciousness.

After the war the German illustrated magazines with high circulations claimed that after the première Hitler wanted to present me with a diamond necklace and that I gazed so deeply into his eyes that I blacked out.

IN DAVOS

In Davos where I went to rest, the season was over, the town was almost deserted, and on 1 April the Parsenn Line even stopped running. I didn't care. I was much too tired to ski, and my appearance had evidently altered so thoroughly that the desk clerk at the Hotel Seehof, where I stayed again, didn't recognize me. I had lost a lot of weight and hardly dared look in the mirror. My face was ashen, my eyes hollow with dark shadows underneath. I was in that state when Hitler saw me once again at the Hotel Kaiserhof, where I had an appointment with Sven Noldan, who designed the titles for *Triumph of the Will*. Hitler, who was sitting in the hotel lobby with several men, waved me over to his table. I was far from pleased, since I was badly groomed and felt wretched. He said, 'You look as if you work too much. You shouldn't do that.'

I could only reply, 'Do please excuse me!' and went back to Herr Noldan.

The next day, when I was in the editing room, I received a bouquet of red roses from Hitler. The card said that he had been taken aback by my appearance at the Kaiserhof yesterday: I shouldn't work so much, and it didn't matter when the film was completed. He told me to take care of myself. The signature read: 'Respectfully yours, Adolf Hitler.'

He had written these lines by hand, and they were the only ones I ever received from Hitler, aside from telegrams of congratulation or condolence.

All this and many other things went through my mind as I lay, wrapped in blankets, on a deckchair on the balcony, inhaling the wonderful fresh winter air. There's no air like it anywhere else in the world.

I had great cause for grief after my arrival in Davos, for I was forced to break off with my lover, Walter Prager. Because I was so busy with my film, he had had an affair. When I was working on the editing I had asked him to go to Davos, his home town, until I was done. We phoned one another often, but the time of separation, six whole months, was too long – at least for him. No sooner had I arrived in Davos than someone told me that Walter had been living with a girl throughout our separation, but intended to come back to me once my work was completed. I wasn't broadminded enough to put up with that, even though I was still in love with him. Hard as it was for me, I ended our relationship.

On the afternoon of 1 May, I received several congratulatory telegrams. *Triumph of the Will* had won the National Film Prize. Hitler also sent me a telegram, but my joy at this award could in no way make up for the strains and intrigues I had endured.

AT THE BERLIN OPERA

When I arrived home and went through my mail, I was surprised to find a personal invitation from Dr Goebbels for a gala première at the City Opera. I believe it was *Madama Butterfly*. The minister probably wanted to be seen in public with the 'Laurette of the National Prize' in order to scotch the rumours about our enmity. Perhaps Hitler had asked him to do so for that reason.

I was greeted by Goebbels and his wife Magda in the centre box. He offered me the seat to his right, while his wife sat behind us with Cerrutti, the Italian ambassador. To the left of the minister sat his aide, Prinz

Schaumburg-Lippe. I remember that seating arrangement so precisely because we were photographed, and the picture appeared in many newspapers. That was probably one of the reasons behind the invitation.

When the theatre darkened and the orchestra began to play, I was dismayed to feel Goebbels thrusting his hand under my gown; it touched my knee and was about to move up my thigh. Indignant, I grabbed his hand but couldn't scratch it because it was covered by the cloth of my gown. What an appalling man he was!

I would have given anything to leave during the intermission, but I was afraid of a scandal. So I remained with Magda Goebbels, who told me that she was expecting another baby. With what struck me as surprising *naïveté* she also described the things she had to do for her appearance, so that she could hold her own among the beautiful actresses who swarmed around her husband. Her husband's amorous escapades were the talk of Germany.

Poor Magda, I thought. She doesn't realize she's married to a devil.

OLYMPIA

Penthesilea still lurked at the back of my mind, but I did not feel I was ready for such a gigantic film project. I focused on various ideas, such as 'Gustav Adolf's Page' by the Swiss writer Conrad Ferdinand Meyer; 'Michael Kohlhaas', the most gripping of Kleist's stories; and *The Life of Druse* by E.A. Reinhardt.

To keep physically fit I went to the Grunewald athletic stadium every other day and did various kinds of light atheletics. I felt I was in good condition and I prepared for the silver sports medal.

I was practising high-jumping when a middle-aged man walked over to me and introduced himself. He was Professor Carl Diem, secretary general of the organization committee of the Eleventh Olympic Games, scheduled to take place in a year, on this very site.

'Fräulein Riefenstahl, I've been planning to ambush you,' he said with a friendly smile.

Brushing the sand from the high-jump pit from my legs, I asked, 'An ambush? What do you mean?'

'I have an idea,' said Diem. 'I'm supposed to prepare the Olymic Games in Berlin, and I would like to launch them with a huge torch race straight across Europe, from ancient Olympia in Greece to the new Olympia in Berlin. It will be a wonderful Olympics, and it would be a great pity if we couldn't record it on film. You are a great artist, you know a lot about sport.

With your *Triumph of the Will* you created a masterpiece, a film without a plot. You must make a film like that about the Olympics.

I threw up my hands in alarm. I had sworn to myself that I would never make another documentary. 'Impossible,' I said.

But Diem persisted. As organizer and president of the German Sports Commission for light athletics, he was a stubborn if diplomatic man, and he explained at great length how important it was to film the Olympic idea. At first I couldn't imagine how one could make a film out of more than a hundred athletic events.

'Naturally one can't show all the contests. It's more important to express the ancient idea.'

'So far as I know,' I said, 'there has never been a film about a summer Olympics. The Americans tried to shoot the Los Angeles games in 1932, but despite their best efforts it turned into nothing more than a teaching aid. And this abortive film was made by a famous director, Dupont. You remember *Vaudeville* with Jannings and Lya de Putti? That was one of Dupont's films.'

I then told Professor Diem a little bit about the great difficulties I had had with the Ministry of Propaganda when I was making *Triumph of the Will*. 'Ultimately,' I said, 'everything will be under Dr Goebbels' aegis again. I would have endless trouble.'

'I don't think so,' he assured me. 'The International Olympic Committee is in charge of the Olympic Games. No one can enter the arenas or the Olympic village without their permission. Only the committee can allow cameras to be used inside the stadium. Even the newsreels can be shot only from the spectator area. However, Otto Mayer, a Swiss, and chairman of the IOC will be certain to grant you special authorizations. He empowered me to make you this offer. He is as convinced of your abilities as I am. May I send you some material, to give you an idea of the coming games?'

I shook my head. 'First of all, much as I would like to,' I repeated. 'I can't imagine turning all those events into a film. Secondly, I swore to myself that I would never make another documentary under any circumstances.' Diem, obviously still not convinced by my refusal, said in conclusion, 'Well, but I can still introduce you to the chancellor of the IOC. He's coming to Berlin in the next few days.'

'I'd like that,' I replied, and said goodbye.

The meal with the chancellor of the IOC and Dr Diem took place in a restaurant near the Kaiser Wilhelm Memorial Church. Both men were rapturous about *The Blue Light* and promised me all sorts of things in order to tempt me with the Olympia project. I didn't feel able to accept, but I said I would think it over.

The idea attracted me more than I cared to admit. I began to wonder how to tackle the job, but I foresaw only difficulties. I could see no way of turning the countless Olympic disciplines into a motion picture that would be satisfying in both artistic and athletic terms, and also on an international level. I therefore decided to discuss this problem with Fanck. Perhaps he, a master of documentaries and sports movies, could take over this task. In 1928 Fanck had made a film about the Olympic winter games in St Moritz. Yet, attractive and beautiful as were the shots of the glittering winter landscape, his production was unsuccessful.

When I asked him if he'd be interested in this Olympic film, he brusquely refused. 'If my film on the winter Olympics was a flop,' he said, 'then one about the summer games would be an even bigger failure. After all, the contests in the winter landscape are a lot more appealing than anything happening in the stadium or in the gyms.'

I had to agree, but I wanted to pick his brain some more.

'Let's assume,' I persisted 'that you had to make the film. How would you tackle it?'

Fanck mused for a while, then said: 'I see three possibilities. It could be a full-length film aiming purely at aesthetic and artistic effects – an impression of movements and elements of various sports. However, this approach would have no documentary value, since two hours wouldn't be enough to cover even the most important events. It would be the most useless solution. Another possibility might be six mammoth films. And the third solution, which I consider the most suitable, would be proper reportage, with no artistic status, to be shown in cinemas within six days of the end of the games; at best this would provide above-average newsreels.'

His theories sounded both cogent and disheartening.

'Too bad you don't want to attempt it,' I said. 'Who knows when we'll have another summer Olympics in Germany?'

'No,' Fanck said resolutely, 'I won't do that to myself.' Using a stop-watch and the table of world records, we calculated the time for each individual sport in order to estimate the length of the film. The figure we came up with was ten times the projected running time.

Nevertheless, I was slowly coming round to the idea. Of the three solutions that Fanck saw, none was possible for me. We could never have found a distributor for six mammoth films, and reportage was completely out of the question for me. The newsreel companies would be doing specials, which would come to the same thing. There had to be some way of making a film that would combine the Olympic idea with the most important Olympic contests.

Without my arriving at any definite solution, the possibility began taking shape. In my mind's eye, I could see the ancient ruins of the classical Olympic sites slowly emerging from patches of fog and the Greek temples and sculptures drifting by: Achilles and Aphrodite, Medusa and Zeus, Apollo and Paris, and then the discus thrower of Myron. I dreamed that this statue changed into a man of flesh and blood, gradually starting to swing the discus in slow motion. The sculptures turned into Greek temple dancers dissolving in flames, the Olympic fire igniting the torches to be carried from the Temple of Zeus to the modern Berlin of 1936 – a bridge from Antiquity to the present. That was my vision of the prologue to my *Olympia*.

After experiencing these images, I decided I would make the film – to the joy of Professor Diem and Otto Mayer, the chancellor of the IOC. However, the financial aspect had to be worked out. I agreed to do the project only if they managed to come up with independent backing. First I turned to UFA. I was optimistic despite my falling-out with General Manager Klitzsch. UFA had had a hit in *Triumph of the Will*, which had won a gold medal at the Venice Biennale, so they were not uninterested in my new project. But then they asked the fateful question: 'Why don't you tell us the plot?'

'I can't imagine a plot in this picture. The *Olympia* film is possible only as a pure documentary.'

The UFA people didn't know what I was talking about. They quite seriously told me that a love story would have to be added. Since I failed to convince them of my idea, the conversation was at an end as far as I was concerned.

Now I tried Tobis, their competitor, whose headquarters was also in Berlin. I didn't know anyone there, but when I telephoned I was connected to Friedrich Mainz, the head of the company. He listened with some interest when I told him about the *Olympia* project. Then to my astonishment he asked whether he could see me at once. A short time after he arrived at Hindenburgstrasse.

We quickly reached an agreement without any fuss or bother and without any tasteless love story. Unlike UFA, Mainz instantly realized the tremendous potential of this film. He accepted my proposal that the film should consist of two parts. I had reached this conclusion after mulling it over for a long time. There was no other way to cover the most important contests.

An experienced screen producer like Friedrich Mainz could also make a rough estimate of what such a project would cost. However, the crucial thing was that he knew that a film like this could be completed and shown only long after the Olympic Games, and I was surprised by his unconditional trust. He was so convinced the project would succeed that, at this very first meeting, he offered me a guarantee of one and a half million marks – a sensational amount in those days. Nothing like this had ever been paid for a documentary in Germany.

When the Propaganda Minister learned that I has signed a contract for the *Olympia* film with Tobis, he summoned me to his office. Two years earlier, he had furiously threatened to hurl me down the stairs. But this time his greeting was cool and aloof. He asked various quesetions – above all, how I envisaged the film and how long I would be working on it. I told him that the film would consist of two parts, and that, given the enormous wealth of material, I expected it to take me one and a half years. He gaped at me, flabbergasted, and burst out laughing.

'Are you quite sane?' he asked ironically. 'Do you really believe that anyone is going to look at an Olympics movie two years from now? It's a joke, you can't be serious.'

I began to feel a few doubts and tried to explain my conception of the film to Goebbels, but he waved his hand as if to brush away my silly, useless idea, and said contemptuously, 'Filming the Olympics makes sense only if the film can be shown a few days after the end of the games.' This was exactly what Dr Fanck had told me. 'The crucial thing here is speed, not quality,' Goebbels went on.

'But that's what the newsreels are for,' I argued. The *Olympia* film has to be an artistic film that will be worthwhile even years from now. In order to achieve that goal, we'll have to shoot hundreds of thousands of feet, then pick over them, cut them, and add the sound. It's hard work, sheer drudgery,' I continued uncertainly, 'and I'm not sure it will succeed. You may be right, Doctor, I still have a lot to think about. I may even decide not to go ahead with it.'

'Fine,' said the minister, 'please let me know what you decide.'

After that conversation I was on the point of not singing the contract, which I had already received from Tobis. The risk seemed too great, and Goebbels' objections had had their effect.

And yet I was already entranced by the idea of this film, and my new project began to monopolize my thoughts. I studied any writings I could dig up on the Olympic Games and racked my brain as to how I could bring the film to life in its individual parts. Strictly speaking, the whole enterprise was hopelessly unreal, even if only half of the 136 contests could be shown. This didn't even include the preliminary and intermediary heats, which are often more dramatic and produce greater athletic performances than the finals. Suppose we devoted just three hundred and thirty feet of celluloid to each sport – a running time of some three and a half minutes. Multiplied by 136 contests that made about 45,000 feet – enough for five very long films. And this didn't even take into account so many other things, such as the prologue, the torch race, the opening of the games, the dance festival, the Olympic village, and the concluding celebration. Fanck's estimate of the running time was not altogether wrong, so it was clear that the film couldn't be made in that way. We would have to select, omit, accentuate, show the essentials and leave out the non-essentials. But how was I to know in advance what would prove important or unimportant and which preliminary heat would break the world record? In other words, everything would have to be shot and from every conceivable angle. And then came the drudgery of making the selections in the editing room.

The vast range of events was not the only problem. One would also have to be familiar with every single sport, research its dramatic potential and work out how to achieve the most effective images. Within a few weeks, despite all my qualms, I was finally ready to make the film.

Now I had to notify the Minister of Propaganda. He was not pleased by my decision, and he warned me about the financial risk. I tried to convince him that the sum guaranteed by Tobis would be large enough, since we wouldn't have to rent a studio or pay fees to stars.

'Do you really believe that the public will be interested,' Goebbels asked incredulously, 'if it has to wait to see the film for one or two years? And two films at that? I don't like the idea.'

'There is no other solution,' I said. 'I have to make it in two parts – just to include the bare bones.'

'Then I wish you all the luck in the world for your venture. I will inform the people in my ministry about your project.'

The conversation was over.

THE STEEL ANIMAL

A short time later, I had to turn to Goebbels again, although very reluctantly. This time it was not on my account, but for Willy Zielke, a brilliant director, and his film *The Steel Animal*. He had produced it for the German Railway in honour of the centennial of the railway. The first time I saw his film it took my breath away. His work was a grand visual symphony, such as I hadn't experienced since Eisenstein's *Potemkin*. Its content: the hundred-year history of the railway, the fate of its inventors, and its development from the oldest steam engine to the modern locomotive. Zielke had turned this difficult material into a thrilling picture. His locomotive looked like a living monster. The headlights were its eyes, the instruments its brain, the pistons its joints, and the oil dripping from the moving pistons looked like blood. This overall impression was intensified by the revolutionary sound montage.

When the officials of the national rail system saw the movie, they were so horrified – according to Zielke – that they left the room speechless. Overcome by resentment, they decided not only to ban any screening, but also to have all prints and even the negative destroyed. The reason for their anger was that the film was a far cry from anything they had imagined. They wanted it to be an invitation to the viewers to travel by train gladly and with great pleasure. For such a film they should have hired a conservative director, but not Willy Zielke, whose revolutionary film art was decades ahead of its time. In his production the railway cars smashed together so violently when they were being switched that the viewers jumped out of their seats. It was a shock for the railway directors who wanted train travel to be smooth and gentle.

Zielke was miserable. He had spent a year on his film, working passionately and obsessively. And now his labour would have all been in vain, and his opus might even be destroyed. I wanted to prevent this and, if necessary, fight for it as if it were my own film. Luckily, I managed to acquire a print for my archive before the destruction of the negative.

So I had to beard the lion in his den for no one but Minister Goebbels, head of the German film industry, could rescind the verdict. I hoped he would be clever enough to see the artistic value of Zielke's film and forbid the destruction of the negative. The minister's secretary gave me a screening date.

That evening, when I arrived at Goebbels' office in the Prince Karl Palace on Wilhelmsplatz, I was amazed to find no guests other than a well-known actress of the stage and screen. I was also surprised by the elegance of the rooms. I recalled how impressed I had been when Goebbels, Gauleiter of Berlin, had been campaigning; he had emphatically promised his voters that after the 'takeover', no cabinet member would earn more than a thousand marks a month. What irony! Goebbels, now a government minister himself, had no qualms about publicly imitating the spendthrift lifestyle of his enemy Göring.

Goebbels was in the best of spirits, as was his actress. Fruit juice and champagne were served. When I entered the large room where the film was to be shown, we sat down on a broad sofa. The actress moved a little away from me, snuggling quite unabashed against Goebbels' shoulder. The lights went out and the film began, but the two of them kept talking to one another without looking at the screen. They paid scant attention to the film, and things got even worse. The actress made mocking remarks about it, giggled at particularly interesting places, and sometimes burst out laughing for absolutely no reason. Goebbels, whom she called 'Jupp' and addressed in the familiar form, seemed similarly contemptuous. I was crestfallen.

When the lights went on again, the minister said, 'The audience will react as negatively as has this lady. I agree that the director is talented, but the film would be incomprehensible to the masses: it is too modern and too abstract; it could be a Bolshevist film, and that is an unreasonable demand to make on the railway directors.'

'But that's no reason to destroy the film,' I replied, in distress. 'It is a work of art.'

'I'm sorry, Fräulein Riefenstahl,' said Goebbels, 'but the decision is entirely up to the railway, which has financed the film. I would not wish to interfere.'

It was the death sentence for Zielke's opus.

DAY OF FREEDOM

Ever since my childhood I had dreamed of a house of my own. Now I found a suitable lot in Berlin-Dahlem, only ten minutes from the Kurfürstendamm and yet in the middle of the woods.

I did a rough sketch of a house and then began travelling through Germany in order to look at houses. Being a lover of mountains, I especially liked the houses of Hans Otler, an architect from Garmisch. He did a few diagrams for me, and I liked them so much that I commissioned him and his partner, the architect Max Ott, to build my house in Dahlem Heydnstrasse 30. During this construction period I began to prepare for the *Olympia* film.

First I had to go to Nuremberg for two days in order to keep my promise and make a short film on the Wehrmacht exercises at the Party rally of 1935. This was the footage that I had omitted from *Triumph of the Will* – to the annoyance of the generals.

I hired five cameramen: Ertl, Frentz, Lantschner, Kling and the brilliant Zielke. The only thing we had to shoot was the army exercises, which took place on a single day. The result was a film lasting some twenty-five minutes, with a very spirited score by Peter Kreuder; we called it *Day of Freedom*, the name given to the rally itself.

My company, which in 1934 had been renamed Reichsparteitagfilm, Reich Party Rally Film, sold *Day of Freedom* to UFA, which used the short as a curtain-raiser for one of its weaker features. My cameramen had done an excellent job. An artistic stature was achieved thanks to the participation of Zielke who, together with Guzzi Lantschner, achieved novel effects, especially in the soundtrack.

When the film was completed I was asked to screen it at the Reich Chancellery. Hoping to bring about a reconciliation with the Wehrmacht, Hitler had arranged a small première, to which he had invited many generals and their ladies. The screening was scheduled for 8 p.m.

At ten to eight I was still at home, struggling with my wild hair, unable to tame it into submission. Jumping into my car, I drove through Berlin like a lunatic. The only thing that prevented an accident was the scarcity of traffic in those days. When I arrived at the Chancellery, harried and with tousled hair, I was twenty minutes late. Hitler and Goebbels were already standing in the lobby, awaiting me impatiently, and the Führer's face was pale, but Goebbels appeared to be grinning. He enjoyed seeing me in such an embarrassing situation. Both greeted me icily. Uneasy and confused, I attempted to apologize.

Some two hundred guests were waiting for me: the generals uniformed and decorated, the women in evening gowns. Here too I was greeted with stony faces. I wished the ground would open and swallow me.

When the film began I was still uncomfortable and felt rather alone, my mind was far away, but within a few minutes I felt a burgeoning interest among the viewers, something like warmth. Anyone who has been on stage a lot develops a sixth sense: you can tell how the audience feels about you. Surprisingly the film made a strong impact. When the lights went on again I experienced a triumph. My hands were shaken, I was hugged. Leni here – Leni there – there was tremendous enthusiasm and I could tell by Goebbels' expression how deeply he resented my success.

Hitler had a sense of humour: at Christmas he gave me a Meissen porcelain alarm clock.

OLYMPIA FILM INC.

It was time now to obtain the financing of the Tobis contract for the Olympic movie. This was no problem *per se*, since the Ministry of

Propaganda had created a bank for film loans in order to promote the cinema. Producers and distributors obtained low interest rates, but only for feature films.

Negotiations had already taken place with Dr Goebbels, who surprisingly was becoming interested in the Olympic film. He had even offered to help me with the pre-financing and pointed out that if the film were a success, it would be good publicity for the Reich, and that was the responsibility of his ministry. His unexpected helpfulness was a great relief to me. Nevertheless, there were difficulties in the further negotiations between the ministry officials and Herr Traut and Herr Grosskopf, who represented my firm.

It took them several months of endless study and conferences with financial and fiscal experts to come up finally with a solution. I had been advised that my most expedient move would be to establish a special firm for the Olympic project, so that the loans which the Ministry of Propaganda was ready to grant could be paid to the new firm rather than to me. In December 1935 the Olympiade-Film GmbH – Olympia Film Inc. – was registered legally, with my brother Heinz and myself as the two stock-holders. To avoid paying enormous taxes, Dr Schwerin, the lawyer of our corporation, advised me to transfer all shares *gratis* to the Ministry of Propaganda until all the loans and accrued interest had been completely paid off. I agreed, since this was only a formality undertaken for fiscal reasons. The crucial issue for me was that my artistic freedom would not be restricted. However, I was not totally free. My corporation, like nearly all German films studios, was under the financial control of the film bank which, in turn, was under the aegis of the Ministry of Propaganda. As managing director of the new company I was responsible for every mark loaned to us. There were other conditions; for example, a limit was set on my personal withdrawals. Furthermore, I had to tell the press that Dr Goebbels had commissioned me to make the Olympic film, even though this was not true. But at the time I didn't care.

All these matters concerned me only peripherally. I was already up to my ears in pre-production work and didn't realize until far too late that the Ministry of Propaganda kept trying more and more to gain control of me. The results were to cause considerable difficulties.

HITLER IN PRIVATE

On Christmas Eve 1935 I went off to the mountains as I had done every year.

Shortly before my departure I received a phone call from Schaub: could I visit Hitler in his Munich home the morning of the first day of the Christmas holiday? Schaub could not tell me the reason for this surprising invitation but, since I would be passing through Munich anyhow, there was no difficulty.

At 11 a.m., this time punctually, I stood outside number 16 Prinz-regentenplatz, an unobtrusive corner house next to the Prinzregenten Theatre. When I rang the doorbell one flight up, a middle-aged woman opened the door. I later found out that this was Frau Winter, the housekeeper in Hitler's private apartment. She led me into spacious room where I was greeted by Hitler. As always when I was summoned by him, I was apprehensive. Would he keep his promise and commission no further film projects from me?

Hitler wore plain clothes and seemed totally at ease. The room was modestly furnished and not very cosy. It had a large bookcase, a round table with a lace cloth, and several chairs. As though reading my mind, Hitler said, 'As you can see, Fräulein Riefenstahl, I set no store by comfort or property. I use every hour to solve the problems of my people and property is merely a burden. Even my library robs me of time, and I read a great deal.' He interrupted himself to offer me a drink. I asked for apple juice.

'If one "gives",' Hitler went on, 'one must also "take", and I take what I need from books. I have a great deal to catch up on. In my youth I did not have the wherewithal or the opportunity to obtain an adequate education. Nowadays I read one or two books every night, even if I go to bed very late.'

I asked, 'And who is your favourite author?'

His reply was unhesitating, 'Schopenhauer – he was my teacher.'

'Not Nietzsche?' I threw in.

He smiled and said: 'No, I can't do very much with Nietzsche. He's more of an artist than a philosopher. He doesn't have a crystal-clear mind like Schopenhauer.' I was surprised, for Hitler was generally said to be a Nietzsche follower.

He added, 'Naturally I admire Nietzsche as a genius. He writes perhaps the most beautiful language to be found in German literature today. But he is not my model.'

Trying to change the subject, I asked Hitler, 'How did you spend Christmas Eve?' There was sadness in his voice: 'I had my chauffeur drive me around aimlessly, along highways and through villages, until I became tired.' I looked at him, amazed. 'I do that every Christmas Eve.' After a pause: 'I have no family and I am lonely.'

'Why don't you get married?'

'Because it would be irresponsible of me to bind a woman in marriage. What would she get from me? She would have to be alone most of the time. My love belongs wholly and only to my nation – and if I had children, what would become of them if fate should turn against me? I would then not have a single friend left, and my children would be bound to suffer humiliation and perhaps even die of starvation.' His words were bitter and he seemed agitated. Becoming calmer, he went on, 'I have tried to express my gratitude wherever I can, for gratitude is a virtue insufficiently valued. I have people at my side who helped me in my bad years. I will remain true to them, even if they do not always have the abilities demanded by their positions.' He then gave me a searching look and said quite abruptly, 'And what about you, what are your plans?'

My heart leaped. 'Hasn't Dr Goebbels told you?'

He shook his head. Relieved, I told him that after a long period of reluctance, I had decided to make a film about the Olympic Games in Berlin.

Hitler looked at me in surprise. 'That's an interesting challenge for you. But I thought you didn't want to make any more documentaries, that you only wanted to work as an actress?'

'That's true,' I said, 'and this is definitely my last documentary. I thought it over for a long time. But I finally said yes because of the great opportunity that the IOC offered me, the wonderful contract with Tobis, and, last but not least, the realization that we won't be having another Olympics in Germany for a long time.' Then I told Hitler about the difficulties of the project and the great responsibility, which made me uneasy about doing it.

'That's a mistake: you have to have a lot more self-confidence. What you do will be valuable, even if it remains incomplete in your eyes. Who else but you should make an Olympic film? And this time you won't have any problems with Dr Goebbels if the IOC organizes the games and we are merely hosts.' To my surprise, he said, 'I myself am not very interested in the games. I would rather stay away . . .'

'But why?' I asked.

Hitler hesitated. Then he said, 'We have no chance of winning medals. The Americans will win most of the victories, and the Negroes will be their stars. I won't enjoy watching that. And then many foreigners will come who reject National Socialism. There could be trouble.' He also mentioned that he didn't like the Olympic Stadium: the pillars were too slender, the overall construction not imposing enough.

'But don't be discouraged,' he added. 'You are sure to make a good film.'

He then began to talk about Goebbels. 'Can a man who laughs as heartily as the doctor be bad?', and before I could say anything, Hitler answered his own question: 'No, a man who laughs like that can't be bad.' I felt that Hitler was nevertheless not very certain about Goebbels.

I stood up, sensing that Hitler wanted to end the conversation. I have never understood what happened next. Hitler looked at me for an instant, hesitated briefly, then said: 'Before you leave me, I would like to confide something to you. Please come with me.'

He then led me through the corridor and opened a locked door. In the room there was a bust of a girl; decked out with flowers. 'I told you why I will never marry. But this girl,' he said, pointing at the bust, 'is Geli, my niece. I loved her very much – she was the only woman I could have married. But fate was against it.'

I did not have the nerve to ask what she died of. Only much later did I learn from Frau Schaub that Geli had shot herself, here in this apartment. The previous evening she had found a love letter from Eva Braun in the pocket of Hitler's coat. The Führer never got over Geli's death.

Confused, I took my leave, and Hitler said, 'Good luck with your work. You will not fail.'

WINTER OLYMPICS IN GARMISCH

On 6 February 1936, the Olympic Winter Games opened in Garmisch-Partenkirchen. I had put up at the Garmischer Hof in order to watch the games, but also to observe and learn the best ways of capturing athletic events on celluloid. Some of my cameramen tested cameras, optics, and stock.

Surprisingly, Goebbels had also decided to make an Olympic film. The task was given to Hans Weidemann, a member of the cinema department in his ministry. There was no doubt in my mind that Goebbels wanted to prove to me how well and how quickly an Olympic picture could be made. I have often been asked why I didn't also produce the film on the winter Olympics. I would have been tempted, but I considered it impossible to make two films in one year, so I didn't do it. The summer Olympics were more important to me.

The Olympics in Garmisch were such a tremendous success that when the International Olympic Committee met on 8 June 1939, just a few months before the start of the war, the members voted by secret ballot on the location of the 1940 winter Olympics even though the Germans abstained, the choice was again Garmisch-Partenkirchen.

The Goebbels film on the winter games, heavily subsidized by the Ministry of Propaganda, was unsuccessful, even though I had to make available some of my best cameramen, such as Hans Ertl, to Herr Weidemann. Despite some fantastic shots, it was hissed and booed at the Olympic village when it was first screened to the athletes there in July 1936; which shows how hard it is to make a good sports film, even with the best cameraman and all kinds of technical aids. I was still faced with the problem.

MUSSOLINI

The winter games were over, and I went to Davos. No sooner had I arrived than I received an invitation from Mussolini. It came from the head of the cultural division at the Italian embassy in Berlin. I had received the same invitation two weeks earlier, but had been unable to accept, since I was in Garmisch and didn't want to miss the games. The Italian embassy had informed me that Mussolini wanted to talk to me about my film work.

When I left Davos, my Austrian friends, who wanted to go skiing with me in the Parsenn area, jokingly asked me to tell the Duce that they did not wish to become Italians, they preferred to remain Austrians. This was a reference to the South Tyrol issue.

En route to Rome I had to spend the night in Munich, where I usually stayed at the Hotel Schottenhamel by the railway station, and there, in the lobby, I ran into Frau Winter, Hitler's housekeeper. I told her about my invitation to Rome, and when, only an hour later, the telephone rang, it was Frau Winter. She said, 'The Führer is in Munich. I told him that you had been invited by the Duce, and he would like to know when your plane is leaving tomorrow.'

'I have to be at the airport at 12 noon,' I said.

'Could you possibly get up a bit earlier so that you could be at the Führer's apartment at 10 a.m.?'

As always I was afraid. What did this mean? My Austrian friends had told me that Italian troops had been stationed at the Austrian border, and that the South Tyrol problem was highly explosive. Was that why Hitler wanted to see me?

At Prinzregentenplatz the next morning, Hitler apologized for asking me over so early in the day. 'I have heard,' he said, 'that the Duce has invited you. Will you remain in Rome for a long time?' I said no. Hitler did not talk about the Duce as I had expected. Instead, he spoke about his construction plans, and about architecture, and various foreign architectural landmarks which he admired, and which, to my surprise, he described meticulously. I can no longer remember their names. None of this had anything to do with my visit to Rome. It was only when I was about to leave that Hitler said casually, 'The Duce is a man whom I highly esteem. Even if he were ever to become my enemy I would greatly respect him.' That was all. He did not even send his regards. I was relieved that I didn't have to transmit any message. Hitler had told his chauffeur to drive me in his Mercedes and get me to Oberwiesenfeld Airfield on time.

In Rome planes still landed on Via Appia Antica in Ciampino, and there I was welcomed by members of the Italian government, some of them in black uniforms. Even Guido di Parisch, the cultural attaché at the Italian embassy in Berlin, was present; he was the one who had twice extended the invitation. When he sat next to me in the car, whispering in my ear: 'You will see the Duce today,' it struck me that this might not be a normal audience. It was an alarming thought. Within a few short hours I entered the Palazzo Venezia. I had been told to address Mussolini as 'Your Excellency'.

Slowly the heavy doors opened and I stepped into an imposing room. At my back, far from the door, was a huge desk from which Mussolini rose and came towards me. He greeted me and led me to a sumptuous armchair opposite his desk.

Although the Duce was not especially tall, he looked strong, full of concentrated energy, but also rather like a Caruso in uniform. After saying a few amiable words – incidentally, in astonishingly good German – he began to talk about my films. I was amazed that he remembered so many details, and he could scarcely believe that the dangerous scenes in the Alps and Greenland were made without a stuntwoman. He also expressed his admiration for the visual technique, and then he came to *Triumph of the Will*.

'This film,' he said, 'has convinced me that documentaries can be extremely effective. I have invited you because I would like to ask if you would be willing to make a documentary for me.'

I looked at him in surprise.

'It would be a film about the Pontine Marshes, which I am now having drained in order to gain new land – a huge undertaking for my country.'

'I thank you for your trust, Your Excellency, but I am now in the process of making a large-scale film about the Berlin Olympics, and I'm afraid that this project will keep me tied up for two years.' Mussolini smiled, stood up, and said, 'Too bad, but I understand. Your present task is more important.'

Then he walked around the giant desk, came towards me, and said grandiloquently, 'Tell your Führer that I believe in him and his mission.'

'Why are you telling me this?' I asked.

'Because the diplomats, both German and Italian, are doing everything they can to prevent a *rapprochement* between me and the Führer.'

At that moment I recalled the greetings from my Austrian friends and I asked, 'Won't you have any problems with Hitler because of Austria?'

Mussolini frowned, then said, 'You can tell the Führer that whatever happens with Austria I will not interfere in Austria's internal affairs.'

I knew little about politics, but I fully grasped the drift of his words. They indicated no less and no more than that. If it came to the point, Mussolini would not prevent Hitler from annexing Austria to Germany.

The instant I got back to Berlin I was summoned to the Reich Chancellery where Herr Schaub took me to a small audience chamber. Soon Hitler came in and greeted me, and as Schaub left the room, he asked me to be seated. He himself remained standing.

'How did you like the Duce?' he asked.

'He is very interested in my films, and he asked me if I would make one for him, a documentary about the draining of the Pontine Marshes.'

'And what did you say?'

'I had to turn him down, since I'm busy filming the summer games.'

Hitler gave me a penetrating look and asked, 'That was all?'

'Yes,' I said, 'except that he asked me to give you a message.' After my audience with Mussolini I had written down his words and I now reported them verbatim: 'Tell the Führer that I believe in him and his mission, and also tell him that the German and the Italian diplomats are trying to prevent a friendship between me and the Führer.'

Hitler looked down at me as I spoke, but he remained completely unmoved.

I went on: 'Then I said something that perhaps I oughtn't to have said . . .' Here I faltered.

'Please go on.'

I told Hitler about the message from my Austrian friends to the Duce. Hitler looked at me in surprise. I said, 'I didn't tell the Duce quite literally what my friends said. I only asked him whether he wouldn't have problems with you about Austria, whereupon the Duce answered: "You can tell the Führer that whatever happens with Austria, I will not interfere in Austria's internal affairs."'

Hitler paced up and down the room. Then he halted in front of me with an absent gaze. 'Thank you, Fräulein Riefenstahl.' Relieved to have delivered the message, I left the Reich Chancellery.

No sooner had I arrived at my apartment than the phone rang again. Göring was on the line. 'I heard that you saw the Führer and that you saw the Duce in Rome before that. I am very interested in what Mussolini said.'

'Nothing that could interest you.'

Göring went on, 'Would you care to have tea with me? I would like to talk to you a bit.'

Göring's apartment was in the government district, near the Brandenburg Gate. He showed me his rooms very proudly. They were sumptuously appointed, overloaded with antique furniture, expensive paintings, and heavy carpets. I couldn't have endured all that pomp for even a day. Göring was in mufti and in a jovial mood. I was embarrassed when he listed the enormous sums he had paid for his paintings and antiques.

During tea he came straight to the point. 'What did the Duce want from you? What did he say?'

'He offered me a film project.'

'That was all?'

'He sent his regards to the Führer.'

'That is not all! You are hiding something!'

'Ask the Führer! I can't tell you anything else.'

'Göring kept trying to prise more out of me; but finally he gave up and dismissed me, rather ungraciously.

On 7 March 1936, a week after my return from Rome, Hitler declared the Locarno Pact to be null and void and ordered the Wehrmacht to march into the demilitarized zone of the Rhineland. A short time later I found out that he had been encouraged to take this step by Mussolini's message, and that it was the Italian ambassador, Attolico, who had planned my trip to Rome.

THE OLYMPICS FILM

From now on I concentrated exclusively on the Olympics film. Geyer had expanded and modernized our offices and cutting rooms and they were fitted out in exemplary fashion. Aside from four large editing rooms, all equipped with translucent glass walls and the latest sound tables, we had our own screening room, dark room, reproduction room, a comfortable lounge, and our own canteen. This was necessary, since our project was expected to last for two years and we had a staff of roughly eighteen or twenty people.

As we were about to move in, a man in Party uniform prevented me from entering my rooms. He had been sent by Hans Weidemann, the vice-chairman of the Reich Film Chamber, who had been commissioned by Dr Goebbels to make the winter Olympics films. He wanted to confiscate my rooms for his work. I had already experienced all sorts of things with Party members, but this was the height of impudence.

I refused to argue with him. Instead, together with Waldi Traut, my executive producer, we went to the nearest police station and reported the incident. I had signed a lease with Geyer, and thus I was legally in the right. Fortunately the police official was not afraid of Weidemann, the Party member. He accompanied us back to our offices and ordered Herr Weidemann to clear out there and then. Raging and threatening to report this to Dr Goebbels, Weidemann left. I had made another enemy.

Now I began to assemble my staff. Along with my two assistants, Traut and Grosskopf, it consisted chiefly of cameramen. Once again I found myself in the same situation as with *Triumph of the Will*. Most of the good cameramen were busy, and the German newsreel photographers, who would have been the most suitable for such work and who were made available to me by my agreement with the Ministry of Propaganda, were practising a boycott: they refused to work for a woman. They probably couldn't have squeezed my film into their schedules anyhow, since they had to concentrate primarily on the daily newsreel reports.

It was a great shame that Sepp Allgeier, who had shot most of *Triumph of the Will*, was not free. Nevertheless, I managed to get Willy Zielke for the prologue. Of all the cinematographers I had worked with, he was the most brilliant and also the best for these sequences. For difficult and experimental athletic shots, I hired Hans Ertl. He had taught himself with the help of manuals; and without any practical experience he had made an excellent full-length picture about Professor Dyhrenfurt's Himalayan expedition. He had never even held a camera before our Greenland venture, in which he had participated as a mountain-climber. Not only was he one of the best, but he was also the most ambitious of the cameramen, and he would have much preferred shooting the entire film by himself. Naturally this made him unpopular among some of his colleagues, and it sometimes took a lot of diplomacy to smooth things over. He was a workaholic who also had original ideas. For instance, he had invented an underwater camera, something entirely new in those days. He had built it himself, and he used it for the diving footage at the swimming stadium – shots that later became so famous. He was also involved in building the steel towers, which were set up inside the stadium for the first time, and from which he photographed breathtaking panoramic sequences.

Many other people deserve mention. None of these men acted like stars. They were thrilled with the project and devoted their creativity to making possible the often impossible. They worked out how to make cunning soundproof hoods for the cameras, so that their humming wouldn't disturb the athletes. They designed a track system which allowed the cameras to follow the athletic contests. They thought up free balloons, captive balloons, airplanes, motorboats – anything in order to shoot the Olympics more closely, more dramatically than sports had ever been captured on celluloid. Along with those men, I hired some two dozen others. This sounds impressive – but most of them were amateurs and assistants. I needed them in order to get enough snapshots of spectator reactions; some of these men worked only with cinecameras.

In May we started doing test rushes of the most diverse athletic events. The cameramen had to practise, sometimes without film in their cameras, in order to learn how to catch the rapid movements of the athletes. Without that training they would never have succeeded in the later shooting. We also wanted to find out which stock achieved the best image quality. In fact we performed an unusual experiment. The possible brands were Kodak, Agfa and the still almost unknown Perutz stock. They were all black and white, for in 1936 there was still no decent colour film. We chose three different subjects: faces and people, architecture, and landscapes with lots of green. The results were staggering. The portraits looked best on Kodak, because it retained the most shades, while buildings and architecture came out the most vivid on Agfa. But the biggest surprise was the Perutz stock: images of subjects with lots of verdure had a striking radiance. So we decided to use all three brands. Each cameraman could choose the stock that he felt was the most suitable for his subjects.

Once, together with some members of my staff, I went to Bad Harzburg for three days; there, in total isolation, we discussed the marathon. While driving I racked my brains about how to dramatize a twenty-five mile race on film. And I hit on the answer during that very drive. I tried to project myself into the heart and mind of the runner and to feel what he feels: his fatigue, his exhaustion, the way his feet cling to the ground; his efforts to get to the stadium with his very last drop of willpower. I also heard the powerful music that drives his weary body along, forcing him not to give up until the sound turns into the cheers of the spectators when the runner enters the stadium and reaches the finishing line with his final ounce of strength. These were all still visions which we had to turn into realities.

Other pre-production work was more strenuous and often unpleasant. We had to struggle against a mountain of red tape, months before the games even began. We had to deal with the officials who were responsible for the many athletic organizations. The main issue was the location of the cameras. Actually, any camera inside the stadium was disruptive. I had to muster a lot of patience and self-control not to give up in my fights with the officials. Once a location was finally granted, new protests came, mostly from foreign sports functionaries and, during these negotiations, I often found it advantageous to be a woman.

It seemed almost hopeless to obtain permission for the pits inside the stadium. To get good shots of the athletes we had to film them against a calm background, the most suitable being the sky. But we could do so only by stationing the cameras as far down as possible. This was the only way of keeping out anything behind the athletes' heads – poles, number signs, or other objects that could disrupt the image and its effect. In no way was my aim – as some journalists wrote – to 'beautify' the athletes. The cameramen were supposed to shoot from the pits in order to disturb the contenders and the spectators as little as possible. However, there appeared to be no hope of obtaining the requisite permission: they refused to grant me even one pit. I had to fight literally for weeks with every single athletics official. But finally, with the help of Professor Diem and the IOC, I managed to obtain permission for the six most important pits. We had to follow the rules laid down by the Athletics Organization Committee. To give some notion of this problem, I shall list a few of those rules.

They approved the following: one pit each at the high jump, broad jump, and pole vault, one pit five yards away from the hundred-metre starting line, one at the side of the finishing line, and one next to the triple jump; plus two towers at the centre of the stadium, one tower behind the starting line of the hundred-metre track. No more than six cameramen could set foot inside the stadium; no more pits could be dug; and no cameras could be used that ran automatically on tracks.

We also had to cope with other problems that no committee could solve; for instance, Hitler's opening speech, which could consist of only a few words, in accordance with Olympic tradition. There was no room for the huge sound camera on the rostrum. No matter where we set it up, it would block the view of the honorary guests. They would not allow me to build a tower in the spectator area, so I had no choice but to discuss it directly with Hitler. This proved difficult. I hadn't seen him since my return from Rome, and his adjutants said he was swamped with appointments. However, I did manage to have a brief talk with him.

I had brought along a plan showing the positions of the sound cameras. For lack of space they could only be set up next to the rostrum area, so that the honorary guests could barely manage to squeeze past. After studying it, Hitler said, 'You can put your cameras there. I'll approve it. They'll only be in the way for a few minutes.'

I heaved a sigh of relief. Then we exchanged a few words about the games. As in Munich Hitler again stated that he was not interested.

187

'I'll be glad,' he said, 'when the entire Olympic commotion is over. I'd much rather not visit the games at all.'

I was speechless. And I was also astonished that he didn't show the slightest interest in my film. Nevertheless, Hitler did visit the stadium. His entourage had convinced him that his presence would inspire the German athletes. Then, when Hitler saw that two gold medals were won by Germans on the very first day, he came back daily.

Indeed, Germany was, surprisingly, the most victorious contender. The German athletes won thirty-three gold medals, twenty-six silver medals, and thirty bronze medals – a record that they never achieved again.

ANATOL THE TORCH BEARER

I still didn't know how I could film the torch race of 4,300 miles through seven countries. On 17 July 1936, eight men left Berlin in three Mercedes automobiles, to accompany the torch racers. Several days later I myself took a JU 52 to Athens with a small crew in order to shoot the lighting of the Olympic fire in the grove of Olympia, and also to photograph the first runners *en route* through Greece.

Our motorcade arrived in Athens in the midst of a scorching heatwave. During the drive to Olympia we were welcomed by cheering Greeks lining the road. Exhausted and bathed in sweat, we reached the classical Olympic site under a white-hot noon sun. Reality surpassed my worst expectations. Cars and motorcycles marred the landscape. The altar where the Olympic fire was to be ignited looked duller than dull. Nor did the Greek youth in athletic garb quite fit the image that I had in mind. I was bitterly disappointed.

Our cameramen tried to catch a glimpse of the altar, but the throng was so dense that their efforts seemed hopeless. Then, loud cheers announced that the Olympic fire was about to be lit and, in between cars and motorcycles, we saw the bright glow of the torch and recognized the first torch bearer as he jostled through the crowd and dashed out to the highway. When we tried to follow him in our cars we were stopped by a chain of policemen who wouldn't let us drive on. Even the IOC stickers on our windscreens didn't help. I leapt out of the car and pleaded with the policemen. They finally relented and, a bit stunned, waved us through. Our cars sped off and we caught up with the runner several minutes later. I realized that this was no way to get useful footage. What we were shooting was pure newsreel: we had to try to film our own torch race, beyond these roads; shoot subjects consistent with the character of my Olympic prologue.

It was the fourth runner in this relay who resembled my image of the bearer: a young, dark-haired Greek whom we came upon in a village several miles from Olympia. He must have been eighteen or nineteen, and as he stood in the shade of a tree, he looked very photogenic. One of my people went and spoke to him. They boy's reaction was hostile. We didn't give up however. Since none of us spoke Greek, we tried to communicate in pantomine but it turned out that he had a smattering of French. We made it clear to him that he should come along with us, and when he again refused, we said we would drive him back again. Finally he indicated that he couldn't join us in his running shorts; he first had to go home and change into proper clothes. After we promised to fit him out, he climbed into our car. I tried to get more out of him, and with the help of a few French words, my classical Greek youth revealed that he was not in fact Greek, but the son of Russian *emigrés* and his name was Anatol. He gradually became used to us. We took him along to Delphi where he proved skilful in the stadium shooting, and seemed to enjoy his role more and more. In fact he soon acquired movie-star airs and refused to run the way we wanted him to; instead, he showed us how he pictured it. We were delighted by his enthusiasm and in the end we got along famously.

When our work was done we drove him to the German embassy and gave him enough money to go home to his parents. When we said farewell he wept and didn't want to leave us. Later, at the request of his parents, we had him come to Germany, where he was to be trained as an actor at Tobis. Unfortunately, his voice was cracked, and so his plan didn't work out. Nevertheless, he didn't want to leave Germany and mastered German perfectly within a very short time, worked as a draughtsman in an aircraft plant, and volunteered for the Luftwaffe when the war broke out. He was inconsolable because they wouldn't accept a foreigner. However, his wish came true in the navy and Anatol wound up in the dangerous one-man U-boats. Luck was with him, however, and he survived the war.

RUHWALD CASTLE

After my return from Greece we all moved into Ruhwald Castle, an old, uninhabited building in a park on Spandauer Chaussee, near the stadium. An endless commuting took place between Ruhwald, the stadium, and the Geyer Printing Laboratories, so that we could check the rushes on the very same day, discuss the work methods of the cameramen and draw conclusions from any defects in the footage.

Before the shooting began I hired Ernst Jäger, former editor-in-chief of *Film-Kurier*, as my press chief, although I knew I'd have trouble with Goebbels. Jäger, an inveterate Social Democrat, had been expelled from the Reich Literature Chamber, partly because his wife was Jewish. I had been able to help him a year earlier when he was in financial straits: my firm commissioned him to write a brochure on the work involved in *Triumph of the Will* for UFA's publicity department. Jäger called the text *Behind the Scenes of the Reich Party Rally Film*. My help, which was well meant, brought me numerous attacks after the war. Jäger, otherwise an excellent journalist, wrote a ludicrously overblown text, perhaps hoping that it would get him re-admitted to the Reich Literature Chamber, and unfortunately, because of all my work, I didn't read his brochure before its publication. Jäger had put it together with UFA's publicity department, which brought it out under my name.

In Ruhwald we set up a model of the entire sports field, which enabled me to establish good camera locations. My film couldn't include any events outside the precincts of the games, such as the dance festivals on the Dietrich Eckart Stage or the functions in the pleasure garden. We focused purely on the Olympic events, and already everything was going full blast. From now on we could sleep only a few hours a night.

Meanwhile Olympic fever had broken out in Berlin. The city was decorated with thousands of flags, and hundreds of thousands of visitors were pouring through the streets. More than eighty theatres were playing, the nightclubs were jammed, and the cinemas were screening films like *Traumulus* with Emil Jannings, *Modern Times* with Charlie Chaplin and the unforgettable *Broadway Melody*.

I had no inkling of the human tragedies taking place behind all that gaiety.

OLYMPIA – BERLIN 1936

On 1 August, 1936, the great moment came: the start of the Olympic Games in Berlin. We were ready to go at 6 a.m. as I gave my final instructions for the distribution of the cameramen. The subjects of the first day were magnificent: the entrance of the nations, the arrival of the torch bearer, the lighting of the Olympic fire, Hitler's opening words, the hundreds of doves soaring aloft, the anthem composed by Richard Strauss. To capture everything, we had added thirty cameras. A total of sixty photographers shot the opening celebrations.

A big problem was setting up the two sound cameras on the rostrum; for lack of space we had to tie them to the railing of the podium. The cameramen and his assistant were similarly tied; they could stand only behind the railing. As I dashed from one cameraman to another, giving final instructions, I suddenly heard someone shouting my name. One of my men was yelling frantically: 'SS men are trying to take down the two sound cameras from the rostrum.' I ran over in alarm, and indeed they were untying the ropes. I saw the desperate face of my cameraman and I had no choice but to stand in front of his camera in order to shield it. The SS men declared that they received their orders from Reich Minister Goebbels, who was in charge of the seating arrangement on the rostrum. Furiously, I tried to make it clear to them that the Führer had approved the siting of the cameras and that they must remain. The SS men were rattled, and they hesitated. When I told them that I was going to stay there until the games began, they left the rostrum, shrugging their shoulders. I didn't dare budge, for fear they might come back.

The first guests arrived, mostly foreign diplomats, while the rostrum and the stands were filling up. I felt somewhat embarrassed standing there, tied to the railing, and I grew more and more nervous since I couldn't give my cameraman any further instructions. This was especially important at the opening ceremony when a lot had to be improvised.

Now Goebbels entered the rostrum. When he saw me and the cameras, his eyes flashed with rage, and he screamed at me, 'Have you gone mad? You can't stay here! You're destroying the whole ceremonial tableau. Get yourself and your cameras out of here immediately!'

I was shaking with fear, fury, and indignation, and the tears were streaming as I stammered, 'Herr Minister, I asked the Führer for permission way ahead of time – and I received it. There is no other place from which we can film the opening address. This is a historic ceremony, it cannot be left out of an Olympic film.'

Goebbels wasn't the least bit impressed and yelled all the more, 'Why didn't you set your cameras on the other side of the stadium?'

'That's technically impossible! The distance is too great.'

'Why didn't you build a tower next to the rostrum?'

'They wouldn't let me.'

Goebbels seemed to be almost incandescent with rage. At that instant Field Marshal Göring in his magnificent white uniform entered the rostrum. For insiders this encounter was intriguing, for they knew that the two men couldn't stand one another. I was especially unhappy that Goebbels was in charge of arranging the guests on the rostrum – and our cameras were standing on the very spot that he had reserved for Göring, one of the best seats in the first row, and they were blocking the view. In order to justify himself to Göring and demonstrate his innocence, Goebbels screamed at me even more loudly, but Göring raised his hand – and Goebbels fell silent. Then the Field Marshal turned to me and said in a conciliatory voice, 'C'mon, my girl, stop crying. There's room here even for my belly.'

Luckily, Hitler hadn't yet arrived. But many of the guests were witness to this embarrassing scene.

THE LEGEND OF JESSE OWENS

From now on I was utterly engrossed in my work, so much that I barely watched the Olympic Games. Often I had no idea what was going on. For example, I didn't witness the tragedy of the German women's relay, when Ilse Dörffeld, with a ten-yard lead over the American favourite, dropped the baton after grabbing hold of it – I didn't hear the yells of the spectators. I had to be in too many places at once. I didn't manage to view that scene until I saw it in the editing room.

We wanted to create something new with this film, and that meant that we had to do technical experiments. Hans Ertl had developed an automatic catapult camera, which could move alongside the hundred-metre sprinters. We could have obtained footage such as had never been shot before, but one of the umpires prohibited it. There were no helicopters in those days and so, in order to get a bird's eye view of the stadium, we experimented with a balloon. Every morning, after equipping it with a small hand camera, we sent it up. By advertising in the *Berliner Zeitung am Mittag* and promising a reward to the finder, we got our camera back every single time.

In order to shoot the victory in the rowing regattas in Grünau we built a jetty one hundred yards long and mounted on rails. In this way the camera, tied to a car, could follow the dramatic final spurt of the boats until they crossed the finishing line. Since we also wanted to shoot this culminating struggle from the air, we borrowed a captive balloon from the Luftwaffe. But our plan was frustrated. A few minutes before the start of the race we were told we couldn't use the balloon because it might cause an accident. Our balloon with our cameraman was already in the air, hovering directly over the finishing line. Now it had to be moved away at once. I wept with rage.

We tied our small cameras with seventeen feet of film to the saddles of the three-day event horsemen. This helped us achieve particular effects. Of course most of the rushes were blurred by the movements, but the bit of useful footage made the whole experiment worthwhile. Walter Frentz came up with another cinematic innovation. He built a wire basket for a small camera and hung it on the marathon runners in training, so that they could start the camera themselves, which resulted in unusual shots of this discipline.

With four gold medals and two world records, Jesse Owens was the athletic phenomenon of the games. One of the legends is that Hitler refused to shake hands with the great champion for racist reasons. Karl von Halt, a member of the IOC and president of the German Olympic Committee, who was in charge of the light athletic contests, told me the true story. It is also recorded in the official American report on the Olympic Games. This, it appears, is what really happened: on the first day of the games, Hitler received the winners on the rostrum, but this was then prohibited by Count Baillet-Latour, the French president of the Olympic Committee, because it was against Olympic protocol. That was why Hitler did not shake hands with any more athletes.

I nearly caused Jesse Owens to have an accident. One of our pits was located some seventy yards behind the finishing line of the hundred-metre sprint, and a cameraman and an assistant were standing in the pit. It happened during the second preliminary heat. Owens swept along the cinder track with incredible grace and ease; he broke the previous world record with 10.2 seconds – but his feat wasn't recognized because of the tail wind. At the run-out, Owens couldn't slow down, and he almost plunged into our pit. It was only because of his swift reaction that he managed to leap aside in time to prevent a mishap. After that the inevitable fuss was made, and we had to fill in not only this pit, but all the others. I begged and begged, and I also pleaded with Count Baillet-Latour to let us work in the pits again. Finally we obtained permission from the IOC.

The cameramen were organized as follows: every evening at ten, two editors handed me the printing lab reports on the results of that day's rushes. Roughly fifty thousand feet of film were printed daily, then viewed and evaluated. In this way, depending on the results, I could relocate the cameramen every day. The ones who worked well got the most difficult shooting spots; the less gifted ones got the less important spots. When I gave them my instructions for the next day I had only five minutes per cameraman. These conferences never ended until two in the morning.

SCANDAL AT THE STADIUM

The two things we really didn't need in our work were trouble and harassment, and we got more than enough of both – once again from Goebbels personally. For the hammer-throwing Germany had two hot contestants: Erwin Blask and Karl Hein. We had built tracks around the hammer-throwing cage in order to get first-class footage, and they had been approved by the organization committee. Moreover, the hammer-throwers themselves were agreeable.

The dramatic duel between Blask and Hein was to be one of the climaxes of our film. Anxiously I watched Guzzi Lantschner shooting as his camera slid along the track. Suddenly one of the judges charged towards him, yanked him away from his camera, grabbed his arm, and pulled him off the lawn. I was so furious that I ran over to the judge, seized his jacket, and yelled: 'You bastard!' The man gaped at me and then instantly complained to his superiors.

It wasn't long before I was handed a note summoning me to Goebbels on the rostrum, and I feared the worst. The minister was already waiting for me in the corridor outside the rostrum, and again frantically yelling, 'Just who do you think you are! Have you taken leave of your senses! I forbid you ever to enter the stadium again! Your behaviour has been scandalous throughout!'

'We were given permission,' I exclaimed, flustered, 'and from the hammer-throwers too. The German judge had absolutely no right to pull the cameraman from his place.'

Furiously Goebbels retorted: 'I order you to discontinue your filming here immediately.' Leaving me there, he stormed back to the rostrum, while I sat down in despair on the steps and cried bitter tears. It was more than I could bear that it should all have been for nothing.

After a while Goebbels – surprisingly enough – came back. Somewhat calmer, he snapped at me, 'Stop crying. There's going to be an international scandal. I order you to apologize to the judge immediately.'

Having no choice, I went down and looked for the judge, and when I found him, I told him I was very sorry.

'I regret the incident,' I said. 'I didn't mean to insult you – I lost my head.' The judge merely nodded, and for me the case we closed. But the scene did not go unnoticed. Several foreign newspapers ran front-page stories about it. Goebbels' hostility towards me had been no secret for a long time now.

The contests became more and more exciting. They were about to post the results of the hundred-metre sprint – a high point of the Olympics. The stadium was deathly still. A hundred thousand people were almost afraid to breathe. Metcalfe, a black athlete, crossed himself before kneeling down at the starting line; Jesse Owens had the inside track. In his white coat, Miller, the starter, gazed in unshakable calm at the runners kneeling in their starting holes. Once again my eyes darted across to the cameramen. The shots of this fantastic race had to succeed. Owens' legs muscles tensed. Then the starting shot cracked through the hush of the stadium – ear-splitting yells broke out, and rose to a crescendo as Jesse Owens streaked ahead to become the winner. Smiling happily, he gazed around at the people, who cheered a superb athlete.

I don't have room here to describe even the most important events. But I remember Lovelock very clearly. He was the only athlete representing New Zealand. He won the fifteen-hundred-metre race – even setting a new record. It was a spectacular event and my film shows his entire dramatic run, not a single frame was omitted. Imagine what Lovelock, the sole bearer of his country's flag in the entrance march, must have felt when he was given the gold medal and the laurel wreath.

The ten-thousand-metre race had to be tackled in an entirely different way. Here I could show only the dramatic high points. The intervals had to be bridged by shots of the audience. As in the long-jump duel between Lutz Long and Jesse Owens, there was a duel here between the three Finns, who were considered unbeatable, and Murakoso, the small, tough Japanese, who fought like a lion. He pulled off an incredible feat – passing the Finns and leaving them behind, cheered on by his compatriots. But eventually he had to yield the victory to the powerful Finns. Nevertheless, Murakoso had won the hearts of the spectators.

A dazzling sun shone over the stadium when the runners gathered at the starting line of the marathon, the classic event of the Olympic Games. Twelve cameramen were stationed along the twenty-five-mile stretch. Zabala, an Argentinian, the victor in Los Angeles, wanted to win again, but the Japanese were his most dangerous opponents. Nan was the favourite, but Son, the second Japanese, was very strong, as were the Finns.

I didn't experience the drama of this race (which the cameramen accompanied in a car) until I cut the rushes. They were so excellent that the marathon became the high point of the film. A poignant moment occurs when the Japanese are honoured as the winners: lowering their wreathed heads, they listen to their national anthem with almost religious devotion.

GLENN MORRIS

I was inside the stadium. The decathlon was in progress. Germany's champion, Erwin Huber, who was a good friend of mine, had already helped me with the pre-production work and introduced me to various athletes. He was to play the discus thrower of Myron in the prologue of the film. Today he wanted me to meet the three leading Americans in the decathlon. It was the second day of this event, and the American, Clark, was ahead of his countryman Glenn Morris. Huber was in fourth place.

With a towel over his head, Glenn Morris lay relaxing on the grass, gathering strength for the next event. When Huber presented Morris to me, and we looked at one another, we both seemed transfixed. It was an incredible moment and I had never experienced anything like it. I tried to choke back the feelings surging up inside me and to forget what had happened. From then on I avoided Morris, with whom I exchanged barely a dozen words, and yet this meeting had had a profound impact on me.

Glenn Morris won the decathlon, achieving a new world record. It was already quite dark when the three American champions stood on the podium and received their medals. The dim light prevented any filming of the ceremony, and when Glenn Morris came down the steps, he headed straight towards me. I held out my hand and congratulated him, but he grabbed me in his arms, tore off my blouse, and kissed my breasts, right in the middle of the stadium, in front of a hundred thousand spectators. A lunatic, I thought. I wrenched myself out of his grasp and dashed away. But I could not forget the wild look in his eyes, and I never wanted to speak to him again, never go anywhere near him again. But then I couldn't avoid him because of the pole vault.

The vaulting contest was perhaps the most dramatic event of those Olympics. The jumping began in the morning and by the afternoon five jumpers were still engaged in a fierce struggle to win the victory for the United States or Japan. Two short, almost delicate Japanese were fighting tooth and nail against three Americans who were as strong as oxen. The sky grew darker and darker, the air grew cold. The waiting jumpers wrapped themselves up in wool blankets, while the absorbed spectators followed this dramatic spectacle. After five hours the decision came. Earle Meadows, a young American, won over the two Japanese, Nishida and Oe.

The big loser that evening was Riefenstahl. For I had no footage of this fantastic event. It had been too dark. There was only one chance – to repeat this nocturnal pole-vaulting the next day, amid spotlights. Would the athletes agree? It was highly improbable after that strenuous day and the preceding weeks of renunciation. Erwin Huber, our decathlon champion, said, 'As far as the Americans are concerned, only Glenn Morris could help you.'

I spoke to him, and he was willing to try and convince his friends. But they had already left the Olympic village and fled to some nightclub. It was their first free day after weeks of abstinence. The Japanese, however, readily agreed to jump again for the camera.

Morris found his friends in a dance hall and dragged them to us in the stadium, but they weren't exactly enthusiastic. In an attempt to create a better mood, I paid them compliment after compliment, while the Japanese waited, smiling their unfathomable smiles. Eventually all the athletes participated – they vaulted. And suddenly they began to enjoy it. Soon it turned into an almost genuine contest, and they reached the same heights as on the previous day. It was fantastic – we got wonderful shots, for the light was excellent. Slow motion, close-ups – everything worked perfectly. And so that evening became one of the happiest moments during my work on the film.

In exchange for his mediation Glenn Morris asked a small favour. He wanted to visit me in my editing room after the games and see the rushes he'd appeared in. I gave in to his request, but otherwise avoided him, for I sensed that I was in love with him and must struggle against it. I knew he was returning to the United States, and besides, I wanted to resist any emotional complications.

On the evening of 16 August, the Eleventh Olympic Summer Games came to a glorious end. Floodlights had been set up around the stadium – in accordance with an idea of Albert Speer's. Pointing vertically at the dark heavens, they locked into a cathedral of light. Then, as the Olympic flame slowly died out to the sounds of Richard Strauss's anthem, a voice sounded forth: 'I call the youth of the world to Tokyo.'

Who could have imagined on this evening that just a few short years later, those same searchlights would be combing the Berlin sky for enemy pilots, and that the young people who had competed here so peacefully would be manning the searchlights and the aircraft.

THE ARCHIVE

When the final rushes were delivered to the Geyer Printing Laboratory we registered the overall amount of exposed celluloid; nearly one hundred and forty-seven thousand feet. Now we had to edit, and add sound and a commentary. An enormous task lay before us.

The tremendous mass of footage made filing it a special problem. The speed at which you have to work at athletic contests doesn't leave the cameramen enough time to film the clapperboard – which contains an identifying number – before each take. How were we to sort the individual scenes without numbers? Some method had to be devised for tracking down any specific shot as fast as possible.

The solution I hit on was for every sport to have a block number so that, including the prologue, the opening celebration and the closing celebration, we ended up with one hundred and fifty blocks, often with as many as one hundred subdivisions. Thus the block 'Audience', which bore the number 10, was subdivided into: 1a, Audience in Sunshine; 1b, Audience in Shade; 1c, Audience Applauds; 1d, Audience Disappointed; and so on. Moreover, the audience rushes were also subdivided by nation and arena. This method enabled us to find any scene very quickly.

To facilitate the matter even further I introduced a colour system, which proved to be efficient and time-saving. The uncut rushes were kept in orange boxes, cuts in green, reserves in blue, discards in black, and sound rushes in yellow. The edited reels wound up in red boxes. It took us a month to box the rushes, and it took two months of screening them ten hours a day to view them all.

Sorting the negatives was a difficult chore, since thousands of feet of rushes had no edge coding. This refers to the small numbers on the lower edge of the negative. A sequential number appears every twelve inches. Hence the German term *Fussnummer*, 'foot number'. The edge coding allows us to find any image very speedily. If these numbers are missing which, alas, was often the case in the early days, then finding specific shots is a difficult and time-consuming procedure. Fortunately I had Frau Peters to assist me. She worked the miracle of tracking down every single scene.

If anyone came into the editing room and asked, say, for the shots of the Italian horseman Lieutenant Campello leaping across the village ditch in the three-day event, I checked the list: three-day event was block 70, 'Village Ditch' was block 22. And in less than a minute the visitor could check the footage at the cutting table. Some cinema experts were astonished by this system. Even Hitler, who once paid us a surprise visit with several escorts, was amazed that I could show him all the footage he wanted to see.

GRAPHOLOGIST

One morning I noticed that the nocturnal fifteen-hundred-metre sprint was missing from the decathlon shots. In those days our lenses weren't fast enough for such takes. However, along with the marathon and the hundred-metre race, the decathlon was one of the most important gold-medal events in the field of light athletics, so the footage had to be as complete as possible.

Erwin Huber and Klein, a Czech, who had both reached these finals, were still in Berlin, so it might therefore still be possible to reshoot a few scenes, but only if Glenn Morris, the winner, could be located. We found out that the American athletes hadn't gone home yet; they were in Stockholm, participating in the Swedish light athletic championships. We managed to get hold of Morris by telephone, and he immediately said he'd be happy to cooperate. The thought of seeing him again made me very uneasy.

When we picked Morris up at the airport, we both had to behave so that no one would notice anything. But we couldn't control our feelings. They were so powerful that Morris did not rejoin his team in Sweden, and I imagined that he was the man I could marry. I had lost my head completely. I forgot almost everything, even my work. Never before had I experienced such a passion. Then came the day of Morris's departure and, to my horror, I realized that I had forgotten to do the shooting of him that we were supposed to do.

We had only one night left, for the next day Morris and his team were to board the steamer in Hamburg and sail to America. We finally had to say goodbye and, though Morris asked me to forget about the shooting, I couldn't. It was difficult for me to say no to him, but reason was stronger than passion and I hurriedly told my people to prepare everything for the scenes to be shot at the stadium. How it could all be arranged that same night was a mystery to me. But we did it. The filming didn't end until after midnight.

When Morris had to leave me at the crack of dawn, a sense of great sadness overwhelmed us. He had to go to New York; as the winner of the decathlon he couldn't miss the confetti parade for the victorious American team.

Then I learned from the press that Glenn Morris was engaged to an American teacher. That was my first small shock. The next one came within a short time, when, for the first time, I received a letter from him. When I saw his handwriting, I almost dropped the letter. I know nothing about graphology, but I felt uneasy when I saw the strangely convoluted strokes. Nevertheless, I sent to America many photos of him in action which were a big help in getting him the part of Tarzan in Hollywood. I still believed I loved him.

Around that time I spent a few days in Kampen, on the island of Sylt, with my friend Margot von Opel, having a brief vacation before I started working in the cutting room. We were sitting on a café terrace one day when we saw a graphologist going from table to table. Margot handed him a letter and I was struck by his accurate interpretation; this reminded me of Morris's letter, which I had with me. The graphologist peered at it briefly, then said abruptly: 'I won't interpret it.'

'Why?' I asked in surprise.

'I can't.'

I had to pester the man for a long time, and it was only after giving him a large note that I persuaded him to interpret the handwriting. He was obviously very reluctant. Hesitantly he said, 'This is a man who is unstable; he's dangerous, uncontrolled, ruthless, inconsiderate, brutal, and even has a sadistic streak . . .'

I couldn't believe this, yet I couldn't get it out of my mind, and after a prolonged struggle and on the basis of my painful experiences, I made up my mind, difficult as it was, to end this relationship. My chief fear was of going through the kind of suffering I had experienced in the past. It took me six months to get over Glenn Morris and not until much later did I learn something about his sad fate. His life went rapidly downhill, and, after divorcing his wife, he died of alcohol and drug abuse.

PROBLEMS AND WORRIES

In early September 1936, at the daily press conference of the Ministry of Propaganda, Berndt, a ministerial councillor, officially announced on behalf of the minister that for the time being the press was not to report on my Olympic film or on me personally. This ban lasted for more than one year and was not lifted until a few short weeks after the première of *Olympia*. There were only two exceptions. The ministry felt obliged to deny foreign press reports that Dr Goebbels had been slighted in connection with me. Moreover, they couldn't hide the fact that I had been awarded three gold medals at the Paris World Fair in early summer 1937.

Harassment from Goebbels went on and on. During an audit of my firm by the Film Credit Bank, our accounts showed a deficit of eighty marks. Because of that tiny sum, Goebbels ordered me to fire Walter Grosskopf, who had been my loyal employee for years and who had a wife and three children to support. I refused to bow to what I considered to be a typical example of Goebbels' insolence.

There was another demand that I also disdained, and which Goebbels transmitted to me through Herr Hanke, his secretary. He wanted the Olympic film to consist of only one part and not show too much of the 'niggers'. I took it upon myself to ignore this order. Just a few days later the Ministry of Propaganda informed me that at the behest of the minister I was to dismiss my press chief, Ernst Jäger, without notice, because of his marriage to a 'non-Aryan' wife. Once again I dared to ignore Goebbels' demand but it was clear to me that they wouldn't put up with my resistance much longer.

What I feared came true. Goebbels tried to oust me once and for all and to get my Olympics film placed under the aegis of his ministry. On 6 November he issued an order that his ministry, through which the financing of the Tobis contract had been taking place, was to pay no more money to my firm. That spelled the end of my work, for we had already used up the Tobis guarantee of one and a half million marks, and any cost overrun was not covered by the distribution contract. We needed a loan of half a million marks for the four projected foreign-language versions and a series of short subjects on sports. We were in the red; our coffers were empty, and so I had applied to the Ministry of Propaganda to approve a loan. The situation was such that I could barely sleep a wink, and I seriously considered giving up the film and moving abroad.

I saw only one way out of this: to talk to Hitler. But I couldn't get an appointment with him. The Führer had no time, he was always out somewhere, but I kept trying week after week. At last, on 11 November, I was given an appointment, and the date happened to be Frau Goebbels' birthday. I was supposed to be at the Reich Chancellery at 5 p.m.

Hitler greeted me as warmly as ever and asked about my work. My nerves were in such a poor state that I began to weep unrestrainedly. I said that I could no longer work here and that under the circumstances I would have to leave Germany.

Hitler was obviously nonplussed. 'But why?' he asked.

'Dr Goebbels hates me!'

Now Hitler became angry. 'What kind of nonsense is that? Why should Dr Goebbels hate you?'

It was not in my nature to mention the sexual advances Goebbels had made to me. I listed only the harassment with regard to my film, and Hitler's response to this was: 'You're overworked – you're a bit hysterical. None of this is possible. Why should Dr Goebbels instigate a vendetta against you?'

I was upset to hear Hitler defending him as firmly, and apparently not believing me at all. Only one thing could help: I would show him the police report which I had planned to use only in an extreme emergency – and this was it. The report described what had happened in Nuremberg when Hans Weidemann, who had a leading position in the cinema division of the Ministry of Propaganda, had ordered the arrest of my cameramen when they refused to work for him. During the light athletics championship we had to wait until after the hammer-throwing event to film important close-ups of Hein and Blask, the winners, since the judge had prevented the cameraman from taking them during the actual games. Weidemann, intent on making the 1936 Party rally film, wanted to surpass *Triumph of the Will*, and tried therefore to annex my people. When Hans Ertl and the others refused, he ordered SS men to arrest them.

Until this point Hilter had sided with Goebbels. Now, reading the police report, he grew very quiet, and his face paled.

'Very well,' he said tersely, 'I will speak to Dr Goebbels. I can say no more to you for now. Go home. You will be hearing from me.'

His goodbye was almost brusque, after his adjutant Brückner reminded him twice that he had to go to Frau Goebbels' birthday party. I drove home in a state of numbness, not daring to hope.

A few days later Brückner called me up and told me the following on behalf of Hitler: 'From now on you will no longer be working under Minister Goebbels or the Ministry of Propaganda. You will be responsible to Rudolf Hess and the Brown House. That,' said Brückner, 'is the result of a discussion between the Führer and Dr Goebbels after the minister declared that he could not work with you any more.'

At first I didn't grasp the drift of this news. Relieved as I was that I could continue working and no longer be subordinate to Goebbels and his ministry, I was still worried about any complications that might arise in the future. It soon became obvious, however, that this arrangement was a boon for me: there was no more harassment or interference, a liberation not only for me, but also for my staff. From now on we could work undisturbed. The loans were approved, our relationship to the Ministry of Propaganda was limited to statements of account and audits until the loans and the accrued interests were completely repaid. But I personally had nothing to do with all that. Traut and Grosskopf shielded me so effectively that I could now devote myself exclusively to working on my Olympic films.

WILLY ZIELKE

We were busy sifting, selecting and labelling the rushes, when we received some shocking news. Willy Zielke's mother told us in despair that her son had been taken to Haar, the asylum for the insane in Munich. We learned from Zielke's wife that in a fit of madness he had destroyed the bulk of his photographs and smashed up the chairs and tables in his home. He had also shot himself with a rifle and tried to set the apartment on fire.

Although we had had previous indications of rather bizarre behaviour, we were devastated by this news and the very next day I went to Munich with Waldi Traut in order to speak to the director of the asylum. We knew that Zielke couldn't be measured by ordinary standards, but even to us his conduct had often seemed irregular. He had frequently telephoned me at three or four in the morning to discuss a camera angle; and eventually I had to hit on some excuse in order not to offend him. I recalled Frau Peters telling me how afraid she was when she had visited him once, because Zielke had used an airgun to shoot at flies flitting about in the room. He was extremely sensitive, but I always got on well with him, and besides, I really liked him.

My interview with the director of Haar was depressing. To judge by their initial observations, Zielke was suffering from a very serious form of schizophrenia. Unable to believe it, I asked the director to take me to him.

'That's impossible,' he said. 'Zielke refuses to receive anybody – he won't even see his mother or his wife.'

This really alarmed me. 'Please do anything you can,' I said, 'to make Zielke healthy again. He must be given excellent treatment. I'll pay for it.'

It was agreed that we should be kept abreast of his state of health, but the news from the institution was discouraging. Eventually though, we received letters from Zielke himself; the handwriting could be read only if we held the writing paper against the light but even then it made no sense. He had formed the words by perforating the paper with a needle.

Several years went by before I was finally allowed to visit Zielke; so far as I remember, it was during the first year of the war. His appearance had barely changed but he had an absent expression, and he did not react to my words at all. Then I asked him, 'Wouldn't you like to be holding a camera?' And he murmured, 'No camera, I'd like to stay here; I want to stay here – don't make me leave.' He became utterly distraught and anxious, and I tried to calm him. 'You can stay at my place, I'll take care of you.'

'I'm not ill – I'm with God here.'

I went to see Zielke again, and the visit was a repeat of the first. It was only in 1944 that I managed with great difficulty to get him out of Haar – but only on condition that I sign a document agreeing to assume personal responsibility for him. Rolf Lantin, our photographer, who brought him to our place in Kitzbühel, took care of him and tended him. We all did our best for Zielke, hoping always that we would rekindle his interest in working with the camera. But his conduct was still too irrational.

In December 1944, when I did the final filming for *Tiefland* in Prague, we took Zielke along and let him do some test shooting in the studio – things like titles and small scenes of plants and grass. Remarkably enough, he still had his technique at his fingertips, but the images were symptomatic of his disease: examples of extreme alienation.

After the war I was unable to continue my efforts on Zielke's behalf. But nevertheless I managed to get some money so that he and a woman friend (whom we had also taken in) could travel to his mother. I was greatly saddened by things I heard about him later. Film people who spoke to him during a Berlin film festival reported that Zielke allegedly claimed that I had handed him over to the Haar Insane Asylum and even ordered his castration. Several members of my staff, who are still alive, can confirm what I have written here about Zielke. Years ago I learned that he married his friend, whom we had taken in at Kitzbühel.

Willy Zielke is not the only person I have helped and who has eventually disappointed me. But at least Zielke, whose abilities have always fascinated me, whose *Steel Animal* I fought for with Goebbels, and whom I got out of the mental home by assuming responsibility, had an excuse: his tragic illness.

THE EDITING ROOM

It took us four months of working an average of twelve to fourteen hours a day to view and sort the rushes. I couldn't start the actual creative work, the editing of the two films, until early February 1937. Of the selected three hundred thousand feet of rushes, not quite twenty thousand were to be used for the final cut. It was a seemingly impossible task.

During this period I was often asked: 'Why don't you let other people select the footage, why can't various editors work on a few blocks, why can't another director take care of the sound – couldn't the film be completed several months earlier? Such questions are understandable from a layman who has no notion about this kind of film-making, but try to imagine the uneven, disharmonious result! What would a house look like if several architects divided up the work; one doing the façade, a second the staircase, a third the interiors, a fourth the rooms. The end result would be very peculiar.

There was no overall plan for the Olympics film, there simply couldn't be one, for athletic events are unpredictable. Nobody could tell which of the numerous intermediate heats would produce a world record, and whether the cameramen would succeed in capturing it. The creation of a documentary actually takes place in the editing room. Creation in this context means first of all that the architectural design has to be established. How does the film begin, how does it end, where are the high points, where are the major suspense elements and the less dramatic parts? A crucial factor is the length of the takes, which can be short or long, thereby determining the rhythm of the film. Equally decisive is the way in which each motion replaces the previous one. It is like composing music, and just as intuitive.

In order to work effectively, you have to remain as secluded as possible from the outside world and my staff kept all distractions away from me. No telephone call, however important, was put through to me. I was out of reach even for my parents and friends. I lived in utter isolation. It was necessary to concentrate entirely on editing.

My staff included two young women who did the splicing – a profession that modern technology has replaced with a machine, which can operate much more quickly. We also had a young man in the editing room who had to label and file every bit of film that I cut. Today the use of splicing machines prevents any loss of images; but in those days every cut meant losing an image, which had to be replaced by black frames. However, my problem was not technology; it was the overall shaping of the film that demanded all my energy.

It would certainly have been tempting to create a purely aesthetic visual composition from the wealth of images and movements – a symphonic paean to motion that ignored the sporting values. But I had opted for an athletic form. The only sequences that I shaped according to aesthetic and rhythmic laws were for sports in which the competitive elements are not so visual, for instance, gymnastics, sailing, springboard diving and high diving.

The prologue too could be edited only according to this approach. I began with this part, and cutting it was so difficult that I nearly gave up. It cost me two months. The prologue had no plot and, since the images all resembled one another, I had to forestall any possibility of boredom by increasing the effect from one take to the next. Often I felt so hopeless that I wanted to toss it all away or to jettison a portion of this beginning. I spent sleepless nights turning over ideas for a satisfactory solution. I kept rearranging the images, trying out new combinations, removing shots, inserting others, until the day when I finally liked what I saw in the screening room.

After that the work advanced more smoothly. Now at last I could watch the Olympic competitions, and they were so exciting that I enjoyed the editing more and more. Usually I couldn't tear myself away until long past midnight. And my staff also endured this for months on end without stopping – not even at weekends and holidays. We were all spellbound by the work. Without this team spirit *Olympia* would never have achieved its final form.

'THE FALLEN ANGEL OF THE THIRD REICH'

It must have been May or June 1937 when Waldi Traut softly tiptoed into the editing room and whispered something in my ear. Since I was totally absorbed in trying out a cut, I didn't understand what he said. Removing the film scrips curled around my neck, I went outside with him. It had to be something urgent, for this was the first time that I had been disturbed while working. Traut repeated, 'The Reich Chancellery telephoned, Hitler would like to see you. You have to come right away.' What in God's name could have happened?

'Didn't they tell you what they want?' I asked him.

The answer being 'no', I peered into the mirror: ungroomed hair, haggard eyes and a pale face looked back at me. I hadn't been to the hairdresser for weeks. Pulling off my editing smock, I told our chauffeur to drive me to the Reich Chancellery just as I was, in my sweater and coat. Six months had passed since my last conversation with Hitler, when I had poured out to him my problems with Goebbels. Since then I had worked in peace.

I entered Hitler's office in my usual state of nervous apprehension, but my fears vanished when he greeted me smilingly.

'I'm sorry to call you away from your work, but it's an urgent matter, for which I have to ask your help.' I was surprised – and even more so as he went on, 'Can you invite Dr Goebbels and me to tea at your home tomorrow?'

I was totally bewildered. 'My house isn't completed yet. I still live on Hindenburgstrasse.'

Hitler was disappointed, 'Isn't it furnished?'

I told him that the interior decorating wasn't done, at which he laughed and, rubbing his hands, exclaimed: 'Why, that's wonderful.' Then he took a newspaper from the table and showed it to me. It was the Swiss *Weltwoche*. The front page said: THE FALLEN ANGEL OF THE THIRD REICH.

'Just read it,' Hitler exclaimed, 'read the shameless lies that they're spreading about again in foreign countries. I usually pay no attention to such rubbish, but this is going too far. For Dr Goebbels' sake I can't take this lying down.

I skimmed the long article which said more or less:

During a dinner given by Reich Minister Dr Frick for domestic and foreign guests, including Dr Goebbels and the actress Leni Riefenstahl, a scandalous incident allegedly occurred. During the meal, we are told, Dr Goebbels stood up and declared that Fraülein Riefenstahl was of Jewish extraction. He demanded that she leave the house immediately, whereupon she was driven to the Reich Chancellery. The next day a removal van picked up her belongings from there, and Leni, now utterly disgraced, had to leave Germany and is in hiding somewhere in Switzerland as the 'fallen angel of the Third Reich'.

Hitler was furious. 'This nonsense will certainly go through the entire international press, and that's why I'd like to deny it officially by publishing a current photo. Tomorrow morning, if you allow us to visit you for tea in your new home, Herr Hoffmann will photograph us together. Dr Goebbels will hand you a bouquet of roses as a housewarming gift.'

I can't say I liked the idea of being photographed in my garden with Dr Goebbels, but I understood Hitler's purpose. How could I have guessed the role that these pictures would play for me after the war!

However, their visit to my house brought an unexpected boon to one of my friends – Bollschweiler, a gifted animal painter and an eccentric, who was very popular in art circles. His love of animals was so great that he actually managed to turn my dislike of snakes into something approaching love. Usually he drew at the Berlin zoo where he could walk into any cage and never be attacked. I had learned how unhappy he was that none of his paintings had been selected for the first exhibition to be mounted at the House of German Art in Munich, but the jury didn't know his work. On the eve of Hitler's visit I decided that, with my secretary's help, I would gather any Bollschweiler paintings I could get my hands on to cover the empty walls of my house.

The next day Hitler, Dr Goebbels and the photographer Heinrich Hoffmann appeared punctually, as agreed. I had also invited my mother and my brother, plus several friends, and everything went as planned. Smiling, Dr Goebbels handed me a huge bouquet of red roses, and Heinrich Hoffmann kept snapping diligently. He also took group photos of us looking at the garden. When Hitler inspected the house he at first didn't notice the Bollschweiler canvases, but as he stood in one of the still unfurnished rooms, he paused at my favourite painting: a white horse's head against a light azure background.

'Lovely,' said Hitler.

'A wonderful painting,' I added, 'I love it.'

Hitler turned to Hoffmann. 'Do you know whether the painter is represented in the show at the House of German Art?'

Hoffmann, very embarrassed, said 'I don't think so, my Führer.' Whereupon Hitler did what I had hoped he would do. He told Hoffmann to request some Bollschweiler paintings for the Munich exhibition.

PARIS WORLD'S FAIR

Tobis had asked me to go to Paris, where three of my films were to be screened: *The Blue Light* and *Triumph of the Will*, as well as the short on the making of *Olympia*. The wildest rumours were circulating about me in the French capital, so I didn't travel under my own name. At Le Bourget airport I got out of the regular plane as Madame Dupont, while the reporters dashed over to a second arrival, a special plane, which landed at the same time. They thought I'd be in it. Only the well-known journalist Roger Feral of *Paris Soir* discovered me and followed me to my hotel. He showed me a newspaper with the headline: LENI RIEFENSTAHL IN PARIS. Underneath it said: 'Is the fallen angel of the Third Reich no longer in disgrace?'

'It's all nonsense,' I said, showing him the photos of Hitler and Goebbels in my garden. He had already seen them, but wanted to discuss them with me personally. The next day the front-page headline of *Paris Soir* blared: MADAME DUPONT, POMPADOUR OF THE THIRD REICH, IN PARIS.

New gossip, I thought, picturing Goebbels' face.

I had far too little time to enjoy Paris – the city I'd been drawn to for years. I was very dejected and so exhausted that I spent most of the day sleeping at the hotel. I slept so soundly that I didn't hear the alarm, and when I awoke, it was already 8 p.m. The film theatre was at the Fair, and I should have been there to greet the French audience prior to the screening of *Triumph of the Will*. I have never dressed so fast in my life; I combed my hair in the car, which had been waiting for some considerable time. Utterly dishevelled, I arrived at the auditorium, where I was welcomed with hisses and stamping feet, as well as with clapping. The spectators had been waiting for twenty-five minutes. I was so embarrassed that when the lights went out I would much rather have slunk away.

But then came the surprise. A short while after the film began there was a burst of applause, and the applause was repeated many times. At the end it was louder than any I had ever heard. The audience went wild. The French lifted me to their shoulders, hugged and kissed me, and tore at my clothes. I was dazed, for the film had not been this successful in Berlin or any other German city.

The next day *Triumph of the Will* was awarded the gold medal, which Edouard Daladier, the Prime Minister of France, presented to me. A documentary was being honoured, not in any way a propaganda film. What interest would the directors of the World's Fair and the French Prime Minister have had in honouring Nazi propaganda?

AT THE BERGHOF

On my way back to Berlin I was supposed to visit Hitler at the Berghof and report on my impressions of the World's Fair. I was told this by the German ambassador Count Von Welczek, who gave a dinner in my honour to celebrate my three gold medals: as well as *Triumph of the Will*, *The Blue Light* and the film on the making of *Olympia* had won gold medals.

This was my second visit to the Berghof. I had first been there in September 1934 after the Reich party rally in order to report to Hitler about my work in Nuremberg. At that time I had asked him what we should call the film, whereupon Hitler had impulsively replied: 'Triumph of the Will', which was of course the name of the rally of 1934.

In the morning a black Mercedes picked me up at my hotel in Berchtesgaden. The road up to the Berghof was very steep and full of twists and turns. This time I could get a close look at Hitler's own home, so beautifully situated in the midst of a mountain landscape. An adjutant took me to the empty entrance hall where, oddly enough, a film was running but with no audience, and I recognized Marlene Dietrich on the screen. Hitler came down the stairs and greeted me as warmly as always. He congratulated me on my triumphs in Paris, asked what I would like to drink, and then sat down with me out on the terrace where I was served coffee and cake. Hitler, as usual, stuck to mineral water.

'How did you like Paris?' was his first question.

'I must confess that I saw very little of Paris. I was too worn out and, unfortunately, I slept through my few leisure hours.'

'A great pity,' said Hitler, 'I'd give anything to see Paris just once. But I'll probably never be granted that in my lifetime.'

'My hotel was on the Champs Elysées,' I said, 'a gloriously beautiful boulevard, and I was also deeply impressed by the Place de la Concorde, and by the churches – La Madeleine and Sacré Coeur.' That was all I could tell him about Paris. Hitler, however, had a lot more to say.

'Paris,' he told me emphatically, 'is the most beautiful city in the world. How ugly Berlin is in comparison. I know every historic building in Paris down to the last detail, but, unfortunately, only from pictures and plans. You must visit Paris again and take time to view those unique architectural monuments.'

Then I asked him, 'How do you feel about the French people?'

'The people have my sympathies,' he replied. 'I met several French soldiers during the war and respected them. But the French nation, which has produced one of the world's greatest cultures, has become decadent. I am afraid its best days are over, and it will gradually perish.' Reaching out for his mineral water, he continued: 'Only a great political leader can save France from ruin. I would be glad to have a sound, strong neighbour at my side.'

After talking more about French history, Hitler asked me to come for a walk. I could understand why he liked retreating here. The wonderful forests and the panorama of Lake König were breathtakingly beautiful.

At one spot Hitler halted, pointed, and said, 'Look, that's Austria over there. Every day that I come up here, I gaze across and beg the Almighty to allow me to live until the day when Austria and Germany will be united in a single great German Reich. That is the only reason I bought this house, because from here I can look at Germany *and* Austria.' He gazed westward for some time, apparently forgetting that I was standing next to him.

How odd, I thought, that for all his interest in my work, he has never asked me a personal question. He has never inquired about my family or my friends, never asked what I like to read, what something means to me, or what are my dislikes. Hitler always spoke only about his own ideas, and as a result remained essentially alien to me, despite the admiration and gratitude that I still felt for him at that time.

As we strolled on, he abruptly began to talk about religion. Although after my visit I made notes on our conversation, I can only summarize his remarks. He thought that religion was necessary for the populace, since most people could not cope with the burden of life on their own. In his eyes the Catholic Church was a lot more successful than the Protestant, which he considered too sober. The Catholic emphasis on ritual and ceremony, the use

As Junta in *The Blue Light*, 1931/2

This film was pivotal in my life, not so much because it was my first successful effort as a producer and director (it won the silver medal at the 1932 Venice Biennale and ran continuously for fourteen months in Paris and fifteen months at London's Rialto), but because Hitler was so fascinated by this film that he insisted I make a documentary about the Party rally in Nuremberg. The result was *Triumph of the Will*.

A photograph of our location work high up in the Brenta group
of the Dolomites

In *The Blue Light* I had to climb unsecured. Since mountain climbing was a passion of mine, I also did my own stuntwork.

Storms over Mont Blanc, 1930
One of Dr Fanck's most hazardous and perilous mountain films
in which I had to walk across a ladder over a deep crevasse.

SOS Iceberg, 1932/3, a German–American co-production
(Universal). Knud Rasmussen, the uncrowned king of the
Eskimos, accompanied the film crew to Greenland.

Arnold Fanck, head of the expedition
and director of this film

On the tip of an iceberg. Playing the role of the female pilot, I
am searching for my husband who is lost in the Arctic.

One of Udet's flights which often terrified me

Eskimos rescue me after I am thrown into
the sea from a moving iceberg

of incense, for example, was more effective than Protestant austerity. At the same time he deplored the history of the Catholic Church, and denounced its historical crimes, the witch burnings and other atrocities committed in the name of the Cross.

I felt perplexed, for it was impossible to talk to him about the things that were most on my mind, for instance, his anti-Semitism. Whenever I knew I was to see Hitler I resolved beforehand to raise the subject, and I prepared my questions accordingly. But the moment I broached the topic Hitler cut me off, saying he hadn't invited me here to talk about things that were not open to discussion.

'I know you, and I know how obstinate you are,' he said, 'as obstinate as I can be. But there are certain things about which we will never see eye to eye. Believe me,' he said, relenting a little, 'I do not reach my decisions lightly. Before making up my mind I do a lot of soul-searching. I spend days and nights thinking of nothing else. I test the very foundations of my beliefs,' he said, 'I view them with the most critical eyes and consider all the arguments against them. I keep attacking my own convictions until I am certain that black is black and white is white.'

I ventured to object. 'But what if you are mistaken?'

'I believe I am not mistaken. One has to be convinced of the rightness of one's own principles. Otherwise one can achieve nothing of value.'

'Do you believe in God?' I asked, gazing at him directly. Hitler looked at me in surprise, then smiled and said: 'Yes – I believe in a divine power, not in the dogmas of the Church, although I consider them necessary. I believe in God and in a divine destiny.' He turned away then and, folding his hands, gazed into the distance. 'And when the time is ripe, a new Messiah will come – he doesn't have to be a Christian, but he will found a new religion that will change the world.'

'Only if he loves all human beings,' I said, 'and not just the Germans.'

I don't know whether Hitler had taken my point. In any case, he didn't say another word to me and we walked slowly back to the Berghof, where he said goodbye rather distantly, and had me driven back to my hotel in Berchtesgaden.

THE DAY OF GERMAN ART

In Berlin I received an invitation for the gala opening of the House of German Art in Munich. Just about everyone who was anyone was there, including sculptors, painters, and architects, as well as writers, actors, and famous conductors like Furtwängler and Knappertsbusch, and also members of the diplomatic corps – all of them as guests of the German government. I shared a sleeping compartment with Elisabeth Flickenschildt, an actress whom I greatly admired.

On entering the House of German Art, I discovered my friend Bollschweiler, the painter, sitting on the stairway and smiling in sheer delight. When he saw me he charged over and said, his voice choked with emotion, 'Leni, you won't believe this, my paintings are sold out.'

'Why, that's wonderful,' I said, amazed.

'But it's true,' Bollschweiler beamed. 'The Führer and Göring fought over your favourite picture, the horse's head. But Hitler purchased it and Göring paid ten thousand marks for my tiger. Then everyone wanted my paintings, and now they're all gone.'

So it had not been a bad idea to hang Bollschweiler's works in my empty rooms. I embraced my happy friend.

That evening the banquet was followed by dancing. I discovered Luis Trenker in the central hall. Ten years had passed since our falling-out and our UFA film *The Great Leap*. We hadn't met in all that time, but meanwhile he had made several good pictures, *The Rebel* and *The Prodigal Son*. I had wanted to bury the hatchet with him long ago, and had in fact written him a few lines congratulating him on his successes. He walked towards me, beaming, and hugged and kissed me in front of everyone. 'I was damn glad to get your notes,' he said, 'and I've come here only for your sake, all the way from Zermatt – I'm doing a picture there on the Matterhorn.'

I was pleased to see that bygones were bygones, and we danced a few times. Later he told me about the problems he was having with Goebbels in regard to his film *Condottieri*.

'Just imagine,' he said in annoyance, 'they cut out very important scenes.'

'What kind of scenes?'

'Some of the most important ones,' Trenker raged. 'A high point in the film, the shots of Condottieri and his knights kneeling down before the Pope in the Vatican.'

'You could have guessed that Goebbels wouldn't be very enthusiastic about that,' I said, amused.

'But I had submitted the screenplay, and it was approved by the Ministry of Propaganda. They could have told me in advance. Then I wouldn't have had to shoot that scene – I wouldn't have given a damn.' Impulsively he grabbed me about the waist, and we danced a waltz together. I never dreamed then what I would eventually experience with this man.

Living as we were, on the periphery of turbulent times, I remember an episode which achieved later significance. I was on Ludwigstrasse, *en route* to the Feldherrnhalle, when I happened to notice a young man in a phone booth who looked very photogenic. Whenever I saw anyone – young or old, male or female – whom I considered a possibility for the screen, I would write down his or her name and address. When the young man left the booth I asked him who he was and where he lived.

'Why?' he asked, bewildered.

'Excuse me – perhaps you know me, I'm Leni Riefenstahl.'

The young man laughed and said, 'My name is Henri Nannen and I can be reached through the Bruckmann publishing house in Munich.'

I remembered him while post-synchronizing the Olympic film. We had to cast the small part of the German announcer who opens the Games. I asked a member of my staff, Herr Bartsch, to contact this young man and do a test shot against a back projection of the stadium, a short scene with only one line. I couldn't come along as I was too busy in the cutting room.

I didn't see Nannen until fifteen years later, and by then he was editor-in-chief of *Stern*. There are prominent journalists who had the audacity to claim that Henri Nannen must have been a Nazi since he played an important role in my Olympic movie in 1938. I have described this minor episode in order to set the matter straight.

But one more thing about the Day of German Art. It was celebrated in public with as much festivity as there had been during the weeks of the Olympic Games two years earlier in Berlin. Munich artists had decorated the route of the procession with extravagance, but also with taste. A Night of Amazons was celebrated in Nymphenburg; and at the English Garden, all around the Chinese Tower, huge multi-coloured balloons hung in the lofty trees, transforming the scene into a midsummer night's dream of fairyland.

In contrast to this splendour, the art works on display were embarrassing. Visitors thronged round Adolf Ziegler's four naked bodies as *The Four Elements*, round Hitler as a 'knight' on a white charger, and another dozen heroic or allegorical Führer portraits. Where were 'my' German artists – Klee, Marc, Beckmann, Nolde, Käthe Kollwitz – whom I had revered since childhood and admired so often at the Crown Prince Palace?

Because of my huge workload I had been living inside a kind of egg, completely isolated from everyday events, and cut off from the outside world. I saw even my parents and Heinz very seldom, and I never listened to the radio or read any newspapers. As a result I didn't have the faintest idea that the works of 'my' artists were vanishing from museums and galleries, defamed and exhibited as 'degenerate' art and/or auctioned off to foreign buyers.

Not only was I shocked by the sight of the new German art, I was irritated by the speech Hitler gave on art in front of thousands of spectators. I had no opinion on politics, but I had definite views on anything involving art. I was horrified therefore when Hitler announced his determination to wage a 'relentless war of purification' against 'so-called modern art'. At the time I still believed that a politician doesn't necessarily have to understand art; but the passion with which Hitler asserted the exclusive truth of his views, and the ardour with which he tried to influence his audience made me much more aware of the danger of his powers.

This was the first time that I realized how greatly Hitler could be mistaken. From that day on I listened to his speeches more and more critically, though I couldn't distance myself completely from him until a few short months before the end of the war. Shortly before the macabre fall of Germany, Hitler was presenting Iron Crosses to children in front of the battered Reich Chancellery and calling them 'brave soldiers'. By then I hated him.

GUGLIA DI BRENTA

By August 1937 I had finished editing *Festival of Nations*, the first part of *Olympia*. Its running time was two hours. Now I allowed myself a holiday in the mountains. I was hoping to carry out my dream of climbing the Guglia, that sharp needle in the Brenta group, which played a leading role in Fanck's movie *Mountain of Destiny* and changed my life forever.

Since that time I had often dreamed of the Guglia. It drew me irresistibly and now at last I wanted to try climbing it with Hans Steger, one of the best mountain guides in the Dolomites, who was willing to take me up.

But when I arrived in Bolzano a disappointment was waiting for me. At the Hotel Greif, where we were supposed to meet, I found a telegram: Steger apologized for not being able to come; Leopold, king of the Belgians, with whom he had been climbing for years, would be arriving earlier than expected. Steger suggested that I climb with his friend Anderl Heckmair, an outstanding mountain guide.

I never regretted meeting Heckmair, the first person to climb the northern wall of the Eiger. With him I experienced my most adventurous climbing tours, and I liked him from the moment we shook hands. He was somewhat coarse-grained, but I instantly sensed his basic sincerity. He had a reputation as one of the most daredevil climbers, yet during our first tours together, he turned out to be extremely cautious and prudent. He climbed with the self-assurance of a cat, so I lost all my fears. The third man on our rope was Xaver Kraisy, one of my skiing comrades.

The weather was marvellous, and I enjoyed climbing so much that I completely forgot the Olympics film, the cutting room, and everything else involved. I had no problems climbing even the steepest parts. I never fell once, for my ballet and dance background was an ideal training for climbing; it had given me strong toes and a sense of balance. Now Anderl no longer had any doubts that I could take on the Guglia as well, even the most difficult route, the Preuss Road across the eastern wall.

At last the exciting moment came when we stood in front of the Guglia – a bit late, unfortunately, for the hut keeper had neglected to wake us. We had wanted to tackle the wall very early in order to get to the top by daylight. But now the sun was already at its zenith and we really should have given up the idea, but it was our last day.

The first parts went smoothly, with no problems. The hardest part was the upper third of the wall, which had already claimed several lives. Even Preuss, for whom this route had been named, turned back at this point during one of his first climbing attempts. When we stood at the top we could scarcely contain ourselves, so delighted were we to have made it, for twilight was setting in, and flashes of lightning heralded a storm. We had to descend as soon as possible, but because of the darkness and the difficulties in finding places to rope down, the descent was far too slow.

The lightning came closer, and the storm reached us. The night was now pitch-black, the thunder rolled and as we lowered ourselves the weather became worse. Anderl looked in vain for a place to rope down further. Finding none, he descended a yard or two, but felt it would be too dangerous to traverse to the other side of the tower with us. We were to wait for him here. The place where we stood was precarious and far too small for us to hold out for long. Meanwhile the storm was raging like a hurricane.

We waited and waited, but Anderl didn't return, and when we got no answers to our shouts, we feared the worst. Now our situation deteriorated further because it began to hail. The hailstones were so large and sharp that they ripped our clothes and injured us. My solid windbreaker, which had survived several blizzards on Pitz Palü was now pierced by the hail within minutes. We couldn't stand there any longer, we had to try to descend without Heckmair, even though we could move downward only during flashes of lightning. We had been descending for a while when, without warning, Anderl stood before us. Illuminated by lightning, he looked like a glowing ghost and I thought it was a hallucination. But then we heaved sighs of relief and continued climbing down under his guidance.

215

The hail stopped and the storm abated. Meanwhile our eyes had grown used to the darkness, and we were slowly groping our way down. Xaver was far below me, unrecognizable in the darkness, and Heckmair was overhead; he came last during the descent in order to protect us.

Then I heard a noise and was horrified to see a dark body plunging towards me. In that fraction of a second we all fell. Above me, perhaps only six feet away, Anderl was hanging on a rock which had broken his fall by an inconceivable stroke of luck. If it hadn't been for that rock, the three of us would have plummeted into the abyss, for we were all tied together and neither Xaver nor I had managed to secure ourselves in the darkness. Only later did we find out what had caused the fall. A knot had loosened when Anderl had lowered himself, precipitating his fall.

Our adventure was not yet over. When finally there was solid ground under our feet and we were happy to have escaped the rockfall, new difficulties awaited us. The very long, narrow and precipitous ice gully, which was covered with old snow during the day, had frozen rock-hard during the night. A step had to be smashed into it for every pace we took, and so we descended in endless zigzags. If anyone of us had slipped he would have been shattered on the huge boulders down below, but, as if protected by good spirits, we finally reached the bottom of the gully. Our hands bled, but we barely felt the pain.

Although we couldn't be very far from our shelter hut, we were unable to find the way in the darkness, and we crawled about on all fours amid boulders and detritus. Then, when it started to rain, we sought shelter under a boulder and fell asleep, exhausted. When morning came, we realized that we had bivouacked scarcely a hundred yards from the hut. A radiant day had begun, and in the sunshine nothing looked so bad any more. For a week my bruised fingers couldn't hold a comb, but I now loved climbing more than ever, and I don't think I have ever felt as healthy and vital as I did after that tour.

BACK IN THE EDITING ROOM

I returned to Berlin having been given a new lease on life. All my mental stress had vanished and I could sleep again at night. I found the work in the editing room so easy that I finished cutting the second part of the film within two months – after spending more than five months on the first part. I could now proceed to the dubbing ahead of schedule, and Herbert Windt could start timing his music. When he played his themes for me I was very impressed by the wonderful rapport he had achieved with the Olympic atmosphere, the way he made everything come alive. I was overjoyed and threw my arms round him. I began to believe in my film for the first time. And I was not the only one. Our cutting room received a surprise visit from Dr Goebbels, accompanied by Magda and by Frau von Arent, the wife of the famous set-designer. Luckily I could screen a few clips, albeit without sound. Goebbels was obviously stunned, and I hadn't expected this. He was enthusiastic, and this time his enthusiasm seemed genuine.

Next came the work with the announcers. Two of the best-known sports announcers of German radio were hired, Paul Laven and Rolf Wernicke. Technology has changed greatly since then. The work, child's play today with a magnetic tape, was an arduous process. Our old shots were only just being developed and we were working purely with sound-on-film. Only the expert knows what this means. In order to listen to the sound, we first had to develop the light-on-sound negative and then turn that into a sound print – a process requiring several hours, often a whole day. Furthermore, defective takes couldn't be omitted, whilst today, with magnetic sound, a correction means only a matter of seconds.

Diction has also changed greatly. In those days athletic events were described very bombastically. Today the commentary is more matter-of-fact and by comparison the diction of those days sounds very odd. The most difficult part was creating a sound background without magnetic tapes. Aside from Hitler's brief address, everything was post-synchronized. The breathing of the horses, the padding of the athletes' feet, the banging of the hammer and the discus, the sounds of rowing and sailing, could be recorded only on light-on-sound negative, as were the noises made by the crowd, which gave the film its living atmosphere. The quality of the original sound recordings that we had made in the stadium wasn't good enough; they were adequate only for newsreels. Our spectator background noises had to be finely tuned, from pianissimo to fortissimo.

This work took six weeks. Four sound editors did their best to attain the finest quality, and all the sound tapes were cut by Christmas. The music was to be recorded in early January and then the sound was to be mixed. My staff was able to take a vacation during the Christmas holidays before undergoing this final stress.

NEW YEAR'S EVE IN ST MORITZ

I spent Christmas and New year's 1938 at Fritz von Opel's beautiful chalet in

St Moritz. I had met him several years earlier through Udet and he had once invited me on a balloon flight, my first, and, unfortunately, also my last. We had taken off in Bitterfeld at dusk for a trip in the moonlight. I went on many plane flights with Udet, and I recall unforgettable ones in Greenland and across lofty mountain peaks; but this balloon trip surpassed all those flights. We drifted through utter silence. Often we hovered only a few yards over the forests and now and then we heard the barking of dogs. But otherwise the night was filled with a ghostly hush. Sometimes, when the bottom of our gondola grazed the treetops, Fritz von Opel tossed down a sack of sand. When I think back to that balloon experience I can compare it only with deep-sea diving; both make you feel utterly remote from reality.

On New Year's Eve I was surprised by the arrival of Josef von Sternberg. We had corresponded, but not seen one another in years. The last time had been a few weeks before Hitler's takeover. Sternberg showered me with questions, especially about Hitler.

'What's he really like?'

How often I had been asked that, and how hard it was to answer. 'I don't know,' I said. 'Hitler strikes me as unfathomable and full of contradictions. The unusual thing about him is his hypnotic power, which can make even an opponent change his mind.'

'In America people think you're his mistress. Is that true?'

I had to laugh. 'What nonsense,' I said. 'If a man admires you it doesn't necessarily mean you're having an affair with him. I'm not his type, and he's not my type.'

'I didn't believe it,' said Sternberg. 'The press writes a lot. But the film you made for him, *Triumph of the Will*, is first class.'

'Where did you see it?' I asked in surprise.

'In New York, at the Museum of Modern Art.'

'Do you really like it?'

'My dear girl,' said Sternberg, 'it will make film history – it's revolutionary. When we met,' he went on, 'I wanted to turn you into a great actress, mould you as I had Marlene. But now, instead, you've become a great screen director.'

'I would much rather be an actress and most of all under your direction. *Olympia* is going to be my last documentary. It was an obligation which I took on only half-heartedly. Once all this is finally behind me,' I said, 'I'll be free to carry out my dream. I want to play Penthesilea and never make another documentary.'

Then I told Sternberg about the conspiracies I had been exposed to and the technical difficulties we had with the Olympics film, the problems of shaping it, and how depressed and dejected I often felt.

'Fame doesn't bring happiness,' I said.

'That's true for me, too,' Sternberg replied. 'But let's have a great New Year's Eve.'

We celebrated it at the Palace Hotel with Margot and Fritz von Opel and their guests, including Prince von Starhemberg with his girlfriend, the beautiful Hollywood actress, Nora Gregory. When a photographer came over and snapped pictures of us, Sternberg asked whether I wouldn't have problems if these photos were published.

'Why?' I asked.

Sternberg motioned at our circle. 'You're partying with those who are not friends of Hitler. Won't that be held against you?'

The thought had never struck me. I felt completely free and saw nothing wrong with having friends who were opponents of National Socialism, especially Prince von Starhemberg.

Sternberg told me he had discovered a young actress in Vienna, named Hilde Krahl, and he prophesized a great career for her. She was to play the lead in his next movie, *Germinal*, based on the novel by Zola.

'And when will you and I be working together?' I asked jokingly.

'As soon as we have no other obligations,' said Sternberg, 'and if there's no war.'

'War?' I asked in alarm. 'Why should there be war?'

That was the last time I saw Sternberg before the outbreak of the war. I didn't meet him again until twenty years later, at the Venice Biennale.

IN THE SOUND STUDIO

The recordings of the Berlin Symphony took place in early January 1938. This was a great joy for us. Now came the final task – to mix the tapes into a single soundtrack. I had no idea what problems awaited us. In Berlin-Johannistal, UFA had built a modern sound studio, a dark, windowless room with a sound mixer in which seven tapes could run simultaneously with the film. For that era this was a sensational apparatus, but it was not technically advanced enough for our needs. Usually only two or three tapes were mixed, so that the static – the crackling noises made in photographic sound-film recordings – was endurable. But it was different with seven or more tapes. Interference was abolished by magnetic tapes, which we didn't have in those days. The first time we inserted seven tapes, all we heard was a roaring like a waterfall. My sound engineer, Sigi Schulz, was desperate. He declared that there was no way of mixing the tapes into a usable soundtrack. The sound quality was so lamentable that he refused to go on with the job. The technicians tried to work out how to solve the problem, and finally one of them had a brilliant idea. He had screens made that filtered all the static without reducing the volume of the sound. This invention allowed us to make the experiments we had in mind and, after managing to hire Hermann Storr, the best German sound editor, we hoped we could add the soundtrack that I envisaged.

Even today the memory of that drudgery is a nightmare. My sound engineer was often utterly bewildered when I told him what I wanted. He would say: 'It won't work.' But each time we kept testing until it finally did work. Frequently we saw that the speaking interfered with the music; then the tapes had to be altered, shortened or lengthened. We tested whether the sounds or the commentary and music should dominate. The sound structure was essential to the film, since this was not a feature, but a documentary; image and sound had to replace dialogue.

Sometimes, when the results of several days' work were unusable because the sound negative was developed wrongly, or the mixings were poor, and everything had to be repeated, I was on the verge of despair. We had only one desire; to get done.

During those months we exprienced moments of crisis when we believed we couldn't go on. I spent two months at the sound mixer with the sound engineer and the splicing girls in a windowless room, and did nothing but listen to sounds from dawn till night, for up to fourteen hours a day. I often doubted whether after that I still retained any sense of judgement or critical aptitude.

I might not have been able to get through that period if I hadn't made a good friend in our sound engineer, Hermann Storr. He was not only a highly sensitive expert in his field, satisfied only with the highest quality, but he also understood my ideas and my personality. Our friendship deepened and then, when the sound mixing was successfully completed, we decided to stay together.

THE DELAYED PREMIÈRE

Tobis informed me that the première of *Olympia* was scheduled for mid-March. I could breathe freely. The great moment had finally come. Would the film be a success? I had no way of knowing.

Since the big night was only two weeks away, I rented a small mountain cottage in Kitzbühel in order to relax there with my staff, but no sooner had we arrived than we received some bad news. Tobis notified me that the Ministry of Propaganda was delaying the première indefinitely. This was devastating. In order to finish earlier we had been labouring overtime for a year and a half, working through the night. Some of my people had fallen ill – unable to endure the pace. And now it was to be all for nothing? I was already derided throughout the industry because no one could understand why I had been working on this film for such a long time. Jokes were even made about me in the cabarets on Kurfürstendamm, and the most malicious were my so-called 'friends' at the Ministry of Propaganda. From the bottoms of their hearts they wished me the worst failure of my life.

We soon learned why the première had been cancelled. German troops had marched into Austria on 12 March, and Hitler, in Vienna, announced Austria's annexation by the German Reich. The Austrians on my staff were out of their minds with joy.

While I realized that these events had had an effect on the première date, I wouldn't hear of delaying it until the following autumn. No distributor would begin to give a good film its first showing in the summer. My despair was so great that I had the crazy idea of meeting Hitler at some point during his journey through Austria and asking him to let the film come out that spring. Recklessly I took the train to Innsbruck, where Hitler was expected, and I stayed with friends, for all the hotel rooms were booked. My experiences in Tyrol may sound incredible today, even if I greatly tone down the account. The Innsbruckers were delirious. They stretched their arms and hands towards Hitler in almost religious ecstasy. Elderly men and women were crying. The universal jubilation was simply beyond belief.

Could I trouble Hitler with my personal problems in this situation? Uncertain what to do, I stood in front of the barrier outside the Tiroler Hof for a long time. It was already evening, but masses of people were still gathered in the square, shouting for Hitler, who appeared at the window now and then.

It was cold, and I began to shiver. At a propitious moment I succeeded in getting through the blockade and into the lobby of the hotel, which was mobbed, and somehow managing to find a seat. The craziness of my plan became more and more obvious to me, and I already regretted that I had even begun to make this foolish attempt. I was discovered by Schaub who, gaping, asked me, 'What are you doing here?' Without waiting for my answer, he said rather nastily, 'No one can speak to the Führer today.' And in a trice he was gone. This confirmed the folly of my undertaking. Yet after a while Schaub came back: this time he was somewhat friendlier. 'Please come along,' he said.

Now at last I was afraid. What should I tell Hitler? I had lost my nerve. I couldn't tell him about my private dilemmas at this momentous time.

When Schaub knocked at the door, a group leader whom I didn't know emerged from the room. Hitler was euphoric. Coming towards me and holding out both his hands, he said, 'How delighted I am that you can witness these great moments here – you can't imagine my feelings.' Then he looked at me as if he had read my thoughts. 'You have something on your mind. Tell me what it is!'

'My Führer,' I stammered, 'it is embarrassing to talk to you now about my small problems.'

'Well, you've caught me at a good time. What is troubling you?' he asked so cheerfully that I took a deep breath and said: 'My problem is the date of the première of *Olympia*. It was set for mid-March and then delayed indefinitely. People are laughing at me, they are already making fun of the endless work I've put into this film. What will become of it if it doesn't get shown until autumn . . .?'

Hitler looked thoughtful. 'This is bad luck for your film, of course, but if the première took place at this time it would be overshadowed by political events. I feel that your film should have a good première date. But there won't be one before the autumn.'

I looked at the floor and thought about the possibility of the next month – not an ideal date, but a lot better than one in the autumn. Suddenly I thought of Hitler's birthday and I said impulsively, 'Wouldn't 20 April be a good date?'

Hitler, quite taken aback, exclaimed. 'A good date, yes, a very good date – but on that date I'll have too many obligations, I'll have to review the parade, receive well-wishers. I wouldn't have time to attend the première, and that would be a pity.'

'I didn't think of that,' I said.

'You know,' said Hitler, 'we'll schedule the première for 20 April after all, and I will come, I promise you.'

Incredulous, I stood there, unable to utter a single word. Suddenly there was a knock at the door. Schaub announced Herr von Ribbentrop.

'Ask him to wait a moment,' said Hitler, 'I have to talk first to Dr Goebbels, for I have just promised Fräulein Riefenstahl that the première of her Olympics film will take place on my birthday, and that I will be there.' Schaub, startled, voiced some obligations and ran through the birthday programme. He pointed out that the film première would turn the whole schedule upside down, but Hitler waved him off, saying only, 'Leave it to me, the doctor will organize it all properly.'

I sat in the lobby again, as if in a trance. There was no one whom I could tell about my good fortune. Had it all been a dream? I don't know how long I sat there like that, but then Schaub came up and jerked me out of my reveries. 'The Führer told me to tell you,' he said, grumpy as ever, 'that following the première, a reception will be held in the hall of the Ministry of Propaganda. You and your entire staff are invited.'

WORLD PREMIÈRE OF *OLYMPIA*

At last 20 April 1938 arrived. I had returned from Davos only the previous day after tanning myself in the spring sun in order to look good on this gala day, but I had overdone it. My back was so badly burned that the skin was peeling, and I had to wear a small jacket over my evening gown to conceal it.

Together with my parents and my brother, I drove to the UFA Palace at the Zoo. The theatre was attractively decorated, and Speer, the architect, had designed a new façade: giant Olympic flags with gold ribbons covered the entire front of the building, while the area around the theatre was blocked off. Crowds of people were waiting for Hitler. Everyone who was anyone was invited to the première: the Reich ministers, the diplomatic corps, leaders in industry and sports, as well as artists like Furtwängler, Gustav Gründgens, Emil Jannings, and many others, but above all, the German Olympic athletes.

The excitement of the public infected me. How would the film be received? So far no one had seen it apart from my staff. No member of the IOC, not even the secretary general of the Olympic Games, Professor Dr Diems, who had, after all, initiated the project. I would have found it unendurable to show an inferior work. I am, alas, an incorrigible perfectionist.

Would the viewers love the film, or would they be bored? I was worried about the long running-time, since the two parts together added up to nearly four hours. I was against showing both in the same evening, but the distributor had insisted. A half-hour intermission was scheduled, however, after part one. My thoughts were interrupted by shouts of 'Heil!' from the throng. Hitler had arrived and, together with several other men, including Dr Goebbels and Ribbentrop, he sat down in the centre box. As the lights slowly faded, the 'Heil!' shouts died down, and the orchestra began. The overture was Herbert Windt's score for the marathon, which he conducted himself. When the curtain parted, and OLYMPIA appeared in huge letters on the screen, I began to shake.

The round of images began, the temples, sculptures, statues, and the torch race, the lighting of the Olympic flame at the stadium in Berlin. I shut my eyes and experienced again the labour it had cost to put all this into shape, and I couldn't hold back the tears. I began to cry, heedless of my make-up and mascara.

There was already some clapping during the prologue, and it was repeated over and over. Now I knew the film would be a success, but in my frame of mind this changed nothing. I felt utterly burned out.

After the end of Part One, the applause swelled into a crescendo, and Hitler was the first to congratulate me: 'You've created a masterpiece, and the world will be grateful to you.' The Greek ambassador, on behalf of his government, presented me with a diploma and an olive branch from Olympia.

It was past midnight when the second part ended. The applause had grown ever louder. Again I was taken to Hitler, who didn't seem at all tired, and who congratulated me again. Now Dr Goebbels appeared: he took me aside, saying: 'I have to tell you on behalf of the Führer that you may ask for something for your great achievement.'

Unprepared, and without thinking, I asked for something foolish. 'I would be grateful to you, Herr Minister,' I said spontaneously, 'if you could take Herr Jäger, the former editor-in-chief of *Film-Kurier*, back into the Reich Film Chamber and allow him to accompany me as my press chief on my planned trip to America.'

Goebbels was clearly irritated. 'I cannot do that, for I would then also have to readmit others, who were expelled for the same reason.'

I pleaded: 'Herr Jäger is an unusually gifted journalist. Please grant my wish.'

'You will be letting yourself in for a lot of trouble with Herr Jäger. Don't let him fool you. I warn you.'

'I will accept full responsibility for Herr Jäger,' I said, totally convinced. 'He is a man of absolute integrity.'

If only I had an inkling of what I had done to myself by expressing that wish!

The reception at the Ministry of Propaganda was the conclusion of that festive première. It was already very late when Hitler shook hands with each and every member of my staff, praising them all for their work. When he asked me about my future plans I said that at the request of Tobis I would be touring Europe with *Olympia*, and after that I would fulfil my great wish to get to know America and travel through the States for a few months. But then I hoped to make my *Penthesilea*.

'You have taken on a large programme,' said Hitler in a friendly tone. 'I wish you luck.'

THE GERMAN FILM PRIZE OF 1938

I didn't have much time to relax after the world première of *Olympia*. My distributor absolutely insisted on my presence at the opening nights in various European capitals. During the few days I had left I went to the Schulze-Bibernell Salon for my tour wardrobe.

The next première took place in Vienna. I took along some members of my staff, and we were greeted with unparalleled jubilation. Never in my life, before or after that, have I received so many and such wonderful bouquets of flowers. But we were able to stay for only two days before going on to Graz, where the enthusiasm was even more wild – if that was possible. Hundreds of young girls in Styrian costumes formed a guard of honour from our hotel to the cinema.

The very next morning, at the crack of dawn, I flew from Graz to Berlin. I was scheduled to attend the festive session of the Reich Culture Chamber at the German Opera House, where the national film and book prizes were awarded every year. It was fairly obvious but not certain that *Olympia* would win the prize. I was accompanied to the ceremonies by Hubert Stowitts, an American painter, with whom I had been friendly for years. Although he preferred having young men rather than girls around him, we got along marvellously. We had met during an exhibition of his works put on by the American embassy in Berlin during the Olympic Games. He painted chiefly American athletes who participated in the games: realistic, yet over-lifesize paintings. We shared artistic interests, for Hubert was not only a painter but also a dancer and choreographer. He had been a partner of the famous Anna Pavlova for five years and had also painted Russian dancers and ballerinas. During this period in Berlin he arranged Lillian Harvey's dance scenes in her UFA film. He was the only person outside my staff who was allowed to visit me in my cutting rooms.

As expected, I received the German Film Prize of 1938 for *Olympia*, but I was surprised that no one greeted me or congratulated me at the German Opera House. What a contrast to the Berlin première and the welcome I had received in Vienna and Graz. Nor was any seat reserved for me. So I sat with Hubert, unnoticed, somewhere in the dress circle. The cool atmosphere was oppressive – it could only have been because here Goebbels was the boss and this function was organized by my 'friends' at the Ministry of Propaganda.

However, Goebbels didn't hint at anything in his speech. He was much too clever. He lauded my work and I even think he really meant it. The film and I as a person were quite separate for him. I recalled the many embarrassing things I had experienced with this man, so I was not surprised at his play-acting now. He was a master of disguise.

We left the German Opera House unnoticed and drove to my villa in Dahlem, where many congratulatory wires had already arrived. I had not yet had time to settle into my new house. The fact that it was at all a comfortable place to live was due to Stowitts, who, during my sessions in the cutting room, had had furniture, paintings and carpets brought to the house, where I could make a selection after my daily editing quota. Now I hoped I would at last be able to enjoy my home and my garden. But it was only for a brief time, alas. Within a few weeks I would have to go on tour with *Olympia*.

UNEXPECTED VISIT

In June, shortly before my première tour, I received an unexpected visit from Hitler. When the Reich Chancellery called me up to ask whether I could receive the Führer, I was surprised, and I wondered what was bringing him to me. Helene, my cook, and Mariechen, my maid, were very excited, and fought over who should serve the tea. At 4 p.m. Helene told me that a black Mercedes had driven up. In my vestibule I greeted Hitler and his companion, Albert Bormann, a brother of Martin Bormann. Both men were in plain clothes, Hitler wearing a navy-blue suit.

Before entering my living room Hitler asked Bormann to wait for him elsewhere, so my maid took him to the rustic bar in the basement. Meanwhile Hitler and I went into the living room, which was also my screening room. As a precautionary measure I had asked Herr Kubisch, my projectionist, to come in case I had to show a film.

Hitler seemed to be in a wonderful mood. He admired the house, the garden, and above all the interior decoration, which surprised me since it was such a different style from his own rooms. Somewhat awkwardly, I asked, 'Wouldn't you care for coffee or tea?'

'As an exception, tea, but weak, if you please, I have to be considerate of my stomach.'

Out in the gazebo, where Helene had set up a table and decorated it with flowers, she now proudly served her home-made apple strudel.

'It seldom happens,' said Hitler, 'that I can take time to be a private person for a few hours. I know that you too are a hard worker and have almost no private life.'

Embarrassed, I stirred my tea in silence.

'I believe,' he went on, 'that you work too much, just like me. You should take better care of yourself.'

That was my cue. Now I was able to talk about my work, about disappointments and sleepless nights, as well as the feeling of happiness when a work is successful.

'People like you,' said Hitler, 'must often be lonely. You probably don't have an easy time of it.'

Again his words surprised me, for Hitler had never spoken to me in such a personal way, and since I didn't know how to reply, I was irritated. Hitler praised Helene's apple strudel and then said, 'For a woman you are unusually active and dynamic. That seems to be a challenge to certain men, and you must make enemies. Many people, and not just men, will also resent your triumphs. You probably know that it was difficult even for me to facilitate your work.'

I thought of Goebbels: perhaps today I could speak to Hitler about him, but a sudden wind interrupted our conversation, forcing us to go back indoors. Hitler sat down on a sofa by the fireplace and leafed through several books of pictures that lay on a small table. Then, abruptly, he said: 'You know that I admire you greatly and enjoy your company, but unfortunately my obligations do not permit me to indulge in seeing you more often.'

His compliments simply added to my confusion.

'I don't know another woman,' he went on, 'who works as singlemindedly as you do and is so obsessed with her mission. I am just as devoted to my mission.'

'What about your private life?' I asked.

'When I made up my mind to be a politician I renounced my private life.'

'Was that difficult for you?'

'Very difficult,' he replied, 'especially when I meet beautiful women whom I like having around me.' After a pause, he continued: 'But I am not the sort to enjoy brief flings. When my feelings are involved they are deep and passionate; how could I assume responsibility for that, given my duties to Germany? How greatly I would be bound to disappoint any woman, no matter how much I loved her.'

It surprised me that Hitler was once again speaking of his personal feelings. After a brief silence, his expression changed and he said with bizarre grandiloquence. 'It is my intention to create a strong and independent Germany – a bulwark against Communism – and this is possible only in my lifetime. After me, no one will come who could do this.'

I ventured to ask, 'What makes you so convinced of this?'

'It is my calling, which I sense daily, an inner compulsion that forces me to act in this way and not otherwise . . .'

With these words Hitler seemed to become impersonal, just as I had seen him speaking at his rallies; then, noticing that I wasn't very interested in politics, he was quite suddenly an utterly charming private person again.

Meanwhile Helene brought us some salad, as well as toast and fruit. I drank a glass of wine, but Hitler was content with his water; then I had my maid light a fire, and when we were alone again, I asked Hitler, 'Have you always been a vegetarian?' He said no to this, and told me falteringly that he had been unable to eat after a deep shock he had suffered. I regretted my question, but Hitler went on: 'I loved Geli, my niece, so much that I thought I couldn't live without her. When I lost Geli I couldn't eat for days on end. Since then my stomach has resisted any kind of meat.'

Perplexed that Hitler told me all this so frankly, I hazarded another question. 'Was Geli your first love?' And he began to tell me about women he had loved before Geli.

'My romances,' he said, 'were mostly unhappy. The women were either married or wanted to get married.' He did not mention Eva Braun. He was bothered, he told me, when women threatened suicide in order to tie him down, and he repeated that he could have married no one but Geli.

I asked him what he thought of Unity Mitford, the pretty Englishwoman who, as the whole world knew, was so in love with him. His reply surprised me. 'She's a very attractive girl, but I could never have an intimate relationship with a foreigner, no matter how beautiful she might be.' I thought he was joking; but Hitler assured me. 'My feelings are so bound up with my patriotism that I could only love a German girl.' Amused, he said: 'I can see that you don't understand. Incidentally,' he went on, 'I would be completely unsuitable for marriage, for I could not be faithful. I understand great men who have mistresses.' The tone of this was lightly ironic.

Our strange conversation was interrupted when my maid knocked. She wanted to know whether my projectionist would be needed, and although it was already quite late, Hitler wanted to see a film. Looking through my list of titles, he picked *The Big Jump*, a farce directed by Fanck. In this silent film I play an Italian goatherd, Trenker's 'goat', who clambers barefoot around the Dolomites. Schneeberger plays a ski acrobat who flies over the mountains in a blown-up rubber suit. It was almost eleven when the film ended, and Hitler, much amused by it, said goodnight and left with Bormann, who had been waiting patiently in my basement bar.

I couldn't fall asleep for a long time. The tensions of the day were too much. Why had Hitler visited me, why had he stayed on for such a long time? And why had he given me such an intimate glimpse of his private life?

That evening I felt that Hitler desired me as a woman.

TOUR OF EUROPE

The next major première was in Paris. A few days before my departure there was some agitation at Tobis, and my trip was almost called off. I was told that the French distributor, who had bought the rights for France, was under pressure not to show the film in his country, or at least to omit certain scenes. For example, I was asked to snip out the shots of Hitler and several German medal winners. However, just as I had defied Goebbels by refusing to omit the sequences showing Jesse Owens and other black athletes, so now I refused to delete the shots of Hitler. The situation worsened and Tobis advised me not to go to Paris; but I was convinced that by meeting personally with the French distributor, I could overcome his anxieties. I had no inkling as yet of the incipient boycott of the Hitler regime. Instead, I remembered the three gold medals I had won at the World's Fair and the passionate enthusiasm the French had shown just a year before for *Triumph of the Will*.

In Paris I was cordially received by the managers of the distribution company. They had reserved an elegant apartment for me at the George V and took me out on the evening of my arrival in order to show me Paris by night. I liked this world of glitz and glamour, as I passed from one delight to another. The beautiful women in the musical reviews were an aesthetic joy: never had I seen such expensive decor and such fantastic costumes, and above all, so much charm and imaginative staging.

My French hosts planned on getting me to change my mind by exposing me to this atmosphere and by giving me lots of champagne. I was in an excellent mood when I listened to their suggestions and arguments, but I remained adamant, and these good gentlemen were desperate. During the evening before the première, when they still couldn't win me over, they began to bluster and threatened not to show the film in France; but I didn't believe them, for they had already paid such huge advances to Tobis. I wasn't willing to go back on my resolution to show the film everywhere only in its unabridged version. If Goebbels hadn't succeeded in getting me to change my mind, then neither could the French.

On the day of the première the film was widely advertised for the Normandie on the Champs Elysées but, unlike in Berlin, they were going to show only one part at a time; the second would follow in a few weeks. With a few exceptions it was handled the same way in all cinemas, including those in other countries.

At 12 noon I was to have a final meeting at the distributor's office where I was convinced they would make all sorts of last-ditch efforts to browbeat me into giving in. When the two managers begged me one last time, I declared that I'd be willing to make a single minor compromise. I agreed to remove two sequences. In one sequence Hitler and Italy's Crown Prince Umberto greet the Italian team with the Fascist salute at the opening celebration of the Games. In the other sequence a German tribute to winners involves some swastika flags.

Now it was certain that the Olympics film, which the French titled *Les Dieux du Stade*, the Gods of the Stadium, would have its French première that day – albeit only at a test screening in the afternoon and without the presence of leading French officials. Since they feared protests, I was advised not to attend. My curiosity was stronger than my fear, however, and, before the screening, I walked up and down the Champs Elysées, wearing sunglasses in order to remain incognito. I wanted to witness whatever happened with my own eyes. The theatre showing was sold out, and so I could sneak in only later to avoid being noticed. However, when the usherette asked to see my ticket I had to identify myself. She looked at me in surprise and then brought me a stool.

The scene of the final torchbearer sprinting into the Berlin Stadium with the Olympic fire was spontaneously applauded. From then on the viewers kept clapping; even to my amazement, during shots of Hitler. Where were the protests they had feared? Relieved, I stayed on until the end. While the audience applauded enthuiastically, I tried to leave the cinema unrecognized, but I was identified and enclosed by the throng within a few seconds. Delighted at this turn of events, I answered many questions in my almost forgotten school French and signed autographs.

After that unexpected success the French distributors put on a dazzling evening showing to which all the important people in Paris were invited. It was quite simply a triumph, just as the Party rally film had been at the Paris World's Fair one year earlier. I was hugged, kissed and besieged.

Contrary to the distributor's anxieties, the Parisian newspapers outdid themselves in praise. I would like to quote a few lines, written fifty years ago. Reviews today are seldom this exuberant.

The gods of the Stadium have given the earth their second promise – eternity. *Le Journal*
Olympia is more and better than a film or even a spectacle. It is a glowing poem of images, light and life; it is ageless and almost without nationality. *L'Ordre*
. . . the Olympic flame rising into an atmosphere that has never been more favourable for peace on earth. *Le Figaro*
The film *The Gods of the Stadium* is so grand, so poetic that those of us who are the hardest to stir left the screening deeply impressed . . . An influential film whose nobility, if I may use this word, will make better people of those who see it. *Liberté*

After that triumph I was supposed to attend the première in Brussels, and here too I had to face some distrust. Tobis was notified by the German embassy that the première could be allowed only after the film was viewed by a representative of the Belgian royal house. I anxiously waited for the verdict, which was favourable, but nevertheless the German embassy advised me not to attend the première. Again it was said that protests were expected.

With my self-confidence boosted by the success in Paris, I travelled to Brussels where the organizers greeted me warmly. Their anxieties had apparently been another false alarm and the latest news was that the Belgian king would probably come to the première. Having no experience with court etiquette, I was given a crash course in proper curtseying.

A few short minutes before the start of the festive screening at the Palais des Beaux Arts, Leopold III arrived, accompanied by Belgium's Prime Minister Spaak and the German ambassador, Baron von Richthofen. I made a deep curtsey before the king and, as we entered the centre box, Leopold was greeted by long cheers. I was allowed to sit at his left, a countess sat at his right and Henri Spaak sat behind us.

After the cheering died down and the lights went out, I was again overcome by doubts; but, as in Paris, I felt that the viewers were responsive. When Hitler appeared for the first time applause broke out, which I had not expected, and it was heard again every time he reappeared. There were neither protests nor disturbances. The unpolitical shape of the film conquered all prejudices. More than two thousand viewers watched *Olympia* enthralled and at the end the audience clapped for several minutes. As in Paris the press outdid itself. One of the most enthusiastic reviews said:

> This document is a triumph of poetry, a triumph of pure and sensual lyricism. It bears the precious stamp of pulsating passion, technical mastery and unshakeable faith – that is the threefold secret of its dreamlike greatness. *Le Vingtième*

The next day Prime Minister Spaak gave a champagne breakfast at which I met Belgian artists, diplomats and well-known journalists. The admiration and affection that I experienced on all sides made me very happy.

Next came a tour of Scandinavia, accompanied by my mother. Our first stop was Copenhagen, where the Danish royal couple attended the festive screening at the Old Fellow Palace. That morning King Christian X had received me in audience. The monarch, who seemed likable and modest, conversed with me for over an hour, mainly about my future film projects. The triumphal progress of my film continued as it had done in Berlin, Vienna, Paris and Brussels. A Danish newspaper wrote:

> It is difficult to write an objective article if one is profoundly moved by the subject matter, and we openly admit that the film on the Olympic Games has deeply moved us. It is a drama of very great stature, a film at the acme of art – a visual poem. *Berlingske Tidende*

Such comments were repeated in the newspapers after the première in Stockholm, Helsinki and Oslo. In Stockholm I was received in audience by King Gustav Adolf V, who was amazingly well informed about the international cinema. *Svenska Dagbladet* wrote something remarkable:

> It would be regrettable if the spirit of international brotherhood represented by *Olympia* could not smash through the barriers of political antipathies.

That came out one year before the outbreak of World War II.

At Lund, Sweden's oldest university, I gave a lecture on my work, and it was enthuiastically received by the students. At the evening banquet in the great hall of the Academic Association, they paid me a special homage by rising to their feet to sing 'Deutschland Über Alles'. A few months later I was awarded the Swedish Polar Prize.

My days in Finland were unforgettable. My mother and I were the guests of the mayor of Helsinki, Von Frenckel, who personally took time to show us the natural beauties of Finland, a marvellous country.

I probably had the most unusual experience of my tour in the Finnish capital. The day of the gala première I went to the light athletic championships, which are something like a national holiday for the Finns. I was in my seat in the stand, watching the events, when, after a short while, one of the sports officials came over and asked me to follow him. He led me to the inside of the stadium, picked up a megaphone and shouted something that I couldn't understand: but I managed to catch my name among the unknown words. The competitions were halted, the spectators in the crowded stadium stood up, and they sang the Finnish national anthem. This tribute was too much for me, I couldn't hold back my tears and, when the anthem was over, I was still standing speechless in the middle of the stadium. Deeply moved, I accepted a huge bouquet of red roses.

The next morning we said goodbye to our Finnish friends and were about to board the plane when, at the very last second, a Finnish athlete, breathless from running, brought me a going-away gift which I still have in my possession today. It was a leather-bound book containing the official Finnish account of the Olympic Games in Berlin. During the brief days of my visit in Helsinki, all the Finnish Olympic participants, including those who lived in the far north of the country, had autographed the book. Not a single name was missing. Even Nurmi, the Finnish racing wonder, had signed.

After these triumphs our last stop in the Scandinavian countries was Oslo where we could scarcely expect the cool Norwegians to show anything like the Finnish enthusiasm. The Tobis people were of the same opinion and again urged me not to go to Oslo. They said that Norway was a Red country, despite its popular king, and the Norwegian government would be anything but friendly to the Germans. I wavered, but then my optimism triumphed. What did 'Red' mean anyway? I'm not prejudiced against people whose political ideas differ from mine.

While editing my film I had tried to shape it in such a way that one and the same version could be shown in all countries. I had not emphasized the many unexpected German victories, or even mentioned that Germany had won the most medals. I wanted to avoid having Germany, as host of the games, preen itself on its victories, thereby belittling nations whose athletes were less favoured by fortune. Instead I chiefly showed the winners of the smaller nations, for instance Lovelock, the only representative of New Zealand.

The German embassy in Oslo was not exactly delighted at my arrival, but I was confident. In the train taking me to the Norwegian capital I had been intercepted by a reporter of *Aftenposten* and, reading this interview today, I must revise my then opinion that the Norwegians are cool. The interview was a prose poem. With this 'overture', I felt I was well armed against any possible attacks.

All my qualms proved groundless. On the very first day, to the utter amazement of the German ambassador, I was invited to an audience by Norway's King Haakon. This was my longest conversation with any of the Scandinavian monarchs. He honoured me by having me join his family at the festive première of *Olympia* at the Colosseum. He sat there in the middle of the German guests of honour – something that no Norwegian would have considered possible.

Here too the film was accompanied by storms of applause, and in Oslo, as in all European capitals, there was clapping when Hitler appeared. Anyone who doesn't believe me can check the newspaper archives. I have often wondered about the significance of such sympathy for Hitler in Europe one year prior to the outbreak of the war.

In Oslo I experienced another high point of Norwegian tolerance. One day before the première the Norwegian prime minister gave a banquet in my honour at the lavishly decorated Rococo Hall. All the cabinet members and government representatives were present – some three hundred people. The situation was unusual in that the magnificent table was surrounded entirely by men in evening dress. My mother and I were the only women.

In their speeches a few government officials advocated cultural cooperation with Germany. Then the prime minister expressed his appreciation of my work, calling *Olympia* a 'messenger of peace', *Aftenposten*, Norway's biggest newspaper, wrote: '*Olympia* is a document that, no matter what may happen, justifies maintaining our faith in a better future for mankind.'

VENICE BIENNALE

After the strenuous première tour I wanted to relax a little before the Venice Biennale. Because of my obligations I had been neglecting my boyfriend Hermann Storr, and I decided to have a seaside holiday with him in the sun. Not far from the Venice Festival House there is a small fishing village on the Lido, and there we hid, far from the swelling tide of publicity.

A few short miles away the jury had begun their work, but we enjoyed the simple life in this tiny village where I knew nobody, and could sunbathe undisturbed amid the sand dunes. I didn't show up at the Festival House until the very last moment, which caused considerable anxiety to the German delegation and to the Italian committee who had no idea as to my whereabouts. *Olympia* was a strong contender for the prize. Its main rivals were Walt Disney's *Snow White*, England's *Pygmalion* and Marcel Carné's *Quai des Brumes*.

There was surprise and annoyance when Marshal Balbo, the Italian governor of Libya, appeared unannounced in his private aeroplane and expressed his desire to sit next to me during the showing of the film. The festival directors turned him down because, according to protocol, the Italian minister, Alfieri, and the German ambassador, von Mackensen, were to sit near me. Balbo, a friend of the Duce's and the aviation minister of Italy, was offended and left the Lido that very same day. I was quite unhappy about this incident as Balbo had made me a wonderful offer in connection with the *Penthesilea* project: he was going to make a thousand white horses with Libyan horsemen available to me for the battle scene. These sequences about the Amazons and the Greeks were to be shot in the Libyan desert; but now this was put in doubt.

At the Lido I witnessed the crowning point of the success of *Olympia*. My film was awarded the Golden Lion, thereby triumphing over both Walt Disney's and Marcel Carné's entries.

At the ceremony I ran into an old friend, Carl Vollmoeller, who had discovered me as a dancer for Max Reinhardt fifteen years earlier. He was staying at the Palazzo Vendramin, where Richard Wagner had spent the final days of his life. Vollmoeller asked us to dinner, and there, in that old and venerable palazzo on the Grand Canal, I spent my last evening in Venice, enjoying the candlelight, the splendid wine, and the company of friends.

PREMIÈRE IN ROME

Before returning to Berlin I had to accept an invitation to Rome where *Olympia* was to be screened in the presence of the Duce. At the Supercinema, the site of the gala première, a surprise awaited me. The German ambassador, Herr von Mackensen, whispered to me that Mussolini couldn't come as he had been unexpectedly called to Munich. This sounded alarming. During my trip to the Dolomites Belgium's King Leopold had also been forced to leave abruptly, even though he was going to climb with me and Steger, a famous guide. The reason he had given us was the political situation caused by the Sudeten crisis. He had spoken of a partial mobilization in England and France after Hitler had terrified the world with an ominous speech at the Reich party rally. We had paid very little attention to all this in our mountain huts, dismissing it as merely one of the usual rumours. Now I was worried that Mussolini's sudden trip to Munich might be linked to that.

I felt very uneasy and no longer enjoyed the festivities, even though the première was dazzling. I also received many invitations and would have loved to spend a few more days in Rome, a city I adored and in which I would be happy to live. Hard as it was on me, I turned down all the invitations, and the next day I flew to Berlin via Munich. It was 29 September 1938, the fateful day on which Chamberlain, Daladier, Mussolini and Hitler convened in Munich to negotiate the German takeover of the Sudetenland and conclude the 'Peace of Munich'. I didn't realize how great the threat of war had already become. Otherwise I wouldn't have chosen America for the vacation that I had been looking forward to for such a long time. For years I had dreamed of getting to know the United States, and now I had the chance finally to make my wish come true.

AMERICA

Two men accompanied me on my trip to America: Werner Klingenberg, secretary to Professor Diem in the German Olympic Committee, and Ernst Jäger, even though Dr Goebbels had jibbed so long at his participation. The Minister of Propaganda approved it only at the last moment and with many qualms. I could not share his distrust of Jäger, for I was convinced that I had never had a more loyal and devoted employee.

From Bremerhaven, during the first few days of November, we set sail on the *Europa*. It was a special experience for me, my first voyage on a liner of this class. The crossing was a dream; I enjoyed everything – the wind, the sea, and not least the shipboard luxury.

When the silhouette of Manhattan loomed out of the fog we were surprised by the arrival of many small boats full of American reporters, who badgered me with questions. Some of them had brought carrier pigeons in the hope of sensational scoops from me which they wanted to publish as fast as possible. They kept asking me over and over again whether I was having a romance with Hitler.

'Are you Hitler's girlfriend?' I laughed and answered the same way each time: 'No, those are false rumours. I only made documentaries for him.' I was pestered and photographed on all sides.

Suddenly a journalist shouted, 'What do you say to the report that the

Germans are burning down Jewish synagogues, destroying Jewish shops and killing Jewish people?'

Shocked, I protested, 'That is not true, it cannot be true!'

Aboard ship we had read American newspapers that printed a lot of nonsense about Germany, stories that I thought had to be libel. We had been reading only old papers for the past five days and had no idea of the latest news. We couldn't know anything about the dreadful events of Kristallnacht.

I saw the results of my denials on the front pages of American newspapers in New York: 'Leni Riefenstahl says that what American newspapers write about the Nazis is untrue.' A parallel article ran on the same page: 'Synagogues are burning in Germany. Jewish shops are being destroyed, Jews killed.' My holiday trip to America was overshadowed by those terrible developments, and had I believed the press reports I would never have set foot on American soil. It was only on coming back to Germany three months later that I found out things that I would never have believed possible.

Immediately after my return I looked up Captain Wiedemann, an adjutant of Hitler's who during World War I had been his superior. Since his relationship to Hitler was now more distant because of his half-Jewish girlfriend, I hoped that Wiedemann would tell me the unvarnished truth, and I was deeply shaken by what he said. He explained how those atrocities on 9 November had come about. On 7 November a young Jew had shot and killed Ernst von Rath, an official at the German embassy in Paris. When this became known, Hitler and all the leading men in the Party were in Munich; on 9 November they were planning to celebrate the anniversary of the 1923 march to the Feldherrnhalle. 'The news hit them like a bomb,' said Weidemann. On 8 November Hitler, in a state of extreme anger, had given a speech in the beer cellar, demanding revenge for the assassination. Meanwhile, in Hitler's absence, Goebbels had addressed an assembly of Party functionaries in Berlin and delivered a fanatical and inflammatory speech against the Jews. Next, synagogues were burned down in German cities, Jewish shops were destroyed, and Jews were thrown into concentration camps. According to Wiedemann, Hitler had been outraged by Goebbels' unauthorized procedures, not out of sympathy with the Jews, but because he feared foreign reactions. The 'Peace of Munich' was only a few weeks old and, as so often before, Hitler covered for his ministers.

This news had not yet triggered an anti-German reaction in New York. Carefree and unaware, I accepted all the tributes paid to me. King Vidor, the well-known film director, came from Hollywood to greet me in New York. Even the press was, on the whole, benevolent.

We also visited the phenomenal Radio City Music Hall, the biggest cinema in America. Indeed, with its seating capacity of six thousand, it was the biggest in the world. During the intermission the manager handed me flowers and took me backstage where he introduced the world-famous Ziegfeld girls. They performed prior to every showing. Hearing that I was a dancer, they surrounded me, and all of them wanted to shake my hand and get my autograph. In this cheerful atmosphere I had no inkling of what was brewing for me. Everything seemed so delightful. The manager, a Dutchman, would have loved to sign a contract with me on the spot: he wanted *Olympia* for his theatre. There could not have been a more favourable start for my tour of America, and we agreed to meet in Hollywood and work out the contract in the presence of a lawyer.

Our next stop was Chicago where we were guests of Avery Brundage, the president of the IOC. The English-language version of *Olympia* was first shown in his house, where it was enthusiastically received by some hundred visitors. In Chicago, we also received an invitation from the American automobile king, Henry Ford, who greeted us in Detroit, and quickly made us realize how sympathetic he was towards Germany. He praised the elimination of unemployment in our country and in general seemed to have a soft spot for Socialism. He proudly told us that when his firm introduced the assembly line in 1914, the minimum wage of $2.50 a day had been doubled, and that he shared his profits with his workers. He said he had always striven to manufacture cheap cars, not just for the wealthy. Thus, in 1918, when he was producing over half a million cars a year, he had lowered the price of an automobile from nine hundred and fifty to five hundred and fifteen dollars.

When we left, Ford said to me, 'When you see the Führer after your return, tell him that I admire him and I am looking forward to meeting him at the coming Party rally in Nuremberg.'

En route to California we interrupted our trip for several days in order to visit the Grand Canyon, where Indians sold me silver jewellery, decorated with genuine turquoise, as presents for my friends at home.

I was disappointed by our next stop – Los Angeles, which I had pictured quite differently. It looked bleak and ugly, so we hurried on, renting a spacious bungalow at the Beverly Hills Hotel in Hollywood. The swimming pools, the gardens and multi-coloured flowers, the orange and grapefruit trees, were delightful; but the best thing of all was the marvellous climate. One could feel so wonderful there.

My holiday mood vanished overnight, however, for the press ran ads by the Anti-Nazi League calling for a boycott against me. The text said: 'There is no place in Hollywood for Leni Riefenstahl.' Such signs were also posted on the streets and Hollywood gave me the cold shoulder. This is not surprising after the terrible events of Kristallnacht, but it was a dreadful shock after the warmth with which I had been previously received. I had been greatly looking forward to meeting my American colleagues and viewing the studios in Hollywood, but I soon experienced the first effect of this boycott. My appointment with the manager of Radio City Music Hall was cancelled without notification, and I heard later that he had been abruptly dismissed because he intended to première the *Olympia* film in his theatre. I wanted to leave immediately, since it was no fun remaining in Hollywood under these circumstances.

Ignoring the appeal of the Anti-Nazi League however, many Americans begged me to stay on. The League, they said, represented only a minority and I had lots of friends here. We were up to our ears in invitations and I let them talk me into remaining. Then a well-to-do American woman asked all four of us, including Stowitts, to her luxury villa in Palm Springs, where we could stay as long as we liked. We visited her for a week.

In those days Palm Springs, which was chiefly inhabited by Hollywood stars and other rich Americans, was still a small community. In the midst of a desert landscape, a South Sea paradise, created by artificial irrigation, blossomed behind tall fences. I had never seen such beautiful swimming pools.

To my surprise I received an invitation from Gary Cooper, who, as I read in the press, had returned very excited from a trip to Germany. I was told he would call for me at my hotel, but then the invitation was withdrawn. Cooper, I was told, had had to leave for Mexico unexpectedly and regretted that he could not meet me. I had no doubt that he had been pressured to break our appointment.

My experiences with Walt Disney, who also invited us, were different. Early in the morning he welcomed us at his studios and we spent the whole day with him. Patiently, but also proudly, he demonstrated how his cartoon figures were made. He explained his unusual technique and showed us sketches for his new production 'The Sorcerer's Apprentice' (in *Fantasia*). I was fascinated. For me Disney was a genius, a magician, whose imagination seemed boundless. During lunch he mentioned the Venice Biennale, where *Snow White* had competed with *Olympia*. He wanted to see both parts of my film, which would be no problem. The prints were at my hotel and only had to be brought over. Disney reflected, then said, 'I'm afraid I can't afford to do that.'

'Why?' I asked in surprise.

Disney: 'If I see your film then all of Hollywood will find out by tomorrow.'

'But you have your own screening room here.' I protested, 'No one will know about it.'

'My projectionists are unionized,' he said, 'people would find out from them. I'm an independent producer, but I don't do my own distributing and I don't have my own theatres. There's a chance I might be boycotted. The risk is too great.'

Three months later, after leaving America, I found out from the American press how powerful the Anti-Nazi League was. Walt Disney was forced to make a statement to the effect that when I had visited him he hadn't known who I was.

It was only later that I found out about the paid detectives who followed me through the streets of Hollywood in order to prevent me from making contact with actors and directors. Every Hollywood artist could have risked losing his job if he had met with me. Nevertheless, reporters plagued me, wanting to see my Olympic films. After some hesitation, I agreed. It wasn't without its danger, but I relied on the effect of the films.

The closed screening took place with an audience of about fifty people. To avoid being recognized, several well-known directors arrived only after the lights went out. As in Europe, the viewers were spellbound. It was a huge success. Even the reaction of the press was unusually positive, despite the boycott. Thus, Henry McLemore, the UP correspondent, wrote in *Hollywood Citizen News*: 'Last night I saw the best motion picture I have ever seen. I've heard that the film is never going to be shown here because of the Anti-Nazi League boycott, and because it is said to contain German progaganda. The film contains no propaganda, it is so outstanding that it should be shown wherever there is a screen.' And the *Los Angeles Times* said: 'This picture is a triumph of the camera and an epic of the screen. Contrary to rumour, it is in no way a propaganda movie, and as propaganda for any nation, its effect is denifitely zero.'

Now came offers from various parts of America. Most interesting of all was the inquiry from San Francisco, where the World's Fair was being held. This was also a good opportunity to visit the most beautiful city in America, so, renting a car, we drove north up the magnificent coastal highway through Santa Barbara. The drive alone was unforgettable.

The directors of the World's Fair were so enthralled by *Olympia* that a contract was presented to me within twenty-four hours, a stroke of luck which I could scarcely believe. The contract only had to be checked by a lawyer, and I was so overjoyed that I got a bit tipsy with my two escorts that evening. Yet immediately on my return to Hollywood I received a wire from San Francisco – another cancellation. I now gave up all hope of ever finding an American distributor who would be willing to risk showing *Olympia*.

Maria Jeritza, the great Viennese opera singer, who had one of the most beautiful voices of her time, was married to Mr Sheehan, an American movie producer, who worked for MGM. They invited me to dinner in their baronial mansion, and Maria asked me to bring along two reels of *Olympia*, if I could, so that her husband could look at it, but only if no one found out. I was the only guest, and after dinner Mr Sheehan went down to his basement with a projectionist in order to view the two reels by himself. However, as a precautionary measure I had shown up with a complete print of each part, and he didn't come back up until four hours later. My hunch had paid off. Contrary to his intention, he had viewed the entire film.

'I just couldn't stop,' he said, still completely dazed. 'It would really be a loss if this film couldn't be shown in New York. It is truly unique and would certainly make a fortune. It would be such a pity.'

'Are you sure there's no possibility?' asked his wife.

'Very sure,' he said. 'Nevertheless, I'd like to show the film to Metro Goldwyn Mayer.' Then, resigned, added, 'But it's hopeless.'

A SPY

On the day of my departure, my two escorts travelled on ahead to New York. Before we left the United States, Ernst Jäger wanted to give a reception for the press. His idea was to invite the journalists directly on board. A few hours before my train left, however, Maria Jeritza rang me up. 'Can you come by this afternoon?' she said in some distress.

'I'm sorry,' I said regretfully, 'but I'm leaving for New York.'

'Only one hour,' she insisted.

'Could you at least come for a few minutes? It's very important for you,' she said, almost pleading, 'I'll send my car over.'

'Dear Frau Jeritza, I would love to come, but I have to leave my hotel in a few minutes. Can't you tell me on the phone?' I was already very nervous.

Then she began to speak, at first hesitantly, then increasingly hurried and insistent, 'Dear Leni, if I may call you that, I have to warn you of a great danger.' After a pause, she went on, 'You have a spy with you. He receives dollars to report everything you do and intend to do.'

'That's impossible,' I cried, 'My two escorts are devoted and loyal to me.'

'That's what you think, but you're mistaken. With my own eyes I saw my husband hand over huge sums to Herr Jäger for copies of your correspondence and for the information that he kept bringing him.'

'That's impossible,' I said, horrified.

'Herr Jäger was in constant touch with the Anti-Nazi League; he also called them from San Francisco after the directors of the World's Fair saw your Olympic film. He kept them abreast of all your plans, daily, sometimes hourly, so that all the offers you received were then cancelled. No matter where you go in America no one will dare show your *Olympia*.'

I was so stricken that I couldn't reply. 'Are you still on the line?' I heard her ask. 'That was why I wanted to see you, my dear child. Herr Jäger, whom you trust so greatly,' she went on, 'made copies of all the letters you sent to Germany with you. I've heard that after you leave he intends to start a newspaper with the film director Dupont and run mainly scandalous tales about you.'

I felt so faint that I could barely whisper 'Thank you' into the phone.

For five days the train rolled from Los Angeles to New York, five long days and nights. And all I could think about was Ernst Jäger. I still couldn't believe what Maria Jeritza had told me. I thought of all I had done for that man. I had even told Dr Goebbels that I would guarantee Jäger's integrity.

When I got out of the train at Grand Central Station in New York, Ernst Jäger was waiting for me with a bouquet of red roses. Smiling, he greeted me as always, so that I wanted to shake off the thoughts that troubled me, but in the hotel I found certain things that seemed to confirm my suspicions.

In the lobby I ran into Mrs Whitehead, the wife of one of the rich owners of Coca-Cola, with whom Heinz and I were friendly. During their last visit to Berlin they had given me a splendid young sheepdog, which I had trained so well that the dog obeyed my every word. Mrs Whitehead came up to my room and told me that Herr Jäger had made several attempts to borrow large sums from her, apparently for me, but, distrusting him, she had given him no money. She too warned me about him since he had said he was not returning to Germany no matter what.

Then a special delivery letter arrived which made me turn pale when I read it. A well-to-do American, whom we had met on the liner, wrote that in response to urgent wires, he had sent Jäger the ten thousand dollars he had asked for. Jäger had claimed that I desperately needed the money after my arrival and would repay it in a very short time.

That was too much. I rang up the German embassy and was told that Jäger had tried to borrow money there too, allegedly for me. As I hung up, Ernst

Jäger walked in. He looked at me guilelessly and said that everything was arranged for tomorrow's press reception on the *Hansa*, the ship taking us back to Germany. I lost my temper. 'What kind of a monster are you!' I yelled at him. 'How could you trick me like that after all I've done for you. You not only spied on me, lied to me, cheated me, extorted money out of people, but, as Mrs Whitehead has told me, you don't even intend to go back to Germany . . .' If I believed I would see a contrite and penitent man I was greatly mistaken.

He waited until I couldn't speak anymore. Then, raising his hands beseechingly, he said, 'My dear Leni Riefenstahl, please don't get upset, stay calm. I could never do something like that to you. Of course I'm accompanying you back to Germany. I know you've acted as guarantor for me – I'd be a rat if I tricked you like that. You know how much I've admired you for years; these things are all misunderstandings, and I can clear them up. I'd give my life for you.' He stood before me like a saint.

I wavered. 'What about the money?' I asked, flustered.

'We've nothing left,' he said, 'and that's why I planned ahead. You'll still need money in New York.'

'But you can't borrow money without my permission,' I said, incredulous. 'It's hard for me to believe you. If any of the things I've been told about you are true, I couldn't bear the sight of you.' Then I went over to him, looked him straight in the eye, and said, 'Can you give me your word that you are returning to Germany with me tomorrow, that you haven't betrayed me and slandered me, and that you will give me back the money you've borrowed?'

Ernst Jäger gazed at me openly and calmly, bowed, and said in a deep and seemingly emotional voice, 'My word of honour.'

Once again everything appeared all right, yet I couldn't entirely shake off my suspicions, despite Jäger's 'word of honour'. I was impressed by his apparent candour and I believed that everything could still be patched up, for he had so frequently given me proof of his deep respect. My mood was more optimistic now because I had a last-ditch opportunity to license the right to *Olympia* to a large distributor in New York who was willing to brave the boycott. Jäger knew nothing about it and, being forewarned, I said nothing to him.

They had been waiting for me impatiently at the offices of British Gaumont – the firm that hoped to buy the American and also British distribution rights to *Olympia*. Gaumont could do so despite the boycott because it was an independent British distribution firm with eight hundred of its own cinemas in the United States. It was therefore free of any influence from the Anti-Nazi League. Their offer was an excellent one, and the preliminary contracts, which I was supposed to deliver to Tobis, had already been worked out. This was a last-minute victory.

The next day I stood on the deck of the Hansa. The German cultural attaché, whom I had informed of my suspicions concerning Jäger, escorted me and tried to calm me down, but I was very flustered. The first guests, especially the invited journalists, were coming on board and Ernst Jäger was nowhere to be found. What should I do? The cultural attaché also became nervous. Perhaps Jäger really was a spy, who could wreak further havoc. While I attempted to field questions from the reporters, I kept watching the gangway, hoping that Jäger would show up at the last moment. What could I say to Goebbels if I returned without Jäger? But far worse, and more painful, was my personal disappointment.

After the captain shouted 'All aboard!' several times and the last visitors left, I was in despair and succumbed to a fit of crying. The cultural attaché took me to my cabin and tried in vain to calm me. Unwilling to leave me alone in this state, he remained on the *Hansa* and accompanied me all the way to Canada.

IN PARIS

The storm raging in the Atlantic Ocean had slowed down the *Hansa* so much that I arrived in Cherbourg on 17 January, half a day late, to find the French correspondents already waiting. They wanted to interview me about my experiences in America and my impressions of the USA.

In Paris it was the German ambassador, Count Welczek, who was waiting for me, for I was to give a talk within the framework of German-French cultural cooperation at the Centre Marcellin Berthelot. The topic was to be 'How I Make My Films', and the auditorium, which held more than two thousand people, was sold out.

Abel Bonard, a writer and member of the French Academy, gave an introductory talk. I spoke in German, and my lecture was translated by a young Frenchwoman. After expressing my joy and gratitude for the invitation, I said that our ancient cultures and common spiritual values could unite France and Germany and both nations could complement one another perfectly. I then came to my actual topic: *Is Cinema Art?*

> I say yes to this question. Cinema is an art just like other arts, but it is still in its swaddling clothes. It has all the prerequisites for an artistic experience, just as much as the works of a Rodin, a Beethoven, a

Leonardo da Vinci or a Shakespeare. However that will not happen in the cinema that we know today, but in the cinema of the future. Even the best motion pictures that we have seen so far can only hint at the possibilities of the film as a work of art.

This new art is independent of the other arts. It would be incorrect to state that cinematic art is tied to painting or music or literature. No. It may not touch these genres, but the word that characterizes the art of cinema is 'cinematic'. By 'cinematic' I mean, above all, pictures in motion, which no other genre can offer. Only the cinema consists of moving images. It has its own laws and in an artistic film everything has to be created according to these laws: the theme, the direction, the performances, the photography, the sets, the sound, the editing. An absolutely sure sense of style is the most important quality a film director should have.

A further important requirement for a film director is a sense of dynamics, construction and rhythm. The distribution of the high points in a film is of major significance – tension and relief have to alternate properly. The sequence of images can be altered in a hundred different ways by the editing. If the director, who should always edit his own work, is musically gifted, he will compose with images and sounds, the way a musician composes according to the laws of counterpoint.

The editor can make the images dance in a wild rhythm or drift by in dreamlike slowness. He can turn the images into an orgy of random absurdity, or he can use the same images to construct a clear, logical plot.

Ideally the director – the shaper of the whole – should be in control. A painting cannot be painted by many hands; a symphony cannot be composed by a number of musicians. The control of all means is the first requirement for creating an artwork. Passionate visions are more instinctive than rational – a balance of the two is ideal. In the creative process the birth can be chaotic; the later shaping, the realization, and the execution, can be conscious.

Once these requirements are present, it is possible to practise this youngest of all arts in order to create great works, as one does in architecture, music and painting.

What distinguishes cinema from the other arts? It is primarily a moving image. This means that the basic elements are pictures annd motion, which are inseparably interwoven. That is, a film can be art only if it consists of these two elements. Neither colour nor sound is necessary. I am not saying that sound films or colour films cannot also be artworks; but the silent black-and-white film is the True Film, because it is made up of the basic cinematic elements: image and motion. The talkie is merely an expansion of this new genre, though a lovely and wonderful enrichment. If the silent black-and-white film consists of two elements, then the sound film is made up of three. As a result it is more difficult to make an artistic sound film than an artistic silent film.

The director of a good silent film must be doubly gifted. First of all, he must be able to make an optical translation of everything perceived by his eyes. Secondly, he has to be musical – not specializing in any area, but cinematically musical. This has little to do with normal musicality.

For example: someone may be highly musical, yet fail to sense that a given music does not fit the images. He is not bothered if some sort of classical or modern music is inserted as a background for certain scenes in a film. However, this will turn the stomach of the talented film creator. In shaping a film he senses what kind of music belongs to the images, even if he himself is not a practising musician. He unconsciously takes part in the musical composition. He senses that certain shots will not endure just any music; it would only destroy the visual effect. Or else, realistic sounds belong here. Or here, the music can have only a specific rhythm, expression, instrumentation and volume. He cannot bear a sound that is too loud or too soft. Incidentally, there will be fewer good sound films than good silent films. Very few people possess this threefold gift and are able to harmonize their individual elements. That too is crucial. None of these elements must outweigh the others. Any disharmony in the distribution of forces will prevent the genesis of an artwork.

The colour film is a far more difficult problem, for it requires a fourth talent. Contrary to what many people believe, a sense of colour or a knack for painting does not suffice. The director who feels capable of making an artistic colour film must also possess, along with the other three gifts, a talent for manipulating colours 'cinematically'. He can then greatly increase the dramatic effect, since colours arouse different emotions. For example, blue is a feminine, romantic colour, while red, in contrast, represents *joie de vivre*, vitality, and passion. On the other hand, too many or too gaudy colours can destroy the effect of images. The colour should integrate harmoniously and, in artistic reciprocity, complement the other elements in the film. This new four-part combination of image, motion, sound and colour, can turn cinema into an art.

If someone were to invent a three-dimensional film, the difficulties of creating an artistic motion picture would increase *ad infinitum*. These five elements would not get along with one another. They would snuff out the life of a film as an artwork. The result would be a super-reality, far removed from art.

My lecture, which lasted for almost two hours, was rewarded with several minutes of applause. Happy over the recognition and sympathy shown to me by the French, I finally dropped off into a calm sleep after the troubles of the past few weeks.

Before leaving Paris, I inadvertently took part in an embarrassingly funny scene. My friends wanted to show me some French film companies, so we visited Pathé, where the director took me through various soundstages. In the biggest and last a remarkable set was being constructed and, as we approached, the workers – stagehands, lighting men and technicians – stopped working. They grouped themselves into two rows and launched into a song, which I assumed was in my honour. Delighted and attentive, I listened to their song, unaware that it was the 'Internationale'. It was only when I headed towards the group in order to thank them that I noticed that their right hands were clenched into fists. Before I could even hold out my hand to the first worker, the studio director dashed towards me and pulled me out of the place. The workers, displaying no emotion, remained as they were, immobile. They looked like a church choir that had just finished singing its chorale. It was only when the director apologized to me for this incident that I realized it was anything but a tribute.

I had never heard the 'Internationale', nor witnessed the clenched fist as a Communist symbol. It may sound incredible today. But almost half a century ago my political ignorance was forgivable.

SCANDAL STORIES FROM HOLLYWOOD

In Berlin a small package arrived by post from the German embassy in Washington, containing a letter and a sheaf of newspapers. Maria Jeritza's prophecies had materialized. Ernst Jäger and the screen director Dupont were publishing a primitive scandal sheet in Hollywood which ran the most outrageous gossip about me. They reported that I was not only Hitler's mistress, but also the playmate of both Goebbels and Göring. They even described the lace lingerie that I picked out for my amorous interludes. These articles included passages that were true, sections that Jäger had copied from my letters. Such mixtures of facts and infamous lies must have sounded believable to outsiders.

What I read was repugnant, to some extent pornographic, and also politically dangerous. Jäger had secretly jotted down some of my not always flattering remarks about Goebbels, and skilfully blended them with all sorts of lies. My staff had told him about some of Goebbels' embarrassing affairs, and Jäger had embellished them very freely. If the minister got hold of these articles there would be such a scandal that I would have no choice but to leave Germany and seek work in some other country. Even Hitler would not be able to help me.

What could I do? I had no friends at the Ministry of Propaganda to prevent Goebbels from obtaining those gazettes. On the contrary they would gleefully make a point of presenting those gutter reports to him as soon as possible. Goebbels had probably already received them. The letter from the German embassy had a footnote stating that copies of the scandal sheets had also been dispatched to the Ministry of Propaganda. The disaster could no longer be warded off.

I didn't have a moment's peace and expected to be summoned to the Ministry of Propaganda at any instant. Out of the blue I received an invitation to the Day of German Art in Munich. I knew I would run into Goebbels there and I couldn't make up my mind whether or not to go. But being in suspense was so agonising that I preferred to bring the situation to a head as soon as possible.

When I arrived at the banquet in the House of German Art I looked around for my place card, and I couldn't believe my eyes. Goebbels would be sitting next to me. I couldn't leave, the hall was already filled with guests, and only now did I notice that Adolf Hitler and the Italian ambassador, Signor Attolico, were placed opposite us, while my right-hand neighbour was Dr Dietrich, the Reich press chief. I felt as if I were going to my execution.

At that moment Goebbels entered the room and greeted me icily and distantly, yet I couldn't tell from his expression whether he had read the stories. I expected a disaster any second. The Italian ambassador, however, must have said something nice about me to Hitler, for the two of them drank to my health, and I was astounded to see that Hitler's glass was filled with champagne. At that moment I had a sudden inspiration. Turning to Goebbels, who eyed me askance, I said, 'I have something to confess.'

'Do you remember, Doctor,' I said with a genuine sense of guilt, 'you warned me about Herr Jäger when I defended him and guaranteed his integrity?'

'Well?' Goebbels snapped, but I thought from the expression on his face that he was not yet informed about Jäger's scandal stories. I breathed a sigh of relief and spoke very softly, so that the others couldn't hear me.

'Something awful has happened. Herr Jäger has published unbelievable scandal stories about me in Hollywood. Have you read them?' I anxiously waited for his reaction.

With a dismissive gesture, Goebbels sneered, 'I told you right away that you couldn't trust that slimy hack.' I nodded in agreement, and after that remark I felt it was unlikely that Goebbels would take the time to read Jäger's articles.

I must surely have had a guardian angel. I had escaped a great danger but by the skin of my teeth.

PENTHESILEA

From then on I saw only one mission for me: the *Penthesilea* film. After my return from the United States I started Leni Riefenstahl Film Inc. for that project. The Olympia Film Inc. had been established purely for the production of *Olympia*, and my Studio Film, which I had rechristened Reich Party Rally Film, could not produce an expensive project like *Penthesilea*. Since it was a general partnership the risk would have been too great. The unparalleled international success of *Olympia* helped to facilitate the backing for my new picture, and the Ministry of Propaganda notified me that *Penthesilea* had been entered into the title registry as No. 1087. That was the starting shot for me.

I realized that the filming of this material involved tremendous difficulties. The style of the film would be crucial. The subject teetered on the razor's edge between the sublime and the ridiculous, and there could be no happy medium. It would be either a great work or a complete flop.

In order to cope with this undertaking I had to be as unencumbered as possible. In particular I couldn't be bothered with organizational details, but there I was lucky, for my staff had learned a great deal and qualified themselves in their professions; and they were also my friends whom I could trust; above all I could depend on my two executives, Waldi Traut and Walter Grosskopf.

Before gearing up for the pre-production work, I took speech training, since my role would make great demands on my voice. Moreover, as queen of the Amazons I had to have the expertise of a circus rider. Despite my versatile athletic activities, I had never had an opportunity to learn how to ride a horse (aside from my abortive attempt in California): I now took lessons every day. Riding came as easily to me as other sports and it was lots of fun, even when I had to learn how to jump on to a galloping horse and ride bareback. I was soon able to go riding in the Grunewald with my colleague Brigitte Horney, an experienced horsewoman, who lived nearby in Dahlem.

My figure also had to look like that of an Amazon, which meant that I had to train hard, and my coach came over every morning to put me through the necessary exercises. During the day I focused mainly on writing the scenario. At the same time I had to select the most important production people. The only composer I wanted was Herbert Windt, and for the sets I hired Herlth and Röhrig, the gifted art directors who had designed the sets for nearly all the the films made by Murnau and Fritz Lang.

My life was so thoroughly monopolized by this project that I had no time for social obligations. Nor did I miss them. Since my adolescence I had never been very interested in socializing. I never once went to the Comradeship of Artists Club, a meeting-place of the VIPs, often visited by Goebbels and other cabinet members. If I felt like getting to know an artist I would invite him to my home. I much preferred a *tête-à-tête*.

In order to write the screenplay in peace and quiet I had rented a cottage with a thatched roof in Kampen on the island of Sylt. I went there with my mother, my secretary and, above all, Märchen (Fairytale), my white mare, which my riding instructor had purchased at the stud farm in Hanover. I wanted to continue my horseback training on the island. After riding I did my Amazon gymnastics and then turned to the script. No work had ever come more easily to me. The scenes loomed before my eyes, and all I had to do was write them down.

I wanted Jürgen Fehling to direct the acting scenes. Undeniably one of the greatest stage directors in Germany, he had mounted wonderful productions at Gustav Gründgens' Preussisches Staatstheater – the best theatre in Germany. I had written to Fehling and was anxiously awaiting his reply when he telegraphed: 'I'll jump up on your horse. Fehling.'

What luck! I rejoiced, and very soon he arrived. Since I had no experience as a stage actress he inspired my deepest respect and I felt like a beginner. But working with him was not so easy. When we talked he kept straying from the topic. He loved talking about sexual deviations, which he claimed he had experienced, while I was completely fixated on my film. I was also bothered by his ugly way of putting down Gründgens as an actor and theatre manager. The opinions he expressed of Gründgens were so devastating that I found it unprincipled of Fehling to keep working with him. Although a brilliant stage director, Fehling remained alien to me on a human level and I soon wondered if we could get on well in the long run.

On the other hand I couldn't imagine a better director, so I tried to overlook many things. We did not differ about the casting or the style I had in mind, and Fehling was also enthusiastic about the locations I had picked out. The battle scenes between the Amazons and the Greeks were to be shot in the Libyan desert, not only because of the support I had been promised by Marshal Balbo, but because of the eternally blue, cloudless sky against which the classical figures under the high sun would stand out like reliefs carved in stone. In no way was the film to resemble Hollywood Technicolour spectacles. I wanted to use the colours sparingly. These were to be subtle nuances between beige and brown, like the colours of the pyramids on the Nile.

The sombre tragedy of the final battle scenes, the duel between Penthesilea and Achilles, contrasting powerfully with the early grand battle scenes in the sunny Libyan countryside, were also to be visually expressed. That was why I wanted to shoot these sequences at Sylt or the Courland Spit. There we could film them against dark cloud banks. However, nature was not to look realistic; it would be stylized by the angels, the light, and superdimensional views of things like the sun and the moon. It was a fascinating task for the camera to create such unreal images of rainbows and clouds, plunging waters and uprooted tree giants. Kleist's language would harmonize with these visions.

That was the only way that I could imagine *Penthesilea* on the screen.

ALBERT SPEER

In Berlin the pre-production work for the film was going full steam ahead. Amid the hectic pace I had forgotten to call up Albert Speer. He urgently wanted to speak to me. One afternoon in mid-August I visited him at his studio on Pariser Platz, where he showed me a gigantic model of the projected reconstruction of Berlin. At first I thought that this was simply an architectural fantasy. I could not imagine a city like Berlin being rebuilt from scratch; but Albert Speer explained that the construction would begin very soon.

'That's why I wanted to talk to you,' he said. I would like to document all this on film – these model constructions which have been designed not only by me but also other architects. And so I thought of you.'

Unfortunately I had to disappoint Speer, since I was preparing *Penthesilea*. I suggested Dr Fanck who, because his last two films had been unsuccessful, wasn't doing anything. Speer was agreeable, but asked me to back Fanck up with my experienced staff, and to organize and supervise the production within the framework of my firm; the documentary would be financed by the Todt Organization.

Unexpectedly, Hitler showed up, wearing his Party uniform, a brown jacket and black trousers, with no coat or cap. He had entered Speer's studio through a back door leading to the gardens of the Reich Chancellery. I wanted to take my leave immediately, but Hitler said, 'Please stay, Fräulein Riefenstahl, you can see something unique here.'

While he looked at the models, I heard Speer say, 'My Führer, I can give you the delightful news that on the basis of the soil inspections the new constructions of Berlin will be completed in fifteen rather than in twenty years.'

Hitler looked up, astonished: raising his hands and staring upward, as he had done at our first meeting by the North Sea, he said in a joyful, excited, somewhat grandiloquent tone of voice: 'God grant that I may live to see it and that I will not be forced into a war.'

I was frightened by the word 'war' and when the war broke out two weeks later I often recalled Hitler's words in Speer's studio. I have never been able to explain them.

While Hitler and Speer discussed the details of the model, I noticed a large, vast thoroughfare running from south to north, linking two railway terminals, and I gathered from their conversation that these would be the only two railway stations. Wide stretches of water were to surround the terminals, which would be lined with lawns and planted with trees and flowers. Hitler declared, 'If guests visit our capital they should come away with an overpowering impression of Berlin.'

In some parts of the city there were universities, schools and educational institutions; in others, museums, galleries, theatres, concert halls and cinemas. A further district consisted of hospitals, clinics and old people's homes. The most noticeable constructions were government and Party buildings in the classical style that Speer had already practised in his design of the New Reich Chancellery. One in particular, a gigantic domed building, struck me as bombastic: its enormous height (the cathedral of Cologne could have fitted into each of the four corner towers) overwhelmed the rest of the townscape. So far as I understood, this building was reserved for special mass functions, and the gigantic corner towers were to contain the burial sites of worthy Party members.

Hitler asked me, 'What kind of trees should we plant on our new main street?'

Unhesitatingly I said, 'The trees I saw on the Champs Elysées in Paris. I believe they are plane trees.'

'What do you think, Speer?'

'Fine with me,' said Speer drily.

'Well, so let's have plane trees,' said Hitler, good-humouredly. Then he took his leave.

HITLER SEES STALIN

According to my journals I see that my conversation with Speer took place in mid-August 1939 – just two weeks before the outbreak of war. Several days later I happened to witness a scene that struck me as having immense historic importance. From time to time artists were invited to film-viewing evenings at the Reich Chancellery, which I was usually too busy to accept, but this time I wanted to go. After visiting Speer I sensed that something was brewing, and it made me uneasy.

As so often, I arrived late when the screening had already begun. Various newsreels were shown, and one which featured Stalin reviewing a military parade in Moscow had a few close-ups of his profile. I observed Hitler leaning forward during these parts and viewing them with great concentration. Surprisingly, at the end of the screening, he asked to see the newsreel again, but didn't indicate why. When Stalin reappeared on the screen, I heard Hitler say: 'That man has a good face; one should be able to negotiate with him.' After the lights went on Hitler excused himself and left.

Just two days later (I remember the date precisely; it was my birthday) the German foreign minister, Joachim von Ribbentrop, flew to Moscow with a retinue which included Walter Frentz, one of my cameramen, and, at the request of the Reich Chancellery, he took along prints of my Olympic films. Now I thought I understood the significance of the screening and Hitler's call. Just one day after Ribbentrop's arrival in Moscow, Germany and Russia signed their non-aggression pact.

When Ribbentrop came home a reception was given in Berlin to celebrate the Hitler-Stalin Pact, which had stunned the entire world, and I was invited. They gave me a handwritten letter from Stalin expressing his admiration for the *Olympia* film.

It was my impression that Hilter's sudden decision to negotiate with Stalin was made when he saw his close-ups in the newsreel.

AT THE TOP OF THE SKY

Before shooting began on *Penthesilea*, I wanted to relax a little, so on 30 August I got into my sports car and drove off to Bolzano where Hans Steger was expecting me. From there we would head to the Sella shelter hut as a starting-point for our first few tours.

The next morning we climbed the Himmelsspitze, the 'Top of the Sky', as training. Since I was in excellent shape this climb was a mere stroll for me – and, as usual, a great pleasure. Standing on the peak, happy and filled with dreams of the future, I had no idea that everything would be destroyed the next day.

When we returned to the hut in the afternoon Paula Wiesinger, Steger's companion, was in a dreadful state. 'Leni, you've got to get back to Berlin right away. Your friend Hermann called up. It's terrible news, there's war! Hermann is in a barracks, just like Guzzi and Otto and other members of your staff. The mobilization is in full swing.'

Insanity, I thought. It can't be true. The world collapsed for me.

Steger drove back with me along the almost deserted autobahn. We tried to fill up with petrol, but none was to be found anywhere, and we reached our destination exhausted and down to our last drop of fuel. The official declaration of war was expected at any moment, and when I learned that all the men on my staff had been mobilized, I went to see them right away and found them all in a barracks (I can't remember the name). In the hope of going to the front lines as cameramen, they implored me to start a newsreel company.

I sympathized, but from whom could I obtain permission so quickly? I tried to inquire at the Reich Chancellery and was lucky enough to get past the sentries. There I ran into a colonel and told him what I wanted.

'If you hurry,' he said, 'you can hear the Führer at the Reichstag where he will be making a statement on the possibility of war.' He wrote a pass admitting me to the building and, on entering the mobbed room, I could hear Hitler's voice from very far away: 'We have been returning fire since 5.45 a.m.'

WAR

WAR IN POLAND

War to me was a dreadful, an incomprehensible thought. I couldn't fathom Hitler's declaration of war against Poland. After all, just a few days earlier, when he and Speer had been discussing the reconstruction of Berlin, Hitler had said: 'God grant that I may live to see it and that I will not be forced into a war.'

Once, during a meal, Hitler had spoken very appreciatively about Marshal Pilsudski, head of the Polish government. The gist of what he said was that, as long as the marshal ruled, any problem between Poland and Germany could be solved. But meanwhile, Pilsudski had died. I was convinced however that only serious reasons could impel Hitler to decide to go to war. The German radio and press had kept reporting that Hitler wanted only to have a land link to East Prussia and to reincorporate Danzig into the German Reich, but that the repeated efforts of the German government to get Poland to agree remained unsuccessful. At least that was what the public was told. Hitler, it appeared, was convinced that England would remain neutral despite her guarantees to Poland, and probably he risked war because he believed he could end it in a short time.

I wondered how I could make myself useful in a war, and at first I thought I could be trained as a nurse, but some members of my staff kept urging me to organize a film crew for combat reporting. When I tried to implement this suggestion there was no response from the Wehrmacht, so I decided to make a concrete proposal. Together, we drew up a list of suitable people (including Allgeier, Guzzi and Otto Lantschner, Traut and, as sound engineer, Hermann Storr) and wrote a brief description of the project. Then I drove back to the Reich Chancellery, hoping to submit the list and the description to one of Hitler's army liaison officers. I had to wait for a long time before I was able to present my plan to a high-ranking Wehrmacht officer who promised to turn my documents over to his superiors. Within twenty-four hours I was notified by telephone that the Wehrmacht had approved our project.

A major took us to Grunewald and taught us how to use a gas mask and a pistol. Two days later we received blue-grey uniforms – later worn by war correspondents – for Germans were not permitted to wear civilian clothing in combat areas. We had to take Sepp Allgeier along in mufti, however, as he couldn't get a uniform in time.

On 9 September our little film crew left Berlin and headed east to Poland where we were supposed to report to Colonel General von Rundstedt, head of the southern army group. By the afternoon we reached headquarters, where we were greeted by von Rundstedt, and told to drive on to Colonel General von Reichenau, whose command post was further east, in Konskie. This small Polish town was in a rather chaotic state, with soldiers in every street and jeeps and motorcycles racing past us. Colonel General von Reichenau was billeted in a sidetracked railway car and I recognized him as the man who five years earlier had complained to Hitler about the Party rally film. His greeting was terse, but friendly; he appeared to hold no grudge against me, but he was rather at a loss about where to put us up. Reichenau advised us to remain with our car as close to the Wehrmacht car park as possible, for we were very near the combat area and might easily stumble into the firing line. The next day we would receive suggestions for possible filming, and since all we knew for sure was that a cameraman was to drive a jeep to the combat area, Guzzi volunteered. Luckily I had brought along my tent, so I was able to spend the night in the parking lot, protected against the cold and the wind, while the others tried to make themselves comfortable in our two vehicles.

Shortly before dawn, as Guzzi was driven off for the film work, we heard gunfire, and bullets suddenly ripped through my tent. I hadn't imagined it would be this dangerous. Meanwhile some of my people had made contact with the soldiers. The day before our arrival Polish civilians had killed a high-ranking German officer and four soldiers, maiming them dreadfully. They had gouged out their eyes and sliced out their tongues. That was the second horrible incident within just two days. In the first incident six soldiers had been butchered in their sleep by Polish partisans. Their remains were transported to Berlin while the victims of the previous day's massacre were laid out in the church and were to be buried here.

We walked over to the marketplace, where a large number of German soldiers were gathered, and in their midst some Polish men who were digging a pit, the grave for the dead German soldiers. Our soldiers were extremely excited and the faces of the Poles exhibited a deathly fear. They understood no German and were terrified that they were digging their own grave. Now a German police officer appeared, stood at the edge of the grave, and ordered the soldiers to maintain calm and discipline. He gave a brief speech: 'Soldiers, cruel as the deaths of our men may have been, we do not want to return like for like.' Then he told the soldiers to send the Poles home and to bury the dead.

After the officer left, however, several of the soldiers dragged the frightened Poles out of the pit, and not very gently. An extremely angry group stood right beside me, and, ignoring the officer's orders, they brutally kicked the men who were pushing their way out of the pit.

I was outraged, I yelled at them, 'Didn't you hear what the officer told you? Are you German soldiers?' The angry men now faced me menacingly. One of them shouted, 'Punch her in the mouth, get rid of the bitch.' Another yelled, 'Shoot her down!' As he aimed his rifle at me. I gasped in horror at the man, and at that instant I was photographed.

When the gun barrel was levelled at me my colleagues jerked me aside, but suddenly we heard a shot in the distance, then several more. Everyone ran from the grave site in the direction of the firing, while I went to Reichenau in order to protest against the undisciplined conduct of the soldiers. Only then did I learn what had happened. A shot fired by a Luftwaffe officer had started a panic that in turn had led to a senseless shooting spree. Soldiers had fired at the Poles who were dashing away because they assumed that some of them were the ones who had committed the massacre.

More than thirty Poles fell victim to this shooting, and four German soldiers were wounded. Reichenau was as furious and disgusted as the rest of us. He said that such an outrage had never occurred in the German army, and the perpetrators would be court-martialled. I was so upset by this experience that I asked the general to allow me to terminate my film reporting and he was very sympathetic to my request. I wanted to get back to Berlin as soon as possible.

While my colleagues continued to work as war correspondents, I, accompanied by Knuth, a cameraman, who did not wish to remain in Konskie either, drove west to the southern army group where a military plane, a Heinkel III, going to Danzig, took us aboard. There was room for five people and I lay on a small carpet next to the pilot in a transparent cockpit. Behind me were Knuth and the flight mechanic.

Being still in the war zone, our plane was violently attacked by enemy guns and we could see the shell holes in the wings of our Henkel. As the din of the artillery grew louder and louder, we plummeted straight down towards the ground for a few terrifying seconds. I still remember the pilot's tense look and, as I glanced around, I saw the cameraman behind me, his face distorted by fear. He was trying to pull himself up on some belts.

By a miracle, however, we were still alive. There was no crash, no bursting into flames, we had not been shot down. The quick-witted pilot had nose-dived when the plane was hit and, to escape the anti-aircraft fire, pulled out only a few yards above the forest. However, we still weren't out of the danger zone, and, as the firing continued, our plane slalomed along like a skier, the pilot frequently changing direction and altitude. He flew so low that we nearly grazed the trees and the telegraph wires. I had gone on some thrilling flights with Udet, but this was the most hair-raising flight of my life.

We reached Danzig in stormy weather, but our several attempts at landing on the small airfield failed. Eventually the pilot managed to touch down, in a crash landing. We had to remain in Danzig, there being no transportation to Berlin, and then we heard that Hitler was expected. After his arrival he gave a luncheon at the Kasino Hotel in Zoppot, to which I was invited. Frau Forster, the wife of the gauleiter of Danzig, sat at Hitler's right side while I sat at his left. Roughly a hundred people, mostly officers, were at the simple table.

I used the opportunity to tell Hitler about the events in Konskie, but he had already been informed and said the same thing I had heard from Reichenau: such an offence had never occurred in the Germany army, and the guilty would be court-martialled. During the meal Hitler received a wire which I heard him rereading to himself several times, and since I was next to him I managed to catch a few lines. The telegram was signed with the letters OKH, Oberkommando des Heeres (Supreme Army Command), and the gist of it was an urgent request to Hitler for permission to launch the attack on Warsaw. Turning to the assistant adjutant who had brought him the wire, Hitler said angrily, 'This is the third time we have asked the Polish government to surrender Warsaw without a fight. As long as women and children are in the city I want no shooting. I would like to make them another capitulation offer and try to convince them of the senselessness of their refusal. It is madness to be shooting at women and children.'

Those were Hitler's words which, if someone else reported them to me, I would consider unbelievable; but I am writing the truth, difficult as it may be for me. To the descendants of the millions of Hitler's victims, these words must sound like mockery, yet perhaps this episode may contribute to an awareness of his schizophrenic ways.

Before leaving Danzig I heard a speech given by Hitler at the Artushof in the Long Market in which he tried to justify his war against Poland. He talked about how Polish mistreatment of Germans had increased intolerably since the death of Marshal Pilsudski; then he accused England of driving Poland into war and passionately voiced his desire for peace. 'Never,' said Hitler, 'did I intend to wage war against France or England – we have no military goals in the West.'

After my return from Danzig the radio announced the occupation of Warsaw. Udet, who had become general aviation master of the Luftwaffe, offered me a chance to fly to Warsaw in a military plane as I wanted to meet my crew there. They were safe and sound, and convinced that the war would be over within a short time. However, I was amazed by what they told me about the first friction between the German and the Russian armies. My colleagues had gathered from telephone calls between officers that the Russians were demanding territories conquered by German troops in Galicia. The issue was oil. The Wehrmacht leaders protested, but at Hitler's personal orders, the German generals resentfully yielded to the Red Army. After Hitler's decision, the tiny flags marking the front lines on the huge map at army headquarters had to be shifted westward. One of our cameramen had to film this scene and, while shooting, he heard one of the officers curse: 'German soldiers conquered this territory with their blood; now Hitler is handing it over to the Russians.'

The next day Hitler's fighting troops had a parade in Warsaw which was filmed by Sepp Allgeier and the Lantschner brothers. I stood next to Allgeier, near Hitler, and saw how the marching soldiers gazed at him as if hypnotized. Each and every one of them appeared ready to do anything for Hitler if he ordered them, even to die for him.

After those experiences in Poland I never visited any combat area again, nor did I ever do any war filming.

TIEFLAND ONCE AGAIN

In Berlin I was surprised to see that despite the war the film industry was producing almost as much as in peacetime; but a *Penthesilea* would have no chance owing to the huge budget required. Goebbels now concentrated chiefly on patriotic subjects in order to make the viewers adjust to the war, and on any kind of entertainment in order to make them forget their troubles.

When I read in *Film-Kurier* that Tobis was planning to do *Tiefland*, I was electrified. After all, I had worked on that film years ago, but had been forced to stop. Should I take it up again? The idea had its pros and cons. On the plus side, the subject had nothing to do with politics or war, and I believed it would be an easy job, requiring only a few months. On the minus side I no longer felt close to it, but I thought it better to do *Tiefland* than to be compelled to turn out a propaganda or war film. I would have been unable to escape such an obligation, for Goebbels' power had been much increased by the war.

If only I had an inkling of the insuperable difficulties involved in this project! More than twenty years passed before *Tiefland* could finally be shown, but no one could have foreseen this. War, illness, and an almost ten-year confiscation of the rushes were to blame. The story of the making of this film is an odyssey which could be turned into a film of its own.

All the other good scriptwriters were 'booked solid', as they say nowadays, so I had no choice but to take a stab at it myself. I rented a small mountain cottage in Kitzbühel on the Hahnenkamm (Cockscomb) and holed up there. Since it was located right by the start of the renowned downhill course, I was strongly tempted to put on my skis. Every day I would draw the red gingham curtains across my window to avoid looking at the winter landscape.

The work was not easy, and I wouldn't have managed if chance hadn't helped me out; I ran into Harald Reinl on the Hahnenkamm. An outstanding skier, he had been involved in many of Fanck's pictures and had also worked in my company as Guzzi Lantschner's assistant. Our encounter proved fateful for him. Reinl had obtained his law degree at the University of Innsbruck and was now preparing to start his career as a government employee. During conversations he inadvertently remarked that he'd much rather work in films, and then he let me read one of his manuscripts. After reading just a few pages I had no doubts about his cinematic talent.

On impulse, I asked, 'Would you drop your government career if I hired you as assistant director for *Tiefland*?'

Staring at me incredulously, he replied, 'But I don't have any first-hand experience.'

'It doesn't matter,' I said, 'you're gifted, and that's more important.'

And so Harald Reinl went into the film business. Soon we began working together in the mountain cottage, and our collaboration went well. I had someone to talk to, which was such a great help with the dialogue that the script was completed within six weeks. Deviating from the opera, we had inserted a social theme: the uprising of the serfs against their lord.

I discovered our Pedro in an unusual way. Reinl and I were in St Anton on the Arlberg, watching the Kandahar race, when I happened to glance at a group of skiers waiting at a closed railway barrier, and noticed a young man among them. I knew instantly: this is Pedro. At that moment the barrier went up, the skiers poured towards the cable car and I had lost my Pedro. I saw him again at the starting line of the Kandahar race, and now I sent Reinl to talk to him, but their conversation was disappointing. Reinl reported that the young man had such a strong regional accent that he couldn't understand him, even though they came from the same area. Bad luck. His appearance made him ideal for the part. I didn't give up however, and asked him to tea.

He was bashful and tongue-tied, but his expression fitted in with my image of the character, and if necessary his lines could be dubbed by someone else. He was twenty-three, an army orderly, and the Wehrmacht had posted him to the Arlberg area as a skiing instructor. I was still uncertain whether to cast such an inexperienced amateur as the male lead; it was a considerable risk, but I kept the young man in mind.

The outdoor shooting was to be done in Spain, as far as possible at the same locations as the first time, six years ago. In spring 1940 we sent the cameraman, the director and a costume designer to Spain, while I remained in Berlin to continue casting. Tobis was not too thrilled by my idea of using a beginner for the lead. However, I was willing to screen-test a few well-known actors who might be right for the part, but very few of them were the Pedro type. The problem was not so much their looks as the genuine *naïveté* that the role demanded. He had to sound believable when he said: 'I've never had a woman.' If the actor couldn't pull off that line, then he'd be wrong for the part and the audience would just laugh. As I feared, the screen-tests were unsatisfactory, and I kept thinking about my Arlberg Pedro. Bernhard Minetti was the favourite for Don Sebastian. At Gustav Grundgens' theatre I had admired Minetti as Richard III and as Robespierre in *Danton's Death* by Büchner. I also tested Gustav Knuth and Ferdinand Marian, but finally opted for Minetti whose ascetic features alone made him look more suitable for the part of a northern Spanish aristocrat.

A major problem was the female lead, Martha, the gypsy dancer whom I had wanted to play myself the first time round, but this time I only wanted to direct. I felt there were only two possibilities for this part: Brigitte Horney or Hilde Krahl, but neither was available and we were at our wits' end. When Tobis and my people pestered me to do it, I gave in, but only on condition that we hire a second director for the acting scenes.

Will Forst, Helmut Käutner, and others I'd had in mind were busy. *Tiefland* seemed to be ill-starred; but at last there was a glimmer of light. G.W. Pabst returned from Hollywood, where he had been working for several years. He wanted to work in Germany again, no simple matter, for despite his film successes, he was unpopular with Goebbels. Pabst was classified as 'left-wing' because of what was perhaps his best picture, *Kameradschaft*. We had been close ever since the days of *The White Hell of Piz Palü*, and he instantly agreed to direct the acting sequences.

Except for Pedro, all the parts were cast; along with Minetti we had such outstanding Berlin performers as Marie Koppenhöfer, Frieda Richard and Aribert Wäscher. Now I resolved to try out my Pedro. His home base in Vienna approved long leave for him, and then one day 'Pedro' stood before us. I wasn't mistaken. Franzl, as we called him, was simply marvellous in the screen test – aside from his diction. I had already been giving that some thought, but unfortunately G. W. Pabst didn't like him and, although he was surprised at how expressive the young man could be, he too was put off by Franzl's diction. What could we do? We still didn't have a male lead. Then we suffered another setback. Astonishingly enough, Goebbels, who so greatly disliked Pabst, made him a generous offer to do two major features, which were actually to be subsidized by the Ministry of Propaganda: namely, *Actors* with Käthe Dorsch and *Paracelsus* with two great stars, Werner Krauss and Harald Kreutzberg. I didn't have the heart to hinder this wonderful opportunity, and Pabst was grateful to me, but I was once again without a director. Then I remembered Mathias Wieman, Pabst's partner in *The Blue Light*. After that project he had demonstrated his directorial talent in his production of *Faust* at the Deutsches Schauspielhaus in Hamburg.

In the midst of these drawn-out preparations, I received a telephone call from Veit Harlan, who asked if we could meet, though I didn't know him personally. Throughout his visit he was very nervous and apparently depressed, but coming at last to the point, he said, 'You have to help me, Fräulein Riefenstahl – you're my last hope.' Then he told me that Goebbels wanted him to do an anti-Semitic film *Jud Süss*. He said he had tried everything to get out of it, even volunteering for combat, but Goebbels had called his efforts sabotage and ordered him to make the picture.

I felt sorry for Harlan, for I knew Goebbels all too well and realized that there was no possibility of opposing him, especially now, during the war, so I had to disappoint him. I couldn't fulfil the hopes he had pinned on me, being the very last person who could have helped him with Goebbels. Yet Harlan was convinced that I had a friendly relationship with the minister and could influence him. He was incredulous when I told him about my own conflicts with Goebbels, but so desperate was he that he burst into tears. I tried to calm him and advised him to move to Switzerland. 'You mustn't make the film,' I urged him.

'They'll shoot me as a deserter and what will become of Kristina?' (He meant his wife.)

I have mentioned this conversation only because some time ago I saw a TV talk show about the film *Jud Süss* and about Veit Harlan, in which one of his colleagues scornfully alleged that Harlan had not been forced to make *Jud Süss*, but had done it purely out of careerism.

On 10 May 1940, the radio announced a special piece of news that had been feared for months: the war on the Western front we had been waiting in suspense for had begun. People now generally realized that there was no going back and, recalling World War I, everyone reckoned that the fighting would last for years; thus they were all the more surprised by, and enthusiastic about, the special Wehrmacht bulletins transmitted day by day: Holland surrendered just five days after the invasion; two weeks later, Belgium; and, though no one believed it possible, France, just seventeen days later. When the first German troops reached Paris on 14 June and the military report also announced the victorious end of the fighting in Norway, the bells rang in Germany for three days, and a sea of flags billowed from windows and rooftops. Berlin was delirious. According to the radio, thousands of people cheered Adolf Hitler in the streets, and I too wired him my congratulations. But everyone who believed in a speedy peace was mistaken. The fighting was not yet over.

Although the French had capitulated, Mussolini declared war on France and sent Italian troops into the South of France; hardly an impressive action.

In the shadow of these events, the *Tiefland* shooting, scheduled to be done in Spain, had to be relocated to Germany. Instead of the Pyrenees, we chose the Karwendel mountains. On the hilly meadows in Krün near Mittenwald, the mill, the citadel, and our film village Roccabruna were constructed in the style of their Spanish counterparts.

The first time I saw the sets I was shocked to find that the designers had made a calamitous mistake. They hadn't built the village according to the camera positions we had indicated. The houses stood so far apart that there was no way of getting a long shot of the village with the mountainous background. The sinfully expensive sets were unusable, but far worse than the waste of almost half a million marks was the loss of time. The six weeks it would take to re-do the sets were simply not available. It was almost July and the outdoor shooting had to be over and done with by the start of winter. Tobis, which had already signed preliminary contracts for twelve billion dollars for *Tiefland*, insisted that the film be completed.

Another problem was the tame wolf. Our efficient production manager was unable to find such an animal. We had inquired everywhere, and the answer was always the same: lions, bears, tigers and other animals can be trained, but not wolves. So we tried our luck with trained sheepdogs, but the rushes showed unmistakably that these were dogs and not wolves.

As I was driving along Kaiserallee with Rudolf Fichtner, my very despondent production manager, I saw a young man on the sidewalk with a wolf on a leash. I could not believe it at first but it was indeed a wolf. Fichtner went to ask the man whether it was really a tame wolf, and came back radiant, holding a business card: Dr Bernhard Grzimek, zoologist.

'Well,' I asked nervously, 'can we work with the wolf?'

'Maybe, but at the moment it's too dangerous. Herr Grzimek's wife is in the hospital; the wolf bit her! But he hopes he can tame it,' said Fichtner, sounding a bit less optimistic. 'We agreed to meet with Traut, our executive producer.'

Meanwhile we had sent for Franz Eichberger – our Pedro – who was taking elocution lessons at an acting school recommended by Frieda Richard. I was convinced that he was the only possible choice for the part. Our photographer, Rolf Lantin, took care of him, shielding him against the metropolitan life of Berlin. We were afraid he'd lose too much of his 'innocence' and then be unable to play his role convincingly.

While the village was being rebuilt in Krün, I went to the Dolomites to seek suitable locations. During the train trip from Mittenwald to Bolzano I had my compartment to myself until I became aware of someone staring at me. At first something prevented me from looking up, but when I did, I saw a man's face. The extraordinary thing was that for a fraction of an instant I had a vision, the second one in my life: two comets with gigantic tails sped towards me, collided and exploded. I was as terrified as if it had really happened, and it was only after a while, when I felt less upset, that I saw the same gaze still fixed on me. The stranger who stood in the corridor, pressing his forehead against the glass pane of the closed door, was an officer in a mountain infantry uniform, still young, perhaps in his early thirties, and with something cocky about his expression. His chiselled features were marked by scars, and I felt an unusually powerful attraction as well as fear, and I avoided his eyes. I tried to fall asleep and wipe the experience away, and when the train stopped at Innsbruck I noticed that the place where the man had been standing was empty.

In Ciampedi, in the Rose Garden area of the Dolomites, I found all the mountain locations that we needed. I also discovered an ideal spot for Pedro's hut; the setting of the fight with the wolf. Dr Grzimek had already agreed to help us, but the for the present we could start shooting without the wolf. It was a pleasure working with Eichberger, who surprised us by how natural he was in front of the camera.

After three weeks we stopped shooting in the Dolomites. The sets in Krün were ready, especially for the expensive long shot of the village with the countless extras which had to be done before winter came; but we couldn't start until mid-September, which was much too late.

Luck with the weather could help, but above all, we had to get the shots of the extras. My Sarentino farmers, who had done such a grand job in *The Blue Light* and looked very much like the north Spanish populace, were ready to pitch in again. In August, trying to increase the Spanish flavour, I had asked

Harald Reinl to hire gypsies – young men, girls and children – and he found them in Salzburg, picking them out at a nearby gypsy camp. After the war I was involved in all sorts of trials and, even as I write this, the matter is again the subject of litigation. Irresponsible journalists claimed that I had personally obtained the gypsies from a concentration camp and used them as 'slave labourers'. The truth is that the camp from where our gypsies were selected by Dr Reinl and Hugo Lehner, one of my production managers, was not a concentration camp at that time. I myself couldn't be there as I was location-hunting in the Dolomites. The gypsies, both adults and children, were our favourites, and we saw nearly all of them again after the war. They said then that working with us had been the loveliest time of their lives, though no one compelled them to make this statement.

While we were working in Krün, I had asked Dr Fanck to shoot the wolf sequences in the Dolomites with Dr Grzimek's help, and one month later I saw these rushes in a cinema in Mittenwald. Fanck had shot over thirty thousand feet, but I realized that, except for two takes, none of the footage was usable. Fanck, excessively cautious, had filmed the wolf from so great a distance that the wolf could just as easily have been a cat. I was aghast, but worse was yet to come.

A few days later our production manager cabled: 'Wolf dead, Grizmek desperate – must stop shooting.' We were at a loss, for Pedro's fight with the wolf was one of the main scenes in the picture. Dr Grzimek mourned his Genghis, as he called him; the animal, having eaten too greedily, had choked to death, and we had no choice but to find a new wolf.

Meanwhile, 'Roccabruna' had become such a tourist attraction that more and more visitors disrupted our work. Also, valuable props, such as cast-iron lamps, grates and old jugs that the art directors had brought from Spain were stolen from the village; like it or not, we had to ask for police protection.

When we awoke one morning, snow lay on the mountains, but luckily it soon melted during a warm spell. Another surprise was that when our Sarentino peasants showed up for the filming, they were unrecognizable; their splendid beards had been shaved off, and they revelled in our dismay. The peasants didn't plan to spend much time in Krün, for they wanted to help bring in the harvest at home. We had promised they could do so, but we had suffered delays as a result of the long period of foul weather, and since we wouldn't hear of their leaving, they had hatched this trick. However, they underestimated our production manager, who had the make-up man paste new beards on their faces. I felt sorry for them and let most of them go, but begged them to send us other peasants. As a result, we got twice the number we needed.

We had to dig up a horse for a riding scene and a stand-in for Minetti, who couldn't get out of his stage obligations. Our production manager had already paved the way, and all I had to do personally was to thank General Dietl, the commander of Narvik, who was making mounts and riders available to us. When I arrived outside the barracks in Mittenwald, a dark, spirited horse was standing there, its reins held by an officer who was to replace Minetti in the riding scenes, and he was the man who had stared at me for such a long time in the train. As before, he wore a casually hanging cloak, his cap was askew, and again his expression looked raffish. I shook hands without hinting at what was going on inside me, nor did he reveal in any way that we had already met; after a few cordial words I said goodbye.

Was that encounter a mere coincidence? Somehow I felt danger heading towards me, and I wanted to do whatever I could to keep out of that man's way; I would do anything to avoid what I had experienced eleven years ago, when Hans Schneeberger had left me. I had sworn as much to myself at that time. Before filming the riding scenes, I learned more about the officer. His name was Peter Jacob, he was a first lieutenant in the mountain infantry, a soldier in an army of one hundred thousand men, who had been on active service from the very first day of the war. He had been awarded the Iron Cross in the French campaign and, after being slightly wounded, he was spending his leave in Mittenwald.

Although Peter Jacob was not yet needed for the shooting, he came by every day, but I never exchanged a single word with him. When he started joining us for dinner in the hotel and sought contact with our crew, I had my meal brought up to my room and stopped going down to the restaurant. When my crew noticed my absences, they assumed that I didn't like the young man; quite the contrary, I was fleeing him; but I couldn't avoid him for long. From a distance the officer, in Minetti's costume, looked like his twin brother. The script called for my sitting behind him on the horse, a scene which had to be rehearsed over and over. The horse, unnerved by all the people, often began to rear, and I was happy when these rushes were finally completed.

I believed I would no longer see the young officer, but I was quite wrong, for he remained nearby, even though the riding sequences were done, becoming friendly with several members of my crew and joining them in our hotel every evening. When I learned that he had even rented a room in our hotel I was angry. His pushiness merely increased my resistance.

Mariechen, my maid, was supposed to take care of the film wardrobe near my room on the second floor, and when one day I came up to change clothes after the shooting, she put her finger to her lips and pointed to the couch where First Lieutenant Jacob, in full uniform, appeared to be asleep. Mariechen whispered that she had given him headache pills. I took away my clothes in order to change in my room, while the girl brought me a bottle of mineral water and departed to her room in a different building.

There was a knock at the door, and when I asked who was there, I got no answer. The knocking grew louder, and still there was no response; then it turned into an ear-splitting pounding. Indignant, I opened the door a crack. Peter Jacob stood there. He shoved his boot into the crack, pushed through the door, closed it – and achieved his purpose after some fierce resistance on my part. Never had I known such passion, never had I been loved so intensely. This experience was so profound that in a way it changed my life. It was the beginning of a great love, and when Peter Jacob's leave ended it was like separating forever.

We still hadn't finished the shooting when winter came for good, and we had no choice but to postpone the outdoor filming until next summer in Krün. This would not only be expensive, but would involve a lot of other problems. For instance, no one had costed the winter storage fees for the huge set. Above all, however, the schedules of the actors caused as much anxiety. Most of them were in Gründgens' company and after drawn-out negotiations he agreed to release them only for the subsequent studio shooting.

At the studios in Babelsberg the art directors Grave and Isabella Ploberger outdid themselves with their sets, which were thrilling. The interior court of the citadel was particularly impressive. It looked so authentic that you could have believed you were really in the Alhambra. As we were doing a lighting test on the first shooting day, a message came from the Ministry of Propaganda, ordering us to clear out of the sound stages which were needed for two films essential to the war effort: *Uncle Krüger* and *The Old and the Young King*.

Could there be some mistake? It seemed sheer madness to strike these expensive sets before even one frame was shot. I immediately tried to reach Goebbels, but was unable to get an appointment, and was simply and firmly told that the sound stages we had rented were to be vacated immediately at the personal orders of the minister. The written directive was sent by Dr Fritz Hippler, head of the Reich cinema division. The expensive sets had to be torn down with not a word about compensation. It was outrageous – the revenge of the Ministry of Propaganda and its lord and master, who had told me to make a film about the Siegfried Line after the completion of the Polish campaign. I had refused.

I was so upset that I fell ill. My chronic complaint, which had begun during my mountain films, started up again. Previously I had always responded to treatment, but not this time. My nerves were too shaken and I ended up in the hospital. Professor Kielleuthner, a top urologist, was discouraging, he robbed me of any hope of a cure. 'Your complaint is too far gone,' he said, 'not even an operation could help.' I asked if I could stay in his clinic, but he said it wouldn't do any good: I'd be better off in the mountains than in a sick-room. I received some painkillers and then continued my trip to Kitzbühel.

Fortunately the medical predictions came true: the healthy mountain air really helped. My pains subsided, and after a while I could get up and take short strolls. Then I had some good news. Peter wrote that he would get Christmas leave before returning to combat and wanted to take some holiday with me in Kitzbühel. Again I felt terribly uneasy, but I was still sure I could control my feelings. I kept re-reading his letters, of which I sometimes got several a day. They had an almost magical effect on me, radiating as they did such powerful and genuine emotions.

Nevertheless, the holiday we had been looking forward to so greatly did not make us happy. Tensions arose incomprehensibly – out of nothing; and they grew; yet there was no doubt about the intensity of our emotions. The arguments constantly alternated with happy periods. Something was wrong, and I didn't know what. The days that we spent in the mountain cottage on the Hahnenkamm were very disturbing. Peter's feelings were as explosive as a volcano, which both attracted and repelled me.

Then he returned to his division and I to Berlin, where Waldi Traut had succeeded in renting a small studio in Babelsberg. Within days my illness recurred – one colic followed another and, since I could stand neither morphine nor other painkillers I was at the mercy of these attacks. My staff were desperate, for once again we were faced with the choice of cancelling *Tiefland* altogether or re-scheduling the shooting. It had taken such a tremendous effort to find a studio, and Gründgens had released Bernhard Minetti once again, so I refused to give up. I was kept artificially in working condition with camphor injections, intravenous injections, novalgin, and all kinds of medicaments to build me up. I was swathed in warm blankets, and hot-water bottles were tied all around me. In this way I could at least continue directing. But I couldn't perform. Benitz, my cameraman, was at his wits' end. Soft-focus lenses and veils didn't help; the pain would have marked my face too sharply. I managed to direct a few major scenes, but by then I was at the end of my tether. Again I landed in the hospital, hoping to be cured. The doctors advised me to take peat baths in Bad Elster, which did no good at all. Professor Kielleuthner wanted to re-examine me but until they had a vacant bed in his clinic I stayed at the Rheinischer Hof across from the main railway station. There I was surprised to receive an unusual visitor: Hitler, whom I hadn't seen since Danzig. His housekeeper, Frau Winter, had told him about my sickness and my sojourn in Munich. Hitler was *en route* to Vienna where he said he would be signing the Three Powers Pact with Yugoslavia.

'What mischief are you up to!' he said, after handing me flowers. He spoke encouraging words and offered to have me treated by his physician, Dr Morell. I was in no condition to register everything he spoke about, and only a few things have stuck in my mind. I recall that he said he planned to retire from politics as soon as the war was over, but that he was greatly worried about the problem of finding a successor.

'None of my men,' he said, 'is capable of taking over the leadership, so this task would have to be performed by a committee made up of members of my operations staff.' He mentioned no names. I was speechless when he said he planned to invite me to the Berghof after the war and co-author screenplays with me. At first I thought he was joking, but he was quite serious, and went into detail about how important good films are. 'If they are brilliantly done, motion pictures could change the world. He enthused about a topic that seemed very close to his heart – the history of the Catholic Church, almost going into ecstasies when he talked about this subject.

'It would be fantastic,' he said, 'if today we could see films from the past, films about Frederick the Great, Napoleon, and great historic events.' Breaking off, he appeared reflective. Then he went on, 'Once you are healthy, Fräulein Riefenstahl, you could do me a great service. Please contact the Kaiser Wilhelm Institute in Berlin and discuss the problem with outstanding scientists and scholars. I could imagine a film stock made of the finest metal, which would not be altered by time or weather and could hold out for centuries. Just imagine what would happen if, a thousand years from now, people could see what we have experienced in this era.' Hitler talked as if the war was already over and we were living in peace again. When he left, the optimism he displayed did not fail to have its effect on me.

I spent the next few days at the Josephinum, a private clinic in Munich, where Catholic nuns took loving care of me. The medical findings were depressing and I had no choice but to withdraw once again with many packages of teas and medicaments to the mountain cottage on the Hahnenkamm, where my disease worsened day by day. The attacks kept recurring and the pain was often unendurable. At this point someone recommended a homoeopathic physician in Munich. When he visited me I scarcely imagined that he could help me; he looked so run-of-the-mill. A short man with a roundish face, he could just as easily have been a baker or an innkeeper. I was wrong, however. First impressions are not always correct.

Briefly diagnosing me just by looking, he determined my illness precisely and suggested acupuncture, to which I at once agreed. When I saw the long needles that he wanted to insert deep into my body, I felt dizzy, but oddly enough it was almost painless. Then he rubbed homoeopathic substances into the veins of my arm, and miraculously the pains went away.

I was still free of pain the next morning, and those past few months seemed like a bad dream. For a total cure I ought to have continued Herr Reuter's treatment in Munich for another three months. Incidentally I did not realize at the time that he was also one of Rudolf Hess's doctors. Recklessly, however, I left Munich, and when the colics stopped, I returned to Berlin. I have often regretted it.

The first night I spent in my home, there was a terrible air-raid on Berlin. At first I watched the countless searchlights sweeping the sky like ghostly caressing hands, and the red and yellow of the rockets illuminating the darkness. But then I pulled my head back in, for a dreadful roaring began as if the flak were surrounding my home – the noise was appalling. My house quaked. I believed I could get used to it all, but I was mistaken, for the attacks grew increasingly violent, and more and more people died under the rubble.

The war at the front was also going badly. I read a newspaper story about the mountain infantry in Greece which had been marching for days, through pouring rain, along narrow softened roads and fighting all the while. Was Peter among them or was he no longer alive? I hadn't had a sign of life from him for eighteen days. Luckily, my fears were groundless, for one day I heard his name on the radio. He had been awarded the Knight's Cross for outstanding bravery when the Germans broke through the Metaxes Line. Now that I knew he was alive and had survived all dangers, I firmly believed I was his guardian angel. Our long separation deepened our feelings and overcame arguments and disharmony.

My health had improved after my treatment by the homoeopath, for once I began using his medicaments the attacks stopped. Then I received a letter from Peter. He asked me for the first time whether I would be willing to get married. His question didn't surprise me, but I hadn't thought about it, since I viewed marriage as only a secondary form of living together. I felt it was far more essential for two people to love one another enough to spend an entire life together in harmony. I didn't doubt the harmony of our love, only its strength. Nevertheless, at this point, I was ready to become Peter's wife. Circumstances wouldn't allow it, however, for Peter was about to return to the front, and I had to complete *Tiefland*.

Then the radio reported the sensational news of Rudolf Hess's flight to Scotland. Anxious as I was to learn more about it, I couldn't ask Hitler's adjutants in time of war, but I could ask Frau Winter, the Führer's housekeeper in Munich. She said Hitler had been so beside himself with frustration and anger that he had absolutely raged. I was and still am convinced that Hitler knew nothing about Hess's plans. From a personal conversation with Hess prior to my European tour, I knew how he suffered from what he considered to be a thankless job. As 'deputy Führer' he had to settle all the disagreements and quarrels among Party men and was not satisfied by this chiefly bureaucatic work. Unlike Göring, Goebbels or Ribbentrop, he had not been given a specific assignment. He would, for example, have loved to become foreign minister, and he considered himself capable of that position, not caring very much for Herr Ribbentrop's performance. I could therefore well imagine that Hess wanted to prove his value to the Führer by a courageous mission that would help to bring peace.

Meanwhile a sound stage had become available, and G.W. Pabst had also completed his obligations, so he was my only hope. Then, on the very first day I sensed that he was not the same man as twelve years earlier, when we had worked together so ideally on *Piz Palü*. His personality had changed. Previously he had radiated warmth and enthusiasm; now he seemed dour, almost cold, and nothing was left of his excellent eyes. Obviously Hollywood hadn't agreed with him; his present approach was a routine more consistent with run-of-the-mill commercial movies and I tried in vain to discover traces of his once pronounced originality.

Tensions arose, making our work increasingly difficult, almost impossible. I suffered so badly from his despotic direction that I could barely perform, and our collaboration became more and more intolerable. I saw no other solution than for us to go our separate ways, but at this point, fortunately, Pabst was summoned to make another picture for Goebbels, his new patron.

Now, along with the job of performing, I also had to direct our film, which went more easily than I thought. The rushes came out exactly as I had envisaged them. My crew livened up, and the oppressive atmosphere gave way to more pleasant working conditions. Then, shortly before the completion of the studio shooting, I was again afflicted by violent colic, and again another director had to be hired. Fortunately, we got Arthur Maria

Rabenalt, who was the antithesis of Pabst; extremely empathetic, calm, almost gentle, he handled even such a difficult actor as Minetti with a smile. Working with Rabenalt was an important experience for me. I learned a lot from him, especially with regard to handling actors. Alas, our indoor shooting was interrupted once again. The huge sound stage required for our citadel set was not available.

Before we left for Krün, Berlin suffered a heavy aerial attack, and within a few days the British returned to renew the assault. The bombings grew more and more violent.

Then I had a delightful surprise – a telegram announcing that Peter had been granted leave which neither of us had counted on. It was a reward for his participation in the heavy fighting in Greece and his successful raid, for which he had been awarded the Knight's Cross; but above all, it was because he was being transferred to the north coast of Russia, near Murmansk. Once again, however, it was not the holiday together that we had been yearning for. I was unable to get out of my commitments as producer, director and performer; it was too much. During those days I cursed the film. Peter was very understanding about my work, but we had to make great sacrifices for our love. And then, sure as fate, came the day that separated us, like so many hundreds of thousands of other people, for an indefinite length of time and with no certainty of our ever meeting again. We parted as two people who had experienced a great deepening of their love in those few short weeks.

Work was the best solace. We were about to shoot the wolf scenes in the Dolomites, for which in desperation we had borrowed an untamed wolf from the Leipzig Zoo, a huge, wild-looking creature. We were all anxious to see how he would behave in front of the camera, but the animal proved to be too tame. No matter what we did he wouldn't bare his teeth; he was as gentle as a lamb. And then one morning his cage was empty; he had vanished. The wolf had dug a tunnel through the stony ground. It was quite a predicament for, gentle as he had been with us, hunger could make him dangerous. A search began, but we were soon informed that the wolf couldn't be caught and had been shot dead.

Tiefland without a wolf was out of the question; yet we could not cancel the film. Seeking help, we turned to Grzimek again, who laconically recommended that we wait one year, until Katya, his young wolf had grown up.

The *Tiefland* saga was by no means over.

PETER AND I

In Berlin I once again experienced the war first-hand. The RAF raids had inflicted great damage, but people still went about their work even though train rails were ripped up and they had to walk long distances to their jobs. However, my house, which I loved so much, was still unscathed, and even before I started unpacking I locked myself in my bedroom in order to read undisturbed, for I had found a huge bundle of mail from the front. Since our parting in Mittenwald I hadn't heard a thing from Peter. I had not arranged to have his letters forwarded, since I was so terrified that they would be lost.

Peter's letters were wonderful therapy for me. They exerted such a powerful effect that they always managed to dispel my fear that we could lose one another. In September 1941 he wrote:

Dearest, dearest Leni,

Now I have been at sea again for a week, and I am painfully aware of how awful it is for me when I cannot communicate with you. You know, Leni, during the many hours when I am all alone and see only the vast ocean, I often think about the two of us and our life together, and I always come in the end to the realization that if I were to die on this mission or in this war I will have had an unfulfilled life . . . You know I do not fear death, but now that I have you, I have developed a fanatical will to live. Everything must turn out all right. Some day I would like to tell you how much I love you, but all the languages in the world would not suffice. I know you feel everything, and I can only keep telling you over and over that I am all yours.

Your loving Peter

There was never a word about the quarrels that had darkened our time together; only love spoke from his lines, and I never doubted that his feelings were genuine, as I read one letter after the other. In them he described his combat missions, the battles with the Russians; how everything was progressing as planned. He said that the mood of his men was excellent despite the enormous physical demands. 'Now and then meagre news trickles through from other parts of the front, and of course we wait for it anxiously – not quite as anxiously as for the army mail, which at present is treating me poorly . . .'

A few days later he wrote: 'Today, I have a day off. I'm sitting in a so-called ground bunker; in plain language, this is a big hole in the ground, covered with birch trunks and a top layer of soil. Unfortunately I've had no mail from you: I only hope that nothing has happened to you. I'm on the move day and night, and sometimes I don't even know when I'll get a chance to sleep for a couple of hours . . .'

Two days later: 'The worst of it is that I'm not hearing from you. If only I could get some mail so that I could know where you are. I expect I'll be having a few hard days, starting tomorrow, and I may not be able to write. Are you still with me as my guardian angel?'

Another letter: 'I haven't been able to write you for five days. I've been on the move night after night, and then in the morning I came back bruised and frozen to my ground bunker, which seems to me like a *de luxe* hotel. Then I fall into a death-like sleep. Tomorrow I'm going forward again, perhaps you will write before that.'

Two days later I received a further letter, which touched me deeply: 'My dear little guardian angel, you protected me again the day before yesterday.' While reading these lines I recalled a strange experience that I had noted in my diary. It took place on 29 October, the day on which Peter had called me his guardian angel. While writing to him I suddenly felt nervous and terribly frightened. As if in a dream I saw two Russians leaning over Peter, who lay on the ground; they were trying to kill him with their rifle butts. During this vision I heard a noise – a large cactus blossom had broken off and dropped to the floor. When I told Peter about this several months later, it turned out that he had been in mortal danger at the very time that I had had that vision and the blossom had fallen. He had been fighting for his life against two Russians who had attacked him.

UDET'S LAST TELEPHONE CALL

One morning the telephone woke me out of a very deep sleep.

'You're still asleep,' I heard a familiar voice from far away.

'Who is it?' I asked drowsily.

'It's me – Erni. Don't you recognize my voice?'

'Udet,' I exclaimed, growing more alert, 'what's wrong, why are you calling me at such an ungodly hour? What is it?'

'Nothing special, I just wanted to hear your voice again.'

'What do you mean?' I asked uneasily.

'Goodbye, Leni, get some sleep,' he said quietly, and the conversation was over.

Just a few hours later I heard on the radio that Colonel General Ernst

Udet had had a fatal accident while testing a new weapon. Horrified, I understood why he had called me. It was a farewell forever. Despair must have driven him to suicide. I remembered several converstations with him which hinted that he saw no other way out. One of the countless victims of that dreadful war, he was a wonderful friend whom we all loved. Only those closest to him knew that Udet had taken his own life, by shooting himself in his Berlin apartment.

Although I hadn't met Udet so very often during the past few years, our friendship had remained unchanged, and he had discussed his problems with me several times. He had especially complained that he could never see Hitler alone in order to discuss the level of production for the Luftwaffe and the difficulties involved. Göring was alway present, and Udet said that Göring never gave Hitler the true facts about output figures; he always juggled with higher numbers than were actually produced. Göring, Udet explained to me, had contrived to deceive Hitler, and the consequences could be devastating. Udet was powerless against Göring and, as he admitted to me, his honour as an officer prevented him from approaching Hitler on his own. I myself had no image of Göring, since, during the twelve years of the Third Reich, I had spoken to him only once, after my visit to Mussolini, when Göring had asked to see me.

Udet must have suffered greatly because of that situation. In earlier times we had known him only as a cheerful man, bubbling with life; but later he had changed greatly; he had become serious, and his famous sense of humour now seemed an unconvincing front. Among his friends he had made no bones about the fact that his appointment as a 'general aircraft master' had not made him very happy. Udet was anything but a pen-pusher and was only forty-five when he shot himself. We were deeply shaken by his death and the circumstances surrounding it.

Carl Zuckmayer caught Udet's character accurately in his play *The Devil's General*, but the motives he comes up with for Udet's suicide are pure fancy. Udet was not, as Zuckmayer shows him, a victim of the Gestapo; and it is also wrong to present him as an opponent of Hitler. By no means was he one of Hitler's uncritical admirers, but, as Udet himself told me, he greatly respected the Führer. Udet deserved to have an important writer like Zuckmayer come up with a more realistic portrayal of his tragedy.

A BAD DREAM

The war was devouring more and more. German troops had already occupied vast portions of Europe. They were shelling Leningrad and, having advanced all the way to the Crimean Peninsula, they were now eighteen miles from the centre of Moscow. In Asia, the Japanese were battling with the Americans and the British in a theatre of operations which reached from Singapore to Hong Kong and Borneo. In North Africa, Rommel's army was fighting the British. The war had turned into a gigantic prairie fire blazing across the entire globe.

In Germany we experienced the hardships of war more and more intensely. We suffered not only incessant air-raids with sirens howling their warnings and all-clears night after night, but also the utter darkening of the entire country, the rationing of food, and of anything and everything that human beings need to survive. Nevertheless, stage performances and film premières still took place; though I never attended them. I had withdrawn from everything, including my friends. My thoughts and feelings were focused exclusively on Peter and his fate. I neglected the people around me; I seldom communicated with my parents, although they meant so much to me, and I adored my mother. I had little contact with my brother, even though we had been close since childhood. My only obligation was to finish the *Tiefland* film. My illness seemed cured, and so, since the script called for me, as a gypsy girl, to do Spanish dances, I could finally start practising the choreography with Harald Kreutzberg, who ran a dance studio in Seefeld. As a dancer, I found working with Kreutzberg a wonderful experience.

During this period I was troubled by a bad dream in which a telepathic anxiety vision conjured up the horrors of war again. I saw surrealistic images of snow, ice and human bodies, disintegrating and then re-assembling like a jigsaw puzzle. I saw an ocean of crosses on white cemeteries and death masks covered with layers of ice. The images became fuzzy and then sharp again; sometimes they were close, sometimes remote, as if photographed from a wobbling aeroplane. Then I thought I heard a dreadful shriek. Hours after I awoke the radio reported that the German advance in Russia had been halted by a sudden onset of Siberian cold, which had claimed many lives. This news gave me an eerie feeling. There was obviously a psychic relationship between my dream and the tragedy in Russia. Even though I had supernatural experiences earlier, I have never been able to forget these visions of horror in my dream.

When the press and the radio announced that Hitler had dismissed several of his generals, appointed himself commander-in-chief of the army, and declared war on the United States, I no longer believed in a German victory. More had happened than the onset of Siberian cold, which brought untold suffering to the Germans fighting in Russia. The profound confidence that the Wehrmacht had placed in Hitler as the victorious commander was shattered. His order to hold the front by Moscow in that Arctic cold, despite the tremendous losses of lives and equipment, triggered protests and distrust among several generals and numerous soldiers. Thus the winter cold that began in Russia on 5 December 1941 could have been the indirect cause of the subsequent débâcles.

THE YEAR 1942

In December Peter paid me a surprise visit. His rheumatism was cured, and after his release from the field hospital his commander had ordered him to perform some important courier services in Germany. In fact his recall to the front line was delayed over and over again, so we were able to spend a few weeks together, and for the first time there were no scenes or arguments. I was very happy. But it was all the harder to say goodbye when Peter had to return to the Russian front. We couldn't bear to part. Peter kept tearing himself away, only to come back, hug me tighter – and then finally, dash out of the house without looking back.

He returned three days later. 'The Arctic Ocean is frozen,' he said, 'the ships are stuck. We have to wait until ice channels allow them to leave.' So our painful farewell ceremony was repeated several times. By the last farewell – 24 January 1942, according to my diary – our nerves were shattered. Peter was going to telephone me from Sassnitz before the ships left port.

I waited in vain. No call – no telegram – no letter. I waited for two days – three days – four days, so unnerved that I couldn't sleep, and after getting no news for nine days, I went to pieces. I was afraid that Peter was no longer alive; perhaps his ship had gone down or hit a mine. Even in the heaviest fighting and from the most remote places, Peter had always managed to transmit messages to me or to notify me of his whereabouts via special couriers.

In my despair I tried to find out the location of his ship from Wehrmacht headquarters; but to no avail. Then I turned to the mountain infantry in Mittenwald. After several telephone calls I learned from an officer that the ships still hadn't put out; they were anchored in the harbour. I was flabbergasted. Where was Peter? I thought I'd lose my mind. Then I received a call from a friend of Peter's.

'I heard that you'd like to know the whereabouts of Peter Jacob,' he said.

'Yes,' I said holding my breath.

'I was with him just a few days ago and we talked about you.'

'You were with him?' I stammered.

'Yes,' he said in his rather booming voice, 'we got plastered; we took a few drops of Dutch courage.'

'Where is he now?' I asked.

'He must be in Berlin.'

'Yes, in Berlin. He's been staying at the Eden Hotel for the past week, with a very beautiful woman, whom you probably know.' I felt faint, the receiver slipped from my hands and I lay on my bed, numb.

At dawn the phone rang again. I didn't want to speak to anyone but it kept on ringing. Finally I picked up the receiver and heard a voice from far away – Peter's voice. I thought my heart would burst. 'Leni, can you hear me?'

'Peter? It's you – where are you?' The connection was so bad that I could hear almost nothing. 'I'm in Sassnitz; I'm still here and we're sailing in a few hours, so please come; I have to see you before I leave.'

'Impossible – I can't come,' I said in despair.

'Come, you have to come. I can't leave until I explain everything.' I was so upset I couldn't talk. 'Leni, can't you hear me? Please, please, come!' his voice was hoarse and it sounded desperate. 'If you hop into your car right now we can still see each other; the ships will wait. I'll keep them from sailing before you arrive – you have to come!'

'I'll try,' I said.

After that conversation I felt as if a great weight had dropped from my shoulders. I had only one wish: to see Peter before he left for the front and to find out what had impelled him to deceive me in that incomprehensible way.

I couldn't get out of Berlin until that afternoon, when I finally took off in my little Fiat with two members of my crew. It had taken us hours to find the necessary petrol and I was almost crazy with fear that I wouldn't ever see Peter.

The day was icy, it was snowing, and driving became more and more difficult; I could barely see through the windscreen. Worst of all, darkness was setting in far too early, and within a few hours the snow had piled up so high that we only crawled along, and finally got stuck. Traut wanted to go for help while I waited in the car, but I couldn't be stopped; and so we trudged through the blizzard and the pitch-black night. Sometimes we sank into the snow up to our bellies. At midnight we reached the docks of

Sassnitz. In the total blackout nothing could be seen, but luckily we had a small dimmed torch. The harbour was deathly still with no one in sight. The storm had died down and it had stopped snowing. Now and then the clouds parted and in the moonlight, on the docks, near the water, I sighted the silhouette of a man. As we approached him he moved and started towards us. It was Peter. He clasped me in his arms and stammered: 'Leni, Leni . . .'

Waldi Traut had managed to find us a room for the night in a small hotel, where at last I was alone with Peter and learned how he had been able to delay the sailing of the ships. He had told the captain he was waiting for an important courier mail from Berlin, which he had to take along. We had only a few hours left until our final parting, but tenderness was not our sole concern. I wanted to find out everything from him, and I hoped he would tell me the truth. I was willing to forgive if I could only understand. 'How could you possibly spend ten days only a few minutes away from me, living with a woman, and make me believe that you had started out long ago, to the front line?' Peter denied it; not that he had stayed at the Eden, he couldn't deny that, but he wouldn't admit that he'd been living with a woman. I was ready to forgive, but I wanted to understand his behaviour. I begged him to tell me the truth. 'We can't encumber each other with such lies. It would be terrible if I couldn't trust you any more. It would destroy my love.'

Peter held me tight, ran his hands over my cheeks, looked into my eyes, and said, 'My dearest, how could you possibly imagine that I could do such a thing – deceive you? That would make me a scoundrel, and I wouldn't deserve your love. I wouldn't be capable of such base conduct.' And he pleaded with me not to believe anything I heard from other people.

I looked at him and I knew he was lying. Perhaps I should have been generous enough not to ask, not to want to know anything, but I didn't have the strength. 'Peter,' I said in despair, 'you're not telling me the truth.'

'How can you think me capable of such actions?' he asked. 'I swear to you on my mother's life, I was not living with a woman; I did not touch any woman or think of any woman. You're a silly, jealous girl!' We parted at dawn, and I watched as he stood on the dock, waving for a long time. With one hand he tossed coins into the air, catching them with a playful gesture, but something had shattered inside me.

During the trip home I was attacked by colic with an unbearable intensity, such as I had never known; yet stronger than my physical pains was my emotional suffering. In Berlin I was taken to the hospital, where I was given injections and painkillers, but nothing helped; I couldn't sleep.

As my mother and my brother told me later, I was in a kind of delirium; I rejected everything – even food – and they were at their wits' end; they took me to see Professor Johannes H. Schultz, who was famous throughout Germany for his relaxation through self-hypnosis. But he couldn't help either. He kept telling me: 'You can be cured only if you separate from that man.' I protested that with love one can do anything – even change another human being. But he disagreed. 'That man will never change, he will always remain as he is.' And he warned me, 'If you do not break off with him, you will remain in constant danger. It is as if a brick could unexpectedly fall on your head while you were taking a walk.'

I couldn't stand it any more. I began disliking Professor Schultz, and stopped my treatment. Despite everything I was still too strongly attached to Peter.

Now came a period of passivity and depression. I was sent to the mountains – the mountains which had so often brought me healing. One day, in Zürs, I found an army letter lying on my breakfast tray . . . the first sign of life from Peter. I had been feverishly longing for a letter, but now, as it lay in front of me, I didn't have the courage to open it. According to the postmark it had been *en route* for several weeks. I held out until that evening; then I read it:

Dearest, dearest Leni,

I spoke to you just two days ago, and now I feel such profound longing for you, as if we had been separated for weeks and months . . . I firmly believe that I can be with you again soon, and we could then remain together for always. You too must have the solid faith that destiny is on our side, consistent with the depth of our love. Earlier I was never able to believe in providence, but your love has filled me with a profound belief in an Omnipotence . . .

His letter raised a storm of mixed emotions in me. Could a man write like that after what had happened? My instinct for self-preservation told me to break off with him, but his words affected me like a drug. Wasn't the war to blame for everything? Yet jealousy was stronger than reason.

LETTERS FROM THE FRONT

After that Peter wrote to me regularly and I was shaken by his letters, since they left no doubt that he had been thoroughly transformed by his overwhelming experiences in action. I shall quote some of them; otherwise my subsequent life and sufferings with Peter would be incomprehensible.

2 March 1942

... Tonight, three hours ago, I finally received your letter and I am deeply shaken by the suffering I have caused you. My dear little Leni, you mustn't suffer any more, do you hear? You're the only woman I've ever loved, for I am part of you – inextricably bound up with you. Perhaps it is our destiny that we must both suffer before we can attain the peak of our happiness. I can feel in my own soul what you are going through and I am torn apart and miserable, for I am so afraid of losing you. You must be able to tell from my letters that I belong completely to you alone; nothing has ever come between us, believe me. And I firmly believe that not even a spark of distrust can ever come between us again ... At the moment, when my life is at crisis point, you know why I want to go on living, you and you alone are the reason.... I was so confused by all the unhappiness that came about from those ten days that I cannot tell you and express everything as I felt it ... And you know, Leni, that I need you a lot more than you need me ... I'm sure you feel and you know that you have never lost me and can never lose me, except through death.

13 March 1942

Today, when I returned, I again found no letter from you. I don't even know whether you'll write at all, and I mustn't think about it; I'm in a state that doesn't fit in with my responsibility here. You know what it would do to me if I lost you, and the thought that you no longer love me is gradually becoming a dreadful certainty ... Since you are so well informed about the ten days, I cannot assume that there could still be anything between us. You do know, Leni, that I did not and do not love you any less for even a minute ...

9 April 1942

Yesterday I returned from an important mission in which everything went well. I then immediately visited several wounded men and returned to my battalion command post early this morning. Unfortunately I again received no mail from you and this eternal waiting and the subsequent disappointment are almost unendurable. We are on the move a lot now, so that there is a possibility that I may not write to you for a couple of days. But there's no cause for alarm ... Dear Leni, don't you know or don't you feel that you're torturing me with your silence? But I'll put up with anything so long as you're healthy again – everything then is sure to turn out for the best. I will always be yours forever and ever ...

20 April 1942

I last wrote to you ten days ago, several hours before a mission . . . I've got ten heavy days behind me with my battalion, and now I've been taken out for six days for rest and recuperation after we bore the brunt of the fighting here. I'm so worn out that I can't even scrape off the filth of ten days before getting twenty-four hours of sleep. I have to write to you quickly so that you won't worry. This time, my dear, dear guardian angel, you were terribly necessary. But now it's over and I don't want to think about it any more . . . But I do know one thing: I'm sure that no human being has ever loved as much as I love you.

22 April 1942

Now I've slept soundly for thirty hours and feel fit again. We had fairly hard fighting for the last two weeks, but one doesn't realize it until later; after all, while you're in it you're so tense and concentrated that you can't even feel the stress of battle. I believe that this is one of the last desperate attempts of the Russians to break through in my sector, and they have had to pay for it with heavy casualties. Naturally we've also had our share of losses, and I have been withdrawn now with my battalion to our original position. I've been replaced by – of all people – my only friend, Captain Meyer, with his battalion. I hope however that I can replace him in a few days. Now the spring is starting to come here too very timidly; the reindeer moss, the only vegetation, is starting to peep out here and there on the boulders. The light is also very quickly undergoing a marked change . . . I believe that each new life-and-death struggle matures us spiritually; and if I can ever again believe that you and I will be one as we used to be, that I won't lose you, then I'll be able to live without anxiety or disquiet, and everything will be fine. I have done a lot of thinking about the two of us and examined myself to see whether I can ever relapse into my old weakness, and I know today that this will never again be possible. Destiny and providence will decide whether I will return to you from this war or die in action. But in any event you have to know forever that in all my life I have loved only you and can love no on else.

25 April 1942

For several days now I've been flat on my back with my old rheumatism; I'm laid up now, all bundled up, at my command post, and I only hope that I can be reasonably fit again by the time the next attacks come. In my last letter I wrote to you that the spring is already making itself felt a little here too, but I was counting my chickens too soon, since snow has been falling here hard and fast. I understand it'll go on like this until June. This means that there's a lot less chance of joining you soon. I don't know how I can endure this constant separation from you any longer; it's all so difficult. If I didn't have Captain Meyer, I wouldn't even know how I could get through this. He always coaxes me as if I were a sick horse, and he has proved to be a friend in a million. I very much hope that you've recovered your vitality and that joy and success is in store for you. You're going to Spain this summer, and from here in the tundra, I'll be with you in spirit wherever you go and wherever you work. If only I could really be with you again very soon, but perhaps this frustration and the impossibility of being granted my only wish and my entire hope are my punishment. I often wonder whether we can forget all the ugliness and rebuild our life together from the beginning . . .

6 May 1942

Nowadays I can only write to you briefly, since both my hands are packed in cotton, and the bandages are removed only in the morning for washing. I can get up for only a couple of minutes when my bed is being made, and I will use the time as often as possible in order to write to you. Unfortunately there has been no improvement, and I don't know when I'll be getting out of here. We've had cold weather and blizzards again. I hope I'll get through this soon, for I'm living in a state of nerve-wracking anxiety. Everything is coming together at once, the heavy fighting and attacks, in which I cannot take part even though I am urgently needed. Most of all, there are my great worries about you. Today, when the roads are partly negotiable, another three hundred wounded men are expected here, and I hope Meyer is among them; it would be unbearable to think that something has happened to him because he replaced me. If everything goes well, I'll try and make sure that he no longer has to go to the front lines . . .

13 May 1942

Yesterday Captain Meyer died in action. Now I'm all alone again. In him, one of our best and bravest has perished and his wife is now alone with the four children . . . Maybe he wouldn't have died if I hadn't fallen ill. This fact oppresses me all the more because he was my only friend – Leni, you are the only person whom I have and whom I need in order to go on living. Sooner or later this road of suffering and misunderstanding on which we travel must come to an end. I believe that I have passed through the ordeal of our life together to reach a better life . . . I know today that, despite my great love for you, I was not mature enough. After this dreadful experience, I do not believe that I will relapse in the future . . . You've made a new man out of me, and I can see now what is true and valuable in life. You are the fulfilment of a life that has previously been false and shallow. Do not leave me alone now, Leni, for I can be your helpmeet and the support that you need. I love you more than I can say . . .

25 June 1942

My Leni – today I venture for the first time to call you that again. A couple of hours ago your twentieth letter reached me and this is the first time in an eternity that I feel free and cheerful, now that I know you are determined to rebuild our life together from the beginning. You have given me a new lease on life. I have suffered terribly, and in my despair and hopelessness I believed your love had died; and that is the worst thing that fate could have in store for me. Today, after your letter, the heaviest burden of my life has been removed from me. In the past few days I met Division Commander Herr General von Hengl, and he told me that I could probably go on leave in late July. I want to beg Providence every day to make this, my greatest wish, come true again. I am desperately looking for an officer to stand in for me during my leave. In my new position as independent battalion commander I am answerable directly to the division, and thus have a greater responsibility. You can have a rough idea of my new position if you can imagine that I have occupied an area of three hundred square kilometres. I am now the most northern German commander . . . If only Schörner, who, incidentally, has become general of the mountain infantry, gives me permission for leave . . . Dearest, the fact that you still love me is the most beautiful gift that you gave me in your letter, and the knowledge that you can work again – let me experience it with you, for everything you do is of tremendous importance to me too now . . .

ENGAGEMENT

After my return from Zürs my health got worse. I was bedridden, I barely ate, and I lost twenty pounds. During this period Peter's letters were my only glimmers of light. I clung to his every word, drew hope from them for a new life together; but I could not snuff out the past completely, and I was haunted by tormenting images. Yet stronger than my jealousy was my fear of losing Peter. If several days passed without a letter, I panicked, always fearing the worst. I was a prisoner of my emotions.

Peter's last letter, in which he wrote about a possible leave, worked a miracle, I felt as if I were awakening from a state of coma. I started eating more, took walks and gradually blossomed, to the surprise of my doctor. Several weeks later I was even able to resume my work on *Tiefland*. The large studio in Babelsberg had become available. We filmed my Spanish dances there. Then we remade Pabst's unsuccessful scenes in such a good work atmosphere that we finished ahead of schedule. This meant that we had completed all the studio shooting aside from the final take, but we still had to film the wolf sequences in the Dolomites and the bull sequences, which could be done only in Spain.

By now Dr Grzimek's young she-wolf, which he had raised with a great deal of love and effort, was an adult. But before we could shoot her scenes, we had to find a major location, the small mountain lake near Pedro's shack. At this point we had neither water nor a lake.

After two days of hunting in vain for a spring to make an artificial lake, we hired a dowser who was recommended by a crew member, Hans Steger. Luck was on our side, and Herr Moser, the dowser, pulled off an amazing feat. With his rod, which was wood and not metal, he detected a small spring, but it trickled so meagrely that it took a lot of patience just to fill a single pail.

Meanwhile we dug a small pond, measuring ten or fifteen yards across. The cemented bottom was painted aquamarine, and the banks were so picturesquely decorated with rocks and rhododendrons that the pond looked like a real lake. In order to get the water up to the lake, we hired some fifty Italians in the valley, and they formed a bucket chain up to the high plateau, which took hours and hours; then we finally had our lake. At this point, however, we had a setback. According to the script, Pedro's herd of sheep is supposed to rest on the shores of the lake, but when our sheep, numbering about eighty, were driven to the lake, none of them so much as paused; they sauntered on. Then one of our people had a brainwave: we must scatter salt, then the sheep wouldn't wander from the lake. It was the most self-defeating thing we could have done! By licking the salt, the sheep got so thirsty that they soon lapped up the entire lake and it had to be refilled three times. Each time, we scattered less salt, but it didn't help; the lake was drained yet again. We were at a loss until finally we tethered every single sheep by the water.

On the first day of shooting, Peter appeared in Ciampedi and held me in his arms. He arrived just as we were doing the Katya takes and after that, everything went marvellously. Dr Grzimek had trained his wolf very well. She wasn't too wild or too tame. Nevertheless, great caution had to be exercised.

The shots of Pedro strangling the wolf were very risky. The animal couldn't be drugged since she had to defend herself; Franzl rolled about on the ground with her until she lay on her back, and he could kneel over her and clasp her by the throat. We trembled, for these minutes were extremely dangerous. He couldn't let go for even a second, otherwise the wolf would have ripped his face to shreds. However the wolf's 'death' had to be faked with the help of an injection, and we all heaved a sigh of relief when this shooting was completed. Later on the wolf was as lively as ever.

One of the most difficult scenes still lay ahead. The wolf had to break into a flock and carry off a sheep. We needed the reactions of the sheep as they sensed the stealthy approach of the wolf and grew alarmed, but our attempts to do the scene failed; no noise managed to induce fear in them. We distributed every last cooking utensil from the shack and formed an earsplitting orchestra, but even firing a scatter gun had no effect. Then Hans Steger suggested hiring an explosives expert: the detonation would finally terrify the animals.

We hired the best Italian blaster in the area, a man who had been practising his trade for years without a single incident. Early one morning when the sun shone in a cloudless blue sky, everything was ready for shooting. Three cameramen were supposed to start cranking the instant the blaster signalled. He had buried the explosive charge on a small grassy hill near the herd, and all eyes were fixed on him. He hurried away from the hill, signalled, and the cameras hummed, but there was no explosion. I was alarmed to see the man running over to the place where the dynamite was buried, and as he bent down, it went off. To my horror I saw his hands reach for this throat, where blood was spurting out. The man was beyond help and he bled to death within seconds. We were so shocked by the accident that we couldn't go on working; the shooting was interrupted for several days.

By the time we had finished in the Dolomites, Peter's leave was nearly over, yet not even this period together was free of tension. This time I blamed it on my work, but it was difficult to understand why the contents of Peter's letters and his behaviour here were such worlds apart. It became more and more of an enigma, which I tried to solve. Before his departure, which happened to fall on my birthday, he placed a narrow gold ring on my finger and said, 'Now you're officially my fiancée.'

I was rather taken aback, for the thought had never occurred to me. Nevertheless, I liked the idea. 'And where's your ring?' I asked.

Peter looked at me in surprise and then said indifferently, 'I'll have to get one.'

We climbed up to a mountain lodge to relax a little. Those were our first hours alone, and it was also the day of our engagement; but Peter didn't stay with me, he spent hours talking to the old lodge-keeper, a stranger, playing cards with him and downing one beer after another, until dark. I felt hurt, and I was assailed by new doubts. Was this the man who had written me those wonderful letters?

I was unable to find an answer.

TOTAL WAR

After my return to Berlin, I experienced the war in all its relentlessness. The air-raids wreaked havoc, and more and more people were killed. The Battle of Stalingrad was raging, and no end to the war seemed in sight. Peter's letters from the Russian front were also depressing. His first letter reported that, one day before his return, the Russians had conquered two bases, killing all the troops and officers, even the wounded. Only one German soldier had survived the massacre.

Now my brother was also fighting on the Eastern front – at times in a punishment battalion. His best friend, who also worked in my father's firm, had denounced him for allegedly buying meat on the black market and making disparaging remarks about Hitler. I was in despair because I couldn't help him. In the middle of the war, it would have been impossible for me to approach Hitler with a personal request.

All this made me fall ill again and as usual I hoped to find relief in the mountains. But ever since Dr Goebbels had declared 'total war' in February 1943, one could travel to a mountain village only with a medical certificate approved by the Ministry of Propaganda. Two physicians had filled out certificates for me, urgently recommending a stay in the mountains. Nevertheless my applications were turned down by the Ministry of Propaganda, and I was forced to stay in Berlin.

During a series of aerial attacks, I suffered one of the worst in my home, on the night of 1 March 1943. Doors leaped out of their frames and all the windows shattered. The explosions were so violent that I thought my eardrums would burst. My maid and I managed to put out seven fires and, when the bombers flew away, we went out of doors to see that all the houses in the neighbourhood were burning. We heard shouts for help from next door, the home of my friends, the Geyer family. Together with their maid, we were able to rescue two children from the flames. The sky that night blazed red for a long time.

The next morning we counted almost two hundred fire-bombs on my property, and, near the balcony of my house, the tattered corpse of a British pilot dangled from the branches of a tree. I couldn't stand these horrors any more; I didn't want to remain in Berlin another moment and Albert Speer came to my rescue by offering me a room at the Todt Home in Kitzbühel. Since Dr Fanck, working within the framework of my company, had filmed the model constructions of Berlin for the Todt Organization, I had the right to stay there briefly, so I accepted his offer. I will never forget the night before my departure. It was like the end of the world.

SPAIN 1943

After a recess of nine months which demanded great patience from us, we hoped we could at last shoot the final takes for our ill-starred film. Because of the bullfight sequences we couldn't do this filming anywhere else, but we had nearly given up all hope of ever completing *Tiefland* after the Ministry of Economics refused our repeated requests to take currency abroad, on the grounds that our film was not vital to the war effort. Yet Tobis had already sold the distribution rights in Spain, so the necessary pesetas were assured.

My two assistants, Traut and Grosskopf, then decided to appeal personally to Reich Leader Martin Bormann, who had been living at the Brown House since Hess's flight to Scotland and now had supreme authority ever since the row with Goebbels. Whenever Bormann wanted to get anything done, he would, as was generally known, cite an order from Hitler; and so by these means we got our currency.

The flight to Madrid seemed short because I was exhausted. Immediately before take-off there had been an air alert, and I had been forced to spend the final night working in the cutting room. We had a one-hour stopover in Barcelona. Here we had real coffee, bananas, oranges, chocolate, simply everything the heart desired. What a feeling it was, coming to a land at peace after four years of war; I thought I was dreaming. My first impressions of Spain were chaotic; it had recovered well after its Civil War, and at night huge neon signs illuminated the streets of Madrid.

Almost ten years ago I had been impressed by the people, the country, the customs, the art – indeed, the Spanish way of life in general – and I was impressed again, my response heightened by the pro-German attitude of the people, and by their kindness.

Our search for locations took us now to Salamanca, where over a thousand bulls gazed at the largest *finca* in Spain. At first there appeared to be no hope of inducing the owner to lend us his valuable animals. After endless conferences we finally managed to win him over, but only because he had a soft spot for Germans. However, we had to agree to take out an enormous insurance policy on these huge creatures which are raised for the best *corridas*. It would be costly, since we wanted six hundred bulls, but Gunther managed to solve this problem too.

The worst was yet to come, for we had no idea how complicated the shooting would be. The bulls, led by several drivers, had to be driven to the locations for many hours a day; then they had one day to rest before we could begin. With the help of mounted specialists everything had been prepared for the bulls in front of Las Pedrizas, a small mountain chain thirty miles outside Madrid. The temperature was over one hundred and forty degrees in the sun when we did our first takes of an incredible tableau: against the background of yellow plains, hundreds of black animal bodies galloped straight towards us, then were stopped by horsemen and driven back. Luckily, there were no accidents.

About this time Bernhard Minetti arrived. Since Gründgens had been unwilling to release him, we had been forced to delay our schedule for nearly a year. In contrast to his behaviour in the studio, he was a lot more relaxed here, and working with him was easy and pleasant. When most of the takes were completed I had a tremendous surprise. Peter, who was supposed to be at the Russian front, stood before me. I thought I was dreaming. None of his letters had mentioned the possibility of leave, and we were speechless. How was it possible for a German officer to travel to Spain in the thick of war? But Peter had managed to pull it off. He had earned this short leave only after the most dangerous combat missions, because he wanted to wipe out any doubts I had in him and win me over completely. His plan worked.

SEEBICHL HOUSE

In contrast to Spain, Berlin was a dismal sight when we returned; nothing but ruins and bombed houses. The Ministry of Propaganda had ordered numerous firms to evacuate, so we too decided to leave Berlin with several staff members. We found a house near Kitzbühel, which, having no heating system, was considered uninhabitable. We had to put one in.

In order to protect our archive against bombings we took along anything we could: negatives, positives, lavender prints, duplicate negatives – not only of *Tiefland*, but also foreign-language versions of *Olympia* and *Triumph of the Will*, as well as *The Blue Light* and many short subjects and sports films. Half the material was stored in two bunkers in Berlin-Johannisthal.

Albert Speer, named Minister of Amusements after Todt's death, would sometimes visit me after an air raid, and we would try to relax over a cup of strong coffee brewed by Helene. Speer was always one of the first to go out during aerial attacks and guide the fire brigades calmly and prudently. I admired his fearlessness and his unassuming nature. Once, when I asked him to sign a permit for some construction material for an air-raid shelter to safeguard valuable film prints, he refused, explaining that he couldn't allocate any material for such a purpose until all people had safe air-raid shelters. This also applied to Dr Fanck's footage of models of Speer's Berlin of the future. Speer spoke disparagingly of certain cabinet members and Party bigwigs, such as Dr Funk, the Minister of Economy, who, as he put it, lived as if it were peacetime, thinking only of themselves and not of the suffering population. He also criticized Hitler: 'If the Führer weren't so weak in some of his decisions I could sharply increase the output of urgently needed material.'

'What do you mean?' I asked.

'The air-raid warnings are sounded too early. We could save a lot of time at each warning and, given the increasing number of aerial attacks, the time saved would add up to a huge number of working hours in the armaments factories.'

'Why can't it be done?'

'Because I can't win the Führer over. He insists on this long advance warning so that everybody can reach an air-raid shelter in time, which is understandable on a human level, but,' Speer's voice sounded annoyed, 'we can't afford it.'

'But don't you feel it's right all the same?' I asked, taken aback.

'Yes,' he said, 'but it's more important for us to win the war. If we don't, the loss of human life will be a lot greater.'

'Do you still believe we can win?' I asked, anxiously.

'We have to win,' said Speer drily, showing not a trace of emotion.

Since the start of the Russian campaign I had been unable to believe in victory.

In November 1943 we moved to Kitzbühel where I hoped to complete

Tiefland at Seebichl House. We had fitted out a larger screening room, a sound-mixing studio, several editing rooms, and, above all, enough rooms for the staff. In an old ruin, Castle Münichau, just a few miles away, we were able to store our film archive, where it was safe from fire and bombings.

In Seebichl House we were temporarily shielded against air raids; but I couldn't work because I suffered colics as violent as they had been on the Hahnenkamm, and Reuter, the homoeopath who had been such a great help, was not to be found in Munich or anywhere else. My doctors did all they could to help me. Every day grape sugar and cardiac stimulants were injected into my veins until they could take no more. I went to Salzburg twice to be examined by Morell, Hitler's personal physician, but he achieved no improvement. In those days there were no antibiotics to combat such diseases.

LAST MEETING WITH HITLER

In 1944, 21 March was the first day of spring. I was in Kitzbühel with Peter Jacob, now promoted to major and granted a short leave. We were standing in front of the civil magistrate, a man who had been Peter's messenger at the front and had transmitted his letters to me. The fact that he was now the magistrate joining us in matrimony was an improbable coincidence, like so many other things about this war wedding, which I had resisted for so long. That morning we had left Seebichl House, riding a sleigh through very deep snow, and after a few yards the sleigh capsized. When I dug myself out of the snow an old horseshoe lay at my feet. According to popular superstition a horseshoe brings luck, so I picked it up, and I still have it in my possession today; not that it brought me luck.

My parents, who had come to Kitzbühel for the small wedding reception, were not very happy about my choice. My father had been very ill and was worried about Heinz. When he was alone with me he had tears in his eyes – something I had never witnessed. Deeply moved, he said, 'My child, I hope you will be happy.'

A dinner had been prepared at the Grand Hotel in Kitzbühel, but as we entered the lobby, an embarrassing incident occurred. A Luftwaffe officer, obviously drunk, dashed towards me with outspread arms and shouted, 'Leni, do you remember our nights of love – you were as tender as a kitten!'

I stared speechlessly at this lunatic – in fact, we all halted in our tracks. Then Peter lunged forward and punched him so hard that the officer hit the floor, and while several people attended to the drunken officer, we sat down on the table. I was happy that my husband, who was extremely jealous, behaved well and believed that I had never before set eyes on the man.

A few days before Peter's leave ended I received a basket of flowers from Hitler with congratulations and an invitation to visit him at the Berghof on 30 March. He had learned about my marriage from Julius Schaub, whose wife lived in Kitzbühel. I felt uneasy, almost alarmed at the thought of facing Hitler whom I hadn't seen for three years during the most dramatic stage of the war. Would he reveal some of his thoughts to us? In what frame of mind would he be? When the black Mercedes picked us up at the hotel in Berchtesgaden, General Schörner stepped out of the car. He had been sent by Hitler, who held him in high esteem.

How often I have been asked about my impressions of Hitler. This question has always been the one that everybody asks, especially when I was interrogated by the Allies, but it is not easy to describe my reactions to Hitler in those days. On the one hand I was extremely grateful to him for protecting me against enemies like Goebbels and others, and for respecting me as an artist; but I was indignant and ashamed when I returned from the Dolomites in the autumn of 1942 and, for the first time, saw Jewish people forced to wear a yellow star. It was after the war before I learned from the Allies that they had been taken to concentration camps and exterminated.

Although my earlier enthusiasm for Hitler had cooled off, the memory of it was still alive in me, and my feelings during our meeting were very mixed. Many things about him bothered me; when Hitler spoke of the Russians as 'subhumans', for example, I was deeply offended by this blanket condemnation of an entire people, who had brought forth such great artists. I also considered it terrible that Hitler found no way of ending this hopeless, murderous war, and wanted very much to ask him why he never went to look at the bombed German cities; but I held my tongue.

Hitler kissed my hand, and having tersely greeted my husband, paid no further attention to him. I noticed Hitler's shrunken frame, the trembling of his hand, the flickering of his eyes; he had aged years since our last meeting. Yet despite these external signs of decay, he still cast the same magical spell as before, and I could see that the men and women around him were still following his orders blindly.

During this final meeting it surprised me that Hitler did not ask my husband a single question. I had assumed he would want to know in which sectors Peter had fought and why he had been awarded the Knight's Cross. Nor did he ask me any questions. Instead, as on that night at the Kaiserhof, he began to talk immediately after greeting us, and he talked for almost an hour. Again, it was a monologue. And all the while he kept restlessly pacing back and forth.

He seemed preoccupied chiefly with three topics. First, he spoke in detail about the reconstruction of Germany after the war; about how he had commissioned many photographers and specialists to do shots of all artworks, churches, museums, historic buildings, so that they could be precisely reconstructed. 'Germany,' he said grandiloquently, 'will rise from the ruins more beautiful than ever.'

On the subject of Mussolini and Italy, he accused himself on making the unforgivable mistake of esteeming Italy as highly as he did the Duce. 'As an Italian, Mussolini is an exception. His qualities are far above average, while the Italians as a rule wage only wars that they lose. Except for their Alpine troops none of them can fight; they are just like the other Balkan nations, apart from the courageous Greeks. Italy's entry into the war has been nothing but a disaster for us. If the Italians hadn't attacked Greece and needed our help, the war would have taken a different course. We could have anticipated the Russian cold by weeks and conquered Leningrad and Moscow. There would then have been no Stalingrad. The front in southern Russia collapsed only because the Italians and the Balkan soldiers couldn't fight, so we had to bear the entire brunt of the war alone. Mussolini is waging a struggle as leader of a nation which has disgracefully betrayed him.'

Growing more and more agitated, Hitler now began to talk about England. Trembling with rage, and clenching his fists, he shouted: 'As sure as I'm standing here, no Englishman will ever set foot on German soil.' Then he launched into a diatribe of hatred against England. Hitler spoke like a rebuffed lover, for everyone in his entourage knew how much he had admired the British. His liking for them was so great that, as several of his generals reported, he had kept coming up with all sorts of excuses to delay the German invasion of the British Isles, until finally he had given up the idea altogether. The thought of razing England to the ground would have been intolerable to him, and apparently he never got over the fact that England had declared war on the German Reich, thus destroying his political dream of joining forces with the British to build a world bulwark against Communism. That was the source of his hatred of England.

As if awakening from a trance, Hitler suddenly returned to reality and, clearing his throat, made an unmistakable gesture that the visit was over. He said goodbye and when I looked back from the end of the corridor, I saw that Hitler was still standing in the same place, watching us.

I had the feeling I would never see him again.

20 JULY 1944

At the exact time of the attempted assassination of Hitler, I was at the Dahlem Forest Cemetery, attending my father's funeral. My father had died far too prematurely, aged only sixty-five.

After the funeral I wanted to visit Speer, hoping to hear something about the miracle weapons people had recently been talking about so much, but when I entered his office on Pariser Platz, he was just hurrying out of the room. As he flew past me with a quick hello, his secretary told me he had been urgently summoned by Goebbels, but we still knew nothing about the attempt on Hitler's life. Through the windows I saw soldiers marching up in front of the Ministry of Propaganda, which had moved to the other end of Pariser Platz. A bit later the radio reported that an attempt on Hitler's life had failed, that the Führer was uninjured and healthy. This news upset us deeply. Wherever I went people were horrified by the attempt on Hitler's life, and when I left for Kitzbühel that same day the train passengers, mostly soldiers, many of whom were wounded, were tremendously agitated.

In Kitzbühel more terrible news awaited me. My brother had been killed in Russia. His death was gruesome – a grenade had torn him to bits. The disaster occurred at the very same time that the bomb exploded at the Führer's Headquarters and I stood at my father's grave.

I have never really recovered from my brother's horrible death, and still cannot forgive myself for failing to approach Hitler just once in connection with a personal matter; all because I felt inhibited about turning to him in this difficult phase of the war. My brother had fallen victim to internal intrigues. Charged with buying meat on the black market and making pejorative remarks about the war, he had in fact been denounced by a colleague employed in my father's business and the accusation stuck to Heinz like a curse. Despite his valour, he was never promoted and, as he wrote to me, he was constantly detailed to 'death commandos', for a while even to a punishment battalion.

As head engineer for my father, who manufactured installations for armament plants, Heinz had been exempt from military service for a long time. His wife, who was friendly with SS General Wolff, planned to divorce him, taking full custody of their children, whom he adored. One day, on behalf of the general, an envoy came to my brother and said verbatim: 'This time, Herr Riefenstahl, your life's at stake.' My brother's papers include two letters from General Wolff in which he threatened to appeal to the Führer if my brother refused voluntarily to give up custody of the two children after the divorce. Since my brother would not be intimidated or blackmailed, he soon paid the penalty. Heinz had a foreboding of his death, for one day, just a few days before the outbreak of the war, he told me about a terrible vision he had had: he saw himself lying dead in a pool of blood.

'I'm going to die young,' he said to me. He was thirty-eight when he met his death in Russia.

COLLECTIVE PUNISHMENT

In the autumn of 1944, in Prague, the final scenes of *Tiefland* had been shot. Our film was not 'vital to the war effort', and so we had been forced to wait for two years until the Ministry of Propaganda assigned us the necessary studio time. We had only one take left, the final scene, for which we required an enormous sound stage. Isabella Ploberger, a young art director whose great talent had brought her success even though she was a lot younger than her experienced colleagues, had built us a marvellous set – a stylized mountain landscape with a beam of light, something not to be found in nature.

We were not the only film people working in Prague. I met many actors and directors there, including G.W. Pabst, Willy Forst, Geza von Cziffra, and others. There was something eerie about the fact that new film projects were still being implemented during this phase of the war; yet our relationship with the Czech stagehands was amazingly good. Not a word was uttered about war or politics, though one could sense in many people their hatred of the interminable war. Almost no one believed in a German victory.

While working on my last footage I learned that my brother's children, who were in my custody according to the terms of the will, had been kidnapped from my house in Kitzbühel on the instructions of his ex-wife. I was extremely distressed. In accordance with my brother's wishes, I had managed to get a friend of his, a kindergarten teacher, to take care of the children, who were three and four years old. The children loved her very much. I interrupted my work in Prague and went to Kitzbühel, but despite my efforts I did not succeed in getting the children back; nor were my later endeavours any more fruitful.

After the war, my brother's wife, who had meanwhile remarried, successfully challenged my brother's will, thus depriving me of the legal custody of the children. Her justification for this was that the name Riefenstahl would constitue a defamation for the children. Another kind of collective punishment.

BEFORE THE FINAL CATASTROPHE

Every afternoon thousands of American bombers now roared over Kitzbühel *en route* for Munich, and we trembled for the lives of our friends and relatives there. The inferno caused by the aerial attacks grew more and more dreadful, and the populace became more and more depressed; it was a miracle that trains were still running and that food was still available. Yet, incomprehensibly, we still wished to complete *Tiefland*, and in Prague we shot the very expensive final takes.

Meanwhile, as the front lines kept shifting closer and closer, and every day the Wehrmacht report announced more bad news, I felt as if we were on a ship that was slowly sinking into the waves. Even though the end appeared inevitable, none of us attempted to escape this fate. I was especially worried about my mother who refused to leave her home in Zernsdorf, twenty-five miles east of Berlin, and I was equally anxious about my husband who thus far had survived all the fighting, though most of his friends were dead.

Fortunately his unit was now located on the Italian front rather than by the Arctic Ocean, but my hopes that the fighting would be less hard there proved false. Peter wrote: 'The roads lie deep in mud, which makes it a lot more difficult to send supplies, so the enemy is superior to us in manpower and equipment. We've barely had a wink of sleep for days now; my new company commander has been killed. The Americans are fighting very tenaciously, and we have to admit that they're very courageous. The constant enemy air-raids are bad; they're causing high casualties.'

I experienced my first strafings during a trip to Berlin, where I had to spend a few days because of my problems with my sister-in-law. We had two alarms, the train stopped, and we all had to get out and lie on the ground. A few women and children were wounded, and medics carried them away. I also experienced a heavy aerial attack the first night I spent in Berlin, during early November 1944. I was staying at the Adlon, since friends were billeted at my house, and in the air-raid shelter, various prominent artists and politicians found themselves thrown together. Among them was Rudolf Diels, who claimed to know who started the Reichstag fire and who at that time had been responsible for my safety. I hadn't seen him since that time. Göring had transferred him to Cologne, then to Hanover. During that night of bombing he told me about his arrest after 20 July, and about how Göring, who held him in high esteem, had obtained his release.

The next morning Berlin offered a bleak spectacle, yet people came trudging to their jobs from far away. It was amazing to see how disciplined they were, going about their work as a matter of course. I had to consult my lawyer, Dr Heyl, with regard to my brother's children; it was the last time that I went through the destroyed streets of my home town before the end of the war.

The trip back to Kitzbühel was an ordeal. The train was packed with soldiers and refugees and, having no hope of getting a seat, I stood for almost the entire ride, wedged in between people. Suddenly my bladder colic attacked me so violently that the blood ran down my legs. A soldier, noticing it, placed his steel helmet between my feet. It was a terrible situation and I was writhing in pain. In Munich I found a seat and fell into a deathlike sleep.

Once again the work on *Tiefland* had to be interrupted because of my mental and physical state, although all that was left was the final cutting and the dubbing. I had received no news from Peter for a long time now and for days on end I tried to call the headquarters of General Field Marshal Kesselring, the German commander-in-chief in Italy. At last I reached an officer, and I inquired about Major Peter Jacob. A few days later I was notified that he was no longer at his command post, but was probably in a field hospital somewhere in Italy.

I made up my mind to look for my husband and in November 1944 arrived in Merano where I succeeded in getting to a liaison officer who was willing to help me with my apparently senseless hunt. After futile telephone calls he permitted me to ride to the front with a supply column, though I can no longer remember all the places I went to. I only know that the trip was hazardous, and often, because of strafings, we threw ourselves into ditches and were soon filthy from head to foot. One week later, after this wild goose chase, I returned to Merano, where I discovered my husband in an army hospital, all wrapped up and barely able to stir. Luckily, he had no bullet wounds and was there because acute rheumatism had attacked all his joints.

Peter was astounded when he saw me, and considered it frivolous of me to have ventured into the combat zone. I have not prayed very often in my life, even though I believe I am deeply religious, but on that day I had to pray; I thanked God that my husband was still alive.

RACE AGAINST THE END

Today it is completely incomprehensible to me why we insisted on completing *Tiefland* while everything was collapsing around us. It was absurd and inexplicable. Perhaps it was my Prussian sense of duty. I was not the only one however; everybody else was doing the same. We no longer believed in the miracle weapons, despite the many rumours circulating about them, but we were all very worried about the 'Morgenthau Plan', about which Frau Schaub had told me horrible things, especially the punishments that the Germans could expect after the war. Wilma Schaub, the wife of Hitler's senior adjutant, had been living at the Todt Home in Kitzbühel for several months, and during the final period she was our life-saving connection with Berlin since she had a direct telephone line to the Reich Chancellery. She would call her husband every day, and in this way we received news about the fate of our nearest and dearest after the air-raids on Berlin.

Frau Schaub also helped us with food – eggs, milk and sometimes even bread. Neither I nor my staff had any links with the black market, and so we were all pretty famished. I weighed about one hundred pounds. Frau Schaub, whom I had first met in autumn 1944, was initially very aloof and began to trust me only gradually. It was she who first told me about Eva Braun, about whose existence I had known nothing.

She told me about the suicide of Geli Raubal, Hitler's niece, whose room he had once shown me. Frau Schaub had been with Geli on the evening of her death. They had gone to the theatre in Munich and Frau Schaub had noticed how exhausted Geli looked, so she accompanied her back to Prinz-regentenplatz where Geli lived in a room in Hitler's apartment. She asked Frau Schaub to stay with her for a while, then, noticing Hitler's coat hanging in the hallway, Geli reached into the pocket and pulled out a letter. After reading it, said Frau Schaub, the girl turned chalk-white and handed her the letter. It was a rapturous effusion from Eva Braun, and Geli, who had for some time been a prey to jealousy, had shot herself a few hours later. 'There was no doubt,' said Frau Schaub, 'that that letter was the trigger for Geli's suicide.'

Frau Schaub also appeared to know about Rommel's death. Hitler, she said, had been deeply shaken upon learning about Rommel's connections with the officers of the July plot, and especially that Rommel had been chosen as his successor. When I asked her whether she still believed in a German victory, she shook her head. Tearfully she said she knew that she would never see her husband again. He refused to leave the Führer, and intended to remain at the bunker in Berlin.

'If my husband dies,' she declared desperately, 'then I want to die with my children.' I tried in vain to calm her down. For my part suicide never even crossed my mind. I was convinced that hard times lay ahead for us, but nevertheless I wanted to go on living. I had this obligation above all towards my mother, who had no one but me after losing her husband and her only son; and I also had an obligation towards Peter, for whose life I had feared during the past four years.

However, the war still wasn't over, and every day brought futher terrible news. In late January 1945 the radio announced that the *Wilhelm Gustloff*, a steamer with German refugees from East Prussia, had been sunk by a Russian submarine, causing the deaths of over five thousand people. A few days later an air raid on Berlin claimed more than twenty thousand lives, yet my mother still remained in this dangerous area, and the Russians were only twenty-five miles from her house.

No day passed without fear and terror. In February 1945 we heard the news of the destruction of Dresden, in which over one hundred thousand people had died. How much longer would this killing go on? Why didn't this era of senseless murder come to an end? Because of the intensity of my pains and the powerful painkillers that I kept using, I perceived the events only as tortured dreams.

Unexpectedly, my mother arrived in Kitzbühel, and deliriously happy, I threw my arms around her. She had escaped from Berlin because, not hearing from me for a long time, she had gone to see Speer, who was just about to drive to Obersalzberg. Without a moment's hesitation, he told her to get into the car. It was her last chance.

I asked her whether she had found out anything from Speer about the imminent end of the war, but she hadn't brought it up and could only report about the drive. Speer was at the wheel, while an assistant sitting next to him took down his instructions, which my mother couldn't make out. She was sitting in the back seat and managed to catch only fragments of sentences.

'I noticed,' she said, 'that Speer seemed active and confident, and I inferred from several of his remarks that he still believes the war will have a favourable end.' I was astonished. It was mid-February 1945, and Germany was shattered. I assumed that Speer, like everyone else in Hitler's entourage, was still under his hypnotic influence, or perhaps he had been unwilling to reveal his true feelings.

Meanwhile my husband had been detailed to the infantry school in Döberitz, near Berlin, which he had to leave in order to stand by his troops. He wrote: 'I was supposed to take over a naval infantry regiment on the Oder, but my commander noticed in time that I am a mountain infantryman.' He was trying to gloss over his precarious situation with his sense of humour, but between the lines I could sense the danger he was in. A further letter was written on 11 February 1945 but did not arrive until much later: 'Except for very strong restrictions and the conscription of the populace for digging trenches and building barricades in Berlin, life here goes on normally. In my opinion, the city is not in immediate danger.' I couldn't believe it, and Peter couldn't possibly have believed it either. He had written those lines purely for my peace of mind.

Later I was surprised by a phone call from the Obersalzberg, and by a familiar voice which said to me: 'Leni, we've just come from Berlin, from the bunker of the Reich Chancellery.' It was the voice of a cameraman who had once worked for me and who had then been summoned to Hitler's headquarters during the war. He had brought me bits of news from there when he occasionally visited me during vacations.

'Thank God,' I said. 'Then you're all saved.'

'What are you talking about? The Führer lied to us. He said he would follow using the next plane, and now the radio says that he's staying on in Berlin.'

'Do you want to die with Hitler?'

'Yes,' he cried, 'we all wanted to die with Hitler; no one wanted to abandon the Führer, not even Hanna Reitsch, who came to the bunker with Ritter von Greim. Hitler ordered them too to leave the Reich Chancellery.'

'You've all lost your minds,' I said. Then I heard no more. We'd been disconnected. What I had just heard was beyond belief. The caller was not a Party member nor did he sympathize ideologically with the racial theories of the National Socialists. He was a thoroughly liberal-minded person. Hitler, now a shadow of his former self, must still have exerted enormous powers if the people around him preferred to die with him rather than save their own lives. We all reckoned daily with the possibility of Hitler's suicide.

During the final dark days of the war, we tried feverishly to dub our film. This work became a race against time. Come what may, we wanted to complete *Tiefland* before the end of the war. Although we did not realize the scope of the tragedy, and knew nothing about the crimes that took place in the camps, we were aware of the abyss into which we would be swept. I wondered what meaning life would have in a world in which our fate would be years of shame and humiliation.

Frau Schaub brought us medicaments and news. 'Tomorrow at the crack of dawn,' she said, 'a car is coming from the Brown House with important documents for Gauleiter Hofer in Bolzano. If you want to get any valuables to safety, you can send along a few things.' We prepared three metal boxes containing the original negatives of the two Party rally films, *Victory of Faith* and *Triumph of the Will*, as well as the Wehrmacht short *Day of Freedom*. As we eventually learned, the boxes never reached their destination. Apparently they arrived in Bolzano, but even the inquiries made by the American and French film officers remained fruitless. The original negatives were not to be found, and they have been missing ever since.

In mid-April I received a cry for help from my earlier lover and cameraman Hans Schneeberger in Vienna: 'Leni, you've got to help me, I've been drafted into the territorial army, and the Russians are already outside the city.' In Berlin, where Goebbels was 'combat commissar', I couldn't have helped anyone, but perhaps I could in Vienna. I wasn't personally acquainted with Baldur von Schirach, the Gauleiter of Vienna, but I heard that he was a tolerant man. After several conversations with a few of his closest assistants, I managed to get a week's leave for Schneeberger, who was already over fifty, on the grounds that he was to shoot the titles for *Tiefland*. Since unpolitical films were also being made until the end of the war, this was not so unusual. A couple of days later my help was needed in a far more difficult matter. It concerned Gisela, Schneeberger's wife, a vivacious redhead, who had been on my staff for years as a photo lab worker. She had been arrested on the train to Kitzbühel and was now imprisoned in Innsbruck. Her husband, utterly desperate, rushed there from Vienna, for her situation was critical. During the final days the death penalty could be inflicted for the kinds of things that Gisela had been foolish enough to blurt out. In a train compartment where wounded soldiers were sitting, she had cursed them and shouted: 'You bastards, why do you keep fighting for Hitler?' An officer in the same compartment had ordered her immediate arrest.

I knew that she was an enemy of the regime and also half-Jewish, but calling wounded soldiers 'bastards' at this point was tantamount to suicide. I tried to help her through Uli Ritzer, whom I had once worked with, and who was now head of the culture division in Tyrol, under Gauleiter Hofer. Ritzer spoke to the head of the Gestapo, but without success, since three witnesses had incriminated Gisela far too seriously. I made up my mind to go to Innsbruck, where I succeeded in getting her out of prison after a long conversation with the Gestapo chief. I told him that Frau Schneeberger had suffered a nervous breakdown in Vienna because of heavy bombing, and so she couldn't be made responsible for her utterances. The Gestapo officer was also impressed by the fact that she was my employee and that I wanted to put her and her husband up at my Seebichl House.

Things there were getting more and more difficult for us. Mattresses and blankets lay in the corridors, and strangers came seeking refuge. Signs were already suspended in the streets: 'We Welcome Our Liberators', yet no one knew whether it would be the Americans or the Russians who would be marching in. Even before the occupation we watched as once enthusiastic followers of Hitler turned into 'resistance fighters'.

Gisela and her husband wanted to go to the Tyrol where a cousin of Schneeberger's owned a boarding-house, and they urged me to join them.

'They'll set your house on fire,' said Gisela.

'You'll jeopardize everyone if you stay here,' said Hans. 'Come with us, you'll be safe there; we'll stay up there until the worst is behind us.' My staff and my mother also urged me to join the Schneebergers, but I didn't want to leave my mother alone, and I was uncertain also about my husband. There was a total blackout on news and information, and there was no prospect of locating Peter now.

When the Schneebergers left, Gisela said, 'You can follow us, I'll wait for you at the hotel in Mayerhofen. Don't forget to bring along your valuable things – clothes, furs, and especially your films – you must save them.'

Eventually, anxiety that my presence could harm my staff contributed to my heeding Gisela's advice. Adolf Galland, the fighter-pilot general, with whom I was not personally acquainted, gave us twenty litres of petrol – a priceless gift in those days. Willy Zielke, brilliant but mentally ill, had been living here with his wife after I had got him out of the asylum at Haar, and before my departure I made sure that they were taken to safety. They were given food and money and were supposed to try and find shelter with Zielke's mother. When I said goodbye to my mother and my staff, we didn't know when or if we might ever meet again. The atmosphere was doom-laden. That night I had a strange dream, almost a vision. In a small German town I saw many swastika flags hanging from the houses of a long, narrow street, but in my dreams their blood-red colour slowly lightened until all the flags turned white.

When I arrived in Mayerhofen, a small Tyrolean village, I ran into an UFA film team that included Maria Koppenhöfer and the director Harald Braun. Work was still progressing on film-making even in the final days of the war – a grotesque situation. Mayerhofen was jammed with German soldiers; returning from the Russian front, they marched through the streets. Drained and dead tired, I collapsed on the bed in the small hotel room, and woke to find Gisela Schneeberger standing before me. Grumpily she snapped, 'Is that all your luggage?'

Amazed at her attitude, I was about to ask her what had happened, when suddenly there was uproar in the restaurant underneath us. Gisela ran downstairs and returned an instant later, did a dance of joy and shouted, 'Hitler is dead – he's dead!' What we had been expecting for a long time had finally come, and I cannot describe what I felt at that moment. A chaos of emotions raged in me. I threw myself on the bed and wept all night.

When I awoke the next day, I was alone, and the innkeeper said that Frau Schneeberger had left the previous evening, on a farmer's wagon going to the boarding house, and left no message. I was faced with the mystery of why she had talked me into leaving Kitzbühel to join her. I felt quite sick; something was obviously wrong, but what could have changed? Hans and Gisela were two of my best friends; they had even come to my wedding in Kitzbühel and spent a week as my guests at Seebichl House. Also, I had helped both of them – rescuing Hans from the territorial army and getting Gisela out of prison in Innsbruck. What should I do? I couldn't remain here. Every room in the hotel was occupied, and there was no prospect of finding a room anywhere else in Mayerhofen. On the other hand I couldn't return to Kitzbühel. I had no petrol left, and I couldn't possibly walk the seventy miles back; there was no alternative but to go up the mountain to find them.

Late that afternoon I found a farmer who brought me up in a small hay wagon. It was already dark when I stood at a door with a brightly painted wooden sign which read 'Hotel Lamm'. I took a deep breath and rang, but no one responded, the door remained locked, so I rang again, this time longer. An icy wind was blowing and I was trembling with cold, but no one came. In my despair I banged my fists on the door until finally it was opened by an ill-tempered elderly man who eyed me distrustfully.

'I am Frau Riefenstahl,' I said. 'Herr Schneeberger asked me to come here.' Eying me up and down, he said nastily, 'You are not entering my house!'

'Aren't you Hans's cousin?' I asked, startled. 'I'm supposed to stay here for a couple of weeks.'

'Sorry,' he said, 'you're not entering my house. Hans apparently didn't realize that I won't take any Nazis.'

I lost patience and, shoving him aside, ran into the house and shouted: 'Hans! Hans!' but there was no answer, though I ran through various rooms and opened every door. I assumed there must be some kind of misunderstanding and I decided to wait, despite the innkeeper's resistance. Then I discovered them in the final room – the kitchen. Gisela stood there and shrieked like a fury, 'Are you here? Are you crazy? Did you really think you could stay here with us?'

I was speechless. All I could do was gaze open-mouthed at Hans, who didn't have the nerve to look at me and crouched on the floor in a corner, hiding his head in his arms. Was this the man with whom I had lived happily for four years, and who had been one of the bravest soldiers in the battles in the Dolomites during World War I? Could he be the man who had remained my friend even after our break-up and who had enthusiastically worked with me on *The Blue Light?*

'Hans!' I shouted. 'Help me!'

Gisela stationed herself protectively in front of him and yelled at me, 'You thought we'd help you? You Nazi slut!'

She's gone crazy, I thought to myself, so now I shouted: 'Hans, say something! I saved your lives a few days ago. I didn't want to come here. It was your wife who persuaded me . . .' Hans trembled in agitation, but didn't say a word, not a single word.

Leaving my luggage, I stormed out, unable to utter a sound. I had never experienced anything like this, and the scene repelled me, disgusted me. A world had collapsed inside me and the landscape seemed deathly still as I slowly trudged down the mountain. The farmer who had driven me up had long since gone, so I looked for another rooming-house, any kind of shelter to sleep in. I found one within a few minutes, but 'We're fully occupied,' they said; I knocked at another door, asked the same question, received the same answer. A third door – always the same.

As I continued downwards, I thought, 'Maybe I'll find a barn, I mustn't sleep out in the open.' In my state of ill health I had to avoid the cold; I had to walk as far as I could. Then a man came towards me. 'Frau Riefenstahl?'

All I could say was: 'Yes?'

'I don't know if you remember me, but I know you. I once worked for you, and I've heard you need a place to stay. Come along, I'll help you!' He took me by the hand, saying he had a small room that I could use, and he would spend the night somewhere else. Then he spoke to the innkeeper who allowed me to stay for one night.

THE FIRST ARRESTS

The next morning I walked down to Mayerhofen in the valley. All I had with me was a small cosmetic case containing medicaments and some cash. For the time being I had to leave the large pieces of my baggage with the Schneebergers. This included the original negatives of *Olympia*; but in my condition it was all meaningless. I had only one wish: to go back to my mother.

En route I hitched a ride in a farmer's wagon filled with men in civilian clothes. Roughly one hour later we were stopped by Americans who demanded our ID cards. I showed mine, but we all had to get out and go with them to a camp which had been set up a couple of miles away, out in the open. We were under arrest.

The first people in the camp to help me were Communists, Austrians from Vienna who had recognized me and who were so friendly that I felt relieved and grateful, especially when they gave me some food. Slowly my spirits revived, I no longer felt so lonely, and we conversed like sensible people, without hatred or vindictiveness. They took care of me by making me familiar with camp life, telling me where things could be obtained and what should be avoided. They also showed me a hole in the enclosure which didn't interest them so much since they were getting enough to eat. It did interest me, however, and I sneaked out the very next day. It was my first escape; but my freedom lasted only a couple of hours before I ran into some more Americans who locked me up in another camp without recognizing me. Since this camp was also poorly guarded, I broke out again: my second escape.

My third imprisonment was near Kufstein, where I remained several days in order to eat my fill and rest up. I was amazed at how loose and casual the Americans were about guarding their prisoners; so it was no problem slipping out of this camp too. Again I walked on, although it was harder and harder to do so, as the columns of soldiers choked the roads, while jeeps and tanks advanced at a walking pace. I was exhausted, but I knew it was no longer very far to Seebichl House, for I was already past Wörgl. After that it was only fifteen miles to my destination, but my feet were so sore that every step was painful. I halted at a farmhouse after spotting a bicycle near the front door. Biking would be helpful, though I remembered a bad accident during my first attempt at learning how to ride. However, at that moment, it seemed to be the only way to get home. I negotiated with the farmer's wife who wouldn't at first give up the bicycle – certainly not for money. Then I noticed the admiring looks she gave my small crocodile valise, so I offered to swap it for the bike, and she agreed. I first tried to ride a few yards outside the farmhouse before I ventured out on the highway, then I snaked past the trucks and jeeps – my desire to see my mother greater than my fear.

As I pedalled up the narrow path from the small railway station at Schwarzsee to my house, my heart began to race. An American flag was waving on the roof, and the shutters were open. As I wondered whether to go in, an American officer came towards me and greeted me so amiably that my fear vanished.

'Frau Riefenstahl?' he asked in broken German. 'We have been expecting you for a long time.' He came with me into the living room and asked me to be seated.

'My name is Medenbach and I am happy to make your acquaintance,' he said with a smile. 'You don't have to speak English, I understand German very well; I studied in Vienna for a while.'

Were these our enemies? I pictured my German 'friends', the Schnee-bergers, and grew uneasy. The officer, who had the rank of a major, noticed my anxiety and said reassuringly, 'You needn't be afraid, you're in luck; we have confiscated your house, but nothing has been removed, except that we had to relocate everyone who was living here.' I didn't have the nerve to ask about my mother. But Major Medenbach read my mind and said, 'Your mother and all the people who were living in the house have been lodged just a few miles from here, on an estate that belonged to the Ribbentrop family. Do you know the property?'

'My mother is alive and nearby?' I asked, incredulous.

He nodded. 'She's doing well,' he said. At this point I collapsed in tears; the joy, the shocks I had suffered, the awful strain, the days of walking, were all too much. The major placed his hand on my shoulder and said, 'Prepare yourself, I have some more news for you, good news.' There was a pause while the American waited for me to stop crying. Then he said gingerly, 'Your husband is also alive.'

I looked at him in disbelief. Peter alive – I couldn't grasp it. Again I burst into tears and couldn't stop. 'Please calm down – calm down,' the American officer said. He informed me that my husband, who had been taken from the POW camp and hired as a driver, was now living with my mother on the estate. The major led me outside, put me in a jeep, and drove up a narrow forest road that was unfamiliar to me. Within a mile or two, we stopped outside a group of low houses in a forest clearing, the property of the Ribbentrop family. First I hugged and kissed my mother, then my husband. It was simply unreal.

Shortly afterwards I found myself in a bed, at my husband's side. For how many years, when Peter was stationed at the front and I was enduring the torrent of bombs in Berlin, had I been longing for this moment. Was it all over now; would we now live in peace? But this happiness was too brief and illusory. Within a few short hours we were wakened by the sound of tyres screeching, engines stopping abruptly, orders yelled, general din, and a hammering on the window shutters. Then the intruders broke through the door, and we saw Americans with rifles who stood in front of our bed and shone lights at us. None of them spoke German, but their gestures said: 'Get dressed, come with us immediately.'

This was my fourth arrest, but now my husband was with me, and we got to know the victors from a very different aspect. They were no longer the casual, gangling GIs; these were soldiers who treated us roughly. Putting us into a jeep, they took us down to Kitzbühel and billeted us in a house where several other people had already been placed but where, since Peter was with me, I remained calm, holding his hand. They told us we could sleep with all the others on the floor of one room. The next morning we were given a breakfast of ham and eggs and we hadn't eaten anything so good for a long time. Nothing that I feared came true; there were no interrogations and we were released as suddenly as we had been apprehended.

'You may go,' said one of the guards, who had pushed us around so crudely just a few hours before. He motioned with his thumb, twice, three times, because we didn't understand him and couldn't believe it. Then we returned to the estate, this time on foot.

Again my mother threw her arms around me. She asked nothing and we didn't speak, for we were too exhausted. The next day I again felt frightened and queasy, imagining I could hear screeching jeeps every moment; but nothing happened. My husband told me that they had had to go on fighting near Regensburg even after Hitler's death until nearly all of Peter's friends had been killed, and he, one of the very few survivors of his unit, had been captured by Americans. Peter tended to understate things and spoke about it without emotion. He was what the military call a 'trooper' – an officer who is appreciated by his men. His calm attitude affected all of us during those days, especially me. We waited to see what lay ahead, and now and then Major Medenbach came up, bringing things that delighted us: oranges, chocolate, cookies.

Then one day a jeep with two Americans in uniform stopped at our door; I was arrested again and this time, Peter wasn't with me. I was told to pack a few small items – soap, a face-cloth, toothbrush and comb. Desperately I looked about for my husband, but Peter was out somewhere with Medenbach, so I couldn't say goodbye to him. My poor mother; once more, she didn't know when she'd see me again.

The jeep raced along the autobahns until, a few hours later, when it was already dark, I was brought to the Salzburg Prison; there an elderly prison matron rudely pushed me into the cell, kicking me so hard that I fell to the ground; then the door was locked. There were two other women in the dark, barren room, and one of them, on her knees, slid about the floor, jabbering confusedly; then she began to scream, her limbs writhing hysterically. She seemed to have lost her mind. The other woman crouched on her bunk, weeping to herself.

I found myself in a prison cell for the first time, and it is an unbearable feeling. I pounded on the door, becoming so desperate that I eventually smashed my body against it with all my strength, until I collapsed in exhaustion. I felt that incarceration was worse than capital punishment, and I did not think I could survive a long term of imprisonment.

For hours on end I rolled about on my bed, trying to forget my surroundings, but it was impossible. The mentally disturbed woman kept screaming – all through the night; but even worse were the yells and shrieks of men from the courtyard, men who were being beaten, screaming like animals. I susequently found out that a company of SS men was being interrogated.

They came for me the next morning, and I was taken to a padded cell where I had to strip naked, and a woman examined every square inch of my body. Then I had to get dressed and go down to the courtyard, where many men were standing, apparently prisoners, and I was the only woman. We had to line up before an American guard who spoke German. The prisoners stood to attention, so I tried to do the same, and then an American came who spoke fluent German. He pushed a few people together, then halted at the first in our line. 'Were you in the Party?'

The prisoner hesitated for a moment, then said: 'Yes.'

He was slugged in the face and spat blood.

The American went on to the next in line.

'Were you in the Party?'

The man hesitated.

'Yes or no?'

'Yes.' And he too got punched so hard in the face that the blood ran out of his mouth. However, like the first man, he didn't dare resist. They didn't even instinctively raise their hands to protect themselves. They did nothing. They put up with the blows like dogs.

The next man was asked: 'Were you in the Party?'

Silence.

'Well?'

'No,' he yelled, so no punch. From then on nobody admitted that he had been in the Party and I was not even asked.

The men were led away, but I had to wait. Then an officer came towards me, his chest covered with decorations. He looked at me, took my hand in his hands, kissed me on the forehead, and said: 'Buck up, my girl, you'll be all right.'

I looked at him confused. He was middle-aged, with hair greying at the temples, and his eyes were kind and earnest. 'Don't give up,' he said, 'see it through.'

Eventually the men and I were loaded on to heavy open trucks on which guns were ranged. Nobody knew where they were taking us.

AT AMERICAN HEADQUARTERS

For hours on end we drove north along highways and autobahns. When we were unloaded, we found ourselves in a vast camp: a huge square surrounded by one-storey houses. It didn't look like a prison. I subsequently learned that it was the headquarters and prison camp of the Seventh American Army.

Before being billeted we had to furnish our personal data, and then the Americans took me to one of the small houses where I was put in a room with three other women. We introduced ourselves. The oldest was Johanna Wolf, Hitler's senior secretary. I didn't know her or the other secretaries. The second woman was a secretary of Von Frauenfeld, the Gauleiter of Vienna; the youngest was a German-French woman from Alsace, who was under suspicion of espionage. The room was furnished with four beds, a table, chairs and a lamp. I was agreeably surprised. There was nothing of the prison atmosphere in this environment.

Nothing else happened the day of my arrival, and I was so exhausted that I fell asleep on the bed without even undressing. The next morning, when I looked out of the window, I saw a great many men strolling in the courtyard. I spotted Hermann Göring, Sepp Dietrich (general of the Weapons SS), Franz Xaver Schwarz (treasurer of the Nazi Party), Julius Schaub and Wilhelm Brückner (Hitler's adjutants), and several generals. Over one thousand prisoners were in this camp, the so-called 'Bear Cellar'. Major figures were interned here and, for the time being, we four women were the only female inmates. Eventually we joined the men in the daily stroll, which took place regularly according to a precise schedule.

Two days later I was taken to my first interrogation. Dreadful photos hung on the walls of this room, of emaciated figures lying on bunks, their gigantic eyes helplessly peering into the camera; I saw piles of corpses and skeletons. Then I hid my face in my hands; it was too horrifying.

The CIC officer asked: 'Do you know what that is?'

'No.'

'You've never seen it?'

'No.'

'And you don't know what these are? They're photos taken in concentration camps. You never heard about Buchenwald?'

'No.'

'What about Dachau?'

'Yes, I've heard about Dachau. It was said to be a camp for political prisoners, traitors and spies.'

The officer gave me a piercing look. 'Go on,' he said sharply.

Faltering, I continued. 'I was curious about it and I consulted a high-level officer. That was in 1944, when I visited my fiancé Peter Jacob on the Heuberg. I even remember the official's name, because he was the brother of the cabaret performer Trude Hesterberg. He assured me that every inmate was given a proper trial, and only those who were incontestably guilty were punished with the death penalty for high treason.'

'Do you know the names of the other camps?'

'Terezin.'

'What do you know about it?'

'I heard that Jews who hadn't emigrated were interned there.'

'Go on.'

'At the start of the war, I personally asked Reich Leader Bouhler in the Reich Chancellery about the place and the treatment of Jews.'

'What did he answer?'

'He said that the Jews had to be interned there because we were at war, and they could commit espionage, just as Germans and Japanese were interned by our enemies.'

'And you believed him?'

'Yes.'

'You had friends who were Jews?'

'Yes.'

'And what happened to them?'

'They emigrated. Bela Balazs went to Moscow; my physicians emigrated to America; Manfred George went first to Prague, then to New York, and Stefan Lorant to London.' I couldn't go on speaking, I felt nauseated and I lost my balance.

The American supported me and gave me a chair. Then he said, 'These are pictures that the American troops took as they advanced across German territory, occupying and liberating the concentration camps.'

He asked me whether I believed it.

'It is incomprehensible,' I said.

'You will come to understand it,' said the American. 'We will continue to confront you with such photos and documents.'

Deeply shaken, I said, 'Ask me anything you like, hypnotize me, I've got nothing to hide. I will tell you everything I know. But I have nothing sensational to reveal to you . . .'

Then I was brought back to my room, but I was so intensely affected by the macabre pictures that I could only toss and turn on my bed, unable to fall asleep.

During the following days I was tormented by the need to learn details about how those gruesome things had come about, and whether Hitler had known about them. I tried to talk to Johanna Wolf, thinking that she must have been informed about many things, since she was close to Hitler until his death. If only she would talk, but she held her tongue. She was so tense that it took days for her to relax, and then hesitantly to answer a few questions. It was clear that she was still under Hitler's spell.

Eventually she said that she hadn't wanted to leave the Reich Chancellery, but Hitler had urged her to go for the sake of her eighty-year-old mother. He had forced her along with others to board the last plane out of Berlin. Julius Schaub, Hitler's senior adjutant, who had also refused to leave Hitler, had to fly on that same plane. Hitler ordered him to do so, and Schaub couldn't refuse a direct order. He was to go to the Obersalzberg and destroy private documents of Hitler's before the arrival of the enemy. Fräulein Wolf said that the people close to Hitler had been unable to escape his magnetism until his death, even though he was quite emaciated. Then she told me about how Magda Goebbels had taken the lives of her five children along with her own, though Hitler apparently tried in vain to dissuade her. She wanted to die with him, like Eva Braun, who adamantly refused to leave the Reich Chancellery and whose sole wish was to become Frau Hitler before her death.

I asked Fräulein Wolf: 'How do you explain these extreme contrasts? On the one hand Hitler is so worried about the fate of his people; on the other hand he is inhumane and tolerates the crimes we have learned here, or even orders them?'

Fräulein Wolf sobbed, 'He can't have been informed about those crimes. He was surrounded by fanatics; people like Himmler, Goebbels and Bormann exerted more and more influence on him. They issued orders which Hitler knew nothing about.' She couldn't go on, and succumbed to a passion of weeping. I too clung to that straw because it seemed incomprehensible to me to connect Hitler, as I knew him, with those crimes. As doubts began stirring in me more and more, however, I wanted to know the truth, no matter how much it hurt. I simply couldn't imagine that orders of such a vast scope could be carried out without Hitler's knowledge. Yet how were these cruelties to be reconciled with the indignant words that I heard him speak in Zoppot, at the beginning of the war: 'So long as there are still women and children in Warsaw, there will be no shooting.' Or that time in

Albert Speer's office, just a few days before the outbreak of the war, when he exclaimed in my presence: 'May God grant that I am not forced into a war.'

How did this fit in with the inhumanity in the concentration camps? I was totally confused. Perhaps, I thought, Hitler changed so much because of the war, perhaps because of the isolation in which he lived from the beginning of the war. From that moment on he was out of touch with the people beyond his own entourage. During his earlier rallies he had been infected by the emotions of the cheering crowds, absorbing them as a medium receives messages; positive impulses were transferred to him, suppressing the negative in him. After all, he wanted to be honoured and loved, but in his voluntary isolation there were no more human relationships. He became solitary, spiritually anaemic and finally inhumane when he realized that victory was no longer possible. That was my attempt at finding an explanation for his schizophrenic nature.

From then on I was taken daily to interrogations that lasted for hours. Everything I said was written down in shorthand, and I also had to fill out numerous questionnaires, but I was allowed to sit and I was treated correctly. My statements were confirmed by witnesses who were also in the camp, and I soon realized that the CIC officers knew more about me than I did. They were extremely well informed, which had a beneficial effect on the way I was treated. After a while I no longer felt like a prisoner, and several times I was even invited to afternoon tea with the commander of the camp and his officers. They talked very freely there, especially about several of the prisoners, and their favourite was almost always Göring. I was astonished at how popular he was. They had given him IQ tests, and they admired him. They had weaned Göring off morphine, and this apparently restored and sharpened his intellectual faculties. He looked as if he had lost weight, but he always seemed very cheerful, and almost none of the Americans believed that he would be condemned to death as a war criminal. I was surprised, for I didn't doubt it for an instant. New prisoners were brought in every day.

Once I had an unpleasant experience in the camp, when a doctor visited me and my room-mates had to leave. When we were alone, he said, 'I have to ask you to tell me a few intimate things about Hitler.'

I stared at him, astonished. 'But you know that I can't tell you anything "intimate" about Hitler.'

'Frau Riefenstahl, I understand that you do not care to speak about such things, but I am a doctor, and you can trust me. It is no crime if you as a woman slept with Hitler. I will not report it any further. We want to know if Hitler was sexually normal or if he was impotent, what his genitals looked like, and so on. These things are important for understanding his character.'

I lost my temper. 'Get out,' I ordered, 'get out!'

The physician gave me a terrified look as I opened the door and shoved him out; then I threw myself on the bed, my nerves worn to a frazzle.

Surprisingly, after just a few weeks, I was released, on 3 June 1945, and I was given a document certifying that there were no charges against me. Here is the original text:

HEADQUARTERS SEVENTH ARMY
Office of the A.C. of S.G.–2
APO 758   US ARMY

TO WHOM IT MAY CONCERN   DATE: 3 JUNE 1945

This is to certify that Leni Riefenstahl has been examined at Headquarters Seventh Army and has been released without prejudice on this date.

BY COMMAND OF LIEUTENANT GENERAL PATCH:-

WILLIAM W. QUINN
Colonel, G.S.C.
A.C. of S.G.–2

On leaving the camp I was assured by the American commander that this document was valid for all four occupation powers. When he saw doubt in my face, he said, 'You don't have to be afraid. The document confirms our inquiries. You are rehabilitated and you don't have to fear any further curtailment of freedom.'

Overjoyed, I thanked him.

An American jeep brought me back to Kitzbühel – to freedom, as I thought at the time.

THE POSTWAR YEARS

BACK IN HÖRLAHOF

My mother wept with joy when she embraced me again at the Hörlahof, von Ribbentrop's estate. It really seemed that we could start a new and better life. I saw my husband almost daily, though he was out a lot with Major Medenbach. It was June, the loveliest month of the year; fresh greenery was sprouting everywhere and the mountain meadows were bright with blossoms.

I remembered that I had left the valises with the original negatives of the Olympic movies at the Schneebergers', but I never wanted to see that house again. Our friend Medenbach offered to drive me there and pick the baggage up personally. In those days, all Germans had to stay within a radius of three and a half miles of their villages, so none of us could have gone for my things. Medenbach was outraged when he learned what had happened to me and intervened to spare me any further upset. He took me as far as Mayerhofen, left me at a hotel there and drove alone up the mountain. When he returned with my trunks, he said, laughing, 'What a nasty bitch. Do you know what Frau Schneeberger said to me when I asked for the baggage? "I thought the Americans would string the Nazis up on the lampposts. Instead they're rescuing their belongings."'

That was 'my Giesela' the woman who, only a few weeks earlier, had tearfully thanked me for saving her. When we checked the baggage later on, we saw that my clothes and furs were missing, but luckily the *Olympia* negatives were all there, unscathed.

During this period, I met Hanna Reitsch, the famous pilot. It was a brief meeting, since she was still in American custody, on an occasion when, guarded by two soldiers, she was being allowed to visit a grave. This young woman, universally admired for her unique talent as an aviator, was the first female flight captain, and she had broken many world records. After the war, she went through a dreadful time. Shortly before Hitler's death, she had pulled off a miraculous flying feat when her friend Colonel General Ritter von Greim was ordered to report to the Reich Chancellery. It was suicidal. Berlin was already being shelled by the Russians and Greim refused to take Hanna Reitsch along, even though she begged to be allowed to accompany him. However, she managed to hide in the small two-seater plane and Greim did not discover her until after they had taken off. When, as they soared through the Russian barrage, the general was seriously wounded and blacked out, Hanna Reitsch, sitting behind him, grabbed the controls

319

and actually managed to land under fire on Charlottenburger Chaussee. She also succeeded in reaching the Reich Chancellery with her injured friend.

After appointing Greim as Göring's successor, Hitler ordered the general and the pilot to leave the Reich Chancellery. They refused, for, like the others, they wanted to die with Hitler, but he insisted that they follow his orders. It was then that Reitsch did the impossible: she took off amid the artillery barrage and flew the wounded Greim out of the surrounded city. After they landed near Kitzbühel, Greim, her best friend, shot himself right in front of her. A short time later, she learned about the terrible deaths of her family. Her father, an inveterate National Socialist, had taken a rifle and killed the entire family, then turned it on himself.

After these experiences, which were only a few weeks old, I was amazed that she had the strength to tell me other things. Reaching into her pocket, she pulled out a crumpled letter, handed it to me, and said with some urgency, 'Read this letter. It may be taken away from me, and then no one but me will know what it says. It's from Dr Goebbels and his wife Magda to their son Harald, who's thought to have been imprisoned by the Americans.'

The letter was four pages long, the first two pages written by Goebbels, the last two by Magda. I was embarrassed by the contents. I could not understand how, given the situation in which the Goebbels family had found themselves, they could write about 'honour and a heroic death'. The text was bombastic in the extreme and I felt that Hanna Reitsch thought so too.

The American soldiers pestered her to finish the conversation. While one of them took her by the shoulder, she said, 'I have to tell you one more thing. The Führer mentioned you too; it was several months ago, when I finally managed to get to see him. I had to speak to him because I was the victim of the most incredible intrigues – having so many colleagues who resented my success. Hitler told me that this was unfortunately the fate of many women. He named several women and then said, "Look at Leni Riefenstahl. She has so many enemies. I've been told she's sick, but I can't help her. If I did, it could mean her death."'

When I heard that, I thought of Udet's warning. In 1933, shortly after I completed the work of the first Party rally film, he said, 'Be careful, there's a group in the SA that's after your life.'

I recall something else from my meeting with Hanna Reitsch. She told me that she had submitted a proposal to Hitler on behalf of a large group of German fighter pilots who were all prepared to dive into the British navy in order to prevent any landing of the Allies. Hitler, she said, very firmly rejected this idea with the words. 'Every person who risks his life in the battle for his Fatherland must have a chance of survival, even if it's small. We

Germans are not Japanese kamikaze.' This was another contradiction of the horrors perpetrated during the war.

I asked Hanna Reitsch, 'Did you really intend to do that?'

'Yes,' said that small, frail woman in a determined voice. We hugged. Then she was taken to the jeep by the American soldiers and I never saw her again.

MY BIG MISTAKE

My freedom had scarcely lasted a month, when it came to an abrupt end. Medenbach told me one morning that the Americans would be withdrawing from the Tyrol the next day in order to leave the occupation to the French, and he advised me to move to the American zone. That day, I committed one of the biggest mistakes of my life. Despite Medenbach's warning, I couldn't bring myself to leave Kitzbühel – the reason being that I still had the obsessive idea of completing *Tiefland*.

It wouldn't have been possible to move all the footage and the technical facilities to the American zone in the brief time that the French demanded. Over three hundred thousand feet of film were stored in Kitzbühel, and my completed sound studio and cutting rooms were in Seebichl House. I also felt safe because of the document from American headquarters, which guaranteed my freedom. Moreover, my greatest film successes had been in France, and I had won the most awards in Paris, so I felt no apprehension while I waited for the French; on the contrary, I looked forward to their arrival.

Major Medenbach was very uneasy about my decision. He said that the French were unpredictable, and once he had left the Tyrol, he would no longer be able to help me. If only I had gone with them! I was under American protection. My big mistake was to assume that the French would treat me as fairly as the Americans had. Before the Americans left Kitzbühel, they rescinded the confiscation of Seebichl House and everything was handed back to us in an impeccable state. Absolutely nothing was missing. We could once again live in our own house. However, this meant another separation from my husband whom Major Medenbach took with him to Gastein as his chauffeur in order to protect him from possible imprisonment by the French.

At first, everything seemed to go well. The changeover was smooth and uneventful as American uniforms and flags were replaced by French ones. But, within a few days, I was visited by several Frenchmen, who introduced themselves as cinema officers. They were friendly and inquired about

Tiefland. Nothing indicated that I would have any trouble. I also received an invitation from the French military govenor of Kitzbühel, Monsieur Jean Reber, who chatted with me for a long time and offered to help me. It was perhaps two weeks later that a French military vehicle pulled up at Seebichl House and a uniformed Frenchman gruffly ordered me to get some toiletries together and come along with him. When I asked what this meant and where we were going, he didn't answer.

This time, I really was afraid. But it had come so suddenly, so unexpectedly, that surely it must be a mistake. The French commander had offered me his help with such warmth.

The Frenchman drove recklessly; when an old peasantwoman was crossing the road, he raced towards her at top speed and grinned when, terrified, she jumped aside at the last moment and went sprawling. The pig she was leading dashed across the road, and since the driver couldn't brake, he ran over it.

In Innsbruck, I was brought not to a prison, thank goodness, but to an elderly couple who lived in the centre of town. They were informed about my coming, but knew little more than I did; they were told only that I was not allowed to leave their home until I was called for. These people, who were intimidated but friendly, served me food and tried to calm me. I was called for the very next day and brought to a building with a French flag waving on it which proved to be the office of the feared Deuxième Bureau.

I was taken to a garret in which there was a camp-bed and when I stretched out on it, my pains returned; I was so afraid of what lay ahead of me. A few hours later, I was taken to a lower room, where several uniformed Frenchmen were sitting at a long table, having a meal. I had to sit down and watch the soldiers eating their lunch but I was given no food and, even worse, nothing to drink, despite my request. Then I was taken back to the garret. The same brutal procedure was repeated that evening and the next day. My hunger was bearable, but my thirst tormented me dreadfully.

This torture didn't end until the following day when I was given a cup of tea and a piece of bread. Then I was taken to a small room, where a girl, who didn't even deign to glance at me, was typing. After what seemed like an endless wait, a uniformed Frenchman came and handed me a document in French. It was an order issued by Lieutenant Colonel Andrieu, head of security, informing me that I had to leave the French zone within twenty-four hours, by the evening of 4 August. I was allowed to take personal belongings, my money and my film *Tiefland*, as well as all films I had made before 1933.

I breathed a sigh of relief at his decision, which I hadn't expected. It meant I had a great deal to do – and my husband and Medenbach were in Bad Gastein. I had to pack the films and objects, withdraw the money from the bank and find transportation in order to get everything across the zone boundary by the next evening.

I wanted to say goodbye to Lieutenant Colonel Andrieu and thank him, but I wasn't permitted. They took me outside and left me in the street without a word. In the train to Kitzbühel, I had such a violent attack of colic that I couldn't leave the compartment on my own. Other passengers helped me, and once at the station, they notified the small Kitzbühel hospital where I was put in a single room and given some injections by Dr Von Hohenbalken, the hospital chief. When the pain subsided, I could sit up in bed and look out of the window. I was alarmed to see that the hospital was guarded by several French policemen. I had been ordered out of the French Zone just a few hours before, but apparently I was once again a prisoner.

When the physician returned he said a French officer urgently wanted to speak to me but I insisted I couldn't see anyone in this condition because I felt too wretched. But the Frenchman simply walked into my room, hugged me, and said exuberantly, 'Leni, mon ange, nous sommes très heureux!' I looked at him, bewildered. He was a young, good-looking man, who introduced himself as François Girard, the officer of the French Film Division in Paris.

'Don't you know that I have to leave the French Zone by tomorrow evening?'

'I know,' he said. 'But you mustn't leave, we mustn't lose you. Don't go over to the Americans. You've got to stay with us.'

It was maddening. I showed him Lieutenant Colonel Andrieu's document. Skimming it, Girard said, 'I know, but this is from the Sureté; they're ignoramuses when it comes to cinema. They don't realize what they'll be doing if they hand you and your *Tiefland* film over to the Americans. I'm not responsible to the Sureté; I work for General Bethouart, the head of the French military government in Austria, and I'm here on his behalf.'

I was at a loss. Who had the supreme decision, the Sureté or the military government? Whom should I believe? My freedom was at stake. Girard tried to explain the situation. He said, 'The French military government and the Sureté are at odds. The Sureté people are Communists and the military government people are nationalists.'

I was so confused that I wanted to get advice from Major Medenbach and my husband and I managed to telephone them with the physician's help. Both of them warned me, saying it could only be a trap, and I absolutely must follow Andrieu's order. They would call for me tomorrow morning and move everything in two cars.

Relieved, I repeated this to Monsieur Girard, who was desperate. He promised me that I could complete *Tiefland* in Paris under the protection of the military government and would be free to work on other films. This was tempting. I even believed him. But the die was cast, I could change nothing.

'Then at least grant us one great wish,' Girard begged. 'We know you're sick. But with the doctor's help, could you possibly screen your *Tiefland* film for us?'

'But why?' I asked. 'It is unfinished, and the sound track hasn't been added. I only have a silent work print.'

'Please grant us this favour. We're your admirers.'

I yielded, just to have a little peace. The physician gave me another injection and we drove to Seebichl House with two uniformed Frenchmen.

Again, something unbelievable took place. As we sat in the screening room, watching *Tiefland*, the door was suddenly smashed open. In came two French soldiers, holding machine guns, who gruffly demanded the print I had of Willy Zielke's film *The Steel Animal*. This print was the only one still in existence. I had wanted to rescue Zielke's unique film after the management of the German railways, which had commissioned the project, had destroyed all the prints as well as the negative.

I have never managed to learn how the French knew that I had a print of *The Steel Animal* or why they so brutally wrested it from me. The incident was very embarrassing to the Frenchmen who had come with me; but now they understood why I wanted to leave the French Zone as soon as possible.

TRAPPED

At the crack of dawn, I was packing the films into boxes and trunks with the help of my mother and several assistants when my husband rang me with bad news. On the way to pick me up, he and Major Medenbach had had a car accident. 'I'm only slightly hurt, but Medenbach is seriously injured and I have to take him to the military hospital in Gastein. But I'll still get to you in a couple of hours and bring you here.

I was dazed. What would happen to me if I couldn't meet the twenty-four-hour deadline? Extremely nervous, I waited for my husband. With only two hours to go, Peter arrived. Time was running out. We could take along nothing but the essentials. The *Tiefland* material had to be left in Kitzbühel. We managed to say goodbye to the French commander of Kitzbühel, who, like Monsieur Girard, regretted my departure from the French Zone.

Just a few minutes later, at the edge of the village, we were stopped by a French military patrol and, despite our protests and my screams, we were forced into their car. All we were allowed to take along was one hand bag. Two armed Frenchmen sat in front while we sat in the back. My husband tried to calm me. At one point, one of the Frenchmen turned around, grinned, and said to my husband in broken German, 'You too in prison.' Unlike me, my husband managed to remain calm and composed even when he was indeed taken to the penitentiary in Innsbruck. I was greatly distressed by this abrupt and unforeseen separation.

I was taken to another building, which had been heavily damaged by bombs. When I desperately asked what would happen to my husband, I received no answer. They brought me to a room in which there were many women, most of them sitting on the floor, a few on chairs; I crept into a corner. My colic started up again and for a while, I lay all rolled up on the floor trying to hide my cramps. Then I heard voices and became aware of people bending over me, but then I must have blacked out. When I came to, I found myself in a small room with a straw mattress on the floor, and a young man in mufti, who proved to be the prison doctor, was standing in front of me. He gave me some tablets and a glass of water; then I lay down on the mattress and fell asleep. When I woke up, I tried to recall the previous day, but of what happened after I had been forcibly separated from my husband I could summon only the vaguest of images. The cell I was lying in had only a stand with a basin, aside from the straw mattress. I lay there apathetically, unable to eat and careless of what happened to me. It was only when the doctor walked in and asked me how I felt that I ventured to ask where I was.

'You are in the sick ward of the Innsbruck women's prison. Unfortunately, we don't have any better rooms to put you up in. I'm sorry, I'm only the prison physician. In case you need me, my name is Dr Linder.'

'I can only have been brought here by mistake,' I said.

The doctor broke in. 'We have no influence on the orders of the occupation forces. You were brought here on the instructions of the Sureté, who were acting on orders from the highest level.'

'What about my husband? What's happening to him?'

The doctor shrugged. Behind him stood a French guard.

'Come along,' said Dr Lindner, 'the toilet is outside your cell. You'll have to get used to having a guard accompany you there.'

I believe two or three weeks passed before the guard left me alone with the physician for a moment and I was able to ask him to inform Major Medenbach at the military hospital in Gastein that my husband was at the Innsbruck penitentiary. The physician nodded. Within a few days, my cell door was opened, and I recognized Medenbach through the crack. I wasn't even allowed to shake his hand. 'Leni, Peter is free, I managed to get him out of prison, but not you. Be patient, you'll be released as well. Unfortunately, I have to return to the States tomorrow but Peter has my address and we'll stay in touch. Be brave. Goodbye.'

What a relief that at least Peter was no longer in prison.

Of all my post-war experiences, the weeks I spent in the Innsbruck Prison were the most taxing. Apart from going to the toilet, I was never once permitted to leave the cell and for hours on end I dozed on my straw mattress lost to all feeling. I had no communication with the other prisoners. Except for the doctor, who was always accompanied by a sentry, the prison guard who brought me food was the only person I could speak to. He was an ugly man of indefinable age whose ears stuck out and whose small, grey eyes were strangely blurred and expressionless. This man always stared at me whenever he brought me food. One day, he said, 'Today, someone else jumped out of the window – a famous actor from Vienna. That makes three.'

'Do you know his name?' I asked, aroused from my lethargy, but the man merely shrugged.

After I told him one day that I felt like dying because I couldn't stand the pain anymore and my will to live was broken, he smuggled a brochure into my cell which detailed all the methods of suicide. I read that when tobacco or cigarettes are soaked in alcohol for a long time, a poisonous fungus is produced – but unfortunately I had neither tobacco nor cigarettes. My yearning to die increased every day, and I pestered the guard to bring me some kind of poison from the poison cabinet he said was sometimes left open. The reward he desired for this macabre service was so grotesque that only a lunatic could have hit upon it. He said with an earnest face, 'I'll bring you the poison, but only if you dance a tango in this cell before swallowing it.' His weird, crazy words shook me out of my lethargy. My reaction was to call the physician, but my voice failed, and I couldn't produce a sound. It was at that moment that three men wearing dark uniforms and steel helmets entered the cell. Wordlessly they walked up to my mattress and thrust a document at me which I was obviously supposed to sign. One of them said something in French but I understood nothing and couldn't even ask what the paper was. One of the men handed me a pen while a second propped me up and pointed to a place at the lower edge of the paper. After signing, I was left alone again to wonder whether I had signed my death warrant or a petition for mercy. In a kind of stupor, I fell asleep.

Presently I became aware of a shadow bending over me. It was when I heard her voice that I realized it was my mother. She was sitting on the floor next to my mattress, stroking my forehead. We embraced tearfully, for a long time. A guardian angel must have brought her to me.

On the train to Kitzbühel, she told me about all her efforts to get me out of prison. After a week of trying and failing to learn anything about my whereabouts she had gone to the French offices in Innsbruck. Since one was not allowed to go more than three and a half miles from my town, the journey was a difficult undertaking and she had to walk long distances. In Innsbruck, she tried to see Colonel Andrieu several times, but never got past his anteroom; there she was told, 'A petition for mercy is hopeless. Your daughter was the mistress of Satan. She will never again see the light of day.'

Refusing to give up, my mother visited a different French office every day, at last she met with success. She never knew who was responsible for my release – it was probably the military government and not the Deuxième Bureau. All she was told was that she could pick me up at the prison.

Under my mother's care, I gradually recovered my physical strength, but mentally I was still in a state of dull imagination. All my hopes had been dashed far too often. Even when I received a document from the French military commander of Kitzbühel, I remained sceptical. The document said:

At the orders of General Bethouart, Commander-in-Chief in Austria, Frau Leni Riefenstahl-Jacob has the right to remain in her house on Schwarzee in Kitzbühel, where she is to complete her film *Tiefland*.

After everything I had gone through in the French Zone, I could only view this as mockery, but my husband, who was now back with us again, was optimistic. According to this notification, he said, I was now under the protection of the French military government in Austria.

He was mistaken. After a short respite, French policemen suddenly reappeared and surrounded our house, justifying my chronic paranoia. A police officer declared that his orders came from a high-level agency in Paris and applied to all the people living in Seebichl House at that time. None of us was permitted to leave the place and this house arrest included not only my mother and my husband, but three of my staff members who happened to be there. Neither my husband nor my mother nor any of my three assistants had ever joined the Nazi Party, nor had any of us been politically active. No charges had ever been filed against us, yet we were at the mercy of the French and had no legal protection of any kind. We were not told the grounds for this new arrest nor anything about its likely duration. We were simply told to order food by telephone and it would be delivered to the house, but we were not allowed to receive visitors. This was my fourth arrest in the French Zone since I had received a written confirmation from the highest level that we could remain and that I was to be allowed to work. All our attempts to reach the commander of Kitzbühel were futile.

A telephone call from Uli Ritzer in Innsbruck made the new harassment more understandable. He said he had run into Gisela Schneeberger at the Sureté office several times, and she had testified there that my film equipment at Seebichl House consisted of personal gifts from Hitler. The French had then appointed the Schneebergers as trustees of my firm and of my assets.

As if that were not enough, a French newspaper sent to me ran a photomontage of myself in General Bethouart's arms. The caption said, 'Leni Riefenstahl, Hitler's former mistress, is now the mistress of our General Bethouart.' I had never even met the general. Clearly, this smear campaign was directed not only at me, but also at the general, to whom I probably owed my release from the prison in Innsbruck. The general's political adversaries, the Deuxième Bureau – the French secret police – were so powerful that, some time later, the general was temporarily removed from his post as commander-in-chief of the French military government in Austria. His opponents were also my enemies.

We were isolated more and more. Our telephone was cut off and my bank account seized, as were my husband's and my mother's. The next step was the confiscation of my film archives and all my personal effects – including clothes, linen, jewellery, etc. – and, finally, our home itself. We all had to leave Seebichl House, each being allowed to take just one hundred and twenty Reichsmarks and one piece of baggage weighing no more than fifty kilograms (one hundred and ten pounds). We were taken to a farmhouse several miles away and a French soldier was left to guard us; a decision as to our fate wasn't reached until weeks later and it was communicated to us by a member of the Sureté who informed us that, on the orders of the French government, we had to leave Austria and were being evacuated to Germany. I asked if I could take along my films and my money, but my request was denied.

We left the Tyrol in an open truck, escorted by three Frenchmen clutching rifles. As we drove through St Anton, I heard that several of my staff were filming there. They had started a company while I was imprisoned in Innsbruck and were making a mountain film with my cameras and equipment. My Pedro was cast in the lead, my assistant, Dr Harald Reinl, was the director and Waldi Traut was in charge of the production. They were all my disciples, and I was glad that they at least had been able to get back to work – and I wanted to say goodbye to them.

Our French driver was sympathetic and went to notify them at the Black Eagle, where the group was having lunch. But I was to suffer a painful disappointment. Of all these people, who had been on my staff for years, only one came out to say goodbye to me: the youngest one, Franz Eichberger, the Pedro in the *Tiefland* film. My best friends would not come out – not one of them. I had helped them and their careers for years, and now they refused to have anything to do with me. As we drove off, 'Pedro' watched us tearfully.

Shortly before reaching the border, our truck somehow got stuck; as a result of the violent lurch, my husband broke his leg and it had to be put into a cast at the nearest hospital. Once back on the road, we drove to the German border. The Frenchmen stationed there had not been informed about what was to happen with us. They asked me what city I would like to go to.

'Berlin,' I said.

'Impossible,' they said. 'It has to be a city in the French Zone.'

I named Freiburg, remembering Dr Fanck, who had had a house there. Of course, I didn't even know if he was still alive.

Since no shelter could be found in Freiburg, which had been almost destroyed by bombs, we were quartered in a prison that first night. The next day, I tried to reach my former director, and actually managed to find him. However, Dr Fanck was another who refused to have anything to do with me; when he brusquely told me not to call him any more, I stood by the telephone, aghast. I had always been there for him. When he was unemployed, I had persuaded Speer to hire him to film the model buildings of Berlin and as a result he had not only received a good salary, but had been exempt from military service for the entire war. I had confidently counted on his help.

Since the French couldn't find a place for us in Freiburg, they drove us to Breisach, a small town not too far away, but here too there was nothing but ruins and rubble. Breisach was the German city that had been bombed most in the war; eighty-five per cent of it had been destroyed. The mayor, a helpful man, didn't know what to do with us but finally assigned us the badly damaged rooms of the Hotel Salmen. We were still under arrest and were ordered to report to the French police twice a week.

IN BREISACH

During the dismal period we lived in the ruins of Breisach, we suffered most from hunger since almost nothing could be obtained with the food cards. With the bread cards, one could get a daily ration of fifty grams – a thin slice – but not always, and the only thing we could smear on it was a little vinegar. There were no vegetables, no meat, no fat, not even skimmed milk. How happy I was when a farmer once gave me a bunch of carrots!

The French were very harsh. I had met a young girl in Breisach, Hanni Isele, who later became my live-in maid. Her parents had a vegetable garden and fruit trees, but she was not allowed to pick a single plum or apple there, not even the fruit that had fallen to the ground. French soldiers even checked the allotment gardens and hit old people and children on the hands if they tried to remove fallen fruit.

My staff fell deeper and deeper into despair. Frau Steffen, who had worked in the cutting room with me for years, was still a young woman, but her hair now turned white. She almost lost her mind, because she was not allowed to go to Berlin, where her husband, who had returned from a POW camp, was waiting for her. She was not permitted to leave Breisach, had no money, and went hungry – as did Fräulein Lück, my secretary, and Herr Hapke, my bookkeeper. I couldn't help them for I had nothing myself.

As for my husband, the separations we were forced to endure had been causing tension between us for a long time. Peter was oppressed by my illness and by the repeated arrests, especially since after almost five years of combat he deserved a better life. He did many things that made me suffer and our affection turned increasingly into a love-hate relationship but circumstances did not allow us to have even a trial separation. We had to live together in a very narrow space, and in the most undignified circumstances.

As our life in Breisach became more and more intolerable, I wrote a desperate letter to General König, the supreme commander of the French zone of occupation in Germany. The reaction came five months later, in August 1946, when a French police car picked me up and took me to a military building in Baden-Baden. There I was given a room together with another woman, a foreigner who, as I eventually realized, was planted there to pump me. During my interrogations, I often failed to understand what they were driving at. For instance, I was asked to describe the hair colour of some actress or other or the colour of the eyes of a well-known German film star or answer other such trivial and ludicrous questions. Then suddenly everything changed and I was ordered to tell them which artists had believed in Hitler and which had been friendly with him.

'I'm no informer,' I said. 'And I couldn't tell you anyway, because I had little to do with my professional colleagues. Apart from Emil Jannings,

Gertrud Eysoldt and Brigitte Horney, I was personally acquainted only with the actors and actresses who performed in my films.' The French response to this was to tighten the screws. They fed me less and subjected me to relentless mental torture.

Then they hit on a different line of questioning. 'Which of your acquaintances were National Socialists out of conviction, and not just artists?' It went like this, day after day. They asked me about people like Ernst Udet and others. 'We will reward you for every item of information. You can get a house on the Riviera and work freely again as an artist.' I was so repelled that I obstinately refused to answer any more questions at all.

Again they changed the subject and brought up the concentration camps. This led to more and more violent arguments since they wouldn't believe that I knew of no camps apart from Dachau and Terezin. 'And you never heard of Buchenwald and Mauthausen?' one of the Frenchmen yelled at me.

'No,' I said.

'You're lying. We don't believe you. Tell the truth.'

Trembling with distress, I shouted: 'No, no, no!'

'If you cherish your mother's life, then . . .' That was too much. He got no further. I pounced on him and dug my teeth so hard into his throat that it bled.

At last they stopped tormenting me and I was taken to my room and left in peace. Several days later, I was brought before a French general in a prison. When I tried to shake his hand, he jerked it behind his back and with an icy stare said, 'We have decided to take you away from here. You will be taken to Königsfeld in the Black Forest where you will stay with your mother and your husband. Your assistants can go to Berlin, they are free. You, however, must report weekly to the French police in Villingen.'

I asked him, 'What are we supposed to live on? What about my money, my films, and the rest of my property?'

'That does not concern me, I have nothing to do with that,' he snapped.

'Please understand,' I pleaded, 'what are we supposed to live on? We have absolutely nothing.'

He did not condescend to answer. Instead, he rang and had me taken away.

KÖNIGSFELD IN THE BLACK FOREST

Before leaving Breisach, we received an unexpected visitor – my husband's sister – who came from Bavaria with a hamper full of food a farmer had given her for helping him with his work. What a banquet! Even today, after more than forty years, when I see the wealth of food in a supermarket, I still recall that day.

Königsfeld, surrounded by dark fir forests, is a quiet resort village in the Black Forest and it seemed like paradise to us. We were allocated a two-room apartment in an old villa belonging to a Frau Fanny Raithel, a member of the well-known Mendelssohn-Bartholdy family of musicians and bankers. The problem was the rent. The mayor couldn't offer us a place under three hundred marks a month. Frau Raithel, a likable elderly woman, was willing to trust us for a few months.

In Villingen, half an hour away by train, my husband found a job as a truck driver and, a short time later, as a wine salesman at the Voll Winery. This was a big help, for the farmers traded us food for wine.

I was further helped by Hanni, the girl from Breisach who had come along with us. I liked her from the first, not only because of her looks – she was extremely pretty – but also because of her warm and cheerful nature. She was nineteen years old and hoped to go to university. After my release, I wanted to have her trained as a secretary or film editor. For the time being, however, she became our live-in maid.

We soon realized that the poverty was as great in Königsfeld as in Breisach. There was nothing to buy, the shops were bare, and no black market existed. Only one kind of wealth remained: the mushrooms. It was autumn, and we went mushroom-picking in the woods every day. Although I had never seen so many mushrooms in a forest before, it wasn't just the mushrooms that we enjoyed so much, but the whole experience of the woods. During every stroll, I had a wonderful sense of freedom. No interrogations, no policemen. I enjoyed the relaxation.

By the time the first snow fell, our situation still hadn't changed. I had sent various letters and appeals to all possible French agencies, but had received no answers.

Now letters from friends and acquaintances in America began to reach me, and even a few CARE packages. Whenever a parcel arrived, it was like Christmas. Just a bar of soap or a jar of instant coffee was a treasure. Clothes, especially warm things, came from my friend Stowitts, from Major Medenbach, and from other Americans whom I didn't even know personally. Stowitts even sent me copies of letters he had written about me to the president of UNESCO and the IOC as well as the chairmen of the various national Olympic committees. Although he never managed to obtain any positive results, I couldn't have had a better advocate.

To our consternation, we discovered that the French had put all my material on trucks and carried it off – including editing tables, sound equipment, mixing desk, movie film cameras and all the office files together with my trunks, clothes and personal effects. According to Willy Kruetschnig, a friend in Kitzbühel, everything had been transported to Paris. I thought I'd lose my mind. My life's work seemed destroyed.

The Americans had rehabilitated me and returned most of my assets. They hadn't kept a single film print. But the French . . .

More bad news came from Innsbruck. Dr Kellner, a lawyer, wrote: 'Captain Petitjean, the head of the French cinema office in Tyrol and officially appointed administrator of Seebichl House and the Munich film storage, has withdrawn all the money from your accounts at the Kitzbühel Savings Bank prior to the removal of the material to Paris.' This added up to three hundred thousand marks from the company account, thirty thousand marks from my private account, four thousand marks from my mother's account, and two thousand marks from my husband's account. It was an endless chain of misfortune.

Two years had passed since the end of the war, and no proper court trial had been approved for me as yet. Nevertheless I had been deprived of my rights and my freedom. The depressions I suffered were intensified so greatly by my conflicts with my husband that I decided to leave him. I also needed medical attention at that time and a young physician in Königsfeld, Dr Heisler, hoped to get me into a sanatorium on the Feldberg, which was willing to accept me without immediate payment. He and another physician from Königsfeld appeared to have succeeded in this when, in May 1947, a French military vehicle stopped in front of our house, and I was told to get ready and come along. We didn't doubt for an instant that I was being taken to the sanatorium.

But I never got there. If enough witnesses weren't still alive to confirm that this 'episode' – that's what people call it – really happened, I could be accused of having made it up. After a two-hour drive we should have reached the sanatorium on the Feldberg, but to my horror I realized that we were driving through the town of Freiburg. We stopped in front of a large building and the two Frenchmen who were escorting me told me to follow them. After that everything happened so fast that I can no longer reconstruct the sequence of events in any detail. All I remember is that I was received in a bare hall by a physician and a nurse; that the Frenchmen signed papers; that I was then left alone with a nurse, who took my case and led me into a small room. When she left, I saw that there were iron bars on the window, and that the washbasin was also behind bars. I has obviously been brought to a closed institution. My protests were useless. The nurses shrugged, and the doctor who examined me the next day said, 'You have been brought here at the orders of the French military government to be treated for your depressions.' In despair, I asked the doctor to let me go home; but it was hopeless. I was locked up once again, this time in an insane asylum.

I have retained very little about this black episode. I recall being led through long, dark corridors, hearing loud shrieks, and one of the nurses saying: 'That was Paula Busch, the one from the circus.' I was taken to a room, where a skinny girl with a pallid face lay strapped to a bench. She let out blood-curdling screams while her body twisted up and down.

Then I was given electro-compulsive therapy, which I remember only dimly, perhaps because I was first given tranquillizing injections. Why had I been locked up in a mental institution? Was I to be certified or even done away with? A long time later, a French film artist sent me a letter, which is still in my possession. He explained that influential groups in Paris were fighting over the ownership of my films, and I was to be kept in safe custody as long as possible.

To my surprise, however, I was freed after three months. It was early August 1947 when I left the asylum with my small case and slowly trudged down the stone steps leading to the street. I had received a document that I was to present to the French office. It said that my confinement in the closed ward of the psychiatric clinic in Freiburg had been necessary because of my depressive frame of mind. A shadow fell across my path and I saw that someone was standing waiting for me. It was my husband. I was taken aback, for after beginning the divorce proceedings, I hadn't expected to see him again so soon. He took me by the arm and said. 'Herr Voll lent me his car. I'm driving you to Königsfeld.'

During the drive, we were too inhibited to talk much but Peter hesitantly told me that the divorce had already been granted – in Constance, by the state court of Baden. He had raised no objections to it, but he hoped this would not mean a complete separation.

'I wouldn't like to lose you,' he said. 'I know I've done a lot of things to you, but you have to believe that I've always loved you.' After a pause, he went on, 'Please, Leni, give me another chance. I promise you that I'll change.'

I couldn't listen to him. He had made me this promise far too often, and I had believed him far too often. 'I can't stand it any more, I'm going crazy,' I said, weeping. I was so afraid that I would give in again that I felt like jumping out of the car. I still cared much too much for him. Peter tried to calm me down.

'I want to help you,' he said, 'You need help now and you need a friend. I'll wait, and I'll always be there whenever you need me.'

Two hours later, he delivered me to my mother, who was overjoyed, and then he drove back to Villingen.

THE STRANGER FROM PARIS

Had I been free and not forced to report weekly to the French military authorities in Villingen, or had I been allowed to practise some profession or at least known when my freedom would be restored, then I would have been able to enjoy our sojourn in Königsfeld. This village, set deep in the splendid forests, had a special atmosphere, but it was the inhabitants who gave the resort its true character. They were very religious, spiritual and artistic, and Frau Raithel was a charming, warm-hearted landlady.

The intellectual life of Königsfeld was nourished by the Christian Brothers, who organized poetry readings, church concerts and interesting lectures. There were also numerous followers here of the anthroposophic teachings of Dr Rudolf Steiner, and the famous religious scholar and African-based physician Dr Albert Schweitzer had owned a summer cottage here. The town had beautiful parks, sanatoriums, boarding houses and small hotels. No blocks of flats or ugly concrete buildings disfigured the landscape. But this peaceful atmosphere did not help me. Every day, I waited for the postman more and more impatiently – waited for some kind of news of my freedom.

One foggy autumn day, a stranger came to visit me who introduced himself as Monsieur Desmarais from Paris. We were disinclined to trust him but he seemed to read my mind and said in a soft, ingratiating voice, 'Don't worry, I have good news for you.' He spoke with a French accent and I guessed his age to be about forty-five or fifty. His face was somewhat spongy, and his eyes had an indefinable expression. 'Before I tell you what brings me here,' he said, 'I would like to tell you something about myself.'

We had just received a CARE package, and so my mother could offer him tea and biscuits.

'I come from Paris, but I was born in Germany and lived in Cologne until 1937. Then I emigrated to France. My French name is Desmarais, my German name is Kaufmann.' There was a pause. None of us dared to ask a question. We were too intimidated by everything we had gone through.

'I know all your films,' he said, 'and I am a great admirer of yours. So is my wife.'

'Please tell me your profession,' I said. 'Are you from the press?'

Smiling, he shook his head. 'No, you're not dealing with some nasty reporter, or with a secret agent in disguise. I am a French film producer.'

He handed me a business card from his wallet. It read:

L'Atelier Français, Société Anonyme
Capital de 500 000 Fr.
6, Rue de Cerisolos
Paris 8e

Far from being impressed by his card, I only grew more suspicious. The stranger went on. 'My wife and I are the sole owners of this firm.' His tone of voice was the kind used by card players when they are about to place their trumps on the table. 'I have acquired French citizenship, that is why I changed my name. My wife is a native Frenchwoman and has excellent knowledge of the film business. Please permit me,' he said, 'I have brought along a few little things from Paris.' He handed me a small package.

'I will unwrap it only when I know what brings you to me,' I said coldly.

The stranger leaned back and, looking at my mother, at me, and at Hanni, he said with an air of complete confidence, 'I hope to bring you freedom and to rescue your *Tiefland* film.'

I jumped up and left the room, unable to hold back my tears; I had to cry. I hadn't believed him for a moment. The thought that I was being deceived again, that everything would only go wrong again, was too much for me. My mother tried to calm me and brought me back to our visitor, who was startled by my reaction. I apologized.

'I know,' said this Monsieur Desmarais whom I had never heard of. 'You've been through a lot. I know that everything's been taken away from you, and you were put in a mental institution. But listen carefully. Soon, I hope, you'll be able to put all that suffering behind you.'

We listened in great suspense to what he had to say.

'I was working at the Paris Cinemathèque. In the basement, where a vast number of film prints are stored, I discovered boxes on which *Tiefland* and your name were written. I was curious. I realized I would not be permitted to view the material all that easily. So I tried the storage administrator. Once his palm had been greased, he was able to have several reels of the film screened for me in one night. It was an edited work print without a sound track.'

When I heard that my *Tiefland* still existed and where it was, I breathed a sigh of relief. 'You saw my *Tiefland* film?' I asked, astonished that he should have done so.

'Yes,' answered Desmarais, 'I don't know if it's the print that you cut, for in the course of my inquiries, I learned that Captain Petijean had a French film editor work on your print for over a year. A French group wanted to complete the film and exploit it without your collaboration or approval. These people have very good relations with the Deuxième Bureau and Colonel Andrieu. Naturally, they were intent on keeping you incarcerated as long as possible, so that they could make use of it without interference.'

'Then it was their idea to put me in an institution?'

'Possibly,' said Desmarais. 'I have to be very careful. No one in Paris must find out that I have visited you here.'

'But how do you intend to help me if nobody can know about it?'

'Let me explain it to you. My wife and I have a very good friend. He is one of the most honourable and most prestigious lawyers in Paris and an honorary member of the Sorbonne. His name is André Dalsace and he has declared his willingness to take your case without payment since he is deeply moved by your fate.

'If you give him permission – and I'm here to obtain it – he will take Colonel Andrieu to court.'

'That's impossible. The head of the French state police can't be sued because of a German.'

'It is possible if you assist us. What we need from you is an affidavit that contains a truthful account of everything that has happened to you in the French zones of Austria and Germany. If you have appropriate documents, you've got to make copies and have them notarized.

'I've got important certifications from the headquarters of the American Seventh Army and from Colonel Andrieu. I'll show them to you. But what are your motives for championing me like this?' I asked.

Desmarais grinned. 'Well, I'm a businessman. I'd like you to complete the *Tiefland* film for me, so that we can share the profits . . .'

'Ah,' I broke in euphorically, 'if I could only regain my freedom. I don't care about the money. You can have it all.'

Within a week of his visit I received my first letter from Desmarais pressing me for my affidavit and the notarized papers and enclosing a package of chocolate, sugar and medicaments. Then a long time went by without a word from him and my patience was put to a hard test. There was only silence from Paris. I became increasingly resigned. I spent Christmas 1947 and the start of 1948 in a dejected mood. But then came the first letter from Professor Dalsace, and it made me confident. He sent me various forms, applications to the French national court and powers of attorney for trials, which I had to sign and return.

In mid-January, Desmarais visited us again. He brought along two contracts, which I signed regardless – I would have signed just about anything to regain my freedom. The first contract stipulated that his firm, l'Atelier Français, would have exclusive worldwide use of all my films, including *Tiefland*. We would share the net profits fifty-fifty. In addition, I had to agree to submit to Monsieur Desmarais any film projects that I initiated or that were suggested to me.

The second contract specified that l'Atelier Français would negotiate any film deals proposed to me, whether as a director, actress or in any other capacity. Furthermore, my written works were to be published and sold worldwide by Desmarais's company. The contract would run for a period of ten years. Moreover, I signed a power of attorney saying that after the release of my property, all my confiscated film material could be handed over only to Monsieur Desmarais.

Given my situation at that time, I would have agreed to even more unfavourable conditions without giving it a second thought.

In early February 1948, sooner than I dared to dream, the postman brought me my freedom in a document issued by the French military government of the state of Baden. After nearly three years' arrest, I was once again a free woman. Monsieur Desmarais had not been making empty promises.

TRENKER AND EVA BRAUN'S DIARY

Professor Dalsace had managed to have my arrest rescinded and now he made efforts to have my property released. This meant not just the films, but also the cash that Captain Petitjean had withdrawn from our accounts in Kitzbühel. Without money, we couldn't even leave Königsfeld.

Then new problems cropped up. My French lawyer wrote that although he had obtained confirmation of the release of my property, everything had then been revoked by orders from above. The reason for this was that sensational stories by certain French newspapers had caused a great stir in Paris. Eva Braun's diary had been published, and Luis Trenker had vouched for its authenticity. The front pages of the gutter press sported huge headlines like LENI'S NAKED DANCES FOR ADOLF, MARLENE TO PLAY LENI over the claim that 'Eva's Braun's diary, published by Luis Trenker, is being

On the rally terrain in Nuremberg, 1934.
This was my final attempt to persuade Hitler to release me
from making a film about the rally.

One of the mass demonstrations at the Luitpoldhain. Albert Speer
helped me construct a small lift on the flagpole which allowed motion
shots and made for dynamic footage of the demonstrations.

Hitler receiving artists at the Reich Chancellery.
I am third from the right.

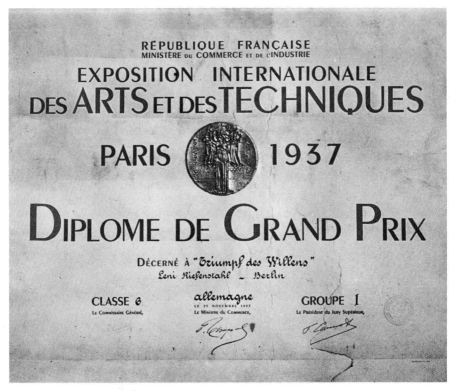

The certificate accompanying the gold medal won by
Triumph of the Will at the 1937 World's Fair in Paris. My
medal was presented to me by Edouard.

Prior to the start of the Olympic Games in Berlin in 1936. I was
looking for suitable camera sites with Guzzi Lantschner.

With Waldi Traut, executive producer of my Olympic film

With cameraman Walter Frentz in one of the pits which I had to
fight so hard to have built

Lovelock of New Zealand (in the black shirt) broke the world record in the 1500-meter race. In this photograph Cunningham of the USA is still in the lead.

Jesse Owens of the USA, the star and favourite of the
Olympic spectators and winner of four gold medals

filmed in Hollywood. Marlene Dietrich has been cast as Riefenstahl.' There was more of the same.

Many lies have been spread about me, but these defamations were the nastiest and also the most stupid. And they came at the very moment when, after years of effort, the French government had finally rescinded the confiscation of my property.

Professor Dalasce wrote: 'While I personally do not believe the news stories and consider the diary a gross fabrication, I cannot do anything for you at the present time. I can resume my efforts only if you succeed in proving that the diary is a forgery.'

I couldn't and wouldn't believe that Trenker had had anything to do with this horrible forgery. After 1933, I had shaken hands with him by way of reconciliation, telling him that I wanted us to be friends, and I remembered how cheerfully he had agreed. He had interrupted his location work on the Matterhorn especially to come to the House of German Art, and had written enthusiastically about my picture book *Beauty in the Olympic Struggle*, which came out in 1938: 'These are photographs such as have never been seen – a paean to beauty and a thank-you to the gods of Mount Olympus!'

Could a man who had written those words publish a forgery that libelled me so wretchedly? I would have to ask him personally to clear the matter up. It occurred to me that a French newspaper had already said a year earlier that Luis Trenker would be publishing Eva Braun's diary and, although I regarded this item as a canard I had written to Trenker asking him to explain. His reply completely ignored my question; he did not so much as mention the diary.

Gries by Bolzano, 25.7.47

Dear Leni,

Please forgive me for not finding time to get back to you until now. I've been in Venice for three months, working on a film, and because of various other obligations, I've been unable to take care of my private correspondence. The collapse of the National Socialists was bound to cause you problems and anxieties during the past two years; and their downfall was probably too horrible for you to get over it all that readily . . . It is not easy; there is a hard, austere future to overcome, in which few will ask about those who believed in the false doctrines of that 'Leader'. Thus, you too must go through the purgatory that many of you have earned, a time of penitence and soul-searching . . . More than anything, I wish you spiritual recuperation and an end to all your worries, and I still think of the lovely time of our working together. With best greetings from me and also from Hilda,

Luis

I was stunned by his letter – not only because he didn't even mention the diary, but because I was offended by what he said. His words sounded so hypocritical. In no way was Trenker persecuted by the Nazis, as he liked to represent himself as having been after the war. He had only temporarily fallen out of favour with Dr Goebbels because of his 1936 film *Condottieri*. On the Day of German Art, in 1937, Trenker had told me he would have simply cut out those scenes if the Ministry of Propaganda had asked him to do so. After *Condottieri*, Trenker had made several more great films in Germany – *The Mountain Calls* in 1937, for instance, and *Love Greetings from the Engadin* in 1938. And if he had been unpopular with the Nazis, they wouldn't have allowed him to make a national film like *The Fire Devil*, which he both directed and starred in. Then, in 1942-3, he played the male lead in *The Germanic Woman*, which was directed by W. Kimmich, Goebbels' brother-in-law.

But still, I never had the impression that Trenker was a friend of the National Socialists, something I have emphasized when interrogated by the Americans and the French. I knew there were two sides to his character but I didn't want to hurt him. Even now, I have qualms about bringing up that repulsive diary affair. But it had such a crucial effect on my life that I cannot omit it from my memoirs.

Before I could undertake anything in this matter, I received a surprise visit from Monsieur Desmarais and his wife and the news they brought was extremely upsetting. The diary publication had exploded like a bomb among my adversaries in Paris. These sensational 'revelations' were new ammunition to be used against the release of my property. Just a few days after the publication, a session of top-level French government officials rescinded the release of my property and ordered a new confiscation.

'You must,' Desmarais and his wife pleaded, 'do everything you can to prove that this diary is a fabrication. We've had our problems too ever since it became known that we have been helping you and are planning to complete the *Tiefland* film. The Frenchmen employed at the Cinemathèque Française – the institution where your film material is stored – have told the Sureté that we are Nazi collaborators. It will be difficult to finish the film in Europe. Canada or the USA would be better. Would you be agreeable to that?'

My head swam.

'If I were unable to prove that the diary is forged, would *Tiefland* then remain confiscated?' I asked anxiously.

'We've considered that,' said Monsieur Desmarais. 'It would make the situation more difficult, but not impossible. What would the French do with the uncompleted film if you cannot manage to finish it yourself? I would try to buy it through a third party. But,' he added, 'nothing will work out if you fail to prove that the diary is a fabrication.'

After the departure of the Desmarais, I felt utterly dejected. The goal of completing *Tiefland* after all had once again receded into the distance. In addition, I was burdened by new conflicts with my ex-husband who kept trying to talk me into remarrying him. Despite my common sense and my painful experiences of several years, I agreed. My mother, who liked her erstwhile son-in-law, also urged me to take him back. Peter was so filled with genuine remorse that after hesitating for a long time, I finally said yes, but on one condition, which he accepted. We agreed on a trial period of six months, during which time Peter had to prove to me that he could be faithful. I would have been happy if this experiment had led to a harmonious marriage.

At first, everything went well. Peter was considerate, visiting us frequently and helping us whenever he could. Since he received only a small monthly salary at the wine company and gave us every last mark of it, he could do nothing else for us financially; however, he took over my petitions and correspondence and I really believed a new, belated happiness was possible. But Peter was incapable of keeping his promise – and he broke it in an almost brutal way. Leaving no address, he suddenly vanished, and it was only by chance that I learned he was in Hamburg, living with a young woman whom he had promised to marry. When this woman wrote me a letter about it, everything was over. And more was destroyed than just my love and my marriage.

After returning from Hamburg, Peter tried to force me to discuss everything with him but I never wanted to see him again. Whenever he came to Königsfeld, my mother hid me in order to save me any further upset. He pestered her, trying to find out my hiding-place, but my mother came up with new excuses every time. I would not have survived a meeting with him and it was to avoid the possibility that I decided to leave Königsfeld for a long period.

In Villigen, I obtained a pass to enter the American Zone. Before leaving Königsfeld, I wrote my mother a letter which reveals my state of mind better then my memory can do today.

Dearest Mother,

I have to leave for a while, for something awful is bound to happen if Peter and I try to live together again. Because of my shattered nerves, his irascibility would, I believe, lead to serious consequences. Don't worry about me, dearest Mother. I'll find people everywhere who will be good to me – and a guardian angel is always nearby whenever things are really bad. I am going through an awful ordeal at the moment, and I have to be all alone until I find the inner strength to struggle through this life no matter what fate may have in store. I have written a detailed letter to Peter. Do not treat him bitterly. During the past few months he really has tried to keep his promise and take care of us. I am grateful to him for his efforts – and you should be too – but it was just too much for him. It is not his fault that he cannot live with me as he would have to for us to be happy. His relapse came at just the right time, before a new marriage bound us together and destroyed us both. My renunciation of him is the greatest sacrifice that I can make, for I love him with all my soul but what good is that if I cannot make him or myself happy. My yearning for a life without lies is far greater than the dubious happiness of being loved but deceived. We have been forced to bear so many heavy strokes of fate over the last few years but we shall get through this too. It is my earnest desire, dearest Mother, to bring some joy into your hard and often unhappy life, but I cannot do so if I am mentally crushed. The loss of my *Tiefland* film and our property, my illness and the collapse of my career – none of this means anything to me compared with the disaster of my marriage. But don't be too sad, my dearest, I will soon be with you again, and we will not despair, God protects us.

Your Leni

I was given a lift in a truck driving from Villingen to Munich, my first trip out of the French Zone in two years. When we stopped to rest in Augsburg, in the American Zone, I couldn't believe my eyes. The people I saw here were so cheerful; they were singing German songs together with American GIs. I felt as if I were on a different planet. Nothing here recalled the hostile atmosphere of the French Zone. I had seen no laughing faces during the whole of my two years there. The Germans seemed careworn and apathetic while the French often looked forbidding or wore expressions of arrogance.

In Solln near Munich, I was able to stay with my mother-in-law, a very nice woman whom I called Mama Jacob. She was delicate, almost fragile-looking but had an iron will which no one could break down.

She did only what she considered right, often to the distress of her daughter, who lived with her. Both of them spoiled me, even though they knew that my marriage to their greatly loved 'little boy', as they called Peter, had foundered. Their house had been damaged by bombs, but it was already repaired; here too, people acted as if there had been no war. Only the ruins throughout the town recalled the nights of bombing.

Supplied with a bit of money and food, I took the train to Rosenheim where, shortly before the end of the war, things from my home in Berlin and from my mother's home – chiefly rugs, books and a few valuable paintings, to which my mother was extremely attached – had been stored with a farmer. Through the local registration office, I managed to track down the farmer, but not our belongings. After the end of the war, the mayor had allowed the released prisoners three days of looting – but considering everything else we had lost, this disaster scarcely bothered me.

In a restaurant, I fortified myself with a liver-dumpling soup, and again I was captivated by the atmosphere. As I sat at a round table in a corner, observing the people, a healthy looking farmer came over and asked if he could join me. He introduced himself: 'I'm Hermann Grampelsberger, the proprietor of this restaurant, and you are Frau Riefenstahl, aren't you?'

'You recognized me?' I asked, somewhat anxiously.

'Of course I recognized you, I know your films. But,' he went on after a pause, during which he quite openly eyed me up and down, 'you look pretty awful, and you've become very thin too.' After some further conversation, the friendly man said, 'First you have to be fed. I would like to invite you to stay at my mountain lodge where you can remain as long as you wish.'

'And where is your mountain lodge?' I asked, surprised.

'Up on the Wendelstein.'

The news soon spread that I was on the Wendelstein and, much as I liked giving autographs and conversing with people, I was worried that Peter might track me down. For the time being, however, I enjoyed the wonderful spring sunshine and the snow on the northern slopes, and borrowing skis and ski boots, I tried my first curves after a hiatus of years. While skiing, I met Paul Grupp, a cameraman who talked me into staying at his nearby mountain lodge for a while. I gratefully accepted his invitation.

One day, I received an unexpected visitor: my ex-boyfriend Hans Ertl, one of the top cinematographers of the Olympic film. After catching up on each other's news for hours and hours, we began to talk about Trenker and the Eva Braun diary.

'You know,' said Ertl, 'something has occurred to me. Some time back, I visited Gorter – you know, the cameraman. He's a mountain enthusiast.'

'I don't know him personally,' I said.

'He showed me a letter from Trenker, asking him to obtain information on Eva Braun which he needed for an Italian newspaper. I don't recall everything,' Ertl went on, 'because at the time it didn't interest me, but when I read what the press is saying about the diary, it rang a bell. If you could get hold of that letter, you could show up Trenker and easily expose the forgery.'

'That's incredible,' I said, genuinely amazed. 'I always believed that Trenker was innocent. I thought that the Paris press was fabricating something that he had nothing to do with. This is awful.'

Yet just a few days later, I was given further evidence that the diary was fraudulent and that Trenker had lied to everyone. Mr Musmanno, one of the judges at the Nuremberg Trial, had learned of my whereabouts and asked me to meet him in Garmisch. There, we spoke for several hours and when we came to Trenker and the 'diary', he said, 'You can take it from me: the diary is a forgery and Luis Trenker is a liar. We are familiar with the documents, and the American agencies are informed about it. Not only do you have my assurance but you can also obtain information from the War Department in Washington.'

This chance acquaintanceship with Mr Musmanno turned into a friendship of many years. Once aware of my financial plight, he sent me dollars every month. I also received unexpected help from other sources. Walter Frentz, one of the best cameramen on my Olympic film, had visited me in Königsfeld several times and he suggested that I get in touch with the Braun family. He himself would be meeting with Frau Scheider, Eva Braun's best friend, who was as incensed as were Eva Braun's parents about the forged diary.

Meanwhile, I had contacted the Gorter family in order to get hold of the Trenker letter and they had invited Frentz and myself to visit them in Kochel. Little did I realize what this visit would mean. First we talked about Fanck's and Trenker's mountain films. Gorter loved mountains more than anything else in the world, and his great wish was to work with us as a cameraman. Towards evening, we started talking about the 'diary', and upon learning that this publication had caused the French to hold back my *Tiefland* film, Gorter himself brought up Trenker's letter. He was appalled for, as a friend of Trenker's, he could not believe him capable of perpetrating a forgery. On the other hand, he greatly respected my film work and couldn't bear to think that a motion picture like *Tiefland* might be discovered. Nervously, I asked him to show me Trenker's letter.

Would he allow me to read it? Gorter stood up, hesitated for an instant, then left. It was a tense moment for so much hinged on this letter. When Gorter turned, holding the letter, my heart pounded. Then I read it:

Bolzano-Gries, 19 November 1946
Via Mazzini 16

Dear Herr Gorter,

An Italian newspaper will be running a series of articles on individual personalities of the Third Reich, including Leni Riefenstahl and Eva Braun. I have been asked to provide data on the latter's childhood, schooldays, home and parents. The newspaper is especially interested in Eva Braun's girlhood and where she spent it, her relations with her sisters and her parents, the living conditions at home, a little about her fellow students, what school she attended, plus a few brief anecdotes; friendships, romances, when she came to Heinrich Hoffmann, where she was employed by him, how she related to her fellow students, where the sisters are, what she was like at school, whether she learned something, whether she was an intelligent child, when and where she was born, where her mother comes from, and so forth. You would have to answer these questions reliably and in great detail. You could send copies of the letters to Kitzbühel and Bolzano respectively. They have to be fifteen to twenty pages long, but don't send everything at once, just four or five pages at a time. If you can enclose a few pictures of her house or parents, I'd appreciate it. So far as I know, her parents live in Ruhpolding. The newspaper will be paying me a fee of thirty thousand lira, and I'll send you half in the form of food packages, in case you need them. If you want a different manner of payment, please write to me. Please let me know very soon whether you can possibly take care of this matter for me but, whatever happens, you must not say anything about it to anyone.

With best wishes, I remain
Yours truly,
Trenker

P.S. If you go there yourself, you needn't indicate the reasons. Just talk to the people in general terms. You could send me your personal impressions of them.

What sort of venture had Trenker embarked on? Yet at that moment, I had only one thought in mind: to take this letter along in order to have the required proof that the 'diary' was a fabrication.

'What a tragedy,' said Gorter, breaking the silence, 'Trenker is ruining his life and work with such nonsense. That man once brought sublime beauty into millions of lives and people have the highest opinion of him. Why is he doing this? What does this *Son of the White Mountains*, this *Rebel, Carell* and *Fire Devil* care about the men and women of politics?' Gorter grew more and more heated as he went on, 'And he sullies everything. This isn't the old Trenker whom we esteem and love – this is a completely different, distasteful, unscrupulous fellow whom we never knew. It is very sad. But there's no changing it. Ultimately, the truth will out.'

Gorter had made up his mind. He lent me the letter for a few days so that I could make notarized copies to send to the appropriate French offices. This I did although I had no intention of filing charges against Trenker.

I didn't want to remain with my mother-in-law in Solln in case Peter tracked me down there, so I gladly accepted the Grupp family's invitation to spend several days at their home in Harlaching. My mood was almost euphoric, since I now had no doubt that I would finally get my films back.

One day, the doorbell rang insistently and as no one else was at home, I cautiously asked, 'Who is it?'

'It's me, Peter.'

What a shock! No one but the Grupp family knew where I was, not even my mother, and I made a point of picking up my letters at the post office in Munich.

'Open up,' Peter shouted impatiently. 'I've got important news for you.'

Feeling very tense, I opened the door and let him in. 'How did you find me?' I asked.

'I'll find you anywhere, no matter where you hide – anywhere in the world.'

'Who gave you my address?'

'It was very simple – the registration office.'

Tentatively, I asked. 'What sort of news?'

'Do you have anything to drink? I've come from Villingen on my motorcycle.'

'Should I make some tea?'

'No, don't bother, water will be fine.'

'Are you bringing me bad news or good news?' I asked, even more hesitantly.

'Good news, or at least I think it is. Dr Kellner, your lawyer in Innsbruck, has written to say you're to get in touch with him as soon as possible. The

French are willing to hand over some of your confiscated things to the government of the Tyrol but an Austrian trustee has to be appointed and Dr Kellner says it's important for you to speak personally to the appropriate agency in Innsbruck.'

'Is the film material also coming to Innsbruck?'

'I don't know,' said Peter, 'Dr Kellner will tell you all about it. We can get to Innsbruck in three or four hours on my motorcycle if the back seat isn't too uncomfortable for you.'

I agreed at once.

The conversation with my attorney was certainly useful, but hardly as crucial as Peter had made it seem. All I found out was that the German-language material confiscated in Austria might possibly by transferred to the Austrian government, though Dr Kellner had been given no date; I could at least give him various powers of attorney towards this end. Thus, the trip was not altogether in vain, especially as Peter agreed to take me to Königsfeld on his motorcycle. He said a lot of post had accumulated there, and my mother was missing me terribly.

I was in Königsfeld the next day, after an absence of two months, and I found my mother in poor health. The most important letter waiting for me was from Monsieur Desmarais, and it was also the most disturbing.

17.6.48

My wife and I are leaving for the United States in a few days since we are encountering far too many obstacles here. But do not worry, we will complete *Tiefland* in America with you, and we hope that you and your mother can join us there soon. Enclosed is a picture postcard of the ship on which you will sail. It is the *America*, the biggest and most luxurious liner ever built in the United States. Please be patient, and do anything you can to prove that the diary was forged. The release of your property hinges on that. Once we have taken up residence in America, we will notify you.

It all sounded like a fantasy. I was determined to have one last try at getting Trenker to tell the truth so I decided to write to him and appeal to our earlier friendship. I didn't receive his answer from Rome until three weeks later:

Temporarily in Rome, 1.8.48
Hotel Inghilterra
Via Rocca di Leone 14

Dear Leni,

. . . I'm sorry you believe that I have compromised you with the publications in *France Soir*. Two years ago, I submitted the notes to the American consul in Switzerland to have him verify them. Subsequently, these documents, so far as I know, were released in America . . . That's all I know, since they were published without my first being notified or being asked for permission. Since you as an artist were very prominent during Hitler's regime, it is understandable that positive and negative things are being written about you. Artists simply have to put up with criticism and attacks . . . As I once wrote to you, I have long since buried any personal grudge against you and I sincerely wish you the very best. Don't worry too much about the rumours circulating about you, for, as I have already mentioned, people in the public eye are always exposed to distortions and defamations. I myself had the same bitter experiences during the last seven years of the Nazi regime.

With my best greetings and wishes,

Your Luis

Friedrich A. Mainz, the former director of Tobis, wrote to tell me that his friend Emil Lustig, also a film producer, had told him in Paris that Luis Trenker had offered the publishing rights to Eva Braun's memoirs for fifty thousand dollars. However, after a thorough examination, the American military government in Germany and Austria had ascertained that the manuscript was a gross fabrication and a pornographic concoction.

Another letter, on the same subject, from Hans Steger, the mountain guide with whom I had gone on many tours, affected me even more deeply.

Bolzano, 23 July 1948

Dear Leni,

Herr Trenker's publications have caused a great stir here too. Some time back, that same gentleman wanted photos that had been taken ages ago, during the Polish tour, with you and your film crew. Trenker wanted them for publication in America. You can imagine that I sent him packing. I am telling you this only so that you can see that he will stop at nothing to cause people even greater problems than those he has already inflicted on them.

Who would have thought Trenker capable of such treachery? Now I had to do every thing I could to expose the forgery in a court of law. It would be difficult in Königsfeld so I simply had to return to Munich.

A new situation – the currency reform – occurred overnight. It went into effect on 21 June 1948 and decreed that every citizen, no matter how great the assets he had salted away or deposited in bank accounts – even millions – could receive a *per capita* replacement of only forty marks. A new economic era began – but only for people who had a job or owned such valuables as stocks, shares, furniture and other commodities. For us, the new era changed nothing. We had nothing before or after the currency reform.

With my forty marks, I took my second trip to Bavaria. Again a truck gave me a lift to Munich, while my mother and Hanni remained in Königsfeld. I was amazed that my mother endured all this so calmly. Where did she get her strength?

In the window of Humpelmayer, a luxury restaurant in Munich, I read the menu: 'Roast goose with red cabbage and potatoes, 6 marks.' Some irresistible force drew me into this expensive, exclusive restaurant. It was midday, there were very few patrons, and a waiter silently handed me an elegant menu. No meal has ever tasted as good as that one and I have never regretted the expenditure, high as it was for me at the time.

In Munich, I learned that Eva Braun's family had retained a lawyer named Dr Gritschneder to prove in court that their daughter's alleged diary was a fraud. The attorney's office informed me that Eva Braun's eldest sister wanted to speak to me. I knew no one in the family; I had never even seen Eva Braun.

Initially, at least, our meeting was rather unpleasant. Eva Braun's sister accused me of being in league with Trenker, but my dismay soon made her realize her error. 'Why don't you sue Trenker?' she asked, still fairly suspicious.

'I have no money, that's why I can't sue.'

'Then join our case as a co-plaintiff. Maybe you can apply for legal aid.'

That was how I met Dr Gritschneder, the lawyer who has defended me against libel for decades. He has never lost a single one of my cases, has won over fifty, and has helped me apply for legal aid for every single suit. I owe it to him and to his colleagues, Dr Karl Beinhardt and Dr Hans Weber, that I have not sunk under the burden of endless libel suits.

On 10 September 1948, the trial began in the ninth civil division of the Munich State Court. Unfortunately, we could not sue Luis Trenker, who preferred to remain in Italy. In those days, Germans were not allowed to sue foreigners, so for the time being, we could litigate only against the Olympia Publishing House in Zirndorf near Nuremberg, which had started running the forged Eva Braun diary in its magazine *Wochenende*.

The trial caused a sensation. Within a few short hours, Dr Gritschneder proved that the diary was forged and, on that very same day, the court issued an injunction against the publisher. The evidence presented by our lawyer was so irrefutable that the publisher didn't appeal and I too, as joint plaintiff, won my case.

The alleged diary, which Trenker claims he obtained from Eva Braun in Kitzbühel, consisted of ninety-six typescript pages without a single correction. Not even Eva Braun's signature was by hand. Let me offer a few samples of the text that Trenker maintains was written by Eva Braun:

Dr Ley, the head of the Workers' Front, had prepared a choice entertainment for the guests. For several days prior to their arrival, a bull had been exposed to the intense summer heat without being given a single drop of water. Then, on Saturday afternoon, the animal was taken to a shady fenced-in place and given unlimited amounts of water. The bull, whose intelligence was plainly not up to its strength, began to drink greedily; soon, the effect that Ley had planned came about: the animal's innards exploded, and it fell to pieces before an amused audience. Hitler and Himmler in particular found the idea 'original'.

Dr Beinhardt, the lawyer, made a wonderful discovery: parts of the Eva Braun 'diary' had been lifted from Countess Larisch-Wallersee's revelations about the imperial court of Vienna – published in 1913.

Entire passages had been taken over almost verbatim from the countess's book. A further example from the 'diary':

The recipes he sent me seem to be good – twice weekly a facial consisting of raw veal and once a week a full bath in warm olive oil. Reluctantly I got used to the leather lingerie that he [Hitler] wanted me to wear.

The text from the countess's book read:

Empress Elisabeth was not committed to any specific facial care. On some nights, she would wear a mask filled with raw veal. The empress often took warm olive-oil baths. She loved snug blouses, her trousers in winter were frequently made of leather . . .

Many more examples could be cited. Several passages in the 'diary' were about me:

Page 9, paragraph 2

Yesterday the house was full of guests. Most of them, however, had to return to Berchtesgaden after the early dinner. Several remained, including Leni. We did not see each other. She did not know that we are meeting here today. He [Hitler] ordered me not to go down. I have to wait in the bedroom, in my nightgown, until he comes. Is she down there, performing the nude dances which people always talk about and which I am never allowed to watch because I am a 'little girl' and she is the 'secret queen'? I always have to think about Leni. 'She bitches about people,' he told me, 'and I don't care for that at all.' Yet he is somehow fascinated by her all the same, and I wonder whether she might not oust me someday.

Another passage on page 19 reads:

We spoke earnestly about Leni for the first time. Previously he had always smiled whenever I tried to get anything out of him about her. Now he told me: 'But she is a great artist and an important person.' I couldn't care less so long as she keeps her hands off him. 'She does not interest me as a woman,' he maintains, and I believe it. They can't possibly have been intimate. I asked him whether she has a beautiful body. He said 'yes' thoughtfully as if he first had to think about it. 'She has a beautiful body, but she is not graceful and delicate like you, she is all instinct. And that has always repelled me.' Yet it torments me all the same: Did he or did he not have an affair with her? Will I ever find out? Naturally, he has given me no power, nor will I ever want anything from him. I have never asked him for anything – I am probably the most easy-going mistress he could have.'

A final sample, from page 32, last paragraph:

Leni gives herself airs and graces and, if one didn't know better, one could believe that she is the star. She was surrounded by some thirty men with cameras, all of whom wore bizarre clothes as if they had come straight from a studio. I hate that woman. She can't help wiggling her behind – but that can make a woman famous. I would give anything to know whether it is true that she danced naked at the Berghof. She is extremely friendly to me, but perhaps she feels utterly indifferent to me. What she mainly cares about is that people *believe* she is having an affair with him. She has a bad influence on his decisions regarding so-called cultural issues. Thank goodness he ridicules her whenever she talks politics. If it were otherwise, that would be the last straw.

These criminal texts, which were published not only in France but also in other countries, helped to defame me for decades, making it impossible for me to practise my profession as a film director. Not even the court verdict that the diary was a fabrication could ever make up for the damage I suffered.

Trenker remained silent about the trial and all the serious charges and, significantly, brought no lawsuit against anyone and stayed away from Germany for five years. In October 1953, *Münchner Illustrierte* ran his article, 'My Heart Still Beats for the Tyrol'. Having been absent from Germany for so many years, he assumed that the diary affair was forgotten, and he actually dared to justify himself with regard to the forgery. Apart from him, few people know the truth about the diary, and they prefer to keep silent.

DENAZIFICATION

The court verdict about the diary was also valid for the denazification tribunal. My first trial took place on 1 December 1948 in Villingen in the Black Forest. After hours of exhausting discussion, the investigating committee certified that the law did not apply in my case. 'After a thorough investigation, no political incrimination has been ascertained. [Frau Riefenstahl] was not a member of the National Socialist Workers' party or any of its subdivisions.'

This verdict was appealed against by the French military government, so that on 6 July 1949 I had to submit to the same procedure, which again lasted several hours. This time it took place not in Villingen, but in Freiburg, at the tribunal of the Baden State Commissariat for Political Purging. The procedure, during which I had to defend myself alone, without counsel lasted all day. I had to respond to every rumour that was circulating about me. The decision was finally announced towards evening and again it was unanimous.

The statement of justification included the following passage:

The investigation of Frau Riefenstahl's relationship with the leaders of the 'Third Reich' has determined that notwithstanding the rumours and assertions widespread among the public and in the press there is no evidence of a relationship between her and any of those people that did not arise from normal commercial intercourse during the execution of the artistic projects assigned to her. Not a single witness or document could be found that would indicate a close relationship between Frau Riefenstahl and Hitler. On the contrary, we are in possession of affidavits from Hitler's entourage that confirm that there was none. The idea of being a propagandist for the National Socialist Workers' Party was alien to her. Her making of the Party rally film and the production of the Olympic film do not prove the contrary. The Olympic film was an international matter, which already excludes it from incriminating her in any way. Frau Riefenstahl steadily and persistently refused to accept the assignment of the Party rally film and made it eventually only at Hitler's express and unyielding instructions. She had neither the intention nor the awareness to execute this project as propaganda for the National Socialist Workers' Party. Her assignment was aimed at making not a propaganda film, but a documentary. The maker of this film cannot be blamed for the fact that it subsequently proved to be an effective means of propaganda for National Socialism and was exploited as such by the Party. Moreover, before the outbreak of the last war, this motion picture was not regarded in other countries as a propaganda film, as was proved by the various high distinctions awarded to it by international prize juries; for instance, the gold medal at the World's Fair in Paris in 1937. It must also be pointed out that when the Party rally film was made, the Jewish laws had not yet been issued and the notorious Jewish pogroms had not yet taken place. Hitler's war preparations were not recognizable to outsiders at that time, and the true character of the 'movement' was still concealed. Thus, no incriminating promotion of the National Socialist dictatorship can be determined. It is contrary to the facts to claim that Frau Riefenstahl was 'incontestably a propagandist' for the National Socialist theories. Furthermore, she constantly maintained friendly relations with Jews, and during the National Socialist regime, she employed non-Aryans in her film work and supported victims of the Nazis. The giving of the Hitler salute was not customary in her firm.

The French military government protested a second time, arguing that the classification 'law not applicable' was in itself unlawful. So six months later, the Baden State Commissariat had to classify me *in absentia* as a fellow traveller. And I preferred that.

Of the many affidavits that I could submit to the tribunal, the most unusual was probably Ernst Jäger's. After he so shamefully abandoned me in New York in 1939, I had heard nothing from him apart from malicious attacks in the press. Now, reading his letter nine years later, I was confronted by a mystery. How could someone who had treated me so dreadfully, who had misused my name for illegal money dealing, now defend me so emphatically? This is his affidavit, which he sent to me without being asked:

Hollywood 28
1385 North Ridgewood Place
11 July 1948

I, the undersigned, Ernst Jäger, residing in Hollywood, hereby make my sworn statement in the matter of the denazification of Frau Leni Riefenstahl-Jacob:
I have known Frau Riefenstahl for twenty years. As the former editor-in-chief of the Berlin *Film-Kurier*, I had ample opportunity to witness her unique rise to being the most important film-maker in the world. During the years of the Nazi regime 1933–8, when I travelled to America with her, I had even more intimate insights into her character and her creativity, since I was involved in some form or other in all the films that she made during that period.

Because of allegedly all-too-glorifying articles about Hollywood that I published in Germany in 1935, I was expelled for life from the Press Chamber; the explusion text was published in many newspapers. Frau Riefenstahl not only was aware of this explusion, but defied it for many years. She did so not because she expected any advantages from my writing ability, but out of a desire to make some form of protest, in my case as in so many others. It would take many pages to describe how Frau Riefenstahl always induced me to stand up for other similarly censored writers and to help them materially. Frau Riefenstahl spent huge sums towards this end, even though privately she was by no means wealthy in those days. Before the entire world, I can demonstrate her attitude in favour of and not against Jews or Frenchmen or technicians or workers or officials or artists in general; and I can do this because, for many years, I kept a kind of journal about her personality and her artistic development. Very few people know, for example, that she kept her Jewish physician. The great majority of the most powerful representatives of the Third Reich hated Frau Riefenstahl, especially Dr Goebbels and his satellites, as well as the 'veteran Party members', who saw her not as a 'veteran', but, at best, as an ambitious artist and as a woman who refused to act obsequiously.

But since she was and is a woman, the legends naturally found nourishment. Her enthusiasm for the screen is unique and has always had unique results. At present, her *Olympia* film is showing all over the United States of America – a proof that her works were simply good films and not propaganda. Even *Triumph of the Will* was screened in America in 1947 because it shows the true face of an era and its influence that has now been overcome.

I have not had any personal news from Frau Riefenstahl for ten years now. I am writing these lines spontaneously and from the bottom of my heart. Her artistry was there for all to see long before Nazism and now that it [Nazism] has been overcome, she will reach her full maturity. I can swear with a clear conscience that she deserves it more than anyone.

Ernst Jäger

Months later, Ernst Jäger tried to explain his incomprehensible change of heart. He wrote: 'After 1933, fear and qualms of conscience twisted me, made me an awkward liar, confused and boastful . . . I believe I can finally state what I think.' In another letter, he said of himself, 'Jäger, as we know, then fell into muddy waters.' I must admit that I let myself be swayed again and I forgave him.

Even though I was rehabilitated and the rumours were exposed, no end seemed in sight for the smear campaign. No newspaper mentioned my rehabilitation by the denazification tribunal and more and more lies were spread about me. How could I defend myself? I was sick and penniless, and most of my friends had abandoned me. Worst of all, I couldn't practise my profession. No 'work prohibition' was inflicted on me, but I had been slandered and libelled so thoroughly that no one dared offer me work. Trenker was not my only enemy. Others lurked in the shadows, waiting for an opportunity to harm me.

Yet even in this period, there were glimmers of light. In Königsfeld, the postman brought me a huge cardboard cylinder from the Internal Olympic Committee in Lausanne: it contained an Olympic diploma. I was delighted. It was a replacement for the Olympic gold medal that I had been awarded in 1939 for my Olympic films. More good news came from the United States. As Ernst Jäger had written, my *Olympia* film, distributed by United Artists, was having a highly successful run there under the title *Kings of the Olympics*.

Although the reviews were so enthusiastic, I was not helped materially and I impatiently looked forward to the decision in Paris. Weeks passed with no news; all my assets were still confiscated.

MY NEW LIFE

It was at about this time that I made my mind to leave Königsfeld for good since I was too secluded there. Accompanied by Hanni, I hitched a lift on a truck going to Munich, and there we stayed temporarily with my mother-in-law. For the time being, my mother had to remain in Königsfeld.

After all my efforts to find work proved futile, I thought I'd have a go at earning some money by selling wine supplied by my ex-husband. It was harder than I imagined, for I had no means of transportation, not even a bicycle, and I had to do everything on foot. We could take along only a few sample bottles in our knapsacks.

When I ventured to try to make my first sale at Munich's luxury hotel The Four Seasons I had to alter my hairdo and put on dark glasses to avoid being recognized; in spite of our efforts, we couldn't place a single bottle. Next we approached Humpelmayer, the elegant restaurant where I had frivolously spent six of my forty marks' quota on roast goose, but we had no luck there either. Then we tried major food stores and managed to get rid of a few bottles, but the profits were so tiny that I lost heart and wanted to give up. Hanni, however, dug in her heels and suggested that we try the surrounding countryside.

The next day we thumbed a lift to Starnberg where we had a small measure of success, in hotels as well as in grocery stores. Thus encouraged, we hitched on to Weilheim, stopping at a small restaurant where we consumed our profits. By now, Hanni too had realized that we could not possibly earn a living this way. We got as far as Murnau, where, rather exhausted, we sold a couple of bottles. In one shop, a salesgirl recognized me and, flabbergasted to see me as a peddler, asked us to wait until she had taken care of the last consumer. After locking up, she invited us to supper, and learning that we had no place to spend the night, she offered us her sitting-room. Nearly always, it was simple, often poor people who lent us a hand. The next day, having decided to give up this arduous business, Hanni returned temporarily to her parents in Breisach while I stayed in Partenkirchen, where a former assistant let me have a small room.

Freed from interrogations, prisons, and slander, I recovered more and more from day to day.

THE GYPSY TRIALS

As so often before my joyful sense of freedom was short-lived. On 1 May 1949, *Revue*, an illustrated magazine in Munich, ran a hair-raising article on me and my *Tiefland* film, forcing me to sue Helmut Kindler, the owner of the periodical. Once again, I had to apply for legal aid and Dr Gritschneder agreed to handle the case. On 23 November 1949, the trial opened at the Munich district court.

Most offensive material published by *Revue* included the photo of a Gypsy woman with the following caption: 'Spaniard from a concentration camp. Finding real Spaniards for the film was impossible during the war but Leni Riefenstahl knew what to do – she selected Gypsies from concentration camps.' Another picture was captioned: 'Film slaves. Sixty Gypsies from concentration camps near Berlin and Salzburg played the Spanish populace. At first they were delighted to be making a film instead of working in a munitions plant . . . How many survived the concentration camp?' Along with these untrue statements, the article had further nonsensical captions. Thus a photo of the male lead was accompanied by the following: 'A Viennese bank teller, selected from two thousand mountain infantrymen in Mittenwald who had to parade past Leni Riefenstahl several times, played Pedro.' In his affidavit, Franz Eichenberger, who in fact played Pedro, stated: 'I have never been a bank teller, nor do I come from Vienna. I was never in the mountain infantry and therefore could not have been selected from among mountain infantrymen. Nor is it correct to say that two thousand Mittenwald mountain infantrymen had to march past the director of the film. Frau Riefenstahl first saw me in St Anton, where she discovered me for the role of Pedro.'

During the trial, Herr Kindler's counsel struck a theatrical pose, pointed his finger at me, and cried into the courtroom: '*Tiefland* must never be shown

on a screen, for you are the devil's own director!' I collapsed and was no
longer capable of defending myself – but fortunately I didn't have to. The
court was already convinced that the magazine article was untrue since this
had been confirmed by all the witnesses. Except, that is, for the Gypsy
Johanna Kurz, who testified for *Revue* claiming she personally had seen
several of the *Tiefland* Gypsies being gassed at Auschwitz. When the judge
asked her if she remembered any names, she mentioned the Reinhardt family
and that was her undoing. The witness Dr Reinl, my then assistant director,
who had selected the Gypsies at a Gypsy camp in Salzburg, had seen the
Reinhardt family after the end of the war and he stated this in an affidavit. In
fact, I too had bumped into many of my *Tiefland* Gypsies several months
earlier when I took the train from Kitzbühel to Wörgl. They had greeted me
with great joy and told me that the Reinhardts were well. Antonia
Reinhardt, supposedly gassed at Auschwitz, read a newspaper story about
the trial and wrote to me from Weilheim:

> My dear Leni Riefenstahl,
>   I will do everything in my power to help you. Please let me know
> immediately when I should come and whether I should bring along any
> members of my family or my mother, who also appeared in the film. Or
> would it be enough if I came alone? Please write to me in plenty of time,
> so that we can arrive punctually at the appointed hour. Apart from me,
> my mother and a brother, who were also in your film, can testify on your
> behalf. We are looking forward to seeing you again. With the friendliest
> greetings, I remain yours truly
>
>   Antonia Reinhardt

The court found that the German government's systematic persecution of
the Gypsies did not begin until March 1943: the *Tiefland* shooting had taken
place earlier, between 1940 and 1941, in Krün. The Maxglan Camp in
Salzburg, said the court, was not a concentration camp. The various
affidavits confirm this beyond any reasonable doubt, as does the statutory
declaration by the actor Bernhard Minetti, one of the last great members of
the Berlin Gründgens Ensemble who are still performing today. Minetti
stated:

> The treatment of the Gypsies in Krün was very loving. Frau Riefenstahl,
> like most of her crew, was in love with the Gypsies. People were
> generally enthusiastic about the natural talents of old and young, their

quickness of response and the whole Gypsy way of life. The overall work atmosphere was particularly good, indeed cheerful, and I was incensed by the assertions of the magazine, which were factually incorrect!

Dr Reinl testified that: 'The claim that the Gypsies were brought from concentration camps is a deliberate lie, since any child in Salzburg can tell you that no concentration camp ever existed in Maxglan; it was merely a reception camp for wandering Gypsies. I make this statement under oath.'

At the end of November 1949, the district court of Munich decided against the publisher of *Revue*, which had a high circulation in those days. Herr Kindler was found guilty of libel and sentenced to a fine of six hundred marks or a prison term of twenty days. He also had to pay the costs of the litigation, though his lawyer, Dr Bayer, filed an appeal.

To my astonishment, several days after the verdict was announced, Dr Bayer asked to see me. I wavered, for I had not forgotten the words he had hurled at me during the trial. Even today, I am amazed that I managed to receive him in my apartment. However, he had something sensational to tell me: 'I am no longer acting for Herr Kindler. I have withdrawn from the case.' He then went on: 'Before I go any further, I must ask your forgiveness a thousand times for what I did to you in the courtroom.'

Dr Bayer assured me he had learned the truth only during the trial and was especially incensed at the testimony given by Johanna Kurz, the witness for *Revue* – whom, incidentally, the judge had instantly convicted of perjury.

Unfortunately, the court verdict could not prevent the *Revue* lies about *Tiefland* and myself from persisting, even down to the present day. Therefore, I would like to quote from unsolicited statements I received from Josef and Katharina Kramer and their family, proprietors of the Hotel Zugspitz in Krün, who were in direct daily contact with the Gypsies during the filming. Maria Kramer owned the barn in which the Gypsies had been quartered and she had been instructed by me and my production manager Fichtner to attend to their welfare. Frau Kramer wrote to me after the verdict was issued:

The Gypsies received the same food as the hotel guests. The food was very good and more than ample, and the Gypsies had double meat-rationing stamps. Eventually, they also received an additional two hundred kilograms of clarified butter. Sheep were repeatedly slaughtered illegally . . . Furthermore, two calves, over and above the rationing stamps, were slaughtered and used for feeding the Gypsies.

The Gypsies enjoyed full freedom. The radio was switched on early in the morning. Breakfast included whole milk, butter and marmalade. Guards were absolutely necessary, since the Gyspies showed a marked tendency to steal; that was the reason the inhabitants of Krün refused to take in Gyspies. It was unequivocally ascertained that they were never guarded by the SS or the SA, but only two constables, who had come with the Gypsies from a camp in Salzburg. Frau Riefenstahl was very popular indeed with the Gyspies, who repeatedly emphasized that they had never been so well off in their lives. The Gypsy children were particularly enthusiastic. Frau Riefenstahl, incidentally, had exactly the same food as the Gypsies who, in bad weather, were even served hot wine.

Since certain journalists unabatedly continued their attacks and libel, I began to doubt whether I had done the right thing in going to court, but Dr Gritschneder commented:

For your later professional work, it was absolutely necessary to have a legally binding court judgement to make it absolutely clear that no prisoners were used for *Tiefland*. Otherwise you would be subject to the greatest difficulties because of the malevolence of large numbers of influential people in the cinema and the press and of public opinion. It is very easy to say now that we shouldn't have gone to court, but just imagine the practical consequences if you had put up with that slander about concentration-camp slaves. You could not possibly have worked in the near future, despite [your] denazification!

How right he was. Whether I wanted to or not, I had to keep facing attacks but I was so wounded by the persistent allegations that I must have known about the dreadful crimes in the extermination camps that I found it harder and harder to cope with those lies. I never dreamed that almost forty years after the *Revue* trial, I would once more have to defend myself against even more serious charges.

Although I had sworn to myself that I would never again sue anyone for making such statements, I was deeply upset by a TV film made by a Frau Gladitz for Westdeutscher Rundfunk and I couldn't ignore her new accusations. I had to go to court for these lies were intolerable. Once again, the issue was the *Tiefland* Gypsies. This time I was aware of how upsetting and expensive a lawsuit would be, but I had to defend myself for the sake of the credibility of these memoirs, which I had begun to write. Since most of the falsehoods had been refuted decades ago, I assumed that the court would straighten the matter out very easily. I was wrong. The new trial became an affair that is still going on four years later, even as I write these lines.

Along with the old accusations, three new claims were made: 1. Allegedly, I was personally present in the Gypsy camp and selected the extras myself. 2. Allegedly, I knew about the imminent extermination of the Gypsies in Auschwitz and had been informed of this by the thirteen-year-old Gypsy boy Josef Reinhardt. 3. The [film] viewer is given the impression that I knew about the imminent extermination and promised to help our Gypsies and save them from the transport to Auschwitz, but that I didn't help them and simply left them to their fate.

It was all beyond belief! I was never in Maxglan, nor did anyone speak to me about Auschwitz during our filming. Indeed, it wouldn't have been possible, because at that time, nothing was known about Auschwitz as an extermination camp and therefore the thirteen-year-old Joseph Reinhardt could not have spoken to me about the imminent extermination of the Gypsies there.

Dr Gritschneder, who had pleaded the Gypsy case so successfully, took over my new case. He asked the court to issue an injunction against any screening of this outrageously mendacious film, and in mid-June 1983, his petition was granted by the district court in Freiburg. However, Frau Gladitz would not cut out the scenes containing the untrue assertions from her film, which she entitled *The Time of Silence and Darkness*, and because of her refusal, my lawyers brought charges in Freiburg.

The methods used by Frau Gladitz can be seen in a letter that was signed 'Anna Madou'. As I found out several years later, Anna Madou and Frau Gladitz were one and the same person. She wrote:

Kirchzarten, 5.12.81

Dear Frau Riefenstahl,

May I remind you with this letter of the conversation we had at the small coffee bar in the Rombach bookshop in Frankfurt where you were kind enough to give me an appointment to see you to discuss your appearing at length in my film about great artists of this century.

You agreed with me, I believe, that one must make time for such a conversation, since I by no means wished to interview you in the usual style, convinced as I am that this kind of interview has never done you justice.

361

You asked me to tell you once again in this letter which television companies would be involved in the production and/or were already interested in purchasing the film.

They are: First German Television Programme, West German Radio, the BBC, Swedish Television; and the American network NBC and possibly French Television have already indicated interest.

Thus you can see that a great deal of interest exists in a motion picture about the artist Leni Riefenstahl.

You were able to suggest early April as a possible time for this conversation, and you asked me to remind you of this in my letter. But this week I had a meeting with the West German Radio and I was told that there is great interest in seeing or telecasting the film in March.

Even worse, I received a wire from NBC, New York, asking me to come to New York in mid-February in order to screen the film.

Now I am really somewhat desperate, since I do not know what to do. I realize that you have a tremendous amount to do at this time and are under pressure, as you told me, because of your new book, the memoirs, and the pre-production work for a film in the Maldives. Nevertheless, I would like to ask you once again whether you see any possibility of granting me an earlier appointment for our conversation. For you can imagine that the interview with you would be the very heart of the film which would be basically worthless without it. You can understand that, given the great international interest in the film, the lack of this conversation with you would be very unfortunate.

If you could find some possibility for receiving me earlier than April, I would be tremendously grateful. Please forgive me once again for the 'tenacity' with which I have already pursued you and be assured of my admiration and veneration for your great art! May I wish you a happy and contemplative pre-Christmas, and allow me to sign off with my highly respectful greetings.

Anna Madou

Such treachery! I had first met her one year before receiving this letter in which she claims to be a great admirer of 'the artist Leni Riefenstahl'. In late September 1980, I gave a slide lecture on the Nuba at the University of Freiburg. Before I began, a woman, who introduced herself as Frau Madou, asked me whether she could film me during the lecture and I innocently agreed. But I was not the only person she wanted to film. As we can see in her film, she had planted in the audience her 'star witness', the Gypsy Josef

Reinhardt, now forty years older. While the spectators applaud me, the camera pans over to the man with the careworn look, in order to present him – a boy during the *Tiefland* shooting in 1940 – as one of the abused *Tiefland* Gypsies.

Frau Gladitz clearly had the specific intention from the very start of producing a slanderous concoction about me. She placed her 'star witness' in the audience in Freiburg; yet she never asked me a single question about *Tiefland* or about the Gypsies employed in it – either at the lecture or, the next day, at the Rombach bookshop, where she filmed me during a book-signing party and then chatted with me. Nor did her letter, written one year later, so much as mention my film, when absurdly she had supposedly been working on what she called her 'documentation' of the making of *Tiefland* for some considerable time.

That it was her precise aim to slander my work is obvious from the blurb accompanying the cassette of her film. It says the following about me and my work:

Is it legitimate, for the sake of art, to use the slaughterhouses of a barbaric system for artistic aims? And is it legitimate to love the cinema so much that one violates human rights for the sake of art?

The trial dragged on for years, through two appeals. The principal witness for the defendant Gladitz was Josef Reinhardt of the Gypsy family Reinhardt. He was thirteen years old in August 1940, when Harald Reinl and my production manager Hugo Lehner came to Maxglan. Josef Reinhardt was tried for perjury in 1955 and escaped sentence only because of an amnesty. However, this court also found that he 'had made false assertions under oath'.

The court believed other witnesses who had been children in Maxglan, one of whom had been only four years old. On the other hand, it dismissed the testimony made by Dr Reinl, who had a law degree, as being merely a 'counterstatement'. Furthermore, the Freiburg court refused to acknowledge that among all the numerous accusations levelled at me by the Gyspy Johanna Kurz at the *Revue* trial, she had never once alleged that I had personally selected the Gypsies at Maxglan. She had spoken only of 'two men'. Had I been at Maxglan myself, as was now suddenly maintained after decades, she would never have concealed it in court. Moreover, the files of the Salzburg State Archive list the name of the man who negotiated at Maxglan and there is not a word about me. I was the producer, director and leading actress of a million-mark film, on which I had been working for a long time; had I been in Maxglan, my presence would doubtlessly have been mentioned in this file, and the Salzburg press would have reported it. Actually, I wasn't even in Germany at that time. I was in Italy, scouting locations in the Dolomites.

In March 1987, the Supreme District Court in Karlsruhe issued the final verdict, and no appeal was allowed. Its finding was the same as that of the lower court. It prohibited the defendant Gladitz from screening her film unless she cut out the Auschwitz statements about me. However, she was still permitted to maintain that the Gypsies were 'forced to work' and not paid, and that I myself selected them at Maxglan. Although this latter charge could not be proved in court, the judges nevertheless decided in her favour on the grounds that her imputation was not likely to damage my public image.

This incomprehensible judgement made it easy for the press to run head-lines like LENI RIEFENSTAHL'S MOVIE SLAVES – EXTRAS FROM AUSCHWITZ; RIEFENSTAHL'S EXTRAS FROM NAZI CONCENTRATION CAMP; RIEFENSTAHL PERSONALLY SELECTED EXTRAS IN A CONCENTRATION CAMP, and articles like 'From the Concentration Camp to the Film – and Back', a newsreel report by Erwin Leiser in *Die Weltwoche*.

Characteristic of the climate in Freiburg was the fact that my lawyer, Dr Bernt Waldmann, who politically was close to the Socialist Party of Germany, was attacked in two newspapers for being willing to represent me.

This litigation and the tormenting anxiety about whether I could again find fair judges cost me four years of my ninth decade – while I was trying to concentrate my strength on a new task. I received well-meaning assurances from many friends that justice would prevail, but I was sceptical after the verdict issued by the lower court.

Thus, until the end of my life I will be thought to have been at Maxglan Camp, even though I never saw so much as a blade of grass there.

LIFE GOES ON

I have interrupted the chronology of my life story because the accounts of the two Gypsy trials belong together. After my conflicts with *Revue*, my life went on – in spite of despair, depression and illness.

Day after day, I kept busy, fighting for the release of my assets by sending more and more petitions. I was given my greatest assistance by Otto Mayer, the chancellor of the International Olympic Committee, who not only sent me food and medicaments, but also championed the release of my films in Paris by getting the French Olympic Committee involved. Even though more and more VIPs, including Avery Brundage, the president of the American Olympic Committee, appealed to the French to release my films, all efforts remained futile. My lawyer in Paris, Professor Dalsace, had filed a suit in the French national court against the French agencies; but he told me we would have to wait a year or two for the verdict.

Since more and more people wanted to see me, I tried to live in Munich, but without money, I couldn't even afford a cheap furnished room; imagine my delight when a friend of mine managed to get me a room at 114 Hohenzollernstrasse, in the home of the Obermaier family, who owned a small auto repair shop.

Around that time, autumn 1949, I received my first post-war offer. The president of the Finnish Olympic Committee, Von Frenckell, asked me to produce and direct a film on the 1952 summer Olympics, which were scheduled to take place in Helsinki. This was a surprise and a marvellous opportunity. But though I felt honoured and yearned for a project, I regretfully turned it down. The obstacle was my first Olympic film which I knew I would be unable to surpass – and I didn't want to make a weaker picture. When subsequently the Norwegians asked me to make a film about the Olympic winter games in Oslo, I refused for the very same reason.

LETTERS FROM MANFRED GEORGE

In April 1949, I received a letter from Manfred George. I hadn't had a sign of life from him since his farewell letter from Prague. But meanwhile, I had found out that he had become editor-in-chief of *Aufbau*, a German-Jewish newspaper in New York. Hesitantly I opened the letter and read:

You have to forgive me for omitting the salutation. I confess quite sincerely that I am at a slight loss to come up with a suitable one . . . Naturally, I remember all the days and evenings of mutual walks and mutual searching – I remember them very clearly, as if a long and dreadful time did not lie between then and now. After all, when our paths separated, more happened than our saying 'adieu' – and it is not easy to know what you (and also what I) have gone through since then. Some of it is well known, of course, to the extent that it regards our destiny as members of different groups and people of different views. But this strikes me almost as inessential – more essential are the things that have happened to us and changed us. Let me therefore begin in a rudimentary way:

My memory of you has always been that of a person seeking perfection. You know that in those days I regarded the path you were taking as wrong, but you were too young and too ambitious to see this. Not that I believe that I own exclusive rights to my way, but the fate that struck me – and I have lost many, many people – has only strengthened me and increased my faith. And I am writing to you because I know a faith was at the bottom of your route . . .

I was deeply moved by the nobility of soul speaking to me from those lines, which I kept with all his subsequent letters as one keeps a great treasure. In my reply, I said:

You cannot imagine what turmoil your words have caused in me. I have already torn up several letters to you; there is so much to tell you that I fear you might not understand. I am basically still the same person as I was then, except that my hard struggles of the past ten years have left their mark. Almost every item the press publishes about me is entirely made up. Absolutely none of it corresponds to the facts. Although my enemies are invisible and anonymous, they are adversaries who intend to destroy me at any price. But I must continue to fight this battle if I want to live.

The greatest charge that I can level against myself goes back to the time when we were seeing one another. In those days, I really believed that Hitler was a man who would champion social justice, an idealist who would strike a balance between rich and poor, and who had the strength to eliminate corruption. As you know, I never agreed with his racial theories, and that was also the reason why I never joined the [Nazi] Party. I always hoped that these fundamentally erroneous ideas would disappear after [his] coming to power and I have never denied that I was spellbound by Hitler's personality. The fact that I was too late in recognizing his demonic nature was, no doubt, my fault or the result of my bedazzlement. The crucial thing, after all, is our own inner experience, and the fault we charge ourselves with depends on what we knew and didn't know. No one believes that many of us didn't know about the terrible things that happened in the concentration camps, or that I learned about them only after the war, as a prisoner myself. For months on end, I could not believe that such horrors had taken place. In accepting the truth I almost lost my mind, and I feared I could never again be free of the nightmare of that tremendous suffering. These lines are in a sense a brief confession. I am telling you this because I always had the feeling that you can look inside a person and understand him.

Manfred George replied:

Rest assured that the account of your feelings, your anxieties, your struggles has been read with great sympathy. Your letter was very sad. On the other hand, it gladdened me a bit, precisely because I never made any concessions to you that might have resulted from my lengthy knowledge of your character and life or, last but not least, from our shared memories of the sunsets as we walked together in Wilmersdorf. It is greatly to your credit that you have never misread me, either then or now. Naturally, I remember that whole bizarre period, which was eventually to end in such a dreadful catastrophe – with us on two utterly different sides. It is strange that, despite all the experiences you must have lived through, you have not been corroded by the acid of bitterness. I hope we can meet again in the near future, somewhere in Europe, perhaps in Germany . . .

When I saw George again, he said he had never doubted me for even a moment. We remained friends, and he wished to help to rehabilitate me – but this was prevented by his far too premature death on the last day of 1965. That summer, I had been with him daily during the Berlin Film Festival.

HARRY SOKAL AGAIN

In 1949, another *emigré* visited me at my apartment on Hohenzollernstrasse; it was none other than Harry Sokal, my co-producer on *The Blue Light*. While as a friend he was not to be compared with George, he was an interesting person. However, I was very angry with him because he had taken off with the original negative of *The Blue Light*, and claimed that it had been accidentally burned in Prague. At the time, I had no proof that he was lying. It wasn't until twenty years later that Kevin Brownlow, the British film director, told me that the original negative was in the United States, in the possession of a friend of Brownlow's, George Rony, who, just before the outbreak of the war, had bought it from Sokal along with the US distribution rights. Rony was able to prove this and, after some negotiating, he told me he'd be willing to return my negatives to me for six thousand dollars; unfortunately, I didn't have the money.

I hoped that Sokal would now pay me my share of the foreign receipts, of which I still hadn't seen a penny, but I was wrong. Instead he offered me three thousand dollars for the remake rights – in those days, a high sum. The money would have freed me from my straightened circumstances, but the contract included a stipulation I couldn't agree to: my *Blue Light* could no longer be screened. That would have been the death knell for my version and I was not prepared to sacrifice my favourite film no matter how high the sum.

Sokal had once been rich and before leaving Germany he had managed to transfer his assets to Baer, a Zurich bank, just in time. He was a passionate gambler, however, and even before the outbreak of the war had lost everything at French casinos, including my fifty-per cent share of the foreign receipts for my film. He then emigrated to the United States, where he was so poor during the war that he had to earn his livelihood by selling vacuum cleaners.

He had saved only one thing: a skiing film that he had produced in France before losing all his money. Since he knew no one in the German film industry, he asked me to help him sell his picture and this I managed to do very quickly. One of the largest German movie companies in that period was Union, whose lawyer, Dr Kraemer, had contacted me about the *Tiefland* film. I introduced the two men to each other, and the contract was signed within a few days. Sokal received one hundred thousand marks for this very mediocre picture and in the circumstances I thought I might get a small commission for my assistance; but Sokal disappointed me once again. He didn't even send me a bunch of flowers.

I received unexpected help, however from a different source. One day, Friedrich A. Mainz, the former head of Tobis, who had been courageous enough to sign a contract with me one year before the Olympic Games, dropped in at my flat. Clutching his head in his hands, he asked, incredulously, 'You live here?' Unprompted, he went on urgently, 'You really mustn't – this is no good – I'm going to help you.' Pulling a cheque book out of his pocket, he wrote out a cheque and handed it to me; it was for ten thousand marks. 'You can get a flat for this,' he said. 'You'll be successful again, just don't lose courage.'

I was speechless with delight, I could only thank him in a letter.

AN APARTMENT IN SCHWABING

After living on Hohenzollernstrasse for more than six months, I was able to move into a new flat, which I got quite by chance.

In Munich, I ran into an old acquaintance, Maria Bogner, the talented founder of the now world-famous Bogner Fashions. Her husband, Willi Bogner, was still a POW in Norway, and she was trying, entirely on her own, to keep their small sports shop afloat. She generously gave me a few items of clothing and several yards of material – dark-brown ribbed velvet – from which I wanted to have a coat made. I took it to the Schulze-Varell Salon, which had once done a lot of work for me, and when I went to pick up the finished coat I noticed an elegant gentleman sitting opposite me in the vestibule. After staring intently at me, he finally said, 'You're Leni Riefenstahl. My name is Ady Vogel. You don't know me, but I know you. We had a mutual friend, who told me a lot about you – Ernst Udet.' Then he mentioned that he was constructing a building in Munich, on Tengstrasse in Schwabing, and when he noticed my interest in the project, he produced the blueprints from his briefcase. After looking at the groundplans and location of the building, I knew I had to live there.

The very next day, we were able to come to terms on a small flat on the fifth floor, thanks to the generosity of Herr Mainz. With the help of friends and workers who agreed to delay their bills, I was able to furnish the three rooms without delay. Now at last I had a home for my mother too.

On the whole, things appeared to be looking up for me. My lawyer in Innsbruck notified me that the French had released certain of my private possessions – some furnishings, paintings and rugs, as well as suitcases and clothing – and friends brought these to me in Munich. Unfortunately I could enjoy living in my own place for only a few months for we had no money for the rent. To avoid losing the flat, I had no choice but to sublet two of the rooms but one. I even had to give up the bathroom and the kitchen. My mother and I now shared a small room, which had a wash-basin, but no bath or cooking facilities, and we had to use the toilet out in the corridor.

My mother was admirable in that she managed to face every situation with great good humour. She prepared our meals on a small alcohol cooker, ironed and patched my clothes – and all this while parties were often being held in my subleased rooms. They had been taken by a Hollywood director and well-known performers like Hildegard Neff and others came in and out without realizing that I lived there too, separated only by a wall. To remain incognito when I went out, I would wear dark glasses and a scarf over my hair.

However, the court trials revealed my whereabouts, and soon I had difficulty warding off the tidal wave of reporters and photographers, who were not always friendly.

MEETING HANS ALBERS

Reconstruction in Germany advanced at an incredible pace. Dust and ruins vanished almost magically. New urban districts arose from ashes and rubble as the survivors of the war tried to forget the past by working fanatically. During the war, many Germans, inspired by their faith in a false doctrine, had done inhuman things in their sacrificial devotion. Then, when the moment of truth came, all that remained was the naked drive for self-preservation and the will to survive. West Germany now had a federal president and a chancellor – Theodor Heuss and Konrad Adenauer – and the 'East Zone' had become the German Democratic Republic. New political realities were established.

During this period, I was repeatedly hurt by other people. When I ran into certain earlier acquaintances, they snubbed me and turned away. I had an embarrassing experience at a sound stage in the Bavaria Studios in Munich-Geiselgasteig where Sokal and Mainz were shooting scenes for a remake of *The White Hell of Piz Palü*. Sokal asked me to watch the screen tests of young actresses, since we wanted to know which of them I liked best for my role. My choice was Liselotte Pulver, who was still unknown at the time, and Sokal wanted to introduce her to me personally.

In the sound stage, I discovered an ice wall made of *papier maché* and artificial tinsel snow. Sokal, seeing my expression, said, 'You're surprised. But, unfortunately, we can't shoot the acting scenes on the ice walls of Piz Palü. Our leading actor is no mountain-climber, he's a sailor. We need a famous name, a star, even if he can't ski or climb. Guess who it is!'

I didn't have the faintest idea until he came towards me and I saw that it was Hans Albers. Recognizing me, he froze in his tracks, pointed at me, and cried out, 'If that woman doesn't leave the studio immediately, I won't do another scene.' Then he turned on his heal and walked out.

Sokal dashed after the furious actor and I stood there alone, somewhat shaken. Many years earlier, in 1926, I had experienced another extremely embarrassing scene with Hans Albers. I found his present conduct incomprehensible since he was reputed to have been one of Hitler's favourite actors.

In contrast to this sort of unpleasantness, I was comforted by more and more fan mail arriving from abroad, most of it from the United States. There, my films, prints of which had been taken away as spoils of war by the Allies, were being screened in university courses. I was encouraged not only by letters, but also by positive articles in American periodicals. The correspondence became so vast that I hung a map of the United States on the wall and attached tiny flags to mark the schools where my films were shown. Letters of appreciation were also sent from England and France. But in Germany, I was still a non-person.

One letter made me very angry. It was a summons from the Villingen tax office to pay fifty marks or go to jail for five days; this was because I was unable to pay the taxes on my house in Berlin, which had been damaged by bombs and was still confiscated. The tax office wanted to seize the few furnishings there and auction them off, so I asked my lawyer to step in. Since several newspaper reporters wrote indignant articles because I, as the owner of a 'luxury' villa, was allowed legal aid to pay my lawyer, let me quote several lines from his brief. They may illuminate the true facts of the case:

Frau Riefenstahl's house in Berlin is in an indescribable condition. Five tenants are living in this house, which was severely damaged by aerial attacks. All the plumbing is shattered, the heating system does not function, and the rooms, to the extent that they were not demolished by fire bombs, are inhabited by people who are destroying whatever is left in the house. Ten dogs have been counted there, as well as cats and chickens, which are kept in the former bathroom. Sackcloth is bedding for human beings and animals and coal sacks serve as doors. By a conservative estimate, the house is so dilapidated that it would take at least fifty thousand marks to do any sort of restoration.

That was my 'luxury villa'. The tax office granted me a delay.

RELEASED AND ROBBED

The American Motion Picture Branch in Munich-Geiselgasteig gave me permission to do an inventory of my film depot in Berlin-Schönefeld, which by sheer chance had not been wiped out by bombs. This meant that my films, except for *Tiefland*, were saved. The storehouse contained the duplicate negatives and lavender prints of them all, plus over a million feet of rushes of all the Olympic events that had not been included in the final version. The material, stored in 1,426 canisters, was all safe and sound. This was verified by the inventory carried out by my assistant, Frau Peters, in June 1950, under the supervision of the American agency. At the time, not a single reel was missing, but many years later, when the American Motion Picture Branch decided to release the material, the bunker was empty. Not a single frame of the extensive *Olympia* footage was left and the duplicate negatives of every single one of my films had vanished. All that remained was an old print of *The Blue Light*, plus several cans of takeouts from this movie. I was shattered by my loss and it was only in the 1980s that American doctoral candidates who were writing dissertations on my Olympic films discovered vast amounts of this material at the Library of Congress in Washington DC and at other places in the United States.

After giving up all hope of ever getting my films back from the Americans, I concentrated on saving the material stored in France. Five years had passed since the end of the war, my property was still confiscated, and I was still unemployed and with no means of support.

IN ROME

At this point something happened that changed my life. The young French actor Paul Müller, who had visited me in Königsfeld many years earlier, kept his promise. He notified me that he had found an Italian producer who would be interested in working with me. Indeed, I soon received a phone call from Signor Alfredo Panone whom I knew from Berlin where he had been at the Italian embassy before the war.

Signor Panone, who was head of Capital Pictures in Rome, was the first person to expect new work from me. He was no cold, matter-of-fact businessman, but highly enthusiastic, like so many of his compatriots. He invited me to come to Rome and suggested that I enjoy some peace and leisure there, in order to formulate my ideas. The prospect seemed so improbable that I couldn't believe in such happiness. But Paul Müller encouraged me.

In Rome, Signor Panone and Paul Müller were waiting for me at Stazione Termini. I was in a state of euphoria. The blue sky, the warm air, the laughing people helped me to forget the greyness that I had left behind in Germany. They had found an elegant apartment for me, and next to the flowers I found an envelope containing a thick wad of lira.

We spent the evening at a restaurant in Trastevere, talking about future projects. Signor Panone suggested that I write down my ideas in Fregene, a resort near the ocean, not far from Rome. This seemed a good idea, since the weather was very hot in Rome. However, my peace and quiet were short-lived since at the weekend, Signor Panone arrived with his secretary and several reporters. Intimidated by my experiences with the German press, I was very cold towards the journalists, and it came as a great – and pleasant – surprise to me when their accounts, translated for me by new secretary Renata Gaede, turned out to be very favourable. The headlines greeted me – OLYMPIA IN ROME, VENTURA IN ITALY.

All this warmth and kindness was so inspiring that I began to write, and more and more ideas came to me with every passing day. After a long fallow period, I was teeming with ideas and within two short weeks I had written three different treatments. One was entitled *The Dancer of Florence* and was a cinematic poem for my friend, the dancer Harald Kreutzberg on a theme that had been on my mind for a long time, since whenever I saw him perform, I was overcome with emotion. His dance recitals were the greatest that I had ever seen.

My second theme was a mountain one for a film to be shot in four countries where Alpine sports were loved and practised. The title was to be *Eternal Peaks*, and the plot consisted of four historic first climbs, culminating in the climax of the ascent of the highest mountain on earth, Mount Everest.

The third project was my favourite: *The Red Devils*. The idea went back to the winter of 1930, when I was on location with Fanck's film *Storms over Mont Blanc*. One day, in Arosa, as I emerged from the hotel I was dazzled by an unforgettable tableau: in the glittering white winter landscape, I saw a group of some fifty students whom Fanck had hired for his 'fox hunt' on skis. They all wore red sweaters and as they streaked down the slopes with the red colour flashing in the sunlight it was a fascinating sight: red against the white snow. I had a vision of a skiing film in colour, though in 1930 colour film did not exist. In my mind's eye, I saw not only red, but also blue – a feminine colour for the ski amazons – a race between red and blue against a white background.

Two weeks later, when Signor Panone visited me in Fregene and read the treatments, he was so enthusiastic that he offered me a contract on the spot. I was delighted. First, we would do *The Red Devils*; the pre-production work would get underway that winter in Cortina d'Ampezzo in the Dolomites. The press ran banner headlines about *I Diavoli Rossi* and the preparations advanced at a surprising rate.

Capital Pictures, engaging me as director, was given good discounts for our crew by the major hotels. Meanwhile, Panone had registered the title and the subject matter in Rome. It was 13 October 1950.

THE LANTIN CASE

A telegram from my mother called me back to Munich where my lawyer was already waiting to help me deal with an unpleasant issue which had just come up. My property, which had been released in Germany in January 1950, had been reconfiscated by the Bavarian Reparations Office. At stake were merely the few furnishings in my Schwabing flat and in my heavily damaged house in Dahlem. I owned no other property in Germany.

One of my long-time and, as I thought, most loyal staff members was Rolf Lantin, who had spent twelve years in my firm as a photographer. He had written to the supreme tax office in Frankfurt, and it was his letter that had triggered this new confiscation of my property. My lawyer instantly filed an appeal, and since I had to name new witnesses, I was summoned back from Rome. The whole matter was completely incomprehensible to me. Before the arrival of the French, I had lent Herr Lantin, in Kitzbühel, film cameras and several crates of darkroom equipment, chemicals and photographic paper. He had hoped to use this equipment in order to start a new life for himself in the American Zone – and evidently, his plans had met with dazzling success.

When we were going through such a terrible time during the years of starvation in Königsfeld, I had asked him to return the material I had lent him. I wrote to him, describing our situation and telling him that I desperately needed money in order to buy medicaments for my mother, but he never replied. Instead, several illustrated magazines ran picture stories on *Tiefland* and I learned that Lantin had smuggled the pictures out of Kitzbühel without my permission and sold them to magazines. In order to protect my copyright, my lawyer had to step in and demand the return of the borrowed material and the *Tiefland* photos. To avoid having to return them, Lantin denounced me instead. With deep hypocrisy he asked the supreme tax office in Frankfurt whether he was obliged to return everything since he didn't know whether funds from the Nazi Party had gone into my firm. He claimed that he had qualms and didn't care to risk being made responsible for replacing the borrowed items.

However, he had no luck with his denunciation for the tax office questioned important witnesses, such as Franz Xaver Schwarz, the former Reich treasurer of the Nazi Party who was responsible for all the financial affairs in the Brown House, and Dr Max Winkler, the head of the Film Credit Bank who was in charge of German film finances and as a result, the confiscation was rescinded for good. Herr Lantin could not ignore this verdict and was forced to return my property. And I was richer by one more bitter experience.

THE ROMAN ADVENTURE

I couldn't remain in Munich and left before the verdict was handed down. In January of 1951, I was supposed to begin pre-production work in Cortina – my contract with Capital Pictures had been notarized in Rome, which made it legally binding – but because of my sudden trip to Munich, I still hadn't received my fee. Signor Panone promised to bring the money to Cortina, where we would meet at the Hotel Majestic Miramonti. I took along my mother, since I found it hard to do without her. In Cortina, we were warmly welcomed by Signor Menaigo, the owner of the hotel, but Signor Panone had not yet arrived. I was glad, for I needed to relax after my strenuous weeks in Munich.

It snowed uninterruptedly and soon the snow was several yards deep; the roads had to be cleared, and within just a few days only the tips of the telegraph poles peeped out of the masses of snow; it hadn't snowed this much in years. Meanwhile Panone wired that he would be several days late.

Since the Italian headlines had reported that *The Red Devils* was to be shot in Cortina, the whole town was in a state of excitement. Wherever I went, I was pestered with questions, but there was still no sign of Panone and I was growing uneasy. My situation became more and more embarrassing as I had relied on the money from Panone and couldn't even afford a lemonade or a cappuccino outside the hotel. All my attempts at reaching him were unsuccessful: no one answered the phone at his office or his flat and my telegrams also went unanswered. Unfortunately, my friend Paul Müller was not in Rome; nor could I get hold of Renata, the secretary I had been given there. Again I spent sleepless nights. I had been waiting in Cortina for three weeks when I decided I had to find out what was going on – but this meant travelling to Rome and how was I to get there?

Signor Menaigo noticed how worried I was and he was dismayed when I described my situation. He was not so concerned that I couldn't pay my hotel bill, but he was deeply upset by the loss Cortina would suffer if the film was never made. He instantly began thinking about other possible ways of backing the project, which was one that had impressed him deeply. He wanted to contact some of the major film producers who were spending their Christmas holidays at his luxury hotel. He consulted Gurschner, the influential transport director of Cortina, who had expressed great interest in my project, and together they turned to Otto Menardi, who, as owner of the mountain hotel Tre Croci, also knew many rich Italians. These three men made intense efforts to find backers for my picture.

I had almost given up all hope when Gurschner told me he had had some favourable phone conversations with one of the greatest Italian producers. This man, he said, was keenly interested in the project and wanted to talk to me. He asked me to come to the Grand Hotel in Rome at twelve the next day – the only time he had available. I was at a loss to know how I could manage this but Signor Menaigo agreed to wait for the payment of my hotel bill and to let me leave. Eugen Sipaes, my mountain guide, who had been assigned to me gratis by the skiing school in Cortina to help me find suitable locations, instantly offered to take my mother to Munich. Luckily for me, I had return tickets and Herr Gurschner, who was also head of SAS, the Italian bus company, gave me a free ticket to Rome.

I reached Rome early in the morning, without a lira to my name. Furthermore, I had been in such a hurry to leave that I had forgotten to take any food with me, and now my stomach was growling. I arrived at the Grand Hotel hours before our appointment and exhausted from my nocturnal bus ride.

In the lounge, I picked up a magazine. What wouldn't I have given for a good breakfast! A waiter came over and handed me the sumptuous menu for which I thanked him and, somewhat embarrassed, ordered a glass of water.

At last, the hands of the clock moved to twelve and only then did I realize how much hinged on this meeting. I forced myself to keep calm, but I couldn't prevent my fingers from trembling. We had agreed on two things for him to recognize me by: my then Titian hair and my strikingly green raincoat, which I had bought shortly before my trip.

Hour after hour dragged by. It was long past the time of our appointment and I felt like putting my head on the table and crying my heart out; it seemed futile to wait any longer. I was just about to stand up when a man came over and asked me in broken German: 'Signora Riefenstahl?' Uneasy, I nodded. Then this short, slight man introduced himself, but I can no longer recall his name. He said, 'We owe you a great apology for making you wait for such a long time. A terrible misfortune has occurred in our firm, and we are all very upset.' He hesitated, and his face looked even paler. Then he went on, gazing past me, 'The manager of our firm shot and killed himself last night. My boss asked me to notify you. He is truly sorry that he cannot speak to you now.'

Long after the Italian had left I still sat there, completely numb. I no longer remember walking out of the hotel, but I can see myself aimlessly roaming the streets. I halted at a newstand and was about to buy a Italian paper when I remembered I did not have a single lira on me. Suddenly I came to myself with a start. Someone had addressed me in German using my full name. I peered into the laughing face of a woman, a stranger, and I heard her say, 'How nice to run into you here. How long are you staying in Rome?'

I shrugged, embarrassed; I had never seen her before. All I said was, 'I don't know.'

'Wouldn't you like to stay with me for a few days? We would be so happy.' Impulsively, she took me by the arm and said, 'In any case, I'm taking you along to tea. I can't miss out on such an opportunity.'

I didn't resist as she led me to her car.

During the drive, she told me that she had been an admirer of my films for many years and that she had also seen me dance. She herself had studied dance in Munich, and spoke almost perfect German. The car climbed up Via Aurelia Antica, a steep, twisting road, until, high above Rome, we stopped at a huge iron gate behind which stood an old, romantic looking palazzo surrounded by tall pines.

'You live here?'

'Yes,' she said, smiling, 'You'll like it.'

Before we entered the garden, I halted for a moment to gaze at Rome, spread out far beneath us and marvellously beautiful. I had loved it from the very first.

Inside the palazzo, we were greeted by guests, and now I also learned the hostess's name. She was Baroness Myrjan Blanc, a Roman celebrity. Tea was served in the interior courtyard. At last, I could eat something but I tried to conceal how famished I was. Looking round, my eyes delightedly took in gaudy birds and tropical flowers. Green plants wound up the ancient walls and columns. I gratefully accepted the baroness's invitation to spend a few days here as her guest. It was all like a dream.

A DOUBLE LIFE

I had been enjoying the baroness's hospitality for a week and during that time had been leading a strange double life. On the one hand, I lived in princely splendour. I had a beautiful room with antique furniture, a large, modern bathroom with Sicilian tiles, and I was spoiled with Italian delicacies. But on the other hand, the baroness never dreamt that I was as poor as Cindrella. She didn't know what I endured when I had to find my own way through Rome. She drove into the city almost every day in order to shop and make her visits, and she usually took me with her. She would drop me and then pick me up again on the Spanish Steps, usually in the afternoon but sometimes not until evening. In between, I was on my own. Walking on the cobblestones was tiring but I had no money for buses; when lunchtime came, it was especially awful watching the people behind the restaurant windows as they devoured their pasta or relished their ice cream and cake.

At the palazzo, dinner was usually eaten in great style at around 10 p.m. and it was on such occasions that my situation seemed most grotesque.

During the first few days, I had been fascinated by the romantic, luxurious atmosphere, but now it had begun to weigh on me more and more every day. I wanted to go home to my mother; the problem was that my return ticket was good from Cortina, but not from Rome. I lacked some fifty marks, but didn't dare ask anyone for the money.

My old illness attacked me once again, forcing me to spend a few days in bed. Myrjan (we were already using the familiar form with one another) told me about a doctor who might be able to help me.

AN UNUSUAL PHYSICIAN

I met this doctor just a few days later when Myrjan invited him with several other guests to what turned out to be a very special evening. For one thing, I got to know the doctor, who was quite a personality, and for another, I met Carl Orff, the famous composer, who played his latest compositions on the piano. One of the guests was Edda Ciano, Mussolini's daughter and a friend of Myrjan Blanc. She had brought along the physician, who, as I learned, was the personal doctor of the Italian royal family.

He was a native of Germany, and his real name was Stückgold. In 1928, he had moved to Italy and changed his name to Stuccoli. Professor Stuccoli agreed to treat me and I was at his office the very next morning. He patiently listened to my long case history and read through the documents I had brought along. Noticing that I was afraid of a painful examination, he smiled and said, 'I don't have to examine you. Your case is clear. You have a very advanced chronic cystitis. There is only one way to conquer this disease and prevent any further painful recurrence but the approach is dangerous, and only you can decide whether you ought to run the risk. Part of your bladder was destroyed decades ago by colon bacilli that settled deep within the diseased organ. To wipe out those bacteria for good, you would have to undergo a drastic treatment. For two months, you would have to have daily injections of streptomycin. This and similar medicaments have been in existence only for the last few years so you couldn't have been helped or cured earlier. Today it takes only from three to six days at the most to cure diseases like this, provided they haven't become chronic. But in your case, a normal treatment would no longer help.'

'And what are the risks involved in this treatment of yours?' I asked.

'Your hearing could be damaged, and you might even lose it altogether,' the professor replied.

Impulsively, I said. 'I will run the risk. All I care about is getting rid of these unbearable pains.'

The doctor opened a door in a wooden panel, pulled out several packets of medicaments, and handed them to me.

'Dear professor,' I said hesitantly, 'I cannot pay the fee, nor can I pay for the medicaments.'

'They're a gift. You owe me nothing.'

If I owe my life to anyone then it is to this physician. I underwent his 'drastic cure' without any damage and, for three decades, I haven't had a single relapse.

THE HOROSCOPE

The day of my departure was now set. My train would leave for Munich the next evening. Fortunately, I had run into Renata, and she had lent me the train fare to Cortina. She also told me why the project with Panone and Capital Pictures had failed. One of the major backers of the company, a Swiss banker, had returned to Rome early that year after a long stay in New York. On learning about the contract that Signor Panone had signed with me, he apparently was furious and categorically refused to finance any film made by Riefenstahl. Since Panone insisted on honouring our agreement, the banker had frozen all the company accounts. Renata knew nothing about what had happened after that, except that the firm was insolvent, and Panone had fled abroad with no forwarding address.

It was my last day in Rome and, since my train wasn't leaving until that night, Myrjan and I planned to have a cosy farewell together. I didn't have to pack for I only had a tiny suitcase. Myrjan took me with her for one last visit to town. During the drive, she said, 'Today, you're going to meet one of my best friends, an interesting man, Francesco Waldner; he is the best-known astrologer in Rome. His abilities are extraordinary, and he has made some astonishing predictions. Do you believe in astrology?' she asked me.

'I would not guide my life according to a horoscope,' I said. 'Anything I do, I like to do without influence and without relying on uncertain facts.'

Signor Waldner lived in an ancient Roman house near the Tiber. He hugged Myrjan and then turned to me.

'This is Leni,' said Myrjan, 'Leni Riefenstahl – you must know of her.'

'Yes, yes,' said Waldner thoughtfully. 'When I was living in Merano, I saw some of your films. *The Blue Light*,' he said enthusiastically. 'I remember you sitting in a grotto and playing with moonlit crystals.' Then, without preamble he asked me, 'When were you born?' Before I could reply, he said, 'It has to be August, you could only have been born in August.'

I smiled and said, 'Yes, 22 August 1902.' He stood up, went behind a curtain, and came back after a short time.

'You have a highly unusual horoscope,' he said. 'How much longer are you staying in Rome?'

'Only until tonight.'

'You shouldn't leave,' he said, unexpectedly insistent.

Myrjan cut in. 'Leni has to, Francesco. They're expecting her in Munich.'

'If you leave tonight, you will miss an opportunity that will never knock again, he said very firmly. 'I have a horoscope of one of my clients. His moon lies on your sun, your stars are so compatible that no better partner could exist for you. This man,' Waldner went on, 'is a rich Italian businessman with artistic ambitions – one could call him a born patron of the arts. If you could get together with this man, the results would be very beneficial for you.'

Myrjan backed him up. 'You really ought to think about it. Whenever Francesco makes such a definite statement, then there's usually something to it. Why don't you remain a few days longer. You could ring up your mother.'

I remained. The next morning, Signor Waldner telephoned Myrjan: 'his' Italian, Professor Ernesto Gramazio, would expect me at his office at via Barberini 3, at 5 p.m.. Professor Gramazio was Austrian consul general in Rome.

Although I arrived punctually, I nurtured no great hopes and therefore didn't feel frustrated at being asked to wait, even though I sat for over an hour. At last, I heard voices and laughter – and Signor Gramazio was standing in front of me. He greeted me enthusiastically in Italian, then in French, and finally in English. Just like an Italian straight out of a picture book, he was very tall and stately, with large brown eyes and the patrician features of a Roman in a Hollywood spectacle. Had I been a young girl, I would have been impressed by his appearance.

He apologized for coming late and then began to talk – so much and so fast that I could barely follow him. He showed me pictures of the president of Italy, Maria Callas, Anna Magnani, Roberto Rossellini and Vittorio de Sica. In each case, he told me when he had last been with this particular celebrity. All this made me very nervous, since it wasn't relevant to me in the least. He didn't so much as mention my work, and I was annoyed at having stayed on in Rome to see him. I waited for a pause in the torrent of words then stood up and said I had to be going.

Gramazio looked at me in surprise. 'You're not leaving, are you? I was hoping we could dine in a nice restaurant and sip a glass of wine together. I'd also like to find out a little about your plans. My friend Waldner has aroused my curiosity.'

Francesco Waldner had not exaggerated. This encounter really struck me as fateful. In contrast to his behaviour in the office, Signor Gramazio was now the best listener in the world. I had to tell him the plots of *Eternal Peaks* and the dance film. I also described my problems concerning the French confiscation of my films and the political difficulties I still had in Germany. It was very late when we got up to go – we were the last patrons.

Gramazio said, 'We're going to work together. Tomorrow, we're starting a company.'

'Tomorrow?' I asked in disbelief.

'Tomorrow,' said Gramazio, smiling. 'By the time you arrive, everything will be ready. I'll expect you at twelve noon.'

IRIS FILM

The next morning, I was back at via Barberini 3. Signor Gramazio was already waiting together with a short, elderly, somewhat chubby man, whom he introduced as his manager. After I sat down, Signor Gramazio handed me an envelope. The letter, from the Banca Populare di Roma, said:

> We hereby inform you that Professor Ernst Hugo Gramazio has instructed us to pay you the sum of two million five hundred thousand lira as of 1 May of this year.

I was speechless. This sum was equivalent to roughly fifty thousand marks or twelve thousand dollars. They anxiously awaited some reaction from me, but I could only stare at them perplexed. Then Gramazio's laughter broke the silence. He said, 'Signora Leni, I am delighted to hand you the letter

381

from my bank as the opening capital for the new version of your film *The Blue Light*. I am happy to be offering you my collaboration.'

I was overwhelmed.

At the office of the notary Olinto de Vitaa, a contract for the founding of Iris Film was signed by Signor Gramazio, the notary and myself. The file number was 45381. According to the contract: after the payment of the capital, which had meanwhile been transferred to me by the Banca d'Italia, Signor Gramazio and I would be the sole partners in this company, and its headquarters would be in Rome. The purpose of the firm was the production of motion pictures, for which Signor Gramazio was investing ten million lira to start with.

The pace at which Gramazio worked was breathtaking. He also accomplished things beyond my wildest dreams. The very next day after our meeting at the notary's office, I received an invitation from the director Vittorio de Sica, whose work I admired. De Sica spoke so enthusiastically about mine that I was almost embarrassed. In a small room at the studios in Cinecitta, he screened his still uncompleted film *Umberto D* for me. It showed the same genius as his earlier pictures *Bicycle Thieves* and *Miracle in Milan*. He was also interested in my future plans. Learning that I had been unable to practise my profession after the war, he was so deeply moved that he called together his entire crew, introduced me, and gave a passionate speech to his lighting men and set hands. Unfortunately, I understood only a few words, but his speech was followed by intense applause.

The next day I met Roberto Rossellini and I was deeply touched by his warmth, especially when I thought of my German 'colleagues'. Rossellini knew all my films and was especially impressed by *The Blue Light*. Eagerly, he assured me, 'We Italians have imitated you in a number of ways. You were the first to shoot studio scenes on location. You even filmed a Mass in a church.'

My heart lifted at his words, and, encouraged and filled with new energy, I left Rome in order to seek a German partner for our Iris Film production.

GERMAN-ITALIAN CO-PRODUCTION

In Thiersee, a small village near Kufstein, a newly constructed movie studio was to house my projectors, editing tables, and some of my equipment – which was still confiscated. The French had appointed the Schneebergers as trustees for these things but I wanted to try to get my equipment back by way of Herr Würtele, my new trustee in Austria.

A new negative might be pieced together from the remainders of *The Blue Light*, which the Americans had left in the Berlin bunker. And indeed, the material proved useful. So, in early July, I began working in Thiersee, where I had set up two cutting rooms at the Breitenhof Hotel. I was given a generous hand by Dr Arnold, the inventor of the famous Arriflex camera and we were genuine friends until his death.

After a hiatus of more than six years, I was now about to start again from scratch. I was soon familiar with this material and became absorbed once more in the whole atmosphere of working with film scripts. Dr Giuseppe Becce, who had been orchestra conductor at the UFA Palace for many years and had composed the impressive music for *The Blue Light*, came to Thiersee to write a new score. We had borrowed a piano, so that whenever a film sequence was edited, Becce could instantly compose from those images. It was an ideal collaboration.

I finished my editing in Thiersee and then, in Munich, established Iris Film, an affiliate of the Roman firm. In a German-Italian co-production, we would complete the new version of *The Blue Light* and than start shooting *The Red Devils*. In Italy, Lux Film and Minerva were interested in this latter project; in Germany, National was equally keen. The German firm, which was ready to invest seven hundred and fifty thousand marks, signed an option. Things were looking up.

I got a lot of help from Dr Schwerin, the husband of Grete Weiser and the former lawyer of my firm. He advised me in all matters concerning the film business. No sooner did the news leak out that I was working again than all sorts of people turned up. Everyone tried to get money out of me, including those who, twenty years earlier, had worked in some capacity on *The Blue Light*. One of them was my former boyfriend and cameraman Hans Schneeberger. He threatened to sue me if I did not pay him fifteen hundred marks that he claimed I still owed him. He assumed that my documents were lost, but was out of luck. My files contained the original receipt that Schneeberger had signed for the money which he now demanded a second time. I have never heard from him again.

The next surprise was that Sokal also demanded money. He still hadn't sent me my share of the receipts from the film, and had made off with the original negative and sold it; nevertheless, he demanded fifty per cent of the profits from my new version and hired Otto Joseph, the most successful lawyer in Munich, to represent him with his unjustified demands. I saw little chance of winning against Joseph and Sokal, so I offered to give Sokal thirty per cent of the profits; but this was not enough for Herr Sokal. He threatened to take out an injunction against any showings of *The Blue Light*.

This was too much – not only for me but also for Dr Schwerin. This man, usually so calm and level-headed, completely lost his temper. He slammed his fist on the table and, without saying goodbye, stormed out of Joseph's office. His anger was understandable, for he had been generous enough to offer Sokal fifty per cent on condition that Sokal listed the countries in which he had sold *The Blue Light* and the income he had received. When Sokal refused to reveal his sales and income, my good-natured lawyer exploded and from then on insisted on legal claims and payment of damages. Only after that did Sokal stop his threats, and his lawyer, Herr Joseph, also had to knuckle under.

Meanwhile, I tried to get Italian producers interested in *The Red Devils*. The prospects looked good, especially since Cesare Zavattini, the well-known screenwriter of nearly all of de Sica's movies, was so enthusiastic about the treatment that he agreed to collaborate on the script. And de Sica promised to play one of the leads.

At last, the customs licence arrived and we plunged into our project. Our Italian colleagues proved extraordinarily gifted, with their great sensitivity, artistic empathy and technological skill. Moreover, Catalucci, a printing lab, did a marvellous job. I was amazed at how expertly they manipulated the light for the master print.

On 21 November 1951, a dazzling gala screening took place in Rome. Professor Gramazio had invited renowned artists and politicians; deeply moved, I received congratulations and flowers. It was a highpoint of my post-war life, but it was destined to be short-lived. Enthusiastic as the public and the press were, it was difficult to sell the film in Italy. The conditions offered by several distributors were unsatisfactory to Signor Gramazio for he wanted at least to cover his expenses, but no distributor wanted to assume a guarantee as the market was flooded with new films. So I pinned my hopes on my homeland, where my film had been so successful before the war and so fateful for my life.

A BLACKMAILER'S PHOTOGRAPH

Two days before the screening of my film in Munich, National Film Distributors held a press reception at the Eternal Lamp, opposite the ruins of the National Theatre. Gunter Groll, the most renowned film critic in Munich, had emphatically advocated a re-release of *The Blue Light*. He called it a 'milestone in the history of the German cinema'. Now, twenty years after its première, I again stood in the public light in Germany, trying to hide my inner agitation as I fielded questions from the reporters mobbing me.

The press response was surprisingly friendly. Then *Revue* struck again. On 19 April 1952, it ran a front-page headline announcing BEFORE LENI RIEFENSTAHL'S COMEBACK. On the inside, it ran a story that outdid in infamy their first article. It was a vendetta perpetrated by Helmut Kindler or – as I heard from my friend, the journalist and writer Harry Schulze-Wilde – by Frau Kindler, a former, little-known actress. At the first *Revue* trial, although admonished by the judge, she had, during a recess, conversed at length with Kurz, their Gypsy witness, who subsequently perjured herself in court.

The new illustrated story in *Revue*, entitled 'Leni Riefenstahl Hushes It Up', gave the impression that, several days after the outbreak of the war, I had witnessed a massacre of Jews by German soldiers in Poland. The text said: 'Leni Riefenstahl is one of the few German women who not only knew but also witnessed with her own eyes the terrible crimes from which Germany's reputation is still suffering throughout the world.'

As alleged proof of this accusation, the magazine printed a huge close-up of my face with a horrified expression. A second photo showed people who had been gunned down, lying on the ground in front of the building. The linking of these two photos was designed to make every reader think that I was watching a massacre – in other words, that I had witnessed such crimes.

As I have already detailed in my section 'War in Poland', where I describe the terrible events in Konskie, the true facts were very different. The apparently incriminating picture was snapped at the very instant that a German solider yelled, 'Shoot the woman down!' and pointed his gun at me. Distracted by the sound of faraway rifle fire, all the soldiers standing around us dashed off in the direction of the shots. Only my crew members remained with me.

It wasn't until I saw Colonel General von Reichenau, in order to complain about the undisciplined conduct of the soldiers, that I learned what had been happening. In a senseless rampage, more than thirty Poles had been injured or killed, and four German soldiers wounded. Neither I nor my crew had seen any of it. In fact, I had been so deeply shaken by the episode that I gave up my newsreel assignment that very same day and left the military zone. However, *Revue* said nothing about that, or about the cause of the dreadful event: the massacre of German soldiers by Poles. The alleged photographic evidence that I had watched a shooting of Jews had already been offered to me one year earlier by a blackmailer, who called himself Freitag. After I refused to buy the picture, it found its way to *Revue*.

THE AFTERMATH OF THE *REVUE* STORY

This new libel had a devastating effect. National Film Distributor informed me that most of the German theatre owners had cancelled their contracts. Worse than the boycott of the revival of my film was the impact on my new project. Herr Tischendorf, the owner of Herzog, one of the largest German film companies, wrote to me: 'Unfortunately, we have to notify you that the recent publication in *Revue* has induced us to renounce any participation in your film project *The Red Devils*. We are truly sorry.'

The worst consequences of the *Revue* article were felt in Paris. In March 1952, the tabloid *Samedi-Soir* reprinted the libellous article with the same 'original photos'. Herr Würtele, who happened to be in Paris in order to pick up my films, which had been released after Professor Gramazio's last visit, informed me: 'The transfer of your film material to the Austrian embassy, officially ordered by the French Ministry of Foreign Affairs for 9 May 1952, was halted at the last moment because of the revelations by *Samedi-Soir* which were taken over, in part verbatim, from the Munich weekly periodical *Revue*.'

That was too much. I collapsed.

The *Revue* article became known in Rome too. When Professor Gramazio learned from Paris that the *Tiefland* material had been reconfiscated, his helpfulness and enthusiasm evaporated totally. He showered me with rebukes and, with no legal justification whatsoever, demanded the repayment of all his expenses for *The Blue Light* and for his trips to Paris. Since I was up to my ears in debt, I could pay him nothing for the moment – which led to years of litigation.

All my hopes were dashed and again I stood there with empty hands. Even so, I wanted to avoid another lawsuit against *Revue* for I felt too drained and didn't think I could win against such a potentially strong adversary anyway. All I could do was wire the Berlin Denazification Tribunal to ask that the procedure be scheduled as soon as possible. The tribunal was supposed to denazify me in regard to my house in Dahlem, and I wanted to clear up the Konskie events. I was immediately given a date.

DENAZIFICATION IN BERLIN

On 21 April, 1952, after the presentation of evidence, Dr Levinsohn, presiding judge of the Berlin Denazification Tribunal, confirmed that the accusations made in *Revue* could be refuted in their entirety. The verdict said in part: 'The Denazification Tribunal therefore regards it unimpeachably demonstrated that Frau Riefenstahl is not incriminated by the photographs in question.' After a proceeding that lasted eight hours, the presiding judge announced that the verdict of the Denazification Tribunal of Freiburg of 16.12.49 was valid for Berlin too.

The Berlin tribunal had prepared itself meticulously. I learned that Dr Levinsohn and his two associate judges, Herr Schubert and Herr Will, had viewed *Triumph of the Will* the day before the procedure and also called a witness from the Eastern Zone. His name was Max Striese, a stranger to me. He came from Leipzig and, as a soldier, had witnessed the events in Konskie. His testimony bore out the statutory declarations made by my witnesses.

When I took leave of Dr Levinhsohn, he said, 'If you need advice and help, please come to me. In my profession, I have dealt with libel, but I have never coped with as many falsifications and lies as in your case. You may cite me as a witness in a suit against Herr Kindler in Munich.' He also told me that the material published in *Revue* as well as further 'incriminating evidence' had already been passed on to the tribunal by *Revue* a year and a half before, but Herr Kindler had wanted to hold up the publication until I got a new start.

Heinz Schröter, the officer accompanying Colonel General von Reichenau, wrote me the following letter:

> I hereby confirm that one day before the appearance of the issue in question of *Revue*, when Herr Kindler asked us for information about Konskie, I described the events in Poland, in the presence of his staff member, exactly as those events are known to you and to me; and I stated verbatim: 'I am sorry that I cannot provide you with a sensational item; but Frau Riefenstahl had nothing whatsoever to do with those events. I hope you don't put your foot in it; it was all quite different in reality . . .

I still have that letter in my possession.

THE SECOND *REVUE* TRIAL

Encouraged by the successful outcome in Berlin, I tried to get Herr Kindler to present the true facts in *Revue*. It was my second attempt to avoid litigation with his magazine. I had shown the exonerating documents to his lawyer, Dr Staubitzer, and asked him to mediate. Although Herr Kindler could now see for himself that he was wrong, he rejected any *rapprochement*.

Therefore, on 8 May 1952, my lawyer, Dr Gritschneder, filed a suit against *Revue*, charging it with defamation, libel and calumny. Even after launching the action, my lawyer made intensive efforts to prevent a trial by having *Revue* publish a retraction. But Herr Kindler preferred to track down further 'incriminating evidence'. Former members of his staff as well as other strangers told me that representatives of *Revue* had tried to pump them for information about me. By means of all sorts of shifts, Herr Kindler's lawyer managed to put off the court verdict over and over again, at first for weeks at a time, and then later for months.

My situation grew more and more desperate, and not only financially. Now, three of us – and during the day even four of us – shared a room no bigger than one hundred and sixty square feet on Tengstrasse. My mother slept on the couch, while Hanni and I slept on the floor. During the day, my ex-husband would call in; he had given up his job in Villingen in order to lend me a hand, and he helped me take care of my business correspondence, while my mother cooked our meals in the same room.

One day I had a letter from Paul Müller, a tried-and-trusted friend, who asked me to come to Rome if I possibly could. A few Italian producers seriously wanted to discuss *The Red Devils* with me. I didn't reflect for long. The very next day, I was on the train for Rome.

BACK IN ROME

When I arrived in Rome at the end of June, it was extremely hot – over 120 degrees in the shade – and my tiny room at the Hotel Boston was like an incubator. Even though the summer holidays had not yet begun, anyone who could had fled to the coast at Ostia.

Paul Müller looked after me. He took me to Minerva, one of the biggest Italian film companies, and the upshot of our negotiations was as follows. Minerva was willing, as co-partner, to pay half the production costs, a sum of seven hundred and fifty thousand marks (almost two hundred thousand dollars), their one condition being that the casting of the lead parts had to be decided jointly. I was asked to come back in a few days as they needed time to work out a rough budget. All the men who participated in the negotiations were thrilled by the subject of the film. Meanwhile, Paul introduced me to lots of interesting people, among them Tennessee Williams who lived in the same building as Paul, near Via Veneto; we got together a great deal, and the three of us had some amusing times. I had an opportunity to see Gina Lollobrigida on location in *Bread, Love and Dreams* and thought her outstanding in her role. Vittorio de Sica, who played opposite her, assured me once again that he would be delighted to play Mr Harris in *The Red Devils*. Then I was introduced to Anna Magnani, a unique actress, whom I greatly admired. She complained that no interesting projects were offered to her and she asked me to find her some suitable parts. Later on, together with Hermann Mostar, I wrote a film scenario for Magnani. It was entitled *Three Stars on the Cloak of the Madonna* and had an exciting role for her – that of a Spanish mother – but she turned it down, explaining, 'I'm too young to play the mother, the part has to be sexy.' Given her unusual temperament, I wasn't surprised.

One of the old acquaintances I ran into in Rome was G.W. Pabst. We had last met ten years before, in Berlin-Neubabelsberg, and had gone our separate ways again after a quarrel. But Pabst bore me no grudge. He introduced me to Jean Marais, who was ideal for one of my red devils. Not only was he young and gifted, he was also a good skier.

A LETTER FROM JEAN COCTEAU

Not long after I returned to Munich, I received a miraculous letter that simply bowled me over. It came from Jean Cocteau. I had never met this great artist personally, so I was overwhelmed by the mere fact that he had contacted me at all. Cocteau wrote:

> 36 rue Montpensier
> Paris
> 26 November 1952

My dear Leni Riefenstahl,

How could I not help but be your admirer, since you are the genius of the cinema, and you have brought the cinema to heights that it has seldom ever attained. I would be delighted to make your acquaintance, far away from the terrible practices that plague the present-day world of the cinema . . . I greet you with all my heart and I would be happy to receive a few lines from you about your future projects and yourself.

> Sincerely,
> Jean Cocteau

I was really startled. Such admiration was in stark contrast to the humiliations I had been forced to put up with for years. This letter gave me such a boost that, despite two cancellations by the Herzog studio, I telephoned Herr Tischendorf the very next day and was actually given an appointment to meet him. Nor did I go empty-handed. First of all, I took along the verdict of the Berlin Denazification Tribunal, as well as the promises from Vittorio de Sica and Jean Marais, plus the interest expressed by Minerva in Rome. With my passionate powers of persuasion, I managed to overcome all of Herr Tischendorf's qualms about this doubtless somewhat risky film project, and, within a few days, I received a contract that required me to complete a ready-to-shoot script within six weeks. If it hadn't been for Cocteau's letter, I would never have summoned up the courage to make that telephone call.

THE LAST STRUGGLE FOR *TIEFLAND*

At last, I could start a creative project. After deciding to find a small place in the mountains, I once again chose Kitzbühel and, above the village, at the Kohl Cottage, I found exactly what I was looking for: two cosy rustic rooms with wooden panelling and a small kitchen. The apartment was splendidly located with a view of the entire mountain chain and below lay the valley in deep snow – yet I was only a twenty-minute walk from the village. It was early December when I planned to begin work – but my peace and quiet were disrupted once again.

One morning, who should turn up very out of breath but Otto Lantschner, a member of my old staff. Otto, who was normally so relaxed and phlegmatic, was obviously trying to hide his agitation behind a smile. Without sitting down, he explained, 'Leni, I apologize for dropping in so early in the morning, but it's very important. Uli' (he meant Uli Ritzer) 'called me up from Innsbruck and asked me to tell you you've got one last chance to keep the French from destroying *Tiefland*, which is what they intend to do. You have to try and catch the express train to Vienna and get hold of the Austrian minister of finance, Dr Kamitz, who is going to be on it.'

'What are you talking about!' I cried in dismay. '*Tiefland* is to be destroyed? That's crazy – it's impossible!'

'Didn't you know?' I shook my head. 'That's why Uli sent me here. He thinks you ought to catch the train that's going to stop in Kitzbühel for three minutes.' Otto's voice was urgent.

'When is it arriving?'

'In fifteen minutes.'

'I'll never make it,' I explained, deeply upset.

'You ought to try. You'll never get another chance like this to speak to the minister as calmly as you will in a train compartment.'

I pulled my warm clothes out of the closet and dressed in a hectic rush, almost forgetting passport and money. Then, together with Otto, I took a short cut over the steep meadows with their light covering of snow. In the distance, I spotted the train waiting at the station, and I ran for dear life. It had began to pull out when, at the very last second, I leaped upon the running board.

What was I getting into? Gradually I began to realize how outrageous my situation was. My compartment was almost empty; only an elderly man, absorbed in his newspaper, sat opposite me. When the conductor made his rounds, I bought a ticket to Vienna.

I would have loved to get out at the very next stop for I had no idea how to find the minister on the train; I didn't even know what he looked like; I had never so much as corresponded with him. All I knew was that he had the final say on the release of German property in Austria.

What had happened? Why were they suddenly about to destroy my film material? Monsieur Langlois of the Cinémathèque had notified me twice that my material could be called for.

'Everything is ready to be shipped,' he wrote. 'It's up to the Austrian legation now; you have to urge them to pick up the films.' Monsieur Langlois was most certainly a serious person, I had to believe him. But his words contrasted sharply with what was obviously happening.

After riding for two hours and gradually relaxing, I began to put my thoughts in order. First I must look through the first-class compartments. I opened a door: 'Excuse me, is there a Dr Kamitz here?' Heads were shaken. I felt like a messenger trying to deliver a telegram without a house number.

Sighting the conductor at the end of the car, I got into a conversation with him. It wasn't long before he found out who I was. That made my situation easier. Plucking up courage, I asked him whether Herr Minister Dr Kamitz had already eaten breakfast. The conductor looked at me in surprise. 'Do you believe the minister would allow me to speak to him very briefly?'

'Should I ask him?' said the conductor.

'Oh, please,' I said, 'it would be so nice of you.' He entered the first compartment door. The decisive moment had come.

Dr Kamitz greeted me in a friendly and unaffected way.

'Please forgive me, Herr Minister, for pouncing on you like this.'

He waved his hand and said, smiling, 'I am delighted to make your acquaintance. I've known you on the screen for a long time. By the way,' he went on, 'I have recently been dealing with your affairs. That is probably why you wish to speak to me, is it not?' I nodded. 'Unfortunately, your case is not very simple.' Seeing my distressed expression, he attempted to reassure me, 'But we will try to help you.'

Dr Kamitz then told me about the struggles of the Austrian government with the various French agencies and described the legal situation of German property in Austria. The most sensational news of all was that *Tiefland* and the rest of my material had been in Vienna for a week now. I was speechless. Then I heard the minister say: 'This was possible only after Dr Gruber, the Austrian foreign minister, intervened several times at the Quai d'Orsay in Paris, and Dr Figl, the chancellor of Austria, also got involved. It was only then that the French finally agreed to bring the material to Vienna – it filled an entire box car. And they agreed only on condition that the material should not be handed over to you.'

'Is it true that it has to be destroyed?' I asked, deeply upset.

'Nothing has happened as yet,' Dr Kamitz tried to calm me.

Now I learned why the French had made their stipulation and why they were causing so much trouble. The chief reason was that, on the basis of the Control Council Agreement between France and Austria, my material should never have been confiscated by the French in Kitzbühel. The confiscation also countermanded the orders of the French occupation forces and film officers, who were directly under the Sureté, had been the ones who also had illegally withdrawn the money from our accounts and taken my private belongings to Paris. This had to be hushed up in order to prevent a scandal in France and so I had been deprived of my freedom and locked up in an insane asylum – from which I might never have been released without the help of Professor Dalsace. First, the French film officers tried to use *Tiefland* to their own ends. For a year, they edited and reedited my material and it was only when the international legal situation made copyright infringement too ticklish for them that they gave up their plans; now they were scared that if the material were handed back to me, it would be obvious how many of my films they had destroyed or sold. The Austrian government, as trustee of German property, could not only sue for damages in the French military court, but also press charges of theft and official misconduct. The French agencies were afraid of this and, in order to prevent it, they tried to obstruct the return of my material. To prevent it legally, they told the Austrian Ministry of Finance that the owner of *Tiefland* was not I but the Nazi Party. For property belonging to the Nazi state and the Nazi Party, the French could issue a statement of forfeiture and then legally do whatever they wished with the material. Such was the situation at the time Dr Kamitz described it.

'Can you stop it?'

'I hope so,' said Dr Kamitz. 'The legal department of my ministry is making concentrated efforts. If you can prove that *Tiefland* was not financed by the Party, then we can save the films.'

I heaved a sigh of relief. 'I have all the necessary documents to prove that,' I said. Just recently, after a ten-month investigation by the Bavarian Restitution Office, I had received confirmation that no Party funds had been involved in my firm. I told the minister about Lantin, who to avoid having to return material he had borrowed from me, had brought the same charges against me as the French. Over one hundred witnesses had once again been questioned. The minister said, 'But you have enemies as well as friends. What are your future plans?'

I was happy to change the subject. So I told him about *The Red Devils*. Dr Kamitz appeared interested and said that this might be material for the Austrian film industry.

'Yes,' I said, 'it would be good publicity for tourism in Austria. Most of the shooting would be done in the best known ski centres in Austria.'

The conversation ended with his inviting me to Vienna to discuss the two films. What luck that I had taken Otto Lantschner's advice.

THE RED DEVILS

For years, the Tyrolean skiers were known as the Red Devils. Wherever they appeared, they were unbeatable, and it was they who were the heroes of my film. The best devil was named Michael. The basic idea of this comedy in the snow was a comic modernization of the Amazon legend. Heinrich von Kleist's *Penthesilea* is one version of that ancient tale.

The colours had a specific function in the drama. The ski amazons were to wear blue. The third colour was yellow, to be worn by the Italian team which competes with the Red Devils. I was enthralled by the idea of colour impressions against a white background and I imagined a symphony of colours, rhythm and music – an Olympic dream in snow. The project filled me with enthusiasm. In a small mountain cottage over Kitzbühel, I worked with the authors of the screenplay, Harald Reinl and Joachim Bartsch. I had committed myself to finishing half the script by the end of January 1953.

We made it. I handed the work in punctually. Herr Tischendorf was so impressed that he told me to start pre-production. Above all, we had to limit the budget, otherwise the film couldn't be financed in Germany. The locations would be Garmisch, Kitzbühel and Arlberg, as well as Cervinia, where skiing could be filmed even in the summer months.

The wild card in this film was the weather, but my script had taken those risks into account: the mass descents were to be shot in blizzards. Furthermore, I planned to have the studio sets built outdoors, in Lech on the Arlberg; that way, we could work even during inclement periods.

The best racers of all skiing nations were to be hired for the film though the 'amateur paragraph' would require a waiver from the International Olympic Committee. They gave us permission so long as we only covered the athletes' expenses.

At the International Sports Week in Kitzbühel and Garmisch, we did test shots of suitable skiers, including the well-known downhill racers Molterer and Spies, who were also to be cast in roles. The male lead was to be played by a Norwegian, Marius Erikson, and another part was to be taken by his brother Stein, one of the best skiers in the world. They were recommended to me by Maria and Willi Bogner, who were friendly with them. The Bogners were also willing to lend their support by providing the wardrobe for all the skiers, male and female. Everything was proceeding at an astonishing speed. During the test shooting in Garmish, I was even greeted by Ludwig Erhard, the West German minister of economy, who wished me luck on my first post-war movie.

I did not encounter such good will everywhere.

SETTLING WITH THE *REVUE*

The script-writing had progressed very successfully, but now I found it hard to continue. My creditors would not leave me in peace, bombarding me with court orders, and the fee for the screenplay melted like snow in the sun. Then the enforcement officer of the tax office turned up at my door to collect the back taxes on my house in Berlin-Dahlem – 19,350 marks (almost five thousand dollars) – but since I didn't have a penny to my name, the seizure was useless. To relieve myself of the burden of debt, I was willing to sell my house, but it was impossible to find a buyer. He would have had to find new homes for the nine penniless tenants and this made any sale impossible.

Under the circumstances, I was glad when my lawyer informed me that, after months of negotiation, Helmut Kindler and Dr Hans Lehmann, editor-in-chief of *Revue*, were prepared to make a satisfactory settlement out of court. *Revue* had kept postponing a decision, because it was gathering material for a third series – to be entitled: 'Leni Riefenstahl's Millions'. That move would have led unquestionably to further litigation. The verdict of the Berlin court could not be appealed against.

Herr Kindler agreed to publish no further attacks on me and I received ten thousand marks (two thousand five hundred dollars) in damages; yet the actual damages went into millions, and the moral damage could never be made good.

Still, given my overall situation, it meant a great deal to me that Helmut Kindler and I had made peace.

EXCITING DAYS IN VIENNA

Since the Austrian voters had re-elected the incumbent administration of the Volkspartei and Dr Kamitz had remained minister of finance, I could see him within two days of my arrival in Vienna. Our meeting was successful, for the investigation of the documents and excerpts from the trade register revealed that I was the sole proprietor of my firm. This prevented any further French manipulation of my work.

Now came the great moment when I could go to the printing laboratory and see my film material again after eight years. I was excited and deeply moved when my hands touched the celluloid strips. It soon became obvious that the trustees had been unable to cope with the innumerable cartons without my help. These cartons contained not only the *Tiefland* material, but also the mountain films and the original negatives and lavender copies of *Olympia*.

From then on, I was busy sorting the material from dawn till night. *Tiefland* was in a bad way. The edited prints and one third of the selected negatives were missing, while parts of the extant material were dusty and scratched. Regenerating the film would require a tremendous amount of labour and in order to keep working the thing I needed most was capital. I myself could pay neither the salaries of assistants nor the rent for a cutting room.

I received many promises, but few were kept. So, with a heavy heart, I decided to sell my house in Dahlem. I could scarcely have chosen a less favourable time than spring 1953. My splendid home, which I had barely lived in, was set in grounds of fifty thousand square feet in a wooded area only ten minutes from the Kurfürstendamm. Yet I received only thirty thousand marks (about seven thousand dollars), since the buyer had to find new apartments for my nine tenants. A few short years later I could have sold it for over a million marks (two hundred and fifty thousand dollars) but I was too tightly squeezed to be able to wait. I used the money to found Junta Film Ltd in Vienna on 16 June 1953, together with an Austrian partner, my former crew member Otto Lantschner. But this was still a far cry from being able to begin.

Meanwhile, four women were sifting through the tremendous masses of material at the Vienna printing lab in order to find the important editing print of *Tiefland*. Four reels of the negative were missing and as this virtually irreplaceable material was nowhere to be found, I had no choice but to go to Paris to hunt for the missing reels. My first stop there was the Cinémathèque Française, where I received unexpected help from Madame Meerson who made sure that several bunkers were combed – but to no avail. Through the French Foreign Ministry, I met with Louis François Poncet, who was willing to continue the hunt in France after my return to Vienna. Meanwhile, the lease contract had been signed, but my firm still didn't have a concession. The Vienna trustee, Herr Lorbeck, had to involve Plessner, a film company in Kufstein. It was all very intricate, time-consuming and expensive.

On the other hand, I was glad to hear that, in Munich, the well-known cinema lawyer, Dr Wolf Schwarz, had worked out a favourable distribution contract with Allianz Film, whereupon a major Austrian distributor, International Film, also bought the *Tiefland* rights.

Now I hoped to start working at last, and once again, Dr Arnold lent a hand. Within just one week, he had set up a perfect cutting room at ARRI.

It was already September when the first shipment of my material finally arrived in Munich – and Allianz had already announced the première for late November. We worked at a tremendous pace, the four of us closeted in the ARRI cutting room – often day and night – as in the old days.

François Poncet in Paris notified me that the search for the missing reels had been unsuccessful, so I had to cut a new version from the extant material – no easy task. Important sequences were gone, especially the 'drought' footage that had been shot in Spain, and this seriously detracted from the plot of the film.

The music was recorded in Vienna at the beginning of November. We had wanted Herbert von Karajan to conduct, and he was willing, but we couldn't afford his fee; instead, the music was conducted by its composer, Herbert Windt, and his work with the Vienna Symphony made up for everything.

AT LAST, THE PREMIÈRE OF *TIEFLAND*

In February 1954, after an incredible twenty-year odyssey, *Tiefland* was premièred at the E.M. Theatre in Stuttgart where Allianz Distributors had done everything it could to make the occasion dazzlingly festive.

When the lights went out, I sat incognito in a corner seat in order to view *Tiefland* as an ordinary film-goer for the first time – free of all the problems I had endured since the making of my film. As the first few takes flashed across the screen, I was assailed by memories of all the pain associated with the making of this picture. Were the sacrifices worth it? Would it hold its own in front of the audience, and what would the critics say?

As the film ran on, my doubts increased, for the theme and the style seemed long out of date. But when I saw again some of the highly expressive shots, black-and-white effects of a graphic quality, my feelings wavered. I found the visual form impressive, as I did the music, the faces of the Sarentino farmers and Franz's performance as Pedro – he was a born actor. When I saw myself on the screen, however, I felt quite sick. I was obviously miscast. How could I have been so mistaken? I hadn't wanted to play the part and I tried, unsuccessfully, to get Brigitte Horney and then Hilde Krahl. Nevertheless, I could have imbued this role with more life if I hadn't been so battered by sickness and misfortune.

Would the public and the media share my reservations? I attempted to stifle my critical faculties but, when the lights went on, I was surprised by the loud applause. We had to take countless bows on stage. The Allianz people were satisfied for the film appeared to be a hit – even though the reviews varied. Some were good and some less good; but they were all objective.

Then my adversaries struck. Hateful attacks in several newspapers destroyed any possibility of success; and despite the verdict of the court, the old lies published in *Revue*, were reiterated. '*Tiefland* Gypsies from a Concentration Camp', 'The Doomed of Auschwitz', 'L.R. Watches German Soldiers Massacre Jews in Poland'. No lie was too big to be quoted. As with *The Blue Light*, many theatre owners backed out of their contracts and refused to screen *Tiefland*. Although I had sworn never to go to court again, I could not oppose distributors when they demanded that I force these newspapers to print retractions or sue them. In all instances, my lawyers succeeded in having retractions published; but as always in such cases, the damage couldn't be made good again. Naturally, the tour for the Austrian première was also jeopardized. I was summoned by wire to Vienna. The executives of International Film Distribution, which had acquired the rights for Austria, were in a turmoil. Associations of concentration camp survivors had threatened to burn down the cinemas. I suggested to Herr Zöhrer, the owner of International, that he or his press chief should invite the heads of those associations to come and see my court records but my idea was rejected out of hand. Since no one knew what to do, I said I would be willing to ask for a personal interview with the association leaders.

'You can't run that risk,' said Herr Zöhrer, alarmed.

'Why not?' I asked. 'I see no other possibility, or do you have a solution?'

I was determined to face those people and I sent to Munich for all the exonerating documents, plus my correspondence with Manfred George.

My meeting with the survivors' association took place in their head-quarters, and it began on a stormy note. No one from the distribution company wanted to escort me, so I went alone. Upon entering the room, I was greeted with insults, so loud and vehement that I couldn't speak for several minutes. I estimate that there were some fourteen to sixteen people present and not a single woman among them.

Shielding my face with my arms, I waited until the hubbub subsided. Then they allowed me to speak. It took at least half an hour before I was able to give them some autobiographical information, and by then I sensed that they were starting to believe me. They seemed particularly impressed by Manfred George's letters and by the fact that I did not deny the admiration I had felt for Hitler. An animated discussion developed, lasting for hours, during which the hostility gradually evaporated.

The next day, the Vienna newspapers ran the following:

NEW DECLARATION BY CONCENTRATION CAMP ASSOCIATION ON THE
RIEFENSTAHL FILM

As announced by the board of directors of the Association of Survivors of Concentration Camps: during a visit to the Association, Frau Riefenstahl presented documentary statements and decisions by various government agencies and courts of law to demonstrate that the accusations that she used Gypsies from a concentration camp in her motion picture *Tiefland* were inconsistent with the facts . . . The Association is still of the opinion that it would be more expedient not to screen the film in question at the present time; but it has decided to refrain from any further action against showings of the film.

The distributors breathed a sigh of relief. My tour of Austria with Franz Eichberger, our Pedro, was a roaring success – not only in Vienna, but also in Linz, Graz and especially Steyr – and the reviews, from both the left-wing and the right-wing press, surpassed all my expectations. The most pertinent comment was, I think, the following: 'An operatic subject has become a lyrical painting.'

FILM FESTIVAL IN CANNES

In 1954, Jean Cocteau was president of the jury at the Cannes Film Festival. We had already met personally and become good friends. He saw *Tiefland* in Munich and, despite its obvious weaknesses, the film made a deep impact on him. 'The images radiate a Breughel-like intensity, the poetry of the camera is unparalleled, and the film has style,' he said. Then he went on: 'I would like to have the film for Cannes,' and he was not just being polite, he was quite serious. Despite his many obligations, he offered to translate the dialogue of the film into French, so that it could be shown with good subtitles. Cocteau telegraphed the West German Ministry of the Interior:

> I would be especially happy if Leni Riefenstahl's motion picture *Tiefland* could be belatedly registered for the Cannes Film Festival. Acceptance guaranteed. Please wire decision to Grand Hotel Kitzbühel. Respectfully, Jean Cocteau, president of the jury of Cannes.

The West German Ministry of Foreign Affairs, to which the telegram was forwarded, replied:

> I must inform you that very serious reservations exist here about the nomination of the motion picture *Tiefland*, which appears in no way suitable to represent the cinema of the Federal Republic of Germany abroad. I therefore regret . . . that I cannot agree to your request. I greet you cordially. R. Salat.

Plainly I could expect nothing from the German government. Cocteau determined that *Tiefland* would be shown in Cannes non-competitively, and, according to my ex-husband, who delivered the print in Cannes, it was a success. Most delightful of all were the following words in the letter that Cocteau sent me: 'I viewed two screenings of *Tiefland* at the Festival. That was my reward.'

A POLITICAL DECISION

Encouraged by this success, I now had only one aim in mind: to make *The Red Devils*. Herzog Film had the script translated into Italian and gave me funds for the pre-production. The schedule and all calculations had been worked out, but, unforunately, the large crew and the long period of ski shooting, so dependent on the weather, made the pre-production too costly for a German film in those days. Despite cuts in the script, the expenses would run to one million eight hundred thousand marks (four hundred and fifty thousand dollars), a sum that could be covered only by an international co-production.

Meanwhile, in Austria, the success of *Tiefland* had aroused great interest in my new project. After all, the Red Devils were Austrians, and they were the real stars of the movie. The Ministry of Finance as well as the tourism division of the Ministry of Commerce and the Creditanstalt (a bank) were equally interested, while International Film, which had become so nervous, offered me twice the guarantee they had given for *Tiefland*.

The greatest possibility was still an Italian partner, and so once again, I tried my luck in Rome. I was on the verge of giving up, however, when Rizzoli Film asked to see me and I perceived a ray of hope; at that time, Rizzoli, a newspaper and publishing magnate, was the uncrowned king of Italian cinema.

When I visited his office, I learned that Signor Rizzoli was very anxious to discuss my film project – he was thinking of Ingrid Bergman for the female lead – but that he had left on vacation the day before.

Disappointed, I asked, 'Where did he go?'

'Positano,' said Signor Freddi amiably. 'Everyone there knows where Signor Rizzoli lives and,' he went on, 'you really ought to think about going there. Signor Rizzoli was impressed with the material, and he is also a great admirer of your earlier films.'

Positano is less than one hundred and eighty miles from Rome, so that same afternoon, I sped off in my Opel Rekord, which I had been able to purchase after signing my contract with Allianz. Unfortunately, I didn't realize what such a drive entails in Italy at the peak of the summer.

Ferragosto, the great holiday period, begins on 13 August annually, and that was the very day on which I took off in the direction of Naples.

In Naples, it was impossible to find a place to stay, even the tiniest nook. So I had no choice but to keep driving through the night. When I saw a sandy beach below me in the moonlight, I did not hesitate for an instant but slammed on the brakes, switched on my parking lights and dashed down to the beach, where, exhausted, I keeled over on the sand. Someone came towards me; it was an elderly man, obviously friendly, who bent over me with a worried look and then motioned to me to follow him to a bathing cabin, where I instantly fell asleep.

I spent the next night sleeping in my car and didn't arrive in Positano until the third day. There I was told that Rizzoli had, alas, gone to Ischia, but I was so tired, my mind so numb, that I barely felt any disappointment. All I wanted to do was sleep. Once refreshed, I decided to travel on to Ischia, but, when my boat docked, I learned that the film king had taken off again, this time in his yacht, and that he would be out sailing for several days.

So I gave up and returned to Rome; there I found a letter from Jean Cocteau: 'Jean Marais would be delighted to be your Red Devil; he is the only man I can imagine in the role. Of all the current subjects, your film strikes me as the most important.' For the capricious part of Kay, Cocteau recommended Brigitte Bardot, who was very young and only just beginning her international career. I also found an offer from an Italian finance group, which was ready to put up one third of the production costs – seventy-five to eighty million lira. Furthermore, Titanus and also Lux Film asked if they might negotiate with me again. The day should have had more than twenty-four hours.

Meanwhile, October had come, and time was running out. The promises I had obtained from stars like Jean Marais and de Sica, and, above all, the generous support offered by hotels and chambers of commerce in Germany, Austria and Italy inspired Herzog Film to increase their previous distribution guarantee for Germany to eight hundred thousand marks (two hundred thousand dollars), a dizzying sum in those days. Together with the Italian participation, the backing of the film was as good as certain.

Now the final decision had to be made. In Vienna, I negotiated a refinancing of the German distribution guarantee and the process was not easy. At first, everything went very favourably. The applications had to be processed in departments of various ministries. The Austrians were very keen on the subject, and so everyone did his best to get through all the red tape. I had the most important meetings with Dr Kamitz, minister of finance, and with Dr Joham, general manager of the Creditanstalt and the decisive figure with regard to the refinancing, and both were one hundred per cent behind the project. Prior to signing the contract, they needed only the consent of Raab, the chancellor of Austria, since Dr Leopold Figl, the foreign minister, had personally approved the film one year earlier, during my visit to Vienna.

At last all was ready; the rooms in Zürs and Lech were reserved, the racing drivers notified and the most important crew members hired.

Christmas had come, and we indulged in a little relaxation after all the anxious months. Then the bomb exploded – not a huge bomb, just a tiny news item, which intimidated the Austrian government and killed *The Red Devils* stone dead. *Der Abend*, Vienna's Communist paper, ran the following headline: LENI RIEFENSTAHL AND THE TAXPAYER. THE MINISTRIES OF FINANCE AND COMMERCE TO BACK EXTRAVAGANT FILM PROJECT BY THE GERMAN DIRECTOR. Although demonstrably untrue, this item was the death blow for the movie.

A political avalanche began to roll. For the opposition, the Socialist Party of Austria, this was an excuse to attack the Austrian Folk Party, now in office. Leftist newspapers published long, dishonest stories, which kept exacerbating the situation, and the assaults on the Folk Party administration grew more and more vehement.

Der Abend wrote:

It would be desirable as a matter of urgency for the government to announce whether this sensational financing of the Leni Riefenstahl film has actually been decided. Frau Riefenstahl has failed to find backing for her film project in either Germany or Italy. She has managed to cover only sixty-five per cent of the production budget. The [Austrian] taxpayer is supposed to make up the missing thirty-five per cent. The taxpayer wonders how it is possible that Frau Riefenstahl is so marvellously well connected not only with the heads of the Hitler regime, but with the heads of the Federal Republic of Austria, that her projects are treated with a generosity unwonted in Austrian film production.

It was a bare-faced lie. The production costs were covered one hundred per cent – a fact which could be read in the contracts already signed by the Creditanstalt. Once again, I was caught between the Scylla and Charybdis of political interests. Then I read in the same newspaper: 'Rejected. Leni Riefenstahl will receive no tax money.'

Herr Tischendorf, the owner of Herzog Film, went to Vienna, hoping to bring about a change by meeting personally the members of the Austrian government, to whom he could submit proof that the press accounts were untrue; upon his return he told me: 'Dear Frau Riefenstahl, you have to forget about your film, you have to bury it. The situation is hopeless; the government would rather resign than let us obtain our refinancing. The opposition to you personally is so strong that – forgive me for telling you the truth – you can never practise your profession again for the rest of your life.'

JEAN COCTEAU

Cruel as this blow was, I tried to pick up the pieces after slowly getting over the shock and a serious illness. Herr Tischendorf had prophesied that I would never again be able to work at my calling but fate gave me another chance.

A visit from Jean Cocteau inspired me with an idea which struck me as charming: a film about Frederick the Great and Voltaire, neither historical, nor heroic, but, as Cocteau phrased it, one that would show the human relationship between the king and the philosopher, their love-hate friendship – symbolic of the relationship between France and Germany, although this would only be hinted at as an underlying theme. Characteristic of this film would be the attempt to capture the two antipodes in satirical and effervescent dialogue. Cocteau was tempted to play both parts under my direction – an exciting thought. I was able to win over another talented man, Hermann Mostar, a gifted writer and connoisseur of the subject, who after years of studying the sources had gathered not only a vast amount of historical material but also a number of unknown anecdotes. His book *A Very Private World History* was one of my favourites. But even though the theme was extraordinary and the production would be cheap (since I could imagine it in black and white, and Cocteau and I were willing to work without pay), we were unable to find backers.

Friedrich A. Mainz, to whom I offered the project and who liked it, said, 'Leni, spare yourself further disappointments. You're not going to get financing or distribution for this or any other project. Don't you know that you're black-listed in the United States?'

'I've learned about it from my American friends, but I'm sure this boycott will have to end sooner or later,' I said, resigned but still hopeful.

'You're very naïve,' Mainz replied.

Cap Ferrat, not far from Monte Carlo, was where Jean Cocteau was spending his summer holiday, at the Villa Santo Sospiz. He had asked me to visit him and wanted to show me the work he had done for our Frederick and Voltaire project.

We spent two unforgettable days with him. Everything surrounding Cocteau was filled with poetry. In his rooms on the lower floor of the villa, he had painted all the walls in lively, but not harsh colours – mainly shades of green. The motifs – depictions of plants, animals and divine figures – were partly abstract, partly realistic. Cocteau had created his own world here. He didn't like reality to come too close to him.

'You and I,' he said, 'live in the wrong century.'

The sketches for *Frederick and Voltaire* were delightful, but even more fascinating was the way in which he presented himself in both masks, as the king and as the philosopher. It was astonishing to see how easily he transformed himself from one to the other. This film, starring Cocteau, could have been a precious jewel, but all I have left of the project are his letters to me, which, from that visit until his death, he always signed 'Friedrich-Jean-Voltaire'.

AFRICA

THE GREEN HILLS OF AFRICA

One night, I read Hemingway's new book, *The Green Hills of Africa*, which had only just been published. I read until dawn, by which time Hemingway's lifelong fasination with Africa had taken hold of me. I was enthralled by this world, hitherto so alien to me, and I could almost hear the words Hemingway wrote in his diary during his first night in Africa: 'When I woke up at night, I lay there listening, already longing to come back to Africa.

Was the thrilling atmosphere he described merely the vision of a poet? Could one really breathe more freely and more happily in Africa? My mind soon gravitated more and more towards that unknown continent, which I resolved to get to know, with or without a film project. I started gathering information, first by looking at a great many picture books and before long, despite all my previous disappointments, I was hunting for a film subject. Inspiration came when I read in a German newspaper a headline which screened: MISSIONARY UNCOVERS SLAVE TRADE IN AFRICA. According to the reporter:

A memorandum sent by the Belgian missionary La Gravière to the responsible agencies at the United Nations tells of dreadful atrocities committed by African slave traders. After months of detective work, the Belgian clergyman has succeeded in exposing how through a huge, illegal organization, as many as fifty thousand blacks are captured and sold as slaves in African countries every year. The price for a very strong, healthy Negro is one thousand to two thousand American dollars, but they are also bartered for ammunition and weapons. For instance, a woman costs three rifles, a strong young man a crate of cartridges, a strong adolescent a pistol or a bayonet. Armed gangs of slavers invade African villages at night, take the intimidated inhabitants prisoner and sort out the 'goods' there and then, children and old or sick people being left behind. The prisoners are chained to one another and driven off by the kidnappers like a herd of cattle; any prisoner too tired to go on is mercilessly shot and killed. The centre of the slave trade is in the Tibesti Mountains, the impassable area along the border between French Equatorial Africa and Libya, where the caravans of slave dealers arrive with their 'black ivory', from Chad, central Morocco, Uganda and the Sudan. The buyers, the 'wholesalers', are mostly white, many of them

deserters from the French Foreign Legion. The human freight is
then shipped along secret roads at night, either on foot or on trucks, to
secret bays along the Red Sea, where Arabic dhows ferry them across to
Arabia.

I was shaken by this report, but doubted whether cruelties could really be
taking place. To learn the truth, I wrote to the Anti-Slavery Society in
London, asking for information. The material I received not only confirmed
the Belgian missionary's story but included further important data. Thus I
learned that slavery also existed in Ethiopia, even though it had been
abolished by law and slave trading was now a capital offence. Many of the
blacks who fell into the hands of slave dealers were on the pilgrimage to
Mecca. They had been deceived from the very start, and by the time they
realized the truth about their ghastly situation, it was too late. The worst
part of all was the voyage across the Red Sea when, with chained hands and
feet, they lay crushed together under mangrove wood. Rocks were tied to
their bodies, so that they would sink quickly if they had to be dumped
overboard through the portholes; such dumping occurred regularly whenever the dhows were pursued and stopped by British police boats.

Mr T. Fox-Pitt, the commander of the Anti-Slavery Society, who
promised to assist me in every possible way, wrote: 'Our link with you
would give any film the stamp of authenticity. We could collaborate in
producing a highly valuable documentary.' After that, I was ready to
embark on what I swore would be a final attempt at making a motion
picture.

BLACK FREIGHT

In Munich, I met Dr Andreas von Nagy, a zoologist from the Hunting
Institute of Göttingen, who had been asked by the museum of natural
history in Bonn to carry out a scientific project in Africa and who, in
addition to this assignment, was ready to act as my adviser. He in turn
introduced me to Hans Otto Meissner, a writer and big-game hunter, who
sent me the galleys of his book *Hassan's Black Freight* which contained such
interesting material that I decided to work with him too. This led eventually
to the film treatment *Black Freight*.

Once again I had to tackle the painful business of finding money for a film.
I sent the manuscript to just about every film company that I knew of, along

with the estimated budget and the documents of the Anti-Slavery Society.

Everything looked fine. I was again greatly helped by Dr Arnold's promise to make all the technical equipment – cameras, cinemascope optics and spotlights – available without immediate payment. We obtained the same conditions from the firms that gave us the colour celluloid and agreed to print our rushes. Similarly, all the participants offered to forgo any wages for the time being.

Unfortunately, all this generosity was not enough and, as I had feared, I was swamped with rejections. Most producers felt that making a film in Africa was too risky, but I was obsessed with my project and refused to give up. Despite all the uncertainty, I reserved three places for 27 November 1955 on the *Diana*, an Italian steamer, for the voyage from Naples to Mombasa. I wanted to travel ahead with two other people in order to do the necessary pre-production work.

I was so convinced that the film would work out that I wrote letters from dawn to dusk, negotiated with one person after another, received promises and rejections and lived in a state of suspense that grew more and more nerve-racking as the day on which we were to set sail from Naples came closer. In the end, however, I was forced to cancel the three reservations on the *Diana*. I had been too optimistic, we couldn't afford to pay for the tickets.

I was on the verge of giving up when, to my surprise, Gloria Film contacted me. I felt encouraged, especially as my initial negotiations with Ilse Kubaschewski, head of Gloria, were quite promising; but soon we hit a serious snag. Although they approved the budget, I found the artistic conditions unacceptable, for Gloria demanded that all the parts, including the Arab slavers and African blacks, be played by Germans. At first, I thought they were joking. But the Gloria people were in earnest, and refused to give way. Only Frau Kubaschewski seemed willing to make concessions.

For hours on end, I defended my viewpoint, reminding them of my *The Blue Light*, in which I had cast laymen in most of the roles over twenty years ago. And now white actors were to appear in black make-up – a ludicrous idea, a mockery of responsible documentation, especially when dealing with an ethnological subject.

After days of tenacious struggling, there seemed to be a glimmer of hope. Frau Kubaschewski and Waldi Traut sided with me, and in order to avoid impeding the difficult negotiations any further I agreed not to play the female lead in the film, even though I wanted to. This character is a scientist who, while looking for her husband who is missing in Africa, gets entangled in the slave trade. We narrowed our casting of the part down to Winnie Markus or Ruth Leuwerik, both of whom were very popular stars.

Black Freight appeared to be coming together, especially when O.E. Hasse, an outstanding German actor, agreed to play the male lead. Then, at the very last moment, immediately before the signing of the contract, everything fell through. Herr Adam, the chief executive of distribution, refused to sanction it.

A PERILOUS JOURNEY

It took days for me to get over the frustration and organize my thoughts. I had such a burning wish to get to know Africa that I couldn't think of anything else. Pictorial visions of the place so haunted me that I decided to go to Africa by myself. To this end, I sold some of my possessions: a Bollschweiler painting of a horse's head – which I really loved – an old rustic chest and a Meissen porcelain clock, all items from my confiscated furniture which had been returned to me by the Austrians. I had already written to a hunting office in Nairobi, Lawrence-Brown Safari, which had arranged the dangerous animal scene for the Hollywood films *The Snows of Kilimanjaro* and *King Solomon's Mines*.

In April 1956, I stood in cold, unfriendly rain at Riem airport, saying goodbye to my mother and my friends. Luckily, my mother, a wonderful woman, understood why I had to go on this perilous journey. When a takeoff delay was announced, I did something I had never done before: I wrote a short will. Was it a premonition? Snow began to fall, and I was glad to board the plane. During the long flight, my life ran past my closed eyes like a film; thoroughly overwrought, I was unable to sleep. The night seemed endless.

As the plane took off again in Cairo, there were very few passengers left. Presently, I saw the first light of dawn, a magical veil of colours, through the dark window panes; I hadn't seen such intense hues since my time in Greenland: yellow and green, soft blue and shades of radiant orange all the way to glowing red. The stars flickered and above them hung the sickle of the southern moon, as if cut out of silver. It was a symphony of light – clear and transparent – in Paul Klee colours, to herald my first morning in Africa.

By the time the sun rose, we had landed in Khartoum, but I still had the clamminess of a grey German April in my body; leaving the aircraft, I felt as if I were sinking into a hot bath. The sun, magnified by the haze and fine sand dust, loomed gigantic over the airfield. I was quite overwhelmed.

The world I had always lived in was that of the mountains, the ice of Greenland, the lakes of Brandenburg, the metropolis of Berlin. Here, I felt the start of something entirely different – a new life.

Against the light, I saw black figures in pale garments coming towards me, seeming to hover in the quivering sunlight, detached from the earth as in a mirage. Africa had embraced me – forever. It had sucked me into a vision of strangeness and of freedom which affected me like a drug. Its narcotic effect still hasn't worn off, even today, though I know now the darker aspects and the apparently insuperable problems of that continent.

In the afternoon, when the plane landed in Nairobi, I finally realized how perilous my trip was. I had no information aside from a few hotel addresses from Herr von Nagy and several brochures. Stepping out of the aircraft, I was bewildered and almost disappointed by what I saw.

As far as the eye could see, there were only dry, grassy prairies, and here on the landing field, there were bleak barracks, where the flight passengers were processed. Nothing recalled the dream vision that had enchanted me in the Sudan that morning. In the slanting afternoon sun, everything looked bare and desolate. Approaching the wooden fence in front of the airport barracks were two men, apparently hunters, in cowboy hats straight out of a western, and next to them was a woman holding a bouquet. I didn't know her, and I was surprised how heartily she greeted me and handed me the flowers. The younger man said, 'Welcome to our country. We are delighted you have come. Unfortunately, Dr von Nagy couldn't accompany us; he's still at the Momella Farm in Tanganika.' Pointing to his companion, he went on, 'This is Stan Lawrence-Brown' – he seemed to be teasing slightly – 'Africa's most celebrated white hunter, and this is his wife Ronnie. My name is George Six, and I've known you for twenty years.'

'But I don't know you,' I said, puzzled.

Mr Six laughed, 'At the Olympic Games in Berlin, I watched you every day at the swimming stadium when you and your cameramen were shooting the swimmers during training. I was the captain of the British swimming team.'

I couldn't have wished for a more charming reception in Nairobi.

From then on, everything went at a breathtaking speed. After the customs formalities were completed, I was driven to the New Stanley Hotel. Located in the centre of Nairobi, it was still as Hemingway had described it: the throbbing heart of the city. This was where the white hunters met with their clients to discuss the safaris, and this was where people found out what was going on in Kenya. Usually you had to book rooms at the New Stanley weeks in advance; but for Stan Lawrence-Brown, this was no problem – he always got a room.

We had lunch on the terrace of the hotel. The climate was as pleasant as the summer in Engadin, and, in contrast to the uninviting airport, the streets and squares of Nairobi were filled with flowering trees.

'You've brought along a film treatment?' asked Stan, gazing at me somewhat curiously. 'Can you tell us something about it?'

'Wouldn't you like to see lions first, before it gets dark?' Ronnie asked me.

Although utterly worn out, I eagerly said yes and in no time was completely carried away. Previously, I had known Africa only from books and films but now I experienced everything at close quarters and it was truly unbelievable. Twenty-four hours earlier, I had stood freezing, in a damp, draughty airport, and now I was in the middle of Africa's plains with their umbrella acacias and other beautiful trees. We sighted our first animals – monkeys large and small, already squatting on the roof of our car. I had brought along both my Leicas and I soon used up my first films. We spotted giraffes, first two, then four, then an entire herd; zebras, koodoos, antelopes approached us. A short time later, we saw our first lion, then a group of four more.

When we got back from the National Park, I was invited to spend the evening at the home of the Lawrence-Browns in their beautiful house which stood in such utter isolation in Lagata, some twelve miles from Nairobi. I heard how leopards had killed the dogs sleeping on the veranda. However, the greater hazard for Mrs Lawrence-Brown was that she and her children often spent months in this Mau Mau area alone, with only her black servants around her. Sometimes, her husband was on safari for a whole year. She showed me her revolver.

After dinner, they asked me to talk about my film plans and to read them the synopsis of *Black Freight*. If the German producers had been only half as enthusiastic as my hosts, the financing would have posed no problem. 'The film has to be made,' said Stan, 'the material is marvellous.' Getting to his feet, he paced up and down the room. 'We are going to help you but I have to think about how. We'll talk again tomorrow. Now I'm driving you home.'

Overwhelmed by fatigue, I slept better and more deeply than I had for years. The next morning, I was woken by a noise and was rather startled to see a pitch-black face behind the mosquito net. 'Ma'am,' I heard a voice say, 'it's five o'clock, here is your tea.' Then the figure vanished. I didn't realize that this was a traditional custom throughout the British colonies in Africa: at 5 a.m., a black boy would enter without knocking and place a pot of tea next to the bed.

During the next few days, we worked very hard. Stan could remain in Nairobi for only a few days until the start of his next safari, so we discussed the entire film project thoroughly, making calculations and clarifying organizational issues. The most important and most difficult problem was getting permission to film but our permit was granted faster than had ever been the case previously.

Before his departure, Stan and George Six (also a director of Lawrence-Brown Safaris) talked about scouting locations on the Tana River. Stan considered this landscape in northern Kenya particularly suitable for our film, and – making my heart race – he said, 'Miss Leni, you are our guest for the next four weeks. That's all the time that George has. He is going to take you through East Africa and show you all the places you wish to see. I'm sorry that I can't come along.'

His invitation surpassed my wildest dreams, and we embraced like old friends.

TRIP TO THE TANA RIVER

George Six was at the wheel, and I sat next to him behind the windscreen of his safari jeep while a black boy sat on our baggage in the rear. Then it happened. Two hundred and fifty miles north of Nairobi a small dawrf antelope leaped out of the bushes and dashed across the road as we approached a bridge across a dry river bed. Six tried to avoid hitting the animal. The jeep skidded across the deep, red sand, we hurtled towards two huge bridge rocks, the left front wheel grazed the rock, the car was jolted aloft, our heads smashed through the windscreen, the car somersaulted and I instantly passed out. I can't recall the last few seconds; all I know is that I saw the front wheels of the jeep dangling above the abyss. I came to, in dreadful pain, aware that someone was trying to pull me out of the car. Our bodies were wedged from the waist down underneath the vehicle, while our heads and torsos were outside. I heard a voice shout, 'Petrol, fire!' then I passed out again. The boy, who was unhurt, had succeeded in pulling George out of the jeep. Although seriously injured, George was then able to help the boy pull me out. All the time the petrol was leaking from the tank and a fire could have started any moment.

We owed our miraculous rescue to an incredible stroke of luck. During the rainy season, this road was normally closed; in fact, George Six needed a special permit to use it. Once a month, however, a British district officer drove along this link between Somalia and Nairobi – and today was the day. Half an hour after our accident, he crossed the bridge and saw us lying next to the overturned jeep in the sand of the river bed. He took us to Garissa where, at the time, there was only a police station consisting of three buildings; there was no physician nor even any medicaments, except for a single morphine injection, which George saved for me on the journey.

Occasionally regaining consciousness, I felt excruciating pain. During the war, George Six had been an auxiliary medical orderly in London, and now, without any disinfectant or anaesthetic, he used a darning needle to sew up a gaping wound on my head, from which a huge artery was dangling. It was torture. As for himself, his knee cap was broken and he put his leg in splints himself.

Four days later, summoned by a police radio call, a single-engine sports plane with room for two people touched down. I was given the morphine injection, was wrapped in sheets and carried into the aircraft. The drug worked so fast that I blacked out completely. Later, Six told me that the pilot had said, 'Don't waste my time and your money transporting the woman. We'll never get her to Nairobi alive.'

AT THE HOSPITAL IN NAIROBI

In Nairobi, I was brought to a hospital and placed in the room for the dying because, after examining me and checking my X-rays, the chief physician, Professor Dr Cohn, an Englishman, and his colleagues gave up on me.

When I awoke, it was dark all around me and I could recognize nothing. When I opened my eyes a second time, I found myself in a bright, friendly room. Through the open windows, I saw a blue sky and white cumulus clouds. A tube had been inserted in my mouth, and I had been raised into a sitting position. My eyes fell on George Six.

If God was my heavenly saviour then George Six was without a doubt my saviour on earth. Despite his own injuries and pain, he never left my bedside until I was finally out of danger. Miraculously, my spine and my heart were unhurt, but a lung had been punctured by several broken ribs in the right side of my thorax. What I didn't realize was that my reawakening was a sensational event for the doctors.

My mind, slowly emerging from the world of oblivion, focused on a single problem: how to prevent my mother from learning about my

accident. With great difficulty, I managed to give George the wording of
the telegram: 'Accident during location scouting. Am out of danger, at
European Hospital Nairobi. Write soon.'

George then left, in order to recover at his farm in Arusha, in the care of
his wife who missed him terribly. Now began a time it makes me shudder to
recall. The British nurses to whom I was entrusted seemed to be heartless
creatures. If it hadn't been for uniforms, they would have passed for fashion
models: they wore heavy make-up and hair-dos more suited to the ballroom
than the hospital ward. Often, they placed my food and drink so far from my
bed that I couldn't reach them, knowing the bell was too far away for me to
be able to summon help. If the tube fell out of my mouth and I couldn't ring, I
suffered great distress.

My broken ribs healed quickly, but the doctor said, 'Your lung is
collapsing and you are not in a condition to fly to Germany. We'll have to
operate on your lung here.'

Now for the first time I was really afraid. Professor Dr Cohn and his
assistant were on holiday so I refused to sign the consent form for the surgery
and my condition got worse and worse. Every day, a long, thick needle was
inserted through my back into the lung in order to prevent a thrombosis.
These young, hard-working doctors tried in vain to talk me into having the
operation but all my life I have followed my instinct and very seldom the
dictates of logic and on this occasion my instinct told me to resist surgery.

By the time Dr Cohn returned, my lung had blown up like a balloon again
– all on its own, without an operation. The doctors were mystified but, from
then on, my progress was rapid. Barely six weeks after the accident, I could
already stand up and make my first attempts at walking.

When George Six, still hobbling with the use of a cane, appeared in my
hospital room, my joy was indescribable. He visited me daily, bringing me
fruit and chocolate, and finally suggested sneaking me out of the hospital.
The first time I could walk into the garden, he would whisk me off to Arusha
in his car, and his wife would nurse me back to health. My escape from the
hospital went without a hitch, exactly as he had suggested.

Sitting next to George in a jeep, I forgot all about the accident and my
pain. I absorbed the African landscape even more deeply than during my
first drive; at one point, I grabbed George's arm and yelled, 'Stop the car!'
He looked at me, startled. Two kingly figures were marching at the side of
the sandy road, without so much as deigning to glance at our vehicle. Their
ochre-coloured garments were knotted on one side, they wore a strange
headgear of high, black ostrich feathers, and their hands clutched spears and
shields. Never before had I seen Africans in their native costume; they had

always worn European clothes. Thrilled, I took their pictures and asked if we could stop so that I could meet them. But Six drove on.

'Stop,' I shouted. 'We have to give them a lift!'

His response was dry and contemptuous: 'No, they stink. I'm not picking them up.'

I was furious. When I turned back to look at the two men, I saw only eddies of dust. The figures had vanished in the haze. 'What tribe do they belong to?' I asked.

'Masai,' Six said tersely. He wasn't interested in them. But for me, that fleeting encounter was the start of the long road which led me to my Nuba many years later.

At that time, in 1956, the Masai were regarded as the masters of the East African savannah. They did indeed have an aura of unapproachable arrogance and I couldn't understand why I was so fascinated by them. Hemingway had once described them as follows: 'They were the tallest, best-grown, most splendid people that I had ever seen in Africa.'

In Arusha, as Mrs Six nursed me back to health, I kept begging George to take me to one of the Masai kraals and finally he gave in. I even managed to convince him that we ought to consider involving the tribe in the plot of our film.

However, our first contact with the Masai was not very encouraging. The women hurled stones at me, and the children ran off tearfully, while the men eyed me from a distance. I respected their timidity and refrained from photographing them; but I returned every single day, sitting down on the grass or on a rock and reading a book. In this way, they gradually became used to my presence, the children drew closer, the women stopped throwing stones at me; and then one day, it was almost like a victory when they stood in front of me, and the women and children laughed. The ice was broken. They allowed me to enter their dark huts, they touched me, and they let me drink milk from their calabashes. At last, they permitted me to take their pictures and, a few days later, when I had to say goodbye, they clutched my arms and wouldn't let me go.

That was the beginning of my great love for the African tribes.

BACK IN GERMANY

My mother came to meet me in Rome and hugged me ecstatically. Surprised by my appearance, she said, 'You look so healthy.'

'I *am* healthy, I could uproot trees,' I said in my exuberance. 'Africa restored my strength – it's a fantastic place.'

416

I did not leave that continent empty-handed. During my last days there, I had received a contract from Stan Lawrence-Brown Safaris for my negotiations in Germany, and the terms were so favourable that I was convinced I would get the rest of the backing for *Black Freight*. Stan and George Six were so enthusiastic about the project that they were willing to risk going in on it with us. The company was prepared to lend us the following equipment at a cost of $2,700 a month: two cross-country cars with four-wheel drive and three or four five-ton cross-country trucks; three hunters, including George Six; complete provisions for the entire crew and the African staff consisting of cooks, tent workers, drivers, trackers and rifle carriers; guns, ammunition and carriers for the camp gear; medical supplies, petrol and a complete supply of camp equipment – beds, blankets, mosquito nets, kitchen utensils, refrigerators, including a special refrigerator for film stock – plus non-alcoholic drinks such as Coca-Cola, fruit juices and mineral water.

This contract meant an interest-free investment of at least two hundred thousand marks, not to mention that the safari company was usually all booked up at least one year in advance, and there was no other with so much film-production experience; I had every reason to be confident. I also brought along good colour photos that I had taken in Africa.

Time was of the essence. It was already June, and the pre-production work was overdue. The filming was to be done in East Africa from early September to the end of November. Furthermore, my head injury, caused by the car accident, required surgery since the wound had been sewn up temporarily. So I plunged into a flood of work, which I managed to get done only with the help of my Hanni, who had developed into a perfect secretary. Hanni not only took care of my correspondence, she also typed up my scenarios and scripts even though she had never taken a typing course. No work was too much for her. At least thirty letters went out every day, for I negotiated not only with German companies, but also with American studios such as Paramount, Fox and others. Initially, they were all interested in my project, but every single time my name still aroused qualms. They hesitated and finally said no; even when I offered to have my name left out, it didn't help. The worldwide boycott and their fear of being attacked if they employed me were more powerful then any amount of profit, no matter how tempting.

Waldi Traut knew my capabilities better than almost anyone else did; he knew what I could accomplish and how obsessively I could work on a film. He had his own production line under Frau Kubaschewski and had produced such hits as Paul May's *0815* and *The Physician of Stalingrad*. Traut was quite aware that my project was extremely promising, so, having failed to convince Gloria Film, he decided to assume the risk himself. In July 1956, he founded Stern Film Inc., in order to produce my film; I was to be his partner and an equal manager in the company. I would contribute my rights to the material, my work and the Safari company's payments in kind (equivalent to two hundred thousand marks), and Waldi Traut agreed to invest two hundred thousand marks of his own money.

My head injury healed quickly, and now everything went with the speed of lightning. Vaccinations, medicaments, visa applications, insurance and the assembling of the technical film and photo equipment were taken care of; the optics were tried out and test shots were done. Before our departure, our home on Tengstrasse was in a state of bedlam.

Finally, I had to get a subtenant for my flat and I found an American. Even at the airfield in Riem, I thought of hundreds of things I had forgotten and Hanni, who was to follow with the others, took notes, but could barely keep up. I was accompanied only by Helge Pawlinin. Then the big moment came: takeoff, waving hands – and we were in the air and on our way.

SCOUTING LOCATIONS IN KENYA

George Six was waiting at the airport in Nairobi. He had prepared everything so thoroughly that we could begin searching for locations just two days later. The only thing left was the completion of our safari wardrobe which almost any tailor could deal with within twenty-four hours.

Before I left, whom should I meet on the hotel stairs to my great surprise, but Peter Jacob, whom I hadn't seen for an eternity. What a coincidence running into him in Nairobi; he had been there for several weeks assisting the director Paul May, who was shooting a film in Kenya. Our brief meeting was harmonious as always during the past few years. Ten years had passed since our divorce, and it had taken me nearly that long to get over that very difficult time of my life. I might never have succeeded in doing so without Africa.

George Six had again chosen the Tana River in northern Kenya for scouting locations. The camp was set up in an incredibly beautiful jungle landscape and only an inspired writer or poet could describe the atmosphere of the first tropical night or the subsequent days. The morning was unforgettable. While breakfasting in the early sunshine, we saw the heads of giraffes through the bushes peering at us with undisguised curiosity.

Our search for locations took us further and further north, almost as far as the Abyssinian border, looking for the out-of-the-way villages of the Samburus, the Suks, the Turkans, the Gallas and the Rendilles; but so far, we had only run into individual Africans, who shyly avoided us, full of mistrust. Helge and I were fascinated by these exotic people, while George, just as before during my first encounter with the Masai, refused to have anything to do with them. This was not good for my project.

Our vehicles had long since left the trails, and we were now only creeping through the almost impassable terrain. Every few hours, both jeeps had to be dug out of the deep sand and often they could only be pulled out with the help of ropes slung around a tree. However, one day not even that method helped. For hours on end, Six and the driver tried to haul the heavy truck out of the sand by means of a rope winch, but the wheels kept boring in deeper and deeper until, at twilight, the exhausted men gave up. The situation was serious, for no human beings came into this area, and we were running out of water.

There was only one solution – to drive the jeep back to Nairobi and get help. Mr Byron had to remain behind with most of the blacks, since George took with him only two boys besides me and Helge. Suddenly, as we bumped along the sandy track, there was a crack and the jeep halted; I anxiously peered at George to find out what was wrong.

'The front axle is broken,' he groaned. He sent the boys off to get water and also to look out for any native huts in this deserted territory; meanwhile two tents were pitched. He had lost his carefree laugh. Only Helge retained the enraptured smile he had worn since his arrival in Africa.

The night was cool and starry. Pulling on a thick woollen sweater, I sat down on an iron crate. My eyes swept across the moonlit desert landscape, which stretched out before me in lonely grandeur. Without warning, as if spirited out of the ground, a dark-skinned boy dressed as a nomad stood in front of me. He gestured for me to follow him as he skipped nimbly ahead of me to where I saw the outline of a clump of palms. No voices or sounds other than our footsteps could be heard and it was as if time had stood still. From the shadow of the palms, a tall man came forward and welcomed us into a nomad camp surrounded by densely woven straw mats. Camels, asses, goats and other animals lay or stood around me and I was offered a bowl of camel's milk which had a pungent taste.

The starry sky, the palms, the camels, the Bedouin all looked like biblical images; in the darkness, my eyes made out several tents and my host allowed me to look inside one; on a wide, neatly plaited straw mat lay a young, beautiful woman with long, pitch-black hair. She was unveiled and wrapped in embroidered cloths and she had golden bracelets on her arms; she did not seem at all embarrassed and she and her husband exchanged a few words. Then he led me to a second tent where I saw another woman lying on the straw carpet; older, but still beautiful, she too was richly decked out in gold. Beaming with pride, he showed me to a third tent where a very young woman sat nursing an infant. My host was probably a very wealthy Bedouin and enjoyed displaying his three tents and his three wives. This glimpse into a foreign world was quite bewildering. After offering me dates and figs, he warmly said good-night and the boy brought me back to my tent.

On the morning of the fourth day, George told me that there was no way of continuing our scouting with the car. It could only be managed in a small sports plane and he had radioed to Mombasa for one but the extra cost of this put us over budget.

The tiny aircraft, flown by a British pilot, landed near our tents within a few hours, but it could take only two people and we had to leave Helge behind. George suggested that the pilot should first head west along the Tana River, flying as low as possible so that we could get a good look at the locations.

Within half an hour, George was so airsick that the pilot refused to fly for longer than one more hour and we had to turn back. However, our flight had shown me that the Tana River was unsuitable for our purposes. The script called for a river in a jungle landscape, the kind you see in Indonesia, Brazil or the Congo, but not in East Africa, although I didn't know it at the time. All the same, I still hoped to find the right location towards the eastern part of the river, near the Indian Ocean.

This flight, on which I was the only passenger, was more successful, because I found the native huts, which had to line the riverbank, and I got to know the island of Lamu, where the old harbour with the Arabian dhous – so important for our slave theme – could be located. I also discovered surprisingly suitable water locations with papyrus, palm forests and exotic mangrove trees. On the whole, the island seemed perfect for our film.

A few days later, I again boarded a small sports plane to go in search of further locations. The flight across Murchison Falls was splendid. This was the only place where we could photograph crocodiles, and when we glided at a low altitude across the Victoria Nile, we saw thousands of hippo-potomuses, more animals than water – a primeval sight.

Our chief destination was the small jungle river of Ruts Huru in the Belgian Congo, the only river flowing through a jungle. On Lake Kiwu, we headed down and, by a chance, were able to see the famous dances of the Watusi. I obtained some wonderful shots. The king of the Watusi and his staff were staying at the hotel where we spent the night; he wore European clothing in dramatic contrast to the spectacular dancers we had seen just a few hours earlier.

Back in Nairobi, I waited anxiously to see what sort of casting Helge had done, but when I asked him about the results, he looked embarrassed and said mournfully, 'I haven't found anyone.'

I had expected active help from Helge but now I had to take over his job as well. It was not from lack of goodwill on his part; he was simply too shy, too sensitive to accost strangers because of his rather passive character. On the other hand, he showed me a number of marvellous sketches that he had done of the Masai in Arusha. Whenever he spoke about them, his face assumed that rapt expression.

LAMU

In mid-September, all of us got together on the island of Lamu – including George Six who had recovered from a serious illness. Waldi Traut had managed to get Kurth Heuser, one of our most gifted screenwriters; to agree to collaborate with Helge Pawlinin on the final script. George had found an ideal camping site outside the village, in a palm grove, right on the bay. However, our situation was still critical. We had no actors as yet for the African parts, and we also had to get hold of props, the most important of which was the houseboat of Hassan the slave trader. It was supposed to be a special boat made up of two narrow, forty-foot long canoes held together by a bamboo cabin. George and Lawrence-Brown had assumed we would have no trouble having it constructed at a dockyard in the port of Mombasa but this was a big mistake for the only dockyard willing to accept the job said it would take them six months. In the end, Six decided to build the houseboat himself with the help of Africans in Lamu.

'And how long would you need?' I asked him.

'One week,' he replied.

Wishful thinking, of course. There was no seasoned wood available in Lamu, and it would take at least two weeks for some to arrive from Nairobi. Once again, George had made a promise that he could not keep.

We required straw mats for the cabin of Hassan's houseboat and, improbable as it sounds, there was not a single straw mat in all of Lamu. We got the name of a native village that manufactured such mats, but it was quite a distance from Lamu and in order to reach it we had to rent a motorboat from an English official! On this occasion, the white hunters again made it obvious that they were completely incapable of dealing with natives. They treated them like inferior creatures, which, of course, made it impossible to get anywhere with them. It took me a whole day to order mats through the chieftain and agree on a delivery date of ten days at the earliest.

Pawlinin and Heuser kept working away on the script, while George, after obtaining wood and screws, constructed the houseboat almost alone – an incredibly difficult task, for not even an electric drill was available.

One week later, only a quarter of the work was done, and we couldn't tell whether the boat would be able to carry sixteen people. I took advantage of the interval to look for actors and, within a short time, I found a few wonderful types in the marketplace – but only for the parts of the slavers, not the slaves. The Africans here were too slender and delicate and I had to search elsewhere.

JOURNEY WITH THE BLACK 'SLAVES'

In our film, casting the slave roles was extremely important. They had to be large and muscular, for the stronger a black, the higher his price. I had pictured this casting as being simple but the reality was very different. The natives of East Africa – the Masai, Samburu, Turkana, etc – are usually slender, even scrawny so the slave traders got their 'wares' from the Congo, the Sudan and Central Africa.

Some of the policemen I had seen in Mombasa and Nairobi were massive enough to fit the parts. Speaking to some of them, I learned to my surprise that none of them had been born in Kenya or Tanganika; they all came from a different area, a small village near Lake Victoria, not far from the Uganda border. Most of them were from the Jalau tribe.

Since I couldn't find a single native in Lamau to cast in a slave role, I decided to fly to the Uganda border in quest of my 'actors'. I was accompanied by an Arab interpreter, the son of the mayor of Lamu. This trip turned out to be one of my most exciting adventures in Africa.

In Malini, the English pilot landed briefly in order to fill up and eat lunch. I wanted to take along Abdullah, our interpreter, but the pilot flatly refused: 'The Arab can't eat with us. If he sets foot in the hotel, the owner will shoot him down.'

I was incredulous but, touching my arm, Abdullah murmured, 'Miss Leni, we Arabs are used to being treated like that here. Go to the hotel with the pilot. There's a small Arab restaurant here where I can eat.' Disgusted, I told the pilot to go to the hotel alone; then I turned my back on him, took Abdullah's arm, and went to have lunch with him.

I was deeply upset by the incident. Abdullah had already studied in Mombasa for a few terms and wanted to get his doctorate in Cairo. He told me about the class prejudices of a certain type of Englishman and now I understood why George Six hadn't wanted to give the Masai a ride in his car. My encounter with the young Arab student developed into a friendship, which still endures today.

We were able to fly all the way to Kisumu on Lake Victoria and there we obtained information about the location of the villages where the Jalau lived. Hiring a car, we left the pilot behind in Kisumu and I drove with Abdullah through dense African bush. My experiences in the villages were deeply tragic. The instant the blacks sighted Abdullah, they became terrified, thinking we were slavers. I had no choice but to leave him behind with a chieftain and try my luck on my own.

I thought I was going to be successful in the very first village, where a small feast was in progress. My driver, who spoke Swahili and some English, took me to the chief, a stout, elderly man, who had a gaudy cloth wrapped around his body and held a large fly swatter in his hands. Greeting us amiably, he ordered an old straw mat for me to sit on while I watched the black men stamping in front of me. Dancing to the monotonous beat of the drums, they whirled up so much dust that I could barely make out their faces.

These natives were the very types we were looking for but it took me hours to convey my wishes with the help of body language and my African driver. The chief told me to come back the next day, since he first had to find out which men would be willing to leave their families for such a long time – I had spoken of three months. He was attracted by the high sum I had offered and the presents he coveted: a wristwatch, sunglasses, plus cigarettes, tea and sugar.

Feeling very hopeful, I returned to the village the next day to find, to my astonishment, that far too many men had gathered in the village square. Actually, I needed only eight natives, but I intended to take along twelve just in case. The labour officer, whom I had brought from Kisumu, helped the chief make a note of the monthly salary and the amount of work time for every single man on a slip of paper. Half the entire sum had to be paid on the spot and the second half at the end of the three months.

After I handed the chief one thousand shillings, we agreed that I would fly ahead to Mombasa, while the labour officer would escort the twelve blacks from their village to the Kisumu railway station the next day. From there, Abdullah would take them by train to Mombasa.

Two days later, at 7 a.m., I stood on the station platform in Mombasa to receive the men and as the train approached, my excitement mounted. The people poured out of the train, but I couldn't spot Abdullah with my blacks. Slowly, the station emptied and there, at the end of the train, I saw several figures and heaved a sigh of relief as I recognized my interpreter. He slowly approached me, followed by three figures, whom I couldn't make out because the light was in my eyes. Depressed and exhausted, Abdullah reported what had happened.

The British officer had appeared punctually with the twelve natives at the Kisumu station, but when they saw Abdullah, four of the blacks had taken to their heels. Abdullah and the Englishman had managed to get the other eight into the train, but three more had fled at the very next stop, petrified of the 'Arab'. At the next station, two more ran off, so that it was only by some miracle that the three others had summoned enough courage to ride on to Mombasa. To cheer them up and get them over their fear, I drove to the market with them; there, they ate their fill and were given some clothes. When I asked them in Swahili what their names were and gave them all the reassurance I could, they slowly seemed to lose their anxiety.

By a happy chance, I met a highly intelligent black in the taxi I had hired in Mombasa whose English was good. When I told him about my difficulties, he offered to help and encouraged me to go to the end of the harbour where the cargoes were loaded and unloaded and where I saw gigantic figures carrying heavy loads on their backs. My cabby accosted several men and managed to talk four of them into coming with us right away if I could pay off their bosses and each of them could say goodbye to his family before departing. Since they all lived in Mombasa, this posed no problem.

We were able to leave before sundown, for my driver, whom I nicknamed Coca, had organized everything. As we drove through the town, I saw an unusually tall black man leaning against a house wall. I hesitated for an instant, then asked Coca to stop. The man's clothing was quite ragged, but he had the same build as the dockworkers and we still needed one more 'slave'; so I told Coca to ask the man whether he would come along with us for good pay and the man hesitantly came over to our car. When he saw the other blacks, and Coca handed him a banknote, the man got in but was obviously embarrassed about being so down-at-heels. However, we promised to give him new clothes.

Thinking back to that trip from Mombasa to Lamu with my 'black freight', I can scarcely understand how I could have launched so heedlessly into that venture. Thirty years ago, there was no real road from Malindi to Lamu, only a path through a dense jungle and without motels or petrol stations. We had to avoid breaking down on this stretch, which was roughly two hundred miles long.

By the time we had passed Malindi, I realized – too late – that I had made another big mistake. We had been in such a hurry that I had forgotten to take along food and water – a serious oversight, for we would be driving for at least nine hours. My stomach was already grumbling so how must the blacks feel? After passing the plain area, we found ourselves in such a dense jungle that the tree branches scraped against the car windows and Coca could drive only at a snail's pace. He had to keep his eyes on the ground to avoid the deep holes and the rocks. Tree trunks lay across the path and had to be cleared away with the help of the blacks. Our car, too heavily loaded for this primitive track, often listed dangerously. Coca, Abdullah and I sat in the front, and the blacks were crowded together in the back.

That nocturnal drive for me – the only white woman, alone with unknown blacks and an Arab – was a nightmare. Now and then, we saw animal eyes glowing in the dark and elephants and rhinoceroses lumbered ahead of us. Several times, we had to stop and back so that animals could get past us unscathed. Then, abruptly, we were jerked aloft, the driver had slammed on the brakes because there, in front of us in the glow of the headlights, lay a gigantic, almost white python, several yards along and as thick as a tree trunk. I nervously watched as the snake inched forward, taking forever to creep into the bushes.

Meanwhile, my blacks were growing anxious – still afraid of being kidnapped, and by now also very hungry. I sensed something like a rebellion brewing as they were waving their arms and shouting. The situation was becoming critical when I had a flash of inspiration. Gesticulating energetically, I tried to quiet them and cried in Swahili, 'Sing!' Coca began to sing, then one after another they joined in; the singing actually made them forget their fear and hunger. They sang until 2 a.m. when we reached the inlet separating us from the peninsula of Lamu.

We woke up the boatman who was to ferry us to our campsite but in the boat, the blacks again became frightened. Some of them knew that their brothers and friends had been taken on an uncertain trip, ferried across water and placed on ships that carried them to foreign countries. It was natural for them to think that we were slavers! Coca and I had great difficulty in calming their fears. Finally, at 4 a.m., we reached our camp. Now my black 'actors' could at last be well provided for. Soon everyone fell asleep, wrapped up in woollen blankets – exhausted, but content. I too plunged into a deep sleep.

BELOW THE EQUATOR

The next morning, at breakfast, I noticed that my crew was dejected, but no one would tell me why. I had assumed that they would all be delighted that we had cast our 'slaves'. But they were all as taciturn as could be.

George followed me into my tent and told me that during my absence war had broken out on the Suez Canal: the English and the French were fighting against Egypt and the canal was closed to ships. The vessel carrying our technical equipment would have to take an enormous detour of several thousand miles around South Africa and we wouldn't be getting our equipment for weeks.

'Don't let it get you down, Miss Leni,' said George, 'Stan and I have hit on a solution. We mustn't stop, otherwise we'll lose everything. What happened is an act of God. Our company is willing to extend the big safari for five weeks without burdening you financially. This is a great sacrifice for Lawrence-Brown Safaris, but if we don't go ahead, we'll lose more.'

I still sat motionless on my camp-bed; the generosity of the safari company was certainly an enormous help, but the loss of time would cause other problems which I couldn't solve.

Was another rescue possible? There were still many incalculable risks since we had to wait in Mombasa for the arrival of our ship. However, we could benefit from the hiatus. Our black performers had to be dressed – a job that Helge skilfully attended to, while George finished constructing his boat and took care of all the necessary props. The blacks also had to be taught how to row – a difficult task since the thing they feared most in the world was water. None of them could swim so I had to join them in the boat in order to calm their anxieties. By the time the ship finally docked in Mombasa and we received our cargo, dark rain clouds were thickening in the sky; just our luck if the rainy season was already beginning. A few short hours of rain can turn any trail into a sea of mud so we hurriedly struck camp.

Before heading towards West Uganda, we first had to return to Nairobi to put together the great safari, knowing it would involve three cars with four-wheel drive and four huge five-ton trucks. Anyone familiar with African conditions in those days can understand why all those vehicles were necessary. We had to take along everything we would need for many weeks or even months. There were no hotels *en route*, no motels or stores. Aside from our eight 'slaves', we had six more black actors, who were to play major roles.

Not counting the performers, our crew consisted of only eight people; but George Six, our expedition leader, took along twenty-four boys, which, together with the seven drivers, brought the total to fifty-two people. Tents and camp-beds or at least mattresses and blankets were needed for all of them, plus kerosene lamps, food and medicaments. One truck carried the tanks of petrol and water, another carried the forty-foot canoes of our houseboat, plus our film equipment, a wagon, tracks, machine units, cables, lamps, silver stops, and finally an aluminium boat with two outboard motors for filming on the river.

I had never dreamed that this project would require such an enormous expenditure. I had been wrong to think that one could shoot a feature in Africa on our shoestring budget; that was my misfortune, or perhaps my fault. It began to burden me more and more.

I felt even worse when I read the mail awaiting me in Nairobi. Waldi Traut begged me to send the rushes to Munich as soon as possible so that he could screen them for prospective foreign backers and German distributors. Otherwise, he saw no possibility of sending us further money since he was down to his last penny.

I thought of cancelling the project but now that we had everything together – the locations, the cast, and the new contract with the safari – I believed we must try to see it through. After all, we still had enough cash to pay for the essentials during the next ten days and George had assured me that it would take us no more than a week to reach Queen Elizabeth National Park, where I had found the most important locations during my flight to Ruanda-Urundi.

On the verge of our departure, we had a disagreeable surprise. Our safari car, which had been parked on the lively main street of Nairobi, right in front of the Torres Hotel, had been broken into at dusk. The thieves had stolen not only all the tropical wardrobe, but also documents, journals, and our exposed and unexposed film stock, as well as five cameras belonging to members of my crew. The worst loss of all was Helge's handwritten shooting script, our only copy. Since Kurt Heuser had to leave because of a contract, our only possibility was for Helge and me to do the work again.

I hadn't had a free moment since my arrival in Africa. We got up at 6 a.m. every day and usually worked, with only a short break, until midnight, not only on scouting locations and casting, but also on writing arrangements, schedules, budget proposals, insurance problems, customs declarations, applications for permits to film animals in the national parks and so on. In three months, I still hadn't begun my actual job, the artistic work, and I was dying to start shooting. My patience was put to a severe test as our departure was delayed over and over again while all the vehicles were being overhauled and various spare parts obtained.

Then came a heavy blow. The Safari Company ambushed me. George Six, whom we hadn't seen all day, sent me a letter by messenger informing us that he had conferred with the two other directors of his company, and they had decided to cancel our safari. They had miscalculated the costs and were reneging on all their promises. They demanded their usual prices, which were three times the contractual sums and which we couldn't afford. This was sheer extortion. The only explanation I could think of was that Six had had the best intentions, but that he was having problems with the other directors because of the great losses incurred by the breakdown of the vehicles. Unfortunately, Stan, the most important director of the firm, could not be reached, being on safari in Tanganika, somewhere in the bush. After two hours of arguing with Six and the other two directors, I got them to promise that we could stay in the tents at least until a final decision was reached by Stan.

Our camp was set up on the outskirts of Nairobi. The boys mutinied because they had to sleep without tents in the pouring rain and I could barely manage to quell the revolt. The mood of my own crew was little better and Heinz Hölscher, my cameraman, fell ill with the usual tropical malaise, with fever and diarrhoea. It all looked so hopeless that only a miracle could save us.

No miracle occurred, but there was a stay of execution. Stan contacted the others by radio, and I was able to speak to him. He decreed that our safari would continue. Our agreements would remain in effect and all due payments were to be put off interest-free until the end of the year. A few weeks after the end of the safari, he would join us in Uganda and lead the expedition himself.

We were finally able to set out for Uganda on 16 November but when our motorcade left Nairobi, misfortune struck again. Helge Pawlinin fell ill but refused to stay put in Nairobi, claiming it was only a temporary fit of fever. During the drive, however, he became so much worse – vomiting, a high temperature, heavy diarrhoea and cold sweats – that we were extremely concerned. I had no other artistic assistants, but nevertheless I begged him to fly to Germany and get some decent medical treatment. At this, to our astonishment, Helge leaped up, threw himself on the ground, dug his hands into the earth and shouted, 'No, no, I want to die here!'

Shaken, we stood next to the sobbing man who seemed to be suffering from some kind of tropical madness. We had no choice but to take him with us.

Our motorcade snaked its way along the terrible roads directly below the equator. The nights were so cold that we froze miserably under our blankets, yet the days were hot and steamy.

IN QUEEN ELIZABETH PARK

Before the end of November, we reached our destination: Queen Elizabeth Park. I had the good fortune to meet the governor of Uganda, who, contrary to his usual practice, allowed our entire safari, including all the boys, to pitch camp in the national park. He also did us an unusual favour: we could row our houseboat past the riverbanks in the park, where hundreds of hippopotamuses were frolicking in the water.

At last, here was the sort of good luck which made our work so much easier. Now we were waiting only for the sun, but it refused to come out. The sky was grey, the air was cold, yet these were supposed to be the loveliest and sunniest months of the year. Never, said the English residents, had the weather been so cold and unfriendly at this time of year; their theory was that the nuclear tests had altered and destroyed the climate throughout the world.

We took advantage of the bad weather to repair the houseboat, which had been damaged *en route*; The canoes had become so leaky that they sank immediately. While Six repaired them, we tried to film animals during the rare intervals of sunshine. There were animals galore here: lions, elephants, buffalo, gazelles, hyenas, rhinos. Since we were allowed to drive our Landrover off the trails, we got excellent shots, especially when our car was attacked by a rhino – something which happened frequently. Helge Pawlinin who had recovered from his serious illness, had produced costumes for our black actors and no one could have done a better job.

Once the canoes were shipshape, we prepared to shoot the first test with our blacks but ran into another serious setback. Our film blacks came to us under the leadership of a spokesman and refused to be filmed in the water with hippopotamuses or crocodiles. We tried to make them see that they were in no danger on the boat, but it was useless. At first, we thought they wanted higher pay, but we were mistaken. They would rather have gone home than enter a boat, even if we doubled their salaries. Inevitably, most of the scenes had to take place on the houseboat, and the waters here were filled with crocodiles and rhinos – in fact, we had bought an aluminium boat with an outboard motor in order to drive the animals away during the filming.

We begged and begged, but it did no good. In my despair, I pleaded with Coca to do anything he could to get the blacks over their fears; eventually, after a lengthy palaver, he said they would try if he and I joined them on the boat.

Finally, the sun broke through, and we got our first good shots – the boat against the palm forest, with a herd of elephants bathing in the background; before long, however, a violent storm, heavy wind and pouring rain forced us to break off. Soaked to the skin and trembling with cold, we returned to camp to be greeted by the sight of the backside of a young elephant sticking out of the entrance to my tent. Too bad I didn't have my Leica on me for the sight was unbelievably funny. We were glad we finally had something to laugh at.

After shooting good footage for three days in a row, we unexpectedly found ourselves in a dangerous situation; we had failed to notice that our boat had drifted into a current which was carrying us straight towards some bathing elephants. We were unable to row the boat out of the current and I was horrified to see a bull elephant spread his ears, lift his trunk and charge our boat. In the last second, George roared towards the elephant with a howling motor and the animal fled.

Because of that adventure, the boys again refused to resume work and perhaps it was this nervous tension that triggered a knife fight in camp that evening. One of the victims hid under the bed in my tent until George ruthlessly stepped in, handcuffed two of the main participants to the trucks and left them there outside all night. When I heard them screaming in their terror of being devoured by wild animals, I woke George up and demanded that he release them; he complied very reluctantly. From that day on, the blacks were willing to go through fire and water for me and I could ask anything of them. This enabled us to shoot a few unusual scenes.

At this juncture, out of the blue, I received a wire from Waldi Traut asking me to fly to Munich immediately as all the cash was used up, and work could go on only if we could screen the rushes for potential distributors and induce them to guarantee the financing. This was a dreadful piece of news. Now that we had finally overcome all the problems, we would have to stop! It was too much. I dashed out of the camp and kept running until I dropped. I wanted to die.

A TRAGIC END

Sitting in the plane, I knew that this was the end of a dream to which I had sacrificed every last ounce of my strength. My partner Waldi Traut had sent a proxy to Queen Elizabeth Park to keep the team together during my absence. Dr Bayer, as Traut's delegate and co-business-manager with me of Stern Film, had brought along my return fare plus enough money at least to feed the others during my absence. The tragedy was that I had been summoned back several weeks too early; we had too little footage to gain new backers for such a risky venture.

It was a shock upon my return to Munich to hear that Waldi Traut and his companion, Baroness von Vietinghoff, had been critically injured and were at the hospital in Innsbruck, their Mercedes having skidded on Zirl Mountain and plunged fifty feet down the slope. When I arrived at the hospital, they were both still unconscious. Frau von Vietinghoff's condition was particuarly serious as both her knees were shattered, and her head was almost scalped. What was I to do? What would happen to our people in Africa whom I couldn't recall without money? I wired Dr Bayer about Traut's accident and begged him not to stop work and to wait for further news; I telephoned the physicians daily. At the same time, I had the rushes developed and when I saw the footage, I realized the scope of the tragedy for the rushes were fascinating; it seemed to me unthinkable that this extraordinary film should die. Perhaps there was still a chance.

Day after day, I waited for news from my people in Queen Elizabeth Park to whom I had dispatched several telegrams but from whom I received no answer. My nervousness was such that at night I had to have tranquillizer injections. At last, after three weeks, I received devastating news from Hanni. Following my departure, pandemonium had broken out, camp had been struck and, after being paid by Dr Bayer, the blacks had scattered to the four winds. George Six had cancelled the safari and gone to Arusha while the others, completely penniless, were staying at the Torres Hotel in Nairobi, waiting impatiently for money and instructions.

It would take us too far afield if I went into any further details about the dramatic wind-up of *Black Freight*. Waldi Traut and his companion miraculously survived their horrible accident. Traut was very enthusiastic about the rushes and hoped to save the project despite all our misfortunes. Since he had to go easy with himself, he asked me to show the footage to several firms. They were all impressed by the material, and Bavaria Film came within a hair's breadth of taking it on but in the end, as on earlier occasions, my name deterred them from making a commitment. Traut, unwilling to give up despite the hopeless situation, sacrificed a great deal to prevent the project from being killed. He was already up to his ears in debt because of *Black Freight*, so that he didn't even have the wherewithal to bring back the crew members who were waiting patiently in Nairobi without a penny to their names. The small amounts he transmitted from time to time were far from enough to cover all the return tickets. Eventually Helge and Hanni managed to return to Munich and I finally learned about all the terrible things that happened after my departure, especially between George Six and Dr Bayer. The latter was in no position to meet the legitimate demands of the Safari company and so he could not prevent its directors, Stan and Six, from seizing – as security until their financial demands were settled – all our film and expedition gear, the wagon with the tracks, the machine units and spotlights, the boat with the outboard motor and a quantity of valuable Kodak stock, fifty thousand feet of which were unexposed. None of his would have happened if I had not been recalled, nor would Waldi Traut have done it; he and I were both victims of an intrigue.

I would never have been summoned back if it hadn't been for a Judas in the person of the production manager whom Traut had sent after me. He was very efficient, and we had worked together very well during the first few months; indeed, his reports to Traut praised my dedication. Then, during the critical period when the Lawrence-Brown Company in Nairobi cancelled our safari, plunging us into a cash flow crisis, he changed radically. He insisted that I sign a few blank cheques made out to him and when, naturally, I wouldn't hear of it, my refusal must have kindled his hatred. Although I noticed nothing, since he went about his job as conscientiously as ever, he had revenge on his mind, and this showed plainly in his letters to Waldi Traut, which I later read. He made untrue statements, hoping to turn Traut against me, and he very nearly succeeded. His accounts, strewn with more and more venomous remarks, blamed all the problems on me, saying I was overdemanding and claiming that the film could be salvaged only if I were fired as producer and director.

Traut was so startled and unsettled by these letters that he sent his lawyer, Dr Bayer, to us, and called me back to Munich to speak to me in person. If it hadn't been for his calamitous car accident, *Black Freight* might have been saved.

Any chance of practising my profession seemed to have gone for good; the prejudice against me seemed so insuperable that I broke down and landed up in hospital where Dr Westrich diagnosed a nervous condition. My chief worry was my mother, who had been in the Schwabing Hospital for several weeks. Years of anxiety had affected her heart and triggered other complaints but we had no medical insurance since we couldn't afford the huge premiums. So far the doctors had treated us without charge, but this time I was at a loss as to how to meet the costs.

Since the end of the war, not a single ray of good fortune had touched me. Life had become an almost unbearable struggle for sheer existence in the face of intrigues and political discrimination, and if I hadn't had to take care of my mother, I would have given up. During those weeks in the hospital, the darkest in my life, I vegetated without a single shred of hope. Now and then, a nurse came to give me medicaments and injections, which brought me relief, but, as I subsequently realized, also carried the danger of addiction.

On my release from the hospital, as Dr Westrich handed me a package of two ampules (I was to have injections at specific intervals during a stay in Spain), he said, 'You must be gradually weaned off the drugs we have had to give you here.' During the week before my departure, I had to have a daily injection and each time I could hardly wait. Afterwards I always felt better and no longer so depressed. It was late autumn and usually dark when I drove to Dr Westrich's clinic on Widenmayerstrasse. One evening when the nurse saw me in the waiting room, she said, 'You're really getting quite addicted.'

'Addicted?' I asked. 'Surely not. What are you giving me?'

The nurse looked hard at me. 'Morphine. Didn't you know?'

'No,' I said, 'that's impossible. I'm allergic to morphine, I've never been able to stand it.'

'This isn't normal morphine, she replied, 'it's a different blend, with a different name.'

'Thank you, nurse. I'm leaving. I don't want any more injections.'

At home, I trampled on the ampules I was supposed to take to Spain. The days without the morphine were torture. It took me a week to get even halfway through my withdrawal crisis, and whenever I see drug addicts portrayed on film or television I still feel terrified.

ONCE AGAIN: *OLYMPIA* 1936

Whenever I have gone through a difficult crisis in my life, I have been able to marshall my resources in the mountains or in southern latitudes. In Spain, beside the sea week after week, I grew calm and felt so tired that once more I could sleep. Today I still believe that sleep is a wonderful source of strength.

I didn't even want to read the mail forwarded from Munich for I dreaded more bad news; when I finally read it, I couldn't believe my eyes. I had invitations from three different German film clubs, in Berlin, Bremen and Hamburg, to lecture and to screen my mountain films and also, surprisingly, my Olympic films. But where could I find the prints? They had been in the archives confiscated by the French for eleven years, then had been released immediately before my trip to Africa and sent to Munich. Dr Arnold had stored the material in two editing rooms that he had set up for me at Arri, his printing laboratory, but, after my return from Africa, I learned to my dismay that the editing rooms had been torn down and transformed into a colour-printing lab. My boxes and canisters had been carelessly tossed into baskets and crates, and my sound tables and footage had been left in the courtyard of the printing lab. There, exposed to the elements, they had rotted.

I had fought in vain for an entire decade to save my films and cutting tables – the only valuables that I still possessed – but I couldn't make Arri responsible for the ruined material and equipment. Dr Arnold, one of the main owners of the firm, had always supported me, and I owed him a great deal. He himself was incensed upon learning about the gross negligence. Since his head was always buzzing with plans, he had noticed nothing, but he promised to make up for the damage as far as possible.

My work on *Black Freight* had prevented me from dealing with the problem of the prints, and now I was so weakened by my illness that I didn't have the strength to cope with the tedious and disagreeable business. I was also scared of any inventory. What condition would my material be in? Which prints were damaged or perhaps gone forever?

But after my return from Spain, I finally had to face this task. For weeks on end, I worked deep into the night at the rewind bench. All the personnel at Arri were busy, and Hanni had taken a job in order to earn some money. Now, my seventy-seven-year-old mother was the only person who could help me to rewind the footage and label the reels. Those were the most wretched conditions I have ever worked in. Eventually, an inflammation of my eyes forced me to take a few days off.

Luckily, the mountain film prints were only slightly damaged; but several reels of the Olympic material had been destroyed. However, since I had several prints and duplicate negatives, I could reconstruct the original version. There was another problem, however. The Olympic films had to be 'denazified'! The shots of Hitler as a spectator, the honouring of German champions and the Olympic oath fell prey to the scissors: three hundred feet or three minutes of running time. Only a few feet were snipped out of the second part.

The claims constantly reiterated by the German press that *Olympia* was a Nazi propaganda film are erroneous. Even today, the general public is still poorly informed about the rules of the International Olympic Committee. In this connection I would like to quote a letter from Professor Dr Carl Diem, who, as secretary general, was responsible for putting on the Olympic Games of 1936. He wrote the letter in 1958 to the Voluntary Self-Supervision Board of the Film Industry, in Wiesbaden.

The International Olympic Games are an institution of the International Olympic Committee, which assigns the games to a suitable city, not to a [national] government. This is to ensure that no laws interfere with the orderly mounting of the Olympic Games. In 1936, the Olympic Games were assigned to Berlin. After the [Nazi] takeover, the German government expressly assured the IOC that all races could participate unhindered in the Olympic Games and these promises were kept. I can name the Ball brothers in ice hockey and the fencer Helene Meyer, who won the silver medal. I may add that these non-Aryan members of the German team were not prevented from getting their start in Germany subsequently. Furthermore, Dr Lewald, the non-Aryan head of the German Organization Committee, was never attacked until the collapse of the regime. The fact that the Olympic Games in Berlin were carried out with no breach of Olympic neutrality is proved by the decision that the IOC reached *in London in June 1939* to hold the Olympic Winter Games of 1940 again in Garmisch. This decision was made without any German participation. It was based on a *secret written vote that resulted unanimously in the decision to grant the Olympic Winter Games again to Garmisch-Partenkirchen*. If the view, circulated today by the media, that the Olympic Games in Berlin were politically misused had been correct, three years after the Olympic Games in Berlin and only two months before the outbreak of World War II, then at least *one or more of the fifty-two nations would have abstained or even voted against another granting of the Games to Germany*. The tasks of the Organization Committee included reporting in every form, which was not subject to the [German] Ministry of Propaganda. In this purview, Frau Leni Riefenstahl was assigned [the task of making] the documentary film. The *Ministry of Propaganda had nothing to do with this decision*, and its subsequent protest was ignored.

It was on behalf of the current President Brundage, USA, and the French minister Pietri, that is, not at the suggestion of Germany, that the International Olympic Committee at the IOC session of 8 June 1939 awarded the Olympic gold medal to Leni Riefenstahl for the artistry of the Olympic film. This [award] would have been utterly impossible if the film had had even a tiny bit of footage containing National Socialist propaganda. In 1938/9, despite the then very powerful boycott against Germany, the entire foreign press lauded the neutral and unpolitical form of the Olympic film, and in 1956, in the USA, a board of well-known motion-picture directors called the film one of the ten best films ever made in the world . . .

(Signed) Diem

These reasons gave me the courage to accept the invitations of the film clubs. The success was overwhelming in all three cities, not just with the audiences, but also in the press. At Berlin's Titania Palace, which held nineteen hundred spectators and was nearly sold out, I received any number of curtain calls. I was joined on stage by Herbert Windt, whose music greatly contributed to the success of the Olympic film.

Once again, things had turned out differently from all expectations. Before appearing in Berlin, I had been warned; and I must confess that I wouldn't have gone to Berlin if I hadn't learned that the owners of the Titania Palace had left the city in a great hurry. Other people's fears restored my courage. The worst that could happen, I thought, was that eggs and tomatoes would be thrown at me. There had been talk of demonstrations and organized riots, but nothing of the sort took place and I witnessed only spontaneous enthusiasm. Even the press was fulsome. Radio Free Berlin said as follows:

It was more than just an ordinary reunion when both feature-length parts of this film ran on the screen. It showed even more clearly than in the past how successful the effort was to translate the idea of the Olympic Games into a cinematic artwork. We saw the motion picture again and we were again enthralled.

That was not a unique opinion. I have a sheaf of accounts that were no less enthusiastic and many people expressed the desire to have further showings of the film. This was not all that simple, since these screenings were put on by film clubs – virtually to a private audience. To be shown publicly, the film had to be passed by the German censorship board.

In early January 1958, I brought prints of the two Olympic films to the Voluntary Self-Supervision Board of the German Film Industry in Wiesbaden where, with a sinking heart, I learned that only the second part had been approved. I couldn't understand this decision for my Olympic film was unreservedly unpolitical. I had tried to make a fair sports film, I hadn't even mentioned that Germany had won most of the medals, and I had left out all the celebrations put on by the Third Reich government within the framework of the Olympic Games – an ommission that Minister Dr Goebbels resented greatly at the time.

I desperately tried to win over the censors, and they finally suggested a compromise. They advised me to add a commentary expressing the tragedy of the youth of that period, the generation that had been committed to the Olympic idea and yet, within a few short years, had sacrificed their lives to a war that forced them to fight one another. Worthy of consideration as the idea was, I could not accept something which would turn a purely athletic document into a political film. Indeed, shouldn't such a voice-over be added to any Olympic movie? Today's youth may become the victims of tomorrow's nuclear war.

Otto Mayer, the chancellor of the IOC, and Carl Diem came to my rescue. Because of their letters and testimonials, the board, after a re-examination, also released the first part of *Olympia* with a few minor cuts involving celebrations of German champions. There was, however, one restriction: no one under eighteen would be allowed to see the film. This was an incomprehensible decision since, after all, minors were permitted to see *Olympia* throughout the world, even in Vatican City.

The censorship board justified their decision with the ludicrous argument that the prologue of the film showed a hoop-swinging female dancer with a *bare torso*. In response to my protest, the board 'generously' informed me that the film could be approved for minors if the girl were cut out or a dark shadow were placed across her bosom. It was all simply grotesque. Since I couldn't remove any frames because of the music, I had to shell out a great deal for a trick superimposition of a dark shadow on the dancer's breasts; yet even this did not satisfy the censors. They cabled:

Your submission of a darkened image of the hoop-swinging dancer in front of the cornfield is unacceptable. Stop. We request a new suggestion.

The censors were making bigger and bigger fools of themselves but they left me no choice. I asked Herr Nischwitz, the trick master at the Bavaria company, to make the shadow so black that no bosom could be discerned behind it. It was only after I sent in the new superimposition that the censorship board wired: 'Submitted footage of hoop swinger is in order.' I am not joking. I have held on to the 'bosom cables'.

The struggle for the official quality rating was even more nerve racking.

Since the West German government offers tax breaks to theatres showing films with high ratings, this classification is vital for a good distribution contract. No one doubted that *Olympia* would be rated 'especially worthwhile'. After all, it had not only received the Olympic gold medal, but was also designated as the best film in the world at the Venice Biennale of 1938. However, the Cinema Rating Office notified me that the film could not receive any rating; even Herr Blank, its chairman, was stunned. He had told me that films with strong Communist tendencies and films made in the Third Reich before 1940 had received the highest ratings. In its explanation, the office criticized the frequent use of slow motion in *Olympia*. Yet other nations, for instance the Swedes, were of a different opinion. *Svenska Dagbladet* had written:

> . . . a factual reportage that is heightened into poetry. It shows ways towards a new cinematic world that has scarcely been discovered. This visual symphony is an instructive documentation of cinematic rhythm, composed and edited with the same musicality as that of an orchestral score.

There were hundreds of international reviews along those same lines, but the German Cinema Rating Office ignored them; just as they ignored protests like that of Otto Mayer, president of the Swiss IOC, who, on behalf of the IOC, asked the German Cinema Rating Office to give this film a proper rating, since it was the best depiction ever shown of the Olympic Games. Nor was any heed paid to an appeal from the authoritative German film critic Dr Gunter Groll and countless domestic and foreign VIPs.

Although I barely had a spark of hope, I nevertheless exercised my legal right to appeal against the Office's decision. When my appeal was rejected, I made a final desperate attempt. I turned to the highest authority, directly above the office: I asked Dr Arno Henning, Hessian Minister of Education, to review the decision. When he turned down my petition, I knew once and for all that I would never again get a chance to make a film in Germany.

However, there were still people who tried to encourage me. One of them was Carl Müller, member and later president of the German Gilde Cinemas, who committed himself with great idealism to artistic films. In April 1958, in the presence of Carl Diem, Müller's Bremen theatre, Studio for Film Art, screened both parts of *Olympia* even without an official rating. Müller's courage was rewarded with success. Despite all the prophets of doom, the film managed to keep running, and *Bremer Nachrichten* wrote, 'We would like to describe it as an immortal Olympic poem.'

I was not foolish enough to assume that so much recognition could smooth my path. The very opposite was true. Theatre owners and distributors received anonymous warnings not to show my films. Several newspapers wrote such blatant lies that my attorney had to force them to print retractions.

These repeated defamations were so powerful that almost no cinema dared to show *Olympia*, and all the distributors who had made bids for the film withdrew their offers. Only Rudolf Engelberth, proprietor of several theatres in Munich, had the pluck to screen *Olympia* in his Roxy Film Theatre and it was so successful that both parts had to keep running for weeks on end.

This continual rise and fall of triumph and attack made it difficult for me to reach a decision on my future life. As long as I still found recognition for my work, I glimpsed a slim possibility of a future in the film industry – and there were two rays of hope. A Japanese firm offered me fifteen thousand dollars for the distribution rights to *Olympia*. Mr Kawakita, a Germanophile and president of Towa Co. Ltd in Tokyo, signed a contract with me. He had distributed the film in pre-war Japan, where it had broken all records.

INVITATION TO PARIS

A second ray of hope came from Paris. The Marquis de Cuevas, whose ballet company was world famous, wanted to stage the *The Blue Light* as a ballet in Paris. Rosella Hightower, a famous prima ballerina, was to dance the part of Junta to a score by Vincent d'Indy. Erik Bruhn, first dancer of the Ballet of Copenhagen, was cast as the male lead. The première, to which I was invited, was scheduled for 20 or 21 November at the Théâtre des Champs Elysées.

I was speechless. At first, I thought it was a joke but, this time, it was a serious offer. Immediately I telegraphed my acceptance, Monsieur Camble, the Marquis's ballet master, wrote to inform me that rehearsals had already begun. From then on I was kept abreast of their progress almost daily during the four weeks allowed for rehearsals and I was asked for advice about stage sets and costumes and encouraged to contribute my creative ideas. I was more and more enthralled by the ethos of the ballet. *The Blue Light* was my favourite of all the films I had made. I had studied Russian ballet and begun my professional life as a dancer; and for a long time, I had dreamed of making a dance film inspired by Edgar Degas' paintings. I worked obsessively on the sketches and texts finding that I was virtually overwhelmed by my long-dormant creative powers. Thirty years earlier, I had written the part of Junta for myself and now it emerged from the world of my youthful dreams.

When the ballet company visited Munich, I met Rosella Hightower who was fascinated by the role of Junta; I, receiving the signed contract in my hands, was absolutely delirious. I was supposed to attend the final rehearsals and the première.

Shortly before my flight to Paris, however, a telegram arrived: 'Please do not come. I will write. Camble.' If it weren't for the letters, the contract and the wire, one might think that it had all been a dream. Monsieur Camble and the marquis were nowhere to be found; they appeared to have virtually vanished from the face of the earth. Neither my lawyer nor I ever received an answer to any of our letters and, many years later, I was told by friends that an influential person in Paris had at the very last moment prevented the performance of the ballet.

NEW EDITING STUDIOS

If it is true that adversity gives you strength, I ought to be as strong as an ox by now for my whole life seems to have consisted of nothing but difficulties. However, never give up has always been my motto; how else could I have survived? The money I was hoping for from Japan did not come through because the Japanese import quota for foreign films was already filled for 1959. I could only look forward to the next year.

My greatest anxiety, however, was caused by my mother's state of health. The previous year, she had been hit by a car and had been unable to walk ever since. She was in constant pain, and her overall condition was visibly deteriorating. What would become of me if I lost her! She was the only person I was living for. As for my career, my only chance – and I clung to it – was to receive a government start-up loan for two editing rooms; I had submitted the application three years earlier. If it were approved, I could rent out one room and use the second one for my archival work. In order to obtain the loan, I had to cope with so much red tape, fill out innumerable forms, and find a bank willing to guarantee it. I had little hope, but at last my application was approved. I was granted thirty-five thousand marks at an interest rate of only three per cent, and with a payback period of ten years.

In the building next to my home on Tengstrasse, I rented two empty basement rooms which still had to be finished. They had neither floors nor heating, neither windows nor ventilation; but these disadvantages were outweighed by the fact that the rooms were only a hop, skip and jump from my apartment. When they were finally ready, after many months of work, I felt I had a new lease on life. The rooms were very attractive, and the colour scheme – white and blue – resembled that of my earlier cutting studios in Berlin. Now, after so many years, I would again be surrounded by strips of celluloid, even though my only aim was to put my archive to rights.

BIENNALE 1959

To my surprise, I received an invitation from the directors of the Venice Biennale who were planning a retrospective of my films. Delighted as I was by this unexpected honour, it entailed problems. They wanted the uncut version of *Olympia* and this was difficult since I had chopped up the negatives for the 'denazification' demanded by the censors. Now I had no choice but to restore the cuts and I was assisted in this task by a former member of my staff, a film editor who was in financial straits and had begged me to employ him. To be on top form for the Biennale, I booked a brief vacation with Club Méditerranée on the island of Elba and enjoyed the sun and the sea.

In late August, I arrived at the Lido in Venice. The film festival had already begun and as I booked into the Hotel des Bains, I recalled the glorious days of long ago when my presence had been the focus of the Biennale. After the great honours once heaped upon me, I anxiously wondered what lay ahead this time.

No sooner had I entered my room than I was summoned to the foyer. Several members of the festival committee were waiting for me, and they were extremely worried; it seemed that the prints of my films had, inexplicably, failed to arrive and that the same was true of my luggage. The committee had assumed that I would be bringing my prints with me. Nor had anyone received the package of photos and PR material that I had prepared for the Biennale. A hectic search began at the customs office at the Brenner Pass. My mother assured me that my assistant had called for all the baggage one day after my departure and taken it to the Kroll Shipping Agency in Munich, but the Kroll office claimed they had never received it.

Then we learned the awful truth. My mother tearfully told me on the phone that after hunting for my assistant, she had learned that instead of delivering the prints and my baggage, he had driven off in my car without leaving any message and had vanished without a trace. He had also taken along her postal savings book, her cash and my camera. 'I trusted him,' she sobbed, 'because he was always so reliable and helpful.'

I wanted to leave Venice on the spot, but the Italians wouldn't hear of it. A frenzied search was launched. My anxiety about my prints – the only ones I possessed – my sadness because the films couldn't be shown at the Biennale, and the loss of my wardrobe – all these things left me a nervous wreck. Then I received a surprising phone call. The Munich police had managed to track down all my luggage in the home of my vanished assistant, who was now a wanted man. My suitcases and prints were *en route* to Venice, and the screenings did not have to be cancelled after all.

During a TV interview, I noticed an elderly gentleman staring at me. His face looked familiar, but I couldn't quite place it. After the shooting, the stranger hesitantly came over, smiled at me, raised wide his arms and drew me towards him, whispering: 'Du-Du.' Now I recognized him. It was Josef von Sternberg. He had changed so greatly that I hadn't recognized him. Twenty years had passed since our last meeting – at the Palace Hotel in St Moritz, on New Year's Eve 1938 – and he had become a mature, elderly man with silvery grey hair.

For me, this was more than a reunion with an old friend. After the war, I had thought of him often, but never dared to write; now he was my constant escort throughout the Biennale. Although we saw a number of films together, there was a retrospective of his own work which he didn't want me to attend. 'They're worthless,' he said, slightly resigned, 'let's go to Venice instead.'

There we visited shops and galleries as well as the lively market of this fascinating city. He bought various things and also gave me a splendid violet woollen scarf. He never once mentioned the past and said almost nothing about his life since our last meeting. After the long, difficult crisis of a terrible illness, he seemed to be a happy man again. He had remarried and he showed me photos of his family – a young, pretty wife, and, if memory serves me correctly, two children. I had the impression that this was now his world but, nevertheless, I was curious to find out something about his period with Marlene. He said it had been pleasant working with her, praised her discipline and spoke admiringly about her technical knowledge, especially with regard to lighting and make-up. 'She knows exactly where the spot-lights have to be set up and how she can be lit to her greatest advantage.' Then he showed me a gold cigarette case on which the following words were engraved: 'In gratitude – Marlene'. That was all he cared to say about her.

My reunion with Sternberg eclipsed everything else at the Biennale, so that I attended only one screening of my films. Sternberg sat next to me.

'You're a good director,' he whispered, 'but I wanted to make you a great actress. *C'est la vie.*'

ADVENTURE FILM

Upon my return, I found my mother, unable to cope with the agitation of the last few weeks, had suffered a stroke.

Meanwhile, the police had done their job. They had tracked down my property in Frankfurt – my car in a garage and my camera in a pawnshop. The perpetrator, who had pulled off all sorts of con tricks and harmed many people, was behind bars. He had driven my stolen car some six thousand miles, leaving it full of dents and scratches. But I was happy to get it back.

My most urgent task was to come up with two usable English-language prints of *Olympia*, since several British companies, including the BBC, had asked for them. It was a wonderful opportunity for the films had never been shown in England because of the outbreak of the war. The process involved revealed the great damage done at the printing lab. The bulk of each English-language negative had been destroyed; only an incomplete print remained, and its sound track was partly wiped out. After weeks of meticulous work and with the help of some very generous Englishmen, I used the *Olympia* prints at the London Film Archives to tape-record the English sound track.

Following my successful collaboration with the British film people, I wasn't altogether surprised that a company called Adventure Film made me an unusual offer regarding *The Blue Light*. The firm was willing to pay me the enormous sum of thirty thousand pounds and twenty-five per cent of the profits for the remake rights to my motion picture. I couldn't take the proposal seriously, the writer of the letter sounded like a 'nutcase'.

But the nutcase wouldn't give up. He was called Philip Hudsmith and he came to Munich and stayed for three days. He was an attractive young man, tall, slender, all arms and legs, with blond hair, usually dishevelled. He seemed carefree and cheerful and we got on well from the outset.

He told me that *The Blue Light* had haunted him since his childhood; for years, he had been yearning to remake it and at last had found a solid basis and backers to make his dream come true.

At the Töpchen in Schwabing, he told me how he visualized the remake. Like the French, he saw the plot as a danced fairy-tale, akin to the British film *The Red Shoes*, which had been a worldwide success for years. He had contacted W. Somerset Maugham about doing the script; and Hudsmith showed me a letter from that great author, expressing his interest in the project. I was astonished at these lofty plans – the young man was obviously a dreamer and the technique he wanted to work with was way beyond the norm: the film was to be shot in the new 70-mm technirama process. I pointed out that such an expensive production was possible only in Hollywood, but Hudsmith paid no attention.

Prior to returning home, Philip called on my lawyer to discuss the contract; before saying yes, however, my lawyer wanted to make some inquiries so he gave Philip only a short-term option. Thus I launched into a new adventure.

The usual attacks rained down on me sooner than I had expected. *Weekend*, a Belgian weekly, ran a cover story that was more stupid and nasty than anything that had been printed about me hitherto. Had this tabloid not had such a wide circulation (including Paris and London) I would have paid it no further heed, but with a printing of four million it was one of the most widely read journals in England. To avoid jeopardizing the new project, I could not swallow that libel without fighting back.

Paul Masure, a lawyer in Brussels, took my case. It wasn't difficult. A large part of the article was taken from Trenker's *Diary of Eva Braun* and the *Revue* items, which had already been unmasked as forgeries in court. A certain inventiveness indicates the quality of the journalism:

> Leni Riefenstahl, daughter of a plumber, began her career as a striptease dancer in a shady club in Berlin [. . .] Before meeting Hitler, she married the Hungarian film writer Bela Balasz, who turned her into an ardent Communist [. . .] A Gestapo report claimed that she was a Polish Jew, which was usually enough to expel someone from Nazi Germany; but Hitler saved her from the gas chamber [. . .]

The whole thing was illustrated with a wealth of photos. Laughable as these smear stories were, they could easily have been taken over by agencies and stored in archives throughout the world. No wonder I eventually became a 'Nazi monster' to those who read such publications.

We settled out of court. On its title page, the tabloid ran my rebuttal, which was the same length as their libellous article.

THE BRITISH FILM INSTITUTE

In January 1960, I was driving my restored car through a thick blizzard towards St Anton and a skiing holiday. The British Film Institute had asked me to give a lecture in London, and I wanted to relax a bit first. At twilight, as we arrived in St Anton where we had booked a cosy room at the Haus Seiler, the landlady told me that there had been an urgent call from London.

What bad news was heading in my direction now? No sooner had I undressed than I received another call from the *Daily Mail* whose reporter read me the following bulletin over the phone:

> The British Film Institute has decided to withdraw its invitation to the German film director Frau Leni Riefenstahl who was scheduled to give a lecture on her work at the National Film Theatre. The directors of the BFI made this decision after more than two hours of discussion.

When the reporter asked me what I intended to do, I said I had expressed my qualms at the very start and did not care to go where I was not wanted.

No sooner had I hung up than the *Daily Express* was on the line; and so it went on until midnight. The British correspondents in Bonn and Vienna were among those who rang me and the final call came from the *Daily Herald*.

I could not escape my fate.

Meanwhile, Philip Hudsmith told me what had happened. A member of the British Film Institute, Ivar Montagu, winner of the Lenin Prize, was also supposed to give a lecture there, but he had protested against my talk and withdrawn. The well-known actor Peter Sellers, who was also supposed to appear, did not cancel his lecture; instead, he supported my coming and attacked Ivar Montagu sharply in the press. The decision of the BFI was publicly trounced. The magazine *Films and Filming* wrote:

> The confidence of creative film-makers in the British Film Institute was shaken throughout the world by this act of weak men – men who do not have the courage of their convictions.

Needless to say, Philip Hudsmith was worried about his project and asked me to enlighten the British press to mitigate as far as possible the damage done by the cancellation.

I promptly broke off my 'holiday' in St Anton. Returning to Munich, I made copies of the court verdicts, denazification decisions, and my personal rebuttal to the accusations, and sent the material to all the British periodicals that had spread untruths about me. This task gave me stomach cramps.

Then a very unexpected call came from London. It was John Grierson, the internationally renowned documentary maker. 'Leni,' he said, 'I'd like to help you. It's disgusting what they're doing to you. Give me several reels of your *Olympia* film, and I'll run them on my TV programme with a suitable commentary. You shouldn't put up with this, you ought to sue the tabloids.'

'I can't,' I said in resignation, 'I don't have the money.'

'I'll give it to you – I'll pay you for subsidiary rights to your films. You have to hire the best solicitor in England.'

And just a short time later, John Grierson proved that his promise was not an empty one. On his TV programme *This Wonderful World*, he defended me as no one had ever dared to do before. As a token of my gratitude, I would like to include the complete text of his talk, which caused a great stir among the British public:

There was a remarkable moment in the war. It was 27 January 1942. Those were dark days, and Sir Winston Churchill was speaking in the Lower House: 'I cannot say,' he said, 'what the situation on the Western Front in Cyrenaica is. We have a very courageous and skilful opponent, and I dare say – across the devastation of war – a very great captain!' He was referring to General Rommel, and it was a moment of generosity in the war that became a classic. I believe most of us have understood the significance when generals of both sides have met on friendly terms since the war. It appears that this forbearance is not extended to artists; certainly not in the case of the German film director Leni Riefenstahl. I am interested in this particular example for I am a man of the cinema, and Leni Riefenstahl is one of the greatest film-makers in the world and certainly the greatest female film-maker in history. She was invited to speak at the National Film Theatre, and then she was told not to come. This is understandable at the present time because of all the rumours about her. But I wish that film-makers could be like generals – and I recall Sir Winston's great gesture of generosity. Leni Riefenstahl was the propagandist for Germany. Yes, and I was a propagandist on the other side, and I am fairly certain that I did more anti-Nazi propaganda and more wicked things than any other film man in England. I took Leni Riefenstahl's own films and cut them into strips in order to turn German propaganda against itself; but I never made the mistake of forgetting how great she was. Across the devastation of war, I salute a very great captain of the cinema. There were several Olympic Games in our time, but there is only one true film masterpiece of the Olympiad, and that is, of course, Leni Riefestahl's made in 1936 in Berlin.

I see in a prestigious Sunday newspaper that the film was full of 'close-ups of Hitler and the Nazi leaders'. Do not believe a word of that. It is a great film report of a public event, and no other film has ever been as great as hers in capturing the poetry of athletic movement. The odd and ironical thing about 1936 was that it took place at the centre of the terrible racial theories of that time. It was the year of the Negro, the year of the fabulous Jesse Owens, the American Negro who swept away the records in so many sports disciplines.

Leni Riefenstahl's film shows all this grandly – and generously. The film was the greatest sports report that I have ever seen at the cinema. It was Leni Riefenstahl's marathon. We have seen many marathons, but this time we also have to introduce a great film artist – and you can see something of the strain and agony of the long gruelling miles – and see what no other motion picture has ever described before or since.

After Grierson's talk, they showed the marathon and other excerpts from *Olympia*.

My British friends were delighted by the sensational broadcast, especially Philip, who, for all his optimism, was very upset by the press attacks. He asked me to come to London and once there I was able to thank John Grierson, whom I had never met personally. At an English club, we embraced like old friends; in front of all the artists there, he removed my shoe and breathed a kiss on to the tip of my foot. It was simply crazy – how could I cope with all that! Grierson insisted that I go to court and offered to pay the legal expenses. The *Daily Mail* and other British newspapers had published corrections or interviews with me, thereby fortunately removing any grounds for a lawsuit, but there was one exception – the *Daily Mirror*, one of the most widely circulated newspapers in England, whose well-known columnist Cassandra had written a nasty story about me. He was the one on whom Grierson had set his sights and Grierson wanted me to sue this journalist and his newspaper in order, as he put it, to create a precedent.

Mr Crowe, a distinguished British solicitor, took my case after going through the documents in order to determine our chances of winning. The atmosphere in England was not very pro-German – understandably, since the previous year headstones in Jewish cemeteries throughout Germany had been smeared with swastikas. My British friends were to experience this too when I was visiting a married couple who live in Sussex. Every day reporters who wanted to speak to me waited outside the house and when I could no longer satisfy them the walls of the house were painted with swastikas. I wanted to leave immediately, but my friends wouldn't hear of it.

My initial meetings with the British solicitor were anything but pleasant. In fact, I felt as if I had been transported back to the time of my interrogations. I had to answer hundreds of questions in greater detail than had been demanded by the Americans or the French. Often, I didn't understand the drift of the questions. During the first few hours, I put up with everything but, little by little, I began to lose patience and grew nervous and irritated. Then came an embarrassing incident. When Mr Walters, a member of Mr Crowe's staff, refused to believe that I had known nothing about the extermination camps, I felt so angry and desperate that the blood rushed to my head. I lost my temper and furiously jumped at his throat. The same thing had happened to me many years earlier when the French Sureté wanted to force me to sign a statement that I had been informed about the extermination camps.

The next day, I found a completely changed Mr Walters in the office and, from then on, our conversations were friendly and sympathetic. I was relieved to find that all distrust was gone and that my suit against the *Daily Mirror* was in good hands. Since a decision could come only after many months, I left London and flew to Bremen where Carl Müller had been expecting me for several days. He had the courage to screen *Tiefland* in his Studio für Filmkunst and we were all surprised by its success. The run could be extended by four weeks, a record that Carl Müller had never before achieved with any other film in his theatre.

HOPES AND SETBACKS

For a brief period it looked as if the dark clouds were rolling away. After the success of *Tiefland*, I heard from Mr Kawakita that the Olympic films could now be imported into Japan; and occasionally, there were friendly press comments in Germany. Good news came from England too. Philip sent me almost daily reports about the progress of his work and told me that, unfortunately, Somerset Maugham had withdrawn from our project after the newspaper attacks. However, Philip wrote, he had found a gifted American author to collaborate on the script. 'This American,' he enthused, 'is a brilliant and famous writer, who has written many screenplays for Columbia in Hollywood. He is also the head of a great international organization that is spread across the entire globe and has over a million members. His name is L. Ron Hubbard, he is a psychologist and Scientologist.' I had no idea who L. Ron Hubbard was. But I soon realized that he must be talented for the first part of his work was surprisingly good. Philip had already arranged for Pier Angeli to play the part of Junta and for Laurence Harvey to play the part of Vigo and, in order to commit me solidly to this project, Philip Hudsmith signed half the shares of his firm over to me. This made me a partner of Adventure Film Ltd in England.

Dr L. Ron Hubbard had put his London apartment at my disposal and there I was to translate cinematically the new completed script with him and Philip. Then Hubbard was unexpectedly summoned to South Africa, where he also had a firm. Nevertheless, he allowed me to remain in his home, which was occupied only by a housekeeper during his absence and Philip came to work with me every day. He had to keep hiding me from the reporters and often sent them on wild-goose chases, because in England, a plaintiff is not allowed to give information to journalists during a trial, so that the judges won't be influenced. All my visits had to be secret and I would have loved to withdraw the suit, but my solicitors wouldn't allow it. They were far too certain of our victory.

At this time, I received a surprising offer from one of London's most prestigious film theatres, the Curzon Cinema. The manager, Mr Wingate, was so enthralled by the Olympic film that, without bothering with long negotiations, he signed a contract with my solicitor to bring the film out on a large scale that very same year autumn 1960. At last, a success. I interrupted my script-writing with Philip and, as I did every year, I flew to the Berlin Film Festival. As usual, it was a great experience, for not only did I see internationally important films but I also met friends and earlier colleagues. Manfred George, who came from New York, spent a great deal of time with me, and said he wanted to write my biography.

When one of my English friends wanted to go to the film ball with me, my invitation was blocked by the office in charge. The reason: 'Frau Riefenstahl's attendance at the official film ball is not desired by the German government.' When my friend, a well-known art collector, protested to the press chief of the Bonn government, he failed to obtain the ticket. 'I thought,' said my friend indignantly, 'that Germany was now a democracy.'

'It will change,' Manfred George tried to reassure me, 'when my biography of you comes out.' But it never did. He fell critically ill and died far too young. With him, I lost one of my last and truest friends.

After my return, the BBC commissioned a 'film portrait' of me in my Munich apartment. Derek Prouse, the director, was a member of the British Film Institute, and, in a very fair way, he gave me the chance to counter the defamations in the press. It was very agreeable working with the British film crew.

In order to terminate my endlessly pending lawsuit with the *Daily Mirror*, I asked my solicitors to settle out of court and John Grierson concurred. I was willing to forgo damages if the newspaper agreed to run a correction and the *Daily Mirror* gave in. It was a meagre victory for me. In England, a foreigner suing for damages had to put up a bond equivalent to twenty-five thousand dollars at that time and since this was impossible for me, I had to be satisfied with the correction.

Again a publisher offered to do my memoirs; this time, it was Hutchinson in London. Mr Cherry Kearton, one of the directors of the house, had already paid me several visits in Munich and offered me very favourable conditions; but I seemed to be under a spell: I wanted to, but I couldn't. I doubted my ability to write about myself. I felt an almost insuperable timidity. I also hoped that we could start shooting *The Blue Light* very soon now that Dr Hubbard and Philip had completed an outstanding script. We were waiting only for my British work permit – the final hurdle.

THE FILM *MEIN KAMPF*

It was during this period that I saw Erwin Leiser's film *Mein Kampf* in Munich. When I entered the theatre, the film had already started and I was rendered speechless by what I saw on the screen. I couldn't believe my eyes. It was *Triumph of the Will*, the motion picture that I had made in 1934 about the Party rally in Nuremberg. It was not, as I first assumed, the entire film, but long excerpts in which, for instance, the Work Service footage and other well-known scenes were intercut with dreadful images from the concentration camps. It was a gross infringement of copyright and also intellectual theft. Despite numerous requests, I had never permitted *Triumph of the Will* to be shown in Germany in case it were to be misused towards neo-Fascist ends. However, it could be viewed in museums and film archives throughout the world. American universities also ran the film as a historical document.

At first, I tried to settle the matter in a friendly way by contacting Herr Leiser personally, but he refused to deal with me. When he sent me a gruff response to my letter, I had to get my lawyer involved once again. Dr Weber, who worked with Dr Gritschneder, the lawyer who had attended to all my legal matters during the past few years, was also a friend and an adviser. He not only forced corrections of erroneous press reports, he also managed to keep putting off my creditors and staving off judicial orders to pay.

The case was legally clear, as far as Dr Weber was concerned. Herr Leiser had allegedly obtained the material from East Germany and, according to a ruling of the state court in Munich, films that are obtained in foreign countries or in East Germany and whose copyright is not owned by the production firm cannot be shown without the owner's permission. What

Herr Leiser had done was outrageous. For his purposes, there were enough newsreels and at least four Party rally films which had been made not by me but by the Ministry of Propaganda.

Leiser's film had been produced by Minerva, a Swedish company in Stockholm, and Dr Weber informed Minerva that the copyright of *Triumph of the Will* belonged to me and not, as had apparently been assumed, to the Nazi party. He also stated that I was not only the producer, but also the director and owner of the film.

Minerva refused to recognize my legal rights and so Dr Weber had no choice; he had to threaten them with a restraining order against any further screenings of Leiser's film, which was distributed in Germany and Austria by Neuer Filmverleih. Minerva would either have to remove the sequences taken from my film or else, as was normal, obtain the rights.

Since *Mein Kampf* was a box-office hit – at least partly with the help of my footage – the distributors decided to settle out of court and we reached an agreement. They paid a subsidiary fee of thirty thousand marks for Germany and five thousand for Austria. In those two countries alone, the film took in more than a million marks. On Dr Weber's advice, I settled my debts by signing over to my chief creditor, the producer Friedrich A. Mainz, any further claims that would result from showings of this motion picture outside Germany and Austria. I did not wish to get involved in any further litigation.

However, Dr Weber and I had a difference of opinion about the use of the money. Despite my difficult financial straits, I wanted to donate it to charity, as I had done before. In a comparable situation, I had received payment for the use of my material in the film *Until Five After Twelve* and I had contributed the money to the Association of Repatriated Prisoners of War. But Dr Weber talked me out of it. He reminded me that I had been unable to pay medical and hospital bills for years, that I received reminders almost daily, and that even my former director, Dr Fanck, to whom I owed five hundred marks, was threatening me with a court order. At the time, I didn't realize that by demanding my legal rights from Leiser, I had made a mortal enemy.

On 7 December 1960, Leiser wrote to Herr Mainz that he would not only never recognize my claims, but he would also present the material he had gathered against me to all the world.

TRIAL IN PARIS

The harassment never stopped. One evening, just as I was about to go to bed, my doorbell rang. A French film director, whose name I can't remember, was standing at my door. He had come from Paris and urgently wanted to speak to me. After apologizing for his 'intrusion', he told me what he wanted. 'Madame Riefenstahl,' he said, 'I am making a series of historical films. I need important, indeed indispensable footage from you.'

When he saw the smile vanish from my face, he tried to calm me down.

'I know,' he said, almost beseechingly, 'that you wouldn't care to talk about it. But,' he went on, almost anxiously, 'if I promise you that no one will find out from whom I have obtained the material . . .'

'What are you talking about?' I icily broke in.

'About your filming during the war, the footage that Eichmann appointed you to shoot at the concentration camps.'

'Get out!' I told him. 'Out!'

Shaking his head, the Frenchman got to his feet. 'Don't you know the book *Six Million Dead*, which just came out in Paris? About the life of Adolf Eichmann?'

Paralysed, I stared at the man.

'This book,' the Frenchman stuttered confusedly, 'contains a chapter about you, detailing your activities during the war. Apparently you buried the footage and you refuse to reveal where it is.'

'My God,' I said, 'that's horrible.'

'Don't you know about it – haven't you seen the book?'

'No,' I whispered, sinking back into my chair.

The Frenchman seemed to grasp that something was very wrong. Growing livelier again, he said, 'The chapter in the book is entitled "The Secret of Leni Riefenstahl".'

'Does the book really exist?' I asked, almost helpless.

'It has just been put out in Paris, by Plon, the French publisher.' My visitor was growing embarrassed. He apologized and wanted to leave.

'Wait, stay here,' I cried. 'I want to ring my lawyer. You must tell him everything you've told me.'

I got hold of Dr Weber and in conversation with my visitor we learned that the book was scheduled to come out in Germany any day now. Subsequently – and in the nick of time, Dr Weber managed to prevent its publication in Germany.

I had sworn to myself a hundred times that I would never go to law again, regardless of what was written about me, but I could not allow such lies as these to be circulated. I called Philip Hudsmith in London. He decided to fly to Paris immediately.

'In this case,' he said, 'we have no choice, we have to sue.'

A few days later, I joined him in Paris where my suit was taken on by Gilbert Mativet, a French lawyer recommended to me by my friend Charles Ford. It was not hard rebutting this libel for the French Sureté, in whose custody I had been for over three years, was informed about every move I made during the war.

A man named Victor Alexandrov was the author of the malicious chapter. Let me quote one passage:

> During the first interrogations of the film director Leni Riefenstahl by the French authorities, the name Eichmann was cited, but Leni Riefenstahl refused to give any precise information. Leni Riefenstahl had filmed one of her documentaries in the extermination camps, with the technical cooperation of the head of the 'Jewish office', section A 4. Without his signature and without the express permission of that high-ranking functionary, it was impossible to enter a concentration camp in that period and make films there. When asked by French, English and American agencies, she refused to reveal the hiding place of the famous documentaries that she had filmed for Hitler and Goebbels – a secret that Leni Riefenstahl will take with her to the grave.

How could a publishing house that had a reputation for seriousness spread such outrageous statements about a living person without first checking their authenticity? My French lawyer was confident that I could easily prove I had worked exclusively on *Tiefland* during the war and had never even met Eichmann. I first read about him in the press when he was on trial in Israel. On 1 December 1960, a few days after my lawyer filed his brief, the Paris court ruled that Plon would have to discontinue publishing the book on Eichmann if the passages referring to me were not deleted.

The French press reports on the verdict were objective, except for *L'Humanité*, the Communist newspaper, which ran long articles smearing me and lamenting that I had not been hanged at Nuremberg like other war criminals. I asked my French lawyer to submit a correction to *L'Humanité* even if they refused to print it.

PRESS CONFERENCE IN LONDON

Leaving Paris, I flew to London where Philip, who had paid for my trip and also covered my legal fees in Paris, had set up a press conference at which *Olympia* would be screened for the first time for British journalists. This was also meant as publicity for *The Blue Light* since the filming was to begin very shortly.

The evening before the press reception, we celebrated my victory in Paris. But once again, we were confounded by events. The next day, when Philip introduced me to the journalists, one of them refused to shake my hand. With an expression of profound scorn, he said, 'I cannot shake hands with a person whose hands are stained with blood.' Another shouted at me, 'Why didn't you kill Hitler?' That was gruesome. The press conference had to be broken off.

Meanwhile, the screening of *Olympia* at the Curzon Cinema had been blocked and Mr Wingate, who had signed the agreement at Crowe's office, could not be reached. Like Monsieur Camble in Paris, he too had gone abroad, possibly to the Riviera, leaving no word of where he could be reached. All the letters that my solicitor sent him were returned: 'Addressee unknown.'

LOOKING BACK

At the end of 1960, I took stock of the fifteen years that had passed since the end of the war. I had spent three years in camps and prisons, and four months in an insane ayslum. Then came the confiscation of my property, denazification, trials and the destruction of my livelihood. All my film projects had been thwarted: *The Red Devils, Black Freight* and another remake of *The Blue Light*.

How was I to go on? Was there any hope at all for me? I lost more and more strength, there was less and less hope of my ever resuming my profession, my enemies grew more and more powerful, and their lies more and more vile. Since the end of the war, I had not really lived; I had been crawling about in the dirty mire of human nastiness. The only thing that kept me going was my concern for my mother; yet in contrast to me, she wanted to live and her courage was beyond my understanding.

At this low point, my Paris attorney notified me that Alexandrov had won his appeal. I was not comforted by the fact that his 'victory' was based purely on a technical mistake of the court and not on any new evidence. The court of appeal ruled that a condemnation of Alexandrov was possible only through a criminal trial and not a civil trial, which my lawyer had pursued and won. A different court was responsible for a criminal trial so a new indictment had to be handed in.

This was fresh material for new hateful comments and no newspaper mentioned the real reason for the second verdict. Readers were left to believe that the things written by Alexandrov were true. And so, for the gutter press, I remained a 'Nazi monster'.

They forged anything and everything. French newspapers ran love letters supposedly written to me by Streicher. *L'Humanité* and East German magazines put me on the same level as criminal perverts. There was nothing I wasn't accused of. Other papers claimed that I had become a 'cultural slave of the Soviets', and had sold my films to Mos Film in Moscow for piles of roubles.

A SILVER LINING

Michi Kondo, a young Japanese, visited me in the mountains. I had been friendly with him and his two brothers for several years, having met them in Berlin on the occasion of the new showing of *Olympia* at the Titania Palace. After the screening, these young men had waited for me and they had enthusiastically told me that they had seen these films at least ten times as children in Tokyo. As proof, they hummed several themes from the score, and they could list the sequence of athletic events almost to a frame. That meeting helped to develop my liking for Japan.

On the first day of his visit, Michi revealed nothing about a plan he had in mind. He borrowed some skis and did some skiing with me and all the time I sensed that he wanted to communicate something important. It wasn't until the next afternoon, during tea at the Hotel Post, that he spoke about his project, surprising me completely. He suggested that I start a film company with him and his brothers.

'We were thinking of making documentaries in Africa,' said Michi, 'and we would be delighted if we could get you to collaborate with us.' He looked into my astonished face and went on, 'We would like to take you into our company as an equal partner. All you have to contribute is your experience and your work as a director. We'll take care of the financing.'

'Have you thought it over carefully?'

'Of course,' said Michi optimistically, 'we Japanese are not bad businessmen, and with your name the film will not be a risk in Japan.

The most important thing we need now is a good subject. What do you propose?'

Spontaneously, I said, 'The Nile.'

I myself had already speculated about African themes and had envisaged a film about the Nile. The river and its history were perfect material and Michi agreed. 'First,' he said, 'we'll establish our firm.'

KONDO FILM LTD

Although Leni Riefenstahl Film Ltd still existed, the Japanese wanted to form their own company. So Kondo Film Ltd was founded in Munich, a secretary was hired and stationery was ordered; the letterhead proudly bore three company addresses – in Munich, Berlin and Tokyo – and I was asked to take care of the preparations. The Kondo brothers wanted to start working on the film that same year.

The first thing I did was to visit Hugendubel, one of the largest bookstores in Munich, where I ordered all the literature they had about the Nile. Then I called on Professor Grzimek at the Frankfurt Zoo whom I had known since our days with the *Tiefland* wolves; from his treasure-trove of experience, he was able to give me valuable advice about filming in Africa.

I completed the screenplay within two weeks. The landscape was not to dominate; it was to be only one element in the film. The protagonist was the Nile. The animals, people and religions; ancient and modern cultures; the modern technology of the Aswan Dam; Abu Simbel and the pyramids; the Valley of the Kings; the nomads and Nilot tribes who, still untouched by our civilization, live in the southern swamp areas of the Sudan; the Nuer, the Shilluk and the Dinka – these were all pieces of the mosaic.

Michi and Joshi came back exhausted but successful from their African trip having achieved all they had set out to do; in Cairo, they had even obtained permission to film the Aswan Dam, which the Russians were building. The only place where they had been unsuccessful was the Sudan, the most important country for our shooting, and this was because the appropriate minister had gone on holiday. I was to take a lightning trip and scout major shooting locations. The main thing, however, was to go to Khartoum and obtain permission to film in the 'closed districts' of the southern Sudan; otherwise the film couldn't be shot.

I was lucky. At the last moment, the Marco Polo Travel Agency managed to book me a seat on a seventeen-day flight to Egypt, Uganda and the Sudan. When we landed in Entebbe, it was cold and rainy, but by the time we had spent a day relaxing in a dream hotel surrounded by a park, palm trees and a wealth of gorgeous flowers, the sun was out again.

The next day was strenuous. We spent ten hours driving along bumpy, dusty roads to Queen Elizabeth Park, that beautiful animal reserve in East Africa where I had shot footage for *Black Freight* five years before. I was in the same place from which I had suddenly been called back to Munich – but I didn't want to think about it.

My most important job still lay ahead: getting the filming permit in Khartoum. I was apprehensive since if I were to be turned down, then our film was doomed.

Since our plane was stopping over in Khartoum for only one day, I had very little time. It was August, the hottest month in this town. By post, an appointment had been arranged for me at the old building where the heads of tourism were stationed. Here, I met my first Sudanese – Ahmed Abu Bakr, Director of Tourism – and I liked him at once. He was a man of about fifty with a full head of greying hair and a face which radiated warmth and cordiality. We hit it off instantly, and since his English was very good, we were able to converse without an interpreter.

Ahmed Abu Bakr told me that during the war he had been a colonel, fighting with the British against Rommel, whom he greatly admired. On the whole, he was a Germanophile, so that I felt I could get somewhere with him. He showed me various oil paintings he had done, including portraits of South Sudanese natives; that was my cue to bring up my request. During the repeated military conflicts it was extremely dangerous travelling in the southern Sudan without police protection. The English had declared the southern provinces 'closed districts', to be entered only with a special permit from the Sudanese government. I had to try and obtain such a permit. After a few hours of intensive discussion, our Nile project had made such a deep impact on Sayed Ahmed Abu Bakr that he promised to give me the permit – but with several stipulations: we could never travel alone, we always had to be escorted by a policeman or a soldier and we were not allowed to film or photograph unclad people.

I was ecstatic when I clutched the documents, which were made out in English and in Arabic; as I took my leave of Abu Bakr, I knew that I had made a friend.

THE BERLIN WALL

On 13 August 1961, one day after my arrival in Munich, the Wall was erected in Berlin, separating the eastern sector from the western ones. It was eeply tragic event and I felt quite paralysed with shock at what was happening in Berlin. What would be the consequences for all of us of this separation of German from German. What would it mean for me?

I was unable to reach my Japanese friends by telephone, so I posted them the account of my trip. Michi didn't visit me until two weeks later and his news was dismal. The Wall had struck a lethal blow to their business. They had lost so much money that they had to shelve all film plans for the time being. They didn't even know whether they would remain in Germany or go back to Japan. I had never seen Michi in such a state of depression and we tried to comfort each other. In any case, our Nile film had now become very, very remote, but my yearning for Africa was stronger than ever.

A LAST-DITCH EFFORT

Neither my mother nor I had a pension, and my mother's only property, her house and small plot in Zernsdorf, was now located in East Germany. Relatives from there told us that her house was inhabited by the mayor of Zernsdorf, so we wrote to him several times, but our letters were never answered. Even if we lived very frugally, our savings would hold out for only a few scant months. Our future was written in the stars.

First, I tried to sell our belongings, although I didn't want to part with my two Leica cameras. But I did have some valuable property: the copyright as well as the negatives and prints of my films. However, almost no one had the nerve to screen them because of the systematic assassination of my character. My name was snuffed out in Germany. What good did it do me that nearly all foreign museums owned prints of my films. Here, no one wanted to have anything to do with me. In contrast, I received an invitation from the University of Los Angeles to give lectures on my films, and I was assured that I would not have to fear any protests. It was not my first invitation from an American university, but I had never had the courage to accept, because I didn't want to be exposed to possible demonstrations. Now that I had no chances whatsoever in Germany, however, I seriously considered accepting the American invitation.

A visitor quickly helped me to forget about the United States in that he represented a chance of getting back to Africa. To do so, I would forgo not only lectures in the United States, but also any other work, no matter how tempting financially. Africa had kindled something in me – an all-consuming fire.

My visitor was Herr Luz, head of the German Nansen Society in

Tübingen. I had learned from a small newspaper item that he was preparing a new expedition through the Sudan.

The German Nansen Society was a recognized non-profit-making organization. For years, its members had been going on anthropological field trips, but so far, their findings had been exploited only on a scholarly level. Now they wanted to make a documentary of their next expedition and Herr Luz was convinced that a valuable film could be made under my direction and with my enthusiasm for Africa.

I had resolved to join the expedition whether or not a film was made. Nor was I intimidated by the terrible strain of the trip, as Herr Luz had described it. With my ballet, mountain-climbing and skiing training I was sure I could endure all sorts of strains despite my sixty years. I would be the only woman among five men, but I was used to that from my mountain films. Herr Luz was taking along his son Horst as cameraman, his son-in-law as physician and expedition assistant, plus two young scientists.

We parted good friends. Since the expedition would be starting in just two months, we agreed that I might fly to Khartoum later on in order to have more time for the pre-production work.

GETTING READY FOR THE EXPEDITION

After that meeting, I felt reborn. Now that I had a task once again, an aim in life, I felt sure that any problems could be dealt with. Even my physical complaints vanished and I launched into the preparations with great *élan*. Never had there been such ideal possibilities for making a good documentary in Africa on such a tight budget. The Sudanese government permit that I had received from Abu Bakr in Khartoum was so valuable that, had I not been so thoroughly defamed in Germany, any TV network or film company would have financed this film.

It could not be shot on the basis of a precise script; I wanted to call it *African Diary* and it had to be improvised. Aside from a cameraman and assistants, all we needed was a car with four-wheel drive. Heinz Hölscher, my cameraman on *Black Freight*, was so fascinated by the project that he was willing to put off his fee for the nine months of the expedition; his assistant felt the same.

The production costs were so greatly reduced by similar arrangements concerning the film stock, printing labs and camera rentals that we needed only ninety-five thousand marks. This was a tiny sum for a colour movie about an African expedition, and I hoped we could easily find it.

I recalled a conversation with Abu Bakr in Khartoum in the course of which he had advised me to contact Alfried Krupp von Bohlen und Halbach. Apparently, this German industrialist had visited the southern Sudan on a hunting expedition the previous year and had been enthralled by his experiences. So far, I had lacked the courage to turn to Herr von Krupp, but now I wanted to give it a try and, to my surprise, I received an answer by return of post. In my letter, I had said nothing about money but had simply requested information about his experiences in the southern Sudan. We met at the Continental Hotel in Munich where I was already expected and the receptionist led me to a small salon, where Herr von Krupp greeted me. He seemed somewhat inhibited, but friendly, and I would have recognized him at once from his magazine photographs. Tall and slender, almost scraggy-looking, Herr von Krupp radiated aristocratic aloofness.

We had a long conversation in which, infected by my enthusiasm, he told me about his adventures in the southern Sudan. He told me that, unlike his guests, he was uninterested in hunting; his hobby was filming and photographing. This world-renowned industrialist had spent five years in prison in the place of his critically ill father, who had been condemned at Nuremberg. He seemed shy and modest, not at all like the leader of a gigantic industrial concern.

Shortly after our meeting, I received a package of his films and photos which he had edited himself, adding his own sound track; he asked me for my indulgence, as well as for my criticism and advice.

I was surprised that he had sent this valuable material by post since the films and colour material – almost one thousand slides – were all originals, not duplicates. Some of the shots which were very good, and of particular value to me, showed native tribes that I was unfamiliar with and very interested in. I was fascinated by all the footage and photos, whether good or bad and the thought that I would see all these things for myself in a very short time filled me with elation. Herr von Krupp also wanted to see the photos and slides that I had taken during the *Black Freight* venture in East Africa: shots of animals and Masai. He liked them so much that he asked me to send the material to his friend. Prince Bernhard of the Netherlands. It was then I got up the courage to ask him if he'd be interested in backing the film. But I was out of luck. Herr von Krupp's secretary notified me that the company had recently been supporting too many projects, so that further funds for such purposes were unfortunately not available. I didn't hear anything more from Herr von Krupp and I wish I'd never made that request.

I had the same experience with the German industrialist Harald Quandt, the step-son of Goebbels, and I received from him the same response as I had originally received from Alfried Krupp. Just who was it these rich industrialists were afraid of? The tiny sum, which could be given in the form of a loan, would have been a mere gratuity for millionaires of that class. They couldn't have been uninterested; otherwise Krupp wouldn't have asked me to post my slides to Prince Bernhard. These men too were probably afraid to be linked for even an instant to the name of Riefenstahl in any way. Perhaps they were worried that it might spell losses of millions for their concerns.

I had no choice but to give up the documentary. But since I wanted so much to join the expedition, I saw a possibility: I could shoot a 16mm film about the work and experiences of this field trip, something which would require only a very tiny budget. The Nansen Society had enough film stock for its educational movies, and Oscar Luz's son had some experience as a cameraman. Even this kind of film could be informative and exciting and, if it were good, it might be shown on TV. But first I had to arrange care for my mother during my long absence and for this I would need three hundred marks a month at the very least.

So, for the first time, after many years of separation, I turned to my ex-husband Peter Jacob, who was legally obliged to support me and would certainly have done so had he not had so very little himself; I hadn't ever told him about our financial plight. When I approached him, he readily agreed to help out with at least one hundred marks a month for my mother and I was promised another hundred marks by Carl Müller, who had played my films so successfully. And then, just in time, good news came from the welfare office. Years earlier, I had applied for assistance for my mother, pointing out that she was an impoverished widow who had lost her only son in Russia; as a result, at last, she was granted one hundred marks a month.

My biggest present, however, came from Herbert Tischendorf, who had backed me so generously with *The Red Devils*. He gave me three thousand marks for the round-trip ticket Khartoum-Nairobi and back. Africa was assured.

The expedition was to start by late September. I would follow by air in order to make a final attempt to obtain backing for the film during the weeks when the expedition was *en route*. Our meeting place was to be Khartoum.

After getting all my vaccinations against yellow fever, cholera and so forth, I was invited to a going-away party in Tübingen. All the expedition members were gathered at the Luz home: the scientists Dr Rolf Engel and Frieder Rothe, a teacher, as well as Luz's son-in-law. Aside from Oskar Luz, they were all very young men. I liked their open expressions, and I felt that these men would never abandon anyone in an emergency. We toasted our friendship and celebrated until dawn. We were all 'Africa-crazy'.

THE NUBA OF KORDOFAN

At last, I was sitting in the plane, leaving everything behind me, as though a great load were slipping from me and I was starting a new part of my life. I didn't just yearn to see Africa, I was magically drawn by a very specific Africa – the dark, mysterious and still barely explored continent. All this was very impressively conveyed in a photo with which I couldn't part and which shows a black athlete carried on the shoulders of a friend. Years earlier, when I was at the hospital in Nairobi, I had cut out the picture from a back issue of *Stern*. It was an unusual study, taken by an English photographer, George Rodger; the black man's body looked like a sculpture by Rodin or Michelangelo and the caption read: 'The Nuba of Kordofan'. There was no other information.

I was so struck by these unfamiliar Nuba that they induced me to do things I would otherwise not have done – one reason why I joined the Nansen expedition was in order to track down the Nuba. It took me a long time to find out where Kordofan was, and an even longer time to pinpoint the Nuba Hills on an English map. Kordofan was a province in the Sudan, and the Nuba Hills lay to the south, but I could learn nothing about the Nuba tribe. Anthropologists told me that few Europeans, not even missionaries, had visited the Nuba; no one in Khartoum could give me any information, not even Abu Bakr, who had travelled through all the provinces of his country. The reasons for this seclusion, I was told, were the great distances involved, the lack of lodgings and the scarcity of water.

Nobody, not even a travel bureau, could tell me how to reach the Nuba and I was on the verge of giving up all hope of ever finding them. Everything I heard was discouraging. Perhaps the Nuba no longer existed. Perhaps I was on a wild-goose chase.

KHARTOUM

We landed punctually at 5 a.m. and to my delight, I was warmly greeted by all the members of the Nansen Society and by Herr Krombach, the head of Lufthansa. We had to spend some time in the Sudanese capital until all formalities were settled and our main problem was the customs. We had to pay sixty per cent on the film stock and one hundred to three hundred per cent on cameras, a heavy and unexpected blow. I had to wage a nerve-racking struggle with the customs officials; every day, from dawn till late afternoon, I sat in the customs building, fighting for my photo equipment, although the very agreeable officials could do nothing against the strict laws and the situation looked pretty hopeless. On the fourth day, I lost patience and blew up, weeping and yelling, until they released everything duty-free. I owed my success mainly to my polaroid shots: I had photographed the officials without their knowledge and when I gave them the photos, the portraits worked wonders. However, a very high security deposit had to be put up for the camera equipment, and this money was obligingly advanced by Lufthansa. All in all, Lufthansa was exceedingly helpful. Its director got me into contact with the Sudanese government agencies that were processing our indispensable visa extensions.

I managed to get a room at the old Grand Hotel, which stands directly on the Nile and and has a very special atmosphere. Here one still felt something of the style of the British colonial past during the time of the Mahdi. Since the Grand Hotel was always overbooked, an old, abandoned Nile steamer was used as an annexe for its guests. The steamer floated on the river, separated from the hotel entrance only by a shady tree-lined lane, the most beautiful I have ever seen. The treetops were so vast and dense that they covered the wide lane like a green canopy. The sunlight flickered through the leaves, and the air, which seemed filled with gold dust, flowed into the white garments of the people.

Although I loved staying at the Grand Hotel, I grew more and more nervous about the bill with each passing day; the hotel was not cheap, and my travel budget was modest. Yet I barely had a chance to think, inundated as I was with impressions of the sort of throbbing social milieu to which I had become a stranger. I received invitations every day, chiefly from resident Germans but also from foreign embassies located near the Nile where parties were held in splendid flower gardens. A high point – and an important one for our expedition – was a garden party given for the Nansen expedition by Herr de Haas, the popular and likable German ambassador. The guests included Gottfried von Cramm, the German tennis playing baron, who was dealing in cotton in the Sudan, and also many Sudanese prominent in politics and business, especially the governors and police chiefs of the Sudanese provinces. These officials, who got together in Khartoum once a year around this time, were the people with power; it was up to them alone whether we could stay in their provinces, and – a lot more crucial – whether we could shoot films and take photographs. This gathering gave me a unique opportunity to speak to each and every one of them, making contacts without which we could never had secured support for our work in the closed districts.

I recall an amusing episode in connection with that party. The Nansen people refused to shave for the reception and for traditional reasons the ambassador refused to receive unshaven men. The Sudanese feel resentment towards foreigners who haven't shaved; they believe that they, as hosts, are not being taken seriously. This aversion to beards is also based on their prejudice against missionaries, most of whom wore beards. The main reason, however, is that such men are frequently penniless adventurers who travel through the country exploiting the hospitality of the Sudanese and often failing to pay for their drinks in bars or to settle their hotel bills.

The Nansen people were adamant, despite all my efforts to get them to cut off their beards by reminding them that we were dependent on the goodwill of the Sudanese. There were two exceptions. Frieder, our young teacher, shaved almost daily; and Rolf Engel of the Max Planck Institute understood and got rid of his stately red beard. Luz's son and his son-in-law stayed away from the reception, but Oscar Luz, as head of the expedition, couldn't afford to follow suit since the reception was in his honour. He had no choice – alas, the beard had to go.

During this reception, the ambassador's wife talked him into taking along a camp-bed for me, something Luz had refused to do, pleading lack of space. I was supposed to sleep in the van but since I preferred sleeping outdoors this was an area for conflict. Eventually, I was allowed to buy a camp-bed for forty marks at the market in Omdurman; for me it was the most important piece of equipment on our expedition.

Further conflict followed and I soon realized that the good impression I had had of the Nansen people in Tübingen was not quite accurate. Having struck me at first as idealistic, carefree and merry, they exhibited few of these qualities as time went on. As far as the Luz family were concerned, they were usually grumpy and unfriendly, probably because everything turned out to be a lot more difficult than expected. They still hadn't received the filming permits and were unable to begin their trip to the south on schedule because it was raining heavily and the roads were impassable. The institute in Göttingen had allotted us the job of making a series of scientific shorts about the Nuer tribe who live in the swamp areas south of Malakal.

In Tübingen, we had decided on a 16 mm film just in case. Luz's son was to do the shooting and therefore I had to stay on good terms with him, but unfortunately he was the hardest one to get on with and there was an all-out

fight at the very first shooting. We were preparing a moving shot on the
bridge, where the Blue Nile and the White Nile flow together, when
without warning or explanation the young man refused to shoot. All he said
was that he wouldn't work with me: he took the camera off the tripod,
packed up everything, and left me standing there. A fine start, I thought,
dismayed. But I could do nothing at that moment, since his father wasn't
with us.

When I told Rolf and Frieder about the incident, they explained that there
had been unpleasant scenes between father and son during the trip from
Germany to Khartoum. They were pessimistic, but had hoped that my
presence would improve the atmosphere. When I talked to Oskar Luz about
the incident, he expressed himself very cryptically, trying to make it clear
that Horst was irreplaceable for him. I now realized what lay ahead for me.
If Luz failed to change his son's mood, I would be nothing but undesirable
ballast for him. However, Oskar Luz was still behaving diplomatically. He
knew enough to appreciate the value of my connections with the authorities,
especially the governors of the southern provinces, where the closed
districts were located.

Since we couldn't leave because of the weather, Abu Bakr and I met
almost every day. He showed me pictures and maps of the Sudan and took
me on a tour of Omdurman. This old Sudanese town is simply fascinating,
with its countless mosques, large and small, and the most bizarre minarets.
The marketplace of Omdurman, the largest in Africa, reminded me of an
Oriental market in a fairy tale. Natives come from all over the country to
buy and sell their home-made objects: jewellery, musical instruments,
spears, Bedouin swords. Craftsmen perch in the narrow, shady streets,
making handbags and small suitcases from snake skins and crocodile skins,
and everywhere master goldsmiths and silversmiths are at work. I was
moved by the piety of the Sudanese who kneel and bow towards the East
with fervent devotion. Their hospitality is equally unusual.

The first time I was invited to a meal in a Sudanese home, that of Sayed
Gadalla, a film producer, I discovered finely wrought silver jewellery lying
next to my plate: a necklace, a bracelet and earrings. If you travel through
the Sudan, you must realize that a guest in a Sudanese home should never
admire anything – a picture, a rug, or whatever. Otherwise, they'll give you
the object on the spot or else bring it over the very next day. If you don't
accept the gift, your refusal is a slur on the host's honour.

An unfortunate event increased the tension between the Nansen people
and myself. Smoke bombs, which I had taken along for possible sandstorm
shots, exploded on the campsite. The men sleeping on the roof of the

Unimog were hurled aloft but luckily suffered only bruises and cuts. It was a miracle the petrol tank didn't catch fire. The damage was extensive. No wonder the head of the expedition regarded me as the culprit.

Meanwhile, almost three weeks had elapsed, and it was still raining in the south of the country. Since waiting in Khartoum was becoming unendurable, I ventured to make a suggestion. I had learned from Abu Bakr that there was another way of getting to the Nuer; though Luz's route, southward along the Nile, was certainly the shorter, and the other involved a detour of nearly six hundred miles, the advantages of using the latter would outweigh the disadvantages. The rainy season had already ended along this western route, which also led through the Nuba Hills – a thought that sent my heart pounding. We would thus be able to film the local natives and, if we found them, even the Nuba, until the road leading to the Nuer became passable. Even if we didn't stumble upon the Nuba, it would still be more rewarding to try this route than to spend weeks sitting around doing nothing in Khartoum. The long wait had worn down the expedition members to such an extent that their leader warmed to my idea more quickly than I had expected and began to prepare for our departure.

I was delighted. Now I was quite confident that I would find the mysterious Nuba whom I had seen in Rodger's photograph.

THROUGH KORDOFAN

The time had come. At the beginning of December 1962, our expedition got underway. We had taken care of our correspondence and bought tomatoes, onions, melons and lemons at the market. The 'winter' weather was splendid – a blue, cloudless sky, the air neither too warm nor too cold. Our clothing was lightweight; I wore a short skirt and sports blouse.

No sooner had we left the capital than we found ourselves on a sandy road with deep tracks and holes which forced us to drive cautiously. After one and a half hours, we left the road leading to Kosti in order to find a place to bivouac before dark. Since we had taken no tents because of lack of space, overnight stops were very easily managed.

Several of the metal crates were placed outdoors, the gas cooker was lit and water boiled for tea, and tomatoes and onions were sliced into a bowl. Half an hour later, we sat together on our crates, drinking our tea with relish. I preferred the simplicity of expedition life to the luxury of a hotel.

Soon, the starry sky stretched out overhead and the men turned in early. Each of us had been given a sleeping bag and a woollen blanket and I set up

At the camera shooting *Tiefland*, 1940

As well as directing *Tiefland*, I also played the female lead – a Spanish dancer. Harald Kreutzberg was my dance teacher.

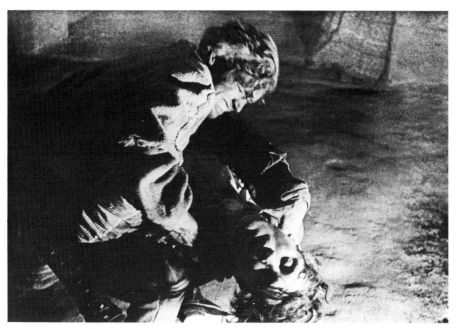

A fight to the death between Pedro the shepherd and the
Marquis (Franz Eidberger and Bernard Minotti)

Here I am rehearsing this scene with the performers

A banquet in Oslo in 1938, given by the Norwegian
government to mark the première of *Olympia*

The banquet in Vienna after the première of *Olympia* in 1938

The Danish royal couple at the première of *Olympia* in
Copenhagen, August 1938. Next to me (almost hidden) is my
mother who accompanied me on this European tour.

With Gina Lollobrigida in Italy in 1953 during the shooting of
her film *Bread, Love and Dreams*

In conversation with Andy Warhol at his factory in New York,
1974

With Vittorio de Sica in Rome, 1953. He was willing to play a
leading role in my film project *The Red Devils*.

Jean Marais shakes hands at the Film Casino in 1954. At my
side is Frau Lonny van Laak.

Robert Schäfer, my publisher at List. I owe to him the
publication of my four photographic books.

my camp-bed between the two vans, placing my torch underneath and snuggling up in my bag. My mind was filled with visions of the Nuba – until I drifted off.

The next morning, I did my first filming. Near Kosti, by the Nile, we saw enormous herds of grazing cattle led by Falata nomads. Gold and silver hoops are worn on arms and legs not only by the women clad in black but also by the children of these wealthy people.

Our second most important station was El Obeid, the capital of the province of Kordofan. It was far out of our way, but it was the seat of the governor and the provincial chief, the only people who could authorize our permits to film in the closed districts, so we had to go there.

Fortunately, the police chief of Kordofan, whom I had feared the most, was enthusiastic about my idea of finding the Nuba but when I showed him the Rodger photo he said, 'I believe you are ten years too late to find them like this. Earlier, you could see the Nuba living close to nature everywhere in the Nuba Hills, but now that roads are being built, cotton planted and schools set up, the life of the Nuba has changed. They wear clothes, work on plantations and keep giving up more and more of their tribal ways.' Not realizing how upset I was by his words, he added comfortingly, 'We normally don't go further than Kadugli and Talodi; that's where the sothernmost police stations of the province of Kordofan are located; but south of Kadugli, there may still be splinter groups of the Nuba.'

We drove further south, through deep sand, towards the Nuba Hills. Our vehicles threw up long clouds of dust, so we had to keep wide intervals between them. If our VW van got stuck in the sand, it had to be hauled out by the Unimog.

Usually, we spent the night under old monkey bread trees. Four men slept on top of the Unimog, one in the van, and I on my camp-bed out in the open. Since there was little room in the two vehicles, the expedition had renounced all modern conveniences. The most important things we took with us were drums of water, petrol and oil, food, medicaments, film gear, scientific equipment, replacement parts for the vehicles, ropes, tools and the like. There were only two washbasins for all six of us, and sometimes they were used to prepare food. My most important item of luggage was the crate holding my photo equipment.

By the time we reached Kadugli, we had been travelling for a week and our search for the Nuba was still unsuccessful. We had encountered a few Nuba families in Dilling and in the side valleys but in their clothing – usually shirts and gym shorts – they looked no different from the blacks in the big cities. We were very disappointed. Our hopes shrank to zero, but we still refused to give up our quest.

Our cars plunged along through tall grass, deep ditches and dried-up river beds. Blocks of stone and age-old trees gave the landscape an almost mythical character. The valley narrowed down, the mountains seemed to converge, and the trail grew rockier and rockier. We had been driving through this valley for hours – no water, no people, not even animals anywhere – when suddenly we spotted small round houses on the mountain slopes, clinging to the rocks like birds' nests. These could only be Nuba houses. A young girl sat on a boulder, swinging a switch. She was naked. Only a string of red beads adorned her black body. She stared at us, terrified, scared, and vanished into the bushes like a gazelle.

Our fatigue vanished and our spirits rose as our vehicles inched forward. We were surrounded by a great hush; the sun faded and the valley seemed virtually lifeless. Stones and roots blocked our way and were about to force us to turn back when we glimpsed a cluster of strangely adorned people in the distance. We left our vehicles and went forward cautiously on foot. Several naked men, covered with snow-white ashes and wearing bizarre headgear, were followed by others, whose bodies were painted white and adorned with white ornaments. Girls and women, similarly painted and decorated with white pearls, nimbly trailed the men, walking straight as candles and bearing calabashes and large baskets on their heads. No doubt about it: these were the Nuba. They clambered precariously up rocky outcrops and over slanting ledges and suddenly were gone. Rounding the boulder that had cut them off from our view, we saw an overwhelming spectacle.

In the light of the setting sun, one or two thousand people milled about in an open area surrounded by many trees. Peculiarly painted and adorned, they seemed like creatures from another planet. Hundreds of spear tips danced against the blood-red ball of the sun. In the middle of the throng, large and small circles had formed, and pairs of wrestlers faced one another inside them. They beckoned, fought, danced, and were carried from the ring as victors on the shoulders of others, just as in Rodger's photograph. I was entranced; I didn't know what to photograph first. A thrilling atmosphere was created not only visually but also acoustically – the ceaseless drumming and above it the warbling of female voices and the shrieks of the crowd contributed to the sense that it was all a dream. Long since separated from my companions. I was among the Nuba at last. Hands reached out towards me, faces laughed at me and I immediately sensed that I was among good people.

468

I had no idea when we returned to Kadugli, the miraculous event had destroyed my sense of time. According to my diary, the Nuba wrestling festival took place on 16 November 1962, and we pitched camp near Tadoro, a Nuba settlement, on 22 December, under a tree with a crown almost a hundred feet wide. I could scarcely believe I was here. After six years, my dream of finding 'my' Nuba had gloriously come true.

AMONG THE NUBA

When I awoke the first morning, the sunlight was already pouring through the foliage above me and I had to think for a moment to recollect where I was. Lying there under the huge tree, I had dreamed that I was actually among the Nuba. Crawling out of my sleeping bag, I noticed that it was very windy; my woollen blanket and sleeping bag were flapping like sails in a tempest, and I had to hold my belongings tight so they wouldn't fly away.

Not far from me stood a couple of attractive naked children observing me curiously. A boy of perhaps ten ambled towards me shyly, offering me my blouse, my skirt and my bra with a bashful gesture; he had retrieved my clothes which the wind had blown away. I produced some sweets from my bag and taking them cautiously from my fingers, the boy ran over to the other children, who sniffed them and put them in their mouths; then they laughed and scurried off. While stowing the blanket and the sleeping bag in a haversack, I watched some women in the distance; they were carrying huge baskets on their heads as they walked towards the fields that stretched all the way to the horizon, glowing yellow in the sunlight and contrasting powerfully with the black figures. I also saw men striding with a springy gait towards the fields. They bore axes on their shoulders and wore only black leather belts with shiny brass buckles at the back. Intent upon their respective purposes, the men and women scarcely noticed us, though a few waved.

In the afternoon, on their return from working on the land, a few of the Nuba stopped at our camp. The women put their heavy baskets on the ground and rested in the shade. The baskets were spilling over with red, yellow and white sheaves of grain, a kind we weren't familiar with. The children slowly approached us. The wind had died down and the air was still.

While the men went about their business, I tried to make my first direct approaches to the Nuba. I sat down on a rock among the women and laughed; they responded by laughing uproariously for a long time. Then an elderly woman came up to me and held out her hand, which I readily grasped. Her hand slowly glided out of mine, and her middle finger snapped, which made the women burst into more raucous laughter. Now the other women came over and held out their hands to greet me in the same way by snapping their middle fingers. I assumed that this was the customary Nuba salutation and since it was accompanied by the word *Monnatu* to me, I realized this must be an important word of greeting. Later on, whenever I wanted to converse with a Nuba, I used it successfully. Sensing that I liked them, they became more trusting. They touched my arms, astonished at the light colour. They also gingerly touched my blonde hair, saying 'yorri' (pretty) and accompanied me wherever I went.

Unfortunately, my relationship with the Nansen people had deteriorated even further and they barely gave me the time of day. During the drive, there had been various conflicts between us and there was no further mention of the film.

After discovering that there was a well less than two miles from our camp, Oscar Luz decided to spend a few weeks in Tadoro. No one was happier about his absence than I – and he could not have found a more ideal place for his scientific work. Unfortunately, Frieder, the nice teacher to whom the Nansens were not much friendlier than they were to me, went off on his own. He preferred continuing his studies at a Sudanese school in Rheika, near the well, mainly because he didn't care for the unfriendly atmosphere among the Nansens. Rolf Engel was less demanding; no deprivation was too great for him, no food too bad. He was the most easily satisfied person I have ever met and nothing upset him. Always helpful and unflaggingly cheerful, he was the mainstay of the expedition. As long as he was nearby, I felt safe.

Gradually, I was able to meet more and more of the Nuba – the mothers and fathers of the children and their brothers and sisters. Every day brought me new experiences, and I liked my new friends more and more. I didn't want to leave them but I realized that I could fully understand them only if I learned their language. Day by day, I picked up more of their words and I always carried a notebook and pencil. *Yoka-i* was the most useful word I discovered. It means: what is this? I only had to point to an object and ask, 'Yoka-i?' and the children would shout the right word. Within a short time, my vocabulary was large enough for me to communicate and, as a result, my relations with the Nuba kept improving. Whenever I appeared, the youngsters would sing; 'Leni buna Nuba – Nuba buna Leni' (Leni likes the Nuba – the Nuba like Leni).

I wrote home about our life among these people and how I felt about it:

25.12.62

Dearest Mother,

Yesterday was Christmas Eve, and I thought about you. You can't imagine how simply we live here, but you can believe me when I say that this life, unburdened by all the comforts of our civilization, has something liberating about it. It is wonderful spending all our days and nights in the fresh air, unbothered by letters or telephone calls, and wasting no time on our wardrobe. And that's not all. The blacks whom we live among here are so delightful that I'm never bored for even a moment. You should have seen what happened here last night. We were sitting on crates, eating supper, unable to move because so many Nuba had settled down next to us on each crate and surrounded by several hundred more who were gathered in a circle. The big attraction was our radio, on which we were trying to receive the German Africa station. This was something strange for the Nuba, but they seemed to like it very much. Men with spears stood in the background behind the older people. The adolescents and the very young children sat on the ground in front of us. It was an odd feeling hearing Christmas carols so deep in the African bush – don't worry about me – I'm happy and healthy.

Your Leni

I neglected to mention that our group had gained a new recruit in Kadugli: a young Sudanese policeman who had to accompany us, not to protect us – which was unnecessary among the peace-loving Nuba – but to prevent us from photographing unclad Nuba. Fortunately, our likeable 'guard' was diverted by the pretty Nuba girls, so that we had few problems taking pictures, if only because a good number of Nuba were already wearing clothes. Now and then, the most remote corners of the Nuba Hills were reached by trucks carrying Sudanese officials who distributed free garments to the natives – usually red, blue and green shorts, as well as shirts and kerchiefs. Since the Nuba had no soap and very little water, these garments soon got dirty and tattered; but they had no money to buy new clothing. Despite the threatened penalties, many Nuba preferred their traditional state of undress.

The Nuba ate twice a day: at sunrise and sunset, 6 a.m. and 6 p.m. Both meals consisted of mush from ground grain, usually unspiced, cooked in water, very occasionally in milk, which was a rare treat.

Our meals too were simple. We had a pot of coffee or tea in the morning and a few slices of pumpernickle on which we could smear honey as long as the supply lasted. Then there was a small wedge of soft cheese which was our only fat since the Nansens hadn't even brought any cooking oil. In the evening, we ate mostly noodles or rice, very occasionally with tough, bony chicken. Because of lack of space, the Nansens had brought no canned goods along. Once, when I asked Luz why he hadn't even included oatmeal, he replied: 'In the Russian POW camp, we managed without it.'

Despite this meagre, fat-free diet, we were all healthy. Although I lost a lot of weight, I have seldom felt so fit in all my life. Despite the increasing heat, I spent hours clambering over rocks with the Nuba in order to visit their homes which were very far away, but well worth seeing as they are unlike the houses of any other African tribe. Each residential complex consists of five or six round houses linked by circular walls. The entrance leads to an inner courtyard, where the hearth is located and it is here that the Nuba eat their meals and go about their business. The walls are decorated with paintings of people, animals and objects, and some shimmer in silvery blue, which looks like blue marble. Soil containing graphite is applied to the clay-coated stone walls and rubbed with palms for days or even weeks, until a silvery blue glow develops.

One evening, when the Nansen people, the policeman, and Rolf were already sleeping and I was busy cleaning my cameras and optics, four young Nuba men emerged from the darkness. I hadn't seen them in our camp for a long time. Their bodies were painted in white patterns and they held guitar-like instruments. Curiously eyeing me while I worked, they strummed their guitars. When I asked them where they were going, I understood only the word *baggara*, the term for nomads who passed by from time to time with large herds of camels. I assumed the Nuba were going to one of the nomad camps and longing to be allowed to take pictures, I asked whether I could join them. They agreed without hesitation.

It was a radiant moonlit night so I left my torch behind and took only my camera and flash unit. As we walked in single file along a narrow path, I realized that the Nuba have an unusually sharp sense of hearing. The first man in our line was a good fifty yards ahead of the last, yet they conversed with one another as if walking side by side.

After two or three hours, the group halted, but there was no sign of a nomad camp near or far. We were standing in front of a thorn hedge, from behind which a sleepy boy emerged after the Nuba called out several times. He moved aside a tree trunk, and we entered a herd camp. In the middle of the kraal, I saw several head of cattle lying in the moonlight and young Nuba men sleeping on round pieces of wood. Next to them, a small fire was burning, tended by several eight- to ten-year-old boys. Tukami, the eldest in our group, pointed at the cattle. 'Baggara,' he said. Now I understood that *baggara* were obviously cattle and not, as I had believed, nomads.

I did not as yet realize how important cattle really are to the Nuba. They are their valuable property and the link to their god. Cattle are sacred to them (as they are to the Hindus), and they keep them for their cult rituals. They can be sacrificed only in honour of the dead, but not for livelihood for the living. Many families have only one or two cows, and anyone who owns more is prosperous. The man who possesses seven or eight is rich, in sharp contrast to the Masai, one of whom might own up to a thousand head of cattle.

Meanwhile, the sleeping Nuba had woken up. They greeted us amiably and settled around the campfire with us. During that night, I learned many new things – for instance, that no Nuba woman is allowed to enter a herder's kraal. They also told me that the young wrestlers who live in the *noppo* (kraal) are not allowed to sleep with a woman during that period – even if they are married. For the Nuba, the *noppo* (*seribe* in Arabic) is a school for training and for arousing their spiritual and religious powers.

That night, I had little sleep since my bed consisted of a few round tree trunks and I had a rock for a pillow; yet I must have fallen asleep at some point. When I awoke, the sun was already shining, the Nuba were busy with their 'morning clean-up' and I was able to take photos undisturbed. Years later, these pictures created a stir around the world for they were biblical images which could have dated back to the earliest days of mankind.

It was noon when Tukami and two other Nuba took me back to Tadoro. I was relieved that none of the Nansens asked me where I had been, for I had no wish to talk to any of them about my experiences – I simply entrusted everything about that unrepeated night to my notebook.

The next day, when we left camp at the crack of dawn to go to the dura fields and photograph the Nuba harvest, the temperature was still bearable, but within an hour it was torrid. I had been following the Nansen people through the head-high grain, but had lost them long ago. I started to feel edgy and was tormented by thirst. In this forest of bamboo-thick stalks of grain, I couldn't see a single bush or shady tree and I ran around as if in a maze. At last I bumped into the Nansen people but they had taken no water pouch along so, remembering that a water pouch was hanging on the Unimog, I asked Luz to point out the direction; I had only one urge – to drink. I tried to find the vehicle as fast as I could, but I must have gone astray again. The heat became intolerable, my blouse stuck to my body and I was beginning to stagger when I discovered some shrubbery amid the gold-yellow stalks of grain and lay down in its shade. Then I blacked out. Upon coming to, I heard laughter and looked up to see Nuba women gazing at me. They had found me on the way home to their village and had poured water on my head and face to revive me. When Nuba work in the fields, they always carry a calabash of water. Luckily for me, the women knew where our vehicle was and they took me there.

After a while, the Nansens showed up. There was only a piece of stale bread in the camp and a few slices of canned pineapple, which were distributed among the five of us. When the others drove to the well to get some water, Luz and I got into an angry argument. Everything that had been bottled up in me during the past few weeks burst out, intensified by my great exhaustion. Luz also lost control and yelled at me. The Nuba around us stared anxiously at this furious scene and when Luz headed towards me with an aggressive gesture, one Nuba put his hand on Luz's mouth and held him back while another grabbed my arm and led me away. It was one of the most gruesome days of the expedition.

After the fight, any relationship between Luz and me was shattered for good and I knew I would be abandoned as soon as there was any possibility of alternative transport for me. This all brought me closer to my Nuba friends who built me a small straw hut where I could sleep protected against the powerful evening winds that swept down from the hills. My hut became the meeting place of many Nuba, who brought me small presents, especially calabashes, made by the boys in the herd camps and decorated with ornaments. I was also given spears, bead jewellery, even musical instruments, and soon my hut had turned into a small museum. The thing they enjoyed most was teaching me their language, and I made good progress with the help of a small tape recorder. Their merriment, which infected me too, was like a fountain of youth.

One morning, Rolf woke me up. 'Get ready, we're driving to Kadugli; we have to pick up mail and a few other things.'

'Will the Nansens take me along?'

'You're coming in my car. Close up all your crates. We're leaving our stuff under the tree. We'll be back in three days at the latest.'

It took us three hours to drive some thirty-five miles because often the cars could only crawl. The deep furrows left after every rainy season had been baked stone-hard by the heat and our cars sometimes listed so deeply that I was afraid they would keel over. When we reached Kadugli, the primitive roadhouse seemed like a four-star hotel. The greatest luxury was the running water in which we could at last wash from head to foot – something we hadn't been able to do for weeks on end.

Kadugli lies in a very beautiful region, spread out amid gently rising hills, and I loved the little town. It has a post office, a garrison, a police station, a hospital, and a large marketplace – known in the Sudan as a *suk* – where among the throng of natives, I saw members of many other tribes, such as Dinka, the Shilluk and the Falata, whose women reminded me of Egyptian queens. Invariably wearing black, they carried their babies, swaddled in cloth, on their backs and wore on their arms and ankles heavy gold hoops.

Merchants, mostly Sudanese, but also Egyptians and Greeks, hawked anything and everything: pots, glasses, kitchenware, tools, ropes, pails, wood and bamboo stalks, as well as colourful textiles and cheap clothing, especially Arab *djellabas*. Several merchants even peddled tinned food, but our expedition leader was such a penny-pincher that he bought only a few tins of pineapple. However, I managed to secrete a few lemons in a pouch.

Upon returning to camp several days later, we saw that all our crates, bags and also my camp-bed had vanished. Not a single object was left under the tree. We were utterly dismayed and our first thought was that passing nomads had stolen everything. But Luz pointed to the hills where a column of Nuba men could be seen climbing down the rocks carrying our belongings on their shoulders. It seemed that, without being asked to do so, they had stored all our luggage in their huts for safekeeping. Laughing and gesticulating, they enjoyed our astonished faces and delighted in the modest pinch of tobacco that each of them received by way of gratitude. At that time, they hadn't yet done anything for money and were used to barter. What little they needed – the small, colourful glass beads which they loved so much, the white cloth in which they buried their dead, and the colourful cloth worn mainly by the *kadumas*, as they called their wrestlers – they 'paid' for with dura grain, tobacco and cotton; the latter, however, was grown only in small patches because water was always scarce.

The honesty of the Nuba amazed us. Once, when I lost my gold wristwatch, the boy who found it in the grass brought it back to me. I discovered this quality only among the Masakin-Nuba, and only until money became a means of payment and doors were added to their homes. They were also extremely hospitable, although the most valuable thing they could offer their friends was a calabash of water and a quantity of peanuts – a rare delicacy for these people.

Their youngsters led a free and happy life. They played outdoors all day long under shady trees and were supervised, washed and fed by their older siblings. Young girls carried the babies on their hips, while the boys tended the cattle. Only the strongest male children came into the herd camp, where they were trained as wrestlers. For the Nuba, wrestling was more than a sport – it was a ritual of seminal importance. Before they could even walk properly, the little boys started imitating the dancing and wrestling positions of the athletes and those chosen were trained in wrestling from their earliest youth. They had matches with one another, adorning themselves like their older brothers and their fathers.

The time and place of a wrestling match was decided by the priest, the *kudyur*, with the council of elders. Next messengers were dispatched to announce the invitation everywhere. The Nansens and I managed to attend some of these wrestling festivals, which often took place very far away, in the remote valleys, each being a great event. Early in the morning, the entire hill community of Tadoro – except for the children and old people – started out, decorated with beads, ashes, fur ornaments and calabashes, which the wrestlers usually tied on the back of their belts. The village flag was carried at the head of the procession; at the rear came the women, balancing heavy pots of water and beer on their heads. Some four thousand Nuba participated in a mass wrestling festival, walking as far as thirty miles to get there.

The matches were inaugurated with rituals. The wrestlers stamped on the ground, emitting dull roars – an imitation of the bellowing of bulls – while dancing and moving their hands, or rather their fingers, as fast as large insects move their wings. As the bellowing, dancing wrestlers approached the wrestling site, the spectators grew ecstatic. The Nuba call this *kaduma norzo*, 'howling'. In this ancient Nuba ritual, the wrestlers incarnate their cattle.

The longer the matches lasted, the more passionate they became. Some took only seconds, others a few minutes. If the spectators came too close to the wrestlers, thus interfering with the match, the referees would drive them away with switches. It was practically impossible to photograph and it was only when the winners were heaved aloft on shoulders and carried out of the ring that with a bit of luck I could manage to snap a few pictures.

DEPARTURE

The day of my departure from the Nuba came much too soon. The Nansen team couldn't spend more than seven weeks in Tadoro, and since I had neither a car nor my own expedition gear, I was forced to leave my black friends. Our farewell was difficult. As the cars slowly moved off, they ran after us; shaking their hands a last time, I shouted, '*Leni basso, Leni robrera*' (Leni will be back in two years). I didn't believe what I was saying, I just wanted to buoy up their spirits.

Two days later, we were in Malakal, a small town on the Nile, where the group and I parted company. I planned to take the Nile steamer which docks there once a week and to sail down to Juba, the southernmost town in the Sudan, about seventy miles from the Ugandan border. Next, I wanted to move on to Kenya, since my return flight to Germany was to be from Nairobi.

As I was buying some fruit and onions at the market of Malakal, a Sudanese soldier came over to me and by his gestures indicated that he wished to show me something. He took me to a house where I was greeted by a high-ranking Sudanese officer, the governor of the Upper Nile Province, Colonel Osman Nasr Osman, who was already informed about my presence in Malakal and who asked me to dine with him. I had to tell him a great deal about my experiences with the Nuba and I found his tolerant attitude towards the natives amazing, especially since he was from the north, and powerful tensions existed between the northern and the southern Sudan.

After my deprivations of the past few weeks, the meal was an indescribable pleasure. During coffee, the governor made an astonishing suggestion. 'If you like,' he said, 'you can photograph the Shilluks. I'm driving to Kodog in several days and visiting the king of the Shilluks. On this occasion, there will be a great festival of warriors. Would you like to come along with me?' I was delighted to accept, but as it turned out I got there before the governor.

As I was thinking over the problem of transport for my trip south, two foreigners arrived at the motel – a German and an Englishman, who were driving an old VW van to Kampala, Uganda. It was a wonderful opportunity for the German was willing for me to join them if I shared expenses. The two men found it boring hanging about in Malakal for a whole week waiting for the Nile steamer, so it was easy to interest them in a drive into Shilluk territory, especially to Kodog, the capital, which is only sixty miles north of Malakal.

AMONG THE SHILLUKS

We had taken the ferry across the Nile, reaching Kodog in less than three hours – one day before the governor was expected – and as happened everywhere else in the Sudan, we were welcomed with open arms. The motel that Sayed Amin el Tinay, the district commissioner, put at our disposal was well furnished, with screens on all the windows to protect us from mosquitoes.

The very next morning, we drove to Fashola, to the residence of Kur, the king of the Shilluks. The Shilluk warriors poured in from everywhere, each carrying several spears and huge, almost man-high shields of crocodile skin. Their torsos and arms were adorned with silver chains, ivory, and colourful glass beads. Several thousand warriors had already gathered in Fashola and when King Kur appeared, his subjects behaved as if he were a god. He was clad in a light-coloured toga, with which his red beret contrasted sharply. His bodyguards wore red shorts and shirts, most unlike the Shilluks who were adorned with leopard skins and jewellery.

Meanwhile, Osman Nasr Osman had reached Fashola with his motorcade, and he greeted the king and introduced him to me; a wild beating of drums began and the warriors formed two groups. First the plump, well-nourished king danced at the head of his bodyguards, so wildly and yet so nimbly that I was simply enchanted, and then his warriors followed him in their dance. Even if the whole thing was just a splendid piece of theatre, it was highly original. The rhythm of the stamping men and their ecstatic expressions of wild enthusiasm demonstrated that the Shilluks – unlike the peaceful Nuba – were a nation of warriors. Their faces shone from the strenuous efforts of the dance, which symbolized a battle: one army represented that of the king, the other that of their demigod Nayakang. Attack alternated with retreat, silvery glittering spears shone from thick clouds of dust, waving leopard skins and fantastic wigs made for a spectacle that could not have been outdone by Hollywood. The wild screams of the spectators egged the warriors on to greater and greater passion and I kept clicking away until I had no film left in my camera.

As we decided to remain for several days, the district commissioner lent me a car with four-wheel drive and a Shilluk driver, who actually spoke a few words of English. If only I had had such an opportunity in the Nuba Hills! Increasingly I thought about the Nuba, and felt more and more homesick for them.

My European notion that the 'savages' must be dangerous proved to be wrong. In daily life, I observed nothing of the savagery that I had seen on the faces during the war dances; I never saw a single unkind look and everyone was friendly towards me. After what I experienced in Africa, the civilized world struck me as far more dangerous. I was threatened by a native only once, and then it was my own fault.

In Malakal, we waited for the Nile steamer, the road to Juba being impassable because of the heavy rain. Under better circumstances, we could have reached our destination in one day, while the steamer took seven days. While we waited, I had a sudden brainwave. I asked the German whether we shouldn't drive to Juba, taking a land detour of several hundred miles. Persuasively, I added, 'You might be able to see the Nuba and their wrestling festivals – something you've never seen.'

Chance came to my aid when the Nile steamer finally docked in Malakal, but was so full that it couldn't load any more people or vehicles. This meant that we would have to wait another week, or perhaps even longer, for the next steamer. Now, the German seriously considered my proposal, aware of the risks involved; anyone who has an inkling of the huge size and tiny population of those territories was bound to be cautious, I was blinded by my love for the Nuba.

For this trip, which included one month's stay with the Nuba, the German demanded fifteen hundred marks, to be paid in advance, but I had only eighteen hundred marks left and this would leave only three hundred for travelling to Nairobi. Besides, I had no guarantee that I would ever reach the Nuba Hills. Osman Nasr Osman urged me not to go on this trip. 'In April,' he said, 'I can take you with me on a very interesting tour of inspection to the Buma Plateau all the way to the Ethiopian border. 'You'd have a marvellous opportunity to photograph animals and natives in unexplored areas.' I hesitated, but it was only February, and I didn't want to remain in Malakal for such a long time without doing something. I was obsessed with the idea of paying the Nuba a surprise visit.

When I tried to get the German to lower his price for the trip, he simply booked two passages on the next Nile steamer. At that moment, I felt that my desire to see the Nuba again was stronger than any rational consideration and I was ready to sacrifice the money. We decided to leave the very next day.

BACK TO TADORO

As we crossed the Nile on the ferry, the sun sank behind the horizon of the endless plain stretching ahead of us. The three of us sat in the VW van, which was packed to the roof. I was sandwiched in between the German and the Englishman, about whom I knew nothing except that he liked to draw. To our right and left, the desolate, treeless savanna glided past us; there was not a hut, not a human being to be seen.

The German drove well, following the still visible trail left by the tyres of our Unimog. He wanted to reach Tonga, a small Shilluk village some fifty miles from the Nile where an American mission was located at which we hoped to spend the night. Suddenly, the car stopped; I thought at first the engine had stalled, but when the two men got out and I heard the German cursing, my dark forebodings were confirmed. We were stuck with all four wheels in a morass. No one spoke a word and the silence was eerie. When would a car ever pass here? We couldn't get free without help, and help could be found only in Malakal. I knew we were only five or ten miles away, so I offered to walk back and get help, but only if one of the two men accompanied me. They both refused because they wanted to stay with the car, but there was no way they could haul the car out of the swamp, in which it had sunk all the way up to the axle. It would be madness to remain here hoping for a miracle and I tried several times to make it clear to them that two of us had to go to Malakal and get help. I offered to stay with the car myself while they went, but they would not budge and in the end I decided to hike back alone. Neither tried to stop me.

Hurrying as fast as I could in order to get as far as possible before nightfall, I saw that the sky in the direction of Malakal was red – perhaps it was a plains fire. In any case, it helped me keep my bearings. As the sky grew darker and darker, I could barely see and had to slow down. Only now did it dawn on me that I had forgotten my torch, having rushed off far too impulsively and heedlessly, but there was no going back – I would never have found the car at night. Slowly, my eyes got accustomed to the darkness and I became aware of animal noises. I halted and listened, paralysed with fear. I remembered that the German had said there were a lot of lions in this area, preying on the large herds belonging to the Shilluk. I was rooted to the spot.

When I could hear only the soft wind, I cautiously moved on again. After walking for about an hour, I made out the silhouette of a man coming towards me. It was a Shilluk and to my surprise he addressed me in good English. He was rather scared at meeting me here all alone and I was positively tongue-tied. He was coming from the Nile ferry and had a tricycle on which he hoped to reach Tonga that very same night. He was employed at the American mission there.

'You can't possibly go on alone,' he said, offering to take me to the Nile; I sat in front of him on his tricycle, and we pedalled back together. When we reached the banks of the Nile, he asked me to wait until he found a Shilluk who'd be willing to row me across to Malakal. By the time my rescuer returned the mosquitoes had all but devoured me. True to his word, he brought with him a Shilluk who would take me across the river. I thanked my saviour and when we parted he gave me a bead bracelet and made me promise to look him up at the mission.

Soundlessly we glided across the Nile in the Shilluk's hollowed-out tree trunk. It was a fantastically beautiful night and the air was filled with chirping and humming, like soft music. The sky was crowded with stars which seemed close enough to grasp and were bigger than any stars I had ever seen. The heavens spanned the nocturnal landscape like a gigantic sparkling canopy.

In Malakal, the Shilluk took me to a police station, where he exchanged several words with the officers. After I gratefully shook his hand and gave him a reward, he vanished into the darkness. The three Sudanese policemen eyed me curiously. It was not a normal occurrence for a white woman to appear here long after midnight, accompanied only by a Shilluk. None of the Sudanese spoke English and I spoke no Arabic, but I caught sight of the telephone and when I tried to convey that I wanted to speak to Governor Osman Nasr Osman, they understood. One of the policemen went to the telephone, and I inferred from his conversation that someone would be picking me up. Although barely able to stay awake, I heard a car arrive. It was the governor's adjutant, a young officer whom I had already seen, and when I told him about our breakdown, he said, 'No problem, tomorrow we'll tow the car out of the swamp.' Then he took me to a small hotel near the airport.

At 7 a.m., three military trucks stood in front of the hotel and the first ferry took us all across the Nile. A short time later, we found the van with German and the Englishman sitting nearby under a mosquito net, eating breakfast. Their faces betrayed neither joy nor surprise. Within a few minutes the soldiers had hauled the van back on to dry land with towropes. In the daylight, it was easy to make out where the road ended and the swamp began. After I had thanked the soldiers over and over again, the military trucks headed back to Malakal.

In the sunshine, everything looked friendlier than it had yesterday in the twilight; nevertheless, the German was tight-lipped as he loaded the mosquito net, the two folding chairs and the food and snapped, 'Get in!' My heart raced. Which direction would he drive in – back to the Nile or towards the Nuba Hills? He took off towards the Nuba Hills and I heaved a sigh of relief.

REUNION WITH THE NUBA

When we arrived in Tadoro one hour before midnight, the van stopped under 'my' tree. The German had made it in less than two days in his old VW van – a commendable achievement. There was a deathly hush, only a few dogs were barking; my exhausted companions went to sleep, the German in the vehicle, the Englishman in his tiny tent, while I set up my camp-bed in the place where it had stood two months earlier. The straw hut that the Nuba had built only a few yards from the tree was gone.

While unpacking, I heard voices, but in the darkness I couldn't make out any figures. Then, out of nowhere, they stood in front of me, and I heard them shouting, 'Leni – Leni, giratzo!' (Leni's come back.) They surrounded me, shook my hands, wept and laughed. At first, there were only a few, then more and more. The men and women hugged me, the children pulled at my clothes; their jubilation was indescribable and I was happy, deliriously happy. I had wanted this kind of reunion, and it surpassed all my hopes. Within a few minutes, Natu and Alipo came, and Tukami, and Napi, and Dia – for the news of my return had spread like wildfire.

That very same night, my Nuba friends led me over a rocky path to Alipo's home, and as we sat together on the rocks outside the entrance, Alipo's wife brought us a huge pot of *marissa* and I felt as if I had come home. The Nuba wanted to know how long I intended to stay, who the two strangers were, and whether I had been in 'Alemania'. We laughed and talked until I was too tired to go on, then they brought me back to my campsite.

The next morning, my two companions were unusually taciturn and after giving me my breakfast – tea, bread and jam – the German told me with a grim face; 'We can't stay here for four weeks, we have to move on in a couple of days.'

I was deeply upset.

'That's impossible,' I cried. 'You have to stay here for the length of time we agreed on. I paid you for four weeks.' My objections fell on deaf ears and I recalled the governor's warning; he had been right. Since I had neither a car nor money, I was at the mercy of these men. Sensing that the strangers didn't feel very friendly towards me, the Nuba, without further ado, carried my bed and my crate up to the rocks and lent me one of their huts.

During the day, while my companions were out driving, I made use of every single remaining minute to increase my knowledge of the Nuba. I made a lot of music and language tapes; in the evenings, there was no greater pleasure for the Nuba than to hear their own music and speech on my tape recorder.

Gumba, who was one of the best wrestlers, came from Tomeluba, a Nuba settlement high in the mountains. He invited me to his home to meet his parents and relatives and I took the Leica with which I recorded everything, virtually in a picture diary.

A NUBA FESTIVAL FOR THE DEAD

It was late when we got back to Tadoro. The German and the Englishman had shot a few birds and prepared them for the pot but while they cooked there was little conversation. I noticed that many Nuba were climbing up the rocky paths with spears; and nearly all of them were covered with white ash. Alipo came over and explained mournfully, 'Napi pengo' (Napi is dead). Shocked, I asked, 'Napi from the *seribe*?' Alipo nodded. I was genuinely saddened, for Napi was one of my friends; I especially liked him because of his great modesty. He was one of the best wrestlers in Tadoro. 'What did Napi die of?' I asked. They told me he had been bitten by a poisonous snake, was dead by the time they arrived in Kurdir with him. They had carried his body to his uncle's home, high in the mountains, where all the Nuba were now congregating. Alipo and I followed the others, hearing in the distance a terrible weeping and wailing which grew louder as we approached. A large, white cloth was stretched over the hut, in front of which, among the rocks, stood hundreds of Nuba, many of them snow-white with ash. The men, including the old ones, carried spears and were ornamentally painted, while the women and girls had drawn white lines and circles on their faces and bodies and I hardly recognized them – especially as they had tied branches with large, green leaves to their backs, which made them look like unreal creatures.

A slaughtered goat lay at the entrance to the hut. Alipo took my hand and led me inside where Napi lay in state in a room crowded with friends and relatives who were weeping loudly and vehemently. The corpse was covered with many pieces of white cloth and three women – the dead man's grandmother, mother and sister – sat on the bier, sobbing and crooning their laments. The young men who came into the hut also wept unrestrainedly and I couldn't hold back my own tears. Two women poured the contents of their baskets over the corpse, a shower of dried beans and dura seeds. I took photographs and no one tried to stop me. Outside, some twenty men were standing on a huge ledge, looking like carved stone statues; they were Napi's wrestler friends from the neighbouring hill community and they clutched leafless branches, the prizes awarded to the victorious wrestlers. Several figures, whom they called 'sentries of the dead', had the lines of skeletons painted on their bodies and looked even more bizarre. They stood on higher ledges in order to keep away any evil spirits of the dead wafting in with the winds, and remained there motionless, leaning on their spears, until the corpse was carried down into the valley. These 'sentries of the dead' were also wrestlers and had lived with Napi in the *seribe*. Everything was so fantastic and unreal that I felt I was on a remote planet. It was difficult for me to take photographs during the solemn proceedings, but I felt compelled to record this ritual of a disappearing culture.

In an open area, a large circle formed around a herd of cattle. Thirty-six head of cattle had been selected as sacrifices for the dead man – an incredible number, considering the poverty of the Nuba. I left the ring before they slaughtered the first animal by thrusting a spear into its heart.

I was so absorbed that I had failed to notice twilight was gathering. In the darkness, everything looked even more spectral. Groups of women, who had decorated their bodies with large tobacco leaves, resembled living plants, and their painted faces were macabre masks. They danced like a ballet of ghosts, moving in circles and lines.

That morning, a grave had been dug in the small cemetery near the lower Nuba huts. From the outside, the grave looked like a round hole, no larger than the small circular entrances leading into the grain houses of the Nuba. This hole was meant to offer protection for the corpse, since an intruder could hardly manage to squeeze into such a tiny space, and was edged with ash. Like the sepulchral chambers of the Egyptians, beneath the ground the hole widened into the shape of a pyramid, so that the dead man could stretch out and still have enough room for quantities of grave furnishings.

Napi's uncle had climbed into the grave and reaching his hands out of the small aperture he slowly drew the corpse, wrapped in white cloth, into the chamber. Calabashes filled with meat, dura, peanuts and even milk were handed to the uncle for the deceased to have with him in the tomb; and not only food, but also his personal belongings: his axe, guitar, knife, jewellery and his wrestling gear.

When the uncle emerged from the tomb, the Nuba scattered ashes into the opening one last time; then the hole was covered with a huge, round rock and earth was heaped on top of it; a pole with a white flag was stuck into the mound. Friends of Napi's broke their spears, kept one half and thrust the other into the mound. Finally, they placed thorn shrubs around the mound –

a symbolic protection for the dead man. The relatives stayed near the grave and mourned all through the night.

I slowly went up to my hut and peered down to the tree where the van was parked. The curtains were drawn, the lights were out and the two men were already asleep. They had taken no notice of the funeral.

TREK TO THE KORONGO MOUNTAINS

The next day, I labelled the films I had shot on the previous day, and made some entries in my journal. Someone came humming into my hut and I knew from the tune that it had to be Tukami. He looked very worried.

'Why aren't you laughing today?' I asked him.

Tukami answered sadly, 'Varibi nibbertaua' (My wife has run away).

'Why?'

Tukami shrugged and only said despairingly, 'Basso veela' (She won't come back).

At this point, some boys ran up, shouting 'Norroo szands Togadini,' and Tukami's problem was forgotten as we hurried outside. There, a group of Nuba surrounded two messengers, one of whom blew a horn, while the other repeatedly banged his *solodo* (leather slapper) on the ground. They had come from the Korongo Mountains to invite the Nuba to a grand wrestling festival in Togadini and I too was infected by the feverish expectations aroused by the invitation. Alipo told me that when the rooster crowed at the crack of dawn, the Nuba would go on a long trek far, far away, 'dette, dette', and he executed a vast, sweeping motion with his arm, 'Szanda yogo' – a big feast. I wanted to notify the German and the Englishman, but the van was gone. They were probably getting water.

It was still night when Alipo woke me up to tell me that the Nuba had already gathered. I ran back into the hut to get my torch, wavering momentarily about whether I should tell the German now, but I didn't care to wake him up. The dawn was wonderful, the temperature pleasant, the Nuba as cheerful as ever, and I felt fine in my lightweight clothing. Alipo carried my bag of optics, but I never let go of my Leica. As the morning advanced, the sky, where the sickle moon was still visible, grew brighter. When the sun appeared over the hills, the yellow fields stretching out ahead of us glittered like gold and the day became torrid. I began to suffer from the white-hot sun earlier than usual and sweated as profusely as if in a sauna. The heat was so fierce that it was too much even for the Nuba, and we rested for over an hour.

485

When we had put the fields far behind us and only shrubs and occasional trees could be seen, I asked Alipo how far we still had to go; he pointed into the distance, 'Dette dette' (very, very far). As so often, I had launched myself heedlessly into a venture from which there was no going back. I simply had to push myself to see it through. On we tramped, mile after mile and I found myself checking my watch more and more often. The trek was endless.

The sun had already long since crossed its zenith when my eyes began to blur and I felt faint. Shadows flitted around me and water was splashed on my head and body, but nevertheless I passed out. I came round rocking as if I were on the back of a camel and I couldn't distinguish between dream and reality – until I realized I was lying in a basket being carried by a Nuba woman on her head.

At last, at sunset, we halted, and the women took me down and placed me flat on the ground; the great heat abated rapidly and I soon felt better. We were in an area outside the unfamiliar village where the great festival was to take place the following day. Never in my experience had the Nuba travelled to such a distant festival and I had brought neither soap nor a toothbrush; but I was even more worried by the fact that the German didn't know where I was.

Meanwhile, darkness had come. Alipo had left in order to find night lodgings for ourselves and our Nuba – roughly sixty. We were eyed curiously by the other Nuba and I was gaped at more than anyone else for they had probably never seen a white woman before. Children who looked at me ran off weeping. The Nuba men here, black giants, were almost a head taller than 'my' Nuba. Their only decorations were the white feathers on their heads and a belt made of curved branches.

Alipo returned to take us to the place he had found for us to sleep – a hut which, so far as I could tell in the darkness, resembled those of Tadoro. The Korongo family retired to the neighbouring huts but one woman stayed behind with us; she lit a fire and put up a huge pot of dura gruel for us. My Nuba couldn't speak to her as the language of the Korongo Nuba is totally unrelated to that of the Masakin. I was too exhausted to eat; so I lay down on the stone floor and instantly fell asleep.

THE GREAT FESTIVAL IN TOGADINDI

When I awoke, I felt thoroughly shattered and was covered with dust from head to foot. Our wrestlers had already begun to cleanse themselves in the middle of our hut and were rubbing ash into their bodies. The tableau was utterly unreal. Sunbeams slanted in through the roof of the hut and the ash whirled and flickered in the light. As if illuminated by spotlights, the white figures moved against the dark background: a thrilling motif for a sculptor.

When I stepped outside, I was blinded by the dazzling sunshine, but as my eyes slowly got used to the brightness what I saw was overwhelming. I had seen thousands of Nuba at their celebrations, but this festival surpassed all the others. I was looking at an army camp of fantastically adorned people – an endless tide of flags and spears.

I dashed into the hut and grabbed my camera, not knowing what to shoot first – the crowds, the faces or the bewildering array of ornaments on bodies and calabashes.

When the procession of the teams begun, I ran as fast as I could, trying to spot our Tadoro Nuba among the marching groups. Alipo spotted them instantly and we pushed our way through the growing human flood. Natu, as flag bearer, was the head of our group with the strings of beads suspended from his helmet covering his face like a curtain. Behind him danced Tukami and the other wrestlers from Tadoro. The morning crowd had doubled in size and I could not begin to estimate the number of people. Circles began to form – a sign that the matches would soon get underway; presently, the wrestlers entered the huge rings like matadors. The drums kept beating incessantly and a vast excitement filled the air; then, as if at an invisible signal, the bouts began. In the circles into which the Nuba had allowed me to slip, some twenty matches were in progress and I felt as if I were in an ancient arena. This wrestling festival was so enormous that it put all the previous ones in the shade.

I was almost knocked over as a pair of wrestlers broke through the ring and nearly plunged on top of me. The match surged to and fro, the Nuba around me yelling like madmen, and one wrestler succeeded in getting his arms around the other man's waist. He twisted him around like a doll and then, amid cheers, lifted his giant opponent high over his head and put him on his back – rather gently. The roar, augmented with drums and fifes, was deafening. Leaving the throng, I ran to photograph the champion, who was being carried from the ring amid great jubilation.

Alipo had been looking for me and, excitedly grabbing my hand, he led me through the crowd. Gogo, the strongest Korongo wrestler, had challenged Natu, his foster-son and the best wrestler of the Masakin Nuba, and – the most thrilling moment for the Nuba from Tadoro – Natu had accepted. When we reached the ring, Natu and Gogo were already facing one another like two bantam roosters. Natu was bending low, thrusting his broad shoulders forward, and Gogo, also leaning forward, was trying in his dancerlike way to touch Natu's head. Almost seven feet tall, slender and fabulously well trained, Gogo looked wonderful – like Michelangelo's David – but so far, Natu had skilfully warded off all of Gogo's attempts to tackle him.

The air was charged with almost unbearable suspense. Suddenly, Natu's arms darted forward, and seized Gogo in a stranglehold; Gogo reacted quickly, throwing his arms around Natu's throat. Intertwined, the two men whirled acorss the ring. The Korongo cheered for Gogo, the Masakin for Natu. I shouted with the Nuba: 'Natu, Natu!'

The match between equally strong opponents went on for a long time, but never became brutal. Now, with the strength of an ox, Natu pushed Gogo toward the spectators, then through the ring, inch by inch, until I could no longer see the wrestlers. Then, I heard the crowd yell and saw the spectators heave Natu onto their shoulders, hand him a spear, and carry him out of the ring. Alipo's eyes were moist; he and all the Masakin Nuba were proud of Natu's victory.

I was about to go over and congratulate him when I spotted the German and the Englishman, like two policeman at the back of the throng obviously looking for me. When they caught sight of me, still euphoric after the most splendid wrestling bouts that I had ever watched, the two men charged towards me and I could tell from their faces that there was to be no reasoning with them. They ordered me to get into the van but this was too much for me. This was no time to leave the festival. I asked if I could stay on for a few more hours, I begged, I wept; but, without a sign of emotion, they demanded that I follow them there and then. I absolutely refused, I dug in my heels, but the German simply said, 'Fine, then stay here. We're going. We're leaving the Nuba Hills tomorrow.'

'No,' I screamed. 'I can't. I paid you for four weeks – it was a lot of money, the last money I had. We left Malakal only a week ago. You can't leave now.'

'Sure we can,' the German said cynically, and they strode out of the ring area. The Nuba standing around us had observed everything and they summoned Alipo. I had to make up my mind – but really I had no choice, I was forced to knuckle under to my travel companions. I couldn't remain here without a car, food or money. I told Alipo that I had to leave, but that I wanted to say goodbye quickly to Natu and my other friends. When Alipo realized I was serious, he told someone else to get the other Nuba, while he stayed with me as if to shield me against something evil. I felt indescribably miserable. Then my Nuba arrived; they seized my hands and tried to pull me away from the van. Thronging around me, Natu, Tukami, Gumba and Alipo clutched my arms and hands, but the German got into the van and switched on the engine. Weeping with rage and despair, I climbed in and didn't look back – I didn't wave. I couldn't endure the sight of my mournful Nuba.

We reached Tadoro at night. The village was fast asleep – only a few dogs were barking. I tossed and turned on my bed, the stars were fading and the day was dawning. Soon the children were in my hut, and several women helped me pack and carried my belongings to the van. Then, without explanation the German declared that we wouldn't leave until the next day. What a nasty trick. I could have stayed on at the festival and watched another day's wrestling bouts. More and more Nuba were collecting around me and the tiny hut could not hold them all. So we sat down under a large tree, joined by youngsters and old people who brought me small going-away presents. The bigger children gave me tiny clay figurines that they had moulded and baked.

It was then that I first thought of having my own house there. The idea began to fascinate me and I started doing sketches. Meanwhile, the sun had set, and the Nuba had withdrawn into their homes. Left by myself, I felt very lonely. I stretched out on my camp-bed and fell asleep.

When I awoke, it was still dark. I stepped out of the hut and listened to the night's deathly hush. Then – was it an hallucination? – I thought I could hear a faint, remote drumming. I scarcely dared to breathe. Again came the faraway sound – closer this time – more and more audible. After a few nerve-racking minutes, I was certain; my Nuba were coming back.

A wave of happiness surged through me as I collapsed on the bed in my hut. It was incredible; they were returning, they had broken off their wrestling matches. The drumming stopped and I heard laughter, voices – and then the first ones were standing in my hut: Suala and Gogo Gorende, then Natu, Tukami and Alipo. Excitedly they told me that all the Nuba were coming back to say goodbye to me. My sudden departure from Togadindi had been followed by a long palaver. Natu and Alipo wanted to leave Togadindi immediately, but the Korongo Nuba wouldn't hear of it. They had prepared a banquet for Natu, even slaughtered a sheep, and the Nuba couldn't refuse without deeply offending the Korongo. After the feast, the Masakin decided to skip the next few days of the festival. We sat in front of my hut for a long time. They played their guitars, and a few wanted to escort me back to Germany. It was an unforgettable evening.

The next day, it was time to say farewell. The Nuba hadn't gone out to the fields. Hundreds of them gathered around the van and held on to me as if unwilling to let me go, but the German sounded the horn and I had to tear myself away. The Nuba ran alongside the van, shouting, 'Leni basso, Leni basso,' and, hanging out of the window, I grabbed a few hands and tearfully called back, 'Leni basso robrera.' This time, I knew it wasn't a promise designed to console. I knew I would come back.

IN WAU

Our destination was Wau, the capital of the southwestern province of Bahr el Ghazahl. It was the most unpleasant stretch of the entire trip but once we got through it, the worst hazards would be behind us. From Wau, it was 540 miles to Juba, the southernmost city in the Sudan. The terrain proved to be very difficult. The rivers hadn't yet dried out, and there was no way to get across them.

The most disturbing problem of all was a shortage of petrol. How far could we get? In the event, we were lucky. After meandering for some fourteen hours, we reached the small railway station of Barbanusssa on our last few drops of fuel. And – what a stroke of luck – several minutes later, the train, which runs only once a week, came lumbering in. Without warning, the German refused to take me on to Juba unless I handed him another three hundred marks, all the money I had left, and I was forced to give in to his extortion.

The ride to Wau seemed endless. We kept stopping, which gave the natives a chance to get out, settle on the ground and cook their meals. The train was so crowded that hundreds of passengers had to perch on the roof and footboards and progress was slow. Instead of going all the way to Wau, we got out in Awiel where we knew we could get petrol.

I saw all the interesting sights in Wau; bazaars, mosques, and a surprisingly large Christian church. The Mass was well attended, and, in a long conversation with the priest, I learned that, in contrast to what the newspapers claimed, no pressure was put on him or his parish. I was also allowed to take pictures during Mass.

Hearing I was in Wau, Osman Nasr Osman telephoned and repeated his invitation to accompany him on his tour of inspection through the Upper Nile Province. Embarrassing as it was for me, I had to own up to my host that I didn't have a penny to my name. The next day, I received an envelope containing a plane ticket to Malakal and some Sudanese money.

THROUGH THE UPPER NILE PROVINCE

On 1 April 1963, at the crack of dawn, Osman Nasr Osman's motorcade left Malakal, led by a Landrover bearing the military governor as well as the police chief and other officers. I counted fourteen heavy trucks. We were escorted not only by those officers, but also by forty Sudanese soldiers – and I was the only woman in this male company. I sat in one of the trucks, next to the driver.

The trip was scheduled to last two weeks and was to be an extraordinary trek during which I was able to snap unique photographs. Interesting as it was, however, it was also extremely arduous, for we drove twelve hours a day, practically non-stop. I couldn't converse with my Arab driver and the dust and the shaking of the vehicle were unbearable. But I managed to endure all the discomforts because of the marvellous sights – especially the animals. We saw gazelles, zebras, impalas (so bold that they kept taking gigantic leaps across our vehicles), hordes of giraffes, gnus and elephants. I had already been to the animal reserves of East Africa, but what I saw here was incomparable, simply breathtaking. In some areas, the herds of gazelle seemed endless – there must have been hundreds of thousands of them.

We reached Akobo, the home of the Anuak tribe on the fifth day. Nowhere else in Africa have I seen such lovely black girls – especially striking were those whose fine facial features revealed a trace of Arabic blood. Their braided hair was oiled and adorned with red clay, which made it look like a wig. Unfortunately, we remained for only two hours, so that I could snap very few pictures. I would love to shoot a film there some day.

After a long drive, we approached the Buma Plateau, near the Ethiopian border, which, with its lush green hills and pleasant climate, looked something like Switzerland. This region, lying ten thousand feet above sea level, is one of the most beautiful areas in the Sudan, but the only safe way to reach it is by air. We remained several days. Unknown tribes still lived in the almost impenetrable green bush which outsiders could rarely enter. I often felt as if we were being watched, but I seldom laid eyes on the natives. Once, for a split second, I saw two black figures, adorned solely with plate-sized metal rings in their ears. Another time, I spotted a group decorated with white heron feathers, which looked like crowns on their heads, but it was impossible to photograph them because they were so timid.

On the way back, we spent a day in Pibor Post, the seat of the Murle tribe whose men are renowned as lion-hunters. The girls and women, who wore headgear consisting of blue beads, smoked huge water pipes like the men and were anything but timid; they were cheerful, enjoyed a good joke and let me photograph them as much as I liked.

In Bor, I said goodbye to the governor who had to return to Malakal. He advised me to wait for a vehicle convoy rather than take the Nile steamer to Juba. The next day, the trucks announced by the governor arrived but I was surprised that the brand-new vehicles had no passengers aside from the drivers. Later, I heard about the revolution that had erupted just a few months after my visit in southern Sudan and I realized that the trucks heading towards Juba must have been military vehicles. The governor's trip to the Ethiopian border had probably been a military reconnaissance mission which I had joined unwittingly.

I left Bor in one of the trucks. With a bit of luck, we hoped to make the last ferry, which would be leaving for Juba at 5 p.m. The road wasn't dry yet, and we often had to drive through deep puddles of water. When I saw three Dinka warriors – very tall, slender men with spears and the traditional, rarely seen wide bead belts – emerge from the bushes, I asked the driver to stop and reluctantly he did so. At the time, I didn't know about the tensions between the southern and the northern Sudanese, which triggered repeated uprisings in the south. All I could think of was the unique opportunity to photograph this unusual group and, clutching my Leica, I jumped out of the truck. Hesitantly, I walked towards the three Dinka, pausing just a few yards away from them; they paused too and when I pointed to my camera, they instantly understood. The tallest one came over to me and held out his open hand for money; I realized that many tourists passed by here on the Nile boat. I nodded in agreement, but somehow I felt uneasy. I did only a few shots and went back to the truck to get some money. Upon opening my bag, it struck me that I had no more money, only a cheque that I planned to cash in Juba. The Dinka watched me angrily, and, suddenly, one of them grabbed my bag out of my hand. I tried to collect everything that had fallen out, but I was surrounded by five or six Dinka instead of three, and more and more came charging out of the bushes. The Dinka rightfully felt cheated. They gesticulated vehemently and were assuming a menacing attitude with their spears when, in that moment of danger, my eyes alighted on a brass snuff box which I had bought in Malakal. The lid had a mirror inside it. I held the box high towards the sun, so that it shone like gold, and then hurled it over the heads of the Dinka into the grass. While they ran towards the box, my driver started the engine and by some miracle the truck made it out of the mud – luckily for us, because the Dinka raced after us for a long time, yelling loudly and brandishing their spears. The driver and I were scared to death, for if the truck had stalled, we would have suffered the revenge of the Dinka. That was the only time during my expedition that I was threatened by natives and the fault was mine.

Twilight came much too soon and we missed the ferry. It was night when we reached the Nile, and since few areas of the Sudan are as dreadfully afflicted by mosquitoes as the southern Nile, we spent an agonizing night.

JUBA

In the morning, we took the first ferry across the Nile, and the driver dropped me off at the hotel in Juba, which was decidedly primitive, with bedbugs in the mattress. My sole desire was to get out of there as fast as possible. But how? I had no car and almost no money. My return flight was valid only from Nairobi, which was hundreds of miles away. At the time, there was no train or bus connecting Juba and Nairobi. I had to find out whether the trucks might be able to take me, but before going into town, I wondered what to wear. Most of my clothes were torn or chewed by ants and were fit only to be thrown out. Luckily, I still had a skirt and a clean blouse.

My first stop was the post office where I picked up my post; at first I was hesitant about opening it because, after all, six months had passed since I'd left Munich. I took the plunge and heaved a sigh of relief; my mother was healthy, that was what I wanted to hear. She had also received my letters. Unfortunately, I had no word from Ulli, the secretary lent to me in Munich by my friend Harry Schulze-Wilde to help me with the preparation for my Sudan trip. This lack of news was unsettling, for he was supposed to have confirmed by telegram the receipt of my exposed films, which I had dispatched from Malakal. Every roll of film was numbered and he had solemnly promised me to report on their condition, listing every unsatisfactory exposure and lack of definition. Had the shaking of the trucks caused defects in the cameras or lenses, making some of the shots useless? A worrying thought!

At the hotel, I ran into Oscar Luz and the Nansen people, who, I thought, had reached Kenya long ago. We exchanged cool greetings, and they avoided saying a single word to me. It was an unpleasant surprise. But I also had the luck to meet a German woman, head nurse at the Juba hospital, who offered to put me up in her home, thereby rescuing me from the dreadful hotel. For the first time since leaving Khartoum, I slept in a real bed, used a real lavatory and sat down on a chair with a back. I particularly enjoyed the huge garden filled with flowering shrubs.

Once again, Rolf Engel, who was still with the Nansens, proved to be my guardian angel. To my surprise, he offered me a lift in his VW van as far as Nimule, a station on the border between the Sudan and Uganda. The next day, sitting next to Rolf in his van, I heard about the difficulties the Nansens had experienced with their film project among the Nuer. The millions of mosquitoes that afflict those swampy regions had made the work unbearable.

We reached the customs border by twilight and it was then the Nansens spotted me with Rolf Engel and were clearly displeased. When Rolf asked Luz to take me along to Kampala he got nowhere and only just managed to keep me from being tossed out of the convoy. When we arrived in Gulu, Uganda, I was dumped with my baggage on the road, where I found a local man willing to carry my belongings to the nearby hotel. There I discovered it was possible to reach Kampala, some distance away, by a bus used by the natives.

At sunrise, I went to the bus stop where a mob of people, all natives, was already waiting. They were mainly women and children carrying sacks, cartons, and such huge baskets of bananas, mangoes and chickens that I doubted whether I could make it aboard with my crates and haversack. Before the approaching bus could even stop, everyone charged towards it leaving me alone with my baggage; but the bus driver, a strong black man, saw my plight and came over, picked up my belongings and stowed them on the packed roof of the vehicle. Then he gently pushed me inside, where buxom African women took me into their midst. As the only white person on board, I occasioned rather a lot of giggling.

IN NAIROBI

Nairobi is the city of my dreams – the only place I could live forever. Its climate is pleasant all the year round – never too hot or too cold – there are gardens everywhere and African fauna abound at the very outskirts of the city. Furthermore, the Indian Ocean with its white sandy beaches is only a few hours away.

I was greatly tempted to stay a while and put off my departure. I wanted to photograph the Masai, being in their vicinity and not knowing if I would ever come back.

My desire was increased by an encounter with Prince Ernst von Isenburg, an elderly gentleman who had been living in East Africa for thirty years. He had lost his farm on Kilimanjaro and was now employed as a tour guide at the German Marco Polo Company. He spoke the languages of the Masai and other African tribes and was willing to introduce me to several Masai chieftains so that I might photograph them; indeed, he made me an offer I couldn't refuse. He would charge me fifty marks a day for his services as guide, driver, and cook, and for the use of his VW van – this would not include food and petrol. The reason for his modest fee was our mutual liking of the Masai; he had allowed them to pasture their herds on his farm in Tanganika and they were his friends from then on.

And yet I couldn't accept his offer for I had no money. What a predicament! Eventually, I decided to ask one of my prosperous friends for a loan and telegraphed Ady Vogel, the 'salt baron' and owner of Fuschl Castle, to send me three thousand marks. The sum arrived within a few short days and, ecstatic, I hugged my 'prince'. Now we could visit the Masai.

THE MASAI

When we left Nairobi towards the end of May 1963, the sky was overcast, the air rather cool. Before our departure, we had gone to the market and bought enough food for several weeks: enormous supplies of produce which we stuffed into every nook and cranny of our vehicle.

The prince was a lively companion and an excellent driver, but, alas, a dreadful cook. When he began to prepare our supper, it was obvious that he couldn't even peel a potato. I was even clumsier; so we decided to have a fruit salad.

Unfortunately, the weather became increasingly cold and unfriendly. Rain made the roads impassable, forcing us to take long rest periods, but I never got bored for Isenburg had endless stories about the Masai and described to me their military lifestyle. According to historical sources, they fought as an élite troop among the Egyptians four thousand years ago and became famous for their fearlessness and extraordinary courage. In ancient times, they were called the 'Mosai', and they remained invincible for millenia, until the start of our century when they were defeated by the modern weapons deployed by the British against them. Yet the Masai retained their pride and arrogance and refused to negotiate with the British military commanders once they learned that the highest authority in England was Queen Victoria. So, in London, at their insistence, the queen received a delegation of the most important Masai chieftains, and a peace treaty was signed there.

Remarkably enough, the Masai are the only African tribe to use no musical instruments, not even a drum. This is because their hard, military training does not allow for the emotions. From an early age, they have to pass the harshest ordeals of courage; they cannot show pain or back away if attacked by lions or other dangerous animals. In this they are the very opposite of the Nuba, and these extreme contrasts are also especially in evidence in the role of the girls and women in the respective tribes. The Nuba have great esteem for women – they can even choose their own spouses – but the Masai women are slaves to the men and have less value than a cow.

When I recall the funeral rites of the Nuba, then I can see how different they are from the Masai. If a Masai father, mother or other relative is dying, he or she is brought to a shady place and there remains until overtaken by death, with only a few calabashes of water and some food. The corpses are devoured by vultures; the remains are not even buried. This emotional coldness, barely comprehensible to us, is viewed by the Masai as part of their religion.

At last, the sun came out, and as the trails dried out very quickly, we soon arrived at our first destination, a Masai kraal in Loitokitok, southern Kenya, near the Tanganikan border. Before I could enter the kraal, Prince von Isenburg had a long palaver with the kraal elders, describing to them his entire family tree: he was related to every dynasty in Europe, all the way up to the British royal house, as well as to Franz Joseph, emperor of Austria and king of Hungary, who had died nearly fifty years earlier. Amazed and filled with awe, they allowed us to enter the kraal, and after a while I was also permitted to photograph them, but though their original restraint vanished, they never became as friendly as the Nuba.

Sometimes I was reduced to despair by their unpredictable ways – they would ignore a promise and often keep me waiting for hours on end – but they could also be disarmingly nice. They showed us how they made their shields, explaining what the designs meant, and even performed fights for us. Many of the young Masai, known as *morani*, had conspicuously fine, exotically beautiful features, almost like those of women. This feminine appearance, contrasting sharply with their virile qualities, was emphasized by their long, red-dyed hair which was skilfully twisted into braids, the tips of which wrapped in goat leather. A *morani's* training lasted nine years and each warrior possessed a spear and a shield. The British administration had outlawed their shields because these could lead to a fight, but they were still permitted to carry spears since a spear was a crucial weapon against wild beasts.

The British colonial officials had long since given up imprisoning Masai for stealing cattle because their love of freedom was so powerful that in gaol they went on hunger strike and starved to death. The British had devised a different penalty: the Masai thief was forced to hand over his favourite head of cattle. The harshness of this punishment can be understood only if one realizes what this means to the Masai who have a virtually magical relationship with their cattle, like the Hindus in India. A Masai's favourite cow is his supreme possession. One young Masai warrior, who had to endure such a sentence, was so desperate that during a public function, at which his cow was rebranded, he reached for his spear and killed the British official, knowing he would have to pay for this crime with his life.

Once, I lost my way when driving through the region and noticing two Masai with spears and shields on the horizon I headed towards them and asked for directions – foolishly enough, in English. To my surprise, one of them replied in faultless English.

'How is it you speak English so well?' I asked in amazement.

'I learned it at school.'

'What school?'

'In Nairobi, then in London.'

'What did you do in London?'

'I got my doctorate. I'm a teacher.'

I was speechless, for the man looked as if he had stepped straight out of the pages of an anthropological picture book.

'Why do you wear the traditional costume?'

He smiled. 'I like being a Masai.'

Not all Masai have the ability to preserve the old customs while integrating the new ones into their lives. At the conclusion of my three-month photo safari through the Masai territories of Kenya and Tanganika, I witnessed an unusual festival which takes place only once every five or six years. At this ceremony, adolescent boys who are to be consecrated as *morani* are circumcised, and the older ones, whose *morani* training is completed, have their plaits cut off. It is a love feast. For three days, young girls and *morani* danced, not to music, but to rhythmic chanting; a lot of mead was drunk, and the festival degenerated into a sexual orgy. We left before it ended but the things I had already seen and photographed were out of the ordinary and I had used up every last roll of film. Bemused by our experiences, we returned to Nairobi. There, I said goodbye to the prince, the most likable of all my travelling companions.

Before my flight, I spent several days in Malindi on the Indian Ocean where the wide, marvellous beach was deserted, I was the only guest at Lawfords Hotel, and the wonderful bay with its huge emerald waves, which always roll up regardless of the direction of the wind, was my exclusive property. Delighted by my experience of Africa, I threw myself into the surf. Forgotten were the harsh years; I felt reborn.

I typed up all that had happened on my small typewriter – and those pages became my most detailed journal. I also wrote reports on the stock, lighting and subjects of all my photos. I had exposed 210 rolls of film in my first job as a photographer.

BACK IN GERMANY

On 8 August 1963, I stood outside my flat on Tengstrasse in Munich where I'd said goodbye ten months earlier. My mother opened the door, and when she recognised me, she shrieked – not a shriek of joy but a shriek of horror.

'My baby, my baby, just look at you!' Tears were streaming down her cheeks.

'I'm fit as a fiddle, Mother darling, I wasn't ill once.'

'Poor Leni, I hardly know you.'

'My hair has been bleached and damaged by the sun,' I said, 'but that's not so awful, it'll recover.'

My mother was in despair. 'For God's sake, you're so skinny; you don't have any arms or legs; you look wretched.'

I didn't feel at all wretched. But after hearing my mother's reaction and looking into the mirror, I realized that the expedition had taken a lot out of me. What's more it wasn't easy to fatten up; no matter how much I devoured, I gained no weight. My body had grown so used to the meagre, fat-free diet that it could no longer absorb protein. It was only after months of injections that I regained my earlier weight.

However, my mother's distressed reaction was not the worst thing that awaited me. Cold shivers run up and down my spine whenever I recall the shock of learning what had happened to the photographs I had mailed back.

It was all because of Ulli. The young man had made a good impression on me: he was quiet, polite and extremely interested in anything to do with photography. He was supposed to inform me as quickly as possible about the technical quality of my shots but I had waited in vain for his report on my first package of exposed film and the wires I had sent him from Juba and Nairobi had gone unanswered. It was only shortly before my depature from Africa that I received an unclear and confused letter. Nevertheless, I knew that the films had arrived and my first question after greeting my mother was, 'Where are my films?'

My mother made an anxious face. 'I'm afraid you're going to have problems with Ulli.'

'What do you mean?' I asked in dismay.

'He has been acting so oddly and always given me such evasive answers.'

'Didn't he hand the films over to you?' I asked in a faltering voice.

'Only some of them,' said my mother, 'the first package, but not the second or third.'

I felt quite faint.

My mother hesitated. 'I found out that he got a job as photographer after you left, and that was why I could never get hold of him.'

My God, I thought, maybe he sold my photos to a photo agency. I was about to make enquiries when at last I heard from him and heaved a sigh of relief. The information he had for me, however, was devastating. The rolls of film he was in possession of were all blank, on clear celluloid. Tersely, he said, 'This could only be the fault of the African censors or customs officials – I didn't notify you because I didn't want to upset you.'

My grief was indescribable, but more than that the whole affair was incomprehensible. I had used up more than two hundred rolls of film, and only the first shipment that my mother had received was salvaged – a mere ninety rolls. I was unable to eat or sleep. How could it have happened? At last, something dawned on me and the implications were dire. Ulli had described shots that supposedly didn't exist. When I tried to get hold of him, he was nowhere to be found, having left Munich with no forwarding address. I submitted the destroyed rolls of film to the detective squad.

They examined them at a special department in Wiesbaden, and the matter was quickly cleared up: Ulli had had the first shipment developed and had then delivered the rolls to my mother. The second and third shipments contained my shots of the southern Sudan, of my trip through the Upper Nile Province and of the Masai. Before having them developed, Ulli had removed them from the capsules and the light had destroyed them. Next, one day before my return, he took them to Agfa, Perutz and Kodak for developing and to the surprise of the lab workers, all the rolls came out blank. After learning this, the police searched his apartment and, in a drawer, discovered four undeveloped rolls that he had forgotten. When these rolls were developed, they were flawless – which proved what had really happened. They are my only surviving shots of the Dinka, Anuak and Murle. I now recalled an incident that should have tipped me off. Shortly before leaving Munich, I received a call from the police: 'Is there an Ulli E. in your employ?'

'Only part time.'

'Did you give him some Kodak colour film?'

'Yes,' I said, surprised at this question.

'I see,' said the police official, 'then the case is clear.' He was about to sign off, but then asked, 'How many rolls did you give him?'

'Ten.'

The policeman repeated, 'Ten? But just this morning, your employee sold thirty rolls of Kodak film to a photo store in Solln.'

This telephone call took place literally minutes before I left for the airport, and there was nothing I could do. In the end, I didn't make a tragedy out of it. I excused the young man – the temptation had been too great for him. But then I should no longer have trusted him; that was my big mistake.

I began to look at my material. The Nuba shots were safe and sound, thank goodness. I viewed them night after night and began to sort them. In so doing, I felt homesick for my Nuba, so much so that everything else seemed unimportant. But how was I to visit them again, given my lack of funds? Friends, who were impressed by the photographs, advised me to give lectures.

Soon I suffered another shock; my friend Frau Sandner, who had been kind enough to take care of my business affairs during my absence, notified me that the West German Network had stopped payment for their use of excerpts from my *Olympia*. They claimed they had been informed by the Federal German Archive in Koblenz that the films were owned not by me, but exclusively by the 'German Reich', and that film rights belonging to the former 'German Reich' were administered by Transit Film.

That was completely absurd – and just at that moment, it spelled catastrophe for me for I desperately needed the seven thousand marks that the Network owed me. What kind of people were they to be denying my ownership of *Olympia* after thirty years! I was forced to hand the matter over to my lawyer and, luckily, he was able to clear it up and thereby avert a disaster. My two former assistants, Waldi Traut and Walter Grosskopf, as well as Herr Dolöchter, the tax consultant of my firm, and Dr Schwerin, my corporation lawyer, who were all still alive, had worked out the contracts with the Ministry of Propaganda. My lawyer demonstrated that the documents cited by the West German Archive and Transit Film were incomplete and proved that our agreement had been purely a matter of form for tax reasons. This was confirmed by Dr Max Winkler, the former trustee of the entire motion picture output of the 'German Reich', and by other ex-members of the Ministry of Propaganda.

Nevertheless, the case dragged on for months and my situation grew more and more critical. My only income – the fees from the various German TV companies – was blocked. My financial problems were acute. To put an end to my predicament and avoid going to court, Dr Weber advised me to agree to a compromise: Transit Film was to receive thirty per cent of all income from *Olympia* throughout my lifetime, and one hundred per cent after my death.

After the war, I had fought for years, with no support from any German agencies, to get back the confiscated original negatives of *Olympia* in Paris. Then, I had laboured for months restoring them, and had spent thousands of marks saving this valuable material. And now I was forced to submit to this compromise. In effect, I was told: Take it or leave it.

I wanted to keep living and to keep working. My friends were enthralled by my Nuba pictures, so I offered them to *Stern*, *Bunte Illustrierte* and *Quick*; but they were turned down by all the editors, including Henri Nannen. The only interest was shown by Axel Springer's Hamburg-based magazine *Kristall*, which had a smaller circulation, but was a very sound periodical. Its editors were so bowled over by my photographs that they not only paid me an advance but they also bought the rights for two title series and for a three-part series for the third and fourth quarter of 1964. It wasn't until years later that my Nuba photos were also published by *Quick* and *Bunte Illustrierte*.

My first slide lecture on the Nuba took place in a small church in Tutzing and was organized by Helge Pawlinin, who lived in that town. I was slightly nervous about how the pastor would feel about the shots of naked people, but he reacted just like all the other spectators by whom I was bombarded with questions. After that 'dress rehearsal', I lectured in a number of cities, always with the same success and, surprisingly, with favourable press reviews. This intensified my desire to go back to the Nuba, and so, in order to earn some money for my trip, I accepted the offer of the Olympia publishing house to work as a photo reporter at the coming Winter Olympics in Innsbruck. Despite my difficulties in carrying out this assignment (the Austrian Olympic Committee refused to give the publisher a press pass for me, so I could photograph only as a spectator), I managed to get a number of good shots. I put by every mark I earned, saving up for my next Sudan expedition. I wanted to make a film about the Nuba.

A NEW EXPEDITION

More than anyone else it was Dr Arnold who gave me the confidence I needed when he offered to equip me fully, without any prior payment. The

Schuster Sports House was willing to give me certain things for the expedition too. But what I needed most was vehicles. During my last Sudan trip, I had learned what it meant not to have a car in Africa. The most suitable vehicle would be a Unimog, a Landrover, or a Toyota, each of which had four-wheel drive; but I couldn't afford any of them. The next best thing would be two VW vans, especially equipped for sandy areas. I approached Professor Nordhoff, even though he had turned me down for *Black Freight*, and this time I had more luck. The VW plant in Wolfburg agreed to help me out: they provided two new VW vans, one fitted out as a living space, the other equipped with freezers for my film material, which could also be used as benches. They lent me one car, and sold me the other at cost. My Japanese friends gave me the money having sold some of my photos in Japan. However, this came nowhere near covering the rest of my budget: for instance, the shipment of the vehicles to the Sudan, the high insurance premiums, my travel expenses, and all the other costs which might arise.

In the midst of my preparations, Carl Müller invited me to his Studio for Film Art in Bremen, where he planned to open his annual Film Art Days with a Leni Riefenstahl Week. This was courageous of him, considering the media image of me as a worshipper of Hitler was still fed to the public year in, year out. Müller hoped to support my expedition with the income from his Leni Riefenstahl Week, which would include every film I had ever appeared in or directed except *Triumph of the Will*.

The festival was as successful there as in Nuremberg. The screenings were sold out and the press was good. At last, nineteen years after the end of the war, I again experienced a few happy days in my profession. But hope for me has always been followed by setbacks. The North German News network ran an item which showed reporters standing outside the cinema in Bremen, interviewing the people who wanted to see my films and asking them whether they felt it was right that 'Riefenstahl's' films were being screened again. In between the answers and reactions, most of which were favourable with regard to me, they showed, without comment, footage of concentration camps. *Die Zeit* also published a vicious and untrue story, which was nothing less than character assassination, and the author must have known he was libelling me for he had previously visited my lawyer and consulted the court documents. Such people were not interested in the truth; they wanted to defame me and to keep me from practising my profession – indeed, to achieve this sublime goal, certain people were willing to use any methods. It was so easy for them for they had money, influence and power.

I felt very sorry for Carl Müller who, delighted at the success of the festival, had written to me prior to the telecast: 'Never before have so many

film-goers come up to me. The spectators kept shaking my hand gratefully.'
He then wrote to his lawyer with regard to the smear campaign:

> The Hamburg TV network has insidiously deceived me. When I was
> interviewed, they led me to believe that the broadcast would be a positive
> one. The thrust of the attacks by the Network and *Die Zeit* is such that
> millions of viewers and readers must believe that Leni Riefenstahl was a
> Nazi criminal and that I am now her henchman.

He, like everyone else who tried to help me, was attacked for doing so.

During this period, my mother's life was nearing its end and though she
fought with great willpower against her illness and desperately resisted
death, I was powerless to help her.

A BIZARRE ENCOUNTER

The preparations for my trip had ground to a halt. I had been waiting for my
Sudanese visa for months and months, while for my last expedition, I had
obtained one right away. Nor had I received a Sudanese permit for the entry
of my two VW vans. Exhausted, my nerves were in tatters, I gratefully
accepted an invitation from Consul Ady Vogel and his wife Winnie Markus
to spend a holiday at their villa. I was almost entirely alone at the Cala
Tarida on Ibiza for the Vogels weren't there and the only people in the house
were their young daughter Diana, the maid, and two friends – a married
couple. I encountered very few people on the beach and the peace and quiet
were balm for my nerves.

One day, I noticed a stylishly dressed woman bathing with her two
children and their nanny. She was an American, as I discovered when I met
her a short time later. To my surprise, she asked me whether I knew the film
director Leni Riefenstahl. I looked sharply at her, and not caring to reveal
my identity, casually remarked that although we weren't personally
acquainted, I was familiar with her films. The woman reacted to this
enthusiastically, saying, 'My husband is a film director and scholar who
teaches at Harvard as head of the film department there. We saw
documentaries made by Frau Riefenstahl before we came here and were so
enthusiastic that we saw them several times over. My husband would love to
meet Frau Riefenstahl because he works in a similar way. He's in Munich
now, trying to meet her.'

I was amused, but held my tongue until she began to describe certain scenes from my films and I could no longer hold back. I said, 'Look, I am Leni.' At first, she wouldn't beleive me and even seemed annoyed, but when I laughed and said, 'I really am Leni – you didn't know?' she hugged me.

Two days later, she introduced me to her husband, Robert Gardner, who had so recently rung my doorbell in Munich to no avail. A man in his mid-thirties, very open like most Americans, he instantly asked me to call him Bob and told me about his work. He had made a film about the Bushmen in southwestern Africa and another film in New Guinea during the past two years; both films had won prizes. I was surprised when he told me he wanted to make a film in the southern Sudan; naturally, he was very interested in my experiences there. He simply couldn't understand why I was unable to obtain financial backing in Germany.

'Come to America,' he said, 'everything is a lot simpler there. You have to make a film about the Nuba, even if its only in 16 mm.'

I smiled in resignation.

'Come and visit us in Boston,' he said coaxingly, 'we have a lovely home, and you can stay as long as you like. We'll support you.'

My head swam. I knew I had to seize this opportunity, but how could I? The VWs were scheduled to arrive at the docks of Genoa in just a few weeks, and I had already taken the precaution of making reservations for the vans and the drivers on the Sternfels. I still lacked the money, the visas and the entry permit for the vehicles, but I had managed to hire the drivers – two young men who were willing to work without fees or allowances.

I had to find a way of taking up the Gardners' invitation. Before leaving the island, I promised to visit them in Boston.

EXCITING DAYS IN THE UNITED STATES

The days leading up to my departure for America were very difficult. Whenever I called up the Sudanese embassy in Bad Godesberg, I was told; 'No visa has arrived. Nor has Khartoum responded to any of our telegrams.' Oddly enough, my two young drivers, a zoologist and an electrician, had received their visas within a week. The embassy people told me that it took longer for artists.

On the plane to America, my head ached: what kind of adventure had I embarked on this time? My New York friends Albert and Joe (the cat-lover) had paid for my ticket and I had also received an invitation from *National Geographic Magazine* whose editors wished to see my Nuba photographs. Finally, James Card had asked me to come to Rochester, New York, to visit the George Eastman House; Kodak had bought prints of mine for its museum.

First I wanted to visit the Gardners. Would they still be the same as in Ibiza? When Lee Gardner called for me in Boston, she was just as enchanting. We drove to their home in Brookline, near Cambridge, and I was given a beautiful apartment overlooking the large park in which the house was set, the trees enchanting in their colourful autumn splendour.

The very next day, I showed my Nuba slides to a group of scholars and teachers at Harvard University and the response was overwhelming. I would have to have stayed on for weeks to have time to accept all the invitations, but I had to visit Rochester. While Gardner was busy trying to obtain funds for the Nuba film, I was welcomed in Rochester as cordially as I had been welcomed at Harvard. James Card, an American film historian, who was a passionate admirer of my films, was the initiator. I owe him a great deal. When I faced the executives gathered at Kodak House in order to see my Nuba slides, I was apprehensive. Nearly all these people were photo specialists, and I felt that I was anything but an expert. I had a queasy sensation in my stomach, but the reaction to the slide show was the same as it had been at Harvard. The viewers, who had been very aloof and only moderately interested, were now converted. They shook my hands enthusiastically and, at the house in which Kodak was born – now a splendid museum – they agreed to screen all my films in the near future.

Gardner's efforts were also successful. The project had been optioned in New York by the American film producer Milton Fruchtman, head of Odyssey Productions. Our contract stipulated that Odyssey would have world rights to the Nuba film, put up 60,000 marks for the shooting in the Sudan, and, after the end of the location work, pay the entire costs of completing the film. The profits were to be split down the middle. It was a rare stroke of luck.

The *National Geographic Magazine* in Washington DC was also interested in my photographs; and here too, my success was surprising. The highly sophisticated members of the editorial staff were so enthusiastic about my work that they arranged a second slide show for the directors of the National Geographic Society. Mr Barry Bishop, who participated in many valuable motion pictures produced by this world-famous institute, was fascinated by my Nuba pictures. He considered having the planned film made on assignment by the Society, which would have been the ideal solution but the shortage of time was an almost insoluble problem. The Society cannot finance a film without the cooperation of a renowned scholar.

Meanwhile, *National Geographic* had decided to buy the Nuba photos and I was so ecstatic I could hardly take in the news. The contract was to be signed at the publishing offices at 5 p.m., and I was to meet the editorial staff and major figures in the Society. Before I could leave my hotel, however, I received a telegram from Munich which, citing no reasons, informed me that my application for a visa for the Sudan had been turned down. The blood rushed to my head and I had to hold on to the staircast bannister. Without my visa, the expedition and the Nuba film were doomed. Then it dawned on me that I might be able to obtain my visa at the Sudanese embassy in Washington. Come what may, I had to make an attempt. My plane was leaving for New York that evening, and from there I was scheduled to fly to Munich the next day.

It was now ten minutes to five. What should I do? The embassy was closing at five, and I was expected at that very same time by the *National Geographic* and the members of the Society. I dashed up to my hotel room, grabbed the Sudanese documents from my case and jumped into a cab. I arrived at the magazine offices several minutes late, completely distraught, and tried to explain what had happened. I told the men who had gathered there that I had to rush over to the Sudanese embassy immediately in order to get my visa. There was an icy silence and I saw that these people were offended. A few began whispering together, obviously discussing me, and I couldn't stand the tension. At length, I was told that unfortunately they couldn't wait, and I knew that I had ruined a unique chance. I was desperate, but what could I do? They politely put a car at my disposal, and a few minutes later I stood outside the Sudanese embassy.

It was already past five and the offices were closed. How awful that I was unable to sign the contract at the Society, and I had also arrived here too late. The embassy was inside a garden; hurrying around the building and peering through the windows, I could see the interior was deserted. In a fit of utter despair, I began wildly banging on the door. Unexpectedly, a shadow appeared behind the glass panes and the door was opened a crack.

'I want to speak to the ambassador,' I told him.

The man, who had a dark face, said that the embassy was closed and that I should come back tomorrow.

'Impossible,' I said, 'I can't, I have to see the ambassador.' The man, an Arab, tried to shut the door but I had wedged my foot in it.

He stared at me in complete astonishment and said, 'I am the ambassador.'

I detected a glimmer of hope. I looked at him, desperate and pleading, and said, 'Please let me in, just give me five minutes.'

He let me in and took me up to an office where he asked me what it was I wanted. I told him about the telegram and the serious consequences if I didn't get a visa. I explained that I had to fly to New York today and to Germany tomorrow.

Politely but firmly, he said, 'Madame, what do you think I can do? You are applying for a visa. It takes at least five days – and that is cutting it rather fine.'

Weeping, I begged. 'Please make an exception.'

Luckily, I had brought along my Sudanese filming and photographing permits from the previous year, as well as the letters of recommendation from the police chief of Kordofan, and letters from and photos of members of the Sudanese government. These documents made the impossible possible and I had my visa within thirty minutes. The price was high for I had lost my chance to see my pictures in the *National Geographic*. I had been in such a rush, and my English was so inadequate, that they had failed to understand why I ran away. They never forgave me.

BEFORE THE START

Sitting on the plane, I was overwhelmed with fatigue. What would have happened if I hadn't obtained the visa at the very last moment? It was only my passionate wish to see the Nuba again that had worked a miracle. But the price was exorbitant. I had been so close to making a great film, and not just going on a photo expedition. Would Robert Gardner manage to sign the contract with Odyssey Productions and transfer the money to me in time? My head was spinning.

The hardest thing that lay ahead of me was my separation from my mother. She was already eighty-four, and her health was steadily deteriorating. Should I leave her alone? She wanted me to. Infinitely selfless, she had only one desire: to see me happy.

In Munich, I still had twelve days' time. The vans were supposed to start for Genoa by late October but first, some attachments had to be installed and additional equipment obtained – you couldn't find screws in the Bush. Then came the vaccinations, the hospital and accident insurance, the bilingual customs declarations, and finally all kinds of food. One of the drivers, Walter, an electrician, had to be trained as a camera assistant; he also had to take a course at the VW branch so that he could tackle any problem with the vehicles. I spent every free moment at Arri, where Dr. Arnold put together the film gear: optics, filters, tripods and diaphragms.

The money hadn't yet been transferred from New York, so I had no choice but to buy on credit. Shortly before the departure of the vans, I held the telegram – my salvation – in my hands: 'Contract signed, 10,000 dollars *en route*, letter follows. Gardner.'

My joy lasted only a few hours. To my great dismay a second telegram informed me that Hölscher, my cameraman from *Black Freight*, was bowing out having caught jaundice in Indonesia. Hölscher was the most important member of my crew, and there was no prospect of finding a replacement in the brief time we had. I would have to send for a cameraman later on.

During that difficult period, I met a young man to whom I owe a great deal and with whom I have been friends ever since. Uli Sommerlath, a young medical student, devoted every free moment to helping our expedition. He did all sorts of chores for us and soon proved indispensable to me and to my crew.

The two young drivers had to start off without me for I had too much to take care of; above all, I had to find a cameraman. I would fly on later and rendezvous with them in Khartoum.

On 25 October 1964, the expedition set off. From my sixth-floor window on Tengstrasse, I kept looking down into the courtyard, where the final crates were being loaded into the vans. We went downstairs when it was time to say goodbye, and I hugged the two young men. They drove out of the courtyard in pouring rain and we gazed after them until we could no longer see them.

Exhausted, Uli and I returned to my apartment to relax over a glass of wine, happy we had made it. Then the radio announced a bulletin about the Sudan. A revolution had broken out in the Sudan, the entire government had been toppled and all its members arrested. What a dreadful turn of events. Those men were my friends and acquaintances, and I had been counting on their help. Uli too was devastated by the news.

Under these circumstances, the project looked hopeless. I knew what the Sudan was like. A trip to the closed districts was extremely difficult even in normal times. Cancel everything, stop the vans! That was my first thought. What would happen if the VWs were set on fire and the drivers arrested. The risk was too great. On the other hand, we couldn't wait for the disturbances to end. Ships were booked up for months in advance.

Uli immediately tried to reach the embassy but no one answered the phone. When I telephoned Sudanese friends and acquaintances in Germany, nobody could tell me anything. We rang up the airport and I learned that all flights to Khartoum were cancelled. Uli tried to get some hard facts from press agencies, but they knew as little as we did; there was no way to reach the Sudan by telephone. It was soon obvious that there was no information.

No one knew the scope of the disturbances and no one could tell if there was any possibility of getting to the Sudan.

By now, our vans were probably beyond the Brenner. Should I stop them or let them go on? We telephoned the captain of our ship in Genoa. In case he couldn't dock in the Sudan, could he possibly bring back our two men? He said no, that the return trip was booked solid. If the revolution hadn't been quelled by the time the boat arrived at Port Sudan, then the vans couldn't be unloaded; there was too great a danger that the vans and the equipment could be confiscated and lost. In that case, the skipper suggested, he would take the vans and the two men along to the next port after Massawa; but he could not carry them any farther.

In Genoa, Walter and Dieter learned about the revolution and both of them were willing to take a chance. I wavered – for many hours.

Calls kept buzzing back and forth. When the final moment came, and my two drivers were nervously and impatiently badgering me for a decision, I took a deep breath and murmured, 'Go on and good luck! I hope we'll see each other in Khartoum.'

REVOLUTION IN THE SUDAN

The turmoil in the Sudan raged on for almost three weeks while my drivers were still on the high seas. Not until mid-November was I able to fly to Khartoum on a plane from London, and it was very eerie sitting in that gigantic empty aircraft with only six other passengers. When we landed in Khartoum at the crack of dawn, only a few people were waiting at the barrier. I showed my visa and found myself outside the airport staring at a ghostly tableau. Overturned, burning cars lay everywhere – all along the road. It was a miracle that any taxis were available but I found one. Since there are no street names or house numbers in Khartoum, one has to know one's way about. After driving through a labyrinth of empty streets and countless burned-out areas, we finally found the house in which my German friends were waiting for me and I learned at first hand what had happened. The governors of all the provinces were in various prisons – not in Khartoum, but some six hundred miles to the west, near Dafur.

Apparently, it had begun quite harmlessly. Several students had demonstrated at the University of Khartoum, demanding that south Sudanese have the same right to study there as north Sudanese. The students were also protesting against alleged corruption in the building of the Aswan Dam. According to an agreement between the Sudan and Nasser's Egypt, a portion of the Sudan near Wadi Halfa was to be put under water, which would mean flooding several villages and towns. Rumour had it that some of the money that Egypt had paid as an indemnity to the Sudan had been embezzled by members of the Sudanese government. Rumour or fact – who could say? In any event, within a few days, the initially small demonstrations had blazed up into a huge conflagration, costing hundreds of lives.

General Abul was named the new head of government, and he seemed to be gaining control of the situation, but street battles kept flaring up in the vicinity of the home of the Weistroffers, my German friends.

I thought of Abu Bakr, my best Sudanese friend, to whom I owed, above all, my access to the Nuba. He had served as a colonel in the African campaign, taking part in the battles against Rommel, whom he greatly respected. Calling a cab, I set out to look for him and drove straight to his ministry. The building was empty but the doors were open. I went from room to room – no one was about. I walked down a long corridor and at the end found a closed door. When I opened the door, I couldn't believe my eyes; behind a desk sat Ahmed Abu Bakr. He had not been imprisoned, he was free, he was here. We hugged, and there were tears in our eyes.

'Ahmed,' I said after a few moments, 'I thought I'd have to visit you in jail, and now I find you here. What luck!'

Abu Bakr, a Sudanese, displayed a degree of calm rarely found in a European; he was composed even in the most difficult predicaments, and now, utterly relaxed, he listened to my experiences of the turbulent past few weeks. Then he smiled, 'Leni, you are a very brave girl.' When I asked him whether I had any chance of travelling back to my Nuba, he said I had to be patient and wait to see the developments. Happy and hopeful, I drove back to the home of my friends where, at last, I had time to relax a bit. The splendid climate did me good for it wasn't too hot at this time of year. The radiant blue sky, the beautiful garden, the generous hospitality – I enjoyed it all thoroughly.

The idyllic atmosphere was deceptive, however. The revolution hadn't yet ended; street fights kept recurring, and more lives were lost.

At last, news came from Port Sudan that the ship had docked, and my people telephoned me. Port Sudan is about five hundred and fifty miles from Khartoum; the road connecting them is a difficult one and can be negotiated only in a convoy. To spare the VWs, they shipped them by rail. On St Nicholas's Eve, I greeted Walter and Dieter at the station. The vans were intact, and the Weistroffers were happy to put my drivers up. The VWs were parked in their garden.

The fighting flared up over and over again and no one was allowed to travel south as the disturbances were said to be more violent down there. Navigation from Malakal to Juba was cancelled for months but, despite this tension, Abu Bakr had obtained my permits for filming and photographing in the Nuba Hills plus the driving permit for our VWs and the extension of our visas. Now we impatiently waited for the end of the uprising, but, after a period of uncertain calm, another storm erupted, changing the situation overnight. This time the fighting demolished the airport, which then had to be shut down, and for the first time, Europeans were killed or wounded. The hospitals were jammed and foreigners prepared to leave. My host and hostess also assumed that they would have to go.

In this apocalyptic atmosphere, I had my first serious conflict with my two companions. Despite our host's warnings and my explicit ban, they drove both VWs into town in order to pick up the post, although they knew there was still fighting in the city. Hours later, when they still hadn't returned and it was already growing dark, we feared the worst. When they finally arrived back very late at night and I confronted them, they arrogantly retorted that I had no say in the matter; they knew what to do on their own. This was a disagreeable surprise and I should have fired them on the spot. When I hinted as much, they said, 'We'd rather go home today than tomorrow.' Were these the same nice young men who had helped me so much in Munich, who had been so enthusiastic about coming? What had caused this change? The Wiestroffers advised me to get rid of them, but how would I manage to replace them quickly? My desire to get to the Nuba as soon as possible made me blind and careless. I hoped that this incident was merely an isolated one.

Our forced vacation in Khartoum also had its positive side. Uli could send me all sorts of things that hadn't arrived before our departure. He wanted to carry out my every last wish. I had asked him to find a tenant for my apartment, take care of my mother, discuss ongoing litigation with my lawyer, and keep me informed about all important correspondence. He was also empowered to administer the funds arriving from the United States in order to pay my numerous outstanding bills.

In mid-December, the Sudan quietened down. There was no more gunfire, the telephone system worked again, and Dieter and Walter behaved more civilly. We decided to risk the trip. Fortunately, a package from Rochester came just in time: it was the film stock that I had ordered from Robert Gardner; now all we lacked was a cameraman. Then Abu Bakr had an idea; he introduced me to a Sudanese cameraman. Thus, after countless apparently insuperable hindrances, my wish appeared to be coming true: I would be making a film about the Nuba.

BACK TO TADORO

It was one week before Christmas, the very day on which I had spent my first night here two years earlier. Again I lay under the huge, shady tree, but this time with my own two vehicles and with good equipment. It was only gradually dawning on me that I was really here. The Nuba greeted me – if it were possible – even more exuberantly than last time, and everything looked the same. Again the children gathered around my bed in the morning looking even more cheerful and the boys ran to the *seribe* to tell the wrestlers that I was back. The first ones came within a few hours: Natu, Tukami, Gumba, they all beamed when they saw me, and they brought me presents: bowls of sesame and peanuts. Nothing of the disturbances in the Sudan had penetrated to the Nuba, and there was no discontent here, no theft, no murder. The Nuba seemed the happiest people created by the Good Lord. Laughing was, without doubt, their favourite occupation.

I had gifts for them too: tobacco and beads, as well as sugar, tea, and even green coffee beans, which they roasted and stamped into grounds. They sometimes traded with them with the Arabs. A sip of black coffee with lots of sugar was a supreme delight for the Nuba. Within a short time, they had built us two huts, one for me, the other for our crates. The two young men preferred sleeping in a tent so long as the weather wasn't too hot. I had hung up the new Nuba photos in my small hut and a small picture of my mother over my bed. Curious, they gazed at the photo for a long time and when they noticed the tears in my eyes they were taken aback, and asked: 'Angeniba bige?' (Is your mother ill?) I nodded and sensed that, in marked contrast to my companions who knew my mother and knew what she meant to me, the Nuba truly sympathized with me. They shook my hand and left the hut.

From day to day, the season grew hotter until the thermometer showed 110 degrees in the shade. The Nuba dug a deep hole, in which we could store the celluloid at a temperature of eighty degrees and shut out the light with double layers of dura stalks and foliage.

I was worried by the lack of interest shown by my two companions and by their apparent indifference to the Nuba. I asked them to pick up the post in Kadugli and when they returned that same evening, they handed me a letter. I recognized Uli's handwriting and, to my dismay, read that my mother had been taken to the university hospital because of a blocked artery in the back of her knee.

'Try to keep calm,' Uli wrote. 'In case the worst happens, please send me the appropriate powers of attorney.'

Now there was no stopping me. I couldn't overcome my agony of mind and decided to interrupt my work immediately. That night, after drawing up a work plan for my crew, I packed my things. I had no idea how long I would be gone. All I knew was that I would remain with my mother until she was completely out of danger. I left Tadoro at dawn. My companions drove me to Kadugli. It was 18 January 1965, a day that I will never forget; when we paused at the post office, I was handed a telegram which read: 'Mother died last night, await letter. Uli.'

I collapsed. I could not envisage a life without my mother. How could I come to terms with the fact that the telegram had been lying at the post office for four days and that Mother had died on 14 January. Friends had done everything to surround her with love until her final breath, but how awful that I was unable to be with her in her last hours. I had to see her one last time, even if she was dead.

I didn't arrive in Munich until four days later. Uli collected me at the airport but I was two days too late. My mother was already buried. This experience had a deep effect on the further course of my life. My only possibility of escaping sorrow, I felt, was to return to the Nuba Hills as soon as possible, do my job, save the film – and, if possible, take back with me a cameraman, since the Sudanese man could only work for a short time. Heinz Hölscher had recommended Gerhard Fromm, a young assistant cameraman who happened to be available. With Abu Bakr's help, he could enter Khartoum without a visa.

Within a week, he and I were standing on the platform of the small railway station at Semeih having arrived there after many difficulties. In Khartoum, we had found no vehicle to drive us all the way to the Nuba Hills, so we had had to take the excursion train, which kept stopping *en route* so that the trip dragged on for thirty hours. Exhausted, we stood on the small platform where not a single human being was to be seen. As far as the eye could see, there was nothing but tracks and sand, although I had telegraphed my men that we were coming. Perhaps the van had stalled on the sandy trail.

We were in a dangerous predicament. Our camp was sixty miles from Semeih and there was no link by rail or bus – just an occasional truck driving to Kadugli. Apart from the station, there are only two or three houses for the railway employees plus a tiny hotel; nothing else. We had no choice but to go to the hotel and wait until a truck happened to drive by.

Again we were helped by a stroke of luck. A droll Englishman, who had something to do with agriculture, lived in the hotel. This man advised us to go to a cotton warehouse and check whether a truck might be standing there. And indeed, a truck happened to be there picking up parts for a car that had broken down on the road. We were delighted that the driver agreed to take us along with him and was also willing, for a handsome fee, to drop me and Gerhard Fromm off in Tadoro.

We arrived at our camp late that evening to find the two men already asleep. When we woke them up, they were far from happy about my speedy return. They grumpily gave me mattresses and blankets for Fromm and the driver, who was staying with us for the night. The two young men had never once driven to the Kadugli post office to find out when I was coming back and so they hadn't received my cable. I now realized how little I could expect from them.

The Nuba were astonished to see me the next morning and their first question was about my mother. When I told them, 'Ageniba peno' (my mother has died), they took me in their arms and wept with me – among them Nuba women I had never seen before. I was deeply moved by the way these people could commiserate with a perfect stranger and it helped me to cope with my grief.

THE NUBA FILM

It was already early February, and my two young men wanted to get home by mid-March at the very latest; we had only six weeks left for our filming. We had to utilize every single minute but our work was hindered by the heat, which grew worse with every passing day.

Our locations were often far away from camp, and if they were beyond the reach of our vans, we had to walk for miles. These strenuous outings were not always successful, but more often the footage we obtained made it all worthwhile. I especially recall a ceremony that the Nuba had already told me about: an adolescent initiation.

A distant drumming had lured us towards a hut inside which we found a snow-white figure illuminated by a ray of sunshine. The figure looked like a statue, not a person of flesh and blood, and the atmosphere was mystical. The Nuba had barely noticed our arrival so spellbound were they by the ritual. They were so mesmerized that, with care, I could photograph the boy at close range. Gerhard Fromm, just as cautiously, set up his tripod and managed to film the scene. Camera moments such as these are few and far between. This ceremony was the most impressive experience I ever had among the Nuba.

We had to hurry in order to get our shots of the harvest. There hadn't been such a bountiful crop in years, which made the Nuba very happy. We couldn't understand why they didn't put aside the excess; unlike many primitive tribes, they consumed everything they reaped, even when they had more than enough. They would use it for their tribal celebrations, even though they knew from experience that bad harvests spelled hunger and even starvation. It would have been child's play to set up rain-proof warehouses in the steep cliffs. When I asked them why they didn't, they merely laughed, saying they were doing what they had always done.

Another problem was water, which was vital to them. The drought, which begins in March, causes a shortage of water. The only well runs dry, and so do the few water holes they have. The Nuba then have to hike for hours to glean tiny amounts of water from puddles. The animals also are parched and waste away to skin and bone. Once the rains come pouring down from late May or early June until October, so much water descends from the sky that the Nuba would never suffer any shortage if they could only store the downpour in containers like most Mediterranean peoples do. This would require raw materials such as cement or certain kinds of thin sheeting, and these, the Nuba do not possess. For years, I tried to help them in this matter. I conferred with well builders, hydraulics engineers and even dowsers, listening to all kinds of suggestions from experts. I kept hoping I could raise the money to help the Nuba store water for the dry spells; but it was no use.

Healthy as the Nuba looked, appearances were deceptive. Many were sick; that was why I had brought with me lots of medicine and bandages. Their most frequent complaints were pneumonia, bronchitis, which could be halted with antibiotics, and the skin sores they got from running barefoot over stones and thorns. Their soles were as thick as elephant hide. Once, when a huge thorn got caught in my sole, and I barely managed to prise off my shoe, a painful splinter remained in my foot. One of my Nuba friends produced a pair of iron tweezers from a sort of knife attached to his arm and skilfully removed my splinter; it was only then I discovered that every Nuba owned such an implement.

Unfortunately, the mood in our camp greatly deteriorated as time went by. The two young men followed my instructions only very reluctantly and though Gerhard Fromm tried to mediate he usually met with no success. Luckily, he was always in a good mood, no job was too much for him.

We had agreed to get up at sunrise every day but they often overslept, and I was embarrassed at having to wake them up. They were abashed, but they behaved as though they were not, often threatening to walk out immediately. I was at their mercy. One morning, there was a particularly unpleasant incident. I had made myself a cup of coffee in my hut while the two young men were still asleep – or so I thought. Without warning, Walter, the electrician, suddenly stood before me, shouting furiously, 'I forbid you to take a cup and spoon, or any sugar and coffee. You don't get any special privileges. We don't drink coffee in our tent.' I recorded his statements verbatim in my diary.

Yet Walter was basically good-natured, and at times he seemed to regret his behaviour. I assumed that he and Dieter were affected by the heat. Once Dieter flew into such a rage that he charged me with his fists because I had reproached him for shooting a Nuba dog. We had all been wrenched out of sleep by the shot and the howling of the dog, and when the Nuba ran up they were very upset at finding the animal dead. If I hadn't calmed them down, the outcome might have been serious. Dieter defended himself, saying that the dog had eaten some of his stuffed bats (which may have been true), but he was obviously trigger-happy. He always took a gun out on our drives, lowering the windscreen in order to be ready to fire. Not wanting to anger him, I soon gave up my protests; as the driver of the second van, he was indispensable.

We still lacked important footage of the wrestling festivals, especially of the final match, mainly because it was extremely difficult to get the camera close enough to the wrestlers, who were blocked off by the Nuba surrounding them. Several cameramen would have been needed to capture all the aspects of such a festival: the faces of the spectators, the wrestlers, the champions, the warbling women and dancing girls – and above all, the fighters themselves.

I was very unlucky at one such festival when, trying to film two wrestlers, I came too close. As I peered through the viewfinder, both of them plunged on top of me and my Leica, and I lay under them with a stabbing pain in my chest. My Nuba weren't angry, they laughed, hoisted me up to their shoulders, and carried me out of the ring. Then they went back to their wrestling. The pain grew worse and that night I could barely sleep. The next day, I had no choice but to go to the small hospital in Kadugli; two of my ribs were broken and I returned to Tadoro all bandaged up.

In order to keep to our schedule, we embarked on a race against time. We already had a lot of footage, but we still needed shots of a funeral celebration and of the *seribe*. Through our friend Natu, we obtained permission to film inside a *seribe*. He shared this shepherds' camp with Tukami, who like himself, feared no opponent, and with Gua and Naju, two boys of perhaps seventeen. The scenario was almost biblical, and we got footage that exceeded my wildest dreams. Even my angry young men were impressed.

Without so much as wincing, the Nuba let themselves be tattooed in front of the camera and as usual painted their bodies with white ash. We didn't spare the celluloid; it was obvious to me that these ancient customs would soon die out.

During our filming, a little boy suddenly turned up with a message, which seemed to alarm the Nuba. Breaking off their work, they talked anxiously and, to our surprise, they decided to return to Tadoro. The news was disturbing. Nuba from the southern valleys had reported that houses were burning in Tosari, only a few miles from Tadoro, and the Nuba living there had already left their huts: invaders had set fire to their homes. I was very alarmed indeed by the news. I thought of the fighting in Khartoum and knew that there were serious disturbances south of us, but I had never dreamed that they could advance this far north.

We hurried back to camp as fast as we could. Our camp was still there, but it struck me that only old people were to be seen, no women or children. Our Nuba in the *seribe* had vanished immediately but we hoped we would see them again soon. Evening came, however, then night, and no one returned. I was quite unnerved.

Near our camp, several elderly people stood with shields and spears, something I had never seen, and when I asked them what it meant, they told us the same thing the messenger had told us: Natu, Tukami and my other Nuba friends had fled to the mountains with their families and cattle. My crew, understandably, didn't want to leave camp in such a dangerous situation and, since I couldn't believe that the homes in Tosari were actually burning, I decided to drive over in one of our vans and see for myself. The Nuba men, armed with spears, piled in. *En route* to Tosari, we occasionally saw groups of Nuba with spears who all wanted to come with us. When we arrived in Tosari, not a single home was burning and there was no fire anywhere; yet a deathly hush prevailed here too. I was relieved to see that the rumours were false, but as we walked from hut to hut we saw that they were all empty. Every single inhabitant had fled and, as in Tadoro, only a few elderly men remained. I tried to calm them, saying, 'Kullo kirre' (it's all lies), 'Killo dette, dette' (it's all very, very far away). We sat down together, made a campfire, and the old Nuba men told me about the things they had experienced long ago, when the British had been here. They believed it was again the British who were threatening them but slowly I managed to relieve their fears.

Meanwhile, an Arab merchant and his family had arrived in Tadoro; he seemed scared to death by the rumours and although the Nuba were very peaceful, the situation could have led to outrages against the Arabs. Scattered Arab merchants lived in the Nuba Hills trading beads and coloured textiles for grain, tobacco and cotton. I drove the Arab and his family to Rheika, where they could be fairly safe at the school; but my well-meant help was ill rewarded. As I eventually learned, the Arab merchant told the police in Kadugli that I was a 'spy', working for the 'enemy', i.e., the Shilluk and Dinka living in the vicinity. These absurd and dangerous accusations found their way into the files of the secret police in Khartoum, so that when I applied for a visa for a later expedition to the Sudan, my application was rejected. To back up his charges, the Arab alleged that we had communicated with the enemies of the Sudanese by means of 'light signals'. He meant the flashbulbs used by Dieter and Walter, who had photographed the armed Nuba during my absence. Furthermore, the Arab claimed that I was setting the Nuba against the Arabs. For evidence, he pointed out that I spoke the Nuba language and had been living among them for months.

The rapidly spreading rumours about the disturbances were not unfounded. Just a few short miles to the south of Tosari, members of the Shilluk tribe had fought with Sudanese soldiers, and Nuba had also become involved. The resulting panic had infected the neighbouring Nuba settlements.

The next day, our Nuba still remained out of sight and didn't return until five days later. We had only a few short days left for filming the *seribe*, yet I couldn't take advantage of the time for all the wrestlers in Tadoro – ten young men including Natu and Tukami – were under arrest in Kadugli.

Luckily, this had nothing to do with the disturbances but was in connection with a crime that the Nuba sometimes committed; though never before had there been so many perpetrators. I had often observed how honest the Nuba were. They seldom stole or broke the law – except in two respects involving activities they considered mere peccadillos; these they persistantly indulged in, despite high penalties. One crime was adultery, whether committed by a man or a woman; for the Nuba this is a serious but common offence. The other crime was the theft of goats, a crime usually committed by young wrestlers living in the *seribe* who wanted to invite friends to a meal. This time, it happened that two young Nuba had run off with two goats and then had invited the best wrestlers to a banquet. Something like this had never occurred before. Usually, only two or at most three Nuba took part in such a feast but in this occasion, given the high number of 'guests', the banquet could not be kept secret and it was reported to the Mak, the chieftain of the Masakin. This matter, which seems to us fairly innocuous, is deemed a serious offence among the Nuba. According to their laws, not only the goat thief, but anyone else who ate so much as a morsel of the goat, is sentenced to three months in prison; inevitably, the entire wrestling élite of Tadoro, including Natu, Tukami and Dia, was jailed. We could not finish shooting at the *seribe*.

The court of law met every Friday in Rheika, the seat of the Mak. There, he passed judgement together with several chiefs of the other villages. The trial, taking place under huge, shady trees, wore on for several hours. I was surprised that all the defendants showed up, unguarded and completely free. None had fled. Their kith and kin also arrived, sitting in circles around the perpetrators, who were called up one by one.

The trial proceeded calmly, appearing more like a conversation than an inquiry, and it was only when Tukami defended himself that gales of laughter erupted. He said he had come to the meal much too late and had eaten only a tiny piece of the innards, since all the good morsels had already been devoured. He claimed he hadn't realized that the goat had been stolen, and his expression was so sad that one couldn't help feeling sorry for him. I was sure he wouldn't be punished, but I was wrong. Three hours later, when the verdict was read, each of the ten Nuba, including Tukami, received the same sentence: three months at the prison in Kadugli. Furthermore, the culprits or their families had to replace the goats.

The prison term struck me as incomprehensibly severe but it was accepted without complaint. The laws and the penalties were determined solely by the Nuba; only the execution of punishments and the prison itself were under the jurisdiction of the Sudanese government.

The delinquents were not allowed to return to their homes; they had to march off to Kadugli immediately, escorted by an auxiliary policeman of the Mak's. It was a sad farewell; I couldn't believe that I wouldn't see them again. At the last minute, there was more drama. When the ten were counted, one of them, Tukami, was missing. He probably felt the penalty was too harsh for a bit of innards; he had vanished and could not be located. Tukami was gone forever – after all, it was hardly likely he would return since he would then have to serve a threefold prison term.

Depressed, I returned to Tadoro. When I arrived, I saw that Walter and Dieter were already striking camp, even though I would have liked to do some more shooting. The end of the expedition had come and our departure was hurried because my men wanted to leave quickly, though, of course, I did not. It was a sad farewell, the most painful I had experienced with the Nuba.

Before driving off, I visited the relatives of the imprisoned Nuba – their parents and siblings. Dividing up my provisions, I gave them all small presents, and was delighted that they did not seem really worried. They knew their men would come back. They would then be welcomed as heroes, and a great feast would be given.

As it happened I did manage to see my imprisoned friends one last time for, as we drove through Kadugli, I saw some convicts doing roadwork and realized it was them. They waved and shouted my name and I asked the driver to stop. It was an unexpected joy and I fervently wanted to help them, but my companions grew impatient and I had to say goodbye.

I kept waving back until they vanished in the dust.

ENDLESS DIFFICULTIES

I didn't arrive in Munich until several weeks after leaving the Nuba Hills, and for various reasons the vans were still on the road. While Gerhard Fromm and I barely managed to catch the train, Walter and Dieter had to remain behind in Semeih. No rail transport being available for the vehicles, which couldn't be shipped until almost three weeks later. By the time they arrived in Khartoum, I had managed to obtain a freight car all the way to Port Sudan, but this time, there had been several incidents. One morning, I was woken up at the home of my friends, the Weistroffers, to find Walter standing in front of me. 'The car was broken into last night, and a whole lot of stuff seems to have been stolen,' he told me, deeply upset.

'The footage too?' I asked, thoroughly alarmed.

He shook his head. 'No, but come along, we have to go to the railway police.' At the Sudanese railway office, I was told that the railway would not replace our losses and that companions were considered to have been responsible. Contrary to regulations, they had left the freight car unguarded for ten hours to have a night out in Khartoum – an unbelievable frivolity. The films and photographs were apparently still here, as were the Arri cameras, thank goodness; but not our various cameras, including my Leica, plus the optics, light gauge, radio, binoculars, and personal belongings. I managed to calm down a little, but my nerves were jangling.

The next day, I flew to Munich. I had lost over twenty-five pounds, even more than two years earlier, and I looked like a scarecrow. Mentally, I had reached a nadir. I couldn't get over the fact that I had not been with my mother when she lay dying.

As I leaf through my journals, reading things I experienced during those two years, I am most reluctant to stir up those memories.

My sole hope was the Nuba film. We had worked with two kinds of Kodak stock: Ektachrome commercial for normal daylight and, for darker locations, the highly sensitive Ektachrome ER-stock, which could not yet be developed in most German printing labs. I wanted to get it developed and printed at Arri; but they weren't yet equipped to handle this new stock. So I turned to Geyer. Everything hinged on the quality of the footage and its development. I handed over a test reel of the highly sensitive ER-stock. The results would decide whether I could develop the film there or be forced to ship it to America.

It took forever for the test reel to come from Hamburg, but at last I sat in the small screening room at Arri, with Fromm and Dr Arnold next to me, and we watched a wrestling scene that had been shot at twilight. I breathed a sigh of relief. The rushes were technically perfect and the colours were well rendered; thus, one of my most difficult problems – the flawless development of ER stock in Germany – was solved. I signed the contract with Geyer and had all the reels of film dispatched to Hamburg.

I waited impatiently for some word from Walter and Dieter for I had been in Munich now for months without receiving any news from them and this was very worrying. Walter's father told me he hadn't heard from them since their departure from Khartoum, but he remarked upon the beautiful films, sixteen colour slide films in all, that his son had sent him from the Nuba Hills. I was staggered; now I understood why the two drivers had constantly refused to take an inventory; even prior to the burglary in Khartoum, I had missed several unexposed rolls of colour stock. The two men had robbed me. As one of them later confessed to me, they had 'divvied up' the films in Tadoro.

At last, the vans arrived in Munich where the expedition equipment was found to be in an indescribable state; it couldn't have looked worse even after years in the jungle. The two men had contacted me only when forced to do so after breaking down on the road. Not only had they destroyed one van in the vicinity of Bolzano because they hadn't put a drop of oil into the engine, but they had never once had the VWs inspected. I appealed to the Volkswagen factory, and without delay specialists were sent from Wolfsburg who repaired the cars in a very short time – a triumph for VW customer service.

It was then that I received a surprise visit from Robert Gardner, who brought me good news. Mr Fruchtman of Odyssey Productions had agreed to change the questionable paragraphs in the contract so that I could count on further backing until the completion of the film. I was vastly relieved, but there was one condition – the rough cut had to be delivered by mid-August.

Anxiously I looked forward to the first shipment from Hamburg. When at last it arrived it contained only one tenth of the footage. I was greatly disappointed, for the colours were not on a par with those of the test reels and there were actual colour faults. The printing lab reassured me, promising that the subsequent reels would have the same quality as the test reels, but the colours of the following shipments were even worse; some had a red cast, others a violet or turquoise one. These samples were unusable and I was growing very uneasy for I had to keep stalling my American partners, who were already impatient. I was at a loss to understand why Geyer was delivering the material at such long intervals, and why its quality was so poor. Something was wrong.

By now, it was mid-July and the situation grew more critical from day to day. It was vital that I meet the deadline, for the financing of the Nuba film was not the only thing that hinged on it. If the film proved successful, Odyssey would let me direct three CinemaScope documentaries in the United States. It was the chance of a lifetime.

After receiving no prints of the ER rushes despite my daily telephone calls, I went to Hamburg. At the Geyer lab, I was faced with utter catastrophe. When the head of the 16-mm film division screened the prints of the ER stock, I stood there, open-mouthed with shock. This was not so much a film in colour – it was a green film, as green as the fir trees in the Black Forest. Now I understood why they hadn't sent me the prints. The highly sensitive ER stock had probably been developed the wrong way; but whatever the reason, the disaster was irretrievable. Those scenes could not be reshot. The division head, whose name I would rather not mention, saw my desperate face and tried to comfort me. 'Don't worry, the green colour is quite normal in ER stock. We can filter it out later on.' Having no experience with ER stock, I took his word. But my doubts remained profound.

After making up my mind to stay in Hamburg until I obtained good prints, I moved into a small hotel in Rahlstedt, near the printing lab. At night, I couldn't sleep; I simply couldn't imagine that this green colour could be normal and that it could be filtered away. Those were nothing but excuses; something must have happened during the developing. The next day, I went back to the lab and asked the man, 'Would you mind if I telephoned a Kodak specialist in your presence?'

'By all means,' he replied calmly and within a few minutes, I was speaking to Dr Würstlin, a Kodak colour expert, in Stuttgart. I told him I was calling from the Geyer lab and that the head of the colour film division was listening to our conversation. This was more or less how it went:

'Tell me, Dr Würstlin, we used your stock on our expedition – not only the normal kind but also the highly sensitive ER film – what should the originals and the final prints look like? Should the sky look blue, a Negro brown and so on or are the colours different?'

'The colours have to look exactly as they do in nature – only, as you know, a bit softer in an original.'

'So the sky has to be blue and a Negro brown or brownish black?'

'Of course.'

'And,' I went on, 'what does it mean if the footage is green, as green as a fir forest or light green like lettuce leaves?'

A pause. Then Dr Würstlin said, 'Well, that means the film is ruined.'

Today, I still cannot find the words to describe how I felt after his unequivocal response. I still couldn't grasp the full scope of the calamity.

'But,' I said desperately, 'we had test reels of both kinds of stock developed before we gave them the job, and they were both flawless, including the ER film.'

'Have Geyer send us the green ER material and we'll examine it.' The conversation was over.

The rushes were ruined. They were green. The scenes couldn't be reshot: the funeral celebrations, the adolescent's initiation, all the other cultic rituals. I thought of the Americans, the contract, and the loans I had had from friends – and all the endless work, which had apparently been in vain. A world collapsed inside me.

I stayed on in Hamburg for five days and was at the printing lab from dawn to dusk every single day. I looked at the originals of the ER stock – so far, I had only seen the prints – but, as I had feared, the originals were also green. I still couldn't tell whether the celluloid had been ruined by heat or by poor development. The former possibility seemed contradicted not only by the test reel but also by the rolls of still film which we had also stored underground and of which not a single roll had the slightest tinge, not even the highly sensitive Ektachrome stock.

I did not care who was at fault; the crucial thing was to save whatever could be saved. Presently, I discovered another major setback caused by the lab. They had printed a large part of the stock without adding edge numbers. If this happens in a printing lab, then the lab is obliged to supply a new print containing edge numbers. However, since this is very expensive with colour film, Geyer refused, and though this subsequently led to grave complications, my years of friendly cooperation with Geyer made me reluctant to go to court. Soon there wasn't the shadow of a doubt that the harm could not be made good again. It took them weeks to produce new prints and the filtering had only turned the green into violet, which looked even less natural. I could not deliver a film to my American partner and the consequences were incalculable. I had lost my final chance to resume my profession. The Americans, on the basis of their partial financing, rightfully demanded all the footage and even the copyright. But I refused to part with my Nuba footage at any price, even if it was incomplete and largely useless. A tough struggle then began with Odyssey Productions, who had already started publicizing the film in the United States. It was only with the assistance of friends who lent me money to repay the capital invested by the Americans that I managed to annul the contract. My goal had been just within reach, and now, like so many other things since the end of the war, it had gone up in smoke.

PROBLEMS WITH NITRO STOCK

For some time, it had been illegal to work with nitro stock except on a very limited scale. Nitro stock is highly inflammable and has caused serious fire damage. As a result, a new, less hazardous celluloid was developed, no other kind could be used and infringement of the law entailed a serious penalty. The situation was especially difficult for me. I had fought for ten years to save at least part of my archive which comprised hundreds of cans, and now they all had to be dumped. What choice did I have but, with an aching heart, to destroy many sacks of valuable film? At any price, however, I was determined to save the original negatives of *Olympia*. Avery Brundage, president of the IOC, advised me to petition the German Olympic Committee or Dr Georg von Opel, the president of the German Olympic Committee.

Although the money would be in the form of a loan, to be repaid from my first income on the film, and although I had offers from the BBC and other sources, my appeal was turned down by every German agency. I couldn't understand it. Money was available for many mediocre films, but not for a German film that had been the only one in the history of sport to receive an Olympic gold medal; a film which, after the end of the war, was counted in Hollywood as one of the ten best films in the world.

Once again, help came from abroad. The George Eastman House in Rochester, which had asked to save the originals, generously offered to produce first-rate duplicate negatives free of charge and also to store the original nitro-stock negatives. In this way the originals of the Olympic films were rescued.

At this juncture, a new incident demonstrated that life in my homeland was being made increasingly unendurable for me. A young man, who was doing some typing for me, indignantly told me one day that he had been with Luis Trenker and several employees of the Bavarian Television Network on the premises of the Network. He remarked to Trenker that it was a pity that his former colleague, Frau Riefenstahl, had been unable to make any films since the end of the war.

Trenker nodded in agreement. 'Yes, it's really too bad – such a great talent. But it's her own fault. Through her connections she once got a friend of mine, Herr Moser, thrown into a concentration camp, where he died. He was working as a dowser on *Tiefland*.'

When the young man, quite taken aback, asked him why Frau Riefenstahl had done that, Trenker allegedly replied: 'Because he prophesied that she would have a bleak future after the war. Apparently, she was so angry that she denounced him and had him sent to a concentration camp.'

I owe it to that odious lie that I was again defamed in the German media, and it wasn't until years later that I happened to learn the truth. During a trip through the Dolomites with my later colleague Horst in search of some of the locations used in *Tiefland*, we looked for a hut near the Vajolett Towers. When our meal was served, the waitress, a large peasant woman, scrutinized me and said, 'Aren't you Leni Riefenstahl?' When I smiled and said yes, she sat down with us and said, 'I'm the daughter of Piaz the mountain guide. My father and Hans Steger once got you down from the eastern wall of the Rosengarten, and I sometimes watched you when you were filming *Tiefland*.'

At once I thought of Moser, the dowser. 'Did you know Herr Moser?' I asked.

'Of course,' she said, 'he visited us a lot and he also talked about you very enthusiastically.'

'What ever became of him?'

'He died a year or two ago, from mushroom poisoning.'

'Where did he live during the war and after?'

'In South Tyrol,' she said, 'with a rich Englishwoman. They often came here.'

'Did you ever hear of Herr Moser being in a concentration camp?'

Piaz's daughter looked at me in astonishment. 'What nonsense! Who'd say something like that?'

'Trenker,' I said, 'Luis Trenker says so.'

'What an idiot! Moser wasn't locked up for even a day. He climbed the mountains with his Englishwoman here throughout the war.'

The witnesses of that conversation are still alive, but it was too late for me to bring charges against Trenker. One isn't always lucky enough to be able to prove the truth at the right moment.

MY BLACK FRIENDS

Working in Germany was obviously impossible; on the other hand. I was no longer young enough to go abroad. Nevertheless, my thoughts and wishes revolved exclusively around my Nuba. These affectionate people had given me so many happy hours that I felt an increasing desire to live among them, forever if possible.

Friends tried to talk me out of it; when they realized that I was in earnest, they appealed to my common sense. But I didn't feel like being sensible or worrying about whether I might fall ill among my black friends. Of course, disease was not to be ruled out and I always took this possibility into account, but if my illness were critical, it would be easier for me to die among my Nuba than here in the big city, where I led a very solitary life. I loved the Nuba, and it was wonderful to be among them. Their merriment, never-failing despite their great poverty, was infectious. How well I understood Albert Schweitzer, the theologian and organist, who had chosen to become a physician in the Tropics.

I was in constant touch with my Nuba friends through Juma Abdallah, a Masakin Nuba, one of the very few who had managed to learn English and who taught Sudanese children at the school in Rheika. I had sent him self-addressed envelopes and stamps so I received letters from him at least twice a month and was kept abreast of everything concerning the Nuba; all illnesses and deaths were reported to me and also the fact that several newborn girls had been named Leni.

At Christmas, I sent Juma a package, through the Weistroffer family, which contained gifts for the Nuba: tea, sugar, sweets, and a coloured cloth for each one. To make sure that Juma distributed them correctly, I glued a photo to each little package. Later on, I learned that each recipient had received his present.

My Christmas gift from my friend Helge was a model of the Nuba house I was planning which he had built himself. An architect friend designed a Nuba fortress for me which consisted of six high round houses with an interior courtyard in the middle. My dreams were taking shape. The courtyard was to have a well surrounded with flowers and flowering shrubs that I would plant. This was no utopia. I hoped to find water with the help of a well digger or a dowser.

SUCCESSES AND FAILURES

During my absence in the Dolomites where I had spent three months, my work had piled up to the ceiling and I didn't know where to start. Fortunately, I had good news, chiefly from the United States. *African Kingdom*, published by Time & Life Books, had run a long photo story using my Nuba pictures, and I had been well paid. Also, an American magazine ran an unusual piece entitled 'Shame and Glory in the Movies' by Arnold Berson and Joseph Keller. Among other things, it said, 'You're a talented director, you work for Hitler? You're a Nazi. You work for Stalin? You're a genius.' The two authors compared my films to the works of Sergei Eisenstein and analysed *Triumph of the Will* and *Potemkin*. With regard to *Olympia*, they wrote, 'This film is not only a masterpiece. It is a testament to German film art.'

I also received an enthusiastic letter from James Card, the head of George Eastman House in Rochester, and when I heard his sensational news, my heart leaped with joy. The House was planning to put on a series, *The Film in Germany, 1908-1958*, and the board of directors had decided to include all the films I had acted in or directed.

For decades, the Germans had remained silent about the worldwide recognition of my work. With a feeling of satisfaction, I would like to quote a passage from the programme of notes George Eastman House's *The Film in Germany* at the Film Department of the Museum of Modern Art, New York, 1965-6.

Leni Riefenstahl's extraordinary film epic of the 1936 Berlin Olympic Games is without question the finest motion picture production to emerge from the entire period from 1933 to 1945 in Germany. It is indeed, in the opinion of some film specialists, one of the most splendid motion pictures produced in any era, in any country.

Olympia is neither a 'documentary record' of the events that took place during the 1936 Olympic Games, nor is it, as it has been unjustly considered, in any way a vehicle of propaganda or persuasion. Comparison of this original, uncut, German version with the English-language version edited especially for the United States and Britain, shows that in all versions no special emphasis was placed on the success of the host-country athletes to the diminishment of others. Nor was any attempt made to understate the achievements of the Negro athletes led by the remarkable performance of Jesse Owens.

Rather than considering *Olympia* a documentary, it should be recognized as a purely creative film which happens to use actualities as part of the raw material wrought by Leni Riefenstahl, with the notable assistance of composer Herbert Windt, into a unique motion picture that forever transcends the petty hatreds and untruths that have unsuccessfully attempted to diminish its heroic stature.

The film was banned for showing in Germany by the Allied Military Government.

Even back in the days of the Olympic Games, I had experienced nothing but fair play from the Americans and my films were shown for instructional purposes at American universities and schools.

The *New York Times* wrote the following under the heading 'Riefenstahl's Film Was Too Good':

The leftwing Spanish filmmaker Luis Buñuel was supposed to rework Leni Riefenstahl's documentary film on the Nazi Party Rally in Nuremberg. The idea was to use it as anti-Nazi propaganda. Buñuel screened the results for René Clair and Charlie Chaplin in New York. Chaplin couldn't stop laughing, but Clair had reservations: Riefenstahl's images were so damned good and impressive, no matter how much they were re-edited, that they obtained the opposite effect of what was intended. It would have been a real boomerang. The audience would have been overwhelmed . . . The matter was taken to the White House. President Roosevelt viewed the film and agreed with Clair. So the film was tacitly consigned to the archive.

The United States and England were not the only countries in which my films were still a draw. *Olympia* was shown on Swedish television and the Swedish magazine *Popular Fotografi* ran a fair interview on its title page. (In Germany, by contrast, my films can rarely be seen.) Such triumphs made it possible for me to summon my earlier assistant, Erna Peters, from Berlin to Munich; new possibilities seemed to be emerging for me, partly because of the Nuba photos, which kept creating more and more of a stir. A tremendous interest was shown in Japan and Michi and Yasu, my Japanese friends, brought me a fabulous offer from Tokyo. But it was questionable whether I could accept it because of what had happened at Geyer. A new TV station in Japan, built specifically for colour and one of the largest in the world, wanted to feature my Nuba material in its opening programme. Not the completed film, which didn't exist, but a rough cut of the most important parts of the unspoiled footage was to be serialized. This offer included an invitation to Tokyo. My fee could go towards a new expedition, and perhaps I could reshoot the 'green' sequences.

I wanted to give it a try in any event. Peterle, as I still call Erna Peters, had taken a few months off, so she looked after me and attended to my needs like a mother. She sorted the footage in the editing room, labelled the cannisters and spliced the strips. She was the hardest-working and most responsible person I have ever met in the film business. Now everything hinged on Geyer. Would the lab be able to produce a usable screening copy?

Meanwhile, the 'photokina' exhibition drew closer and closer, but despite my constant calls and pleas, I still hadn't received the print from Geyer and I was frantic. In my desperation, I had to fly to Cologne without the print. According to the latest bulletins from Geyer, they hadn't managed to finish because of technical problems, but they wanted to try and send the reel directly to the Kodak stand in Cologne.

I waited daily at the Kodak stand in Cologne – but the print didn't come and the Japanese TV executive couldn't wait until the end of the exhibition; he left, deeply disappointed. As for me, these were days of bitter frustration. The print arrived only at the very last moment, a few hours before the closing of the exhibition, which was far too late. What came next was worse. The Kodak projectionist refused to screen the reel because he was afraid it would rip; Geyer had spliced various sections of my work print into the new print, and because the perforations were partly destroyed, the film couldn't go through the projector. They probably hadn't found the originals – an unbearable thought – so no one could view the print and the damage was immeasurable. Not only the Japanese, but also the BBC and French TV were interested in my Nuba material and after 'photokina', I was supposed to screen the sample reel in London and Paris. My hopes of rescuing the Nuba film by going on a new expedition were buried for good.

IN LONDON AND PARIS

Despite the disasters in Cologne, I flew to London after 'photokina'. I had no film reel, only the Nuba pictures, but since I wanted to try and sell them to a magazine, I contacted the editors of the *Sunday Times Magazine*. I had no connections there and, after all my experiences with the British press, I didn't even know if I'd be welcome. I relied solely on the impact of my photos, which proved a sound instinct. Godfrey Smith, the editor-in-chief, was already waiting for me and, after an informal and cordial greeting, several staff members, including Michael Rand, his future art director, joined us in the small office. A projector was set up and, rather nervously, I screened my slides for the group in the crowded space. Within a few minutes, I knew that they liked what they saw. Upon leaving Thomson House, where the *Sunday Times Magazine* was located, I hurried through the streets of London in a state of exhilaration. Godfrey Smith had not only purchased a Nuba series for several full-colour pages, but also paid me an advance without my even asking him.

This success in London appeared to go on. The next day, I was asked to lunch by Mr Harris, the director of the Hutchinson Publishing Group. Again, the subject was my memoirs but I still couldn't bring myself to agree – I was too frightened of such a project. All I could do was ask Mr Harris, whose friendliness towards me was a blessing, to be patient. Fascinated by the Nuba slides, he was the first person to suggest that I do a picture book and he encouraged me to find a suitable German co-publisher at the same time. 'We can't do it alone, unfortunately', he said, 'since we're not specialists in producing picture books.' I didn't tell him how sceptical I was about my chances of finding a German publisher.

The good atmosphere was also in evidence at the BBC where I visited Mr Howden – even though I couldn't screen my footage for him. No sooner had I settled in his office than more and more staff members came in, eager to make my acquaintance. Because of the shortage of chairs, nearly all of us sat on the floor – it was like being in a commune. At office-closing time, I was whisked off to someone's flat and again we were accompanied by so many people that most of us sat on the carpet and every corner of the room was crowded. We remained together until the small hours and met some of England's most gifted young filmmakers, including the host, Kevin Brownlow, with whom I have remained friends ever since.

Success was mine in Paris too. Charles Ford, the French friend who later wrote a book about me, accompanied me to *Paris-Match*, where the office of Roger Thérond, the editor-in-chief, was soon mobbed. Here too, the Nuba won the hearts of the French journalists, and I went back to Munich with several offers.

Was it because of my joy or the bad news awaiting me at home? I will never know. According to my diary, I see that on the day of my return I suffered such a critical circulatory collapse that my doctor, Dr Zeltwanger, spent long hours of the night with me. The examination showed that this time nearly all my organs were affected, even my usually sound heart, conditioned by dancing and athletics. I was forbidden all professional activity for a long time.

My collapse was probably caused by a letter from Geyer, which I found on my return. It contained the heart-breaking news that the sole correctly developed reel and irreplaceable ER sample reel, the chief evidence for any possible litigation, as well as other original stock, were lost for good. Now I knew why the Geyer people had inserted parts of my battered work print into the copy that they had dispatched to Cologne: they had been unable to find the originals of that footage. For me, this was more than a shock – it was a tragedy.

But throughout my life, with its relentless ups and downs, there has been a ray of light to kindle my hopes. And this was true once again. When Rudi and Ursula Weistroffer in Khartoum learned about my illness, they instantly invited me to their home. They knew how good I felt there and how healthy I would become in Africa. Before taking off, I received a surprise visit from Albert Speer and his wife Margarete. A few weeks earlier, Speer had been released from twenty years' imprisonment in Spandau. He was the only person whom I was friendly with from the days of the Third Reich, and so I felt deeply touched when I received his letter just a few days after he came out of Spandau:

8.10.66

Dear Leni Riefenstahl,

I feel that our frienship of many years, uninterrupted even by captivity, now requires an emphatic step forward. I think – don't you agree? – that we can use the familiar form with one another? My wife and I will be in Munich in mid-November and I will telephone you then. I am looking forward to seeing you again and I greet you warmly.

Yours, Albert Speer

Although eager to see him, I felt very worried for I was afraid of finding a broken, careworn old man. It was a surprise therefore when he stood before me at the door, unbroken and with the same penetrating eyes; he was the same man that I had known – except that he had grown older. I could scarcely believe it possible. He seemed a bit inhibited however, so I avoided asking him about Spandau until he himself brought it up. He talked about his imprisonment as if it had been merely a long vacation in his life, which he wouldn't have cared to miss. I was speechless and somewhat ashamed. I recalled my despair in the Salzburg Prison, when I beat my fists bloody on the door of my cell. Speer must have had extraordinary inner strength.

When we said goodbye, promising to see each other more often, my own problems seemed to have much less significance.

CHRISTMAS WITH THE NUBA

In early September 1966, I flew back to the Sudan. This time for only twenty-eight days as my discount ticket was good for that period only. My baggage was light, for I was to stay just long enough to see the Nuba.

Sayed Ahmed Abu Bakr, who was still head of the Ministry of Tourism, had approved my Nuba trip, but I was unable to obtain a vehicle. However, I found solace in his invitation to take part in an unusual safari with five hundred guests, mostly diplomats from various countries and members of the Sudanese government. First we attended the dedication of the Roseires Dam on the Blue Nile, six hundred miles south-east of Khartoum, which had been constructed with German help over a period of six years. Next, the safari was to view Dinder Park, the largest national animal park in the Sudan.

The train to the Roseires Dam took thirty-one hours – two nights and a day. I had a sleeping compartment and was able to have a thorough rest during the long ride. Abu Bakr was accompanied by a young Englishman, who was working in Khartoum and who was also a journalist. He knew my films and was interested in everything I had done and he listened to my stories for hours on end.

When we arrived in Roseires, the sun was radiant. In the intense heat, I could still feel how exhausted I was, and I found it difficult to walk for almost half an hour across the hot sand to the dam – an imposing construction. However, I had taken along my new Leica and, absorbed in taking photos, I forgot my fatigue.

In a large, open tent on the banks of the Nile, Abu Bakr was entertaining friends who were guests of honour and I spent an unforgettable evening at his side. We sat on straw mats enjoying a sumptuous meal, served by blacks, who looked wonderfully picturesque in their colourful garments and wide sashes. One of the most lasting impressions, as always with Africa, is of the deep blue sky with its billions of stars, stretching over us like a gigantic canopy.

The trip of Dinder Park had to be cancelled because the trails had been turned muddy by the rain and were not yet negotiable, so we started back ahead of schedule. During the ride, I was invited by Sayed Ismail Azhari, president of the Sudan, to have tea in his Pullman carriage. This good-looking, elderly man, who reminded me of Hindenburg, asked me about my experiences with the Nuba. Hearing that I wanted to revisit them, he surprised me by raising no objections; he even encouraged me and promised to help in any way he could.

Now there was no stopping me and on the very day of my return I plunged into my preparations. Mr Bishara, the affluent owner of a delivery firm in Khartoum, lent me a truck, which I could use from El Obeid to the Nuba Hills asking only that I pay for the petrol. My German and Sudanese friends equipped me with all sorts of necessities for my brief, one-woman expedition and Abu Bakr even lent me a tape recorder. In the end, I had several crates with me. I had to go by railway to El Obeid, a trip lasting at least twenty-six hours, because I could not afford to fly. This gave me less time with my Nuba friends, for under no circumstances could I miss my return flight to Munich. I had also had to promise to celebrate New Year's Eve with my friends at the German Club.

Late one evening, a week before Christmas, I stepped out of the train at El Obeid and stood alone on the platform with my heavy crates. Using sign language, I found my way to a small hotel where Mr Bishara's driver found me the following afternoon. When I saw the truck, a gigantic five-tonner, I opened my eyes wide. Apart from the driver, a young Arab, there were just two black assistants and myself. Unable to communicate with them, I couldn't find out whether they knew the way to the Nuba Hills or how long we would be driving. I sat next to the driver while the two assistants sat in the back. The sandy trails made it difficult to get our bearings. After three or four hours, I noticed that my handbag, containing my passport, my money, and the indispensable residence permit, had vanished. It must have fallen out of the truck and I was scared out of my wits. The driver halted at once and, understanding my gestures, turned around and drove back. For once, I had the most amazing luck for within an hour one of the assistants had found my bag. Our truck had driven over it and the bag was completely crushed – but, apart from my smashed glasses, everything was saved.

We didn't encounter a single vehicle and although now and then we had minor breakdowns, it was always something that could be fixed. We should have reached Dilling, the small idyllic village located roughly halfway between El Obeid and Kadugli, in three or four hours; by the time we had been driving for nine hours, it was clear that we were lost. The driver grew nervous; I was uneasy, for I had the feeling that we were going round in circles and I wished I had brought a compass. It was dark by the time we eventually reached Dilling. Exhausted and hungry, we spent the night outdoors; the men slept in the truck while I slept next to it on my camp-bed.

The next day, I hoped we would make Tadoro, but we only got as far as Kadugli – and not until late in the afternoon, so that we just barely managed to buy something at the market. The district officer, to whom I was supposed to give the residence permit, already knew me and wished us *bon voyage.* We were just about to climb into the truck when a policeman approached us and shouted something to the driver. I had no idea what he wanted. Mohammed tried to explain to me that we had to follow the policeman. I couldn't understand why, but my driver made unequivocal gestures that I was to come. Finally, with a sense of foreboding, I followed the policeman. We went to a house, where a higher-ranking police chief was waiting for us and I greeted him uneasily. He said something in Arabic, which I naturally didn't understand. Then he spoke furiously to Mohammed, who couldn't translate his words for me. Using sign language unsuccessfully, my driver attempted to make it clear that we could travel no further, we had to turn back. I merely shook my head angrily and, with gestures, tried to make the police chief realize that I had permission from the governor of El Obeid.

It was useless, he didn't understand me either. I grew more and more upset, he grew angrier and angrier, and by now I was afraid, for I realized how serious our predicament was. Outside in the street, I sat down in the sand. I was at my wits' end. Had I come all this way for nothing – only to be turned back when I was so close to my destination? Mohammed tried to calm me down, but I wouldn't budge. They would have to carry me away.

Then I had a brainwave – the little tape recorder I had with me could mean my salvation. I leaped up and ran to the truck – the police chief must have thought I'd gone mad – and hurriedly rummaged through my baggage, until I found the recorder and the tape. When I switched it on, an Arabic voice came out. Mohammed looked thunderstruck. By now quite self-assured, I walked back to the police chief who was still standing by the road. Over his protests, I set the recorder up and watched his face. What he now heard must have bowled him over. It was instructions by the supreme chief of police of Kordofan to all subordinate agencies to help me in any situation and to allow me to shoot films and photographs unhindered. He also described me as a friend of the Sudan.

My recorder had already worked several miracles, and it was no less effective on this occasion. The police chief shook my hand, hugged me and invited me home to dinner. But since I badly wanted to reach my Nuba by midnight, I politely declined. I was happy just to get away from there.

By the time we reached Tadoro, it was already the morning of 21 December. Within a very short time, I was surrounded by my Nuba and their joy and enthusiasm were more intense than I had ever experienced. They carried me on their shoulders, and everyone around me began to dance and sing while my driver and his Arabs looked on speechless.

Nearly all my old friends were there. They hastily conferred as to where to put me up, for they realized that I could only remain for a few days; they had no time to build a hut but didn't want me to sleep outside because of the evening storms. Within a few minutes, the home of Natu, who was staying at the *seribe*, was made available to me, and the men, women and children living in the house moved in with friends. Only Nua, an elderly woman, and two young boys were to remain, so that I wouldn't be all alone.

From then on, the place was mobbed by the Nuba who came from far away to welcome me. I felt as if time had stood still, as if I had been gone for only a few days; nothing had changed. The very next day, I prepared for a visit to the Korongo Hills which was always tremendous fun for my Nuba; anyone who could squeeze into our huge truck did, since it was a distance of some twenty miles and they would otherwise have had to walk. I was boisterously welcomed by the Korongo Nuba when we arrived and I handed them small gifts; they also gave me presents: chickens, peanuts, calabashes.

According to my calendar, it was Christmas Eve; this was my third Christmas with the Nuba. I had brought along candles and an artificial green fir branch from Khartoum, as well as a lot of silver tinsel, for the Nuba like anything that glitters. I had planned to have a small Christmas party – a surprise for the Nuba, who don't know what Christmas is. When I lit the candles in my hut at twilight, it turned out that the Nuba had never before seen a candle.

Alipo and Natu had the children line up in two rows outside the hut. More and more children joined them, and soon there were fifty or sixty. I had brought with me a bag of sweets and I put a few into each tiny hand. The children were thrilled and their joy and laughter were like the twittering of birds. This delight soon spread to the older Nuba when I took out my other provisions – cans of meat, smeared slices of bread – and distributed them among the adults. I noticed that almost everyone who received a slice of bread broke off a few pieces and handed them to the youngsters and the old people standing at the back.

Meanwhile, some women had brought the marisse beer, and the mood became more and more cheerful. But my days were numbered. I had already added one day, and my friends in Khartoum were expecting me in two days. This time, it was easier for me to say goodbye to the Nuba. We had the big truck, and many wanted to accompany me to Kadugli. It was a sacrifice for them, since they had to walk back that night – a distance of over thirty miles – in order to reach Tadoro the next day, in time for their greatest wrestling celebration, which takes place only once a year.

It was already dark when we left Tadoro and the Nuba were very dejected. When the truck stopped some nine miles outside of Kadugli the generator was found to be defective, and since the driver was unable to fix it, we had no choice but to wait for a vehicle that could take us to Kadugli where we hoped to find replacement parts. Only now did I realize how critical my situation was. I had taken things far too lightly; I could not afford to miss the plane. We all got out of the truck and sat down by the roadside together, but my Nuba friends could not wait indefinitely for they had to hike back to Tadoro in order to prepare the great celebration. Indeed, they wanted me to join them but this, of course, was impossible. I would have had to hike twenty-five miles.

Quite soon, we spotted a light in the darkness. A truck loaded with sacks and people was approaching and although it was unfortunately heading in the wrong direction for me, we hailed it in the hope that it could at least take my Nuba back to Tadoro. The driver shook his head, saying he was going further west, but when I gave him nearly all my remaining money, keeping only a small reserve, this helped. But now my Nuba were up in arms, refusing to drive back without me. 'You have to come,' they begged, 'we're putting on our festival for you. You're a guest of honour – you have to be there.' Crazy as it was, I gave in. Since a few of my Nuba spoke Arabic, they explained to my driver and asked him to pick me up in Tadoro as soon as the truck was repaired.

We were back in Tadoro the next day. I awoke out of a deep sleep to find the Nuba already busy preparing the festival; I had never before watched their preparation so closely. The three best wrestlers – Natu, Tukami and Gua – were decked out in the house I was staying in. Tukami, who had fled rather than serve his prison sentence, had returned after two years and been joyfully welcomed. Amid drum rolls, the wrestlers were dressed and smeared with ash. Their wives and mothers attached goatskin ribbons to my wrists and ankles and hung chains of beads around my neck. No one found this strange, and I had already grown accustomed to it. Then, along with their escorts, the wrestlers, taking me in their midst, headed the procession to the site of the wrestling matches. There, in the middle of the space, Natu and Tukami did a dance, reminding me of birds of paradise. They emitted noises like birdcalls and moved their hands like Indian temple dancers. During the dance, which I photographed from every side, the Nuba, who had been waiting in the shade of trees, came dashing in from all directions with whistles and flags and, in less than ten minutes, we were surrounded by hundreds, later by thousands. It was an indescribable spectacle. I tried to capture everything with the camera, unaware of the time, forgetting that I should long since have been *en route* to Khartoum.

In the middle of the hubbub, the truck arrived, much to my dismay. I should have climbed in on the spot, but – how can I explain it? – I wanted to enjoy the entire fascinating celebration. In my optimism, I hoped that we could still make the train. Luckily, my driver and his assistants were so enthralled by the festival with its pretty girls that they were more than willing to put off departure until the next day.

The Nuba usually get up at cockcrow; but this morning, it was somewhat later. As the day grew lighter, the first Nuba arrived. More and more of them came and again they tried to coax me into staying on. As I was packing, the truck drove up and looking at the sight of my crates, I became rather apprehensive. Although Mohammed could drop me off in Semeih, he couldn't possibly wait until the train arrived for he simply had to get back to El Obeid. The train, which stops in Semeih for only a few minutes, is usually mobbed and apart from the station master, there would be no one who could help me load the heavy crates. As these thoughts shot through my mind, one of the Nuba asked me whether I could take him along to Khartoum. It was Dia of Taballa, a young wrestler.

'What do you want to do in Khartoum?' I asked.

'Buna gigi Leni nomandia.' He wanted to watch me climb into the great bird and fly to heaven. I couldn't take him seriously. There wasn't even time to get him dressed – he was wearing only a loin cloth.

I said, 'No, Dia, I can't take you with me, it won't do.'

But he pleaded so insistently that I decided it might not be such a bad idea if he came along and helped me load the crates. As I was thinking about it, several Nuba asked if they could come too and I realized I could not take just Dia or else a lot of the others would be jealous and get even with him afterwards. I would take two Nuba, and the second had to be Natu; he instantly agreed, and although the Arab driver kept pressing me, he was willing to wait while Natu hurriedly said goodbye to his wife. After that, everything went lightning-fast; we didn't even have time to get clothing for Dia and Natu. After shaking many hands and taking our leave from a lot of people, we left Tadoro rather late.

At 2 a.m. we finally arrived in Semeih, hungry, tired and freezing cold. We were in time for the train, which was scheduled to arrive early in the morning; meanwhile, we tried to sleep in the truck. My two Nuba suffered most of all from the cold, so I rummaged through my belongings and found some tracksuit trousers for Dia. They were much too short, but otherwise, because the Nuba have such narrow hips, they more or less fitted him. I gave Natu the jacket, which was far too small but gave him some protection against the cold. I also had dresses and scarves to cover them with and when they were all bundled up they looked like carnival figures.

Mohammed woke us before sunrise and we had to get out of the truck at once since he had to reach El Obeid punctually. Natu and Dia lugged the crates to the station platform, and before I managed to explain that they couldn't come along to Khartoum in their get-up, the train lumbered in. It was mobbed, as I had feared. The Nuba had never seen a train in all their lives and they stood transfixed. For them, it was a large house on wheels, and they showered me with questions while I tried to push my way into the train. It was quite a feat getting the crates stowed away. Natu and Dia each took one and dashed after me, until I found a goods wagon. As were were piling up the various items of luggage, the train began to move, and it gathered speed so fast my Nuba couldn't jump out, nor did they want to. We stood squeezed together in a corridor, stared at by Arabs – a solitary white woman, accompanied by two big, suspicious-looking Nuba dressed only in loincloths. The train had no choice but to take my friends along to Khartoum, but I had managed to catch the train, which was a great relief.

The trip was scheduled to last twenty-four hours, perhaps even longer, and naturally, the Nuba knew nothing about lavatories or the like; they had never even seen a tap. We squeezed our way along the corridor and waited outside a lavatory until it was free; then I showed them how to turn the tap on and off, how to wash their hands and drink, and explained what else one does in such a room. I used pantomime to get my point across – they understood and burst out laughing.

Leaving them to their own devices, I tried to wriggle through to the first-class and second-class cars in order to find some food. I succeeded, for Arabs are very helpful by nature; they had spread out their food packages in the compartments, and when they saw my yearning looks, they instantly gave me things to eat: bread and mutton cutlets. Of course, they assumed it was for me, but I quickly vanished to carry the food to my hungry Nuba. Later, I went into another compartment, made hungry eyes again, and got more food as well as invitations to remain; but I made excuses and left to take Dia and Natu this second ration, which we all shared. We had no seats, but we could perch on the crates. It was good that I had no mirror on me for I must have looked a sight – something my friends in Khartoum subsequently confirmed. I was exhausted, my hair was full of sand, and my body was covered with dust. Nevertheless, I felt fine, because I was now certain to catch my plane, and when an Arab offered me his seat, I was even able to doze for a few hours.

Halfway to Khartoum, I suddenly missed my two Leicas. At Kosti, the next stop, I notified the police. They spoke only Arabic, and so the Sudanese passengers assumed I was accusing them of theft. The Arabs, in turn, suspected my Nuba, who were in the corridor of another car, crushed together as if in an animal freight car. At every station, I was afraid the police would arrest Natu and Dia and I fought like a lion to make sure my friends were not dragged off the train. I was so worn out that my eyes kept closing; and finally, I could no longer make out the faces around me.

We arrived in Khartoum at 6 a.m., exhausted and filthy. My loyal friends, Herr and Frau Plaetschke, were waiting at the station, with a car Abu Bakr had sent with a chauffeur. The Plaetschkes had risen at the crack of dawn every single morning since 29 December in order to pick me up at the station. They had been extremely worried. It was lucky they were here, for policemen were already approaching us, ordering me and the Nuba to go with them. The problem was the theft of my cameras. My friends were able to explain things to the officers, thereby putting an end to the whole business.

I was deeply distressed by how dismal my black friends looked. When I thought of how proud and self-assured they were in the *seribe* or in their wrestling matches, and how intimidated and humiliated they now appeared, I profoundly regretted bringing them with me. Fortunately, the situation changed when we drove to the Weistroffer house and my Nuba could at last wash thoroughly under a garden shower. They kept holding their hands under the stream of water. For them, this large amount of water was an even greater miracle than the railway. Bearing in mind the dirty water that they are often forced to drink from holes, one can readily understand that this pure, clear water was a real luxury for them. Since everyone was nice to the Nuba, they soon got over their shyness. I was eager to learn what impressed them the most, apart from the water. It was not the beautifully manicured lawn or the flowers; it was something else, in the hall of the house. They gaped in sheer delight at Herr Weistroffer's hunting trophies – the huge buffalo horns and the tremendous elephant tusks. The Nuba were fascinated; they were permanently gripped by a hunting fever which was never satisfied since, because of the water shortage, there was little game in the hills of their homeland.

Now we were served good food – bread, fruit, butter and honey. The Nuba also downed several quarts of milk – a miracle in their eyes, for in Tadoro, a small bowl of milk is almost a luxury. Then we had tea and, as a special treat for them lots and lots of sugar.

Soon after breakfast, we drove to the marketplace, to buy them clothes. The most practical thing for them was the *jellaba*, the most common garment in the Sudan, a long robe which shields the wearer against dust and sunshine and is not only practical, but also becoming. Natu picked a turquoise *jellaba* and Dia absolutely insisted on the same colour. But there were no others; the vendor offered Dia a light-green *jellaba* but he was adamant. He didn't want light green, and he almost started to weep like a baby; it was only when I told him that he wouldn't get one at all that he sulkily pulled it on. Fortunately, he soon got over his disappointment.

There was no end to the Nuba's wonderment. For them, the heaps of shoes, clothes and other things were sheer miracles. I bought a few woollen blankets to keep the old women warm at night, as well as other practical articles which I happened to find. I had little time and had yet to notify the police that I was leaving.

While repacking the crates, what should emerge but my Leicas, all wrapped up in towels. During our hasty departure, I must have stuck them into the crate at the very last moment. Embarrassing as it was for me, I nevertheless reported it to the police.

That evening, we received a visit from Abu Bakr and I was overjoyed to see he greeted Dia and Natu as heartily as a father. When he embraced them, the two Nuba beamed with delight and I knew I could entrust them to him with a clear conscience.

Take-off was scheduled for a few minutes after midnight. Natu and Dia insisted on watching me soar into the sky, but they had no intention of staying in Khartoum after I'd gone and they were keen to start back the very next day. Once they were alone, the big city was much too sinister for them; they wanted to get back to their families as soon as possible.

Whenever a foreigner flew out of Khartoum, many friends came to the airport. The passengers could wait downstairs, the friends up on the terrace. Now my two Nuba were standing up there too and in their immaculate *jellabas* they looked like two Christmas angels. The other people enjoyed the way I conversed with the Nuba in their own language, which only we three could understand. The Nuba wanted to know as much as they could – especially about the aeroplane, which they called *nomandia*; in their eyes, it was like a gigantic bird. They also wanted to know when I'd be coming back. At a loss for an answer, I had a sudden brainwave, inspired by the big moon that loomed overhead. I had presented a tape recorder to Khalil, a teacher at the school in Rheika, so that he could tape the language and music of the Nuba for me. Now I tried to explain to Natu and Dia that I would send Khalil tapes on which I would tell them what I was doing in 'Alemania', and how I was getting on. They were to visit Khalil at every full moon to play my tapes and record their answers. It wasn't so easy explaining this to them but at length they understood and beamed their pleasure.

This unusual correspondence was not hard to carry out. It functioned for a long time, since Kadugli had a small post office, and Khalil had business there twice a month. In this way, despite the immense distance separating us, I could remain in touch with my Nuba friends.

These African expeditions left me neither healthier nor younger nor more beautiful – quite the contrary: they demanded the utmost of me. Nevertheless, I very much wanted to return to Africa and, if at all possible, settle there forever.

A DIFFICULT YEAR

I was back in Munich. The sky was grey, the weather cool and foggy. The postman had already brought the *Sunday Times Magazine* with an impressive photo story about the Nuba and an excellent text. The editors also asked me if I could photograph the Olympic Games in Mexico the following year.

As regards my health, however, I was not in good shape. Because of my insomnia, I was always tired and often depressed. I suffered badly from the solitude that I nevertheless preferred; perhaps that was why I was so drawn to the Sudan which I had come to see as my spiritual home. I was convinced that I could find peace only with the Nuba, and to make this dream come true, I first had to create some kind of subsistence for myself. I was burdened more and more by my debts, and since I had never contributed to any pension plan, I was sure to end my days on social security – an unbearable thought. Then I had an idea. In exchange for a monthly pension, I would offer copyright to all my films as well as my rich photo archive and the still serviceable Nuba footage, plus the negatives of my films and the many theatrical prints still in my possession. I was on the point of signing a contract to this effect when the man who was seriously interested in the deal backed out at the very last moment. At the time, I was willing to give up everything I owned for a monthly pension of only one thousand marks. I saw no other way out of my predicament. The fees for the sales of my Nuba pictures and film rentals came too irregularly and did not provide even the most frugal livelihood. And there was also the as yet uncertain outcome of the pending lawsuit that Herr Mainz had brought against Leiser's Minerva Film regarding his use of material from my *Triumph of the Will*. I was in a desperate situation. On top of everything else I had taken on too heavy a work load and I urgently needed a good secretary.

My wish soon came true in an unusual way. When Inge Brandler first visited me in April 1967, I didn't realize how important she would be in my future life. She had been recommended by a young man, Herr Grussendorf, who had done some temping work for me. 'She admires you,' he said, 'I met her at the Munich theology school; she works there as a secretary.'

'Well then, she won't have time for me.'

'Oh, but she will,' he said. 'I've already talked to her. She'd love to type for you in her spare time or do other office work for you. But she refuses to accept any money from you.'

When she stood before me that day, small and delicate, I would never have dreamed that such a tiny creature could be such a bundle of energy and willpower. She began to work for me on the spot, and we have been friends ever since. Nothing was too much for her. She came in the evening and often remained until midnight. Always good tempered, never showing fatigue, she quickly took on more and more responsibilities. She gave me every free moment she had – Saturdays and Sundays and even holidays. Soon she became so indispensable that without her I could never have survived the many terrible crises that I suffered.

Several interested parties in London wanted to view the Nuba wrestling reel Geyer had reprinted for me. The printing lab had had five months' time to improve the print that could have had such positive results for me at 'photokina'. After my previous experiences, however, I hadn't had the courage to look at the new copy. I kept procrastinating until at last I had to face what proved to be a new disappointment. I had long since resigned myself to the likelihood of a mediocre print. But the one that ran on the screen was an enigma. Aside from the 'green' parts, which were now a brown tone, the colours were well balanced – which proved that they could have been printed correctly from the very outset. But the editing was not mine. Frames that I had omitted were restored; some that I had included were missing. The sequences were too long or too short. Nothing was right. The overall result was a mess. And finally, as the culmination of the horrors: half the frames were reversed. What I saw was a mutilation; my film was irreparably damaged.

I cancelled my trip to London. There were other upsetting problems that left me no time to think. I was worried about the originals of my Nuba slides and I didn't have the wherewithal to make duplicates. It was always risky letting original slides out of one's possession, especially sending them abroad. Now, after my last visit to the Nuba Hills, I had posted over two hundred of my slides to Khartoum. The Nuba were supposed to see them through a viewer, which would be marvellous fun for them; but the metal crate containing the slides arrived in Khartoum only after I had left for Tadoro. The crate which my friends had entrusted to a trucker was forwarded to me but never arrived. The Sudanese authorities began a major search, but the crate was nowhere to be found – and it had in it some of my best shots. What a catastrophe! I was in the depths of despair.

Then I received a phone call from New York. I was asked whether I would be willing to sell National Education Television the US rights to *Olympia*. The offer was indeed generous. NET acquired the TV rights to the English-language version for five years and paid for new duplicate negatives and lavender prints on 'non-flame' stock. These new negatives and prints would become my property when the five years were up.

Throughout this period, I remained in touch with my Nuba. Khalil had already sent me several tapes and on the last one, Natu reported on how he had spent the money that I had given him in Khartoum for his return trip. He had bought a shovel and a pail at the market in Kadugli, and they had already dug a wide hole thirty feet deep, but still not found any ground water. They would keep on digging.

Robert Gardner was staying briefly in Khartoum *en route* to the southern Sudan to make a film about the Dinka and the Nuer. Through the American embassy in Khartoum, I asked him to send money to Khalil, so that the Nuba could buy more equipment for the well contstruction. Without shovels, their progress would be very slow and most of them were using only dried pumpkin shells to dig. It was exciting to think that the Nuba might actually come upon water. Day after day, I waited for further news from the Sudan. I made a definite decision to fly to Khartoum in October, after the end of the rainy season, and stay with the Nuba for a long time.

Then black clouds gathered on the horizon. In the Middle East, a war had flared up between Israel, Egypt and Jordan and within six days the Israelis had won a victory that shook the world. The consequences for my trip were grave. Letters from the Sudan informed me that this war had had a serious impact on the position of Germans in Khartoum, and that I too was affected. A sudden and profound change had occurred in the Sudan. The positive attitude towards the Germans had turned into a negative one. Ruth Plaetschke and her husband, for whom Khartoum had become a second home, wrote to me:

> We loved being here, but everything has changed so thoroughly that we no longer feel right. When we used to appear in the marketplace, we had friendly greetings from all our vendors. But now they all frown at us. This is true not only for the Germans; the British and Americans are also undesirables. Many of them are leaving the Sudan. It is believed that this is due to the growing Russian influence.
>
> Your name has also made waves here. An Arab vendor, who lives in the

Nuba Hills, has lodged an official complaint in Parliament, because you photographed naked people – a crime for a Mohammedan. Abu Bakr, who acted as censor for your photographs, has been asked to comment. He defended you and took full responsibility. He said that your pictures are anthropologically valuable and do not defame the Nuba in any way. Abu Bakr has a great deal of influence here, but he has to be cautious to avoid losing his position. I must therefore greatly disappoint you. Hard as it may seem, for the time being you must not count on carrying out your wishes to settle down among the Nuba . . .

I couldn't read on. It struck me like a bolt of lightning. Never see my Nuba again? Have my dreams and wishes destroyed so suddenly? No. I would never give up. Never. Sometimes, the impossible can become possible after all. So many things can change. I was certain of one thing: whether I got permission or not, whether I was locked up or not, whatever they might do to me, I would see the Nuba again – if only for a few days. If I never got a visa again, then I would even marry a Sudanese, just to obtain Sudanese citizenship.

My patience was put to a long, hard test. None of my letters to Abu Bakr was answered. When I asked my friends why Abu Bakr was remaining silent, their responses were evasive. Only Ruth Plaetschke had the courage to tell me the truth. She wrote:

Abu Bakr feels as friendly to you as ever. That is why he doesn't want to give you unpleasant news, since at the present time you have no hope of obtaining a visa or support for your plans. There is no possible way of entering the Sudan without a visa. The airport is cordoned off so that not even visitors or people coming to pick up travellers can enter the building. Ruthless guards with machine pistols are stationed everywhere. They are quick to make arrests . . .

Now I saw that I could not expect to visit the Sudan for the time being and this had a disastrous effect on my mental and physical health. All my illnesses returned and I could not cope with them as effectively as in the past.

One day, some people I met – a married couple from Hamburg and a publisher who was introduced to me as Dr Bechtle – asked me about my future plans. I told him about the Nuba, about my yearning for Africa. I said that all I desired was a car, so that I could travel through Africa and shoot films and photos there. 'Is that all you desire?' the elderly gentleman from Hamburg asked me with a smile.

544

'Quite honestly,' I said, 'this is the only desire I have.'

The elderly gentleman looked at me for a while and then said, 'If that is your only desire, then I believe I can make it come true.'

At first, I thought he was joking, but then he told me how he and his wife very much admired my films, and – what made everything seem more credible – that he was Paul Hartwig, head of the Mercedes office in Hamburg. When he told me that he had several Unimogs, I slowly began to believe him.

Indeed, within a few days, I received a letter, which said, in black and white, that I could get a Unimog gratis. I was electrified. It was almost like a fairy tale. I could already see myself crossing Africa as my mind grasped the possibilities, I felt that I had been restored to life. I would stop at nothing to get the visa for the Sudan and perhaps my film could still be rescued. However, I was realistic enough to understand that the car did not solve everything. A film expedition, no matter how limited, would still cost a tidy sum. And could I drive the vehicle all by myself?

Nevertheless, I held on to the prospect that had now opened up for me. I went to Gaggenau and looked at the various types of vehicles at Mercedes, enthralled by their performance possibilities; realistically, however, I was forced to admit that I could not drive such a magnificent car through the Sudan on my own. Perhaps I could do it with a Landrover? Herr Hartwig was agreeable.

Since I needed certain special features, the Landrover had to be ordered from England. These extras included: protective underplates, super-powerful springs and shock absorbers, an electric petrol pump and a tropical roof. Meanwhile, things kept piling up in my apartment: more and more gear, food, medicine, large and small water tanks, and the excellent katadyn filters to make dirty water drinkable which were almost indispensable for expeditions in arid regions. I also collected gifts for my Nuba, especially the small, coloured beads, donated by someone in Schwäbisch Gmünd.

However, I still hadn't received a visa or a permit to bring my vehicle into the Sudan; uncertainty hovered over my head like a sword of Damocles, for I knew I was black-listed in Khartoum. Nor had I received any reply to the many letters I had written to Abu Bakr.

Despite this risk, I dared not interrupt my preparations which involved having to reserve a ticket for the boat trip to Alexandria months in advance. I was lucky enough to get a booking on the *Cynthia*, a small Greek freighter with the proviso that on 19 November 1968, the car would be loaded in Genoa – it was a deadline I was committed to. The Suez Canal was still closed, so the Mediterranean crossing was the best and also the cheapest solution. Driving from Alexandria to Aswan via Cairo was no problem, but neither the Egyptian consulate nor any travel agency could tell me whether or not I could go on to Wadi Halfa on the Sudanese border. There are two routes from Aswan to the Sudan – one along the Red Sea, the other across the desert – yet neither could be used, since the roads were blocked at various points, even though the Middle East war was over. My only chance was to cover that distance in two days on a Nile steamer sailing from Aswan to Wadi Halfa, but the difficulty would be finding out when the boat was scheduled to leave Aswan and whether it could take my Landrover.

HOW I FOUND HORST

Time whizzed by at a bewildering speed, and I still hadn't found a travelling companion; I knew now that I couldn't undertake this expedition alone, as I had originally planned. On the other hand, given my previous experiences, I did not want to take a crew. It is hard to get on in the bush with other people, no matter how nice they may otherwise be, for not everyone can endure equably the heat and strain. The companion I was looking for had to be stable and healthy and also enjoy the work. Not only did he have to be a good driver, but he also had to know how to fix cars, and, since I couldn't afford a cameraman, my companion would also have to know something about film-making. Such a companion would be ideal, but I realized the possibility of finding him was wishful thinking on my part. Then, once again, chance took a hand.

Whenever I went to the Arnold & Richter Printing Laboratory, I asked a clerk whether he knew of an assistant cameraman who could also deal with cross-country vehicles. The clerk merely laughed and said, 'The person you're looking for doesn't exist.' It seemed he was right; for months on end I had been asking all my friends, but to no avail. Then, one day, a man working in the delivery department came over and said, 'I happened to overhear what you were saying. I think I know just the man you're looking for.'

'Really,' I said in disbelief. 'Who is he? When can I meet him?'

'I can ask him. He comes here a lot to have his films developed.'

'What kind of work does he do?'

'He's an assistant cameraman, and also a mechanic – a motor mechanic, I think. I pricked up my ears.

'Could you introduce me?'

'I can contact him through my mother. He rents a room from her.' While jotting down the name and telephone number on a slip of paper, the man added, 'He'd be just the right man for your expedition.'

Several days later, when I called the number, Frau Horn answered. Her son had already told her about me but I was disappointed to hear that her tenant had left for a vacation in Italy just the day before and wouldn't be back for three weeks. 'But,' Frau Horn went on, 'Herr Kettner asked me to tell you that he will get in touch with you as soon as he returns to Munich. My son Reinhold outlined your problem to him the day before his departure and he thought the whole thing was a joke. But if it really is an expedition to Africa, then he says he'd be interested.'

'And what kind of a person is Herr Kettner?' I asked.

Frau Horn became very enthusiastic. 'A fine person,' she said, 'really a fine person, and so quiet and modest. I've never had such a tenant. His room is always orderly, he doesn't smoke or drink, and he's always so helpful. I can only say the very best things about him.'

It all sounded too good to be true, though it was very questionable whether anything would come of it. I had to find a solution. I needed a companion at least as far as Khartoum; after that, he could fly back from there, and as for the shooting, I would, if the worst came to the worst, hire a Sudanese cameraman. Such makeshift solution would be better than ditching the expedition.

As preparations went ahead, an unpleasant surprise came from my friend Ursula Weistroffer in Khartoum, in a letter I had been looking forward to for a long time. Dismayed, I read:

The political situation is still uncertain, and I don't know whether Abu Bakr can obtain your residence permit for the Nuba Hills. His Arabic politeness prevents him from openly stating whether or not you are still black-listed, which makes it difficult to learn the truth. You certainly have a lot of admirers in the Sudan, but I do not believe that any of them would care to pick an argument with the security police in order to get you a long stay. To be sure, the Nuba, unlike the Dinka and Shilluk, are not hostile to the Arabs; but in the eyes of the Arabs, the Nuba are, nevertheless, 'primitive' people, and if a white person comes along and sympathizes with them, then the simple Arabs, who can't imagine that anyone could love those people, they suspect ulterior motives. I'm sorry that my letter is so contrary to your hopes. I wish you the strength that you need to make your decisions.

For the first time, I was on the verge of giving up the whole idea. But I just couldn't. Then something happened to cheer me up. Late one night, I was dictating letters, when the telephone rang. It was Horst Kettner whom I had forgotten all about. Half an hour later, he was in my apartment. I welcomed a rather shy young man, very tall, slim and attractive, whose face inspired my trust from the very first moment. Tactfully, I tried to find out about his background and in broken German he told me he was the child of German parents, but had grown up in Czechoslovakia; he had been working in Germany for the past two years. My name meant nothing to him, he had never heard of me; it was his interest in Africa which had prompted him to get in touch with me. When I was forced to tell him that I could afford to pay only his travelling expenses and the necessary insurance fees but no salary, he didn't care. He accepted my offer without hesitation.

Horst got to work three days later. There was so much to do: we had to complete the camera equipment, do test shots with the optics and filters, purchase stock and film, and, above all, acquire the tools and replacement parts for the vehicle.

It was already late September, and although our visas and the vehicle entry permit still hadn't arrived – just like last time – we went ahead and had our vaccinations done. It was now time to pick up the Landrover in London, and as Horst had agreed to take care of this, I had to take the risk of giving him the full amount for the Landrover, although he didn't speak a word of English. His trip to England was not altogther smooth for there were problems with the vehicle. A strike prevented Horst from picking it up but, with the help of my British friends, he managed to get the work on it completed and picked it up at the Rover Works in Solihull. Then, since the boat would be sailing from Genoa very soon, Horst drove non-stop from London to Munich. Already my new assistant had done a wonderful job at proving himself.

After that, events followed each other in rapid succession. Horst had water tanks attached to the van, plus a stable luggage carrier that could sleep two. Meanwhile, I drove to Wetzlar to test my photo equipment for Leitz and also to add to it. The next day, I went to the Frobenius Institute in Frankfurt, where I showed my Nuba slides and discussed my expedition with Professor Haberland. One day later, in Munich, I stood in front of a BBC camera; they were making a fifty-minute film about me, directed by Norman Swallow, an extraordinarily nice Englishman, with whom I became friends. I was also the subject of a second film being made at the same time. Its director was an American, Chadwig Hall, a sensitive artist, who was working together with his wife, the well-known German photographer Christa Peters.

Then, a miracle occurred. The visas arrived, literally at the last moment. I couldn't believe it and was delirious with joy, even though I still had no permit for the Landrover; but I could at least enter the Sudan myself and the news gave me a tremendous boost.

Horst, busy as a beaver from dawn to dusk, measured the crates and realized that the van couldn't possibly hold all our baggage. We had to get hold of a trailer as fast as possible and fortunately Inge and Heinz Hiestand, my Austrian friends whom I had met years ago in the southern Sudan, generously lent me their cross-country trailer.

Our preparations were now advancing at a feverish pace. Customs lists, insurance and indispensable medicines were only a few of the things to consider. Nothing could be forgotten, since there was so much that couldn't be obtained in the Sudan. I had invited a dowser from Allgäu to teach me how to detect groundwater. The dowsing rods were made of copper, and they actually started vibrating in my hands wherever there were water pipes.

Next came the packing. Horst declared that we had to leave behind at least forty per cent of the 'most necessary' stuff. But what? The canned bread was just as important as the oatmeal, the bottles of gas for the cooker were just as indispensable as the lighting set for the filming. I just couldn't toss anything overboard. On that day of all days, the lift in my building was out of order, and we lived on the fifth floor. Uli Sommerlath helped us lug the three thousand pounds of heavy crates and sacks down five flights, but we still couldn't make it and it was past midnight when I drove to the main railway station to enlist the help of the lone porter who might still be on duty at this late hour. We were to have started out by noon.

Horst worked away in the courtyard, loading the crates into the Landrover and the trailer, while I gathered everything I considered essential. We hadn't slept a wink in twenty-four hours, and it was already 4 a.m. To make matters worse, it now began to snow. When I looked, I was stunned to see that Horst had unloaded crates which in my opinion were absolutely indispensable. There was simply no room for them yet they contained vital things like presents for my Nuba – pearls, mirrors, necklaces, scarves. Unwilling to leave them behind, I insisted we reload them, but Horst replied, 'If we do, the van will collapse.'

There followed a heated argument in the snowstorm which resulted in my throwing out part of the food and Horst stuffing the bags of gifts into various nooks and crannies.

By 7 a.m., it was all done, but we were so exhausted that we could barely keep our eyes open; climbing into the heavily loaded van, we drove off into the grey dawn. Uli, who was at the end of his tether, remained behind. The streets were icy and as the overloaded trailer made it hard to drive the van, Horst had to be extremely careful. He asked me to keep talking to him so that he wouldn't doze off. We couldn't stop to sleep; otherwise, we would have missed the boat in Genoa.

Horst in his time had driven many trucks, but he had never been as tired as he was now. What's more, he had lost a good twenty pounds during the preparations. We mustn't fall asleep: that was the thought uppermost in our minds.

The customs house on the Brenner presented new anxieties, but, maybe because of the violent snowstorm, the Italians were extremely accommodating and waved us through. In Bolzano, we drank espressos, and then pressed on; soon we were on the brink of total exhaustion. From village to village, we wondered what to do, knowing we couldn't go on much longer; shortly before Lake Garda, we stopped at a small hotel, and allowed ourselves an hour and a half's rest.

At 3.30 a.m., when it was already getting light, we set off again. The road was no longer icy and for the first time we could drive at a decent speed. It was a race against time. Then, forty miles short of Genoa, one of the trailer tyres blew and when Horst pulled out the tools, he accidentally dislodged the tin cans we had distributed throughout the trailer at the very last moment and they rolled across the motorway. While I gathered them up, Horst feverishly changed the tyre; we had hoped we were going to arrive on schedule but couldn't make up the minutes we were now losing; we could only trust to luck.

When we reached Genoa, the next problem was how to find the right dock in this gigantic port. From one section of the harbour to the next we went, asking dockers, policemen, anybody – but nobody could help us and it was already one hour past the loading deadline. In my desperation, I grabbed an Italian by the arm and, using gestures, tried to get him to follow us. He eyed me as if I'd gone berserk – frantically pointing at my watch and then at the harbour – shook his head and walked away. I dashed after him and was encouraged when he paused at the door of a building and signalled that he would soon be back; I waited and waited for what seemed like an eternity. At last he returned, and for a moment I didn't recognize him; he now wore the uniform of a police officer and was ready to escort us to our ship. The hands of my watch were racing along and time was running out when finally we sighted the *Cynthia*, still in the harbour. I heaved a sigh of relief.

The skipper was willing to let us aboard, customs and shipping formalities were expedited, and it was time to sail. We had made it – almost. The men who were supposed to hoist the Landrover and the trailer on deck took one look at how overloaded it was, shook their heads and waved us off. At first, I didn't understand, but the captain explained the vehicle was too heavy and their ropes weren't strong enough to heave it on deck. We stood rooted to the spot. The ship loomed in front of us – surely it couldn't all have been for nothing? I burst into tears, weeping like a child, and the captain took pity on me. He had the trailer disconnected and several crates removed from the van; then up it went. Some twenty men had secured the vehicle very gingerly with the help of a loading net while a huge throng surrounded us, watching the manoeuvre. Would the old ropes hold – or would the Landrover plunge down?

Despite my anxious state, I had the presence of mind to grab our Super-8 and shoot the scene. Through the lens, I saw the vehicle dangling at a drunken angle in the net, slowly rocking through the air. 'Dear God,' I prayed, 'please don't let it fall.' It worked. The crane set the Landrover on the deck without a hitch. Dead tired, we staggered to our cabins.

THE 1968-9 SUDAN EXPEDITION BEGINS

We had five days to sleep our fill during which I saw little of Horst who was seasick and rarely left his cabin. We went ashore in Alexandria, but before starting for Cairo we had to attend to the customs formalities; these, however, were completed within a few hours.

The first thing we had to do in Cairo was go to the main post office but there we found neither a letter nor a telegram. Next, we had to determine how to get our Landrover to Wadi Halfa, and found there was a small Nile steamer twice a week from Aswan. I recalled the advice given me by Herr de Haas, the former German ambassador to the Sudan, and I cabled the speaker of parliament in Khartoum: 'Arriving Wadi Halfa on boat 7 December 1968 – Leni Riefenstahl.' I didn't have the faintest idea who would receive this telegram, or whether it would work, but it was worth a try.

We left Cairo for Aswan, a distance of six hundred miles away, and as the roads were good, we advanced rapidly. Since the steamer wouldn't be sailing until four days later, we spent a few days in Luxor, which for me was a dream come true since I could visit the Valley of the Kings. It was a tremendous experience and I could hardly tear myself away from the frescoes in the burial chambers.

When we saw our little steamer in the harbour of Aswan, I was seized with anxiety for this was no tourist ship; it was a fruit boat, carrying only Arabs and blacks. Where could we stow our van and trailer?

Loading them was, in fact, extremely difficult. The Landrover was too high, so that our heavily burdened luggage rack had to be removed – it took twelve strong dockworkers to do the job. Then, as the ship had no room for our trailer and luggage rack, it had to take an extra boat in tow. Horst and I sat on deck amid the crates of oranges and dug into our provisions for the first time, filtering water and eating pounds and pounds of delectable citrus fruit. This was not the Nile passage I had imagined.

On the third day, as we approached Wadi Halfa, I became very nervous and fearful. Would we get into the Sudan or not? The Sudanese border lay ahead of us and it was there that the fate of our expedition would be decided. I watched several Sudanese officials coming over to the boat, and as one of them headed straight towards me I held my breath.

'Are you Miss Riefenstahl?'

I couldn't speak.

Then a second official in uniform came over and said, in a cordial tone, 'You are welcome in our country.'

Was he making fun of me? Welcome – after receiving no visa for months, and obtaining no permit for my van; there had to be a catch; I was afraid of another nasty surprise. I listened incredulously when the officer told me that Khartoum had notified them of my arrival and asked them to make everything as convenient as possible for me. First of all, they had reserved a railway wagon and two couchettes, thus, enabling us to travel to Khartoum that very evening. Horst and I just couldn't get over it.

No one asked for the vehicle permit. Customs officials filled out our forms and then stamped our passes without so much as glancing at our masses of luggage. For months, I had received nothing but bad news from Khartoum. What was the explanation for this change? We were guests of the district commissioner, a man of considerable charm who entertained us lavishly and, when twilight came, arranged for us to be escorted to the station.

The trip takes thirty-six hours, one day and two nights, and it was pretty late on the second night when the train stopped and I heard a male voice calling my name from the corridor, 'Leni, Leni.' It was General O.H. Osman. Years earlier, the first time I had travelled into the Nuba Hills, he had given me letters of introduction to the governors of various Sudanese provinces, asking them to assist me. He had stood out because of his vivacity and his hospitality.

'It's great to have you back in the Sudan,' he said. I was notified by

Khartoum that you were passing through here. I'd love to invite you to dinner. Do come to my home.'

Disconcerted, I replied that we could not leave the train.

'Don't worry,' he said. 'The train won't go without you.'

Feeling rather confused, we got out and were driven to the general's home where a servant showed us two elegant bathrooms – a welcome sight indeed for we hadn't been able to shower since the steamer passage. During the dinner, which was attended by the police chief and other officers, I learned that all sorts of things were awaiting us in Khartoum. To my astonishment, the general even asked whether I had evening clothes. Parties were the last thing in the world I was prepared for!

'Make yourself nice and attractive, they're expecting you in Khartoum and you will be received like a queen.' It was all beginning to sound uncanny.

The train had been held at the station without difficulty because General O.H. Osman was the highest officer in Atbara. When we said goodbye, he invited us to spend a week with him on the way back. We continued our trip. Wondering what it all meant.

In Khartoum, the Weistroffers, who were expecting us as their guests, were already informed about the honours awaiting me, but they knew no details. The first gala reception took place in a palatial building in Omdurman but was an ordeal for me because I had caught a bad cold, and it was a strain answering the many questions with my hoarse voice. When the host sat down with me, I asked him what this festive welcome meant after my months of waiting for the visa in Germany. Smiling, he leaned back in his chair and said, 'It's a strange story.' I looked at this Sudanese in his elegant, black silk *jellaba* with its silver trimming; he must surely be a cabinet member or the governor. 'I happened to see your Olympic film on TV in New York,' he said, 'and I was very excited. Then I read a *Newsweek* article which said that you were a friend of the Sudan and that you were preparing an expedition. Next, I went to London, and by pure chance I saw *Olympia* once again, on the BBC. And now I'll get to the point,' he went on. 'The BBC then showed another film which was shot in your home prior to your expedition. You talked about your plans, your film about the Nuba and your love of Africa. It was really fascinating. Then, in Bad Godesberg, I learned about your great efforts to obtain the visas and the vehicle permit, so I saw to it that you received everything immediately. Unfortunately, the permit arrived too late; you had already left.'

It was then that I realized that this man was the speaker of the Sudanese parliament, whom I had wired from Cairo. Forgetting where I was, I embraced him, for my joy and gratitude were boundless. He handed me his card: Dr Mubarek Shaddad, Speaker of Parliament.

I felt able to ask him why I had originally been forced to wait so long for the visas. He told me that during my film expedition in the Nuba Hills during 1964-5, a Sudanese merchant had told the police in Khartoum that we had signalled to the enemies of the Sudanese with our torches. It was then I remembered the Arab merchant, whom I had helped so greatly. 'It was thanks to him that I was labelled an 'enemy' of the Sudanese in the police files, and had had my visa applications turned down over and over again. If Dr Shaddad hadn't seen my films, I wouldn't have been granted a Sudanese visa for years.

Cautiously I asked Dr Shaddad questions about the natives in the southern Sudan and was delighted to hear that he was very interested in the ethnological studies on these tribes ever since he had spent several years in the Sudanese province of Equatoria. I asked him whether an expedition into the Sudan would be possible at this time.

'Why not? Would you like to visit the south?' he asked ingenuously.

Surprised, I answered, 'Yes – of course. But I've heard about disturbances there?'

'The disturbances have been virtually quelled for some time now and the area is no longer dangerous. You can see for yourself that the stories spread about the Sudanese are lies.'

'Do you think I could visit the Dinka in Wau and the Latuka in Torit?'

'You can travel wherever you like, even in areas that have been out of bounds for years because of the fighting.'

'And would I be allowed to take photographs and make films?'

'Of course. We will put suitable vehicles at your disposal. All you have to do is tell us where you'd like to go.'

Choking back my excitement, I asked, 'Can I drive back to the Nuba Hills?'

'Why not?'

I was so overjoyed that I leaped up and exclaimed, 'You're wonderful.'

PARADISE ALTERED

Shortly before Christmas, we left Khartoum. Ursula Weistroffer, who wanted to meet my Nuba, came with us, but only for two weeks. As usual, the first thing we did upon reaching El Obeid was call on the governor since it was he alone who decided whether films and photographs could be shot in the Nuba Hills. Thus it was with an anxious heart that I stood in front of Sayed Mohammed Abbas Faqhir, the governor or Kordofan. Imagine my relief when I heard him say, 'Miss Leni, I know how much you care about your Nuba friends. I hope that this time you have the time of your life in the Nuba Hills.' This was not mere rhetoric for he did indeed help me in any way he could.

I went shopping at the market of El Obeid, partly for furniture for my Nuba home. To Horst's dismay, I bought a huge old wooden table, a cupboard and several stools, as well as straw mats, wooden shelves, bamboo poles and, for the Nuba, a whole sack of sugar. We had to hire a small truck to carry all these things.

I had already spent three Christmases with the Nuba and I wanted to reach Tadoro again before Christmas Eve. Kadugli was already behind us and we were some thirty miles from my campsite when the first Nuba came running out of the fields. I knew none of them but when they saw me they kept shouting as they raced alongside our van: 'Leni, Leni!'

There it stood, my tree with its gigantic crown, and it welcomed me for the fourth time. As in the past, we were immediately surrounded by Nuba and greeted with handshakes, hugs, laughter and yet more laughter, as if a long-missed family member had returned and were being embraced by everyone. The first thing I learned was that Natu had built me a house, which he proudly showed off to me and to Ursula Weistroffer and Horst who were speechless with wonder.

The Nuba carried our baggage up to the house and since not everything could be stowed inside, we decided to build straw huts for the rest. The Nuba offered well-considered suggestions and had already worked out where to get the materials. The entire village helped to construct the *rakobas*, which required tree trunks, dura stalks, straw bark.

We worked so hard that we nearly forgot about our Christmas party and it was almost midnight when we unfolded our artificial Christmas tree, trimmed it and lit a few candles before inviting our Nuba friends over. We gave the children the sweets they loved and the older people tobacco; there were beads for the girls and women, and the young men were enthralled by the great variety of lovely fabrics which I had brought. However, the high point of our festivities was a surprise prepared by Horst; at the very last moment, he had managed to get the right materials for building a shower–hose with a shower head, attached to a plastic canister that was pulled up into a tree. On Christmas Eve, we tried out the shower by torchlight and it was an indescribable feeling getting rid of the dust. We had the most fun with the children. At first, they were afraid of it, but as soon as a few of the little tots had a go, they all wanted a turn, screaming with delight. Horst had once again proved himself to the ultimate degree. Assiduous, calm and understanding, he was an ideal comrade. No work was too hard for him, and he managed to deal with every technical problem.

The dowsing rods were tried out, but we soon gave up on them because the rods trembled far too often, and it would have been impossible to dig in so many places. The Nuba had abandoned their earlier efforts after Alipo broke his leg in a thirty-foot hole. Luckily, his fracture soon mended. I saw only one solution to the water shortage: a real well had to be built.

Soon, Ursula had to leave – although the Nuba had grown very fond of her, Horst drove her to Kadugli and from there, the district commissioner took her to El Obeid. Shortly after Horst returned, I heard shouts in the vicinity of our campsite and saw all the Nuba dashing in one direction. I ran after them and found them peering into a deep hole which I had never seen before because it had been covered over with branches and soil after Alipo had broken his leg. Now, a boy of about twelve had fallen in and though they shouted down into the hole, there was no answer. None of them could climb down in this thirty-foot pit since the vertical walls had been washed smooth by rain. They were helpless and the boy's father was in despair. I hurried to get some rope as fast I could and summoned Horst. We let the rope down, hoping the boy could grasp it and be hoisted up, but nothing stirred. I recalled my climbing days and, looping the rope around my body, I had Horst lower me, while the Nuba watched fearfully. I reached the boy who was still conscious and whimpering softly. Tying him to the rope I had them raise him gently; then they sent the rope down again for me. When I surfaced, I saw the father violently beating the boy, even though the accident was not his fault. I was so indignant that I forgot myself and slapped the big Nuba man left and right. He stared at me in amazement, but did nothing, while all the Nuba nodded in approval. The boy's back was rather seriously injured, but Horst treated him, and he soon recovered. I had the Nuba fill in the well hole.

Before we started shooting, we wanted to show the Nuba our slides and some 8-mm films of Charlie Chaplin, Harold Lloyd and Buster Keaton. We had patched together a screen out of pieces of canvas and, with the help of our small dynamo, we managed to generate enough light. Our film shows were a sensation. People who were living practically in the Stone Age, who had never even used a wheel, suddenly saw themselves on the screen. The Nuba laughed very hard but then screamed and wept for they were really frightened at the sight of closeups, unable to understand why their heads were so gigantic on the screen. They sat there from dawn to dusk; every stone was occupied, and in the evening, the young people squatted in the trees.

They were just as excited by the sound recordings, especially those we had done, without their realizing it, of their conversations, their songs, their shouts during the great wrestling festival and their litanies during the funerals; they kept wanting to hear everything over and over again. So many hundreds of Nuba poured in that, to prevent a stampede, we had to stop the screenings.

One important job for us was to help the sick and we set up a regular medical service. The best time for treatment was after sunset and since the Nuba were not accustomed to any kind of medicine, we effected some incredible cures. As for the patients whom we couldn't help, Horst drove them to the hospital in Kadguli. This often led to dramatic scenes when the patients' families refused to let them go. I understood why Dr Schweitzer had opposed his medical colleagues by setting up his hospital at Lambarane in such a way that families could remain with their sick. Our experiences confirmed that he had done the right thing.

When we attended the first wrestling festival, I noticed that now nearly all the wrestlers were wearing gaudy trousers in all sorts of colours, and the lovely calabashes that had adorned the backs of their belts were now frequently replaced with plastic bottles or even empty tin cans. I was saddened and Horst was disappointed that the things he had seen in my photos were no longer here. In the end, we scrapped our plan to film the festival; it would have been a waste of celluloid.

How could this change have come about? Just two years earlier, I had shot mesmerizing footage of these matches, but during the first few days of my return, I had been so thrilled that I had failed to notice these external changes. However, the passing of the ancient customs was even more apparent when I went to a funeral. A rite that had once affected me so poignantly was now embarrassing. The once ghostly figures, covered with ash, now wore dirty, ragged clothing. When Horst and I visited some of my friends, I was dismayed to find the doors to various houses locked. I asked why and they said, 'Nuba arami' – the Nuba steal. At first, I just couldn't believe it. Not only had I never needed to lock my baggage, but anything I lost had always been returned to me. What had caused this change? It couldn't be the fault of tourists, for apart from a British air-hostess who had managed to advance this far with her father, no outsider had ever come here except for myself.

The reason was, no doubt, linked to the fact that civilization was spreading further and further throughout the world affecting others as it had the American Indians and the Australian aborigines. Roads were being built, schools set up and money, root of all evil, came into the lives of people. Money produces greed and envy and was at the bottom of this profound change. Equally disastrous was the fact that the Nuba were no longer permitted to run around naked, but were forced to wear clothes. The Sudanese government had ordered this several years before because, as Moslems, they considered nudity an abomination. Six years earlier, during my first visit, the soldiers driving military vehicles through the Nuba Hills had distributed colourful gym shorts to the natives and this had been the thin end of the wedge. The clothing stricture had deprived them of their innocence, making them ethically unsure of themselves. The economic consequences were just as serious for whenever their garments wore out, they had to buy new ones. They needed to buy soap, and to obtain the necessary money, many Nuba left their lovely homes and went to the towns. When they came back, the childlike laughter had vanished from their faces.

I had experienced the same thing in East Africa where I had encountered members of the Masai and other tribes who were ragged with the sunlight gone from their eyes. Gone too was their natural and charming dignity. They no longer belonged to their tribes and swelled the slum populations of the cities where they saw so many awful things. What had they previously known about the crimes and perversions they could now see portrayed on the screen? Wherever the dark side of civilization spreads out, human happiness disappears. Now, with infinite sadness, I saw these developments among my Nuba.

I had feared this tragedy for a long time, but since the Nuba lived in such extreme isolation, I had not expected it to come about so soon. Now I saw the beginnings of this disastrous process here too and I could discern more changes day by day. Nuba came to me and complained that they had been robbed; someone had stolen a tool or a pot of honey, which was an expensive rarity for them. One day, Alipo was very upset: he told me that his brother's house near the school in Rheika had been completely looted and then set on fire. Just two years earlier, such a calamity would have been unthinkable; now we had no choice but to lock up our equipment and provisions. Horst made a primitive door for our hut and attached a padlock. If we went out, elderly Nuba volunteered to stand guard.

This situation also affected our work schedule. There was no prospect of repeating any of my lost or spoiled film footage. We couldn't even do close-ups at the *seribe* since neither the young men nor the boys were willing to part with their ragged clothing. When Horst asked a boy to slip out of his tattered shorts and cover his body with ash, he smiled in embarrassment and refused. We gave up.

In Tadoro, there was now only one man, an elderly Nuba, who still went about unclad. His name was Gabicke, and he was a real original. Once he came to us to ask us a favour. From an old piece of cloth he ponderously unrolled some torn banknotes, nibbled at by mice, which he said no one would accept. When he cautiously spread them out on my mattress, we saw that they added up to twenty Sudanese pounds – a fortune among the Nuba. Gabicke had saved up this nest egg over years of hard work, by planting more dura than the other Nuba and selling the surplus to Arab merchants. He asked me to trade him new banknotes for his old ones – a request with which I could easily comply. He left our hut smiling radiantly, and the next day, when I saw him going out to the fields, the front of his leather belt sported a pouch containing his treasure. He explained that stored like this it couldn't be stolen.

Oddly enough, the weather had also changed. During my earlier visits to the Nuba Hills, the sky had always been blue, but this time, it was very different. Furthermore, heat constantly alternated with cold, so that sometimes we were so cold that we switched on the heat in the Landrover, only to find, just a short time later, the heat so unendurable that we had to wrap our bodies in wet cloth. An even more peculiar change was that the clear views we had always enjoyed in the Nuba Hills no longer existed. The air was hazy, and we no longer experienced the marvellous sunsets that Horst had so greatly admired in my photos. The Nuba assured us that they had never known such weather.

Although all this made our work more difficult, we spared no effort to get pictures that contained something of the natural work of the Nuba. Nevertheless, we experienced disappointments even in areas where we would never have expected any sort of decline.

The weather grew worse and worse and one morning the air was filled with red dust so that we couldn't see more than a few yards away – a natural phenomenon that had apparently never occurred here before. Although it wasn't even mid-March, an otherwise ideal time for our work, premature rain could spell danger. We spent a few stressful weeks trying to make up for several missing shots but usually we came back empty-handed. In the end, I decided to film only inside the huts, where, aside from a few metal bowls, everything looked the same as the past.

Our first attempt was dramatic, though initially everything went well. Horst had set up the equipment not too far from the hut so that the noise wouldn't interfere with the sound recording. I then told the Nuba what I wanted them to do, but, unfortunately, we couldn't get started because too many onlookers crowded into the hut. It was unbearably hot, my hands were wet and the lamps were knocked over, but I didn't dare to lose my temper. I had to ask them amiably to leave and then try to start again. However, the Nuba outside were making such a racket that recording the sound was out of the question; we decided eventually to shoot without sound and do the sound track later. Meanwhile, so much time had elapsed that the daylight had almost vanished by the time Horst, squeezing into a corner, could begin.

The Nuba were spontaneous and uninhibited when answering my questions and were obviously enjoying themselves. Before long, we were disturbed once again by a Nuba who dashed in with what was evidently a piece of upsetting news since, one moment later, the hut was empty. Grabbing their spears, the Nuba swarmed up the rocks and we learned from the women that a goat had been dragged off by a predator. Now the men were all in pursuit but soon they returned empty-handed but keen to continue shooting. By now, however, the hut had filled up with fumes and smoke because our host's wife insisted upon cooking dinner; nothing would change her mind. Refusing to move, she just kept stirring her gruel. I had to think of something and finally I bribed her with a small mirror. Beaming, she allowed the men to put out the fire, but, by now, darkness had set in, and we had to call it a day. The sky was covered with dark, gloomy clouds such as I had never before seen here and which the Nuba eyed anxiously. Growing uneasy, I asked them whether this meant rain. 'Gnama-birne basso,' they said – Rain may come.

I knew we would be prisoners of the rain if it came too early for we wouldn't be able to drive away even in the best four-wheel vehicle. No outsider had ever spent the rainy season here because within a few short hours the ground turns into a deep morass. Our hearts sank at the thought of our film stock buried in a pit which one hour of rain could destroy. A premature rainfall would be disastrous for the Nuba as well. The harvest hadn't been brought in yet, and the rain would destroy most of it, and this would mean starvation.

The entire village – even the children, the old and the sick – set about bringing in the harvest and we helped by driving the dura to the gathering points. When we consulted the Nuba about how best to save our belongings in case of sudden rain, Alipo displayed an amazing organizational talent.

Even though we had considered it impossible, our worst fears were realized as we sat in the *rakoba* and felt the first drops falling through the straw roof. Then it began to rattle down – the rain had come. Hurriedly, we took the film stock out of the pit and carried it to the vehicle, while the Nuba lugged every single one of our crates from our *rakoba* to their rain-proof huts. Everyone pitched in, and soon our equipment was safe – but our *rakoba* was soaked and half ruined. The rain had come three months early. Not even the oldest Nuba could recall ever seeing rain in mid-March, yet, despite this alarming situation, they remained astonishingly calm and soon their composure affected us too.

When the rain stopped after several hours, the ground was soaked and there was no possibility of driving. I shuddered at the thought of being cut off from the outside world for months on end, especially as we had only enough provisions for a few weeks, and were running out of medicine. What would happen if one of us fell ill? Not even the most powerful car could get us out. A stay during the rainy season ought to be prepared very thoroughly. Special clothes are needed to protect you not only against countless swarms of mosquitoes but also against the many snakes that come out during that time. On the whole, the rainy season is a gruelling period. Large portions of the fields are inundated, and to reach them, the Nuba have to wade through hip-high water and swamp. In places where the water is too deep, they use ropes, which they themselves weave, but as they can't swim, and are afraid of water, many of them drown, especially the elderly.

On the other hand, the rainy season has its positive sides. It brings fish, of which the Nuba did drawings for me in the sand. These fish seem to be a very unusual species, which survives the dry season by remaining in the mud of the ground water. In our *rakoba*, we noticed small frogs suddenly leaping about in the sand under the constantly dripping water bag. During the rainy season everything grows a lot faster and the Nuba plant peanuts, beans and some Indian corn around their huts. In this way, they store up a lot of vitamins, which may explain how they manage to get through the droughts on a diet so poor in nutriments.

The rain had stopped, but it was still uncertain as to when we would be able to leave since the ground was still far too wet. We had loaded the Landrover, ready to make an immediate start, but the heat was once again formidable, and here was a danger that our film stock and food would perish. Every morning, we therefore had to unload the boxes and carry them to the Nuba houses some hundred yards away, a difficult and arduous task.

Our farewell celebration made both us and the Nuba sad, since no one knew if we would be able to come again, but the occasion went off happily enough. There were so many guests that there was soon no room at all either inside or out of our *rakobas* which had been put together again after the rain. Horst and I were not the only givers of presents; the Nuba showered us with gifts – bowls of nuts and marisse which they freely distributed. Mothers brought along even their youngest children, and they couldn't hear enough of their songs and reminiscences on our tape-recorder.

It was late when the last people left, and there was hardly any time for Horst and me to sleep. We spent the night packing and considering in detail how best to divide what we were leaving behind amongst our Nuba friends. It had to be done fairly, but we know there would be no jealousy. Even the smallest thing was valuable to them, every nail, every piece of wood, every empty jam jar: everything was hotly sought-after, though they never begged us for anything. We also wanted to leave toolboxes, saws and other implements, torches and batteries, also sugar and tea, paraffin lamps and water containers. No less valuable were the medicines, bandages, ointments, antiseptic powder, sticking plaster and cough sweets. Most precious of all were our four *rakobas* but we didn't have to think too hard about those: four families had built them for us with special diligence and each of those would now fall heir to one *rakoba*.

Alipo was the first to appear. He arrived before sunrise, followed by Natu, Tukami and Notti. The day hadn't even really begun, and more and more Nuba kept gathering around our *rakobas* and our vehicle. They came from the neighbouring mountains, from Tossari, Tabballa, Tomeluba. In contrast to the previous evening, they were very quiet, but their faces seemed anxious. Natu and Alipo took over the distribution of our belongings and, as we had predicted, there was no fighting. We could barely make our way to our Landrover.

Horst gingerly pressed on the accelerator, for hundreds of Nuba crowded in front of us and at our sides, dashing along beside the wheels, each of them wanting to shake our hands one last time. Horst could hold only one hand out of the window, while the Nuba practically yanked me from the vehicle. They ran behind us for a long, long time, and Horst just couldn't bring himself to drive off.

The farther we got from Tadoro, the darker grew the sky. Any moment, a new shower could make it impossible for us to continue. But my mind was filled with the Nuba. Despite the great chance they had undergone, I cared for them as much as before. Would I ever be able to see them again and perhaps actually spend the rainy season with them as I had so often wished? We hadn't even left the Nuba Hills when I was almost overcome by a strong desire to turn back.

Exhausted from our strenuous drive, we finally reached Semeih, where a nasty surprise awaited us. Our train to Khartoum was not running. We were trapped, for our still overloaded vehicle and the trailer would not be able to make it over the long, difficult road to Khartoum. Our only chance was to reach El Obeid via the north-west, but this route ran across a desertlike terrain, its trails blurred by sand storms, and was dangerous.

I shall never forget that nightmare trip. The vehicle had to keep wallowing through deep sand for there was neither road nor signposts and we could get our bearings only by the sun. In the relentless heat, no man or beast was to be seen, no vehicle came our way, no clue indicated our whereabouts. The upsetting thing was that we didn't dare stop the car for we would quickly have stuck in the deep desert sand. Deep ruts made driving even harder and our eyes were dazzled by the sun since we had to keep driving towards it. I didn't dare speak, I was too afraid of distracting Horst.

We were accompanied by a monkey, a gift from the Nuba, which we hadn't wanted to leave in Tadoro where she certainly would have been killed and eaten, for the Nuba eat anything that creeps or flies. Now she sat there, well-behaved, either on my lap, on Horst's shoulders or on the steering wheel. We called her Resi.

At long last, after sundown, lights emerged on the horizon; it was night by the time we reached El Obeid.

IN THE SOUTHERN SUDAN

I had been lucky enough to get a plane ticket from El Obeid to Khartoum, and for several days I waited there for Horst. When the train finally arrived in Khartoum, he was the last passenger walking from the end of the platform. Horst was filthy, emaciated and carried a distressed monkey. Both of them had inflamed eyes for during their thirty-hour ride Horst had lain in the open wagon behind the Landrover, because he didn't want to leave the valuable material and the cameras unattended for even an instant. The trip must have been an infernal torment for both of them. The flat bed of the wagon, fitted with iron, was so blazing hot that it could burn your skin. The only shade was underneath the Landrover and that was where Horst and the frightened monkey had managed to find protection from the broiling heat.

The house, where we were able to recover from the strain and stress of our trip, was surrounded by a large garden filled with many trees where Resi could let off steam, for she was accustomed to running around without a rope. At night, she slept in some treetop, but from sunrise to dusk she always remained near us.

Actually, we wanted to get back to Germany as soon as possible: but Dr Mubarak Shaddad had long since prepared a trip for me to the southern

Sudan and I couldn't turn down such a generous invitation from the Sudanese government. My plan was to sell the Landrover in Khartoum to pay for my return ticket to Munich. Such a vehicle commanded high price in the Sudan, so we gave it to a colleague of Herr Weistroffer's who would try to sell it for us during our absence.

Shortly before our departure Resi disappeared. When Horst had driven to town, she had probably scurried after the car and lost her way. Since that hellish rail trip, throughout which she had anxiously snuggled against Horst, she would never leave his side and hissed at anyone who came too close. We searched for several days, enquiring in hundreds of homes but to no avail. I promised a large reward, on TV and in the newspapers, but there was no response. The police also made an effort, but the monkey hunt was useless. Our Resi, whom we had grown so fond of, was gone. However, I found some solace in the thought that she'd be a lot better off at home in Africa than in the cold city of Munich, where I would have had to donate her to the Hellabrunn Zoo.

Our first destination was Malakal, the small capital of the Upper Nile Province, where the governor, who was expecting us, had already worked out an extensive programme. I was anxious to see if I could find any traces of the unrest that had brought such turmoil to Malakal. The Dinka and Shilluk villages, however, showed no traces of fighting, no charred huts, though the ruins had probably been removed by now. I again met the Shilluk king, who joined us on an outing; his authority seemed undiminished: every Shilluk respectfully threw himself on the ground in front of the monarch.

Our next stop was Wau, capital of the southern province of Bahr el Ghazal, a fertile territory, inhabited mainly by the Dinka, the largest tribe in the Sudan. Like the Shilluk, the Dinka are a warlike people, and some of them had fought against the north Sudanese; yet here too we found no trace of fighting.

To our amazement, we were permitted to shoot films and take photographs at the Catholic church, which could hold as many as a thousand worshippers. Starting at 6 a.m., four Masses were held, and they were always crowded. This was the biggest church that I saw in the Sudan and it was it was here that we had a strange experience. When Horst, stationed near the altar, was filming the priest giving the host to the faithful, the blacks gazed ecstatically at my cameraman, thinking they were looking at Christ. Horst had already lost forty-five pounds during our expedition and, with his thin arms and legs and his hollow bearded face, he truly resembled the picture of Christ in the church.

I felt that it was important to see how the natives were taught to vote in

Wau. Ballot papers showing symbols – a crocodile, a cow, an antelope and even a tree – were distributed for the candidates of the various tribes. The natives knew which of their chieftains each symbol referred to and they voted by pressing down a thumb to leave a print.

Our trip still wasn't over; Equatoria, the most southern province in the Sudan, still lay ahead and was said to have been the scene of the worst unrest and fighting. Compared with Wau, Juba was a ghost town, and one sensed the presence of earlier turmoil. We were no longer allowed to drive alone and always had to be accompanied by two policemen. When we visited Torit, the last stop on our agenda, we even had to travel in an armoured military transporter, escorted by several amphibious tanks and army trucks occupied by armed soldiers. I must confess that I felt quite nervous, especially a few hours later, when we had to switch to a smaller armoured vehicle. We lumbered through a hilly landscape, crowded with tropical plants, like a jungle, and I could well imagine what it meant to have to fight an enemy camouflaged in this thick bush. We reached Torit, the seat of army headquarters, without incident. It was unusually accommodating of the Sudanese to allow us to visit this place which had been the centre of the fighting.

We were guests of the rather young army chief, who was very candid when answering my questions about the unrest in this area, and we talked until late at night. For the first time, I obtained some insight into the almost insoluble political, ethological, and religious conflicts between northern and southern Sudanese. An outsider has to talk to both sides in order to get an accurate picture of the situation.

We were surprised by a dance of the Latuka, which, unlike the official dances in the Dinka villages, was still very original and unspoilt. The Latuka had large drums which they constantly warmed with clusters of burning straw. Their faces were smeared with red ash, and their hands clutched sticks with long black animal hairs waving at the tips. Leaping and shrieking wildly in these ritual dances, they worked themselves up into greater and greater ecstasy, as they whirled around a kind of pyre made of pieces of wood, they looked like unleashed demons performing not only for the benefit of the spectators but also to release their own primitive emotions.

Just as the dancing ended, there came sensational news. Khartoum radio announced a *coup d'état*, in which the government and its allies had been taken prisoner; the putsch had been led by an officer named Gaafar Nimeiri. We looked at each other in fear and consternation. By now, they had probably arrested the governors and police chiefs who had supported us and whose guests we were. I was surprised at how calmly the officer we were with took the news.

This was the second revolution I had experienced in the Sudan. Without further delay, the commander in Torit had his men escort us back to Juba, where I suffered my first attack of malaria: I ran a high temperature and had pains in my limbs, but, after taking enough resochin, I was up and about within an amazingly short time. Two days later, we flew back to Khartoum airport where it was a relief to see our friends. They had no clear understanding of the situation as yet but their news was upsetting. All the radio stations, bridges and public buildings were occupied; tanks were everywhere, and the streets were teeming with soldiers; then I learned the worst news that evening. A colleague of Mr Weistroffer's who had taken our Landrover to sell reported that the vehicle had been stolen. He had foolishly permitted a prospective buyer to take it for a trial spin, and the man had never returned. According to our host, it was probably in Ethiopia by now.

This upset me so much that a doctor had to give me tranquillizing injections. In this turbulent state of affairs, there was no hope of ever recovering the car, and without it, we had no money for the return trip. I despaired. Several days later, however, still numb from my injections, I saw two figures standing in the open doorway of my room: Horst and a woman who looked like Nora, Weistroffer's secretary.

'The car's here, we found it,' I heard them cry. I thought it was a bad joke, and since I was still in a hypersensitive condition, I had some sort of fit in which I flailed around; when Nora tried to calm me, I bit her hands and scratched my own face and they had to give me another injection.

Later on, I learned what had happened. Nora, an intrepid young woman, had pulled off a really daring feat. On the main street of the city, amid the chaos of innumerable vehicles, she had spotted our Landrover with the sign, 'Sudan Expedition', still attached to its back. Setting off in hot pursuit, she caught up with it and blocked it with her own car. Recognizing the thief as a director of Sudanese TV, Nora forced him to get out of the car and hand her the keys. Then, parking her car off to the side, she got into the Landrover and sped away. She did even more for us by managing to sell the car at a good price, despite the customs problems. She was our guardian angel.

We boarded the aeroplane at last, exhausted but happy to have survived our perilous expedition; despite the *coup*, we had succeeded in getting all our belongings through customs.

A JUDICIAL ERROR

The mail which awaited me in Munich included a letter from Friedrich A. Mainz, which left me stunned. In contained shattering news about the West German Supreme Court verdict on Mainz's years of litigation against Erwin Leiser and the Swedish firm Minerva for using footage from my motion picture *Triumph of the Will*.

I had been dispossessed of the rights to my film. For decades, I had been condemned and persecuted as director and producer of this documentary, but no one had ever doubted that I had made it. That is, until Erwin Leiser turned up and used almost two thousand feet of *Triumph of the Will* for his film *Mein Kampf* without permission either from me or from Transit, which administered the rights to films made by the Nazi Party and the German Reich.

The judgement was based on the arguments that 'countless instances of printed matter contain indications that the Nazi Party was the producer of this motion picture'. This allegation was refuted long ago by Herr Opitz, press chief of UFA, whose statutory declaration states that UFA said such things only in the hope of gaining publicity advantageous to the film. In 1934, the year this picture was made, the relationship between UFA and the Nazi Party was still unresolved. UFA saw this production as a good opportunity for an intense advertising campaign, for and with the Nazi Party which would lead to a better relationship with the Party. A further argument used by the court was meaningless, naïve and had been refuted by numerous witnesses. The judges cited a handwritten entry in a memorandum, taken at the signing of the distribution contract in which one of the UFA people described me as a 'plenipotentiary of the Reich leadership'. This may have been his personal opinion, but it was not consistent with the facts. I had merely explained that I was to make a film about the Party rally at Hitler's wish. Naturally, I could not enlighten UFA about the internal strife in the Party, which prompted Hitler's refusal to let the Party make the film.

It was a bitter irony when the court decided that my film had been produced by the Party film department, which contained my greatest enemies. If the film had been a Party production, it would not have required UFA financing, for the Party had ample funds of its own. Nor were there any contracts with the Nazi Party that commissioned me to make the film. Statutory declarations by responsible members of the Nazi Party confirm beyond doubt that my company was a private firm, which we called Reich Party Rally Film only for the production of the Party Rally film. Even the treasurer of the Nazi Party had confirmed this in a statutory declaration.

The court took a different view, but this did not alter the facts. Judges have been known to make mistakes in serious cases and this verdict could only be a judicial error.

I sought advice from Dr Weber, whose schedule had not permitted him to take over the lawsuit from Herr Mainz, and his comment on the court decision was, 'This is a purely political verdict.'

'Is there anything I can do about it?'

'There is. This verdict is wrong. It is not based on the true facts and the legal situation. It was handed down with regard to the case of Mainz *v* Minerva, and is therefore valid only *inter partes*, but not for the litigating parties. In a new lawsuit, the court would in no way be bound by the findings of this trial. However, you would have to present decisive new evidence.'

I recalled that after Herr Mainz had lost at the court of first appeals, Dr Boele, his lawyer, had suggested calling Albert Speer to testify. Speer was present at the Party rally site in Nuremberg when Hitler had given me the assignment – explicitly declaring that the Party was to be excluded from the film and to have nothing to do with its production. Dr Boele was so certain of winning the case, that he felt he could dispense with testimony from Speer.

I knew of a witness even more important than Speer, but I doubted whether he would be willing to testify on my behalf: Arnold Raether, a former senior executive officer in the government, head of the film department of the Nazi Party, and the man who was, at that time, in charge of all motion pictures made by the Party. I had learned just recently that he was still alive, but I didn't have the courage to have him called as a witness since, during the Third Reich, he was my chief enemy. The first Party rally film had been made under his aegis, and he had boycotted Hitler's orders that I must direct it. Raether's opposition to me had been so persistent that he had even been imprisoned for a short time; that was why Hitler excluded the Nazi Party – which he knew would have caused me insuperable difficulties – from the production of the second rally film. Although the events took place over thirty years before, I still hadn't dared ask Raether to testify, but now that this judicial error had been issued, I was willing to risk it, especially as Dr Weber urged me: 'You have to try. After all, the court refused to recognize many of the statutory declarations obtained by Herr Mainz, because they weren't notarized.'

No one had ever told me to notarize these important declarations, and now it was too late. By now, some of the witnesses had died. With a heavy heart and scant hope, I did as Dr Weber asked and this time I had quite a surprise for Herr Raether replied on 28 December 1966: 'We have all learned that tensions in those times had to do with the period and its men, and should by no means lead to grudges. It goes without saying that I am willing to testify in this matter.'

Despite his advanced age of seventy-four, Herr Raether came to Munich and went to the trouble of making a notarized statement on 29 December 1970. Because of its extraordinary significance for me and for the truth, I would like to quote the most important paragraphs:

> I was head of the Reich Propaganda administration, Main Agency for Cinema, with regard to both production and its cinematic propaganda use. On the basis of this position of mine, I can make the following definite statement: Party films, that is, films in which the National Socialist German Workers' Party was the legal and commercial producer, hence proprietor, could not be made without my knowledge or without my permission. For each one, I always obtained the approval of Reich Propaganda Minister Dr Goebbels. For this reason, I can state with absolute certainty that the motion picture *Triumph of the Will* was neither made by the National Socialist Workers' Party nor commissioned by it.
>
> The case was different with the motion picture about the Reich Party Rally of 1933 *Victory of the Faith*, which Frau Riefenstahl also made. The Party was the producer of this film. Since Frau Riefenstahl endured considerable difficulties from the Party while shooting the film in 1933, Hitler decided that the Party was to have nothing to do with the film scheduled for 1935. *Triumph of the Will.* [His decision] referred both to the production and to the financing. I still remember that the then state secretary in the Ministry of Propaganda, Herr Funk, prohibited me from concerning myself with the organization and the production of the motion picture. Thus, the motion picture *Triumph of the Will* was a project of Frau Riefenstahl, who was also responsible for the financing and the production. I also remember that UFA liked using the Nazi Party as a figurehead, and that alone can be the reason why UFA in its publicity for the motion picture *Triumph of the Will* flaunted the link of the film to the Nazi Party . . .

> Arnold Raether

This document could not be returned by any court of law, but I decided not to sue Herr Leiser. It is enough for me to hold such an important testimony in my hands.

PHOTO-SAFARI IN EAST AFRICA

International photo magazines having asked me for animal shots, I decided to go to East Africa with Horst and take pictures.

How easy it is to fly to Nairobi or Mombasa today! Sixteen years ago it wasn't nearly as comfortable in a charter plane. The seats were so narrow that the flight was agony, and there were endless delays on landing as passports and baggage were processed.

We rented a VW beetle in Mombasa, planning to visit several national parks, and soon I was once again infected with camera fever. There were all sorts of things to photograph, but what fascinated me most of all were the faces of the natives; as before, I felt a strong desire to live in Africa.

After getting some fine shots of animals and also of the Masai in Ambosielli Park on Mount Kilimanjaro, we headed towards Lake Manyara and the famous Ngorogoro Crater. We were lucky with the weather, which was pleasant; there was no rain, and we encountered very few cars on the easily negotiable roads.

One day before leaving Malindi, I read the word *goggling* scrawled in chalk on a blackboard, and I learned that it meant the same as 'snorkling'. In my childhood, I had been a 'water baby' – my parents having taught me to swim when I was five years old – but later on, I had little opportunity for water sports, since I spent all my leisure in the mountains and my hobbies were climbing and skiing. At this point, I never dreamed that my random glance at the word 'goggling' would eventually turn me into a diver.

To pass the time, we joined a group of snorklers, although I had never owned goggles or flippers and this was the first time I'd ever tried them. Had I made this attempt in the Baltic or in the North Sea, I would not have felt the same enthusiasm; but here, in the Indian Ocean, I was enchanted by the mysterious underwater world and Horst had the same reaction. We were delighted by the many colourful fish that circled round quite unconcerned by our presence and we just couldn't get enough of this seascape. The subtle hues and fantastic ornaments were breathtaking as was the splendour of the corals. I wasn't able to remain underwater for as long as I would have liked, because the air ran out so quickly; yet, when the entire group was already back in the boat, Horst and I were still in the water. My first experiences here were so entrancing that I was miserable about discovering this new world on the very last day of the trip. Previously I had seen it only in films by Hans Hass and Jacques Cousteau; but it was so much more exciting to view it first hand. I resolved to get to know the underwater world as soon as possible.

THE NUBA IN *STERN*

Shortly before Christmas, I received a visit from Rolf Gillhausen, art director of *Stern* magazine, famous for his outstanding layouts. I was eager to know whether he would like my Nuba photos of which I had prepared a selection, and was gratified when he said he wanted to see them all. We looked through the pictures for hours on end, and I realized how much he appreciated them when without hesitation he selected the best.

He picked about a hundred slides, including one that I didn't want to give him; it showed two naked Nuba adolescents playing the guitar in the interior courtyard of a house. Gillhausen was fascinated by the photo, but I had to consider the religious sensibilities of my Sudanese friends, whom I didn't wish to offend. When I asked him to omit this particular picture it simply increased his resistance, and the more I argued, the more adamant he grew – until he finally made the publication of the entire story dependent on that single photograph. Unwilling to lose my connection with such a major magazine because of one picture, I finally gave in. Even so, when Gillhausen left, I still had no solid commitment.

'Maybe we can run a series in two or three months, he said. 'I'll be in touch.'

I was disappointed as I had expected more. I was all the more surprised, therefore, by a phone call a few days later from Henri Nannen, the editor-in-chief of *Stern*.

'Leni,' he said, 'please take the next plane and come to Hamburg.' I thought he was joking, but before I could even ask him a question, he said, 'Your photos are thrilling. Our whole editorial staff is enthralled by your wonderful pictures and we want to publish a major series before Christmas; maybe even run one photo on the title page. We need all your information – urgently. One of my editors will be waiting for you tonight at your hotel in Hamburg. Our Munich staff will organize everything for you.' There had to be a catch. I was so used to frustrations and setbacks that I didn't dare allow myself to get too excited.

When I arrived in Hamburg that evening, Herr Braumann, a member of the editorial staff, was waiting for me at the Hotel Berlin and soon I understood the reason for all the haste. After seeing my photos, Nannen had decided to insert a fifteen-page full-colour series on the Nuba in the already half-printed pre-Christmas issue of the magazine; the original cover would have to be changed and to do this they would have to print the texts by the following day at the very latest; since the issue was due to hit the news-stands in one week.

When I heard this I felt a wave of panic. How were the texts to be written in just a few hours? They wanted not just captions, but a detailed account of my experiences among the Nuba. Herr Braumann encouraged me however. 'Tonight, you'll tell me about your most vivid memories, and I'll bring you the text tomorrow morning. You can make revisions before we hand it in to the editorial staff.' We remained together until midnight. I no longer recall whether he took notes or taped what I said; I remember only that we had a good report, for we had been to Africa several times.

Unfortunately, what happened the next morning left me feeling wretched. I had been quite happy after breakfast, because the *Stern* office sent me not only a wonderful bouquet of flowers but also a cheque for twenty-five thousand marks, and I was overjoyed. Finally a bit of luck, I thought. But then, when I read the manuscript that Herr Braumann brought over, I was so displeased with it that I could never have given my consent. The text wasn't bad. On the contrary, it was journalistically brilliant, but the things it said were too sensational and diametrically opposed to my views. There was not time left to alter the text, so I had no choice: hard as it was for me, I knew I had to return the cheque and stop the presses.

Greatly distressed, I tried to get through to Henri Nannen but he was in a meeting, so I handed the cheque to his secretary along with a short note. Before I even left the building, Nannen came dashing after me. 'What's wrong?' he said, half laughing, half angry. 'Are you out of your mind? You can't pull out now. The photos have already been printed.' I felt like a cornered hare, my nerved failed me and I began to sob. Nannen, whom I hadn't seen for fifteen years, tried to propitiate me. 'You can revise the text if it bothers you. That's no reason to keep the series from coming out.' He took me to his secretary's office, where I was to dictate my revisions.

'The main thing,' said Nannen as he left, 'is you must get it done in two hours – that's the absolute final deadline for going to press.' Then he thrust the cheque into my hand and said goodbye.

This incident, hardly an everyday occurrence in a magazine office, took place on 3 December 1969; I received the *Stern* issue the very next week. I couldn't take my eyes off the cover which was marvellous. The photo story designed by Gillhausen was so extraordinary that I am not exaggerating when I say that *Stern* set up a monument to the Nuba.

A MISTAKE IN SPEER'S MEMOIRS

During this period, I received Albert Spear's first book, his memoirs *Inside the Third Reich,* written in Spandau Prison where he had spent twenty years. Speer was the only defendant at the Nuremberg trial who had pleaded guilty, thus eliciting innumerable comments from friend and foe alike. Books were written about him, films made about him and the verdicts on his conduct were extreme. Many of his friends did not understand him and their judgement was harsh. Believing that his inner transformation was opportunistic, they labelled him a traitor. Other people, especially some who had been persecuted, tried to forgive him – and, in my opinion, Speer wanted this forgiveness; he craved it. I truly believe that he suffered the torments of hell, and rather than taking the easier path, that of suppression, he sought confrontation.

So long as Hitler was alive, Speer was virtually in bondage to him. How else, after being condemned to death by Hitler, could Speer have returned to him just before the end of the war to say farewell before his own possible death and yet have the strength to refuse Hitler's 'Scorched Earth' order? Who else in the Third Reich displayed such great courage?

Speer sent me his book with a brief letter:

September 1969

Dear Leni,

Here is the long-awaited book, which I send with some hesitation, since I fear that it will somewhat alter your opinion of me; though not for the worse, I hope. I assume that you will understand how urgently I wished to give future generations a standpoint to help them avoid similar difficulties. I have to admit I have my doubts about the ability of human beings to learn anything. However, one should – each in one's own way – contribute what one can . . .

Sincerely, Albert

I was deeply impressed by these lines and extremely anxious to read the book. Would it contain an explanation of our tragedy? Once I began reading, I couldn't put it down, for it was riveting. I am one of those who believe in Speer's inner transformation; however, I wish he had written more about what made Hitler so fascinating, for that is the question I am repeatedly asked. Speer met with Hitler almost daily, while I saw Hitler only in a few exceptional situations. In my opinion, Speer did not offer an adequate answer.

When Speer telephoned me and asked whether I had any corrections, I indicated a few errors of which the most serious was something he had written about Rudolf Hess. Surprisingly, not a word of what he said about him in one particular context was true:

> I recall, incidentally, that the footage taken during one of the solemn sessions of the 1935 Party Congress was spoiled. At Leni Riefenstahl's suggestion Hitler gave orders for the shots to be refilmed in the studio. I was called in to do a backdrop simulating a section of the Kongresshalle, as well as a realistic model of the platform and lectern. I had spotlights aimed at it; the production staff scurried around – while Streicher, Rosenberg and Frank could be seen walking up and down with their manuscripts, determinedly memorizing their parts. Hess arrived and was asked to pose for the first shot. Exactly as he had done before an audience of 30,000 at the Party Congress, he solemnly raised his hand. With his special brand of ardour, he turned precisely to the spot where Hitler would have been sitting, snapped to attention and cried: 'My Leader, I welcome you in the name of the Party Congress! The congress will now continue. The Führer speaks!'
>
> He did it all so convincingly that from that point on I was no longer so sure of the genuineness of his feelings. The three others also gave excellent performances in the emptiness of the studio, proving themselves gifted actors. I was rather disturbed; Frau Riefenstahl, on the other hand, thought the acted scenes better than the original presentation.
>
> By this time I thoroughly admired the art with which Hitler would feel his way during his rallies until he had found the point to unleash the first great storm of applause. I was by no means unaware of the demagogic element; indeed I contributed to it myself by my scenic arrangements. Nevertheless, up to this time I had believed that the feelings of the speakers were genuine. It was therefore an upsetting discovery, that day in the studio, when I saw that all this emotion could be represented 'authentically' even without an audience.

That whole episode was a figment of Speer's imagination and had nothing to do with reality. I am sure that his intention was not bad; but, during the twenty years of his imprisonment, he had naturally mixed up a few things. When I explained it to him and was able to prove that the events had been different from his portrayal of them, he regretted his mistakes and promised to rectify them in future editions. Yet how could Speer, a fanatical stickler for the truth, make such errors? The scene actually occurred as follows. It is true that Speer rebuilt the speaker's desk of the congress hall in a cinema, but we did not film Rudolf Hess, we shot a close-up of Julius Streicher. During the latter's speech at the rally, the cameraman had run out of stock, and since Streicher as Gauleiter of Franconia was to appear only once, a sentence a few seconds long had to be reshot. During this brief sequence, no one was present other than Speer, Streicher and the technical crew: neither Hess, Frank, Rosenberg, nor I was there and no additional footage of Hess was ever filmed.

I think I can explain Speer's mistake. One day before the opening of the rally, Hess asked for a lighting test at the speaker's desk in the congress hall. He went up to the desk, together with Sepp Allgeier, to check whether the spotlight would be bearable for Hitler, who was to give a long speech here the next day. In those days, the spotlights produced a tremendous heat. During this lighting test, in which Speer and I both participated, Hess delivered no speech. The photos taken of us here convinced Speer of the real facts. Nor wa it true that Hitler ordered inadequate sequences to be reshot in the studio. I can only hope that Speer made no errors of even greater significance.

WITH SPEER IN THE DOLOMITES

I gladly accepted an invitation to Wolkenstein in South Tyrol and, before I left, Will Tremper, who had started a new magazine, asked me to get a few photos of Albert Speer there. I hadn't realized that Speer would be spending his holiday in Wolkenstein, but I was sure there would be no problem, and I looked forward to seeing him.

When we met, I was struck at once by his air of serenity. One would never have guessed that he had just been released from a long prison term. He took daily walks for hours on end, while Margarete, his athletic wife tackled the steep slopes. When Speer learned that I was working on a picture book about my African travels, he offered to help. First he read my manuscript, which he liked very much: his only reservation was that it was too long for a book of this kind, and so we worked together, almost every day, shortening the text. Often we went strolling in the snowy forest landscape, and I asked him questions about the past; something I would never have dared to do before. I was astonished at his calm and relaxed attitude, which seemed to raise him above all petty things. Whatever one may feel about Speer, there is no doubt that he possessed extraordinary strength of character.

The Nuba cast their spell on him too. He suggested a number of titles, among them *My Greatest Love* and *As if on a Different Planet*. The motto he proposed came from Christopher Columbus's journal, from the entry dated 25 December 1492: 'They go about as God created them. Both men and women paint their beautifully shaped bodies. Athough [the Indians] are not Christians, one may say that they truly love their neighbours.'

It's a wonderful subject,' said Speer, 'I really enjoy being involved with it.'

After five weeks of working together, we had reduced the 247 manuscript pages to eighty-eight. Speer had pulled off an architectural feat, and I had learned a great deal from him.

TOM STACEY

The Nuba photos in *Stern* and the *Sunday Times Magazine* had attracted attention not only in Germany and the United States; interested parties also contacted me from France and England. When I visited London, two publishers, Peter Owen and Tom Stacey, offered me immediate large advances. Agreeable as it would have been to work with Owen, a young publisher with a highly impressive list, I opted for Tom Stacey, who was familiar with Africa. He had published a twenty-volume reference work on primitive tribes around the world and had also spent years in Africa as a journalist.

The Nuba book began its odyssey.

My friends Michi and Joshi Kondo, former partners at Kondo Film and owners of the Tokyo, a Japanese restaurant just a few minutes from Piccadilly, had invited Tom Stacey and me to their restaurant in order to celebrate the signing of my contract.

Tom Stacey made a very favourable impression. He was tall and slender, in the prime of life, and also very lively and extremely charming. In Africa, he had mainly worked as an anthropologist, hence his great interest in the Nuba; his twenty-volume encyclopaedia, with its hundreds of colour plates, was almost a definitive work. I could not have wished for a more suitable publisher. I had every reason to be in a good mood that night, for along with the Stacey contract, I had signed another important one that same day: the BBC had acquired the British TV rights to my two *Olympia* films, and wanted to show the original full-length version during the 1972 Olympics in Munich. This was a triumph for me – and not only commercially. In Germany, my Olympic films had never been shown on television even though they had become newsworthy because of the Munich Games; not a single German channel expressed interest.

Before leaving London, I received a third offer. The *Sunday Times Magazine* wanted me to photograph the Munich Olympics. It was a prestigious offer, but a difficult decision. Would I be able to do such strenuous work at the age of seventy? I asked them to let me sleep on it, and when I finally agreed to accept the offer, my reason was quite simple. Having been in Africa during the sales of the tickets to the Games, I had been unable to buy one, but I very much wanted to attend. I decided to accept the *Sunday Times* offer, which would get me into the stadium. I realized that this would be quite an adventure.

TURBULENT WEEKS

I had been in Munich for less than a day when Tom Stacey's picture director, Alex Low, turned up to pick the photographs for my book. This work was fun because Low was an excellent photographer. As a result, we were in complete agreement about the selection.

Then the inevitable happened. This new chance and the growing number of favourable press reports about me galvanized my adversaries. Sometimes I felt as if I were walking a tightrope with no safety net underneath. When I was invited to the UFA Palace at the Zoo, where *Olympia* was to be screened, I never dreamed that this would lead to wild protests; after all, nearly fifteen years earlier it had run at the Titania Palace and been a great hit with both the public and the press in Berlin. But my experience this time could not have been foreseen. Wenzel Lüdecke, head of Berliner Synchron Film, who wanted to show the film in Berlin because of the Olympic Games in Munich, had not counted on these reactions.

Although the theatre was almost sold out, my film was not screened simply because influential groups in Berlin had loudly protested against it. In newspapers, in TV and radio broadcasts, as well as in telegrams to Berlin's mayor Klaus Schutz, they demanded a prohibition of the screening. Their reason was that the film was a Nazi concoction and showing it would be an insult to the victims of the Nazi regime. The senator for Scholarship and Art was similarly pressured, but he saw no way to ban the showing, since the film had been approved, even for children, by the German self-censorship board, and had run in various German cities without disturbances. Yet it could not be screened in Berlin. The head of the UFA Palace was forced by anonymous calls to cancel the film. Otherwise his theatre would have been burned down. I myself received similar anonymous threats, although I didn't necessarily take the death threats seriously I was dismayed and bitterly disappointed when I left Berlin, the city of the Olympic Games; to have experienced these things in my native town was especially wounding.

On the other hand, the BBC Television broadcast was an enormous success. Stephan Hearst, one of the top men there, ended his enthusiastic letter with the following sentence: 'The *Olympia* film will remain a milestone in the history of the cinema.' Norman Swallow, executive producer of the BBC, wrote: 'What is Leni Riefenstahl's sin? That Hitler admired her?'

The rumpus I got involved in before the start of the Games in Munich hardly gave me a chance to think about anything else; and actually, I should have concentrated on the new cameras in order to do my job properly. Leitz had lent me their newest Leicaflex cameras, but each day brought me new obligations. Most remarkable of all was an offer by British TV to make a sixty-minute film which Norman Swallow was to produce and Colin Nears to direct. I loved working with them. We combed my archive and spent hours in the editing studio, selecting footage from my old pictures. I also had to make time for Rolf Hädrich, who was filming Thomas Wolfe's novel *You Can't Go Home Again*: he wanted to use shots from my Olympic films and also have me take part in the project. While I respected Hädrich as a director and liked him personally, I was very hesitant about going to Berlin for the shooting. I didn't care to expose myself to the kind of insults and threats I had experienced a few weeks earlier. Will Tremper, who had introduced me to Hädrich, also tried to get me to change my mind. When I learned that the German historian Joachim Fest and Albert Speer would also be participating, I finally gave in.

The action of the television film Hädrich was making takes place in 1936 during the Berlin Olympics, and Hädrich wanted to give several contemporaries a chance to speak in the film: not only Speer, but also H.M. Ledig-Rowohlt, Thomas Wolfe's German publisher and friend. Incidentally, the shooting in Berlin was never disrupted.

From London, I heard that Tom Stacey, my British publisher, wanted to speak to me urgently. On the day of my arrival, I happened to see the film made about me by the BBC in Munich which I had been somewhat reluctant to view, afraid, likable as the Englishmen had been during the shooting, that I would be disappointed by the results; but my fears proved groundless. Colin Nears and Norman Swallow had made a highly original film without the usual falsehoods, and my friends and I were very happy that evening.

I visited my publisher the next day. Alex Low had already prepared everything for the layout with the designer Tom Deas and the atmosphere was very pleasant. This was the first time that I had watched a book being laid out – a fascinating process. The design showed that this would be a special book, which therefore entailed quite a number of problems, especially financial ones. No co-publisher had been found as yet; but Stacey was optimistic, and he hoped that the book could come out in four months, provided I could write a new, more scholarly text within a very short time.

THE OLYMPIC GAMES IN MUNICH

Three weeks later, I was able to send Tom Stacey my new text. I had been writing day and night and now felt ready for a holiday, but the Olympics were just around the corner, and so I couldn't even think of going away. However, Stacey's enthusiastic telegram made me happy about this, my third manuscript for the book.

Now I had to turn my attention to Leicaflex cameras and, above all, get hold of a press pass. Michael Rand in London had told me how difficult it had been for the *Sunday Times Magazine* to obtain a press pass for a photographer; they had been granted only one, for their correspondent, and as a result they were forced to ask their *Guardian* colleagues for a pass for me.

When word got around that I was writing for an English newspaper, I could barely escape the hordes of journalists. Telephone calls came from New York and Paris, from Stockholm and Rome, and now suddenly, the German press got into the act. I fled from my flat and moved into the Sheraton, but interest in me was intensified by the fact that I had turned seventy just a few days before the opening of the Games. On my birthday, with a group of friends, I saw Hädrich's TV film *Memories of a Summer in Berlin*, in which Joachim Fest interviewed me. We found this powerful film so compelling that we forgot everything else.

I had tried, unsuccessfully, to get Horst a pass from the German Olympic Committee. I urgently needed help with my work, and Monique Berlioux, who was on Avery Brundage's staff, got me some. Shortly before the start of the Games, I again received anonymous threats on the telephone, and the police informed me that there had been death threats against me. Luckily, the events of those weeks and my work schedule left me no time for anxiety.

The Olympic Games commenced on 26 August 1972 with an opening celebration that was extraordinarily impressive. The entrance of the nations and the subsequent dances were a whirl of colour, and the modern Munich stadium provided a striking setting. What a wonderful film could have been made of this spectacle! Thirty-six years earlier, at the time of my *Olympia*, there was no good colour stock, I could shoot only in black and white. Nor did we have the other technical possibilites of the nineteen-seventies. We had no light-sensitive celluloid, no zoom lenses, no magnetic tapes – by today's standards things were positively primitive.

This time, the Olympic film was produced by David Wolper, an American, with the Bavaria company. Wolper, one of the most successful documentary producers in the world, had hit on the idea of having the film made by ten directors from ten different countries. Each director was to be given a portion depending on his individual gift, and Mr Wolper had planned to let me do the opening and the closing celebrations. 'Unfortunately,' he said regretfully, 'I was pressured by Bonn to forgo your collaboration.'

This conduct on the part of official German agencies was nothing new, and it took an especially crass form during these Games. I didn't realize it at the time, but the rules of the IOC specify that the holder of an Olympic diploma can claim a seat in the box of honour for the rest of his life; but even though I possessed such a diploma, no German agency invited me to any of their festivities. I was all the more delighted therefore when the American embassy asked me to a party at Munich's America House. There, I saw Jesse Owens for the first time since 1936, and it was a deeply emotional meeting. As Owens hugged and kissed me, we were both near to tears. Several guests began to clap, then the applause grew louder and louder, intensifying into a storm. Confused and embarrassed, I left the reception.

From then on, I didn't have a moment to myself. Each day, I worked from seven in the morning until midnight and my job was difficult. Very few photographers were allowed to enter the interior of the stadium, yet that was the only place to get really excellent shots of the events. Along with the other photographers, I had to stand in the ditch that circled the stadium.

Even more difficult was shooting the indoor contests, such as gymnastics, basketball, bicycling, swimming, fencing, etc. Because space was tight, a special pass was needed and usually I failed to obtain one.

In the evenings, I went to the press centre, where the films could be developed. Then Horst took them without delay to the airport so that they could be in London the next morning. Since I didn't know whether the photos met the expectations of the editors, I was relieved when Michael Rand called me up and assured me that they liked them. However, I discovered something else, which depressed me: the *Sunday Times* had been attacked for hiring me as a photographer. In a letter to *The Times*, the British Section of the World Jewish Congress vehemently protested against my work. Their reasons were identical to those of the Jewish Community in

Berlin, but while no one in Berlin ever defended me, the *Sunday Times* leaped to my defence. The response it printed went as follows:

> We commissioned Leni Riefenstahl to photograph the Olympic Games of 1972 for us, because, as the pictures we have just received demonstrate, she is the best photographer in the world in this area.
>
> Leni Riefenstahl has been twice checked by German courts of law and declared free of any guilt. Her earlier link with the Nazi Party is no reason for a constant boycott of her work; otherwise, the TV and film companies could never again show her classical films of the Olympics of 1936. Yet in fact, they are repeatedly shown.
>
> No official complaint was made five years ago when we ran her brilliant photographs of the Nuba. We sympathize with your feelings, but do not believe that they have a logical basis.

This recognition was a challenge to me. I must not disappoint the editors; yet obtaining good pictures was tremendously difficult, given the photographers' cut-throat competiton for passes and good seats. Often, I would sit on the floor of an indoor arena for hours on end, trying to get a few special shots.

Then that gruesome and infamous crime was committed. Six days before the end of the Games, Arab terrorists killed two Israeli athletes in the Olympic Village and took nine as hostages. We were all horror-struck. The Games were halted, and there followed hours of unbearable suspense. The terrorists threatened to shoot their hostages if Israel didn't meet their demand to release two hundred inmates from Israeli prisons. The deadline was twelve noon, but they kept extending it throughout the day. Sharpshooters surrounded the house where the murderers held the athletes at gun-point, while negotiators tried to deal with the terrorists. Now and then, one of the masked hostage-takers appeared on the balcony and the photos of these criminals went round the world.

For hours we remained at the press centre, anxiously awaiting news. Then word came that the terrorists with their hostages had been flown by helicopter to Fürstenfeldbruck Airport. After several hours of uncertainty, a sensational report came late at night, when a press spokesman announced that the terrorists had been overpowered and all the hostages freed. The crowded press hall broke into cheers, and, relieved that no further hostages had lost their lives, I went back to my hotel. How terrible it was the next morning when we learned that last night's report had been totally untrue.

During the dramatic attempt to free the hostages on the darkened airfield, the shootout had claimed all their lives.

Despite this tragedy, the Olympics resumed. The IOC reached this decision in agreement with Israeli agencies, and after a pause of one day, a memorial service was held for the murdered athletes. Avery Brundage gave a speech justifying the decision by arguing passionately that a handful of terrorists should not be permitted to destroy the core of international cooperation as embodied in the Olympic Games; he ended with a heartfelt cry to the audience: 'The Games must go on.'

After the tragedy, my work was half-hearted and I completed it more out of a sense of duty.

The Games ended with poignant and impressive ceremony during which, in a moving address, Willi Daume, president of the German Olympic Committee, once again condemned the terrible crime that had blighted these Games, and pleaded most earnestly for faith in the Olympic idea.

I eagerly looked forward to seeing my picture story in the *Sunday Times Magazine*, and, only three weeks after the conclusion of the Games, I held the periodical in my hands. The cover showed two amazingly similar photos of highjumpers: one shot in Berlin in 1936: the other, thirty-six years later in Munich. The title above the pictures said: 'Leni Riefenstahl's Second Olympics'.

Following the example of the *Sunday Times*, more and more international periodicals and TV companies refused to let themselves be intimidated by boycott threats against me. CBS in the United States made a film portrait of me in connection with the Olympic Games, which was directed by Stephan Chodorov and John Musilli of Camera Three. During the four days of shooting, my apartment looked like a soundstage, and the two Americans worked so hard that I was infected by their zeal; it was as if it were my own film. They had the patience of Job and spared no effort. They even travelled up to the Zugspitze with me, because they considered this the most suitable location for interviewing me about my mountain films. The film was shown in two parts in the United States and was such a success that it was repeated several times.

Next, I was approached by Andrew Mannheim, a London-based journalist, who wanted to have a long interview with me for the American magazine *Modern Photography*. Of all my interviews, I felt that this one was the most interesting, because he also covered the question of techniques in all my films.

THE GEYER TRIAL

The new year brought me new setbacks. My creditors, who were suing Geyer for damages, had lost their second appeal; the Supreme Court of Hamburg had thrown out their case because the statute of limitations had expired. This was a dubious verdict; the legal opinion obtained from a specialist by my creditors before starting their litigation had expressly denied any such danger.

Geyer had made such a huge number of mistakes that the company's gross negligence was not covered by their normal conditions, so the statute of limitations could not run out. It was tragic that this judgement should result from a Kodak opinion that was based on an error.

During the trial, the Geyer lawyer skilfully created an atmosphere of hostility towards me, and his efforts left their traces on the judge. He not only brought in political aspects that had nothing to do with the case, but he also described me and my work in a cynical and disparaging manner. Geyer caused enormous damage, saying things like, 'After all, it's only a film about naked Nuba.'

I asked my creditors not to go to a higher court, for I could afford neither the enormous legal costs (of which I had to pay half) nor the time spent writing endless briefs. Furthermore, the vanished reel, which would have to serve as evidence in an appeal had not turned up at Geyer. What tipped the scales for me, however, was the fact that my Nuba material would have been blocked during years of further litigation.

THE PRODUCTION OF THE NUBA PICTURE BOOK

Meanwhile, Tom Stacey had managed to find international co-publishers for my Nuba book: Harper & Row in America. Denoël in France, and List in Germany – an ideal combination.

However, there were still many problems; for instance, Stacey had sent the German publisher not my text, but the English translation, which List had to render back into German, an utterly absurd procedure. List didn't have my address, and when they learned that I lived only fifteen minutes from the publishing house, they were astonished and extremely annoyed. Then, after reading the manuscript, I realized, much to my chagrin, that this was not my text. It contained so many mistakes and distortions of meaning that I had to ask for it back from the American and French co-publishers.

As for the production of the book, they had picked the renowned firm of

Mondadori in Verona, one of the best and biggest international printing establishments. No reader of my book could begin to imagine the great efforts that went into its production. I owe a great deal to List and to Gerda Hiller, Mondadori's representative in Germany, for the publication and quality of my book. Gerda Hiller in particular understood my demands from the very start and supported them in Verona. She also suggested that I go to the printing place so that, through personal contact with its specialists, I could obtain the best possible colour quality in the printing. The first edition ran to twenty-five thousand copies, ten thousand of which were bought by the American Book of the Month Club.

The three days that I spent in the gigantic Mondadori enterprise with its more than six thousand employees opened up a whole new world for me. What surprised me most was that manual work was still being done in such a huge company, which was equipped with state-of-the-art machines. I was amazed at the enthusiasm and devotion of all the people involved in our project. Later on in Tokyo, I had the same experience with the Japanese.

Exemplary as the technical work was, we had a great deal of trouble with Stacey. He suddenly informed me he couldn't honour the revisions and must stick to his text. As if that weren't enough, our French co-publisher Denöel made a serious mistake. They printed the wrong title on the jacket: *Les Nubiens*, the Nubians. But the Nubians have nothing to do with the Nuba, historically or ethnologically. The Nubians come from the ancient kingdom of Nubia, which was once located in what is now the northern Sudan. Since the mistranslated word appeared not only on the jacket but countless times throughout the text, all seven thousand beautifully printed copies of the French edition had to be pulped. It was an unforgiveable mistake on the part of the French translator, compounded by the publisher who had, alas, neglected to send me the galleys. Then, worst of all, Mondadori had to stop its presses, because Stacey was unable to pay, and was already in liquidation. A member of his staff told me that his firm was going through a severe financial crisis. Stacey had apparently overextended himself; of the hundred titles he had published during the past two years, many had sold poorly, and his twenty-volume series *People of the World* has also imposed a very great financial strain on him.

The news was devastating – and for List, too, for the German publisher had already announced the Nuba book and planned to bring it out at the Frankfurt Book Fair. The advances Stacey had obtained from his co-publishers were lost, having been used towards covering debts so enormous that they couldn't even be wiped out by the £300,000 paid to him by Mondadori for the rights to his twenty-volume encyclopaedia. As a result, the Americans and the French provisionally rescheduled the publication date of my Nuba book for one year later; I was in despair. This project was another which seemed doomed until at the last moment the German publisher agreed to risk it on his own. It was thanks to the courage of Robert Schäfer, then head of List, and to his faith despite the many setbacks that my book would be completed and out in time for Christmas. The sensational success of my book, not merely in Germany, vindicated Robert Schäfer's decision.

MY SCUBA TEST

The troubles of that year left their mark on me and, as soon as I could free myself of my obligations, I flew to Kenya with Horst. The Indian Ocean and the mysterious underwater world, which I had first experienced two years ago, lured me like a mirage.

We stayed at the Turtle Bay Hotel, north of Mombasa, where a German diving school was located, and where I could observe the young people, none of them much older than twenty, practising every day in the swimming pool. I wondered if any diving teacher would risk accepting a seventy-one-year-old pupil. My desire to dive with an oxygen cylinder was so intense that I decided to use a trick. Registering as Helene Jacob, I lied about my age: instead of 1902, I wrote 1922 in the application form. My rejuvenation notwithstanding, the scuba instructor eyed me sceptically; he was probably thinking: She'll never make it.

This was the diving school of the Poseidon Nemrod Club of Hamburg. There were ten of us on the course, Horst having registered too. I noticed that even the youngsters had a hard time doing some of the exercises, especially putting on and taking off the diving equipment thirteen feet below the surface. The hardest thing of all for me was swimming three hundred yards in full gear, and the final test had to be taken not in the swimming pool, but outside, in the ocean, thirty feet below the surface.

Unfortunately, on that day, the ocean was very dark and choppy – in sharp contrast to the calm, crystal water in the swimming pool. The diving instructor took us out in a small, violently rocking boat (Horst, who had already passed his test two days earlier, came with us). I anxiously peered into the murky depths into which I was supposed to dive. My teacher said, 'You'll find me down below, at the anchor,' and without further instructions, he leaped into the water. Quelling my fear, I jumped in after him. Then I noticed I had lost my lead belt and I had to go back up to the surface. Diving right into the sea, which was only thirty feet deep here,

Horst retrieved my belt. Although the darkness prevented me from spotting my instructor, I recognized the anchor rope and followed it down. I felt a strong current and was relieved at recognizing the outline of my teacher waiting at the bottom of the sea. With visibility at most six feet, the teacher took my hand, and, hugging the bottom, we swam over to a coral reef, where the current was weaker and we could hold on to the corals. Here I had to perform all the things I had learned in the swimming pool – such as removing and putting back on my lead belt, my oxygen cylinder, my flippers and my mask! Then came the changeover to ordinary breathing and finally an emergency ascent – one of the most important skills that you need to learn to avoid serious accidents in dangerous situations. I was relieved and delighted when I clambered back into the boat. I had passed.

That evening, when the longed-for certificates were distributed, my true age was revealed. After open-mouthed astonishment, there was a gigantic 'Wow!', and we celebrated like mad.

A HOUSE IN AFRICA

After my diving experience, Horst and I flew to Nairobi, where I wanted to look at properties outside the city. They were still reasonably priced in those days, but none of those I liked were for sale. My dream was a garden that would bloom all year long, a paradise for my animals.

That evening, in the front garden of the Stanley Hotel, we were expecting Herr Luedicke, who had been living in Nairobi for years and ran a thriving weapons store. His clientele included the best-known white hunters. I had known him since my car accident in Kenya. Tonight, I wanted to ask him for some advice, for very few people knew the area as thoroughly as he.

When we told him about our plans, his face became reflective. 'If you want to live here,' he said, 'you really ought to think it over very carefully.'

I looked at him in surprise, 'Why, you've always been so enthusiastic about Kenya,' I said.

'The Africa you are looking for,' he replied bitterly, 'no longer exists.'

'But,' I interjected, 'we can still find the old Africa in areas untouched by tourism, and that's where we want to go.'

'You can't travel safely through Kenya; there are bandits everywhere; they waylay people in the bush, rob them and even kill them. Just look,' he said, 'armed policemen are stationed outside all the hotels and most of the businesses, and yet assaults and killings are commonplace.'

I had already heard about these things, but had not realized how bad conditions were. During my last visit to the Nuba, I had witnessed the changes in Africa, but at least no murders had been committed. The situation here was very different.

Just a few years earlier, I had wandered through Africa all by myself, sleeping out in the open and never meeting with danger, except for that one adventure with the Dinka warriors, which had been my own fault. Could all that really be gone forever?'

'Things may be different in the Sudan,' said Luedicke, 'but here it's over and done with. As for me, I'm going to close shop and leave Nairobi. Life isn't fun here anymore.'

'You're robbing me of my most cherished dream,' I said, deeply disappointed.

'I'm very sorry, goodness knows, but it's better this way; you have to know the truth.'

We intended to visit my Nuba friends again after five years' absence, indeed no one could stop me. I wanted to show them my book of photographs and I was eager to see their reactions. We planned to drive to the Nuba Hills by way of Khartoum, but our problem was getting a car there. In the Sudan, vehicles with four-wheel drive are almost a necessity for their owners, yet the customs duties are so high that few Sudanese can afford such a car. Luck was with us, however. From an Arab merchant we rented a medium-sized, somewhat rattling Ford, with Mohammed, a young Sudanese driver.

When I saw the first Nuba houses in the cliffs, my heart missed a beat. How would they receive us after an absence of five years? Would all of them still be there? Natu, Alipo, Tukami and Gumba? Then I heard children's voices: 'Leni basso, Leni basso' – Leni's back, Leni's back.

We drove past little girls who stood in the yellow straw and waved at us, making for the big trees under which I had always pitched camp. No sooner did we brake to a halt than they came running, their sharp eyes having already spotted us from the cliffs. Hands reached towards us, and I kept hearing the shouts, 'Leni basso, Leni basso.'

During my last visit I had seen how greatly they and their world had changed, yet the sight that now greeted us was even worse. Were these 'my' Nuba? I could barely detect the traces of earlier times. I tried hard to hide my disappointment, not wanting them to notice how pained I was by what I saw. Horst, too, was deeply shocked.

PARADISE DESTROYED

After a brief visit, our one desire was to get away as soon as possible. Worst of all, our time was so taken up by the Nuba, who were as dear and trusting as ever, that we didn't have a moment's rest. They surrounded us like a swarm of bees, and for all their affection, it was very tiring. The Nuba, who had never before expressed any wishes, had now changed radically. This wasn't true of our old friends; despite their ragged clothing, they had remained the same. But the others, who came pouring by the hundreds from the neighbouring settlements, had a thousand wishes, and it would have been impossible for us to fulfil them all; they wanted medicine, treatments for injuries, tobacco, beads, shirts, trousers, batteries, sunglasses, anything, and everything. We also had a bad time with the almost unbearable heat. At midnight, it was still over 110 degrees Fahrenheit, and wherever the sun shone, it was so hot that you could scarcely touch anything. In addition, there were gale-force winds so powerful that you could see almost nothing through the clouds of dust and even the sun was hidden.

Our old friends, happy to see us again, put us up in a still incomplete Nuba fortress. As yet it had no roof, so, to shield us against sun and dust, the hut was provisionally covered with dura stalks. First, Horst made a door, since we could no longer ward off the tidal wave of Nuba. Their appearance was lamentable with scarcely a trace of their former beauty. Every last one of them wore filthy, tattered clothes. Even the smallest child wore a dirty rag, worse than the garb of beggars in European slums. It was a picture of woe.

We were eager to see how they would respond to the pictures in the Nuba book and Horst wanted to film their reactions. We allowed only a few Nuba into the hut, and I showed them the pictures I had once taken of them. Their response was astonishing. They laughed and were obviously ashamed of their nakedness. Out of courtesy, we visited some of their wrestling festivals, but now they merely looked comical. A paradise had been destroyed.

A STRANGE DREAM

Despite our disenchantment, we stayed for a month. Shorly before our departure, I had dreamed about a fight between two black figures with sharp rings strapped to their wrists. When I woke up, I recalled that during my previous expeditions, I had wanted to visit the Nuba who fought such duels. Five years earlier, when I had asked the Arabs about them, they had told me these fights were a thing of the past. But my dream triggered doubts.

Perhaps these Nuba still existed after all, and even if they no longer fought these unusual matches, I might still be able to learn something about their life and older customs. I had an irresistible wish to find them.

The problem was time. We had already booked a flight from Khartoum to Port Sudan where we wanted to go diving in the Red Sea before returning to Munich. So there were too few days left for a trip to that tribe.

When I told Horst about it, he thought I was mad, but the more he tried to talk me out of the idea, the more stubbornly I argued, emphasizing that this was our last chance to discover something special in this corner of the world – and we only had to travel a few hundred miles; later, it would be thousands of miles, and it was questionable whether I would ever go on another expedition through Africa.

We talked to Mohammed about this journey into the unknown. Although he had no objections, he pointed out that petrol supply was low and there was no possibility of filling up in this region. Nor did we have any maps for our route. All I knew was that the 'South-Eastern Nuba', as this tribe was dubbed by anthropologists, lived some hundred and twenty miles east of the Nuba Hills. I also remembered hearing the name 'Kau' in connection with this tribe, but I couldn't find it on any of our maps. The only thing that I thought I recalled from some photo or other was that Kau was surrounded by rocky mountains. I wanted to take a chance.

We rationed our petrol and left part of it in our camp for the return drive from Tadoro to Kadugli. According to Mohammed's calculations, we must not travel more than one hundred and fifty miles from Tadoro and, in order to get help in an emergency, we decided to take along Natu and Alipo, who were both good runners. Undoubtedly the risk was great and the prospect of success small; nevertheless, it was something I felt compelled to do.

THE DRIVE TO KAU

We started off in blazing heat; I sat next to Mohammed, Horst and the two Nuba sat in the back with our belongings. We drove due east according to the compass. To ward off the heat, I had wrapped wet cloth around my head and chest. When we drove over hard bumps and potholes, the old truck creaked in every joint and with every crunch, I feared it would fall apart.

Driving across the pathless plains, we encountered no one. We passed a few huts, but they were deserted and our hope of coming upon Nuba diminished the further east we came. At one point, a broad *wadi* blocked our way, and when we finally found a place where we could cross, one of our tyres blew. I began to reproach myself. My limbs ached, and all of us were totally exhausted. Wouldn't it be better to turn back? We decided to keep driving as far as our fuel would allow. There were no mountains, no rocks on the horizon, only a yellow plain stretching as far as the eye could see.

Then the character of the landscape changed; we saw more shrubs and huge ancient trees, and far in the distance, amid treetops, I thought I could dimly make out the vague silhouette of a mountain chain, which vanished when I excitedly pointed it out to Horst and Mohammed. Was it a mirage – or merely a figment of my powerful desire? But presently the others also saw the mountain chain on the skyline, and we could scarcely believe our eyes. The hills drew closer and closer until they seemed to be within arm's reach; how disappointed we were to come a single large stone house with one or two hundred children dressed in white *jellabas* standing in front of it, watching us. 'A school!' said Horst, with bitter irony. 'I told you so, it was stupid going on this trip.'

I too felt frustrated. As we stood under a shady tree, anxious only to slake our thirst and stretch our legs, a giant of a man wearing a clean Arab garment and a small cap approached us and greeted us very cordially in Arabic. Mohammed, delighted that he could speak to someone, chattered away animatedly. Now we knew we had reached Kau, and this almost-seven-foot giant was the *mak* of the local Nuba.

It was odd and unusual that no one approached us after the *mak* left and the children vanished. We were left all alone, something I had never experienced in Africa. Whenever we stopped anywhere, even in the most remote areas, natives would appear after a short time and peer at me curiously.

Far off in the cliffs, I saw many small huts which aroused my curiosity, and as Horst was willing to accompany me there, I got my Leicas out of the crate. Natu, Alipo, and Mohammed had gone to sleep in the shade of the tree. It was afternoon, the sun was on the western side and we were surrounded by an almost ghostly quiet. The landscape was beautiful; the ground was covered with small hollies and their intense green contrasted picturesquely with the yellow hues of the straw.

Soon we were standing in front of the huts, which reached all the way up to the highest cliffs. It was like a ghost village. We clambered up some rocks and ran into two small children, who fearfully scurried away. Where there are children, I told myself, there have to be adults; we had only climbed a little further when, in between the huts, hopping over the stones, I saw two young, absolutely beautiful girls – naked, but oiled from head to foot and painted a shiny red. The instant they caught sight of me, they vanished as if swallowed up by the earth. I was so excited, never having seen anything like this, that I no longer felt heat, fatigue, or exhaustion; all I wanted to do was photograph them. But once again, the area was filled with ghostly silence. I called to Horst, who was clambering about further up and hadn't seen the girls; he was pointing upwards to where the heads of a girl and two children were peering over a ledge. They were painted too and their eyes were timid and distrustful. I managed to get a few shots, but they disappeared lightning-fast behind the rocks. I was very happy, for now I knew that my trip had not been in vain. Since the sun would soon be going down, we decided to continue our search the next day.

Meanwhile, the *mak* had returned to our campsite, and Mohammed had made him some tea and was conversing with him. Natu and Alipo, who knew a little Arabic, now became interpreters and I learned that aside from Kau there were two other villages in the vicinity: Nyaro and Fungor. The *mak* was willing to take us there the next day.

'Are you an Arab or a Nuba?' I asked.

'A Nuba,' he said with a proud smile. Then from nearby, we heard a soft drumming, which grew louder and louder. The *mak* stood up and, pointing in that direction, he said, 'Nyertun' – a dance of girls.

I grabbed my cameras, and Horst got out his Arriflex. Cautiously, I stole over to the dancing place, where I found an unusual and thrilling tableau. In the final rays of the setting sun, very slender figures moved in balletic grace to the beat of the drums. The girls were completely naked, oiled all over, and painted different colours ranging from red to ochre and yellow; their hands clutched flexible switches or woven leather whips. Their movements were seductive and became wilder and wilder, although no man could be seen apart from the two drummers. The dancers hadn't noticed me, since I was concealed behind a tree trunk, photographing with long telelenses. Through the clouds of dust whirled up by the girls, I saw that Horst too was trying to capture these unique images on celluloid without being seen. Unfortunately, we could film and photograph for only a few minutes, for it was already growing dark. For me, this was the greatest visual experience I have ever had during any of my African expeditions.

When we returned to camp, an incredible piece of news was awaiting us: the *omda* – as the *mak* was called here among the South-Eastern Nuba – told us that tomorrow afternoon, a *zuar* would be taking place in Fungor. The *zuar* referred to the matches that I had heard about years before (and recently dreamed about), and in search of which I had come on this perilous trip. So these rituals still existed. What chance had led me here – or was it some sixth sense?

The next afternoon, we drove to Fungor with the *omda*. All I could see at first, other than numerous trees, was a colossal cliff. In the shade of one of the trees, however, I discovered a group of young men who were obviously the combatants, for a few had heavy brass rings around their wrists. Like the girls, they were naked and painted, not only on their bodies, but also on their faces. Each man looked different, with his own individual colours, ornaments and decorations; all they had in common was the way their hair was shaved in a wedge at their temples, and the middle of their heads were emphasized by white feathers or peanuts. This group under the tree consisted of contestants from Nyaro, but presently warriors came charging out of Fungor. With feathers on their heads, they ran in line, then streamed apart in all directions, halted, leaned back, and emitted penetrating cries like birds of prey. Then the Nyaro fighters leaped up, ran towards their opponents, and also let out blood-curdling shrieks. They moved as elegantly as predatory cats. There were no women to be seen and, as I subsequently found out, this was a rule of the ritual bouts.

At first only mock fights were fought; then the actual battle was launched. It happened so quickly that I could barely follow the events. The fighters began by hitting one another with sticks, striking so hard that they could smash a skull, a hand, or a leg if the blow weren't parried with the swiftest reaction and utmost skill. These stick fights lasted for only a few seconds, then the sticks flew into the air and each opponent deployed his martial technique to avoid being struck by the dangerous blow of the sharp brass ring. The referees tried to keep apart the fighters, who, although covered with blood, never let go of the opponent and kept struggling until one man's shoulders touched the ground, or until the referees called it a draw.

Gingerly I tried to approach the arena and managed to shoot my first takes. I had equipped my Leicaflex cameras with motors and teleoptics and slung them around my shoulders. After getting a few long shots, I went up to the fighters, right into the tumult, but was quickly driven away and had to attempt it from the other side. Knowing that these were unrepeatable images, I struggled for every shot. Horst was less lucky with his movie camera, for the referees kept blocking him. Nevertheless, he managed to capture a few scenes.

When the matches were done, I was exhausted, sweaty, and covered with dust, but also very happy when I returned to our truck. The *omda* wanted to show us something before we drove back and pointed to a tree underneath which an old man was sitting with a drum in his hands. I realized that something was about to happen here, and sure enough, I saw a girl approaching, oiled and painted like the ones in Kau the day before. When the old man began to beat his drum, more and more girls came over, their hips swaying, switches in their hands. Then they were joined by the young men from the arena, but now they were almost unrecognizable. Adorned with plumes and beads, freshly oiled and painted in original patterns, they slowly walked over to the dancing girls, eyes averted, and sat down on rocks near the dancers. With grave, unsmiling faces, they held sticks in both hands and they gazed at the ground. Their sole motion was the quivering of their legs, to which tiny bells were attached. Now and then, one of these young men stood up and walked about with dancing steps, almost in slow motion compared with the wild movements of the girls. The dance pantomime grew particularly exciting when the men paused in front of the drummer, leaned back, placed a hand on their mouths and then, just as they had done before the matches, screamed like predatory birds. It looked as if they were drawing these shrieks out of their bodies with the movements of their hands and arms and, in the whirling dust and the pale green twilight, the whole spectacle was strange beyond words.

There followed an exciting roll of the drum, and I saw three girls each raising a leg to swing it over the head of her chosen man and rest it on his shoulder for an instant; during this very intimate ceremony, the girls kept their eyes fixed on the ground and when it was over they danced back to their group. Although I did not understand the meaning of this cultic act, I knew it could only be a love ritual and subsequently I learned that among the South-Eastern Nuba, the girls are permitted to choose their life partners in this way.

We had to leave Kau the next day but before we went the *omda* wanted to show us Nyaro, the third village and perhaps the most beautiful. It was larger than Fungor, but smaller than Kau. Not more than about three thousand South-Eastern Nuba lived in these three villages.

Looking around Nyaro, I came upon an adolescent boy sitting in the shade of a hut who was unlike anybody or anything I had ever seen; his body was fantastically painted, like a leopard, and his face reminded me of a Picasso. To my surprise, he raised no objections to being photographed, and soon I discovered that he was not the only one painted in such an unusual way; young men came towards me from everywhere, with faces like stylized masks. These were no primitive paintings. The harmony of colours and forms revealed a high level of artistry.

Not everyone was willing to be photographed, however, and I sensed that it would require time and patience to make contact with these people or even to become friends with them. My experiences during those two days was so overwhelming that I decided to put off my other responsibilities and return as soon as possible. Meanwhile, I said goodbye to a magical world which filled me with new dreams and yearnings.

THE RED SEA

By the time we arrived in Khartoum after fifty-three hours of uninterrupted driving, we were at the end of our strength. With hollow cheeks and dull eyes, Horst was visibly ill for the first time and drooped about like an old man. For two days, he could keep down no medicine or food, and could barely move. I wanted to cancel our flight, but Horst managed to get through the worst. He even succeeded in getting all twenty crates of our baggage through customs inspection and dispatching it as freight to Munich.

Before our departure from Khartoum, Ahmed Abu Bakr, who now worked closely with President Nimeiri, brought us an invitation from the president, who wanted us to take a few pictures of him. Nimeiri received us in his private residence, and I was impressed by his modest, cordial manners and by his Spartan lifestyle. During a long conversation about the beauties of the underwater world in the Red Sea, I begged him to prohibit harpooning there and, as I later found out, he did issue such a ban.

Nimeiri was quite uninhibited during the shooting. Abu Bakr had told me that the president was religious, so I wanted to photograph him at prayer and to my surprise, he agreed. I took him in his bedroom, which looked like the bare living-quarters of a soldier. Next, he took us for a walk through the well-tended garden leading to the government palace, and there he showed us the staircase on which General Gordon had been killed by followers of the Mahdi in 1885. The president then took us to his office where something completely unexpected occurred. Abu Bakr informed me that in recognition of my services to the Sudan, President Gaafar Mohamed Nimeiri wished to grant me Sudanese citizenship. He added that I was the first foreigner to receive this honour. Finally the president handed me a Sudanese passport. Deeply moved, I thanked him.

AN INTERNATIONAL SUCCESS

After four months' absence, we returned to Munich. Without a doubt, this had been my most strenuous expedition, but luckily, we had caught neither dysentery nor any other tropical disease. This was almost miraculous, when

During the Olympic Games in the summer of 1936

After the war in the autumn of 1945 with my husband Peter Jacob.
We managed to spend a few days together at Seebichl House in
Kitzbühel when we were kept under house arrest by the French.

With my brother Heinz whom I loved as a friend
as well as a brother

With my very dear Hanni who helped me through the hard
post-war years

With my Arriflex I filmed my friends the Masakin Nuba
in 1974 in the hills in the south of the Sudanese province
of Kordofan

Among the south-eastern Nuba in 1975

The Indian Ocean, 1974. I first learned deep-sea diving
at the age of seventy-two and it became my passion.

My colleague Horst filming in the Maldives

In 1986 I discovered the most beautiful reefs
while diving in the Red Sea

I think how we often drank unfiltered water with the Nuba, in order not to offend them, and also drank their *marisse* from a common vessel as was the custom.

Nervously we looked forward to the results of our shooting in Kau, but we were not disappointed; the stills and the rushes were very exciting. Unfortunately, there wasn't enough material for another book of photographs or for a film, but the impact of the pictures was so powerful that Robert Schäfer wanted to do a second book. The people at *Stern* were also enthralled and when Rolf Gillhausen had his first look, he exclaimed, 'Leni, you have no choice, you have to go back. This is simply fabulous.' Ernst Haas, the world-renowned photographer, who attended the showing, encouraged me to do anything I could to go on another trek. List and *Stern* were willing to support a new expedition.

I was uncertain whether I wanted to run the risk of another such project, but a number of things seemed to favour the idea, including my Sudanese passport which would surely facilitate matters. Finally – and this may have tipped the balance – Harper & Row, New York, ordered seventeen thousand copies of my Nuba book from Mondadori and were certain to take a share in the next one. Thus, a new trip was financially guaranteed.

First, I had to take care of various matters, such as the pressing need to buy a new car. My beloved old one had done its duty for twenty years, like an old horse, but by now it couldn't possibly pass any inspection. I opted for a blue Audi 100GL because of its large boot and its colour, which was similar to that of my loyal Opel.

MICK AND BIANCA

One day, Michael Rand telephoned from London and made me a stunning offer: 'Come to London and shoot Mick Jagger and his wife Bianca for the *Sunday Times*.'

'Who is Mick Jagger?' I asked.

'You don't know Mick Jagger, the world-famous rock star?'

Hesitant and unsure of myself, I said, 'No.'

'That's impossible. You must have heard of the Rolling Stones?'

'I've heard of them, but I don't think I'm the right person for the job.'

Michael Rand persisted and eagerly listed all the advantages I would derive from doing the photographs. When he then told me that it was also Mick Jagger's wish, I agreed.

The very day of my arrival, I met the leading member of the Rolling

Stones, the *Sunday Times* having arranged a meeting at Brown's Hotel. I had imagined a very different type – a dozy hippy with unkempt hair, churlish and arrogant. But Mick Jagger was not at all as I had expected. He was clearly intelligent and sensitive; within a short time, we were absorbed in a conversation that grew more and more intense. We spoke about all kinds of things; art, the theatre and films. He told me he was a big fan of mine and was familiar with my films, having seen some of them as often as fifteen times.

I took pictures the next afternoon, on the landscaped roof of a London department store. Meanwhile, I had learned what these photos were all about and why I of all people had been asked to take them. Mick and Bianca had at first refused to pose together because their marriage was on the rocks, but when their manager insisted, the two of them agreed only on condition that he hire Leni Riefenstahl for the job. I was eager to see how I would deal with these two stars, especially Bianca, who was said to be very eccentric.

Mick was the first to appear in the rooftop garden, and I had no problems filming him. He was relaxed, cheerful, open and altogether very pleasant. Bianca turned up very late, accompanied by her hair stylist and her dresser, who were lugging a colossal number of suitcases and hat boxes. Bianca seemed proud and unapproachable and I was sure I wouldn't have an easy time getting a portrait of a loving married couple. I could only marvel at Bianca's wardrobe; she had brought expensive clothes with all the accessories. After being coiffed and made up, she slipped into a white lace frock in which she looked enchanting – a queen. Bianca must have been aware that I liked her, for her aloofness soon melted, and I had no trouble after all in getting the picture that the *Sunday Times* wanted.

By the time we said goodbye, we had become friends.

FILM FESTIVAL IN TELLURIDE

Bill Pence, James Card of Eastman House in Rochester, New York, and Tom Luddy of the Pacific Film Archive in Berkeley, California, had invited me as a guest of honour to the film festival at Telluride which was to open with *The Blue Light*. The organizers planned it as an alternative to Cannes, Venice and Berlin and certainly this was an unusual idea for Telluride, a goldmining town in Colorado, six thousand feet above sea level and surrounded by lofty mountains, had a total population of only one thousand.

The centre of the festival was the old Sheridan Opera House, built in 1914, which Bill Pence had bought and restored. Its interior, a small jewel, had room for two hundred and fifty spectators and when it was lit up, it had a warm atmosphere because of the gold and violet hues in the design. Three artists of the cinema were to be honoured: Gloria Swanson, the queen of the silent cinema; Francis Ford Coppola, who had just had a world-wide hit with *The Godfather* starring Marlon Brando; and, surprisingly, a German film artist. The choice had fallen on me and I had no doubt that this would trigger protests and controversy. Should I stay away or be there? It was a major decision for me, but one which I did not care to evade. This festival could be a touchstone, indicating whether I was definitively 'out' or whether I still had a chance of resuming my profession.

I was put up at the Manitou Lodge, next door to Gloria Swanson who greeted me with a hug. Despite her age, she looked dazzling, and her personality was as pleasant as ever, but I saw that she studied me with her green feline eyes. Paul Kohner, one of the best-known film agents in Hollywood (I still remember him as the production manager of our Greenland film *SOS Iceberg*, forty-two years before) had asked her to boycott the festival if I were present. Paul Kohner had also advised Francis Ford Coppola and the other artists against visiting the festival. But, incredible as it may sound, not a single artist would be intimidated. They all came, and in even greater numbers than the organizers had expected.

Telluride was buzzing like a beehive, feverish with excitement; the facilities were good and there were excellent restaurants with a four-star international cuisine. Yet I felt uneasy. I had learned that the American Jewish Congress had dispatched a sharp protest to the organizers of the festival and also asked Francis Ford Coppola and Gloria Swanson not to go. Dangerous clouds piled up over this small, romantically situated town. I was quite willing to leave, but the organizers wouldn't hear of it and even the Jewish mayor, Jerry Rosenfeld, urged me to stay. He assured me that all security measures had been taken to prevent any violence. I felt wretched, nervous and deeply apprehensive.

When *The Blue Light* began to flicker on the screen of the Sheridan Opera House, there was a full moon outside – a happy coincidence, for in this film the little village of Santa Maria resembles Telluride and its rooftops are moonlit like those of Telluride that evening. The theatre was surrounded by a crowd of people and I was led through a back entrance; I learned that the police were searching every visitor for weapons – something I had never experienced before. Demonstrations were expected, though nothing happened. I sat trembling in my box throughout the screening. When the film ended, tremendous applause broke out and went on and on. James Cord, director of the festival, presented me with a silver medal; Al Miller, a spokesman for the committee, said the film was an eternal testament to the great cinema of the past, while another member enthusiastically added that there was no drug more potent than this film. The next day, *Olympia* received even greater applause and there was a standing ovation.

When Gloria Swanson was asked by a reporter the next day what she thought of the controversies concerning me, she brusquely retorted: 'Why – is she waving a Nazi flag? I thought Hitler was dead!'

Francis Ford Coppola also showed me sympathy by asking me to dinner and inviting me to come to San Francisco, where he was busy cutting *Godfather II*. He was interested in my editing technique and the time I spent with this brilliant film director, who looks like a big teddy bear, was an enriching experience for me, obsessed as we both are with the cinema.

Another film artist who appealed to me was Dusan Makavejev, whose unusual erotic film *Sweet Movie* was premièred in Telluride. Although no greater contrasts could be imagined than those between this highly gifted Yugoslav director and me, he suggested a collaboration.

The festival was a total success; the efforts of the organizers had paid off. Although I had every reason to be satisfied, even happy, I felt only half-hearted about it, depressed as I was by the repeated accusations. Although only eight young people staged a demonstration, they carried a sign saying that my 1934 film *Triumph of the Will* shared the guilt for the millions of victims who died in the German concentration camps and I was deeply upset to see such a sentiment expressed. After all the horrible stories that have been circulating about me for decades, I can understand the demonstrations and protests of young people. Unlike my homeland where it doesn't happen, I always find friends and even strangers in other countries who show me their support, but deeply moved as I was by my sucess in Telluride, I was finally forced to realize that I will never get rid of the shadows of the past. Nevertheless, I have found the strength to come to terms with this fate without bitterness.

HURRICANE FILE

From New York, Horst and I flew to Honduras via Miami. After my troubled days in Telluride, I was eagerly looking forward to diving in Roatan. A few days after our arrival, however, something dreadful happened. The radio warned of an approaching hurricane, something I had never before experienced. Through the windows, I saw the palms bend low and leaves whirl through the air and I dashed outside to get my Leica to photograph the brewing storm, but I had such a terrible time struggling back to the main building that taking pictures was out of the question. When I thrust my hand out of the door, I thought it would be wrenched off. The storm grew wilder and wilder, the roaring of the wind louder and louder, and then the first window panes shattered.

'According to the radio,' said Dee, the owner of the house, ' "Fifi" [that was the hurricane's name] is heading straight towards Roatan. She'll be passing over us in a short time, at a speed of over 120 miles per hour. No one is to leave the house.'

Watching the storm lashing the sea, the waves surging higher and higher, and branches flying through the air, I was really quite frightened. The roaring of the storm grew louder by the second, the door was torn from its hinges and we retreated to the corners of the room. Beams came crashing down from the ceiling, and I was convinced that the two-storey house would cave in on us. Then it began to rain, and soon there was a torrent of water pouring down on us which we tried to catch in all kinds of vessels.

Twelve hours passed before we could venture outside. It was a scene of devastation. Giant old trees were uprooted or else had had their trunks broken like matchsticks. The corrugated iron torn from the roofs had wrapped itself around treetrunks like paper cuffs. The storm had wrenched the roof off the building where we had sought refuge, and the upper storey was completely destroyed. Dee's boathouse was floating on the waves, and a huge yacht that had been anchored in the sea lay on a hillside, badly damaged. The entire area looked as if it had just been heavily bombed.

It was a miracle that we had survived. We learned that this, in September 1974, had been the worst hurricane of the century. The authorities estimated that eight to ten thousand people had perished, a hundred thousand had been left homeless and half a million had suffered all sorts of material losses. Railway lines and bridges had been destroyed and for sixty hours, a heavy tropical rain fell non-stop; dried-out riverbeds had turned into raging torrents and a mixture of detritus, tree stumps, soil and water devastated the town of Coloma. During the flooding, which spread for miles around, refugees were crushed by tremendous landslides or drowned in the raging waters, and the government of Honduras declared a national emergency. There was no way of getting off our island for all the power and telephone lines were torn down. Worst of all for us was that during the next few days, corpses were washed up on the beach. It was as if there had been a war. We couldn't leave until three weeks later, when we took off for the mainland in a tiny plane. We landed in San Pedro de Sula and drove through the half-demolished town, where the air was still foul with the stench of corpses. Later, when we reached New York, it all began to seem like a bad dream, but we had been through a time of great danger, and, at home, our friends and relatives had been extremely worried.

NEW YORK

As Horst and I strolled up Fifth Avenue, we paused in front of Rizzoli's, a large bookstore, and saw in the window the American edition of my book, *The Last of the Nuba*. That wasn't what surprised me, for I knew that its publication was due here at any moment; what amazed me was the fact that the store window was filled up exclusively with innumerable copies of the book; I had never seen anything like this before. Harper & Row confirmed that my book was a great success with buyers and with the press, and when I went back to Rizzoli's late in the afternoon, I was told that every last copy, including the ones in the window, had been sold just hours before. We celebrated Rizzoli's own success at Nanni, one of New York's many fine Italian restaurants.

Word quickly got out that I was in New York, and from then on, I didn't have a quiet minute. Not only was I besieged by journalists and photographers, but artists and friends also appeared, including Bianca Jagger, who invited me to tea at the Plaza, where she was staying. What I had guessed about Bianca at our first meeting was now confirmed. She was not the fashion doll that many people considered her – quite the contrary. She had read a great deal about the cinema and was particularly interested in directing; she was surprisingly well informed about my work. I also had another meeting with Mick, who came in especially from Long Island, and every detail of the evening we spent with him is etched in my mind. He invited Horst and me to dinner with the beautiful Faye Dunaway and her new husband, the rock musician Peter Wolf; Anni Ivil, a young woman who was a business acquaintance of Mick's, was also there. Anni had told me that Horst would have to wear a tie, and I an evening gown – *de rigueur* at La Côte Basque, a smart French restaurant. This was somewhat difficult for us, since Horst hates neckties, and my evening wardrobe was rather modest.

When we were picked up, I admired Faye Dunaway and Anni Ivil, who were beautifully dressed; yet, as we entered the restaurant, an elderly French hostess scrutinized us from head and let us all pass except Faye Dunaway and Anni Ivil. The ludicrous reason was that women in trousers were not allowed in. At first, we thought she was joking, as Faye and Anni were wearing wide-swinging, ankle-length chiffon skirts, but the hostess pointed imperiously to the exit. That was too much for Mick. He swore furiously, strode over to the table reserved for us, grabbed a wine glass and smashed it on the floor. I tried to calm him down. Meanwhile, the manager appeared, sent away the officious hostess and begged Mick to accept his apology. Mick wavered a while, then, still frowning, decided to stay. Faye and Anni, whose divided skirts had not escaped the sharp-eyed Cerberus, went off to change. Naturally, the evening was ruined, for despite caviare, lobster and champagne, we couldn't recover the same mood.

The next day, I met with various American film people and artists. The autumn weather was splendid, almost warm enough to wear summer clothes, and at time like this New York is wonderful; it draws you like a moloch. In my few short days there, I was struck by the immense contrasts between grinding poverty and fabulous wealth, the breathtaking architecture and the bleakness of the Bronx, the countless luxury restaurants and shop windows full of all kinds of priceless objects, the derelict shops and empty lots.

I had a major appointment almost every hour but my most important meetings were with Richard Meran Barsam, professor at New York University, who was writing a book on my films, and Sidney Geffen, owner of the Carnegie Hall Cinema. Geffen took me out to a Czech restaurant, where I enjoyed the best roast duck that I have ever eaten. No less interesting was my meeting with Peter Beard, the well-known photographer and writer on Africa; a friend of Mick and Bianca, he invited us to his farm in Nairobi. Then my publisher wanted to see me, and so did Stephan Chodorov and John Musilli of Camera Three (who had made a TV film about me). I also spent several hours with Jonas Mekas, the 'pope' of the underground cinema, whose film-theatre screens motion pictures with maximum technical quality; he too wanted to show my films. Everything was tremendously exciting and promising; but it was already October, and I wanted to visit the Nuba of Kau in November.

I was very lucky for in New York, of all places, I saw Dr Mahsour Khalid, the foreign minister of the Sudan. We met at Andy Warhol's factory, where I had an appointment with Warhol. His factory consisted of empty lofts containing a few tables and chairs; that's all I remember. I had to wait a long time for Andy, and when he came he looked almost delicate, his pale skin intensified by his white hair and his dark suit, and had a small dog on a leash. Our conversation, which he taped, was very matter-of-fact. Andy spoke slowly, almost monotonously and his face showed no emotions; he seemed a bit shy. This was probably a defence against strangers, since he had already become a cult figure for too many people. I stayed in touch with him for quite a while through Paul Morrissey, the director of his films and a fan of mine: Morrissey often called me from New York, and we had long conversations.

A TELEPHONE CONVERSATION

In Munich, everything was at sixes and at sevens. All the preparations for our trip had to be completed within a few weeks, and this time the arrangements were more complicated than ever before. The Nuba Hills were only two or three hours from Kadugli, where you could buy a number of things; but in the surroundings of Kau, there was nothing, not even markets for the natives. We had to take everything we would need with us.

During this work, we received several phone calls from strangers who wanted information about the South-Eastern Nuba; one of these callers was a travel agent, who was planning a trip to Kau in the near future. We were utterly dismayed and Horst, who had spoken with this man, tried to dissuade him from going. He said that according to his information, this tribe had long since discarded its customs and traditions; apparently, there was even a school there. When Horst asked him how he had heard about these natives, the man said he had recently read an interesting photo story about them in the Swiss newspaper, *Neue Zürcher Zeitung*. The author had written about the great changes and imminent decline of the South-Eastern Nuba. Many of the photos, said the caller, showed that the natives were still naked, which certainly made it an interesting travel destination.

This news didn't bode well.

I finally managed to calm Horst, who had a vision of Kau mobbed by tourists, then I sent for the newspaper article. Entitled 'Artists and Fighters', it was penned by a man nammed Oswald Iten. Hoping to discuss the South-Eastern Nuba with him, I obtained his address and phone number from the newspaper.

Herr Iten was not at home, but I introduced myself to his landlady as Helene Jacob. Before I could even explain the reason for my call, she launched into enthusiastic praises of her tenant. She said he had brought back wonderful shots from the Sudan, but he couldn't sell them, 'that Riefenstahl woman' had spoiled his business. Nor could he find a publisher for his photos; no publisher was interested, the landlady said, because of 'Riefenstahl's' Nuba book.

'Is Herr Iten a photographer or scientist?' I asked.

'He's still a student, and he's very young,' she replied; she told me that when her tenant had returned from his trip to the Sudan, he had been upset because 'that Riefenstahl woman' had visited the South-Eastern Nuba just before him and had worked there with a huge crew and enormous equipment. What foolish lies! No one could have worked more modestly in Kau than Horst and I.

I couldn't guess at the time that this student would eventually defame me everywhere by spreading the most incredible stories about me in newspapers and even in a paperback book.

BACK IN SUDAN

It was early December 1974 when I flew to Khartoum, and as always before an expedition, I was worn out. Horst was to follow me with all our luggage one week later; this time, since I did not want to impose on the hospitality of my friends, I had booked a room at the Sudan Hotel. No sooner had I landed in Khartoum than I became ill with violent stomach pains and a skin allergy which covered my face and body with red spots. A German woman doctor helped me with strong calcium injections so that by the time Horst arrived, I was on my feet again and able to go to the airport.

It was the day before Christmas Eve when our luggage finally arrived, but we couldn't get to our things because all the offices and agencies, including customs, were shut down – and for a whole week to boot; the major festivals of both Christians and Moslems occur during the last week of December and then January brings the Sudanese independence celebrations. The situation was extremely frustrating for us since it meant we were trapped in Khartoum.

That was when Norbert Koebke became our guardian angel; I still can't work out how he did it, but he managed to get our luggage released during the Christmas holidays. To our consternation, however, the haversack containing such indispensable gear as light cables, camera foils, tripods, etc. was nowhere to be found so we had to order replacements from Germany, thereby losing another week. I had wanted to be in Kau by early December, and now it was already Christmas. To make matters worse, we were unable to hire a truck in Khartoum despite my helpful friends and my good relations with the Sudanese authorities. President Nimeiri and some of his ministers were spending those days in Mecca, and Abu Bakr was out of town. Preparing the expedition had been such an arduous task, and now we had been stuck here for three weeks already.

Fortunately, the Sudanese foreign minister, whom I had met in New York and who had promised to help me in any way possible, happened to be in Khartoum. He succeeded in getting us vehicles at least from El Obeid, plus a plane ticket for me to that town and a railway ticket for Horst.

While I dealt with the vehicles in El Obeid, Horst remained in Khartoum until the replacement gear arrived from Munich. With his thirty-five crates, he would then take the train to El Obeid.

I had been waiting impatiently for days when at last the train chugged in and, trembling, I looked for Horst. He was on the train, and, thank goodness, so were the innumerable crates. The trip had been very gruelling for him, mainly because he had stayed awake the whole time, guarding the crates. Whenever the train stopped – and it stopped very frequently, he had dashed over to the baggage car and counted the crates.

We left El Obeid before sunset. General Abdullahi Mohamed Osman had assigned me two vehicles driven by soldiers: an ancient Landrover and a truck for our luggage. Petrol was in short supply even for the army and we were given only two canisters, drums enough at most to reach our destination and spend two or three weeks there. From the state of the tyres, it looked as if we could count on a good many punctures.

In Kadugli, where the new governor welcomed us with open arms, it was impossible to find any petrol. But still, we had the opportunity to get to Kau, and we also had the governor behind us.

It was early January when we finally reached Kau, all of us exhausted. We set up camp under the same old familiar tree and as always its friendly foliage provided ideal shade. No Nuba were to be seen as yet, but that evening, the *omda* came to welcome us. He seemed delighted and again offered us his help. Our most urgent need was a high straw fence around our camp, and so four men arrived the very next morning. By nightfall, our 'house' was as good as completed, and I found it more beautiful than any luxury suite. In early January, the heat was still bearable.

We were surrounded by a heavenly silence, for the Nuba still didn't appear – which was fine with us, for we first had to unpack our crates and arrange the camp. Then, bringing our presents, we visited the *omda*, who lived only a few minutes away. Our gifts were simple, but nicely wrapped, and for the people living in this seclusion, they were almost priceless. We were served tea and got to know the *omda*'s entire family with all his wives and children. Then we gave the *omda* a large torch with many replacement batteries; we gave the women beads and the children sweets. Next, I handed the *omda* several documents. The most important ones came from President Nimeiri's office and from the supreme police chief of the Sudan. These documents asked the Sudanese to give me any possible help. I also had a document from the Ministry of Culture and Information, confirming that I was a 'friend of the country' and that my filming was done under the minister's aegis. I also had my Sudanese passport and the *omda* was deeply impressed by the signatures and stamps.

Before saying goodbye, he proudly showed us a shiny gold Swiss watch that he had not been wearing a year ago. The *omda* asked Horst, who knew a little Arabic, whether he could repair the loose band. Seeing our astonished looks, he explained that last year, after we had left Kau, a 'Swisserer' – as he put it – had come here for only a short time and taken photographs. When the *omda* said the man had come from Malakal, I recalled the story in *Neue Zürcher Zeitung* about the South-Eastern Nuba and the tremendous changes the author had observed between his visits in 1972 and 1974. 'The time is not too far off,' he had written, 'when the South-Eastern Nuba, like their brothers in Talodi and Rheika, will start weighing themselves down with all sorts of rubbish – plastic covers, metal pails, car tyres. The greatest danger to their ancestral way of life is Islam. Torn from their traditional background and now accustomed to money, many Nuba are vegetating in the slums of towns and cities.'

I had experienced the same thing with 'my' Nuba. Could this already be happening to the South-Eastern ones? Only ten months had passed since I had photographed the traditional knife duels in their original town. Could those have been the final pictures? If this was the case, then I could have saved myself the trouble of coming. I had no answer as yet. So far, we had seen only children and old people.

I was soon to know for certain. The *omda* accompanied us to Fungor, to the place where I had photographed the fights one year earlier, and what we now saw was a bitter disappointment. Most of the men had come as spectators or escorts. There were few combatants and those there were wore shorts or Arab costumes. The fights themselves were a chaotic sight, preceded by arguments about who was to fight whom, and, in the end, there was only one bout. The two fighters were so completely surrounded by spectators that we could get neither stills nor footage. The two days of our previous visit had been a unique occasion, which would never come again.

We had to say goodbye to Suliman, the driver of our truck, who had to return the vehicle to El Obeid on schedule. It was our last chance to send letters; from now on, we would be virtually cut off from the outside world. We may have been only seventy to ninety miles from the next village; but for our Landrover, old enough to be put in a museum, this distance would be impossible without an accompanying vehicle and fuel reserves. I wrote to the general, describing our situation and asking him to send back the truck as soon as possible with spare parts plus petrol and oil. Along with the letter, we handed Suliman a large sum of money so that, if the worst came to the worst, he could buy these articles on the black market. Mohammed, our very young soldier driver, was convinced that Suliman would return with all these things within a week at the latest. So far, so good.

But then, we suffered our next big disappointment: we found the village of Kau practically deserted. Whenever we strolled around the houses or scaled the cliffs, all we saw were barking dogs and a few elderly people who waved us off the instant they sighted our cameras. Not a single young girl was in view, not a single one of the fantastically painted men and it was only when I met Ibrahim, the Arab teacher at the school, with whom I could speak English, that I learned the reason. All the able-bodied Nuba were still out in the fields, bringing in the harvest, and they wouldn't be returning to their villages for weeks.

The barometer rose from day to day and soon the temperature hit ninety-five degrees in the shade. On no previous expedition had I had such unpleasant experiences with snakes. We had snake serum with us and even a small petroleum fridge to keep the serum and other medicine fresh. But there is no remedy for the highly venomous boomslangs, and one such snake had slid into the sack in which I had put my bed sheets every morning. Horst heard me shriek when I took hold of the sack and a green snake over two yards long slithered along my arm, and with great presence of mind he killed it with a stick. After that, we stretched two huge sheets over the beds so that serpents and others creatures couldn't drop on us from the overhead foliage.

The next day, I had just finished washing my dusty hair when a huge swarm of bees came buzzing up, attracted perhaps by the scent of my shampoo. Horst shouted: 'Quick! Under the covers!' We had put plastic covers on our beds to shield them against dust, and now, as we lay perspiring under the plastic with thousands of bees humming around us, I could scarcely breathe; sweat came gushing from all my pores. Through the transparent material, I saw hundreds of bees clustering upon it and I heard Horst yell, 'Close the covers, the bees will sting you to death.'

The buzzing of the bees grew louder and louder. Horst kept shouting, 'Tute, tute, Mohammed, Arabi.' But no one heard him. We lay there, bathed in sweat, for a good half hour, until we finally heard voices and sounds. I recognized Tute, a relative of the *omda*, but I didn't dare open the cover. Then I heard the crackling of fire, and knew the Nuba were smoking out the bees. When we rolled out of the plastic covers and staggered along the ground, a yard-long swarm of bees was still dangling from a tree trunk and under it Tute and a pair of other Nuba were holding straw torches. The earth was covered with dead bees, but hundreds more were still flying about buzzing furiously. We all had painful bites, and weren't free of the bees until sunset.

Our chain of bad luck seemed endless. One morning, during breakfast, another disaster struck. There was a sudden bang and in no time flames were licking up our tree, and my clothes, which hung on a line, were on fire. Using sand and blankets, Horst managed to put out the fire, and we discovered that our gas cooker had exploded. Less than an hour later, I banged my head on a low branch, which left me with concussion. Horst, who had scorched his hand while extinguishing the fire, was putting compresses on my head and camomile poultices on my eyelids, when we heard large vehicles approaching and coming to a stop right by our fence. Horst peered through the straw and said, 'We've got company. Two large Unimogs. Look like tourists.'

How in the world were tourists getting here? Horst went out to talk to them and came back with the news that they were nice people who had learned our whereabouts from an indiscreet official and wanted to visit me.

Some of them had read the article in *Neue Zürcher Zeitung* and also a short, remarkable book about the South-Eastern Nuba, illustrated with colour photos and published years ago by James Faris, an American scientist. The strangers were disappointed not to see painted Nuba, and next day the Unimogs drove off again.

We were very unhappy about this visit – and not just because it disrupted our work. Now, suddenly, all kinds of native children and also adults showed up with large banknotes, expecting us to change them, and we realized what the tourists had done. Tute reported that they had used money to lure the timid Nuba in front of their cameras. This spelled disaster for us. With money, you get only posed shots; and once the natives start posing, a real photographer is doomed. This happened with the Masai and other African tribes.

Since there was now little to photograph in Kau, we visited Nyaro, and once again saw the pretty oiled girls who, at our approach, scampered off like timid gazelles. To our surprise, fewer of these local Nuba were out in the fields; nor was their appearance marred by ugly clothing. I felt a vast relief: there was still hope for our shooting.

When I made my first attempt at photographing in Nyaro, an elderly man came towards me; although I didn't understand his language, I caught his drift, since *krush* means 'money' in Arabic. I had never experienced this among 'my' Nuba, and we refused to pay him anything. This was all the fault of the tourists, and it made the situation difficult for us. When I discussed the incident with the *omda*, he merely smiled and said that the tourists in the Unimog had been preceded by others who had paid the Nuba in order to photograph them. James Faris, he said, had also given them money in exchange for taping them.

The *omda* drove to Nyaro with us, and soon we were sitting in a Nuba hut with the elders and sub-chiefs; *marisse* beer was handed around, and then the *omda* showed the chief the documents I had submitted to him. I couldn't tell whether the chief was able to read the Arabic writing, but he was obviously impressed; the letters were solemnly passed around, and the faces of the men lit up. The Nuba gave us permission to film and photograph without paying, but at dances, we had to give the drummers oil. An ideal solution.

Despite our agreement, the work was unbelievably difficult. I often spent hours sitting in the terrible heat, concealed behind rocks, just to snap a few pictures. It was easiest shooting the men painting themselves; very few of them waved me off, most of them being so deeply absorbed in their task that they didn't even notice me, and these were my first good photos. The girls, however, were much more shy. I had often seen an extremely beautiful girl in front of a hut up on the cliffs and had brought some beads to tempt her with; when I showed them to her and pointed to my camera, she understood at once and stationed herself in front of the door, as stiff as a doll – just as I expected. The girl was so beautiful, with the figure of an Amazon, and a wild, defiant expression, that, after taking a few pictures, I gave her the bag of beads. Settling on the rocky ground, she let the beads glide through her hands, making sure that none fell down. She was raptly absorbed in gazing at them when her little sisters came over, and suddenly lots of little girls were sitting around me, every last one of them wanting beads. I couldn't help it – I laughed, and they all joined in my laughter. When I stood up, they combed my pockets for beads, and since they were covered with oil and pigments, I was soon all smeared. I tried to shield my lenses from the oil, for they were grabbing at my camera, but the children hung on my arms like a swarm of bees, tugging at my hair and my skirt, and I had to pull away firmly.

Horst was having a much harder time with his film camera and still hadn't managed to shoot a single foot. Wherever he turned up with his camera, the children loved warning the others, who then hid in the houses or behind the rocks. All he could film was a couple of goats and pigs.

Since I wanted to learn more and more about the customs and social structure of these Nuba, Tute introduced me to the most important Nuba man who could help me, the man who had also aided Faris in his research. His name was Jabor El Mahdi Tora, and he too was related to the *omda*. Jabor was a quiet, intelligent person, both modest and astonishingly tactful. For several hours a day, he obligingly answered my questions with the assistance of Ibrahim, the teacher. I tried to convey all this information in my picture book *The Nuba of Kau*, in which I limited myself to clarifying why he endured these strains and perils in order to get pictures, explaining that it was perhaps the last chance to document these unique and fascinating South-Eastern Nuba for posterity.

Jabor said that apart from Faris, no outsiders had ever spent any length of time here – not even missionaries. It was only thanks to their isolation from the rest of the world that the Nuba could stick to their ancient traditions of body painting, which, oddly enough, exist only in this tribe and not in the hundred other Nuba tribes. Nor do any of the other Nuba tribes do their hair in this way or wear similar ornaments and tattoos.

Jabor told me interesting things about the body cult, about who could go naked and who couldn't. Only those people who were young, healthy, and had what they considered a beautiful body were allowed to be nude. Once the men could no longer participate in the knife duels (they started to fight when they were between twenty-eight and thirty), they stop painting their bodies and going naked. Why bother decorating themselves, they said, once they lose their beauty? They wear clothes even if they have only a minor illness, say a cold in the head. The same applies to the girls. Once they discover they are pregnant, they put on a loincloth and never go unclad again.

James Faris writes: 'There are no laws forbidding the older ones from going naked or adorning themselves. But if anyone tries to do so, he runs the risk of being laughed at. The principal exercise is the celebration and exposure of the strong and healthy body.' A girl who has not oiled her body feels 'bare' and can therefore not participate in village life, including the village dance, which takes place almost every evening at twilight. This also applies to the belts they wear. No girl or man is ever seen without a belt, even if it consists only of a string and a palm leaf. Without a belt, a Nuba feels 'naked' and embarrassed.

The Nuba knowledge of the human body is so subtle that they have a special word for every muscle and every position, and in this their vocabulary is far richer than ours. They have a different name for every position of the shoulder or the belly. Words indicate whether the heels of a squatting person touch the ground or whether his body rests purely on his toes, whether the belly is pulled in or bulging, whether the shoulders droop, whether they are broad or narrow. It is impossible to find a male or female Nuba with even an ounce of fat because they consider fat ugly.

Their favourite occupation is wrestling, which functions as training for the much harsher and more hazardous knife duels. The bouts are fair but hard, and they are fought only between villages, never between the members of one village. There are also large fighting festivals, to which all three villages (the only villages among the South-Eastern Nuba) send their best combatants. This is an ancient tribal custom and these festivals are connected to their love life. The better a fighter, the better his amorous chances. The victors enjoy such great prestige that even married women can sleep with them if they want a child from such a man. The husband adopts the child and raises it as his own. Otherwise, the rules of matrimony are very strict. If a man wishes to marry a girl, he has to spend eight years working in the fields for her family. Despite the strict rules, free love is widespread, but only covertly, as among the Masakin Nuba.

An unusual feature of this tribe is that the girl chooses the man, and not vice versa. This selection occurs annually at the cultic love dances, which usually take place several hours after the great fight festivals. I remembered the dance that I had seen in Fungor one year earlier; after the dance, each girl had placed her leg on a man's shoulder.

'Will I be able to see such a dance here?' I asked Jabor.

'Yes,' he replied, 'once the people return to Kau from the fields.'

'When will that be?'

With a shrug, Jabor replied, 'Soon.'

But they didn't come. Nor did the often announced battle between Nyaro and Fungor take place. To avoid missing this treat, we drove to Nyaro every single day, only to be told that too many Fungor combatants were still out in the fields.

Day by day, the mercury climbed higher, reaching over one hundred degrees in the shade. We were gradually worn down by all those hours of useless waiting behind the hot rocks and lost our appetites completely; all we desired was water, for we were too exhausted to prepare meals. Worst of all we had been waiting for Suliman and his truck for three weeks now and there was no sign of him. We could not drive back without the truck or the replacement parts and the petrol. Then I caught a fever and, without warning, the weather changed: the sun vanished, the sky became overcast and I realized the dangers of our isolation.

When a truck loaded with cotton and grain came our way from southern Malakal, we waved it down and paid the driver to take with him Arabi, our soldier, who was happy to return to El Obeid to see his wife. Like Suliman, he too carried an SOS letter to the general and also a large amount of cash. I begged him to do everything he could to return immediately with a vehicle, petrol and replacement parts. He knew how perilous our situation was – that we had no spare wheel for our Landrover, and were running out of petrol.

After Arabi's departure, the weather grew worse and worse. Powerful sandstorms made us anxious, and so did dark rain clouds which were unusual for this time of year.

During those days, all we could do was wait. Then Jabor informed us that the Nyaro-Fungor fight, which had been delayed any number of times, was now definitely taking place. The storms had receded, the sky was blue again, but the heat was almost unendurable. Tense and eager, we drove to Nyaro, but found no signs of an imminent duel.

Presently, however, from the rocks, I heard the penetrating shrieks of the combatants – the kind I had heard the previous year – and I saw painted men dashing to and fro. The villagers seemed tremendously excited. For the first time, I managed to get some really genuine shots, of the men; they barely noticed us, being too deeply engrossed in thoughts of their imminent struggle. Horst, too, could film unhindered. More and more men gathered, running with lithe, feline movements to the village. We followed them in our car to the arena which was not too far away; many parts of it were lined with gigantic trees, and the fighters of Fungor were sitting in their shade. Here they were, the young men we had been waiting and waiting for, over twenty of them. From a distance, they all looked alike, but as I approached them, I noticed that each man had a knife tied to his wrist, which was adorned with numerous amulets. Clutching their sticks, they gazed unswervingly towards the Nyaro Nuba who were dashing into the field uttering loud battle whoops.

When the first duel began, it was harder to photograph than in the previous year, because too many spectators came scurrying in front of our camera or blocking the fighters. Horst, stealing closer to the combatants, was shooed away by the referees; the same thing happened to me. For us, it was nothing but running, chasing and being driven away.

Then I saw two fighters, who, although losing a great deal of blood, kept on duelling. They grew wilder and wilder and two referees were unable to separate them until finally others came over to help, in order to prevent serious consequences. I couldn't imagine the pain these men must be enduring. Critical as their wounds may have been, no fighter showed any sign of suffering. They were all virtually intoxicated, and the main task of the referees was to prevent an unintentional killing when the duel reached its perilous climax.

The sun was already going down when the fights ended. Filthy, sweaty and exhausted, we were climbing into the car when we noticed a group attending to a fighter with a seriously battered skull. They had applied a small goat horn to his leg in order to draw blood and thereby decrease the flow of blood from his head. They had also strewn sand into his deep head injuries – from our medical knowledge, an impossible method of treating wounds – and seeing this, Horst quickly grabbed our first aid kit and a canister of water from the car. The Nuba offered no resistance as Horst cleaned the injuries, put antiseptic powder on them, and skilfully stapled them shut. The young patient lay there, utterly still, accepting everything without a murmur. Finally, Horst bandaged his head and gave him a few painkillers. He also treated a second patient by the glow of my torch. We didn't return to our camp in Kau until late that night.

At 6 a.m. we had a visitor from Nyaro whom we recognized as our 'patient' by his head bandages. The painkillers seemed to have worked miracles and he wanted more, he also asked for a new bandage, but we told him a change of bandage wouldn't be necessary until three days later.

That was the start of a closer rapport with the Nuba – and also the start of a very strenuous time. From now on, men, women and children came, day and night, with all sorts of genuine medical complaints – and also with the most trivial aches and pains. Many of these visitors weren't even ill but merely wanted some pills to swallow; to these we gave vitamin tablets. Mothers brought their tots even if they had only a harmless scratch, but some were seriously ill, many of them with burns, for they often ran into fires. The medicine usually had a powerful effect. Our prestige grew, and we made friends with many families. After that we were able to film in the villages, taking photographs that would have been impossible if we hadn't treated the sick. At the same time, it made our work more difficult because we were brought to patients almost against our will. The Nuba had the most outlandish notions. One day, they absolutely insisted on getting my sunglasses for a blind man, convinced that my glasses would restore his eyesight. I tried to make it clear to them that these were not medical glasses, but it was only when the blind man tried them on and was still unable to see that they lost their interest in my sunglasses.

What fascinated me most were the young men whose painted faces revealed an incredible imagination and artistic talent. They painted themselves in order to beautify their appearance, each trying to outdo all the others. As time went by, I got to know many of them by name and once they noticed how impressed I was by their face paintings, they tried to astonish and excite me with new masks every day. Some of them were especially gifted and their drawings, figurative or abstract (the latter serving aesthetic rather than cultic purposes), touched upon the origins of art. Painting themselves symmetrically or asymmetrically, with ornaments, lines, or stylized figures, they always produced a harmonious impression. Their use of signs and colours demonstrated so high a level of artistic inventiveness that they looked like living Picassos. Nobody knows where the Nuba get this incredible talent; so far, it has not been investigated, and it will probably remain a mystery.

A few Nuba had mirrors from the days when the British ran the Sudan, and some bought mirrors from Arab merchants. I had brought along a number myself, but knowing what would happen, I had not yet given any away. Eventually, I was foolish enough to give a few to my friends, and it was something I instantly regretted. From now on, they gave me no peace – especially the boys and adolescents, who kept incessantly demanding *mandaras* (the Arab word for mirrors). When I ran out of mirrors – and I couldn't possibly have brought along as many as they wanted – they reached into my pockets, becoming insistent and even nasty. The demand for mirrors spread like an epidemic through Nyaro, Kau and Fungor and wherever I went, they shouted, 'Leni, mandara.' We had experienced something similar after taking polaroids of a few girls and young men. Everybody wanted one. They failed to understand that our cameras couldn't conjure up an infinite number of paper pictures; they thought it was ill will on our part and refused to let us photograph them.

Weeks dragged by, but there was still no sign of Arabi, much less Suliman, and the truck. We had no vehicle to transport our luggage and no petrol. We had to carry water on the back of a donkey. The heat became so intense – one hundred and ten in the shade and not much cooler at night – that we couldn't travel long distances.

Some difficult weeks followed. It was nerve-racking waiting for the truck, and having no petrol made it impossible for us to drive to Nyaro and Fungor. We came down with flu, running high temperatures alternately, and were on the brink of total exhaustion. My lips were so parched that they curled inward like dry leaves and when I lay down, I had to wrap myself in wet cloth. More and more I longed to get out of here and be home again. We dreamed of green forests, sea breezes, and yearned for beer. Yet we were nowhere near having all the film we hoped to bring back – that in itself would have rewarded us for all these deprivations and vicissitudes.

Then, one day, Tute came to tell us that the Nuba of Kau had returned from the fields. These were the magic words that made us forget our condition and we decided to do something special in order to win favour with them. I had brought along duplicates of the pictures I had shot the previous year, and in order to show them, we set up a projector, a screen and lights.

The news that the strangers were planning something out of the ordinary spread like wildfire, and soon many people had gathered nearby. Their reaction to the pictures was indescribable. They went wild when I showed the knife fights of Fungor, the excitement just buzzed through the air; the Nuba seemed to recognize everyone, even on the basis of a mere silhouette. The show was a great event and a great success. Now we were sure we would be able to take new photographs. And we were not mistaken. The very next day, many Nuba appeared at our camp, especially young men from Kau, splendidly adorned and painted. The days following were crammed with activity. Filming, photographing, treating the sick, entertaining countless visitors, and comforting them if we were unable to fulfil their wishes. Thus it went on till late at night. Now and then, even young girls came from Kau, some of them with their mothers; sometimes it was out of simple curiosity, but chiefly it was because they wanted beads. A few of these beautiful girls gave me their metal hair ornaments or bracelets in exchange.

During this period, I had an unforgettable experience. One night, when Horst was sleeping after an extremely hard day, I watched the moon rise over the mountains of Kau. The moon has always cast a great spell on me, even in my youth, but I had never seen one so huge and bright. Too excited to fall asleep. I left our enclosure taking only a stick and a torch. In the distance, I thought I heard drums and the dogs were barking, but otherwise the area was utterly still. The light from the moon was so intense that I could see quite well without my torch as I walked in the direction of the drumming, which became ever louder. After some twenty minutes, I could discern the outlines of a large number of people at the edge of the village: young girls and men dancing in the moonlight – a spectacle of almost unearthly beauty. A grave and reverential mood emanated from the dancers, affecting the onlookers. I sat down on a rock next to a group of girls who recognized me and greeted me warmly. Only four or five girls danced at a time and were then replaced by others. Nearly all of them had perfect figures with very long, slender, well-trained legs. Only one man at a time danced into the middle of the small area, with leisurely movements, almost in slow motion. The men were oiled rather than painted and their bodies looked like living marble sculptures, in contrast to the girls who wore red, yellow, and ochre makeup, as if covered with enamel. No stage production could have created such an atmosphere. The drumming was accompanied by elderly women chanting like a choir. What I witnessed there was like a mystical vision from an ancient myth. I had no camera and even if I had had one, I wouldn't have used it. Unobserved, I eventually returned to camp.

The next morning, we had an earnest talk with Mohammed, which forced us to make a crucial decision. Mohammed had given up all hope of a truck after listening to Khartoum on his radio: political changes had occurred there, and they might have serious consequences for us. The domestic and foreign ministers, whose supports had enabled us to stay in Kordofan in the first place, appeared to have been relegated to other positions, and several generals had been dismissed. Thus, the general to whom I had sent my SOS letters might no longer be in El Obeid; perhaps that was why the truck hadn't returned. We were in a difficult position. The rainy season could start any day now, as we had already experienced in the past. We dared not remain here, yet we could not leave. Mohammed had just enough petrol left to drive the Landrover – with a bit of luck – to the tiny community of Abu Gubeiha, some hundred miles or so to the north. There, he hoped to obtain enough fuel for the trip to El Obeid. It made no sense letting Mohammed go on his own; I had to join him in order to find help in Abu Gubeiha. In any event, Horst had to remain in Kau, for we could never risk leaving our camp untended, with all the cameras and valuable film stock.

I took along enough provisions for several days plus a huge canister of filtered water, a torch, medicine, my Sudanese passport and, perhaps the most important item of all, the letters of permission from the Sudanese government agencies. I planned to be back in two days. In case of breakdowns, I also took with me two Nuba men – and indeed, just three hours later, the car stalled; even though Mohammed had been driving very carefully, the spring had broken. I looked for a shady spot on the vast plain but the sun burned mercilessly.

Within just two hours, we were able to lumber off to a slow start, and shortly before darkness we arrived in Abu Gubeiha, a small town with several thousand Arabs and a police force, a district commissioner, a post office, a market and a hospital. I felt certain I could obtain petrol, oil and spare parts and, above all, be able to telephone or telegraph the governor in El Obeid to send us a truck. I was given a bed in the roadhouse, where the officials also resided. Every single Arab was extremely friendly and promised with many gestures not to leave me in the lurch.

Yet all their promises seemed to burst like soap bubbles. When I awoke, Mohammed had driven to a garage, the two Nuba from Kau had vanished and, within a short time, I was swamped with bad news. No one had petrol or oil, much less inner tubes or other necessary spare parts. The telephone lines were out of order, radio communications were jammed, and no wires could be dispatched.

One of the officials escorted me to every single well-to-do businessman in town in the hope of hiring a truck for all the money I had on me. It was the only possible way of getting out of Kau, but the few businessmen who had cars needed them themselves and all our attempts failed. The only thing I achieved after hours of effort was to buy twenty gallons of petrol from an Arab peddler – enough to get Mohammed to Er Rahad, the only major town (and an important train stop) on the road to El Obeid, where we had the best chance of getting what we needed. However, it is far from Abu Gubeiha – one hundred and fifty to one hundred and eighty miles to the north – and we heard the trails were very bad. It was questionable whether our Landrover would make it all the way to Er Rahad.

I doubted it and I doubted even more that Mohammed would ever come back. Nevertheless, I let him go, with letters, wires and enough money. Meanwhile, the two Nuba had reappeared and we agreed that Cola was to accompany Mohammed and Jabor was to remain with me. Mohammed and Cola said goodbye to me that same night and I felt the young soldier was very keenly aware of his responsibility. He shook my hand firmly, tapped his left hand on his chest several times, and said, as if he had an inkling of my scepticism, 'Mohammed, much Arabi, Mohammed beji tani' – Mohammed is not like Arabi, Mohammed will come back. I would have loved to believe him, but after my previous experiences, I had little hope.

Day after day wore by and there was no news from Mohammed. I was in the throes of despair and wanted to return to Horst in Kau – but this was impossible without a car. Then, one evening, one of the Arabs said that a truck would be passing by in just a few minutes, and it could take me to Kau. It was fully loaded with merchandise for Malakal; I could just barely squeeze in between two Arabs in the front seat and Jabor had to sit on the roof, where many Arabs were already perched on sacks and crates. Uncomfortable as I was in the cramped space, which I shared with three others, I thanked God that I would be back in Kau within a few hours. We were scheduled to arrive by midnight, but, roughly two hours later, the truck stopped somewhere in the pitch-black night. The driver, a giant of a man, got out and the other Arabs jumped down too. I remained alone inside. After what seemed an eternity, the driver returned and motioned me to get out. I followed him and saw several men carrying a mattress into a straw hut; they made signs indicating that I was to stay there. What could I do? I was at their mercy. My torch revealed that the floor was covered with animal excrement; and I was quite unable to fall asleep. Since the hut had no door, they had placed a sheets of corrugated iron across the entrance and when dawn came, and the first light fell through the cracks, I heard not only a rooster but also children's voices. Soon, the metal sheet was pushed aside, and a group of gaping children stood at the opening. Then an old man came with a glass of tea, which I gratefully accepted.

By now, I was quite apathetic; I could only wait. At last, in the afternoon, the truck returned, and again the fours of us crowded into the narrow front seat. My knees, which flanked the clutch stick, felt bruised and battered. What a relief when we reached our camp shortly before midnight.

We prepared ourselves for an emergency situation, since we could hardly expect Mohammed to return, but this time, we were wrong. Two evenings later, we heard the roar of a vehicle and there stood our Landrover. Mohammed leaped out of the car, followed by Arabi and Cola. Gratefully we hugged our rescuer and shook hands with Arabi, who was somewhat embarrassed. Mohammed proudly showed us two cans of petrol that he had brought back. Seldom in my life have I owed anyone so much. He had helped us far beyond the call of duty.

We were all extremely relieved, and during the few remaining days, we tried to film and photograph as much as possible. The greatest enemy we had to endure was the increasingly murderous heat, for it was now April – the hottest month of the year in this region.

I very much wanted to film the tattooing of a girl or a woman and we were lucky enough to get both. Macka, a 'patient' of Horst's, was a specialist in this decorative tattooing, and thanks to her we received permission from a girl and a married woman to film them during this very painful 'beauty surgery'. The work became a torture for us too. It wasn't easy watching Macka pull out the skin with a thorn and cut into it with a knife. First, we witnessed the tattooing of a girl, then, several days later, that of a married woman. Both operations took place high up, among rocks aglow from the sun. The tattooing of the woman was especially painful. Since her entire body was tattooed, she lost a great deal of blood from the thousands of tiny incisions. The procedure lasted two days, and the woman tried to conceal her pain even when her most sensitive areas were being cut. Only an occasional facial twitch revealed how much self-control she was exerting. This ceremony, to which every female must submit after three years of abstinence upon the weaning of her first child, is one of the most important cultic rituals among the South-Eastern Nuba. Once she has endured the tattooing, the woman receives an ample reward. The new adornment of her scars casts a great spell on the Nuba men, making the woman once again desirable in her village.

We decided to spend one day resting, but a sudden compulsion made me want to go to Nyaro in the afternoon and we arrived in the middle of a dancing festival such as we had never experienced. The Nuba had already reached such an intense state of ecstasy that we could work undisturbed as long as we did not mingle directly with the dancers. It appeared as if all the young girls of Nyaro were joining in. The combatants, in contrast, the *kadundors*, all painted and decorated, sat next to the drummers inside the open *rakoba*. With lowered heads, they clutched their sticks, jingling their tiny bells with their trembling legs as they waited for the girls to make their love declarations. The chants of the older women accompanied the wild rhythms of the dancers, while other women, who danced along with their daughters, sang about their daughters' innocence. Then the girls would lie face up on the ground, lifting and spreading their legs, while their loudly warbling mothers praised the virginity of their daughters. Apart from children and mothers, only virgins were allowed to participate in the dancing.

No doubt about it: this was the *nyertun*, the great love festival held only once a year that Tute and Jabor had told us about. Meanwhile, the first few girls had ventured closer to the men. The excitement intensified; the dancers resembled a wild coven of dancing witches; now one girl was only a hair's breadth away from a man and, quick as lightning, one of her legs swooped over his head and rested on his shoulder for a split second, her body swaying to and fro, while her chosen man gazed at the ground. Then the girl, still dancing, left the *rakoba*. When I tried to film this unusual declaration of love, I was surrounded by the mothers, who skilfully prevented me by forming a circle and dancing round me. Meanwhile, two other girls had placed their legs on the shoulders of men and I felt like screaming because they wouldn't let me film the ritual. Tearing myself away from the mothers, I dashed over to the other side of the *raboka*, where a girl was dancing in front of her chosen man. With trembling hands, I adjusted the light and the focus and started the motor – but the woman were already there; this time, I decided to grin and bear it, and instead I tried to imitate their steps and dance with them for a few minutes. Then, panting from the heat and the strain, I settled on the ground to change films. My dancing had gained the goodwill of the women who shook my hands, gave me a whip and asked me to keep dancing. Swinging the whip and dancing with them, I broke loose in order to get a few shots in the final rays of sunlight.

I was lucky and managed to obtain some fantastic footage of two girls vying for the same combatant. One girl had her leg on his right shoulder, the other her leg on his left shoulder. Tute subsequently told me that in such a case, the man has to make up his mind, which can trigger violent scenes of jealousy between the girls. The rendezvous takes place at night, usually in the home of the girl's parents, and the assignation can lead to matrimony, though not necessarily. A girl who bears a child out of wedlock is respected as much as other women. Horst succeeded in filming these rare rites. That night, we stayed in Nyaro for a long time, drinking *marisse* with the Nuba and making new friends.

The next morning, Suliman showed up with the truck and, delighted as we were to be going home, we had a hard time breaking off our work now of all times; it had taken us three months to become friendly with some of the people. But we had to leave for we could scarcely have survived a longer stay.

As a special treat before our departure, I took out all the beads I had. Beads are specially treasured by the Nuba because some time ago to discourage the wearing of traditional ornaments, the Arab merchants had been ordered by the government to stop selling them any. During my first expedition, I had seen in the markets any number of the small, colourful beads, but now they were nowhere to be found. I started distributing them with the help of Jabor and Tute. At first, it went quite properly, but within a short time, there was so much pushing and grabbing that I fled, letting the Nuba fight over the beads themselves. Horst began packing that same night.

The question of whether our film would contain any of the strange and vanishing fascination of this unusual tribe nagged at me during our long trip home. Had all the pain and effort been worthwhile? We still didn't know. Of the five trips that I had taken in the Sudan, this one had been the most arduous. It was nothing short of a miracle that we had survived.

THE TRIUMPHAL PROGRESS OF THE KAU PICTURES

In Munich, I suffered a physical collapse which forced me to seek treatment from Dr Zeltwanger.

Meanwhile, Horst and Inge were attending to work that had been awaiting me for months, and even more important, Horst had the photos and the rushes developed. So much hinged on the outcome that when I held the prints in my hands, I didn't dare look at them, fearing disappointment. For once, however, luck was on my side. I kept examining the stills and the footage which were really wonderful and nearly made me forget my illness.

First, I showed the slides to friends; they were absolutely amazed. Then I notified *Stern*. Of the two thousand pictures, more than half were good, many even very good, and when Rolf Gillhausen saw them, he was extremely impressed. 'I've never seen such photos,' he said. Just a few days later, *Stern* purchased the first publication rights for Germany; and immediately afterwards, Michael Rand did the same for the *Sunday Times Magazine* in England. Thus began the triumphal publication of my Kau pictures throughout the world – not only in Europe, but also in America, Australia, Japan, and even Africa. Not only were they reproduced in periodicals, but new book publishers also showed interest. For instance, Sir William Collins and his publishing house invited me to show my slides in London, and as, so far, my first Nuba picture book had appeared only in Germany and the United States, Collins decided to put out both books. List had acquired the world rights for *The Nuba of Kau* and now France, Spain, Italy, and Japan fell into line. I recall that just a few years earlier, a prominent Munich publisher, renowned for his outstanding picture books, had liked my photos very much, but regretfully stated that they could count on selling only three thousand copies, and only by subscription.

The offers flooded in in such rapid succession that I didn't know which project to start with. I had to write the texts and also do the layouts but as I felt far too weak, I decided first to put everything on hold and take a holiday in the Caribbean where I could indulge my love of diving and underwater exploration.

THE LIBRARY OF CONGRESS

Before returning to Germany from the Caribbean, I flew to New York where I had to take care of some important business. The main problems were the copyrights of my motion pictures in the United States where for decades I had been repeatedly exploited by dishonest firms. My films had been played time and again without my permission and without my receiving a penny.

People were even selling prints of them on the black market, although the quality was abysmal since they had been copied and recopied several times. In other countries, one could go to court but, as American lawyers informed me, the United States copyright legislation is an impenetrable jungle.

For almost thirty years, I had struggled tirelessly, but in vain, to stop these black-market dealings. The reasons for my failure were political. In January 1963, the United States Department of Justice had given me back the American subsidiary rights to my films *Triumph of the Will, The Blue Light, Olympia* and *Tiefland,* and my ownership was respected by serious companies such as NET, Janus Films, John G. Stratford and several others. Non-serious firms on the other hand, continued to pirate my films and many other foreign films too, especially those produced before 1945, to the extent that not even the attorneys in New York could unravel the tangle. I had consulted lawyers, and each one gave me a different story; finally I realized I had to go to Washington and get information at the legal division of the Library of Congress.

I found all the employees there very helpful, but to obtain a clear answer, I had to work my way up to the head of the appropriate legal division. To my surprise, this person was a woman – Dorothy Schröder – who gave me both advice and assistance. Upon checking the archival documents, as she told me to do, I discovered that in 1940, a certain Mr Raymond Rohauer had copyrighted my two Olympic films in his name. His copyrighting of *Olympia* was sheer fraud; a lawyer at the Library of Congress told me that Mr Rohauer had often been charged with similar offences.

I didn't have the money to start copyright litigation in the United States, so I had to try a different tack, recommended by Dorothy Schröder. She told me to make small changes in my films; for instance, to supply English subtitles, and then apply for a new copyright. This was a possibility, but it required a great deal of work and money. Changes had to be made in five films and also new prints produced, since, in order to obtain the certification for the new copyright, I would have to supply a print containing all the changes indicated in the application. Nevertheless, I decided to go ahead.

The day before my return flight, I was able to relax in a wonderful mansion roughly one hour from Manhattan. We had received an invitation from Frank Barsalona, one of the most successful record managers in the United States; he had been awarded countless Gold Albums, especially because of his Beatles releases. His home was surrounded by dense woods as far as the eye could see. I was enthralled. Along with other artists I also met the movie director Martin Scorsese, a highly remarkable man with whom I got on straight away. Here, as everywhere else, my new photos aroused utter amazement, and my visit to America ended with a cheerful party.

A STROKE OF FATE

On my return to Munich, some bad news awaited me. A friend to whom I had entrusted my savings during the past few years had lost his fortune in a very short time and claimed he had lost my money too, despite our express agreement that he would invest it safely. With the added interest, it was to have been my security in my old age for I had no pension. Furthermore, the money included large sums that friends had recently lent me on the basis of my great success, so that I could finally complete the Nuba film. Not only was this dream shattered for good, but I was confronted with such a mountain of debts, that I was desperate. How was I to pay them back without the film? I was already seventy-three and didn't know how long my strength would hold out. Was I to be condemned until the end of my life to struggle for my livelihood, while I yearned more and more for peace and quiet? In this state of pain, weakness and depression I was on the very brink of putting an end to my life.

It took me a long time to get through this crisis, and during it my personality changed. I began to isolate myself more than ever and I tried to drown my sorrows in my work for it was not only my financial straits that overshadowed my life. New attacks against me were mounted by my adversaries, who were intent on defaming my new work too, my successful Nuba pictures. Now that it was foolish to keep condemning me as a 'racist' or to denigrate my films as poor or lacking in talent they found other ways of wounding me. The well-known American journalist and film-maker Susan Sontag wrote a major article for the *New York Times* entitled 'Fascinating Fascism', and it created a sensation there and also, when it came out, in Germany. According to her thesis, I was as much a Fascist as ever. She wrote: 'but if the photographs are examined carefully, in conjunction with the lengthy text written by Riefenstahl, it becomes clear that they are continuous with her Nazi work. [. . .] *The Last of the Nuba* is the third in her triptych of fascist visuals.'

Susan Sontag discovers this 'mentality' in the mountain films that I made with Dr Fanck and also in my *Blue Light*. Thus she writes that 'heavily dressed people strain upward to prove themselves in the purity of the cold.' How simplistic. She thereby brands thousands upon thousands of mountain climbers as Nazis or Fascists. Incidentally, her ideas were not new; she was merely rehashing an opinion that Siegfried Kracauer had voiced in his film catechism *From Caligari to Hitler*, which is respected by a number of cinema enthusiasts and film students.

Susan Sontag is equally outrageous when she writes about my documentaries. For instance, she makes the absurd claim that the Nuremberg Party Rally of 1934 was staged specifically for my film *Triumph of the Will*: 'the historic event serving as the set of a film which was then to assume the character of an authentic documentary. In *Triumph of the Will*, the document (the image) not only is the record of reality but is one reason for which the reality has been constructed [. . .]' What a pity Susan wasn't around when I was working on the film.

Even those American journalists who generally esteem Susan Sontag refused to give credence to this theory. A few of them told me that a possible reason for this absurd attack was that she may have been doing it as a favour for someone who had helped her as a filmmaker, this 'someone' being one of my most dedicated enemies.

Another attempt to defame me was undertaken by Glenn B. Infield in his book *Leni Riefenstahl – The Fallen Film Goddess*. Its subtitle was typical: *The Intimate and Shocking Story of Adolf Hitler and Leni Riefenstahl*. In his pulp work *Eva and Adolf*, Infield had told the wildest stories about me, and now he was continuing the saga. As the title makes obvious, he wallowed in scandals, which he got from Trenker's forged Eva Braun diary and from other legends spread by the gutter press. Infield also used forged letters and documents, even though the archives where he did his research contained the genuine documents. Clearly, any evidence contradicting his published fantasies did not fit in with his plans, so he blended fiction and fact. His only motive was profit through sensationalism, but his concoction was so inferior and unbelievable that little heed was paid to it.

FAME AND DISGRACE

Deeply as this kind of journalism hurt me, it could not prevent my comeback. In October 1975, the major international magazines ran my photos of the Nuba of Kau, and the *Stern* series in particular was a sensation. Never before had any magazine devoted twenty colour pages with more than fifty pictures to a single theme. I could not believe it. One week later, the *Sunday Times Magazine* began an identical series, spreading it over two issues, and causing another great stir. The Art Directors' Club of Germany awarded me a gold medal for the 'best photographic achievement of the year 1975'. I would never have dared dream such a thing. These were my first laurels since the end of the war and a reward for the stress and strain of the expedition. *Stern* was honoured by the same club 'for the best layout'; as always, Rolf Gillhausen had done a superlative job.

Meanwhile, it was already October, and I was supposed to visit my publishers in Paris, New York and London before the end of the year to discuss the details of the co-production of the second Nuba book. Before leaving, I still had to write the texts and design the layout, but luckily I had an ideal working arrangement with List as well as with Mondadori and as they were interested purely in quality regardless of budgetary considerations, they carried out all the colour corrections I wanted without hesitation.

My first stop was Paris, where Monsieur Herrscher of Editions du Chêne was awaiting me. We had never met before, but his calm personality was immediately comforting, and he seemed more concerned with art than with business. After all the problems with the translator had been cleared up, I showed my pictures to *Paris Match* and *Photo*, both of which were interested in the Kau series. For the sake of a better printing quality, I opted for *Photo*, although this magazine had a far smaller circulation than *Paris Match*. I have always opted for quality.

In Paris, I also visited *Table Ronde*, a highly prestigious house which had published Cocteau's books and was preparing a book about me by Charles Ford, a well-known film historian. This was the first book about me that came close to the truth and if it contains any errors, then the fault is mine alone; my African expeditions left me little time to deal with the author and read his manuscript. Nevertheless, his book, entitled *Leni Riefenstahl*, is the only serious attempt to find out who I am and to destroy the endlessly rehashed legends about me.

As I had done during my early visits to Paris, I gave a slide lecture, this time in the silver mirror room of the architect Jean François Daigre, and my French audience was enthralled. The effect was helped by the unusual setting. The screen obtained by the host was the size of the entire wall, or sixteen feet wide, and as the room was barely thirty feet long, the vast surface of the images had a powerful impact. The guests, numbering no more than forty or fifty, sat on the carpet, and included well-known film directors, painters, publishers, theatre personalities and a number of very elegant women. One of the enthusiastic admirers was Pierre Cardin, the 'fashion czar', who owned a theatre in Paris and was deeply interested in art. After my show, he asked me hundreds of questions. No one could believe that I had shot the pictures myself, and even though I presented nearly three hundred slides, they clamoured for more. My French publisher, who participated in this triumph, was radiant.

In Washington, I got met Mary Smith of the *National Geographic* who had already sent me a contract in which the magazine agreed to run twenty pages of my new Nuba pictures. I was to do the layout with Bill Garrett, and I spent several hours a day with him in the big work room; he reminded me of Rolf Gillhausen and Michael Rand, and from him I learned a lot. An excellent photographer, Garrett had spent years taking pictures in Burma, Thailand and Vietnam, and had been employed as the *National Geographic*'s art director for twenty years. I enjoyed working with him. Generally, his staff designed the layouts, since he was always involved in several series at once. However, Bill Garrett was in love with the Nuba photos and attached great importance to our collaboration.

Within a very brief short time, black-and-white pictures of various sizes were made from the colour slides, and the layout emerged on a large magnetic wall. This made it so easy to interchange the photos and shift them around. In Munich, I also worked with black-and-white enlargements, but I had to lay them out on the floor, which limited my space. Here one could see them all at a glance and decide on the best arrangements quickly and confidently.

During our work, more and more members and directors dropped in from the various departments to look at the photos hanging on the wall. Mr Leakey also visited us, as did many other prominent scientists, including Jane Goodall, the Englishwoman who had been living alone with a group of chimpanzees in Africa, publishing the most exciting reports about her experiences. I kept hearing the word 'incredible' applied over and over again to my pictures. Even Mr Grosvenor, the president of the *National Geographic*, was impressed.

Then, something unexpected happened. At 10 a.m. on the last day, I arrived at the *National Geographic* to find Mary Smith and Bill Garrett looking grim; they informed me that the series had been cancelled. I was stunned and deeply disappointed and it was obvious that they were just as flabbergasted as I. Apparently objections had been raised against me from the very start, but several of the leading editors, like Mary Smith and especially Bill Garrett, had spoken up so strongly in favour of the series that the resistance seemed to have been withdrawn. The omnipotent board of the magazine however, which had the final say on everything, was made of some twenty super-rich, old and extremely conservative Americans, who were also the magazine's sponsors and were nicknamed the 'demigods'. They had become involved in vehement debate on the series, and the majority had voted against publication, an outcome which could not be overridden by the chairman, Gilbert W. Grosvenor. One decisive factor in the board's decision was the fear that subscribers who were members of religious sects might be offended by the nudity of the Nuba. When I asked why this decision had come so late, Mary Smith said that the disaster had taken place only after the publication of Susan Sontag's controversial article, which, although attacked by other journalists, portrayed me as a fanatical National Socialist and had apparently shocked and alarmed the board members. A further unfortunate factor was that because of his old age, Grosvenor, who had run the magazine for decades, had turned it over to his son. The latter, I was told, was certainly just as intelligent as his father, but was still so insecure and anxious that he was afraid of losing his position if he went against the will of the board of directors.

I tried to endure this new blow as best I could, but it was not easy. I felt I just wanted to retire somewhere and forget. They paid me my full honorarium plus expenses, but that was no comfort, the shock and disappointment went too deep; but I parted from Mary Smith and Bill Garrett as from old friends.

The Library of Congress made up a little for my setback. Here, when registering my new copyright, I found complete support. My five new prints had arrived, and so all I had to do was fill out the various forms, pay the fees and board the plane to New York with the documents actually in my hands. Now I hoped to be able to block the pirating of my films in the United States.

After taking leave of my American and German friends, I flew to London where something special was awaiting me. Mr Buxton, head of Survival Anglia Films and one of the most remarkable men in the British film industry, had asked to speak to me about the Nuba footage which greatly interested him. With his aristocratic appearance, he looked more like the owner of a racing stable than a movie producer; but appearances are deceptive. He had a thorough knowledge of the entire film business, and the documentaries made by his firm were among the best in the world. I had a chance to view several of the films, and I also met one of his directors, Alan Root, who worked chiefly in Africa and had just returned from Kenya. His films about the animals and about the natives were outstanding, so we had a wealth of subjects to talk about and I would have loved to stay on in London. But, after coming to terms harmoniously with Collins, I had to return to Munich very quickly in order to complete my picture books.

So much work had piled up there in the meantime, that I cancelled all my appointments for the rest of the year. Inge and Horst worked with me every night until very late. We had no private life. The last entry in my 1975 calendar says: 'A strenuous year – no time for Xmas, no time for New Year's Eve – only work.'

MY REPLY TO SPEER

At this point, however, I found time at last to read Speer's *Spandau Diary* which he had sent to me soon after publication, but which I needed peace and quiet to study properly. Speer had written that he was somewhat reluctant to send it to me since he feared it might contradict my view of our common past. 'However,' he wrote, 'you are one of those people who can accept different opinions and this has always been so. In the past, you were tolerant and sympathetic towards other points of view, and I am certain that our friendship will not be harmed by this book.'

I shared his hope: even before reading his memoir, I was sure that whatever Speer wrote, he did so out of innermost conviction, for this was the essence of his character and the reason why I so greatly respected and admired him. Nor would my opinion change if he had taken a different direction from me, but as yet I didn't know whether he had. I replied:

8 June 1976

Dear Albert,

If you have not heard from me for a long time, the reasons are numerous. However, most important of all was that I wanted to read your book before writing to you. In order to devote myself to it, I had to leave Munich, where the climate usually makes me too tired for any degree of concentration.

You are correct in saying that some of my impressions regarding the past, especially of Hitler, are different from those you describe. But this has nothing to do with our friendship, which, at least on my side, is very deep, even though it could never be expressed in its full depth – either before or after the war. Your book – like everything else you have done – is a great achievement. I believe I understand your struggles with the past, especially in dealing with your early relationship with Hitler, and your desire to warn all those who are still unable to free themselves of the fascination exerted by Hitler.

No other member of Hitler's entourage who has written about his experiences has come as close to the truth as you have. It is admirable to see how much trouble you have gone to and one can see how much courage it must have taken. Your refusal to spare yourself is bound to elicit respect even from your adversaries. None the less – and you must forgive me for saying this – you do not provide a satisfactory answer to the millions of questions that will always be asked, like 'What was it about Hitler that impressed, indeed, bewitched not only the German people, but also so many foreigners?' Your failure is this respect is mainly because you have emphasized the negative aspects of his personality more strongly than the positive. A Hitler such as you describe could not possibly achieve unusual things, good or bad, could not shake the whole world to its very foundations, as he very nearly did. Here, our views diverge – but why not? I am not anything like Winifred Wagner, who still says today, 'If Hitler were suddenly to stand before me, I would receive him as a friend.' I too can never forget or forgive the terrible things that were done in Hitler's name, nor do I wish to; neither do I wish to forget what a tremendous effect he had. I would be making things very easy for myself, if I did forget. However, these two seemingly incompatible opposites in his personality – this schizophrenia – were probably the source of the tremendous energies he deployed. Yet can someone who, like you, has spent and survived over twenty years in prison still feel that today?

Perhaps – and I very much hope so – we can meet again – without talking about the past.

Yours, Leni

SCUBA DIVING IN THE CARIBBEAN

After seeing the picture book *The Living Reef* by Douglas Faulkner, whose wonderful underwater photos made a deep impression on me, I felt a growing urge to dive again. And not just to dive; I wanted to try and take such pictures myself. Faulkner's photos affected me so profoundly that I can only describe them as the birth of my work as an underwater photographer.

We were back in the Caribbean, this time in the Bahamas – at the Current Club in North Eleuthera, where I was working with two Nikonos cameras and Horst was filming with a Super-8. The very first entry in my diving log says: 'Fantastic – Super.' And indeed it was. Every dive was an experience, especially now that I was concentrating on photography. The world below the ocean's surface is fascinating, and capturing it on film is especially exciting. There were fish all around but when I wanted them to pose for me, they refused to keep still. You have to have a lot of patience and master the technique perfectly; you must estimate the distance precisely and choose the right aperture, often in a split second. Certain underwater opportunities occur only once – and you're not always ready to shoot at the critical moment.

At times, the search for appropriate subjects was an adventure in itself. Often fish such as perch and morays hid in thickly overgrown caverns, where I could barely see them in the darkness. And when I was shooting, I couldn't aim my spotlight at the same time. I often had to choose between the camera and the spotlight, and each dive seemed far too brief. Time underwater simply flew by, since there was always something new to discover: bizarre sea stars, sea slugs, crabs, mussels. However, the most important thing I discovered was a Nikon reflex camera, which was shown to me by John Schultz, the diving master of the Current Club. Never before had I focused so effectively on a subject. Crucial for me was not just the sharpness, which could easily be adjusted, but, the exact framing. I decided to purchase this camera and the accompanying underwater case before travelling to Montreal for the Olympic Games.

THE MONTREAL OLYMPICS

These were the first Olympic I ever attended as a spectator (not counting the 1928 Winter Games in St Moritz). Since I was holder of an Olympic Diploma, I was invited to Montreal as an honorary guest and I took along my camera; it was a splendid feeling to be able to take pictures without any restraint.

The days I spent in Montreal were unforgettable, though there was too little time to see even the most important things. In the radiant summer weather, Queen Elizabeth opened the Games, and I had an ideal seat from which I could get fine shots with my teleoptics.

Several days later, while watching the events, I was exposed to a new scandal. Members of an important organization sharply protested to the Canadian Olympic Committee and to the Minister of Labour and Immigration, objecting to my participation on the grounds – according to the Canadian newspapers – that my presence was an insult to all Canadians. They demanded that I be expelled from Canada instantly, since, as they claimed, 'her philosophies are a shameful affront to the Olympic spirit.' But, as in 1972, during the Olympic Games in Munich when the *Sunday Times* had rejected the protests of the Jewish community, these massive reproaches did not work to my disadvantage in Canada.

FRANKFURT BOOK FAIR

After another diving trip in the Caribbean, I returned to Munich where no sooner had I unpacked than I was standing in front of a camera. The date for this had been set long ago. The director Fritz Schindler was doing a film portrait for German television – the first German TV film about me since the end of the war. It was pleasant working with Herr Schindler who was interested in my work and was in no way concerned with making a sensational exposé.

Just a few days later, I was interviewed by Dr Wolfgang Ebert for a television programme called *Aspekte* (Aspects). The producers were interested in my book on the Nuba of Kau, which List was going to exhibit as a new title at the Frankfurt Book Fair. This book, an even bigger success than the first, delighted all its publishers, especially Sir William Collins, who absolutely adored it and invited me to attend the book fair in London. That was our last meeting, for he died just a few days before my arrival in London. His unexpected death was a great loss not only for me, but for his entire publishing house and his authors. In the international publishing world, men like him are few and far between.

My book was taken over by Robert Knittel, his editor-in-chief and the son of the successful Swiss writer John Knittel. Robert Knittel's wife, the German actress Luise Rainer, gave a party for me in their London home. The guests included Joy Adamson, known world-wide for her books and films about Elsa the lioness.

CHAT SHOW WITH ROSENBAUER

In London, the BBC ran an interview in which I spoke about my most recent expedition to Africa. The programme included not only photos of the Nuba of Kau but also, for the first time, excerpts from my Nuba footage, which were also supposed to be included in a chat show beamed from Cologne. After long efforts, the producer, Kay Dietrich Wulffen, had finally managed to coax me into agreeing. Having already been burned by the German media, I wanted to be spared any unpleasant surprises. Horst also warned me, but Herr Wulffen, who had discussed the show with me at the Frankfurt Book Fair, so convinced me of the objectivity of the programme that he dispelled my suspicions.

'We promise you,' he told me in Frankfurt, 'that we will not confront you with questions about the past, we will at most lightly touch on them. What we want is to inform the public about your work as a film director and photographer, and we would like to show your new African and underwater shots.' Seeing my sceptical expression, he went on, 'You have to believe me; it will be an interesting talk beneficial to your picture book. That's guaranteed by the name Hansjürgen Rosenbauer, who, by the way, is really looking forward to the interview. It's going to be his farewell show.'

A couple of days before the broadcast, I received Herr Rosenbauer in my apartment on Tengstrasse. He was a good-looking and likeable young man but when he told me that they had at first considered having Rainer Barzel appear with me, I was irritated. A politician would have been an utterly unsuitable partner for me on that show. I found the idea absurd. But anyway Rosenbauer said they had settled on someone else – an elderly working-class woman who had, it seemed, made some favourable remarks about me.

Apparently, she had said that I had been treated unfairly after the war. How could I guess what lay ahead?

Before the programme began, the others were introduced to me: Knut Kiesewetter, a pop singer, whom I didn't know, and Elfriede Kretschmer, the working-class woman. At first everything seemed quite harmless and peaceful, but not for long. Within a short time, Frau Kretschmer started to attack me. 'I don't understand,' she shouted at me, 'how a woman could make films that were against all humanity – I would never have done that.'

'What *did* you do?' asked Rosenbauer.

'I worked.' Huge applause from the claque, which as I subsequently learned, had been bussed to the studio, I had already sensed that the audience was 'ultra-left' and, alarmed, I suspected a trap. Nevertheless, I tried to remain calm as I warded off this assault. I didn't succeed, however, mainly because I received no help from Herr Rosenbauer, who kept losing control of the situation. He was unable to halt the outpourings of Frau Kretschmer, who behaved like a Communist candidate making a party political broadcast. 'How can one make such films? In my opinion, they're pied-piper films,' she said viciously. 'I could never do such a thing. We people already knew by 1930 what we were doing and where everybody around us was heading – you can believe me, we knew.' This was too much. We launched into a heated discussion, during which my accusers grew more and more aggressive.

'I'd be happy,' I said, 'if we stopped. I'm not here because I wanted to be; I was asked to come. I was promised that it would be a fair and non-political conversation.'

What it turned out to be was more like an interrogation in front of a tribunal than anything else. Whatever I said was ignored by the three other participants who bombarded me with the most offensive questions. When we got to the Olympic film, they asked me why I didn't make films about the handicapped, and why my Olympic films showed only beautiful, nobly symmetrical people. I retorted that I hadn't selected the athletes, all of whom had been filmed by thirty different cameramen in very different places, and it wasn't my fault that athletes tend to look very fit. But my arguments went unheeded.

No objective discussion could develop, the other participants were too biased, and, unprepared as I was, I could only struggle to get out of this embarrassing predicament. I could have told them I had often spoken with opponents of the past regime, and I had always been sympathetic towards people of other opinions, including inveterate Communists. In 1944, I had even employed an old-time Communist, very similar to Frau Kretschmer, as an executive producer in my firm. That same year, when he was arrested for insulting the Führer, I intervened on his behalf and kept him in my employ. His name was Rudolf Fichtner, and he was from Munich. It was a great pity he couldn't stand at my side that evening; maybe Frau Kretschmer wouldn't have been so hard on me.

It was not exactly a triumphant farewell for Hansjürgen Rosenbauer. The next day, the newspapers wrote: 'When the spotlights faded, an embarrassed silence filled the studio, and Rosenbauer was left very much alone. Even stage hands avoided him, and the cold buffet arranged as a send-off came to nothing. Hundreds of television viewers phoned the station to protest. They were ashamed of the way an old woman had been treated like a criminal and morally executed. The programme became a scandal and I was told that the station had registered some two thousand phone calls during the broadcast. Nothing like that had ever happened before. Furthermore, the viewers at home had unanimously sided with me. My friends and colleagues Inge and Horst, who had watched the programme in my apartment, told me that just a few minutes after the start of the show indignant viewers started telephoning me, not realizing they were watching me live in the TV studio in Cologne.

I received literally countless letters and telegrams but the press was divided. In *Der Spiegel*, Wilhelm Bittorf found parallels to my earlier films in *Vanishing Africa*. His article, called 'Blood and Testicles', went as follows:

In her search for strength and beauty, Leni Riefenstahl has found her way from the black corps of the SS to the black bodies of the Nuba . . . What's so different about the primitives when the Nuba adolescents with carefully shaven testicles let it all hang out like Wild West cover boys . . .? Like a latter-day Sleeping Beauty, rendered lifeless by the poison of frustration and bitterness, Leni Riefenstahl has awoken once again. And the enthusiasm with which she once celebrated the cults of the Nazi and the bodies of the Olympic contenders is now devoted to the cults and bodies of the Nuba . . . This enthusiasm has fully revealed how incorrigible her passion for strength and health has remained since the days of faith and beauty. For her, the Nuba are, ultimately, better Nazis, purer barbarians, the true Teutons.

This was staggering. I would never have dreamed that pictures of 'my' Nuba could recall the SS. Did that mean that I should avoid photographing 'brown' fish in my underwater films? Bittorf's analysis is quite bizarre. After all, inveterate National Socialists were racists, who regarded everyone else as inferior to blond Aryans. How did that fit in with my friendship and love for the black Nuba?

There are not too many analysts like Wilhelm Bittorf, Susan Sontag, and others, whose prejudices prevent them from judging my work objectively. My compensation was all the letters condemning the kangaroo court, and also the impressive picture stories that were published in magazines after the chat show. The offer I received from Rolf Gillhausen for the magazine *GEO* showed that the broadcast was a boomerang. He asked me to revisit the Nuba of Kau and record the changes that had come about in their world. Although Gillhausen was now working for *Stern*, *GEO* was still his baby – the magazine he had created.

Attractive as this assignment was, I didn't want to accept it. I had not yet recovered from the strains of the previous expedition, and I had also vowed never again to go on such hazardous adventures.

Gillhausen succeeded in overcoming my qualms, however, especially with regard to scheduling, since he promised the Sudan expedition would not interfere with my proposed diving trip. Furthermore, the Sudan expedition would be less demanding because a first-class journalist would be accompanying us to write the text, and this would allow me to concentrate entirely on my camera – and, for the first time, I would be free of any financial burden. All these aspects made Gillhausen's offer more and more alluring; as I wavered, I received an unexpected invitation from Khartoum. Friends informed me that something 'special' was awaiting me there, but they refused to tell me what. Although I was in the middle of preparing for my imminent trip to the Indian Ocean, I decided to fly to the Sudanese capital immediately.

IN KHARTOUM

It was wonderful being back again, if only for a couple of days. My friends picked me up at the airport, but no one could tell me why I'd been invited. I stayed with Norbert and Inge Koebke, who had helped us a great deal during our previous expedition. After all the distress of the preceding weeks, I enjoyed the heavenly peace and quiet.

I still had received no word from Nimeiri or from any of his assistants. Nor did Abu Bakr have any explanation. Then, at a most inconvenient moment, I was notified that President Nimeiri would be expecting me in two hours. When this phone call came from Herr Koebke, I was in the swimming pool at the German Club. How would I make it to the People's

Palace in time? But Inge pulled it off. She dried my hair, helped me dress, and drove me furiously through the streets to the People's Palace where I was expected; a government official led me into the presidential office.

As I walked in, I felt my heart lurch with shock. Along with Nimeiri there waited several ministers and a camera crew. The president welcomed me with a hug, but I sensed a strange, almost solemn atmosphere. Nimeiri signalled, and someone handed him a leather case, which he presented to me with an expectant smile. Hesitantly, I opened the case and inside I found a medal with a broad pink ribbon of silk. At once, the tension dissolved in the room and everyone laughed and talked while I gazed confusedly at the medal. The president talked briefly, explaining why the Sudanese government had awarded me this decoration; he spoke enthusiastically about the content and form of my two picture books, which allowed even Muslims to see the unclad Nuba without being offended. 'For that reason and because the Sudan is your second homeland, we would like to honour you with this medal.' He concluded by saying, 'We all love you very much, may God bless you.'

Deeply moved by so much warmth, indeed friendship, I thanked the president. That evening, the ceremony was shown on television. Remembering how I had begged the Sudanese ambassador in Washington for a visa and how I had lain on the floor in front of a minor police chief in Kadugli, crying my eyes out because he refused to let me drive on, it all struck me as deeply ironic.

The next day, I discussed my new expedition with Khalid El Kheir Omer, the minister of state. He promised that I would not have to endure the same problems I had suffered during my previous expedition. 'Just give me a list of anything you need, you will receive all possible help from us. By the way,' he added, 'you will be pleased to hear that we have ordered several hundred copies of your Nuba books from England and America. Our government is going to send them to the foreign embassies at Christmas.'

At that moment, I was certain that I would revisit the Nuba for *GEO*.

THE CHANCE OF A LIFETIME

Several days before we left Munich on 9 February 1977 – a day I marked in red on my calendar – the three top editors of *Stern* – Nannen, Gillhausen and Winter – came to see me. They offered to publish my life story in ten instalments of words and pictures which would appear at the time of my seventy-fifth birthday; the proposed fee was exceptionally high. Nannen was aware that, so far, all attempts to write my memoirs had failed. The idea was that a writer or a good journalist would write the text on the basis of taped conversations with me over a period of only six weeks. I realized that such an opportunity would never arise again. There was actually only one reason for my reluctance, and it was stronger than any financial inducement: I could not imagine devoting so little time to presenting my long and adventurous life in a comprehensible way and without misunderstandings. With only six weeks to do the job, since I wouldn't be returning from the Sudan until the end of May, the biography would be shallow, and would devalue any later memoirs, which I still hoped to write some day.

'It is simply impossible,' I said, 'to narrate my life in six to eight weeks. It would shatter me physically, and there is no way of telling whether in the end it would depict Riefenstahl as she really is.'

It was almost midnight when we parted. I felt apprehensive, wondering whether I had destroyed the chance of a lifetime; and I also felt sorry to have disappointed my friends so deeply.

MY FINAL SUDAN EXPEDITION

Two weeks later, I was in Khartoum. I had flown ahead to prepare everything *in situ*: vehicles, permits, petrol and food. Nimeiri had kept his promise. We received two almost new vehicles, a Landrover and an eight-ton truck, as well as two drivers from the presidential pool and sufficient petrol, oil and spare parts. Never had I been so well-equipped. I began to look forward to the trek. Meanwhile, Horst had arrived with the baggage and our two companions. One was Peter Schille, who was to write the story for *GEO*; the other was Wulf Kreidel, who was to assist Horst.

The drive to Kau went along sandy trails, through deserted villages, and across increasingly difficult terrain. Now and then, we encountered an Arab, who greeted us amiably, otherwise, all we saw in this rather bleak landscape were occasional camels and goats. In the daytime, we suffered from the heat yet at night we froze in our sleeping bags. After three exacting days, we sighted the first Nuba huts. Our companions were eager to see the Nuba, but Ali and Gamal, our two drivers, couldn't believe their eyes when they spotted the first naked Nuba – a dreadful sight for them as devout Muslims.

Peter Schille was equally dismayed – not by their nudity, but by their appearance which was not at all as I had portrayed it. I had warned him that the Nuba I had known and photographed now hardly existed; but not even I could have foreseen how rapid the change would be. Not more than two years had passed since I had seen them in their primal state.

As we drove through Nyaro, the first and prettiest Nuba village, my vehicle was besieged by the Nuba. They had recognized me and were shouting, 'Leni, Leni!' but their appearance was ridiculously distorted by impossible clothes and glasses. Furthermore, unlike the Masakin Nuba, they were aggressive, demanding goodness knows what from us, even our clothing. Nevertheless, they were overjoyed to see us again.

In Kau, we visited the *omda*, who was as friendly as ever and immediately went with us to find a suitable campsite. Soon, Jabor and Tute came to lend a hand and within two days our camp was fenced in. Our Sudanese drivers had brought with them a huge tent and they settled in, but it was obvious that they didn't feel comfortable.

Jabor and Dr Sadig, the Sudanese physician in Kau, told us that James Faris, the American anthropologist, had returned here after many years, intending to shoot a film, but, unable to obtain a residency permit, he had been forced to leave. What Jabor revealed about Faris made us furious; apparently, he told the Nuba in Nyaro that I had paid eighty pounds for a dance of the girls in Kau and eighty pounds for a *nyertun* dance in Nyaro. Such allegations left me speechless. I of all people had learned how greatly it spoils everything if one gives the natives money to pose for pictures. Aside from the fact that such photographs always look posed, all the natives want to be paid, even if they are not in the pictures, and they keep asking for more and more each time. Instead of cash, we gave the Nuba oil, which was not cheap in Kau, and by treating their sick we had gradually made friends and had been allowed to take stills and films. We had paid money only in very exceptional cases, when we ran out of oil, and we had never given more than one pound. If what Jabor told us about James Faris was true — and we had no reason to doubt it, since it was confirmed by Dr Sadig – then the anthropologist must have been driven by revenge. He had witnessed the sensational success of my Nuba books in America, while his outstanding scholarly work on the South-Eastern Nuba – a small book published in England under the title *Nuba: Personal Art* – was not as well known as it deserved to be. I had already learned from his *Newsweek* review of my picture book that his attitude towards me was not friendly. Two years earlier, in Kau, I had wanted to surprise James Faris by photographing 'his' Nuba, those he had worked with. I took shots of them looking at their pictures in his book and planned to send him the photos. However, when I found out what he thought of my own work, I didn't bother.

I also learned that a Swiss man, whom they called Woswos, was in Fungor and had often been seen with Faris. That could only have been Oswald Iten. Little did I know what lies this young student would spread about me. When we tried to visit him in Fungor to have a talk and clear up any possible misunderstandings, the *omda* told us that Woswos had been picked up by the police. I was glad that I had obtained my permits from the highest authority.

Meanwhile, Peter, Horst and Wulf were trying to make the camp as practical as possible. Peter Schille proved to be an excellent cook, while Horst and Wulf concentrated on the pre-production labour, setting up the film and still cameras.

However, before we could get to work we were dismayed by the arrival of two busloads of tourists. To be sure, the changes in Nuba life were caused least of all by tourism; they were due chiefly to Islamization (although not through missionaries, since none had ever lived here). The reproach that my photos contributed to these changes is foolish. After all, the things that were now happening among the Kau Nuba had already come about nine years earlier among the Masakin Nuba, before even one single tourist group had visited Tadoro and the neighbouring communities.

The tourists, who usually came here without permits, understandably annoyed the Sudanese authorities; but they also felt cheated, since they were not allowed to take pictures here. So they bribed the *omda* or other prominent sheiks with money or whisky. Jabor knew that tourists would pay up to a hundred dollars to watch a dance and secretly photograph it, and the Nuba would come to us with large notes, asking us to change them.

With the departure of the tourists, morale improved and when the *omda* told us that Woswos was back in Fungor, we decided to pay him a visit. He came towards me in the doorway of the Nuba hut where he lived and I saw coldness and rejection in his eyes. No reasonable conversation emerged. He hurled all sorts of accusations in my face, especially that I had corrupted the Nuba with money. Perhaps he even believed his own words, for the Nuba had grown cunning, and they told everyone who wanted anything from them that the 'Allemannis', as they called the tourists, would give them money. Besides this, he was eaten up with envy because of the success of my Nuba pictures. Like Faris, he had failed to obtain a photography and film permit and therefore had to work secretly, which was why the Sudanese police had taken him to Fungor several times.

Luckily for me, I had managed to take my stills and rushes two years ago and just needed a few additional scenes, plus the new photos for *GEO*. In the meantime, a lot of changes had occurred in the life of the natives, and not just externally. During my previous visit, very few trucks drove through

637

Kau, but now trucks often came bringing Sudanese, who hired Nuba men and women for work. Many of the natives went along with them in order to earn money, and often they were gone for months on end. That was why we missed several of our friends this time.

Because Peter Schille had to get back to Germany, we had little time left, but I felt I must revisit 'my' Nuba prior to going home.

After ten hours of driving, we were in the Nuba Hills and there was a great joy in Tadoro when we were reunited with our Nuba friends, Natu, Alipo, Dia and Gabicke. Peter Schille and Wulf Kreidel were able to see how different the Masakin were from the South-Eastern Nuba. Despite their rags, they had remained charming, and were happy that I was still alive for they had been told that I had died long ago.

We could stay only one night as my eyes were badly infected, and I had to reach Khartoum as soon as possible in order to consult a doctor. Ali and Gamal, who missed their wives very much, made it back along the difficult route in just twelve hours. Exhausted, but happy to have completed our job, we arrived in Khartoum without – miracle of miracles – breaking down even once.

While still in the Sudanese capital, Horst saw the familiar red car near the presidential palace and we soon learned from Inge Koebke, our hostess, that a Swiss man who had just returned from the Nuba had told people at the German Club that 'Riefenstahl' had been officially ordered to leave Kau immediately because according to rumour she occasionally withdrew to her tent with very big and 'strong' Nuba men. That was the limit! The slander couldn't get any filthier – it disgusted me. Iten perpetuated his campaign for years, in newspaper articles and even in a book. Apart from libelling me personally, he actually accused me of destroying the traditional customs of the Nuba, whom I allegedly corrupted with lots of cash and whisky, letting both 'flow' freely. According to him, it was I who had brought about their decline. Of course, I had no 'war chest' overflowing with money, as he described (our budget was very modest), nor did we bring with us a single bottle of whisky. I would never have given alchol to the *omda* or to any other Nuba; this would have been utterly irresponsible in my eyes. And it is a lie to claim that my pictures had triggered the changes among the Nuba and the destruction of their values. In fact, in 1974, a whole year before even a single one of my Kau photos appeared, *Neue Zürcher Zeitung* had run Iten's photo-studded article on the Nuba of Kau (or, as they are known to scholars, the South-Eastern Nuba). At that time, his photos drew the attention of travel organizers to these Nuba, while my 'Kau pictures' didn't come out until the following year.

THE JAPANESE

After our return to Munich, so much happened that I was unable to cut my Nuba rushes. A Japanese television crew had been awaiting me for days. Mr Ono of the Tokyo TV Union wanted me to collaborate on a ninety-minute film about the 1936 Olympic Games in Berlin. He had a curious idea: the Japanese athletes who had won medals in 1936 were to compete once again, as seniors, with their surviving rivals at the Berlin Stadium. At first, I thought he was joking, but when he switched on his video recorder and showed me the footage he had already shot in Berlin, I realized he was serious.

A torchbearer, in the same uniform as in 1936, ran through the stadium and lit the Olympic flame. This was not a sequence from my film, it had been shot anew, and Mr Ono proudly told me that this was the same runner who had lit the flame in 1936. They had managed to track down the same torchbearer, Fritz Schilgen, and he was not the only senior survivor invited and filmed by the Japanese. On the screen, I saw the 1936 Olympic contenders from not only Japan but also from Germany, Finland and several other countries. 'Look,' said the Japanese director, 'that's Salminen, the great Finnish runner. You do remember, don't you? He was Nurmi's successor and he won the ten-thousand-metre race. Even though he's seventy-five years old, he's still a good runner; just look at him passing Murakoso – he's seventy-two now – he fought so bravely against the three Finnish winners.' I remembered very well how the diminutive Japanese had been a favourite with the crowd. Nearly half a century had passed since that day.

It was incredible to see how skilfully the Japanese had restaged the events. Most impressive of all was a nail-biting finale in the swimming stadium, where the 1936 winner of the two-hundred-metre breast stroke, Tetsuo Hamuro, a Japanese, swam side by side with Erwin Sietas, the German who had won the silver medal. Now they were both elderly gentlemen; this time, forty-one years later, the German arrived first although, at sixty-two, he was a bit older than Hamuro. The Japanese accepted defeat with a disarming smile.

The Japanese film-makers had invited not only the male participants, but also women like Hideko Maehata, who had won the gold medal in the 1936 two-hundred-metre breast stroke. Now a matron of sixty-three, she again came in first.

The Japanese had something else in mind. They wanted to film me being interviewed by Mr Ogi, one of their well-known film critics; our conversations were to be shot in Berlin and Tokyo. I readily agreed since I loved the idea of getting to know Japan. It was a joy working with the Japanese in Berlin. I had seldom known a film crew to be so calm, so considerate, and yet so enthusiastic.

Late June brought the day on which I was to pay my first visit to the Land of the Rising Sun. I enjoyed the flight, which went via Moscow and was like a precious gift to me. Upon my arrival at the airport, the Japanese gave me a few small presents and surprised me by inviting Kitei Son, the marathon winner of 1936 who now lived in Korea, to greet me. There, Mr Ono introduced me to Noriko, a charming young girl who was to be my interpreter for the entire visit and would also help me in any way she could.

On the very first day, I attended a show at the famous Kabuki Theatre, where following the ancient tradition, the female roles are played by men. It wasn't easy to work out what was going on, but I was deeply impressed by the acting, by the flexibility of the performers and by their masks and costumes. It was an aesthetic delight. When I asked about our programme, they behaved rather mysteriously. One afternoon, we went to a television studio and there the Japanese director took me behind a huge screen and asked me to wait for a moment. I heard prolonged applause from the other side of the screen and finally a speech in Japanese in which I could make out my name. At that same instant, the screen was pulled away and I was suddenly dazzled by spotlights and surrounded by cheering Japanese men and women. The film company had invited all the surviving Japanese contenders of the Berlin Olympics to Tokyo, including those who lived abroad, like Kitei Son. They had screened my *Olympia* for them in this studio, but the spectators hadn't realized that I too would be present; their surprise was as great as mine when the screen was removed and I stood on the stage. That, of course, was exactly what the director had planned and now shot as a scene for his film. I will not hide the fact that I was deeply moved by so much affection and recognition; I dared not think about my homeland or about my treatment there.

The reunion with the athletes of 1936 after a period of four decades turned into a huge celebration. I recognized several contenders, especially Tajima, who had broken the world triple jump record, and Nishida, who had won a silver medal after a five-hour struggle in the pole vault; I had seen them both countless times at my editing table. Mr Ono, who had hit on this wild idea and managed to pull it off, was beaming with joy.

Before I flew back after my two-week stay, the film company arranged for me to visit Kyoto and Osaka with Noriko and the film critic Ogi. What I saw in Kyoto surpassed all my expectations, tradition and modernism blended so naturally. The gardens, the temples and teahouses, all cast such a spell that I understood why Japanese art, which omits the superfluous and is so spare in its lines and forms, has so powerfully influenced Western art in our century.

Our farewells came much too soon and the last two days were chaotic. I saw a different visitor almost every hour – prominent actors, publishers, film-makers and, above all, photographers and newspapermen, who wanted to interview me before my departure.

At the airport, a final surprise awaited me. Not only the Japanese film crew but also several of the 1936 athletes had come to see me off. Once again, I received countless gifts – so many that I couldn't have carried them all myself. Overwhelmed by so much warmth and hospitality, I left Tokyo.

BIRTHDAY CELEBRATIONS

Just one day after my return to Munich, I was interviewed for several hours by Imre Kusztrich for *Bunte Illustrierte*, and by another interviewer every day thereafter; it was because my birthday was just around the corner. I was going to be seventy-five, which was not a happy thought. I had never had time before to think about my age.

List Publishers, for whom I was preparing *Coral Gardens*, my third book of photographs and the first culled from my diving experiences, had arranged a dazzling birthday party. I was deeply moved by Robert Schäfer's speech, and this evening became an unforgettable experience in my not very happy life. I was also very touched to discover my oldest admirer among the guests – my penfriend, Professor Okajima, now eighty years old. He had come all the way from Tokyo, and he now handed me copies of every single letter that I had written to him during the past forty-five years. We started corresponding in 1932, when he had first seen *The Blue Light*; since then, I had received the most beautiful Japanese stamps from him month after month.

My unsettled, adventurous life gave me little time for things that were not connected to my various kinds of work, so I barely had any private life; because of this I enjoyed the day all the more. Forgetting about my problems, I was able to meet friends I hadn't seen for years, and many of them asked me how my 'memoirs' were going. Recently, I had received a number of tempting offers, not only from abroad, but also from Germany. I wavered, but the price would be too high – I would have to give up everything that I enjoyed: scuba diving, working with my camera and, most important of all, my freedom. Ever since my childhood, freedom had always been the most important thing in life for me. It's better to turn down all demands, if by doing so you can stay free. Memoirs? Reliving all those years of pain and worry, suffering again experiences best forgotten? – what a horrible idea! No, on that day, I refused even to think about it. I wanted to put the past out of my mind.

I celebrated with my friends until dawn.

MY DEAREST WISH

For years, I had wanted to move out of the city. The climate was uncomfortable as was the lack of space in my apartment. For years, I had been dreaming about having a small studio house, with a cutting room and a screening room – outside the city and, if possible, surrounded by trees.

I owe the fulfilment of my dream above all – strange as it may sound – to a very nasty article published in a widely circulated newspaper just a few days after the Rosenbauer chat show. The title was 'What Has Become of You?' I had allowed the journalist and the photographer to interview me in my home, with Horst as a witness. When I read the results, I was sickened. I had experienced all sorts of unpleasantness in my life, but the things printed here surpassed everything else in tasteless falsehoods. I have no choice but to quote a few passages:

> What has become of her? In a four-and-a-half-room flat at one o'clock in the afternoon, Leni Riefenstahl is wearing a silk nightgown. She lies in bed. A screen hangs from the window and on to this she projects her slides. Even now, she works all the time. Hitler's film-maker has become a photographer. But what a photographer! Leading magazines all over the world print her photos because they are incredibly beautiful. She photographs Negroes – tall, proud, beautiful Negroes with enormous genitals. A gigantic curtain is behind the bed and behind the curtain lies her big film and photo archive. The man at her side is also unusual: forty years younger – that is, thirty-four – his name is Horst Kettner, and he is a giant of a man, six feet four inches tall . . .
>
> 'Why do you still work so hard?'
>
> 'I have no money, no pension, I have to pay the rent . . .'
>
> And now Leni Riefenstahl talks about her dream. 'I want to have a cottage – a small one, with a garden; something that belongs to me and where no one can throw me out.'
>
> She says this at the age of seventy-four, the age at which most people

think about a different piece of land, a plot six feet deep, with a stone upon it . . .

We select a photo that shows her as she is. A seventy-four-year-old woman with dyed, curly hair. That's all it shows.

People who know my films and picture books can hardly imagine that I am the type of person to lie in bed, wearing a nightgown, when I receive journalists. Once again, everything was a concoction. Should I sue the newspaper? I was tired of all the lawsuits I had been forced to bring, and anyway I had neither the time nor the money. However, now I *was* obsessed with the thought of my own house (which I hadn't even mentioned during the interview) and I brooded over it day and night: How could I get a piece of land and a house despite my burden of debts? I knew that I had valuable property: the copyright to my films, picture books and photos, and the uncut rushes from several Sudan expeditions. Perhaps I could mortage these precious items. I felt like a chess player who can think of nothing but the moves he has to make in order to win.

In November 1977 (this day too is marked in red in my calendar), I found my dream site, only fifty miles from Munich. I stood in front of a green meadow framed by splendid beeches, pines, birches and ash trees. The most beautiful tree was a giant oak, two hundred and fifty years old, with which I fell in love. This, I thought, is where I want to spend my twilight years with a view of that wonderful tree; then perhaps some day I would write my memoirs.

A DISASTROUS ACCIDENT

My financial position improved. *Coral Gardens* had just appeared in Germany as well as in France, England, Italy and the United States. It was to be followed by a book of my African photos. This was a big help, but not big enough. The most important question was whether my friends, to whom I owed a great deal of money, would allow me extended interest-free credit; fortunately, they did.

It was June by the time we stood on my meadow, which was covered with thousands of daisies, to pick the exact spot for building the house. Then the great day came on which my House by the Oak was to be put up; it was an exciting moment when the gigantic crane slowly swung the huge prefabricated sections over the treetops and placed them with centimetre precision on the foundations. It took only two days to complete the job; we were able to celebrate the roofing ceremony on the second evening. It was an eventful and happy day for me – and once again, it was my birthday.

Still, it was a long time before I could move in and I had to delay completion of the Nuba film until my work rooms were set up. Luckily, I had a lot of help not only from Horst, but also from the very gifted young architect Josef Strobel, who helped me decorate the rooms. Before this work was finished, I had a serious accident: while skiing. I broke the neck of my femur. I was in St Moritz, speeding down an icy trail on the Corviglia, when one of my skis got snagged on a rock and I plunged down to an icy ledge. One hour later, I was flat on my back on the operating table in the accident clinic. When I came round from the anaesthetic, I was optimistic; the operation had gone well, I had received no artificial joint, and the fracture had been pinned. I saw no reason to take the accident too tragically. I quickly got used to my crutches and was soon able to leave the clinic for further treatment in Munich, where the X-rays taken four weeks after the accident showed that everything had healed beautifully. I did physical therapy in a swimming pool every day, gradually becoming more supple, but the pain wouldn't go away and sometimes it became almost unbearable. I began to worry for the powerful painkillers left me very tired and this made my work more difficult. When the pain still persisted after three months, the doctor prescribed a cure in Montegrotto, and there, for four weeks, I was treated with mudpacks, thermal baths and remedial gymnastics. Nevertheless, the pain got worse than ever, and, hard as it was, I had to learn to live with it. All the orthopedic consultants agreed that the bone had healed perfectly; no one could determine the cause of the pain, which was especially severe in my hip and my upper thigh. Perhaps, said the doctors, it was the intervertebral disc, perhaps it was rheumatism, perhaps it was nerves . . . I was free of pain only when swimming, so I hoped I would still be able to dive. Taking our film and photo gear, Horst and I flew to San Salvador, an island in the Bahamas with marvellous diving locations.

Luckily, I felt no pain while diving, but as soon as I got out of the water I could only limp and this became a problem. Expecting that I would recover quickly and be rid of the pain, I had contracted to do two films, one Japanese-language production and one English-language production, which were to be shot in San Salvador. I never dreamed I would still be suffering so greatly eight months after the operation, since patients are normally pain-free within two months after hip surgery. My efforts to delay the filming were unsuccessful and before I could stop them, the Japanese arrived from Tokyo – six of them – and were joined by 'my' Noriko who had married a German scientist and was now living in Munich.

I had to try and work on the filming, and so long as we shot underwater there was no problem, at least for me. It was harder for the cameraman with the monster of an underwater case which they had transported from Japan for their video camera. With the help of Horst and several divers, we got our footage, which wasn't all that easy because of the current. It was more difficult for me when, followed by the sound camera, I had to stroll along the beach talking about my life; every step was agony. However, the Japanese were so sympathetic that I could refuse them nothing.

No sooner had they left than Jeanne Soloman, the producer of CBS News, arrived. She was a young attractive and energetic woman who was to do a film portrait of me for the well-known American news programme *60 Minutes*. My interviewer was Dan Rather, a prominent American television presenter who was greatly feared because of his sharp tongue. Friendly as they all were to me, I dreaded the interview, partly because it was to be conducted in English. Although Mr Rather, like others before him, had promised not to ask me about Hitler or politics, he did so anyway, of course, and I was so annoyed that we had to break off. Even though well over a quarter of a century had passed since the end of the war, I still felt inhibited about discussing the past. Eventually, we reached a compromise, whereby I agreed to answer a few of his questions.

This programme in the United States was an extraordinary triumph for me and I received countless letters. I also got film offers, the most unusual from a rich American who wrote that he'd be happy to finance any film that I cared to make, regardless of its theme and length. What an irony! Now of all times, when I was ill and had little hope of recovery, I was getting the sort of film offers I had been waiting for for decades. *GEO* offered to let me make an underwater film and I couldn't imagine anything I'd like more, but I couldn't even think about it seriously. I felt wretched.

However, when publishers once more approached me about my memoirs, I took their proposals seriously for the first time. My accident seemed almost like a stroke of fate in that finally I was able to find time to deal with this task. The most interesting German offer came from Willy Droemer, who was willing to pay me a substantial sum for the German-language rights. Times Books, the publishing house of the *New York Times*, offered twice as much for the world rights (not including the German-language rights), and the two houses were ready to do a co-publication. After a long conference with Mr Sulzberger, head of the *New York Times*, my anxiety vanished and our meeting contributed decisively to my giving up all resistance to the idea of memoirs. He was altogether different from the way I had pictured him: a very charming elderly man, who asked me no upsetting questions. If these plans ever came to fruition – and I felt dizzy at the thought – I would be rid of my debts; I could finance the Nuba film myself, and have no more money problems for the rest of my life.

While my publishers were casting about for a suitable ghostwriter, I flew to Tokyo. I had been invited to the opening of an unusual exhibition of my Nuba photos at the Seibu Museum; this, my second trip to Japan, deepened my impressions of the country. The initiator of the show was Eiko Ishioka; a prominent artist, graphic artist, award-winning art director of films and curator of exhibitions – not only in Japan but also in America where she had learned about me through my Nuba books – she had visited me in Munich and spent three days meticulously selecting over a hundred photos for the show. The presentation of my work was first class. I had always respected the Japanese, but this time they had performed a technological miracle. My originals had been only small slides, but they had used intermediate negatives to obtain wonderful blow-ups as large as four by sixteen feet, the biggest covering an entire wall. These formats were breath-taking – the museum had spent the equivalent of one hundred and fifty thousand marks just on lab work. The Japanese obsession with art is demonstrated by the following story. One day before the opening of the exhibition, Eiko decided that she didn't like the colour of the walls on which the pictures were to be hung and she managed to talk the workers into staying up all night in order to repaint them. Thoroughly exhausted, but ecstatic, she hugged me before the official opening.

These were festive days – the loveliest I had spent since the war – and I was so happy that I forgot my nagging pain. The visitor record was broken fivefold; on some days, as many as three thousand visitors were counted. My slide lectures, which Noriko interpreted simultaneously, were sold out, as were the screenings of all my films. My Japanese publisher, Parco in Tokyo, was surprised by the scale of the success. Within the very first week, people bought over two thousand copies of the Japanese edition of my Nuba picture books. Nowhere else in the world have I enjoyed the enthusiasm and hospitality that I found in Japan.

Before leaving Tokyo, I had a special experience. I had long been fascinated by the Japanes art of tattooing, but I knew it would be difficult to meet the masters of this art. By a stroke of good luck, in Yokohama, Issei Miyake, the famous Japanese fashion designer and a friend of Eiko's, introduced me to these young tattooed men who welcomed me warmly in the home of Mitsuaki Ohwada, chairman of the Japan Tattoo Club. On the walls of the small room I was surprised to see the huge posters of my photo exhibit, and I realized that it was the portraits of the painted or ash-covered

Nuba that had won me the hearts of the 'tattooed'. They let me snap as many shots of them as I was able to take during this brief visit; fortunately, Horst also had a Leica, and so we managed to get a great many pictures. Naturally, my mind was already running on a film and a picture book and hoped I would soon be well enough to make my plans come true.

When my publishers, List, Herrscher and others, saw these tattoo photos, they were so excited that they would have loved to send me back to Japan right away; and I would have loved to go. For the moment, however, I knew my memoirs had to have top priority. Then something happened which made the whole project questionable. Just a few days after the final details of the contract had been worked out with Willy Droemer it was announced that he would be leaving his publishing house, and the new heads of the house would not accept the terms that Willy Droemer had agreed to. Everything had to be renegotiated. At the same time, I was asked to come to New York, but I feared complications since the head of Times Books had left his publishing house almost at the same time as Herr Droemer. Happily, Mr Chase, the new director, was very accommodating and pleasant to deal with and I came to an agreement on all the details with him and his colleagues. Like his predecessor, Mr Chase was so convinced of the success of my memoirs that he was ready to put out my book without a German partner. But problems remained.

Then I was introduced to Dr Albrecht Knaus, a prestigious and successful German publisher. When we met, he so inspired me with confidence that I soon decided I would like him to become my new publisher.

My illness still prevented me from starting work. However, on days when the pain was more endurable, I managed to tell Dr Knaus about my life. During these preliminaries, I realized how important it was to set up an archive of my papers, which, despite great post-war losses, I still possessed in great numbers; they consisted of letters, diaries, calendars, newspaper clippings and countless files containing all the documents regarding my trials, my expeditions and my private life. I shuddered at the thought of producing a book from this abundance of material.

THE MALDIVES

When I couldn't stand Munich or my house because the pain had grown intolerable, I fled. I had tried to work – but it was no use. Despite my pills, I had sleepless nights.

In the dream world of the Maldives, which consist of thousands of islands between India and Sri Lanka and which I now visited for the first time, life looked altogether different. I went to the island of Furana, where Stolli – our diving instructor on the Indian Ocean – had set up his base. Here, after just a few dives, I felt like a new woman, but I couldn't tell whether it was the climate, the peace and quiet or the fascination of the underwater universe. Perhaps it was because I could photograph underwater free of pain. On every dive – and I dived at least twice a day – I took along my camera in search of subjects.

In the Maldives, Stolli, Horst and I were invited by a French producer, who was making a film about shark behaviour in many oceans around the world, to watch him on location. My curiosity outweighed my fear. He was filming at a place in the Waadhoo Channel where the current was so strong that we could only advance very slowly, holding on to the corals. I had never experienced such a powerful current. The film crew was getting ready to shoot at an edge of the reef, and we also had our cameras with us.

Then, everything happened very fast. Michel, the French diver who was supposed to lure the sharks over, opened a sack of fish, took out a big one, and waved it over his head. In the twinkling of an eye, everything around us was black as fish of all sizes swam between us and Michel, who could barely be seen although he was kneeling on the sand only two or three yards away from us. It was only a sudden motion of the fish that signalled the first shark, which was catching its prey at lightning-speed. Nor was that all. Terrified, I watched Michel thrust the next fish into his mouth – I couldn't watch, I looked away. It seemed an insane game with death and I was afraid that disaster would strike at any moment. But nothing happened. The sole indication of the diver's stress was the stream of bubbles rising upwards. Several sharks had materialized but they could only be glimpsed fleetingly because of the numerous fish. The sack was emptied in less than half an hour; Michel had fed them all.

I was glad when we were back in our boat. I hadn't enjoyed the shark feeding, but the French were well satisfied. Without my noticing it, they had used this opportunity to film me as I photographed underwater.

Much later, on the island of Bandos, I witnessed a very different shark feeding. It aroused world-wide attention as well as protests. Herwarth Voigtmann, a magician who performed his shark show twice a week, was one of the leading specialists in underwater filming. His show took place at a depth of approximately sixty feet, and it had to be seen to be believed. While Herwarth, sporting an elegant diving suit and kneeling on a projecting coral head, prepared to feed the sharks, the audience of divers sat on a reef ledge just a few yards away from him. It was like a theatre-in-the-round with rising rows of seats. Everyone peered at the dark water, eagerly waiting with their cameras for the appearance of the first sharks. Horst too was prepared with our 16-mm camera; he wanted to capture the marvellous sight at really close quarters.

Just a few short minutes after Voigtmann produced a fish from his sack and small fish began snapping at it, the first sharks emerged from the deep. Swimming in circles, they maintained a certain distance. As they drew nearer, we could see that they were big ones, almost white in the daylight that seeped in; indeed they gave off a sort of silvery shine. Before I could even register it, a shark leaped at Herwarth and grabbed the fish from his hand.

What followed was a nerve-racking ritual. Some sharks veered off just before reaching him, then returned. Whenever a shark swam towards him, a different situation resulted, yet Herwarth dealt masterfully with the most dangerous incident; even when two sharks zoomed towards him simultaneously he was ready and warded them off lightning-fast with a knife. After viewing the first feeding from a respectful distance, I moved closer to Herwarth, gradually experiencing less terror. In the end, I got so near that, kneeling next to him, I was able to shoot close-ups of the exciting moments when the gaping mouths of sharks grabbed the fish from Herwarth's lips. I even got a photo when a shark accidentally bit into Herwarth's thigh, letting go when it realized this was no fish. Even such incidents left Herwarth unruffled. Calm, without even attending to his injury, he went on with his show; only his blood, which looked green in the water, revealed that the shark's teeth had actually sunk in.

AT THE GROSSHADERN CLINIC

I was awaited impatiently in Munich. List urgently needed the picture layout for *Vanishing Africa*, which once again I was designing myself. A decision also had to be reached about the memoirs.

My hope that I could get down to work energetically was dashed. Within just a few days of my return, I was driven to seek out a specialist who might be able to diagnose the cause of my chronic pain. But Professor Viernstein, who examined me thoroughly, could find nothing wrong, and though he treated me with injections and new drugs I showed no improvement. Nevertheless, I had to complete the new book for List since it was scheduled to appear in Germany and abroad for my eightieth birthday.

The rushes and stills we had brought back from the Maldives were surprisingly good, the best results I had ever had from a diving trip. Horst's footage of the shark feeding and our dives with Herwarth were first class. On the screen, I could see a few of the sharks grazing my flash unit as they swam over my head. Unfortunately, I had no time to edit the rushes, and like my footage of the Nuba, these rushes still lie, unedited, in my cutting room.

Prior to my trip to the Maldives, Rainer Werner Fassbinder had tried to hire me as cinematographer for his film *Querelle*. I would love to have met this unusually gifted as well as controversial director and to have worked with him – especially after he wrote to me about how keenly he looked forward to our collaboration; but notwithstanding the state of my health, I could accept no more offers, not even press or television interviews.

While I was trying to get back to work, the prediction Dr Caveng had made in St Moritz came true. When we landed in Frankfurt, I was unable to get up from my plane seat. Within a very short time, I was back on the operating table, this time in the orthopaedic ward of the Grosshadern Clinic in Munich. A third operation on my hip was unavoidable for tests indicated a necrosis formation; an artificial joint had to be inserted. Professor Dr Zenker, a surgeon experienced in this field, performed the operation and the results, according to the X-rays, were excellent.

I would rather not write about the aftermath. However, both my work and I were so deeply influenced by this that I cannot omit it. When I was released from the clinic two weeks after my surgery and transferred to the Feldafing Clinic for post-operative treatment, I hoped to be free of pain within a few weeks. Day after day, I waited, but to no avail. On the contrary, the pain actually intensified – although otherwise, my stay in this hospital was pleasant. Through the window of my room, I saw green trees, and I could move painlessly in the indoor swimming pool. Dr Bielesch, the exceptional head physician, had time for every one of his patients, and several weeks later, when the pains still hadn't abated, he asked the well-known Munich neurologist Professor Dr Paal to examine me thoroughly – but he found nothing. Soon I could move my leg and my scars healed, but clearly I was going to have to exercise a lot of patience and learn to live with the pain as best I could.

Two months after my surgery, I was able to continue my treatment at home but the pain was worse than ever. No physician could find an explanation and I could endure my condition only with the help of powerful painkillers which left me very tired.

Nevertheless, I had to try and look fit for my eightieth birthday; List and Mondadori were throwing a party for the press and my friends at the Grünwald Castle Hotel to celebrate my birthday and to launch my fourth picture book *Vanishing Africa*. The day was very moving. My joy in greeting so many old friends, some of whom I hadn't seen for a long time, helped me forget my troubles.

I had sworn to myself that after the launch I would start on my memoirs which by this time I had decided to write myself. First, however, I wanted to reduce my pain by taking a cure in Ischia. Sadly, it brought no real improvement.

WITCH HUNT

The success of my books, which extended into their excellent paperback editions, and the increasing recognition of my work inspired my old adversaries to take further action. Their attacks may also have been prompted by several magazine picture stories about my eightieth birthday and a marvellously printed French publication *Double Page*, which included the loveliest of my Nuba photos, and about which the French writer Jean-Michael Royer wrote: 'Leni Riefenstahl, the modern Plato and Michelangelo of the Leica . . .' My enemies prepared a new libel campaign, which I feel is worth mentioning because of its insidious nastiness.

After my experiences with live broadcasting, I was reluctant to reappear on television, but the Swiss network Radio Télévision Suisse Romande was very persistent. For over a year, its head producer Jean Dumur tried to see me and when he finally visited me he persuaded me to change my mind about appearing. My impression of him was so favourable that my doubts were removed; in short, he succeeded in gaining my trust. He assured me both verbally and in writing that they would report only on my work and not touch upon events connected with the Third Reich. The TV crew filmed in my work rooms several times and I found all the participants very pleasant. Marc Schindler, the director, promised that he would most certainly stick to our agreement, and he was so convincing that even Horst put aside his distrust. The TV company obtained sequences from my films, shot interviews with several members of my former staff and even got some footage at one of my birthday parties. The director said that they wanted to present the truth and rehabilitate me. Perhaps the members of the crew didn't realize what the producer had in mind.

Shortly before I was to travel to the live television broadcast, friends in Geneva telephoned to warn me. They told me about a special edition of a Swiss TV gazette, which could be obtained at newsstands. The front page showed a photo of me, and the bold-face caption read: 'Leni, the Nazi film-maker'. Utterly dismayed, I decided not to go to Geneva and telephoned the TV executives, but they assured me emphatically that they had nothing to do with that publication, and that they were sorry it had come out. Their film, they said, had no political footage, and since our conversation was taped and having no evidence to contradict them, I didn't want to break my contract. In Geneva, I was picked up at the airport, and a suite was reserved for me at the Richmond. Everyone made an effort to be very friendly.

Still feeling mistrustful, I insisted on viewing their film prior to the live show, but they refused – just as I had feared. I wanted to leave instantly. Promising me all sorts of things, they tried to talk me out of the idea of seeing their film before the evening showing; they begged me to trust them. It was only when I got into a heated argument with various people involved in the programme and when they realized that I was adamant that they finally gave way.

I sat in the studio's tiny screening room with dark forebodings, and what I saw was totally shattering. It began innocently enough with excerpts from my films, then photos of myself as a child and as a dancer, followed by scenes from the mountain films. Maybe it won't be so bad. I thought, feeling relieved. Then I heard the name Adolf Hitler and on the screen, I saw an old lady, the well-known cinema historian Lotte Eisner, who, before emigrating to Paris, had been a critic for *Film-Kurier*. Aghast, I heard her tell the following story in an interview:

> One fine day – it was either in 1932 or in early 1933 – Leni Riefenstahl came to my office and said, 'Frau Doktor, I would like to introduce you to a wonderful young man.'
>
> I thought to myself, 'Wonderful' man? Strange. That can only be Trenker. But he had said he didn't like the people around Leni. Suspicious, I asked, 'Whom do you want to introduce to me? Trenker?'
>
> 'No, not Herr Trenker, Adolf Hitler,' said Leni.

Frau Eisner spoke with so much conviction that one almost had to believe her. Yet what nonsense! As if Hitler, shortly before coming to power, had had nothing better to do than go to *Film-Kurier* with me to meet a Communist editor. How could an intelligent woman talk such rubbish! I have never spoken to Frau Eisner, have never even met her – not in Berlin or Paris or anywhere else. They could at least have asked me whether her story was true.

There was even worse to come. The subsequent footage had nothing to do with my films; it was taken from Holocaust films, old newsreels of book burnings, Crystal Night, deportations of Jews, all interspersed with photos of me; finally, as the climax of this perfidious assemblage, came the old lie that I had been assigned by the Wehrmacht to film Wehrmacht shootings of Jews in Poland. And all this despite the fact that American, French and German authorities, after years of interrogations, had ascertained that all such rumours about me were untrue.

The Swiss television film also misrepresented my line as a war correspondent in Poland shortly after the outbreak of the war – an experience that I have described here in detail. In the film, the viewer sees my horrified face in the same photo that the blackmailer, who called himself Freitag, tried to sell me before the *Revue* trial. Next, the film shows blindfolded people kneeling on the ground with rifle barrels trained on them; there is the sound of gunfire and then corpses are lying on the ground. The next shot is again of my horrified face, this time greatly blown up.

Anyone watching that footage was bound to believe that I had witnessed an execution of Jews. Such cross-cutting adulterates truth into its very opposite. Back in 1950, when I sued the publisher of *Revue* for printing that very same libel, the Berlin court rejected his story as untrue. In Poland, I never saw a corpse, either of a soldier, or of a civilian.

When I saw this misrepresentation before me on the screen and recalled that the TV people had promised to report only the truth about me, I collapsed and a doctor had to be summoned.

I tried to prevent the broadcast of the film that evening, or at least to have them cut out the scenes incriminating me, but my efforts were useless and it was too late to get a court injunction. The doctor ordered me not to participate in the live programme, so Claude Torracinta, the producer of that concoction, had to go ahead without me. My chair remained empty. I believe that in my state I would have been unable to defend myself against Monsieur Torracinta in a live discussion. When I handed the matter over to my lawyer, so that he could at least block further transmission of the film, Dr Müller-Goerne, who had often given me friendly advice, managed to do this out of court. I decided not to sue for damages for I needed peace and quiet in which to concentrate on my work.

I HAD TO WRITE

According to my calendar, I made my first attempt on 1 November 1982. A white pad of paper, completely blank, lay in front of me. Had I had even the slightest inkling that this work would devour five years of my life, I would not have agreed to do it. I became a prisoner, chained to my desk, forced to give up almost everything else that I would have liked to do; to make matters worse, those years were accompanied by illness that made writing difficult and at times almost impossible.

I was still undecided about where to start. Should I begin in the middle of my life or at an even later point and flash back to my youth and development? Or should I choose the more conservative form and unroll my life from childhood on? I opted for the latter, because I had experienced too much, and if these events were not related chronologically, the result would be an impenetratable labyrinth. Furthermore, I believe, certain features of my character emerged very early, determining the course of my life.

I must confess that initially I felt quite at a loss and I would have given up if Will Tremper hadn't constantly encouraged me to go on. It was in his presence that I made my first attempt at writing. He asked me to talk, and then said, 'That's exactly how you have to write.' Raimund le Viseur was also my godfather. When I let him read the first few chapters, he liked them, and his reaction so boosted my self-confidence that gradually I spread my wings.

When winter came, I felt homesick for the mountains – packing up my binders and documents, I went to St Moritz with Horst. I could work a lot better in the good mountain air and also take my mud baths there. No sooner had I unpacked my bags, however, than the International Olympic Committee invited me to the screening of my Olympic films during the Olympic Week in Lausanne.

Here, I was warmly greeted by many of the guests, including Monique Berlioux, the director of the IOC and a good friend of mine. The elegant apartment that the IOC put at my disposal was decorated with huge vases of most beautiful roses I have ever seen. I have never sought a luxurious way of life but I did enjoy it. It was delightful – although it lasted for only a very short time. When Monique Berlioux came back several hours before the screening, she looked worried. 'Leni, I have some bad news,' she said. 'I'm sorry. We were all so greatly looking forward to your visit.'

I waited, apprehensive.

Monique went on. 'This morning, our president Monsieur Samaranch was warned that protests are expected against your presence at the screening of the Olympic film.'

I remained silent. This was undoubtedly the result of the witch-hunt film that had been beamed over Swiss TV.

'What was the Committee's response?' I asked at last.

'Naturally,' said Monique, 'it's your decision entirely whether you still want to appear at tonight's screening. The IOC has refused to be pressured, but I must tell you, alas, that they have been threatened with demonstrations.'

Dejected and depressed, I said goodbye to Monique; the Olympic film was shown in my absence. I was not comforted by the silver plate with the engraved dedication that was sent to me afterwards by Samaranch, president of the IOC.

All I knew was that I had to write this book.

CLOSING REMARKS

Before completing my manuscript, I asked friends to point out any mistakes or unclear passages in my presentation; I learned that some people were surprised when I gave the exact dates of many events – above all when I quoted Hitler, Goebbels and many others verbatim. I was advised to omit such direct quotations, since I no longer have any documentary evidence of the precise wording. After mulling over these objections, I decide that I had to write in that way. Nevertheless, such criticism had induced me to explain to my readers, who might have similar reactions, how I am able to render these utterances verbatim.

Hitler has so left his mark on my life that I can still remember every single word of my conversations with him and with the most important people in his entourage. Very often I described those meetings later to members of my staff and to friends; even more often, after the war, I had to repeat those conversations to American and French authorities, both military and civil, in the course of repeated interrogations during the years of my imprisonment.

Most of these interrogations were taken down and the transcripts were signed by me. How could I report anything differently now? I have to abide by my earlier detailed statements, if only to protect myself against the possibility that documents signed by me might suddenly emerge from archives in Washington or Paris.

The events of those years run before my eyes like a film, over and over again, and I am repeatedly confronted with the past, even today. Furthermore, when I was young, I made almost daily entries in my diary. After the war, irreplaceable notes and documents were either taken from me or were lost. During the 1950s, the French gave me back a number of documents and files of correspondence which had been confiscated and kept in Paris for many years. In this way, with the help of my friends, many of whom were witnesses to my presentation and who collect everything that is published about me anywhere in the world, I was able to rebuild a vast archive, without which I could never have written my story.

My aim was to tackle preconceived ideas and to clear up misunderstandings and I spent five years working on the manuscript. It was not an easy task since I was the only one who could write these memoirs; it did not turn out to be a happy one.

INDEX

657

659

667